50th Yearbook of the National Reading Conference

Edited by

James V. Hoffman
Diane L. Schallert
Colleen M. Fairbanks
Jo Worthy
Beth Maloch

University of Texas at Austin

With the editorial assistance of

Sarah J. McCarthey
University of Illinois, Urbana-Champaign

Anna Rudolph Canter
University of Texas at Austin

Judith C. Burnison
National Reading Conference

Anthony Cheung
Imprint Publications

Published by
National Reading Conference
Chicago

2001

NRC YEARBOOK is published annually by the National Reading Conference, Inc., 11 E. Hubbard, Suite 5A, Chicago, IL 60611, Tel: (312) 755-0635.

POSTMASTER: Send address changes to NRC YEARBOOK, 11 E. Hubbard, Suite 5A, Chicago, IL 60611.

SUBSCRIPTIONS: Institutions: $60 domestic or $75 foreign (surface), per year, or, $120 or $135, respectively, as part of a combination subscription with NRC's *Journal of Literacy Research.* Foreign subscribers add $20 if airmail is preferred. Individuals who attended the 2000 annual conference receive the YEARBOOK as part of their registration. Members and nonmembers who did not attend may purchase the YEARBOOK for $25 or $60, respectively ($75 foreign), Quantity discounts available for use in university or college courses. Write for information.

Microfiche copy is available from ERIC Reproduction Service, 3900 Wheeler Avenue, Alexandria, VA 22304. The YEARBOOK is indexed in *Psychological Abstracts, Index to Social Sciences & Humanities Proceedings* and *Educational Research Information Clearing House.* The NRC YEARBOOK is a refereed publication. Manuscripts must be original works that have been presented at the Annual Meeting of the National Reading Conference, and that have not been published elsewhere.

ISSN 0547-8375
ISBN 1-893591-03-4

Printed in the United States of America

National Reading Conference

Officers

Board of Directors

Editorial Advisory Review Board

Fiftieth Yearbook of the National Reading Conference

50th Yearbook of the National Reading Conference

PREFACE

AWARDS

PRESIDENTIAL ADDRESS

NRC ANNUAL REVIEW OF RESEARCH

INVITED ADDRESSES

Award Addresses

Articles

50TH NRC ANNUAL MEETING

PREFACE
NRC TURNS 50

At the 2000 conference in Scottsdale, Arizona, the National Reading Conference celebrated its 50th anniversary, and with this issue, we offer to the readership the 50th *Yearbook* of the conference. Fifty years of continuous effort in reading research is something to note and honor, and the evolution of the National Reading Conference into its broad-based focus on research in literacy issues has been nothing short of remarkable. In some sense, as an organization, we are barely recognizable from our origins as the Southwest Reading Conference for Colleges and Universities. NRC has grown not just in numbers but in the diversity of its interests, its membership, and its perspectives on literacy research. In this respect, our evolution as an organization reflects the evolution of reading research itself.

The *NRC Yearbook* has also reflected the continuity and change in our field. The proceedings from the first conference, a slim 48-page volume, comprised seven reports including papers by Oscar Causey, Albert Kingston, and William Eller, responding to the theme "Developing a Reading Program for College Students." By contrast, the 2000 meeting of the conference featured several hundred presentations, from which 96 research reports were submitted for peer review and 40 included in this publication. This year, active areas of inquiry included teacher education, professional development, classroom practice, and policy issues. Diversity, both cultural and linguistic, and its impact on literacy, constituted a major thread woven through nearly all of the studies we reviewed. As in past editions of the *Yearbook,* all of the plenary and award addresses from the conference appear. Finally, we have elected to include a complete list of presentations and their authors from the conference along with a summary report from the current NRC President, Peter B. Mosenthal, to reflect the archival role of the *Yearbook.*

This year, we have also chosen to order the research articles alphabetically by the first author. As we examined the themes and research perspectives represented in the reports, we found it increasingly difficult to place them into a specific category. We found ourselves asking questions such as: Does a study of preservice teachers learning to teach diverse learners go in "teacher education" or "diversity"? And, just as our understanding of literacy has grown more contextualized and more complex, we realized, so has our examination of it. As a consequence, few papers fit neatly into a single category, and a different organizational structure seemed warranted. We believe that individual titles provide the reader with a guide to themes and specific authors and that a short perusal of the table of contents will direct readers to articles of interest to them.

We begin our term as editors in awe and appreciation of all those who have served in this role before us from the term of Oscar Causey to that of our immediate predecessors—Drs. Timothy Shanahan and Flora Rodriguez-Brown. We commend the work of our Editorial Advisory Board, the NRC Publications Committee, and NRC Headquarters in supporting our transition into the role of new editors. A special thanks to Sarah McCarthey is necessary for serving as editor on manuscripts submitted by current colleaques or students from the University of Texas at Austin. We also extend our thanks to Anthony Cheung and Anna Rudolph Canter for their tremendous efforts in the editing process.

Happy golden anniversary NRC!

James V. Hoffman, Diane L. Schallert, Colleen M. Fairbanks,
Jo Worthy, and Beth Maloch
University of Texas at Austin

Lee Gunderson

ALBERT J. KINGSTON AWARD

The annual Albert J. Kingston Award for Service to the National Reading Conference was established in 1985 to honor Alert Kingston for years of dedicated service to NRC. Professor Kingston, an educational psychologist and reading specialist, was President of NRC in 1965-66.

The Albert J. Kingston Award seems to have been designed just to recognize the outstanding contributions of this year's recipient. For more than two decades this member of the National Reading Conference has played numerous roles which have enhanced the welfare of the organization. He first began attending the national conference in 1979 prior to obtaining his Ph.D. from the University of California at Berkeley in 1981. Since that time he has presented regularly at the conference, reviewed conference proposals and manuscripts for both the *Yearbook of the National Reading Conference* and the *Journal of Literacy Research.* The recipient currently serves as Professor and Head of the Department of Language and Literacy Education at the University of British Columbia.

This National Reading Conference member has served in many leadership capacities over the years. He took part in the early planning and organization of the Field Council and served as a representative for several years. He has been a strong supporter for international membership in the organization and served as a mentor for numerous new colleagues in the field. Further, he was instrumental in initiating the joint National Reading Conference/International Reading Association Literacy Research Series.

However, the 2000 Albert J. Kingston Award recipient's most intense and extensive service to the organization has been through his work as NRC's Secretary since 1991. Over the 10 years of his service in this capacity, Lee Gunderson has attended and recorded the minutes of over 30 Board Meetings. His patience, attention to detail, and—most of all—humor has done more than just support the work of the organization. For the past decade, Presidents and Board Members have come to rely heavily on his prodigious memory. He *is* the living history of the National Reading Conference.

Lee Gunderson has served the organization in still another highly visible and critical way. He has contributed to our sense of community and lightheartedness. He began the much-valued annual T-shirt sale and single handedly has continued it every year. On behalf of the Kingston Award Committee and the entire membership, it is with great pleasure that I present the 2000 Albert J. Kingston Award to Lee Gunderson for over two decades of dedicated service. Please join with me in congratulating this year's recipient for all his many contributions large and small to the National Reading Conference.

Presented by Lea M. McGee
December 2000

Michael Pressley

OSCAR S. CAUSEY AWARD

The Oscar S. Causey Award recognizes outstanding contributions to reading research. Dr. Causey was the founder of the National Reading Conference and served as its president from 1952 to 1959.

This year's recipient is highly regarded for his substantial contributions to many areas of literacy research. To demonstrate the scope and depth of his work and the acclaim he has received, I turned to the *Handbook of Reading Research, Volume III*. To begin with, his early research on mnemonic strategies for word learning is cited in the chapter on Vocabulary Instruction. Through a series of studies spanning more than a decade, he approached the phenomenon of vocabulary learning in multiple ways, from a number of different angles, and with learners of different ages and talents. His work is characterized by the sustained pursuit of issues that cumulatively yield important insights into the nature of literacy learning.

He is best known for his many studies of comprehension and metacognition. He is interested not only in psychological processes but also teaching strategies. He examines these for learners of all ages, from the very young to college age. His work on the effectiveness of transactional strategies instruction is respected both for the quality of the content-specific instructional programs and the rigor of their assessment. His recent studies of early reading methods are setting high standards, both methodologically, in using of a variety of research approaches, and conceptually, in recognizing the complexities of instruction.

The work of this year's recipient consists not only of original research, but also of methodological analyses and comprehensive reviews of the research. Through this variety of work, he articulates current ways of viewing phenomena and develops new formulations. He asks the hard questions about what we are doing, what we have overlooked, and what we should be doing.

This year's recipient is highly regarded not only for his scholarly contributions to the field of literacy but also more generally to the fields of psychology and child development. He provided skillful editorial leadership for *Applied Cognitive Psychology* and the *Journal of Educational Psychology*, as well as the *Journal of Reading Behavior*. Last year, he was selected by readers of *Educational Psychologist* as one of three researchers most influential in the field of education.

For him, scholarship means not only the conduct of quality research but also the inclusion of young scholars with him in that research. He has nourished a vast number of doctoral, masters, and undergraduate students who have been marked by his high standards for inquiry and ethical conduct. Most of his research publications are jointly authored, and include students who participate in the work.

He received his Ph.D. in Child Psychology from the University of Minnesota in 1977. He has held tenured appointments at the University of Western Ontario, University of Maryland, College Park, and State University of New York–Albany. He currently holds the Chair for Catholic Education at the University of Notre Dame.

Always meticulous in his research, highly regarded for his outstanding mentorship, a leader who has made sustained and prolific contributions over the past 25 years—by now the identity of this year's recipient will come as no surprise. It gives me great pleasure to present the 2000 Oscar S. Causey Award to Michael Pressley.

Presented by Rebecca Barr
December 2000

Literacy Teaching, Literacy Learning: Lessons from the Book Club *Plus* Project*

Taffy E. Raphael
Oakland University

Late this summer, a front page, *New York Times* article on teacher education led with this statement:

> A growing number of states and school districts are short-circuiting the usual route to teacher certification with their own crash courses that put new teachers in the classroom after as little as three weeks. . . . (Zernike, 2000, p. A1)

The article went on to describe the predicted shortage of qualified teachers if we are held to current models of teacher preparation. The tone of the article was harsh, describing schools and colleges of education as having "done more harm than good," being "cumbersome," and offering "mind-numbing courses." Quoting policy-makers who "express near hostility to teacher education schools," the article called for new programs in teacher preparation to address the projected teacher shortage and concerns of quality.

I am uncertain why the article troubled me so much. Certainly I am used to criticisms of teacher preparation and, too often, I find that some are warranted. Perhaps it was the sheer hostility of the rhetoric and that the article appeared in a reputable public print medium. Articles such as this one signal how high the stakes have become. As a field, we must improve how we convey to the public, and each other, our knowledge about teaching literacy and preparing teachers who are competent and confident in their professional knowledge base. This is the focus of my presidential address.

I begin by sharing my understandings of this public debate about teacher education, and consider its consequences for literacy instruction and the education of literacy teachers. Second, I trace how my understandings influenced what I have chosen to study. I then turn to complexities that characterize literacy teaching and learning, ending with implications for professional development.

Public Debates About Teacher Education

Public discourse about education explores a range of topics, three of which are of direct concern to those of us in literacy education: (a) teacher preparation in

*Presidential Address, The National Reading Conference, Scottsdale, AZ, December 2000.

National Reading Conference Yearbook, ***50***, *pp. 1–20.*

general, (b) early literacy instruction, and (c) teaching diverse youngsters. In terms of general preparation of teachers, we may not agree with what appears in the media, but we can agree there is a common theme: the public's lack of value for current practices. Whether it is the argument for home schooling, the push for charter schools that have less stringent teacher certification requirements, the suggestion that "life experience" is a substitute for formal training, or the push for alternatives to schools of education and reading departments, the role of schools of education in teacher preparation and ongoing professional development has been devalued (e.g., Moats, 2000). Although teacher's knowledge about language and literacy is fundamental to their ability to teach students, especially those in early and middle elementary school, the average number of credits for reading, writing, and language practices, as well as children's literature and literacy assessment averages only 6.36 semester hours (2.23 courses) in typical 4-year undergraduate teacher preparation programs (Hoffman & Roller, 2001).

To counter this tendency to downplay the importance of teachers' preparation and professional development in literacy and closely related areas, our profession can begin by becoming clear and confident about what teachers need to know and by identifying ways they can build this knowledge, in both formal routes in existing schools and colleges of education and through new and innovative professional development programs. A likely outcome of putting inexperienced teachers with little formal preparation into classrooms is a profound need for inservice education—professional development on site as well as through graduate programs. Teacher educators must make the most of available credit hours during preservice education, while becoming ready to meet the increased needs of new teachers in the field.

A second focus of public discourse about teacher education relevant to literacy teacher preparation stems from our own debates about beginning reading instruction. Those in the media have given this topic so much attention that one might think the only knowledge a teacher needs is that relevant to the first few months of school. Yet, I believe our profession would acknowledge that literacy instruction continues throughout students' school careers. Teachers must be able to support the development of critical, independent thinkers who understand the power of literacy as it plays out in all aspects of our lives. Living in a democracy places heavy demands upon our citizens, which I was reminded of throughout the election and post-election processes. We need an educated, literate citizenry for our democracy to thrive. With a projected need for hundreds of thousands of new teachers, coupled with relatively few credit hours to study literacy teaching and learning, inservice teachers new to teaching likely will be inadequate in their understandings of the full range of literacy abilities and literacy content they are responsible for addressing.

A third topic has received less direct attention in public discourse, but arises indirectly in discussions about the increasing diversity of our student population and continued lack of diversity within the teaching force. Current preparation through multicultural education has been inadequate in preparing teachers to work in diverse settings with diverse youngsters (Au & Raphael, 2000; Raphael, Florio-Ruane, Kehus, George, Hasty, & Highfield, 2001). Even more insidious, current preparation makes it easy for teachers who teach students much like themselves to dismiss multicultural study as being largely irrelevant to themselves and their students. This does little to prepare these youngsters to live and work in a diverse society.

This lack of preparation can be attributed, at least in part, to the kinds of texts and how they are used to teach future teachers and school-aged youngsters about diversity. First, social science texts (i.e., textbooks) dominate the curriculum. Treated as "science," they are rarely integrated with the study of genres which would lead to more critical examination of what is presented as science and to analysis into the "whys" and "wherefores" represented in the texts. At worst, such texts may end up promoting the very stereotypes they seek to diminish.

Moreover, textbooks are frequently the primary, if not the only, information source. They are not integrated with other literatures of cultural experience such as autobiographies written by members of different ethnic, racial, and social backgrounds, nor are they integrated with children's and families' experiences of literacy. Literature can provide a rich source of information about culture and humanity. From my experiences working in collaboration with Susan Florio-Ruane, I have seen how autobiography and autobiographical fiction can encourage the study of diversity and multiculturalism in ways that penetrate the reading and language arts curriculum in teacher education and for school-aged students (Florio-Ruane, 2001; Raphael et al., 2001).

Exploring Problems of Practice: A Personal Account

Over the past 5 years, Susan and I have used a model in which we frame our research in terms of "problems-of-practice." We began with today's challenges: a lack of value for teacher education when thousands of new teachers will be hired can lead to too many who will be unprepared to teach literacy, much less to a diverse student population. The problem-of-practice that concerned us is how one becomes a good teacher generally and specifically with respect to literacy. In our project, we have targeted three bases that are foundational for effective literacy instruction: (a) literacy teaching and learning as a complex cultural practice, (b) literature's role within the literacy curriculum, and (c) opportunities and alternatives for professional development. These areas provide the basis for Susan's and my efforts to help meet today's challenges for teacher education through the Teachers Learning Collaborative, a network of classroom- and university-based teacher researchers. Within this group—which networks three teacher study groups across southeast Michigan—we explored teachers' learning through conversation and collaborative inquiry, the influence of these experiences on teachers' design of literacy curriculum and assessment, and how the curriculum supported their students' learning about literacy and culture.

A Little Professional History

My evolving focus on literacy teacher education and its relationship to students' learning parallels that of our field. Like many of us who finished graduate school around 1980, I conducted instructional studies from the late 1970s into the mid-1980s. Studying with David Pearson and others at the Center for the Study of Reading at the University of Illinois, I attended graduate school when research on comprehension instruction was just beginning, and cognitive psychology provided the foundation. I used experimental methods to test particular strategies, such as QARs, and the means and effectiveness of using multiple strategies, such as Carol Sue Englert's and my work in Cognitive Strategy Instruction in Writing. The times were exciting. We were part of a group building a base for teaching and assessing comprehension and hundreds of studies demonstrated the power of strategy instruction on students' abilities to make sense of text. With this work, I began my extended focus on *what to teach* in the name of literacy instruction.

In the mid-1980s, at Michigan State University and the Institute for Research on Teaching, Carol Sue and I began engaging with teachers for more extended periods of time than I had in past research. We met with the teachers working with us at least once a month for most of the academic year. We did weekly observations as they implemented Cognitive Strategy Instruction in Writing. Teachers taught the program and helped with some data collection. However, a pivotal event occurred in the year following the writing work.

A Pivotal Event

In 1989, a year after Carol Sue and I had completed data collection, I bumped into one of the project teachers (whom I will call Marcia) who had been actively involved throughout the project. As we pushed our carts up the grocery store aisle, I asked Marcia how things were going with her current fourth graders. Initially, she was enthusiastic, but then seemed to become embarrassed. She apologetically said something along the lines of "I really liked your writing program, and wish I had time to keep using it." She mentioned her students' gains in writing while in the program, but she said she just could not find time for it in the curriculum.

As we parted company, I was struck by Marcia's comments. First, she called it "your" writing program, meaning Carol Sue's and mine, rather than "ours," including her and the other teachers. Second, she said she had believed her students had benefited from the program, but that she did not have time to use it now that the project had ended. Yet, she taught in a district and school that at the time gave teachers quite a bit of autonomy. This encounter began my process of rethinking how I approached literacy research with teachers, specifically in terms of ownership, engagement, and inquiry as viewed through the lens of sociocultural theory.

Kathy Au (1998) has talked extensively of the importance of *ownership* for students to fully participate in literacy events, and I began to think about how relevant this is to teachers working within literacy education. John Guthrie and his colleagues (e.g., Guthrie & Wigfield, 1997) have written of the importance of student *engagement* with literacy, which also seems crucial for teachers who want to be effective in adapting, rather than simply reproducing, literacy instructional approaches. Gordon Wells (1993) argues strongly for an *inquiry approach* with students and the related changes we must make in teacher education. Yet, such approaches to teaching are challenging when teachers themselves have never experienced inquiry-based approaches in their own learning. Sociocultural theory argues not only that literacy is cultural practice, grounded in language-mediated activities, but also that it is only through an ongoing and iterative process of appropriation and transformation, publication and conventionalization that learning—both teachers' and students'—occurs (Gavelek & Raphael, 1996).

Marcia's comments stood in stark contrast—I believe our grocery store conversation showed she had little ownership. Moreover, though engaged during the project, she was not for the long term. Our inquiry had involved questions of interest to the university researchers, but apparently not at the same level of concern for participating teachers. For Marcia, the writing instruction was frozen in time, lacking connection to her ongoing curriculum. In Vygotskian terms, she may have appropriated what was presented during inservice activities to use as *we*—the researchers—had intended within her classroom, but there was little evidence that she felt the program would address a meaningful problem she had identified within her own practice. And, these problems may have been exacerbated by a lack of collegial support after the project ended.

Despite my own references to constructivist theories, I had not interacted with teachers in the ways that I encouraged them to engage with their students, a striking disconnect between my theory and practice. In retrospect, despite believing strongly in a particular approach for student learning, I had ignored what I believed about learning in my own work with teachers, essentially taking teacher learning for granted. It was from this experience that I began my continuing interest in *how to teach.*

A Different Approach: Collaborative Inquiry and Teacher Research

The Book Club line of research, which I began in 1990 with Sue McMahon, Ginny Goatley, and Laura Pardo, took a substantially different form, becoming increasingly collaborative with colleagues from public and private school settings as well as from the university (McMahon & Raphael, 1997). Based in principles of collaborative inquiry through teacher study groups, we explored how to solve numerous problems of practice. For example, we studied ways to create instructional contexts in which students engaged in discourse around age-appropriate texts, promoting critical thinking, comprehension, and text interpretation (Raphael, Florio-Ruane, & George, in press). We examined the effects of such instructional contexts on diverse learners within the regular education classroom

(Goatley, Brock, & Raphael, 1995; McMahon & Raphael, 1997). We studied the impact of this collaborative inquiry on our own professional development and learning about literacy instruction (Florio-Ruane, Berne, & Raphael, 2001; Florio-Ruane & Raphael, 2001; Raphael, Damphousse, Highfield, & Florio-Ruane, in press). Many members of the original Book Club project team have stayed with the project as it has evolved, serving as more knowledgeable others to support learning within the group. New members brought different perspectives and new problems-of-practice, representing an ever increasing range of districts within southeast Michigan.

Unlike Marcia, the members of the Collaborative have been involved in sustaining, as well as transforming, the Book Club program. For example, in 1991, Kathy Highfield, Laura Pardo, and Julie Folkert developed the content-area links that now characterize the program. At the time, each taught fifth grade in different districts across southeast Michigan; Julie and Kathy were beginning the masters degree program at Michigan State University that Laura had just finished. Kathy and Julie developed a sample unit as part of a project for a course they were taking with me. They also began meeting with the original Book Club Teacher Research Group, where Laura was active. Impressed with Kathy and Julie's curriculum work, Laura modified it to use with her social studies units. The three continued to refine the content-area connections over a 2-year period until it became part of the conventional approach to Book Club (Highfield & Folkert, 1997; Highfield, 1999; Raphael & Hiebert, 1996).

A few years later, MariAnne George, a third-grade teacher, developed the Literacy Block component of Book Club *Plus*. At the time, MariAnne was a member of the Book Club *Plus* node of the Teachers Learning Collaborative where we focused on expanding Book Club to serve the needs of struggling readers. Adding Literacy Block provided a context for guided reading and independent practice on strategies, skills, writing, and other work thematically related to the unit. Nina Hasty, a member of the Literacy Circle Study Group, another node of the Collaborative, heard MariAnne and others talk about Literacy Block at the meetings of the full Collaborative.

Nina teaches in an elementary school in a high-poverty urban setting. The school district has fewer resources and more restrictions on implementing the literacy curriculum than MariAnne experiences, and the teachers' professional development activities there are dominated by district-mandated workshops for which their attendance is required and paid (Florio-Ruane et al., 2001). Working with the support of members of the voluntary Literacy Circle Study Group, Nina adapted MariAnne's work to meet the needs of her first and second graders. Her enthusiasm from her students' successes both within the program and on school assessment measures have led the Literacy Circle Study Group to select Book Club *Plus* as this year's primary focus.

Members of the Collaborative also worked together to solve broader problems-of-practice. As teacher educators and teachers, we are well aware of the importance of accountability for our students' literacy learning. While we were convinced of our students' success based on observational and descriptive data from our pilot studies, we knew that a systematic study evaluating students' progress in reading, writing, discussion, and content learning—using experimental methods—would be potentially more convincing to others. Conducting such a study with minimal resources became a problem-of-practice for the Collaborative to solve.

In the summer of 1999, a subset of seven of us held a retreat in northern Michigan to develop a thorough but manageable assessment system. We represented first through eighth grades, five different districts including high-poverty urban, working-class rural, and middle-class to affluent suburban communities. Drawing on district, state, and national standards, we developed a common set of standards for reading, writing, discussion, evaluation, and related content areas, such as the study of culture, connected to the Book Club curriculum. We then created an assessment system that included a standardized test and informal group and individual assessments such as the QRI, writing samples, and observations. All could be handled by teachers within the context of their own teaching. We brought the system back to the Collaborative for refinement, and it became the basis for the assessments we conducted during an evaluation study of Book Club *Plus* this past school year.

These teachers' experiences differed markedly from Marcia's. In *this* research project, the teachers felt both ownership and engagement. Together, we identified problems of practices to be addressed, and group members were crucial to our success in addressing them. The inquiry stance we assumed enhanced our own teaching as well as the curriculum work in which we engaged with Book Club *Plus* (Raphael, Florio-Ruane, & George, in press). My experiences since 1990 have convinced me that we do not have to sacrifice teacher's ownership and commitment to their own learning in the name of scientific study, nor do we have to sacrifice accountability in the name of collaborative inquiry.

Complexities in Literacy Teaching and Learning

Teacher ownership and engagement are crucial when working in the very complex domain of literacy instruction. To feel and to be professionally competent for creating skillful readers, teachers must have a broad knowledge base. I return now to the three areas that Susan and I targeted as foundational to the professional development of literacy educators: understanding complexities in a complete literacy curriculum, knowledge about literature as humanity's recorded history and values, and opportunity to engage in meaningful professional development.

Complexity in a Complete Literacy Curriculum

Literacy exemplifies what Rand Spiro has termed a "complex domain," with complexity attributed to its highly contextualized, ill-structured, and non-algorithmic nature (Spiro, Feltovich, Jacobson, & Coulson, 1995). In a recent *Educational*

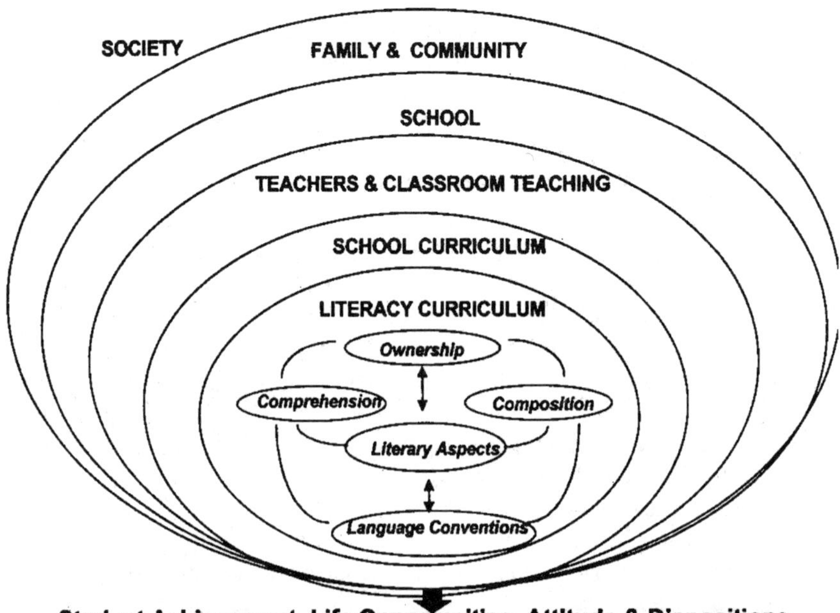

Figure 1. Teaching and learning as cultural practice. Modified from Taylor, Anderson, Au, & Raphael (2000).

Researcher article, Taylor, Anderson, Au, and Raphael (2000) attempted to capture this (see Figure 1).

Grounded in a sociocultural perspective, the figure reflects the many layers that influence and shape a students' literacy development, from family and community values and practices to those of the school; from the specific school curricula and related areas of emphases to those of the literacy curriculum. Effective literacy teaching and learning depend on teachers having a clear understand-

Language Conventions	Comprehension	Composition	Literary Aspects
Sound/Symbol Grammar Syntax Interaction	Background Knowledge prediction Text Processing: summarizing sequencing identifying importance Monitoring clarifying planning	Process: planning drafting revising Writing as a tool Writing from sources On-demand writing	Literary Elements theme plot character setting Response to Literature personal creative critical

Figure 2. Articulating the literacy curriculum.

ing of how these different levels contribute to children's literacy acquisition, practice, values, use, and engagement.

Turning to the school curriculum, literacy teaching and learning involve knowing how the language system works; being facile at creating, comprehending and interpreting text; and most important, insuring each student ownership so literacy can serve his or her goals (see Figure 2).

Debates of the past several decades stem, in part, from limitations in the amount of curricular time devoted to literacy instruction. As literacy researchers uncover areas important to literacy acquisition and practice, educators (and researchers) have taken the bait that pits the new or the timely against current curricular content. In my teacher training program in the late 1960s and in the curriculum materials I used in the 1970s, most of the emphasis in the reading program was about teaching the code and that generally was unquestioned.

With research from the Center for the Study of Reading and others during the 1980s, the importance of comprehension and strategy instruction was unquestioned, but it ended up being pitted against skills related to our language system. Similarly, as the importance of literature emerged, researchers and educators found ourselves pitting related aspects—such as response, interpretation, and appreciation—against comprehension and skill instruction (Stahl, 1999). None of this makes sense. Instead of recognizing that with each passing decade, our field has learned more about how to teach literacy, about the complexity of the literacy processes, and about the ways in which literacy is instantiated and valued across time and cultures; we essentially fell into the trap of assuming that new knowledge somehow replaced or overshadowed previous practice. This is *not* simply my attempt toward reconciliation—that, in some trivial sense, everything matters. Rather, in very important ways, all that we as a field have researched and demonstrated to have an effect on reading progress *does* matter.

To engage in literacy is to engage with the signs and symbols of our culture. A sociocultural perspective highlights the way in which language mediates these interactions, whether the language focuses on text comprehension and interpretation or the literacy curriculum itself. Jerome Bruner (1996) has suggested that curriculum is actually an ongoing conversation. Florio-Ruane makes the point that if curriculum is conversation, the teacher is the interlocutor (Florio-Ruane, 2001). Yet, the boxes illustrating the literacy curriculum, in and of themselves, often end up lending themselves to a hierarchy when, in fact, the whole chart is the cultural practice. Over time, this grows in complexity, feeds back upon itself and leads us to work with all aspects all the time.

Certainly, the curriculum changes over time through dialogic activity in different conversational spaces. Jim Gavelek and I adapted Rom Harré's (1984) work to detail the conversational spaces in which the curriculum is appropriated and transformed, made public; and sometimes changes to that curriculum become new conventional practices (Gavelek & Raphael, 1996, see Figure 3). Notice that this figure conveys conversational spaces that can be public and social, where conventional knowledge can be introduced and explained, as well as private and individual (such as occurs when students read independently or record their

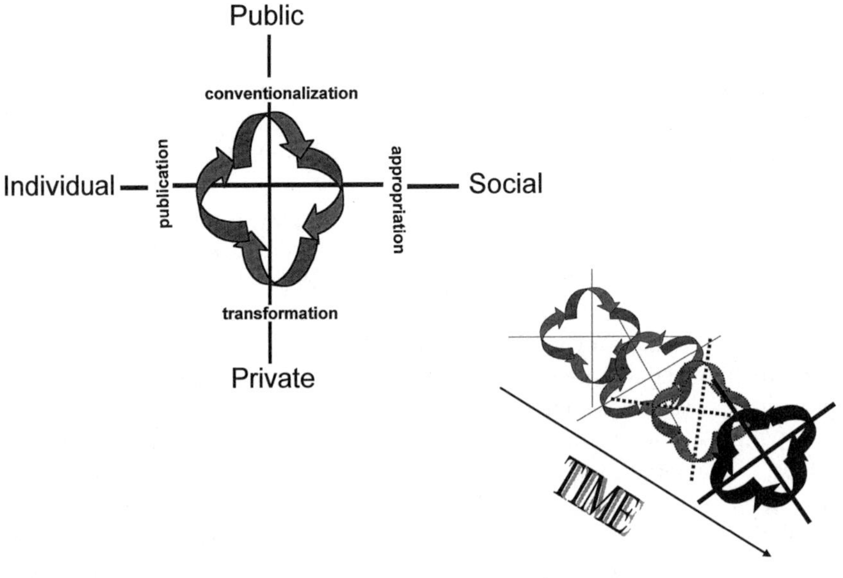

Figure 3. The Vygotsky Space.

thoughts in reading logs, appropriating and transforming what they have learned). Moreover, these conversational spaces are iterative. Over time, they feed back upon themselves in the way that Bruner has described. The work done within these conversational spaces suggests a curriculum that is not static, but a dynamic structure that helps teachers and researchers organize language and literacy processes that we have declared as comprising the curriculum. These conversational spaces and the work done within them are the activities of the language arts; they represent our cultural practices. We—teacher educators, teachers, and researchers—should stop taking the bait that asks us to privilege some aspects of the curriculum over others—it is not in the best interest of students or teachers.

Literacy is the foundation for all other learning, the means by which youngsters develop critical thinking skills. It is the vehicle through which humans can make sense of our world and ourselves. It is a complex set of skills, as well as cultural practice, that both determines the skills that comprise it and the values placed on how the skills are employed. This requires a literacy curriculum for *all* readers—those who struggle as well as the avid and proficient—a curriculum that engages students in meaningful literacy events in which they see the value of the skills, strategies and dispositions directly and indirectly taught. It also underscores teachers' need to understand the depth of literacy practices and ability to adapt instructional programs to insure students can and do participate in literacy practices.

Complexity from our Dual Obligations

This brings us to the complexities related to what I call "dual obligations" of literacy teaching. Keith Stanovich has raised the specter of the rich getting richer and the poor getting poorer with respect to literacy learning in today's schools (Stanovich, 1986, 1998). Students who struggle need to develop a repertoire of decoding skills to read age-appropriate materials. Thus, they require instruction and practice in applying these skills to texts at their reading level. Historically, our field has taken up that challenge. Many programs, as well as resource staff, exist to guarantee that students are taught the basic skills they need to improve reading fluency with reading-level appropriate materials. In addition, the practice of ability grouping for guided reading within the regular education classroom further supports this aspect of instruction.

However, literacy educators have done little to guarantee that when students have caught up on basic skills, they will have had—and be able to draw on—rich experiences with age-appropriate materials. These materials push their text analysis, interpretation, response, and critical thinking about issues in ways that their more successful grade-level peers experience daily. These are the dual, and often competing, obligations of literacy educators: providing sufficient practice with reading-level appropriate materials, as well as access to and engagement with age-appropriate text. Moreover, in both cases, we must identify meaningful ways to ensure that these texts become part of students' interactions with each other through literate conversation. As John Shotter has articulated (Shotter, 1993; cited in Florio-Ruane, 2001), students learn not only the content of the texts, but the social system into which the text is embedded. This social system and associated sorting of students has implications as profound for their life-long literacy learning as being able to read the print.

As literacy researchers and educators, we cannot choose between these two obligations, nor should we view them as being in opposition. Unfortunately, with many approaches, low-achieving readers may conceivably go through school never engaging with texts appropriate for their age level, texts that require higher order thinking and interpretation skills such as those laid out in our national agenda and reflected in both national and state standards documents. Further, these struggling readers rarely have opportunities to talk with peers about such materials and the ideas they contain. When this happens, the classroom becomes stratified (i.e., the social system in which the curriculum is embedded is instantiated). In that setting, it is difficult—if not impossible—for low-achieving readers to join, or for the teacher to create, a functioning community of learners. And it is belonging to such a community that helps motivate thinking and learning (Wells, 1999). Yes, the rich get richer and the poor get poorer, and not only in the area of fluency (Raphael et al., 2001).

Literature's Role Within the Literacy Curriculum

I hope I have now conveyed what I include in knowledge of literacy processes, reasons why it is important for our profession to make this knowledge clear, and challenges that stem from our dual obligations as literacy educators and literacy teacher educators. Teaching the processes that constitute literacy inevitably leads to the texts that we use during instruction. Thus, I now turn to the second area foundational to teachers' successful literacy instruction: literature and its role as literacy's substantive content.

Literature as Cultural Practice

Literature is the "meat" of the reading program, for it includes the texts with which students learn to read, practice learned skills, and develop fluency. Although scholars today in fields from critical literacy to cultural studies debate both what "counts" as literature and whether literature refers to the object itself or the activity in which it is involved, there is little debate about the value of children's reading literature in and out of school. Many suggest good literature is motivational—inspiring students to become avid readers who exhibit the kind of ownership and engagement that scholars such as Au and her colleagues (Au et al., 1997), and Guthrie and his colleagues (e.g., Guthrie & Wigfield, 1997) have described. But literature is more than a tool for bringing students into literacy. Birkerts (1994) describes literature as follows:

> Our entire collective subjective history—the soul of our societal body—is encoded in print. Is encoded, and has for countless generations been passed along by way of the word, mainly through books. I'm not talking about facts and information here, but about the somewhat more elusive soft data, the expressions that tell us who we are and who we have been, that are the record of individuals living in different epochs—that are, in effect, the cumulative speculations of the species. (p. 20)

Literature as Textual Practice

In addition to capturing society's "soul" and history, literature represents a set of textual practices (Golden, 2000). Current work in textual practices is often framed within genre study. In our work, we have found it useful to classify these genres broadly in terms of their goals: scholarship, fiction, and a sort of hybrid, autobiography, recognizing that each has imitations as well as strengths. Bruner's discussion of paradigmatic and narrative modes of thought was helpful as we distinguished between these genres, allowing each to be judged in light of its own criteria for effectively describing or explaining human experience. Although both can result from disciplined inquiry, they create very different texts.

The scholarly record of the society is often recorded using the genres of social science exposition, where criteria such as falsifiability and generalizability are important. These genres, by their very nature, are static and tend to "freeze frame" the knowledge being reported. This writing—biased toward a search for universal truth conditions and characterized in terms of the outsiders' perspective—appeals to procedures for establishing formal and empirical proof and uses arguments to convince readers of their truth.

In contrast, the genres of fiction as well as autobiography are told through narrative where criteria for justification include verisimilitude—that is, the likelihood or probability of an event—and believability. Rather than seeking universal truths, these genres search for likely connections among events, using stories to convince readers of their likeliness. Fiction genres tend to be personal and told in dialogue between insiders and outsiders. These forms invite contact with, and changing knowledge through, comparisons of lived experiences. As such, they stand in contrast to the freeze-frame nature of the literature of social science and invite alternative ways of reading and making sense of the content.

Literature as Cultural and Textual Practice

Thus, through both content and form, literature provides a reflection of and a window into the history and practices of a culture (Galda, 1998). In our work in Book Club *Plus,* we find that framing questions about what is revealed through the literature helps students see and explore the stories of their own lives, their families, and different cultures. To construct meanings from this literature, within the Book Cub *Plus* curriculum, students learn and apply traditional comprehension strategies, as well as analytic and interpretive skills less typical of literacy instruction, especially for early and struggling readers.

For example, in our Book Club *Plus* work in third grades, this played out in an author study of Patricia Polacco, a prolific Michigan author who through her autobiographical fiction shares family stories of her Russian immigrant and her Michigan farmer ancestors. Her stories became the basis of activities for both book club discussions and for teacher-led guided reading. As students read books like *My Rotten Redheaded Older Brother* (Polacco, 1994), they practiced their basic skills as well as explored issues of power and authority within their families and by extension within their classroom and their community.

Teachers must establish the community; select the texts; create the contexts in which the texts are read, written about, and discussed; and provide instruction supporting comprehension, literary response and analysis, composition, and language conventions. Yet, few teachers are immersed in the personal interactions with text that provide background on which to draw or in the scholarly study of literature in preparation for supporting children's response and interpretation of the texts they read. Without teachers having knowledge of and direct experiences with literature's content and form, they are reduced to being the tool of the adopted commercial materials, rather than positioned to use these materials as tools for developing skillful readers.

Like the dual obligations of both reading-level- and age-appropriate texts, balance must be created between readers' aesthetic experiences with the texts and exploring the content related to literature, and between the substantive focus on literature and the instruction in literacy skills that provides readers with access to that literature. As Desai (1997) wrote, "Literature has the power to open eyes and change lives, it is also apparent that this does not happen merely by reading a piece of culturally diverse literature in a classroom" (p. 175). Literature deserves serious attention in defining the knowledge base of an effective literacy teacher.

Opportunities and Alternatives for Professional Development

The third base for successfully developing skillful readers lies in teachers' initial preparation and ongoing professional development. With an increasingly less experienced and underprepared teaching force, we must consider professional development opportunities for new and practicing teachers. So, what are options in light of current policies and practices for teacher education?

Literacy researchers and teacher educators can begin by recognizing that different inservice models have different goals. We can take a minimalist approach—raising test scores on a specific test such as a state assessment or commercial achievement test. We have seen the growth in popularity of these approaches today, and it is not surprising. It can be tempting in the face of great need to look for solutions that give us the greatest sense of control, what Anders and her colleagues (Anders, Hoffman, & Duffy, 2000, p. 732) call a "packaging mentality." Cloaked in the mantle of science, like the social science texts I talked of earlier, they tend to freeze-frame both the content of what is taught and the ways in which instruction occurs, usually through specific delivery systems. Because of their nature, such models are not generative and thus unresponsive as new issues emerge.

More powerful experiences arise using a problem-of-practice approach. As Gordon Wells (1993) has written:

> Knowledge construction and theory development most frequently occur in the context of a problem of some significance and take the form of a dialogue in which solutions are proposed and responded to with additions and extensions or objections and counter-proposals from others. (p. 51)

Dialogic models are, by their very nature, responsive to the problems identified, and because of this, generative in terms of both problem identification and solution. Where can such dialogue occur? I have come to value three opportunities: (a) within-school (e.g., through grade-level or school-wide reform efforts), (b) through magnets such as graduate programs in literacy education, and (c) through creating and sustaining teacher networks dedicated to exploring and solving problems of practice.

School-wide Models of Professional Development

Recently, scholars have researched successful school-wide efforts. For example, Barbara Taylor, David Pearson, and their colleagues studied schools that beat the odds in terms of students' achievement scores relative to what would be predicted given locations in high poverty settings (Taylor, Pearson, Clark, &

Walpole, 2000). Jim Mosenthal, Marge Lipson, and their colleagues conducted case analyses of schools whose students performed well on the state-wide Vermont literacy assessments (Mosenthal, Lipson, Mekkelsen, Russ, & Sortino, 2000). These success stories reveal a consistent pattern in the schools. There is a public and shared vision among the teachers and administrators. Schools have extensive professional development opportunities within the school with stable leaders to support these efforts. There are means of communication that are open and ongoing for all the staff members and respect for the teachers. Teachers are characterized by their high levels of expertise and their ability to be articulate about their work and a variety of approaches to instruction, rather than a "packaging mentality" or single program emphasis.

Yet, not all teachers have access to school reform efforts, and in school-wide efforts, the status quo can be hard to overcome. If buy-in is required from all teachers, passive inaction by a few can be sufficient to derail professional development efforts. How can those of us in university and other professional development settings support teachers interested in becoming part of innovative practices, but who teach with colleagues who may not be interested in reform? And, how can we support those same teachers so they can assume positions of leadership within their professional settings?

Professional Development Through University Graduate Programs

The response to these questions invites us to turn to the context for which we probably have the most influence: our own literacy masters degree programs. In light of the trends predicted over the next decades, it seems timely for us to engage in serious review to create programs with two goals. One is helping teachers develop the expertise needed for effective literacy instruction across grade and ability levels, as well as across cultural and linguistic backgrounds. The second is helping teachers develop the expertise necessary to become instructional leaders within their professional settings.

Rather than trying to fight for undergraduate credit hours, I think we should focus on the practicing teacher, a market likely to grow as new teachers realize how much they need to learn to help youngsters become literate. Moreover, even in the best circumstances, teacher educators' influence on teachers' practices increases greatly with just a year or two of classroom experience. Readers with experience teaching at the preservice and graduate levels are likely to have shared experiences similar to my own. I have taught a course to those preparing to teach and a few years later, some of those former students appeared in a master-level class I was teaching on similar topics. During the latter half of my 15 years at Michigan State University, these students whom I had taught as undergraduates would, in the graduate course, ask something like, "This (whatever the "this" happened to be) was really helpful. Why didn't you tell us about this in the undergraduate course?" Yet, if anyone compared the two syllabi, it would be obvious that the course content was quite similar. Developmental differences between a preservice teacher and even a relatively new teacher are dramatically different. They have more upon which they can build and they know what they do not know.

As much or more than ever before, teachers need more than simply a knowledge base for literacy instruction. They need more than advanced methods in various aspects of oral and written language. They need to be more than reading teachers, clinicians, or language arts specialists. They need to have principled understandings of practice and be skilled at conveying them to all the stakeholders who directly and indirectly affect their decisions and practices. Thus, in a strong masters program, teachers would learn about methods of literacy instruction and literacy as a set of cultural as well as political practices. They would develop a clear vision of literacy instruction and understand its theoretical roots and implications for their own classroom practices. And, they would become articulate at conveying their position with respect to how literacy is defined and taught.

Professional Development Through Teacher Networks

A third professional development opportunity I have come to value is the teacher network helping members solve problems they have identified in their practice (Clark, 2001). Such networks "work against the traditional isolation of teacher from teacher, university from classroom, novice from experienced educator . . . to craft a new professional community with a new discourse for the understanding and improvement of practice" (Raphael et al., 2001, p. 606).

For members of the Teachers Learning Collaborative, experiences within the network mirrored our work as teachers and teacher educators on multiple levels: the curriculum through which we learned about literacy and culture; the texts we read, responded to and discussed; the social organization and power of learning through conversation that we experienced; the border crossing that helped make the familiar strange and provided authentic opportunities for articulating commonalities and differences. Through our research, we have documented changes in teachers' beliefs and learning, changes to curricular practices, and growth in children's literacy learning and understandings of culture (Raphael et al., 2001, in press, a, b).

The power of Networks for enhancing teachers' learning, curriculum development and planning, and ultimately, students' literacy progress suggests an important next problem of practice. The challenge for any successful intensive, dialogic professional development effort is to "scale up," providing the means for other teachers to create their own professional groups, their own networks, and their own efforts to enhance literacy curriculum and instruction for their students. How can we build from the experience of successful networks such as ours to provide tools others might draw upon as they begin new professional networks?

In an ill-structured domain such as literacy teaching, Rand Spiro has argued for the importance of cognitive flexibility and for the power of case-based learning, specifically using mini-cases that, through computer technology, can be juxtaposed to illustrate complexities of teaching. This year, Susan and I have begun collaborating with Rand, applying cognitive flexibility theory to our work with teachers, and with Kathy Au, who has developed professional networks through her work in Hawaii. Our initial efforts and future plans are to develop a series of mini-cases created from artifacts generated by members of the Teachers Learning Collaborative and, in Hawaii, the Kalama Teacher Education Program. Rand describes these mini-cases as "bite-size chunks of real-world complexity" (Spiro & Jehng, 1990) because—to paraphrase William Blake—sometimes the only way to see a world is in a grain of sand.

Concluding Comment

I conclude reflecting on a cross-cultural professional experience that gave me a lot to think about regarding professional development. In October, I led a reading delegation in Cuba to learn about the Cuban approach to literacy education, one of two national initiatives Castro instituted when he rose to power. In Cuba, the illiteracy rate is now under 5% which, according to world standards, means that they have no illiteracy. The Cubans have both national standards and a national curriculum, but allow local control for how the standards are met. Each school has two leaders, one responsible for the curriculum, the other for school management.

While I do not want to overly romanticize what we were able to observe in our limited time there, it appeared that literacy instruction is determined by those involved in teaching—teachers and the curriculum leader. We were struck by the "taken-for-granted" notions of teacher professionalism. All teachers are expected to study their practice. In each of the schools we visited, the notion of the teacher as researcher was so unremarkable as to be mentioned only in passing. This sense of the teacher as respected professional extended to the family and community relationships as well. On the word of the teacher, family and community members could be expected to take action to help a student in need of support beyond school hours.

The Cuban example suggests that treating teachers as professionals can, at the very least, co-exist with—and, perhaps, contribute in important ways to a successful literacy program. I find this encouraging as I think about how well-situated literacy educators are here in the United States for addressing students' literacy problems. We know *what to teach* in our literacy programs. We know *how professionals learn* in complex domains such as literacy education. We know *how to create opportunities* for education professionals from a variety of settings to engage with each other to solve problems in our practices. What I hope is that we can learn from our field's and our own histories, in our search for effective, creative, and generative solutions.

I have used this presidential address as an opportunity to make sense of my own path as a literacy educator and use that understanding to make sense of what is happening within our field. Steven Birkerts (1994) captured the essence of this reflective experience in an essay on autobiography. He wrote:

> There is a path, then, from A to B . . . though of course it neither begins right at A nor ends obligingly at B. As paths go, it is a meandering thing, with many twists . . . each describing some choice made at a crucial moment. Back then, when the whole idea of a path was hazy, I did not think of myself as following or making any sort of track. I wandered to and fro in the realm of the immediate, moving toward what I liked and striking out against whatever displeased me. Retrospect alters everything. Looking through the aperture of time is like watching movement from a great altitude. What felt like blundering starts to look like fate. (p. 34).

May it be the fate of all of us not only to live in interesting times, but to be part of the times when we solve the problems of practice that have plagued us as a profession.

References

Anders, P. L., Hoffman, J. V., & Duffy, G. G. (2000). Teaching teachers to teach reading: Paradigm shifts, persistent problems, and challenges. In M. L. Kamil, P. B. Mosenthal, P. D. Pearson, & R. Barr (Eds.), *Handbook of Reading Research* (pp. 719–742). Mahwah, NJ: Erlbaum.

Au, K. H. (1998). Constructivist approaches, phonics, and the literacy learning of students of diverse backgrounds. In T. Shanahan & F. Rodriguez-Brown (Eds.), *National Reading Conference Yearbook, 47* (pp. 1–21). Chicago: National Reading Conference.

Au, K. H., Carroll, J. C., & Scheu, J. A. (2001). *Balanced literacy instruction: A teacher's resource book* (2nd ed.). Norwood, MA: Christopher-Gordon.

Au, K. H., & Raphael, T. E., (2000). Literacy and diversity in the millennium. *Reading Research Quarterly, 35,* 170–188.

Birkerts, S. (1994). *The Gutenberg elegies: The fate of reading in an electronic age.* New York: Fawcett Columbine.

Bruner, J. (1996). *The culture of education.* Cambridge, MA: Harvard University Press.

Clark, C. M. (2001). *Talking shop: Authentic conversation and teacher learning.* New York: Teachers College Press.

Desai, L. E. (1997). Reflections on cultural diversity in literature and in the classroom. In T. Rogers & A. O. Soter (Eds.), *Reading across cultures: Teaching literature in a diverse society* (pp. 161–177). New York: Teachers College Press.

Florio-Ruane, S., Berne, J., & Raphael, T. E. (2001). Teaching literature and literacy in the eye of reform: A dilemma in three acts. *New Advocate, 14*(3), 197–210.

Florio-Ruane, S., with deTar, J. (2001). *Teacher education and the cultural imagination: Autobiography, conversation, and narrative.* Mahwah, NJ: Erlbaum.

Florio-Ruane, S., & Raphael, T. E. (2001). Reading lives: Creating and sustaining learning about culture and literacy education in teacher study groups. In C. M. Clark (Ed.), *Talking shop: Authentic conversation and teacher learning* (pp. 64–81). New York: Teachers College Press.

Galda, L. (1998). Mirrors and windows: Reading as transformation. In T. E. Raphael & K. H. Au (Eds.), *Literature-based instruction: Reshaping the curriculum* (pp. 1–11). Norwood, MA: Christopher-Gordon.

Gavelek, J. R., & Raphael, T. E. (1996). Changing talk about text: New roles for teachers and students. *Language Arts, 73*(3), 182–192.

Goatley, V. J., Brock, C. H., & Raphael, T. E. (1995). Diverse learners participating in regular education "Book Clubs." *Reading Research Quarterly, 30,* 352–380.

Golden, J. M. (2000). *Storymaking in elementary and middle school classrooms: Constructing and interpreting narrative texts.* Mahwah, NJ: Erlbaum.

Guthrie, J. T., & Wigfield, A. (1997). Reading engagement: A rationale for theory and teaching. In J. T. Guthrie & A. Wigfield (Eds.), *Motivating readers through integrated instruction* (pp. 1–12). Newark, DE: International Reading Association.

Harré, R. (1984). *Personal being: A theory for individual psychology.* Cambridge, MA: Harvard University Press.

Highfield, K., & Folkert, J. (1997). Book Club: The content area connection. In S. I. McMahon & T. E. Raphael (Eds.), *The Book Club connection: Literacy learning and classroom talk* (pp. 286–298). New York: Teachers College Press.

Highfield, K. (1999). Evidence of literacy learning in a literature-based reading program. In T. E. Raphael & K. H. Au (Eds.), *Literacy based instruction: Reshaping the curriculum* (pp. 173–194). Norwood, MA: Christopher-Gordon.

Hoffman, J. V., & Roller, C. M. (2001). Preservice teacher preparation. *The IRA Excellence in Reading Teacher Preparation Commission's report: Current practices in reading teacher education at the undergraduate level in the United States* (pp. 32–79). Newark, DE: International Reading Association.

McMahon, S. I., Raphael, T. E., & Goatley, V. J., & Pardo, L. S. (Eds.). (1997). *The Book Club connection: Literacy learning and classroom talk.* New York: Teachers College Press.

Moats, L. C. (2000). *Whole language lives on: The illusion of balanced literacy.* Fordham Foundation Website, http://www.edexcellence.net/library/wholelang/moats.html

Mosenthal, J., Lipson, M., Mekkelsen, J., Russ, B., & Sortino, S. (2000). *Contexts and practices of successful schools within a standards-based environment* (Final Report Northeast and Regional Laboratory).

Polacco, P. (1994). *My redheaded older brother.* New York: Aladdin.

Raphael, T. E., Damphousse, K., Highfield, K., & Florio-Ruane, S. (in press, a). Understanding culture in our lives and work: Teachers' literature study in the Book Club Program. In P. R. Schmidt & P. B. Mosenthal (Eds.), *Literacy in the new age of pluralism and multiculturalism, Volume 9, Advances in reading/language research.* Greenwich, CT: Information Age.

Raphael, T. E., Florio-Ruane, S., & George, M. (in press, b). Book club plus: A conceptual framework to organize literacy instruction. *Language Arts.*

Raphael, T. E., Florio-Ruane, S., Kehus, M., George, M., Hasty, N., & Highfield, K. (2001). Thinking for ourselves: Literacy learning in a diverse teacher inquiry network. *Reading Teacher, 54,* 596–607.

Raphael, T. E., & Hiebert, E. H. (1996). *Creating an integrated approach to literacy instruction.* Ft. Worth, TX: Harcourt Brace.

Shotter, J. (1993). *Conversational realities.* London: Sage.

Spiro, R. J., Feltovich, P. J., Jacobson, M. J., & Coulson, R. L. (1995). Cognitive flexibility, constructivism, and hypertext: Random access instruction for advanced knowledge acquisition in ill-structured domains. In L. Steffe & J. Gale (Eds.), *Constructivism in education* (pp. 85–107). Hillsdale, N.J.: Erlbaum.

Spiro, R. J., & Jehng, J. C. (1990). Cognitive flexibility and hypertext: Theory and technology for the nonlinear and multidimensional traversal of complex subject matter. In D. Nix & R. J. Spiro (Eds.), *Cognition, education, and multimedia: Explorations in high technology* (pp. 163–205). Hillsdale, NJ: Erlbaum.

Stahl, S. A. (1999). Why innovations come and go (and mostly go): The case of whole language. *Educational Researcher, 28*(8), 13–22.

Stanovich, K. E. (1986). Matthew effects in reading: Some consequences of individual differences in the acquisition of literacy. *Reading Research Quarterly, 21,* 360–407.

Stanovich, K. E. (1998). Twenty-five years of research on the reading process: The grand synthesis and what it means for our field. In T. Shanahan & F. Rodriguez-Brown (Eds.), *National Reading Conference Yearbook, 47* (pp. 44–58). Chicago: National Reading Conference.

Taylor, B. M., Anderson, R. C., Au, K. H., & Raphael, T. E. (2000). Discretion in the translation of research to policy: A case from beginning reading. *Educational Re-*

searcher. 29, 16–26.

Taylor, B. M., Pearson, P. D., Clark, K., & Walpole, S. (2000). Effective schools and accomplished teachers: Lessons about primary grade reading instruction in low-income schools. *Elementary School Journal, 101,* 121–166.

Wells, G. (1993). *Changing schools from within: Creating communities of inquiry.* Portsmouth, NH: Heinemann.

Wells, G. (1999). *Dialogic inquiry: Toward a sociocultural practice and theory of education.* Cambridge, England: Cambridge University Press.

Zernike, K. (2000, August 25). Less training, more teachers: New math for staffing classes. *New York Times,* pp. A1, A23.

Literacy Policy and Policy Research That Make a Difference

Sheila W. Valencia
University of Washington

Karen K. Wixson
University of Michigan

We wrote this review while our country was in the throes of one of the most controversial presidential elections in our history. Although the outcome was unknown on December 2, 2000, what was certain, even on that date, was that education and education policy were at the top of both candidates' agendas. Whereas policy research dating back to the 1970s demonstrated that "policy can't mandate what matters" (McLaughlin, 1990), such findings have not shaken policy-makers' determination to instigate more and more educational policies. In fact, today 49 of 50 states have adopted content standards in reading and writing, 48 of 50 have enacted policies on statewide testing (Education Week, 2000), and the number of phonics bills introduced annually increased 900% between 1994 and 1997 (Patterson, 2000). But what do we really know about the effect of literacy policies and what do we know about the kind of policy research that has been conducted?

That was our assignment for this year's review of research—policy. Although at first glance, this one-word topic seems fairly proscribed, anyone who does policy-related research or reads in it or simply lives in our current educational environment knows this is no small domain. So, in preparation for this review, our first job was to understand and narrow our focus—what is included in policy research, what piece of it should we address, what sources should we use. We begin with a quick sense of the terrain to situate this review in the larger context.

Review Parameters: Dimensions and Sources

Dimensions

Policies vary along several dimensions. First, they vary in terms of *locus of authority*—where a policy originates or who has the real authority over it. So, policies related to national testing such as National Assessment of Educational Progress (NAEP) or special programs such as Title I and special education have their origin and are monitored at the federal level. However, for the most part, states have been the center of educational policy-making over the past two de-

National Reading Conference Yearbook, ***50***, *pp. 21–43.*

cades, since we have had a focus on standards (Linn, 2000; McGill-Franzen, 2000). Add to these policies on standards and assessment, state policies on teacher quality, class size, bilingual education, restructuring, and resource allocation and the power of states is clear. And here, at the state level, is where the pressure point—high stakes—is usually found. There are also policies at the district and classroom levels. At these levels, state policies often get translated into specific policies that influence daily classroom life—mandated curriculum, retention, professional development, special services, and policies on grading and grouping, just to name a few.

Second, policies also differ in *scope*—how far-reaching or ambitious they are. Some policies are fairly narrow, targeting a particular practice, program, or resource allocation, such as implementing new assessments or establishing cut scores for special programs. Others are broader and much more complex, with a systemic focus (Smith & O'Day, 1991), such as the reform package in Kentucky in which school organization, new content standards and assessments, professional development, governance, and finance are all included. The point of systemic reform is to create a coherent set of efforts rather than a series of discrete unrelated policies and actions.

Finally, policies differ in terms of their *focus*—what they target. For example, policies may focus on graduation requirements, organizational issues, specific groups of students, or curriculum. Amazingly, studies show that although the majority of reform efforts are proposed to improve student learning and teaching, most policies do not focus on the classroom. In fact, a study of more than 1,500 school districts found that fewer than 50% had policies focused on both curricular content and teaching (Shields & Knapp, 1997).

Obviously the policy landscape is vast and varied, requiring us to set some parameters for this review. We decided to focus on what McLaughlin (1992) describes as a generation of research on reform that began in the 1980s; it is focused on ambitious standards and has as its goal improved teaching practice. These policies vary in scope (some narrow, some complex) but for the most part they reside at the state level. As a result, the slice we cut for this review is standards-oriented state policies. We will not review specific policies related to Title I or special education—for those we refer you to McGill-Franzen's excellent chapter in the *Handbook of Reading Research* (McGill-Franzen, 2000). We focus here on literacy policies that target the broader population. And, we will not deal with the question of whether research *should* influence policy or the process of policy-making. These topics we leave to our braver colleagues and to different venues.

Sources

With regard to our sources, we did not use stories or newspaper clippings for this review. We relied on published pieces including books, articles, conceptual pieces, and technical reports from research projects and Centers. As a result, we do not deal with some of the "hottest" issues of the hour—the so-called Texas "miracle" (Haney, 2000; Hoffman, Assaf, & Paris, 2000), the impact of Proposition

227 (bilingual education in California), or the new literacy policies in California. There is simply not yet enough high-quality research available on these policies. And, as these new hot topics suggest, the policy ground has shifted and *is* shifting as we speak. Our review therefore is not only retrospective, as all reviews are, but it reflects policies that may now look quite different even though many of the studies we cite are from the last several years. This is simply the nature of a review and the nature of educational policy in this age of reform.

We begin with a brief rcview of the findings and the nature of current literacy policy research—a kind of survey of what we know and the kind of research we have. From there, we offer a model for thinking about policy research that is informed by the research. Then, we present two case studies compiled from the research to support this new and, we believe, useful model for us as literacy researchers and educators. These cases and this model lead to policies that can make a difference and to insights into how to improve literacy policy research.

Overview of Research

This review is informed by an analysis of approximately 50 policies studies related to literacy standards and assessment that we conducted for the *Handbook of Reading Research* (see Valencia & Wixson, 2000, for a complete list of studies reviewed). We begin here because standards and assessment are a major thrust of many state policies from this generation of reform. What did we find?

First, at a kind of meta-level, we found that it mattered whether the researchers were grounded in policy, measurement, or literacy. They targeted different audiences for their work and typically did not publish in the same places (see Table 1). Even their bibliographic citations had little overlap. In addition, they had different research questions, conceptual frameworks, methodologies, and perspectives on literacy. In our view, these are important differences because they ultimately shape what we learn from the research, limit the possibility of learning across perspectives, and influence policy.

Policy researchers, for example, typically focus on broad reforms involving standards, reorganization, governance and the like; literacy is simply one of the subject areas of the reforms they study. In fact, we found it difficult to identify policy studies that had enough information on literacy issues to include in our review. When they did, we often had to search to find the portions that were related to reading and writing. Policy researchers' questions typically focused on the system, and their data were gathered through surveys and interviews. When they focused on teachers, it was typically through self-reports of their practices rather than observations of classroom practice. That said, however, there is a new group of policy researchers who are more focused on subject-specific issues and classroom instruction than we have typically seen in the past. We return to these researchers and their work later.

Measurement researchers, as we might expect, were most interested in the assessment components of reform and were particularly concerned with validity issues and with the psychometric qualities of new assessments that are

Table 1

Sources of Literacy Policy Research

Policy
Educational Policy
Educational Evaluation & Policy Analysis
National Center for Research on Evaluation, Standards, and Student Testing (CRESST)
Consortium on Policy Research in Education (CPRE)
American Educational Research Journal
Assessment
Applied Measurement in Education
Educational Assessment
Educational Measurement: Issues & Practice
National Center for Research on Evaluation, Standards, and Student Testing (CRESST)
RAND
Literacy
NRC Yearbook
Reading Research Quarterly
Elementary School Journal
National Reading Research Center (NRRC)
Educational Assessment
Language Arts

needed for accountability and policy. For the most part, they relied on statistical analysis and, to some extent, self-reports, interviews, and artifacts to address their questions.

Literacy researchers generally asked questions about instruction and learning in relation to literacy research and theory. For example, do new standards and assessments result in better reading and writing instruction? Are reforms consistent with sound research and theory on literacy learning? Just as literacy was the vehicle for many policy studies, rather than a targeted area of study, policy was the vehicle for many literacy studies. Literacy researchers typically looked closely at actual classroom teaching practices and evidence of student learning, but for the most part they did not explore the policy context in any systematic or in-depth way. Policy provided the backdrop to their literacy research.

Looking beneath orientation and focus at the specific content of these studies, we found that, in general, policies that are focused on literacy standards and assessment *do* have an influence on teachers' beliefs and practices. However, the influence is not always in the expected or the desired direction. The effects of policies are mediated by a large number of factors such as teachers' knowledge, beliefs, and existing practices; the economic, social, philosophical, and political conditions of the school or district; the stakes attached to the policy; the specificity of the policy; and the quality of the support provided to teachers and administrators. It also appears that policy by itself is not sufficient to promote desired change; simply implementing new assessments or creating new standards does not insure improved teaching or learning. What is less clear, however, is just what it would take to improve teaching and learning. Although several studies suggest that discipline-specific professional development is important for policy to have the desired effect, we do not know much about successful professional development processes or the quality of those processes.

In sum, these studies suggest the need for more coordinated research on policy issues. There appears to be a trade-off between understanding the broader context of policy and specific understanding of how factors mediate its enactment in classrooms. These studies also clearly suggest the need to address specific subject-matter issues. There seems to be an almost tacit assumption among many policy and measurement researchers that whatever holds true for one subject matter will likely be the case for others.

As we broadened our search for this review beyond policy studies concerned with standards and assessment, we found converging evidence of the need for research to address two areas: (a) specific subject matter in policy research and (b) the tension between policy research viewed from the national, state, or district levels (what we label the "global view") and policy viewed from classrooms (what we label the "local view").

Most of us are well aware of the important role of subject matter in teaching and learning from the work of Schwab (1964) and Shulman (1987). However, several studies support the need to take on subject matter more directly in policy research. One is a case study by Spillane (2000), in which he tracked a teacher's response to both literacy and mathematics reform. Although this teacher was eager to improve her practice in both subjects and was in a supportive environment for learning, there were substantial differences in what and how she taught across subjects. Spillane posits that this teacher brought different resources—different understandings, dispositions, and commitments—to the reform in math and reading, and thus she experienced very different opportunities to learn about her own practice. Two other studies, one by Willingham and Cole (as cited in Linn, 2000) and the other by Linn (2000), demonstrated significant differences across achievement test scores and subtests scores in different subject areas, adding a psychometric perspective to the subject matter argument. In other words, subject area matters in policy work.

As to the tension between global-level and local-level views of policy, we can go back as early as the 1980s (i.e., Elmore & McLaughlin 1988; Sabatier & Mazmanian, 1980) to note that:

> Change is ultimately the problem of the smallest unit. At each point in the policy process, a policy is transformed as individuals interpret and respond to it. What actually is delivered or provided under the aegis of a policy depends finally on the individual at the end of the line. (McLaughlin, 1987, p. 174)

Although there seems to be widespread acknowledgment that teachers play a critical role in enacting policy, much of the policy research has continued to focus on the inputs (i.e., the various policies) and the expected outcomes, or outputs, leaving the working space between them unexplored. When that space is explored, it is often through analysis of surface features such as teacher qualifications, school structure, or time spent on particular activities. We argue that researchers must do a better job finding out what is going on inside that space, inside the "black box," where the effects of policy are studied in terms of the *quality* of teaching and learning (see Figure 1).

We cannot continue to expect that inputs alone will stimulate change or continue to generate more policies, whatever they may be (e.g., class size, restructuring, teacher qualification, curriculum) and expect they will make a difference. The research reviewed above suggests policies cannot stand alone nor are they enacted in a vacuum. Teachers and administrators are not simply conduits for policy. Similarly, we cannot continue to focus only on outputs as the indicators of change, such as student achievement, numbers of students graduating, teacher knowledge, curriculum alignment, or even teacher behaviors such as topics covered, time spent teaching, or self-reported teaching strategies. They are important, to be sure, but to focus solely on these would be missing how real improvement in learning is created. We offer three arguments and sample studies to support why it is problematic to judge policy efficacy by focusing only on outputs.

Focus on High-Stakes Test Scores

We have a great deal of evidence dating back 10 to 15 years which points to the negative consequences of high-stakes testing: narrowing of the curriculum; overemphasis on basic skills; excessive time spent on test preparation; exclusion of low achieving or special education students from testing (Allington & McGill-Franzen, 1992; Nolen, Haladyna, & Hass, 1992; Resnick & Resnick, 1992; Shepard 1991). More recently, Linn (2000) identified new evidence that test scores may not reflect true student learning. Looking at state test scores over 12 years, he found that results can give an inflated impression of true performance when the same

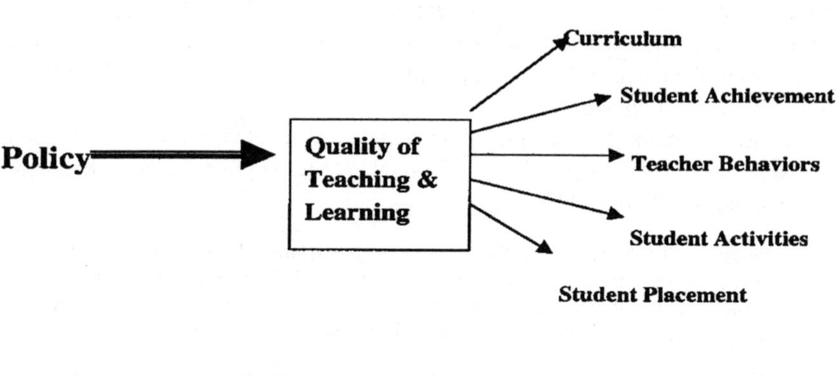

Figure 1

test has been in place for a number of years. Specifically, he found that performance appeared to be increasing when the same form of the test was used over time, but when the test form was changed, student performance dropped off significantly when judged by comparable national norms. Interestingly, just 2 years after the new form was implemented, there was a sharp increase in student performance, a clear demonstration of teaching to a particular test rather than teaching for genuine learning.

Linn (2000) also found that different cut-scores, or performance standards, can send mixed messages about performance. For example, he demonstrated that the percent of students passing state assessments was substantially higher than the percent of students scoring at the proficient level on the fourth-grade NAEP reading test. For example, 88% of Wisconsin students met the state standard in reading but only 35% scored at the proficient level on NAEP. Although the state standard was intended to identify students who may need remediation and the NAEP standard was intended to represent "solid academic performance," which are very different standards, it is obvious that we would draw different inferences about the quality of student learning from each test. This pattern of differences across tests has been replicated recently in a high-profile study of test scores in Texas. Klein, Hamilton, McCaffrey, and Stecher (2000) found that reading gains on the Texas Assessment of Academic Skills (TASS) were several times greater than they were on NAEP. Just what do these tests measure and what do their results mean? However, beyond these problems of validity and generalizability, which certainly merit attention, is the added problem that scores do not reveal what is happening in classrooms to produce the scores. Essentially, a focus on outputs distracts us from looking at the quality of teaching and learning.

Focus on Change

A second reason to question outputs is the tendency of policy-makers to focus on change—for example a change in the curriculum covered, or time students spend on particular tasks, or even teachers' instructional practices such as working with small groups. Change is not necessarily improvement. It can be a sign of "instability, indecision or lack of vision" (Shields & Knapp, 1997). Conversely, lack of change may not be a sign of poor quality teaching or learning.

A good example of danger of focusing on change is found in research conducted in Vermont by Lipson, Mosenthal, and colleagues who examined instructional quality under Vermont's state portfolio policy (Lipson & Mosenthal, 1997; Lipson, Mosenthal, & Mekkelsen, 1996; Mosenthal, Lipson, Mekkelsen, Daniels, & Jiron, 1996). Their classroom observations revealed that some teachers, those who already used process writing and portfolios, changed little under the new portfolio policy; they did not need to change in order to align their practices with the new policy. On the other hand, they argue that what might appear to be fairly small changes (e.g., students developing ownership in writing) set the stage for more profound changes in instruction over time; that a small change may be quite significant.

Sometimes changes appear more meaningful than they are. For example, a longitudinal study of restructuring carried out by the Consortium for Policy Research in Education (CPRE) (Elmore, Peterson, & McCarthy, 1996) found that although all the teachers and administrators in restructured schools had complied with policies and had changed school structures (i.e., grouping practices, more professional development, shared decision-making), classroom observations revealed these changes had little relationship to changes in teaching practices. And several other studies (Cohen & Ball, 1990a; Heaton, 1993; Mayer, 1999) have demonstrated that even teachers' self-reports of change in teaching practices are often at odds with their observed epistemological stances and actual instructional practices. Note that in all these studies, the researchers had to go beyond tallies of time or activities or even self-reports to get at the quality of teaching. They had to go into the classrooms and they had to bring subject matter expertise to their analyses.

The Moral Imperative

A third reason for caution in using outputs is put forward by Black and Wiliam (1998a, 1998b). Using their research on classroom assessment in England and an extensive review of related research, they assert that the prime locus for raising achievement is the classroom. They argue that it is strange and simply unfair to leave the workings inside the black box entirely up to teachers on their own. In fact, their work demonstrates that teachers who are supported in learning how to use classroom assessment to make instructional decisions and to provide feedback to their students actually produce significant gains on tradition achievement tests, especially for their low-achieving students. This call to help teachers focus on the quality of instruction, what we name here the "moral imperative," is also recommended by the recent National Research Council report on Title I Testing and Assessment (Elmore & Rothman, 1999). The report cites several studies that question the effectiveness of policy focused only on standards, assessment, and accountability. They argue that policies must be tied directly to building the capacity of teachers and administrators to improve instruction. The National Commission on Teaching and America's Future (Darling-Hammond, 1997) draws a similar conclusion.

Beyond the Black Box

If our argument for focusing on the black box, on the quality of teaching and learning, seems rather obvious, as it must to those who work in classrooms, let us assure you that it is not obvious to many who do policy research. For example, among the articles we read for this review was a summary of research on new Title I programs that focused on achievement test scores, characteristics of the schools and districts, and organizational structures. Of the 13 studies in this summary, only 2 actually looked at instruction. In another study, researchers asked various people to evaluate test items as a way to judge the quality of what was taught in schools. Clearly, looking inside the black box is not common practice in policy research. It takes time and subject matter expertise, and it is difficult to do on a large scale or under tightly controlled experimental conditions.

Perhaps one of the first close looks inside the black box in our field came with Richard Allington's seminal work on the quality of instruction for Title I students, which called into question the traditional reliance on compliance with the rules and regulations as a measure of effectiveness. Instead, he looked at the quality of the instruction these students received and, as we all know, he found that instruction lacking (Allington, 1983; Allington & McGill-Franzen, 1989; Allington, Stuetzel, Shake, & Lamarche, 1986).

But we do not want to stop here. We want to go further to suggest that looking inside the black box, at the quality of teaching and learning, is not enough. We must look at the contexts in which the teaching and learning exist—the policy environments that surround and filter influences on teaching and learning. This is how we can bridge the divide between the global and local perspectives and between generic and subject-specific teaching and learning that we identified at the beginning of this review.

To make this point, we rely on a model developed by Michael Knapp and colleagues at the Center for Teaching and Policy at the University of Washington (Center for Teaching and Policy, 2000) and recent research that has informed the model (see Figure 2). This graphic, which we have adapted, places the black box of "quality of teaching and learning" in the context of conditions and forces that

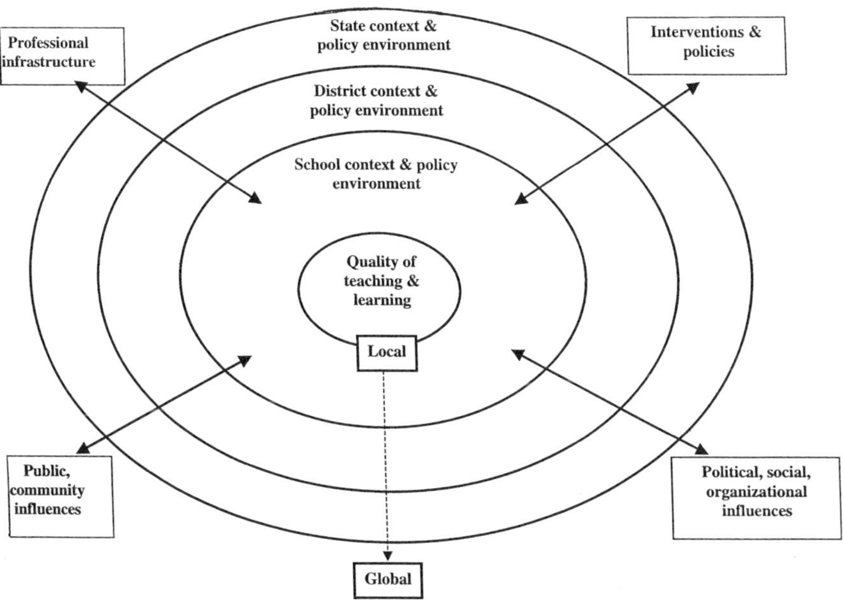

The quality of teaching and learning in context.
From: Center for the Study of Teaching and Policy, University of Washington.

Figure 2

have the most potential to influence what happens in the classroom. Classrooms reside in schools, which reside in districts, which reside in states. Note the term "policy environment" which connotes the array of policies past and present, the contexts from which those policies emerge, the coherence of the policies, and responses to those policies that all come together to create a policy environment. The model also reminds us that policy passes through many filters on its way to the classroom, all of which can have a significant influence on the quality of teaching and learning. Policy is not simply handed over; it is shaped by the events, conditions, and players inside and outside the classroom. Furthermore, the filters are bidirectional and interactive. For example, teachers shape how policies are defined in schools, and districts influence state and community perceptions and support for new initiatives; ultimately practice influences policy itself (Cohen & Ball, 1990b). Taken together, these contexts can support or undermine the policy goals. Consequently, what we need in order to understand the effects of policy is research that considers these contexts, that tries to understand the influence of these conditions and interactions among them on the quality of teaching and learning.

This model reflects much of the research we have reviewed so far. But it is especially influenced by the work of two groups: (a) David Cohen, Deborah Ball and their colleagues and former students (e.g., Cohen & Ball, 1990a & 1990b; Cohen & Barnes, 1993; Cohen & Hill, 2000; Jennings, 1996; Spillane, 1998) and (b) Michael Knapp and his associates (Knapp & Associates, 1995; Knapp, Bamburg, Ferguson, & Hill, 1998). In general, these researchers have merged policy and subject matter expertise, the global and local, to study teaching quality. Their work also reminds of us of the reciprocal relationship between policy and teaching—that teachers are at once the targets and agents of change.

A little thought experiment might illuminate how this model can enhance research on the relationship between policy and the quality of teaching and learning. Imagine research on a first-grade class-size reduction policy aimed at improving reading achievement. Regardless of whether the outputs indicated that student reading achievement improved or declined, we would need to ask questions like the following to judge the effectiveness of the policy: What does reading instruction look like in these classrooms—the materials, curriculum, pedagogy, classroom organization, and instructional discourse? What do we know about the qualifications and background of the teachers—certified, previous experience at primary grades, beliefs about reading instruction, and knowledge? What kind of professional development was provided at the state, district, and school levels? What do we know about the curriculum being implemented (e.g., type, mandated or self-selected)? What about teachers' role in selecting the curriculum? What kinds of assessments are in place—high-stakes tests, portfolios, and so on?

With the review of research and this conceptual model as background, we now move to two case studies compiled from research representing a variety of levels, from a more global to a more local perspective (see broken line in Figure 2). Research at the more global end of the continuum is usually focused more on policy questions than on subject matter analyses and rarely includes classroom observation. Research in the middle of this continuum often reflects a combined interest in policy and subject matter issues and often includes some level of classroom observation. Research at the more local end of the continuum is typically more concerned with subject matter issues than general policy questions and relies heavily on classroom observation.

We examined the literature representing a number of state and district policy contexts before finding two that had a relatively full complement of studies spanning the global-local continuum. The states we selected for our case studies are Michigan and Kentucky. The policy contexts investigated in these two states are also distinct enough to provide some interesting contrasts. As each case study unfolds, what appears are some instances in which difficulties in interpretation arise because research does not situate itself in both local and global contexts. In other instances, there are studies that try to understand the constellation of influences that converge on policy implementation.

Before presenting the case studies, a few caveats are in order. First, when a full range of research is available for a particular policy context, it is likely the policy context has been in place for some period of time. As a result, the policy contexts studied in Michigan and Kentucky are not necessarily those that are currently in place. A related issue is that the layering of studies from the most global to the most local does not always reflect the chronology of findings within a particular policy context. For that reason, it is important to attend closely to the time frames in which data were collected. Finally, as literacy policy researchers who have worked in Michigan, we want to make clear that our only role in the research reviewed here was as informants.

Case Study 1: Michigan

We begin our case study of Michigan with a description of the policy environment at the time of the research we review. According to Goertz, Floden, and O'Day (1995), three key factors characterized the policy context in Michigan at that time: (a) local educators' desire to redirect reading curriculum away from basic skills to higher order processes, (b) state government's desire to make the education community more accountable, and (c) the historical use of organizations outside the state department of education to communicate and implement reform efforts.

The literacy policy context was framed by Michigan's Essential Goals and Objectives in reading and state assessments derived from these objectives. The reading objectives in place at the time of the research presented here were developed jointly between the state and the Michigan Reading Association (MRA) and adopted by the state in 1986. These objectives reflected a "new" vision of reading that was emerging from the professional community at that time, one that recognized comprehension as the ultimate goal of reading and characterized the reading process as interactive, constructive, and dynamic.

Although the education profession in Michigan played a major role in defining the content of the state's standards and assessments, those outside the profession determined which policies should drive education reform and in what direction. For two decades, Michigan used a low-stakes assessment based on the Essential Goals and Objectives to communicate content standards and to encourage changes in local curriculum. This approach of "friendly persuasion" fit the state's strong tradition of local control but did not produce the type of workforce Michigan businesses needed.

Responding to calls from the business community and the governor for greater accountability in education, the legislature enacted Public Act 25 (PA 25) of 1990 requiring local school boards to prepare and distribute annual education reports. PA 25 also called for voluntary implementation of the state model core curriculum and required districts to report on the status of their curriculum compared to the state's model core. In the year following the passage of PA 25, the legislature called for a high-stakes high school graduation test. Although school improvement plans were to include professional development, there were no specific state policies on professional development for reading.

More Global Emphasis

We begin our review of research with a large-scale policy study by Goertz et al. (1995) that looked at reading in Michigan and writing in two other states. The stated purposes for this study included examining district, school, and teacher responses to state reform policies in a small number of reforming schools and districts, and studying the capacity of the educational system to support education reform. The findings are based on data gathered from interviews and surveys conducted in 1993–94 in actively reforming elementary and middle schools located in three states—California, Michigan, and Vermont. Although we can distill information about language arts from this report, it is important to remember that it is about systemic reform, not about language arts per se.

The portion of the study dealing directly with language arts reform in Michigan examines the degree to which teachers' reports on their instruction were consistent with explicit or implicit curriculum recommendations in state policies such as the model core curriculum and state assessments. The data indicate that Michigan teachers emphasized content matching the "meaning-centered" view of Michigan's Essential Goals and Objectives in Reading (1986). For example, both elementary and middle school teachers in the study indicated that they spent over 3 hours per week on comprehension strategies and having students respond to what they read, and barely over ½ hour per week on basic skills, such as phonics and word recognition. They also indicated spending the largest amount of time in whole-class activities. In addition, both elementary and middle school teachers spent close to 50% of their instructional time using literature trade books and no more than about a third of their time with reading basals. Goertz et al. concluded that the call for school districts to incorporate state goals and objectives in their own curriculum led the two districts in this study to review, revise, and/or develop their curricula, and the impending requirement that students pass a test for a state-endorsed diploma made the state assessments a more important aspect of teachers' professional lives.

However, a closer look at the two elementary schools in Michigan revealed important similarities and differences with the general findings. Although both schools described their reading instruction as shifting from decoding to understanding, teachers in School #2 indicated that they relied far more heavily on their literature-based reading series than did teachers in School #1, who reported using other instructional materials such as trade books, book clubs, and subject-area reading an average of 80% of the time. Also, teachers in School #1 reported that half of their instructional time was spent with students working in pairs or doing individual work, whereas teachers in School #2 reported spending two-thirds of their time in whole-class lessons and discussion.

What is important here are the differences between the aggregated data and what was learned upon closer examination of the individual schools. No doubt, these differences are what led Goertz et al. to conclude that when state policy instruments send messages that are in line with what educators are hearing from other sources, they can be used to inform changes in instruction. Although teachers indicated that they had been influenced by state policy instruments such as curriculum and assessments, these state influences were by no means the only, or even the most important, influences on practice. Teachers reported that their own knowledge and beliefs about the subject matter and their students, for example, generally had a larger influence than state policies.

A second global study by Spillane (1996) provides further evidence that state policies play out differently in different educational contexts; however, in this study, the emphasis is on districts instead of schools. Using interviews to examine the impact of Michigan reading policy on both an urban and a suburban district, Spillane found that the suburban district used the revision of the state reading test as a lever to move in a different direction from the basic skills orientation of the central administrators. In contrast, the state's reading policy did not figure prominently in the reading program developed in the urban district. For example, a new basal reading program was mandated accompanied by a traditional workbook that provided students with drill in reading skills. Administrators made no effort to revise district policy on student assessment despite significant revisions of the state's reading test.

Combining Global and Local Emphases

A study by Standerford (1997) represents another layer of investigation and highlights the tensions between classroom and district practice within Michigan's policy context. She studied two small districts from 1988 until 1991. Both districts formed reading curriculum committees in an effort to interpret the state reading policy and design an official district response. To understand what happened in these districts, Standerford observed both the curriculum committees and the classroom practices of the teachers on these committees.

Standerford's results indicated that the district rules, objectives, players, audiences, and time frames made participation in the district effort quite separate from both the state policy and from the classroom changes that individual teachers were making. Districts' responses to state reading reform appeared to be focused primarily on compliance with little attention to the substance of the policy. In contrast, the teachers made changes in their classroom practice based on their individual professional development activities, but were often unsure just how those changes fit with the state policy.

Standerford concluded that state and district policies had influenced the teachers' efforts by making them aware that changes were expected in reading instruction, but had not made clear for the teachers what those instructional changes were, nor offered much support for their efforts to figure that out for themselves. As teachers learned more about the new ideas, they gradually changed the enacted curriculum in their classrooms. Yet, those instructional changes were minimally represented in the written curriculum that they produced as members of the district committees because their roles and objectives were defined differently at the district and classroom levels.

More Local Emphasis

Research by Jennings (1996) and Spillane and Jennings (1997) moves even closer to the local end of the continuum. Looking at nine second- and fifth-grade teachers in the suburban district Spillane (1996) reported on previously, Spillane and Jennings (1997) found that the extent to which teachers' practices reflected the district's literacy initiative depended on how well the reforms were elaborated by the district.

Initial data analysis suggested significant uniformity in language arts practice among the nine classrooms and offered striking evidence that the district's proposals for language arts reform were finding their way into practice. For example, they found that all nine teachers were using literature-based reading programs and trade books, engaging in activities such as Writer's Workshop, and focusing on comprehension over skills-based instruction. However, closer inspection of the observation data suggested differences across classrooms that were not captured by their analytical framework. This led Spillane and Jennings to a revised analytical frame focused on classroom tasks and discourse patterns that revealed important "below the surface" differences in pedagogy. Comparing results using the two analytical frameworks, Spillane and Jennings showed that it is relatively easy to arrive at very different conclusions about the extent to which reforms calling for more ambitious pedagogy have permeated practice.

Jennings (1996) also conducted an in-depth case study of three Michigan teachers, one of whom taught in the suburban school reported on previously. Jennings found that the ideas and practices the teachers brought to their learning influenced how and what they learned from the policy. However, she also noted the complexity of figuring out teachers' prior knowledge as well as how it shaped their learning. For example, two of the teachers brought ideas about reading and reading practices consistent with the reform, yet they learned very different things because they had different dispositions toward the policy. One of the two brought an eagerness to see the policy as something from which to learn and, as a result, did learn new ideas from it. The other did not learn because she was reluctant to see the policy as something from which she could learn rather than a reinforcement of what she already knew.

Spillane and Jennings (1997) argue that if reforms are meant to help all students encounter language arts in a more demanding and authentic manner, then policy analysts cannot rely solely on indicators such as the materials and the activities teachers use. We would add that to be able to explore these issues effectively, one must understand a great deal about the subject matter that is the focus of the reform. Spillane and Jennings have amassed a great deal of knowledge about language arts and language arts instruction over their years of studying language arts reform. We believe that without this knowledge, they might never have even seen the differences that led them to develop new analytical frameworks or to probe teachers' understandings and ultimately to uncover important differences in teachers' learning and classroom practice.

What have we learned through the juxtaposition of studies, from global to local, about the impact of Michigan reading reform in a relatively low-stakes policy environment? Aggregated data from teacher surveys suggest alignment of practice with state policy. However, a closer look at districts, schools, and classrooms reveals important differences in practices. Although the policy clearly had an impact on districts, the response varied from substantive change consistent with the policy, to superficial compliance, to staying the course. Furthermore, teachers' practices within these districts also varied ranging from practices that were surprisingly more consistent with the intent of the state policy than was their district's response, to superficial changes that did not reflect the true intent of the policy. From the more local perspective, these studies suggest that reading policy and recommended curriculum were not uniformly implemented in Michigan, a finding that may have been influenced by the low-stakes nature of the situation and the lack of attention to professional development in the policies. Although districts seemed to have the potential to mediate teachers' practices, they were not automatically influential or helpful; when district response was congruent with state policy and when districts worked to elaborate policy, practice was more likely to be positively influenced. Although there is a relatively full complement of studies in Michigan across layers of investigation, there is also a serious lack of information on how the various responses to the policy affected student learning.

Case Study 2: Kentucky

Now we turn to Kentucky, a state with a very different policy context. In what has become an historic decision, the Kentucky Supreme Court ruled in June 1989 that the public school system was "unconstitutional" because every child in Kentucky was not being provided with an equal opportunity for an adequate education. As a result, the court ordered the state to establish a more equitable system and to monitor it on a continuing basis. The Kentucky Education Reform Act (KERA) of 1990 resulted from this court decision.

KERA represents one of the most comprehensive pieces of educational reform legislation ever enacted in the United States. It was designed to change the state's entire educational system and address nearly every aspect of public education including administration, governance and finance, school organization, accountability, professional development, curriculum, and assessment. The areas that have received the most research attention, at least with regard to literacy practices, are assessment and professional development.

As part of its charge to enact KERA, the Kentucky Department of Education (KDE) developed a multifaceted professional development program to help schools and teachers achieve the reform goals. In 1994, the legislature allocated 65% of all state professional development funds directly to schools. The KDE also developed a new statewide assessment system known as the Kentucky Instructional Results Information System (KIRIS). KIRIS, which has recently been reenvisioned as the Commonwealth Accountability Testing System (CATS), was designed to be both performance-based and high stakes and included year-long portfolios in mathematics and writing. KIRIS assessments were aggregated to determine a school score, which in turn became part of an accountability index used to determine how much gain a school needed to receive cash rewards and avoid state sanctions. The emphasis placed on the accountability index led many to equate KIRIS more with accountability than with performance-based assessment, and, in time, blur the distinctions between KIRIS and KERA that were clear in the early 1990s.

More Global Emphasis

Koretz and his colleagues (Koretz, Barron, Mitchell, & Stecher, 1996) used telephone and written surveys to examine the influence of KIRIS assessments; information about language arts is embedded in the responses of the elementary teachers in this study. The teachers reported that they supported the new assessments and even changed some of their practices such as spending more time on writing, although they felt that more specific curriculum frameworks would be helpful. On the negative side, however, they reported spending considerable time in test preparation activities and a tendency to deemphasize untested material, and they did not support the use of test results for accountability. In addition, teachers' expectations rose for high-achieving students rather than low-achieving students, and they credited student gains to specific test practice and test familiarity rather than to true improvements in capabilities. So, we learn that the assessment policy was having both positive and negative influence on teachers.

A more recent CRESST/RAND study by Stecher, Barron, Kaganoff, and Goodwin (1998) provides more of a subject matter emphasis, but still focuses primarily on general policy questions. Reporting on the results of a 1996–97 survey, this research was designed to examine contrasts between practices that were consistent with Kentucky's view of standards-based education and practices that were consistent with traditional views of education. Responses left little doubt that KERA and KIRIS had effects on writing curriculum and instruction in Kentucky. Writing teachers aligned themselves philosophically with the standards-based approach but continued to combine traditional and standards-based practices. Another interesting finding was that Kentucky teachers rated professional development highly and felt well prepared to teach most aspects of writing.

Stecher et al. (1998) observed that despite the alignment among the standards, KIRIS assessments, state curriculum materials, and training opportunities, there were few associations between KIRIS gains and reported classroom practices. They concluded there was "no convincing evidence that a particular set of actions or policies would produce higher scores. If there is such a pattern it would appear to include both standards-based and traditional approaches" (p. 85). The authors were disappointed not to have found stronger links between reported practices and student performance. They speculated that perhaps Kentucky educators have not found a practice or constellation of practices that consistently promotes higher achievement.

Another global study by McDonnell and Choisser (1997) used interviews and teachers' assignments instead of self-reports as a measure of teaching practice in social studies, math, and language arts; they produced results similar to the Stecher et al. (1998) study. The McDonnell study found that teachers had added new instructional strategies such as having students work in groups, but that they were still using traditional approaches as well and had not fundamentally changed the depth and sophistication of the content they were teaching. For example, few of the teachers' assignments included the state learning goals that stress thinking critically, developing solutions to complex problems, and organizing information to understand concepts.

Combining Global and Local Emphases

In contrast to the previous group of studies, Bridge (1994) combined an emphasis on general policy issues with an emphasis on literacy instruction by examining the reading and language arts instruction in Kentucky's newly mandated primary schools. A structured observation guide was used to determine the extent to which teachers' practices reflected the literacy practices recommended by the KDE. The results supported the Stecher and McDonnell global findings that teachers were using a combination of newly recommended and traditional practices, and they add important detail about teachers' instructional practices in reading and language arts. For example, a finding that teachers combined traditional approaches with newer ones was supported by observational information such as

> . . . in one classroom in which the observer reported that there were about 3,000 books, the teacher had children complete skills charts together and dictate sentences with "T" words. At the same time, children were working on a project related to the Caldecott books.

What is clear from this example is that, as in the Michigan research, the schemes used for analysis and observation, and researchers' definitions of traditional and reform-oriented practices have a significant impact on the findings and conclusions.

Although in a subsequent classroom study Bridge, Compton-Hall, and Cantrell (1997) found changes in the amount and quality of writing activities compared with a 1982 study, the authors were reluctant to attribute the changes to the reform because most teachers had learned a great deal about process writing in the ensuing 13 years. The results of these two studies leave unclear the impact of the policy on classroom literacy practice.

More Local Emphasis

The last set of studies provides more of a local perspective on literacy practices within the context of the Kentucky reforms. Callahan (1997) conducted an ethnographic case study of a high school English department faced with implementing state portfolios in 1992–93, the second year of the mandate. This research demonstrates how local context interacted with the state's emphasis on accountability to work against fulfilling the intent of the mandate to both improve teaching and learning and hold schools accountable for student learning.

Unlike some other districts where the responsibility for enacting the portfolio mandate was shared among teachers and administrators, the principal of this high school charged the English department with this task. This decision, combined with the fact that this was the school's first experience with portfolios, led the English teachers to perceive the portfolio as a test of their competence as a department and of the reputation of the school. Individually, the English teachers acknowledged that they were asking for more and different kinds of writing from their students than they had in the past and were using scoring criteria to discuss writing with their students. In addition, as a department, they recognized that *all* students needed the opportunity to write personal narratives, stories, and poems and were exploring ways to provide these opportunities. The portfolio mandate was not, however, creating the kind of classroom writing experiences envisioned by KDE in which students are engaged in a continual process of goal setting, writing, self-reflection, and portfolio assessment. In focusing on the portfolio content and scoring requirements, the English teachers were responding to KDE's emphasis on these features and their principal's decision to give them the responsibility for this visible element of their school's accountability score. Their individual classroom practices were not under scrutiny, but their ability to follow the portfolio content requirements and scoring guide was. Consequently, teachers put their energy into the visible, procedural elements of the high-stakes assessment rather than deeper level changes in instruction.

Finally, focusing on exemplary case studies in the larger, multi-year CRESST/RAND study by Stecher et al. (1998), Borko, Elliott, and Uchiyama (1999) concluded that the case study schools and teachers provided "existence proof" that

Kentucky's approach to professional development can provide the resources needed to support statewide, standards-based educational reform. Nevertheless, Wolf and McIver's (1999) brief case study of Mr. Bass, an exemplary seventh-grade writing teacher in one of the case study schools, revealed that the basic tension between best practices in the classroom and preparing students for the demands of externally mandated portfolios still existed 5 years after Callahan gathered her data. This comment from Mr. Bass clearly illustrates this problem:

> I'm responsible for the on demand. I'm responsible for the open response. I'm responsible for the portfolio. And doggone it, there are times that—Boy, this is really strange. Because of KERA, I changed my style of teaching to a more workshop-oriented approach. But because of KIRIS testing, I'm not allowed to truly implement that approach. (p. 406)

The juxtaposition of studies focused on different levels of analysis offers insight into the impact of KERA and KIRIS on writing instruction. Within this relatively high-stakes policy context, the research suggests that state policy had an impact at both the school and teacher levels, but not always in ways researchers judged to be consistent with the reform. For example, several studies suggest that although there was change, teachers were not yet "up to speed" in their instructional practices; they combined traditional and reform-based strategies.

The combination of high stakes and an extensive professional development program from the state was likely responsible for the greater impact on teachers in Kentucky than in Michigan. Yet, the collective evidence suggests that the dual goals of the reform for accountability and for improving teaching and learning often worked at odds with each other. Overall, as in Michigan, there was little research on the relation between teachers' practices and student learning; unlike the Michigan case, however, we know little about the district role in the Kentucky reform.

Conclusions and Implications

We focus our conclusions and implications on both what we have learned about literacy policies that are likely to make a difference and what we have learned about the nature of the research.

The literature reviewed here suggests that to be effective, literacy policies need to address several issues. First, policies must be educative (Cohen & Barnes, 1993); that is, they must take into account the learning required of enactors. Policies must be more than mandates; they must attend to the new learning required by people and systems at all levels. Second, policies must also include provisions for in-depth professional development for teachers and administrators that are coordinated at the state level. This means partnering with local educational agencies to ensure the funding, support materials, and guidance needed for local level enactors at district, school, and classroom levels. Finally, policies must also address the problem of developing accountability systems that do not interfere with the desired improvements in teaching and learning. Such systems will most likely involve multiple indicators of achievement and shared responsibility for data collection at classroom, school, district, state, and national levels.

This review also provides some insights into the nature of literacy policy research. The most obvious conclusion is that literacy policy research needs to use a layered approach of complementary studies conducted at all levels, from global to local, within the policy environment. At the same time, such studies should incorporate multiple perspectives, including those of both policy and literacy researchers. If we only have aggregated data, it is clear that we can be misled about the impact of state policy—in either direction. Alternatively, if we only have classroom observation data, we cannot understand the relations between state policy and responses at the district, school, and teacher levels.

The nature of more global research demands that teaching practice be evaluated in terms of self-reports or other proxies for teaching without situating them within the contexts of the classroom, school, and district. From the classroom-based studies we gain much needed detail about what it is teachers are doing within the larger contexts of their classrooms and schools. Looking across the continuum of studies raises questions about researchers' expectations with regard to literacy instruction and the validity/utility of the schemes used to characterize teaching practices or their proxies. It is questionable that counting up instances of somewhat discrete entities representing either more or less desirable practice can tell us much about the effectiveness of the policy in improving teaching and learning. The whole of teaching practice may be more than the sum of its parts.

Literacy policy research needs to probe deeply into the relations among particular classroom contexts, teacher practices, and specific types of student learning rather than simply focusing on test scores or aggregated data. Consequently, it is essential to address what counts as quality teaching and learning in literacy. This review revealed the lack of consensus, even among literacy researchers, as to what constitutes quality or aligned literacy teaching and learning and, as a result, it raises questions about the ways researchers evaluate practice. This is a problem that needs to be dealt with directly and systematically within the literacy domain or it will continue to undermine our ability to say much of anything that is meaningful about the impact of policy on literacy teaching and learning. In our view, the more detailed the research data, the more likely we are to be able to judge for ourselves other researchers' conclusions.

Clearly, finding ways to understand the effects of literacy policy is not simple. We owe it to ourselves and to our students not to oversimplify the questions or answers. Ultimately if we take this difficult road we can discover literacy policy and policy research that make a difference.

References

Allington, R. L. (1983). The reading instruction provided readers of differing ability. *Elementary School Journal, 83,* 548–559.

Allington, R. L., & McGill-Franzen, A. (1989). School response to reading failure: Chapter I and special education students in grades 2, 4, and 8. *Elementary School Journal, 89,* 529–542.

Allington, R. L., & McGill-Franzen, A. (1992). Does high stakes testing improve school effectiveness? *Spectrum, 10,* 3–12.

Allington, R. C., Stuetzel, H., Shake, M. C., & Lamarche, S. (1986). What is remedial reading? A descriptive study. *Reading Research and Instruction, 26,* 15–30.

Black, P., & William, D. (1998a). Assessment and classroom learning. *Assessment in Education, 5*(1), 7–74.

Black, P., & William, D. (1998b). Inside the black box: Raising standards through classroom assessment. *Phi Delta Kappan, 80,* 139–148.

Borko, H., Elliott, R., & Uchiyama, K. (1999). *Professional development: A key to Kentucky's reform effort* (CSE Tech. Rep. No. 512). Los Angeles: National Center for Research on Evaluation, Standards, and Student Testing, University of California.

Bridge, C. A. (1994). Implementing large scale change in literacy instruction. In C. Kinzer & D. Leu (Eds.), *Multidimensional aspects of literacy research, theory, and practice.* Forty-third yearbook of the National Reading Conference (pp. 257–265). Chicago: National Reading Conference.

Bridge, C. A., Compton-Hall, M., & Cantrell, S. C. (1997). Classroom writing practices revisited: The effects of statewide reform on writing instruction. *Elementary School Journal, 98,* 151–170.

Callahan, S. (1997). Tests worth taking?: Using portfolios for accountability in Kentucky. *Research in the Teaching of English, 31,* 295–336.

Center for the Study of Teaching and Policy. (2000). *Mid-term review materials* (p. 7). University of Washington: Center for the Study of Teaching and Policy.

Cohen, D. K., & Ball, D. L. (1990a) Policy and practice: An overview. *Educational Evaluation and Policy Analysis, 12,* 347–353.

Cohen, D. K., & Ball, D. L. (1990b). Relations between policy and practice: A commentary. *Educational Evaluation and Policy Analysis, 12,* 249–256.

Cohen, D. K., & Barnes, C. A. (1993). Pedagogy and policy. In D. K. Cohen, M. W. McLaughlin, & J. E. Talbert (Eds.), *Teaching for understanding: Challenges for policy and practice* (pp. 207–239). San Francisco: Jossey-Bass.

Cohen, D. K., & Hill, H. C. (2000). Instructional policy and classroom performance: The mathematics reform in California. *Teachers College Record, 102,* 294–343.

Darling-Hammond, L. (1997). *Doing what matters most: Investing in quality teaching.* New York: National Commission on Teaching and America's Future.

Education Week (2000). Quality Counts 2000. *Education Week, 19*(18), 72–75.

Elmore, R. F., Peterson, P. L., & McCarthy, S. J. (1996). *Restructuring in the classroom: Teaching, learning, and school organization.* San Francisco: Jossey-Bass.

Elmore, R. F., & McLaughlin, M. W. (1988). *Steady work: Policy, practice, and the reform of American education.* Santa Monica, CA: RAND.

Elmore, R. F., & Rothman, R. (Eds.). (1999). *Testing, teaching, and learning: A guide for states and school districts.* Washington DC: National Academy Press.

Goertz, M. E., Floden, R. E., & O'Day, J. (1995). *Studies of education reform: systemic reform.(Vol. 1): Findings and conclusions.* New Brunswick, NJ: Consortium for Policy Research in Education, Rutgers University.

Haney, W. (2000). The myth of the Texas miracle in education. *Education Policy Analysis and Archives, 8*(41). Available: <http:// epaa.asu/epaa/v8n41>

Heaton, R. (1993). Who is minding the mathematics content? A case study of a fifth-grade teacher. *Elementary School Journal, 93,* 153–162.

Hoffman, J. V., Assaf, L. C., & Paris, S. G. (2000). High-stakes testing in reading: Today in Texas, tomorrow? *Reading Teacher, 54,* 482–499.

Jennings, N. E. (1996). *Interpreting policy in real classrooms: Case studies of state reform and teacher practice.* New York: Teachers College Press.

Klein, S. P., Hamilton, L. S., McCaffrey, D. F., & Stecher, B. M. (2000). What do test scores in Texas tell us? *Educational Policy Analysis Archives, 8*(49). Available: <http://epaa.asu/epaa/v8n49>.

Knapp, M. S., Bamburg, J. D., Ferguson, M. C., & Hill, P. T. (1998). Converging reforms and the working lives of frontline professionals in schools. *Educational Policy, 12,* 397–418.

Knapp, M. S., & Associates. (1995). *Teaching for meaning in high-poverty classrooms.* New York: Teachers College Press.

Koretz, D. M., Barron, S. Mitchell, K. J., & Stecher, B. M. (1996). *Perceived effects of the Kentucky Instructional Results Information System (KIRIS).* Santa Monica, CA: RAND.

Linn, R. L. (2000). Assessments and accountability. *Educational Researcher, 29*(2), 4–16.

Lipson, M. Y., & Mosenthal, J. (1997, April). *The differential impact of Vermont's writing portfolio assessment on classroom instruction.* Paper presented at the meeting of the American Educational Research Association, Chicago.

Lipson, M. Y., Mosenthal, J. H., & Mekkelsen, J. (1996, December). *A close look at teacher change: What gets influenced, who changes and why.* Paper presented at the meeting of the National Reading Conference, Charleston, S.C.

Mayer, D. P. (1999). Measuring instructional practice: Can policymakers trust survey data? *Educational Evaluation and Policy Analysis, 1,* 29–45.

McDonnell, L., & Choisser, C. (1997). *Testing and teaching: Local implementation of new state assessments.* Los Angeles: National Center for Research on Evaluation, Standards, and Student Testing, University of California.

McGill-Franzen, A. (2000). Policy and instruction: What is the relationship? In M. Kamil, P. Mosenthal, P. D. Pearson, & R. Barr (Eds.), *Handbook of reading research* (Vol. 3, pp. 889–908). Mahwah, NJ: Erlbaum.

McLaughlin, M. W. (1987). Learning from experience: Lessons from policy implementation. *Educational Evaluation and Policy Analysis, 9,* 171–178.

McLaughlin, M. W. (1990). The Rand change agent study revisited: Macro perspectives and micro realities. *Educational Research, 19,* 11–16.

McLaughlin, M. W. (1992). Educational policy: Impact on practice. In M. Aiken (Ed.), *American Educational Research Association encyclopedia of educational research* (pp. 375–382). New York: Macmillan.

Mosenthal, J., Lipson, M. Y., Mekkelsen, J., Daniels, P., & Jiron, H. W. (1996). The meaning and use of portfolios in different literacy contexts: Making sense of the Vermont Assessment Program. In D. J. Leu, C. K. Kinzer, & K. A. Hinchman (Eds.), *Literacies for the 21st century.* Forty-fifth yearbook of the National Reading Conference (pp. 113–123). Chicago: National Reading Conference.

Nolen, S. B., Haladyna, T. M., & Haas, N. S. (1992). Uses and abuses of achievement test scores. *Educational Measurement: Issues and Practice, 11*(2), 9–15.

Patterson, F. R. A. (2000). The politics of phonics. *Journal of Curriculum and Supervision, 15,* 179–211.

Resnick, L. B., & Resnick, D. L. (1992). Assessing the thinking curriculum: New tools for educational reform. In B. R. Gifford & M. C. O'Connor (Eds.), *Future assessments: Changing views of aptitude, achievement, and instruction* (pp. 37–75). Boston: Kluwer.

Sabatier, P., & Mazmanian, D. (1980). The implementation of public policy: A framework of analysis. *Policy Studies Journal, 8,* 538–560.

Schwab, J. J. (1964). Structure of the disciplines: Meanings and significances. In G. W. Ford & L. Pugno (Eds.), *The structure of knowledge and the curriculum* (pp. 6–30). Chicago: Rand McNally.

Shepard, L. A. (1991). Will national tests improve student learning? *Phi Delta Kappan, 72,* 232–238.

Shields, P. M., & Knapp, M. S. (1997). The promise and limits of school-based reform: A national snapshot. *Phi Delta Kappan, 79,* 288–294.

Shulman, L. S. (1987). Knowledge and teaching: Foundations of the new reform. *Harvard Educational Review, 57,* 1–20.

Smith, M., & O'Day, J. (1991). Systemic school reform. In S. H. Fuhrman & B. Malen (Eds.), *The politics of curriculum and testing* (pp. 233–268). Bristol, PA: Falmer.

Spillane, J. P. (1996) School districts matter: Local educational authorities and state instructional policy. *Educational Policy, 10,* 63–87.

Spillane, J. P. (1998). State policy and the non-monolithic nature of the local school district: Organizational and professional considerations. *American Educational Research Journal, 35,* 33–63.

Spillane, J. P. (2000). A fifth grade teacher's reconstruction of mathematics and literacy teaching: Exploring interactions among identity, learning, and subject matter. *Elementary School Journal, 100,* 307–330.

Spillane, J. P., & Jennings, N. E. (1997). Aligned instructional policy and ambitious pedagogy: Exploring instructional reform from the classroom perspective. *Teachers College Record, 98,* 449–481.

Standerford, N. S. (1997). Reforming reading instruction on multiple levels: Interrelations and disconnections across the state, district, and classroom levels. *Educational Policy, 11,* 58–91.

Stecher, B. M., Barron,S., Kaganoff, T., & Goodwin, J. (1998). *The effects of standards-based assessment on classroom practices: Results of the 1996–97 RAND survey of Kentucky teachers of mathematics and writing* (CSE Tech. Rep. No. 482). Los Angeles: National Center for Research on Evaluation, Standards, and Student Testing, University of California.

Valencia, S. W., & Wixson, K. K. (2000). Policy-oriented research on literacy standards and assessment. In M. Kamil, P. Mosenthal, P. D. Pearson, & R. Barr (Eds.), *Handbook of reading research* (Vol. 3, pp. 909–935). Mahwah, NJ: Erlbaum.

Wolf, S. A., & McIver, M. C. (1999). When process becomes policy: The paradox of Kentucky state reform for exemplary teachers of writing. *Phi Delta Kappan, 80,* 401–406.

What Do We Say to DeShawn?: Literacy As Social Action in the Middle Grades*

Susan Hynds
Syracuse University

> One of every five children in the United States lives in poverty, an estimated twelve million children, according to the Children's Defense Fund. In cities like Chicago, the rate is considerably higher: one of every three children. . . . By the time they enter adolescence, they have contended with more terror than most of us confront in a lifetime. They have had to make choices that most experienced and educated adults would find difficult. They have lived with fear and witnessed death. Some of them have lashed out. They have joined gangs, sold drugs, and, in some cases, inflicted pain on others. But they have also played baseball and gone on dates and shot marbles and kept diaries. For, despite all they have seen and done, they are—we must constantly remind ourselves of this—still children. (Kotlowitz, 1991, p. xi)

Over a decade ago, I entered the middle school classroom of a woman I called "Meg Andrews," to begin what I thought would be a 1-year study. Three years later, in 1991, I left her city classroom forever changed. Many years later, I chronicled our mutual changes during those 3 years in the book *On the Brink: Negotiating Literature and Life with Adolescents* (Hynds, 1997). Today, this woman (whose real name is Mary McCrone) has welcomed me back into her classroom again. For the past year, we have been co-teaching, researching, and hoping eventually to write a book together about our experiences in teaching literacy as a form of social action with a group of middle school students in her current city classroom. In the fall of 1999, when I was still teaching at the university, I became a regular observer and participant in her classroom as she began the first phase of our work together with her seventh-grade students. By January 2000, I came on board as a full-time co-teacher in her classroom. Many of our students, like those described by Alex Kotlowitz in the opening of this essay, have already contended with more in their short lives than we could have imagined at their age.

One such student is DeShawn. Like so many young men in our city classroom, DeShawn has lived many lifetimes in his few short years. And, as Kotlowitz reminds us, we must remember that DeShawn, like so many of his classmates, is still, at heart, a child. DeShawn would be a stand out in any middle school classroom. A head taller than most students his age, he is many things: an athlete, a

*All names of informants and the names of the schools are pseudonyms. This article is an abbreviated form of a chapter to appear in a forthcoming book (title to be determined) by Susan Hynds and Mary McCrone.

*National Reading Conference Yearbook, **50**, pp. 44–62.*

man older than his years, in many ways, still a child. Most days, his hair is in plaits or sometimes poofed in a kind of bun on the top of his head, his pants drooping dangerously, an earring in one ear, and a captivating smile, "a gentle giant" (at least in our room) who has had his share of scrapes with the authorities. Last year, he got into a major fight with a classmate who, DeShawn claimed, threatened to pull a knife in a playground full of young children. His mother works in our cafeteria. As she told our principal when she applied for the job, she did not want to be one of "those Black moms who didn't know what their sons were doing each day."

Today, I hold in my hand the longest piece of writing DeShawn has ever written. The time I have spent with him as he composed this piece convinces me that these words come from the very center of his soul. DeShawn and his eighth-grade classmates will take the New York State English Language Arts examination this spring. It is a litmus test upon which Mary, her school, and the students in her classroom will be judged. In a few months, their scores will be splashed across the newspaper, and schools will either suffer or celebrate the taxpayers' appraisal of their performance.

To our state department of education, DeShawn will be one of those scores. The numbers they record for him will not reflect the breakthroughs we have witnessed this year and last. The taxpayers and test-makers will not know how many hours he has spent with me on this piece of writing—first, eaking out his story as I scribed a four-page outline, then painstakingly typing it on the computer as I watched from behind, occasionally offering a spelling word or a detail he might have missed. The politicians and the high-stakes test-makers do not see DeShawn as he rereads his piece on the computer screen, reliving each time a devastating experience that, weeks ago, he could not even talk about. He plods right past his spelling errors and his grammatical mistakes as the words seem to wound him again with every scan of the page.

What Do We Say to DeShawn?

> African American children cannot afford the luxury of shielding themselves with a sugar-coated vision of the world . . . parents, teachers, and neighbors need to help arm African American children with the knowledge, skills, and attitudes needed to struggle successfully against oppression. These, more than test scores, more than high grade point averages, are the critical features of education for African Americans. If students are to be equipped to struggle against racism they need excellent skills from the basics of reading, writing, and math, to understanding history, thinking critically, solving problems, and making decisions; they must go beyond merely filling in test sheet bubbles with Number 2 pencils. (Ladson-Billings, 1994, pp. 139–140)

If Mary and I have learned anything at all in our brief time with young people like DeShawn, it is the truth of Gloria Ladson-Billing's statement: equipping these students with the critical skills to confront racism and social injustice extends far beyond helping them to master the list of competencies on our state assessments. On a typical day, DeShawn walks through the hallways of K. T. Dwight School, a

magnet for young African-American children in our K–8 building. "Hi DeShawn," the little girls whisper, eyes turned heavenward. He is a man of few words; he does not seem to need them. Last year, in what seemed a contradiction to his "boy behavior" and his athletic prowess, DeShawn chose babysitting as his community service project. He is always the one to run the projector or the sound equipment when Mary or I have a class performance. We call on him whenever we have large items to carry out to our cars after a school event. As thanks for all of his help, I have been promising him a cherry "Powerade" for months—a fact he reminds me of nearly every time I see him.

So, when Mary called this fall and told me that DeShawn was in the hospital after being beaten by a gang of white high school students, I was devastated. When he came back from the hospital, I asked if he would like to talk with me about the incident. We went out in the hallway, and I turned on my tape recorder. He fingered his unopened Powerade (I finally coughed up the dollar and bought him one) and began to talk about the incident—at first, haltingly, and then, not at all. When he was done, I asked if he saw the act as racist. He looked away: "I don't want to talk about it," he said. "It's over. I just want to go on." There was an invisible string of silence between us that I did not dare to break.

When the interview was over and DeShawn had gone back to class, I felt my own powerlessness in the face of what he had just been unable to articulate. What could I begin to say to him? I decided to put it in writing, scribbling a note in my spiral notebook. I told him how sorry I felt about what happened to him and how much I wish I could take his pain away. I talked about the unfairness of what had come down and invited him to write about it if he ever felt the urge. I folded the letter, handed it to Mary to give to him, and wrote my invitation off as probably a lost cause. The next day she smiled and handed me his reply:

> Dear, Susan
>
> I got your letter thank you for taken your time to write me that letter. I was thinking about what you was saying to me I should write a story about that because it is in the past now so I can talk about it now . . It is one thing I need you to help me on it because I don't think I can do it by my self . . So I guess I will see you in class ok". Bye Bye !!!!!!!!
>
> From,
> DeShawn

And so we began. A week later, I got him out of "study and support" period and took him to the library where the computers still work (those in our classroom work only on-and-off—mostly off). The first day, we took 40 minutes just to get everything down. I suspect it was the first time DeShawn had ever worked from an outline. I remembered how tough it had been for him to talk about the incident a few days earlier, so I offered to "scribe" for him. As he talked, I prodded him: "And then what happened?" "How did you feel when he called you that?" We ended up with four pages of scrawled notes, which he folded and stuck in his pants pocket. For the next several days, every time he saw me, he asked if I was coming to get him during study and support so we could work on the piece. Each day in the library, he unfolded the notes and we began where we had left off. Here is what he wrote:

> It's 6:00 in the evening we are at Carver field with brother and friends. We are about to play football. We started playing then about 15–20 of them they came from the soccer field they was all white 1 mix boy . . A couple of them walk up and said we don't play n - - ger ball we play cracker ball something yall don't know about . . I was thinking just let it go, I did but then they threw a rock and hit me on my head . . I started walking home because I know it is a lot of consequences if I get into a fight with these boys . . I started to walk into Oak wood were I live at . . Why I was up there I did not do anything because up there they would call the police quick up because they see black boys going afthere white people they would come quite . . I started going home because it was time for me to get close to home around that time, I live at 143 Oak wood a.v.e. . . Before I left I ask them did we had a problem they said yeah with you: n*****s. They started throwing more big rocks about a size of a baseball on of them graze my faces . . I walk over to them to try to get around them he try to punch me I did the same . . When we got out of the fence he said he will be back, I was not worry because I never aspect those boys to come they it is usually the black boys to go after them not them to come after us . . I was standen by a friend house I seen a car road by and seen one of he boys in the car so then I know it was going to be a problem then . . There was a car just setting there I seen one of the boys so then I knew it was going to be a big problem, Then as I was walken toward home, they just started coming from ever where. There was 3 to 4 cars of them, So as I seen them they seen me I knew it was a time for me to think real fast because it seem like those boys was not playing.Theses big boys had everything you can name, They had baseball bat tire iron crowbars and the list changes.
>
> When this was going on I was by my self intill I yell for help my words was that "they're back so hurry." I was yell to my friends that was around the coner, Before my friends came they had me conerd around them so I had to think fast, The first thing I was thinking about is don't get hit with anything. And also thinken about what can I pick I did not see anything so I grab one the boys and took the bat from him so they can back up from me, as I was looking they was not scared because it was one of me and about 25 of them. So as when my friends got there we started fighting , So it was about 6 of us. When I turn my back they hit me with the bat in the neck I did not fall I turn around and caught eye contact with him and started chace him as I was running someone threw the tire iron at me and hit me at the back of the head that made me think I was getting hit for fun because, There was so many they was doing it just because I was at the wrong place at the wrong time, "fther I got hit when I whent back to the car he tryed to pull off but before he got away I smash the window out then he got out and ran so then I just totalled the car, I yell call the police. I did not fel the hit intill I got close to Richard house something keep me gonig. When I got there I fel out I was stil up but I was just sitting there. The police and the ambulance came then I seen my mom I tryed to get up but I was to hurt to get up so she came to me, She came to me and ask me what happen and where is my brother. I told her what happen then when we got to the hospital I rember were he was he was at a friends house. Afthere I took my xrays the police came to my room and told me I could go with my mom downtown our they could take me you know what I pick mom. when I got down there they told me to come in the room for I can look

> at some pictures in the year books I look at some and spoted to of them out so they look them up and see where was they at the crim seen . . They had found one of them it was the boy that started it so they brought him down and talk to him then afthere that the police man came in the room and ask me did I smash the windows I could a said no but it was my word against there but I was not trying to keep it going so I said yes I did it, He said thank you because if I would a said no he would need to go and ask questions but I did the right thing because he could a charge me with somethеing about lyeing. They had charge me with second degree felony. Afthere we whent home a couple days later I got some mail abot what happen it said I could go to court to apeal or like I did go downtown to get some hours of community service instead of going in frount of the judge. my mom said we will just go downtown because she wont it to be over. They gave me 15 hours. The other kids got away with a lot of stuff. No charges was pressed on them. I was still thinking about what happen because they play football for the same team I played for . . So I had to wacth my self because it seem like the walls was closen on me . .

Where to Begin?

> In my 25 years of teaching, I have known dozens and dozens of Black boys who say they don't care about school and thinking and learning; who say they don't care about a friend who betrayed them or about an enemy who was killed, or a girl who rejected them, or a baby they don't see anymore; who say they don't care about the soul or love or anything. I have known virtually no one who really meant it. I always believed that these students' pride and posturing held them back from showing emotion and from asking for the help that they really did want. (Shakespear, 1999, p. 83)

All of us are reading this book because we want to touch the lives of young people like DeShawn. We want to give them hope, turn them into lifetime readers and writers, and help them—through their literacies—to negotiate the tricky and confusing world that surrounds their school lives. Most of the time, their "real lives" would astound us if we knew; sometimes they render us mute as we realize what a miracle it is that some of them even come to school at all, much less devote time to reading and writing. Above all, we want to give them the help that all of their "pride and posturing" so thinly veil.

I ask you to stand in my shoes. What would you say to DeShawn? Where do you begin? In the tradition of process-centered teaching, do you say,

> This is very good, DeShawn. But you might want to add more detail or consider using some "action words." You need to "show, not tell." Why don't we take your first draft here through some revisions. A peer response group might help. And while we're at it, let's add a few skills to your "skills to know and use" notebook.

Or, in the tradition of reader-response teaching, do you say,

> DeShawn, I am struck by the way you shared your personal experience. I have some novels about gang violence you might like to read. They could help you to understand your own situation much better, and they're about Black men like

you. Maybe you'd like to write more about your feelings in your response journal.

From your knowledge of linguistics, you probably recognize the markers of what has come to be called "Ebonics" (Perry & Delpit, 1998) in the parlance of our popular press. You may believe, as I do, that DeShawn's writing is not a *dialect* but a *language* with a grammar and structure of its own (O'Neil, 1998; Smitherman, 1998). Recognizing the importance of students' home languages in your multicultural classroom, you might be wary of focusing on DeShawn's language at all. This piece was written to get a painful incident off his chest and come to terms with it. What better language to use than the language of home and family? This is hardly an occasion for a lesson in linguistics.

And then again, what is the cost of *not* confronting the nonstandardized nature of his piece? Some of our African-American colleagues (Delpit, 1995) have warned us about the unwitting marginalization that our generation of mostly white teachers has promoted by not making DeShawn conscious of the social consequences of his language choices. As an African-American colleague of mine at the university once told me: "The world is suffering from too much White liberal guilt." Am I to say nothing about his choice of language, knowing full well that DeShawn may never make it out of high school until he begins right now to *unlearn* years of grammatical nuance and structure that keep his home language relegated to the margins of academic and economic success? It is fine to celebrate difference in our classrooms, but we live in a world that fears and often abhors difference. What is my responsibility to make DeShawn aware of these harsh realities and to help him negotiate their rocky contours in my language arts classroom? And if I take up this responsibility, where do I begin? Bob Fecho (1996) echoes these questions in describing his own teaching:

> [H]ow can we account for a range of dialects in the Black community under one label, "Black English"? This insight sent me hunting for terms to use in their stead. "Home language," "peer language" and "mainstream language," although not without some baggage, seemed more personal and accepting because they credit the influences that affect our language choices. On the other hand, I realize that by denying the direct influence of race, we may lose the opportunity to celebrate a language worthy of pride. On this subject I am torn. (p. 68)

I too am torn; but certainly more disturbing than his language choices is DeShawn's overt denial of the obvious racism behind the attack. I wonder, as I listen to his story, if he is a victim of naiveté or the epitome of resilience. Stephen O'Connor (1996) describes similar survival tactics among his urban students:

> I have never had a student describe him- or herself as anything other than middle class, even though sociologists would label the vast majority of them working class or poor. While all of my students think of racism as one of the great evils of contemporary life, and while many of them tell stories of not being served in stores or of being assumed to be thieves simply because of their skin color, and even while many of them suffer from an extreme lack of confidence that is clearly a heritage of racism and slavery, I have never heard a student admit that

> racism might limit his or her particular opportunities in life to the slightest degree. Sometimes I admire my students' optimism and gumption. Sometimes I shake my head at their innocence—and at the terrifying and tragic experiences they report as if they were merely average events of a normal life. (p. 12)

Our politicians and our popular press would tell us what a crime it is that students like DeShawn have gotten this far without learning *what they define* as "reading and writing skills." The solution is simple, they tell us: test students like DeShawn every year until they graduate or drop out. And, if they do drop out, as many have, so much the better. As they fall out of the testing pool, test scores (and political ratings) rise accordingly. Perhaps that is why, in my state, the New York City School system was challenged by the Department of Education's office of civil rights for improperly placing large numbers of racial- and language-minority students into special education programs, presumably so that their test scores would not be reflected in the larger testing pool. In nine districts, black students were more than twice as likely as white students to be recommended for the "most restrictive" special education classes. These are classes in which students are less likely to be transferred back to the mainstream (NYC schools chief, 1998). In an age when schools are threatened to raise their scores or close their doors, I hope that such events are not destined to be the "average events of a normal life" (O'Connor, 1996, p. 12) for young people like DeShawn.

Those of us who resonate with feminism, poststructuralism, cultural criticism, and other perspectives that challenge the political structures that render young men like DeShawn mute in the face of obvious racism would say that I should make DeShawn and his classmates acutely aware of racism, homophobia, sexism, and other "isms" as a daily part of my teaching (Cummins, 1993; Edelsky, 1994; Fine, 1995; Gee, 1999; Lewis, 2001; Luke, 2000; McLaren & Gutierrez, 1994; Shannon, 1993). Perhaps I can give DeShawn the courage to share his experience with other students, eventually engaging the whole group in an anti-racist or anti-bias curriculum of critical action and social justice, organized around what Giroux (1992) has called "a language of both critique and possibility" (p. 308). What is my responsibility to help students like DeShawn to make the world a place where no child—regardless of race income or sexual orientation—is ever attacked or made to suffer for the color of their skin, the clothing they wear, or the people they choose to love?

I must admit that all of my theories fail me in the moment that DeShawn finally types out his last sentence. I respond not as teacher, facilitator, linguist, anthropologist, or social critic. I respond as fellow human being who cares more about DeShawn, the child/man who sits beside me at this very moment, than I do about my own theoretical loyalties and conflicts. "That's a powerful piece, DeShawn. It's the longest thing you've ever written. Does writing it make you feel any better?" I say, lamely. He turns his chair, wraps his long arms around the back, leans precariously away from the desk and seems to stare at a point beyond my head, out the open window at the high school in the distance. He shrugs and says nothing. I choose not to press him for the moment at least. We both gather our things for the long walk back to the classroom.

Welcome to Our World

> On any given day, most students in any class have watched murder, assault, love-making, war-making and/or competitive sports on television the previous night. For many—especially at the secondary level—their classrooms are located in large schools, 1200–2000 students, sometimes more. Teachers in these schools often cannot distinguish students from strangers on campus. . . . It is not surprising that the single greatest complaint of students in these schools is, "They don't care!" (Noddings, 1992, p. 2)

I open with DeShawn's story, not because I want to imply that the world of the young adolescent is dreary of devoid of hope. On the contrary, he and his classmates have given Mary and me far more to laugh than to cry about. Some days we giggle to the point of tears over something that one of them has said or done. One by one they tumble in to our classroom, a clutter of Fubu and Tommy Hilfiger, of "ghetto" pants, blue braces, hair clips and "dreads." They enter like a shrieking tornado and take their 5 minutes of "free time" before the serious business of class begins. The chaos is deafening: "Ms. McCrone, can I go to the washroom?" "Susan, you sign my pass?" They slap at each other or slouch in their seats, run for the few spaces on the couch, and grab notebooks out of each other's hands. A group of girls sits in a clump, talking about boys or the dance last week. Emma is in her seat, working quietly, as usual. Jovann sits alone, fingering a book. He seems to be in perpetual slow motion. Chloe has settled like a cat into a comfortable chair. Max is unusually agitated. Did he remember to take his meds today or will we have to send him to the nurse? Briana is lounging with a bunch of "groupies," serving up the brilliance of her smile like lemonade to her admirers. Chiquia grabs me in a spine-crunching bear hug. Derek pesters us about losing the novel he has been writing and wonders if I have kept a copy. Mary wrestles with her attendance cards—the bane of her existence—and it seems that nothing will ever be quiet again.

They all come to class and they all sit side by side in the same room. We are supposed to reach them all, collectively and individually. More important than any literacy skills we might give them, our greatest challenge is to create a community of caring that Nel Noddings (1992) writes so passionately about. There are 170 students on Mary's roll because she teaches every seventh and eighth-grade student in our K–8 building on a 6-day rotating schedule of 80-minute-block periods. Mary and I have known each other for 15 years now, ever since she enrolled in our masters program and invited me into her classroom for what turned out to be a 3—no, make that a 5—no, make that an 8-year study of her middle school students. At the end of that project, and in the 8 years it took me to write and publish that book, it became clear to both of us that many of Mary's middle school students saw themselves as what my friend Deborah Appleman (personal conversation) calls "quite literally useless" in today's world. Advertisers of video games and sports equipment love them, but to the rest of the world, they are viewed as what Peg Finders (1998–1999) calls a bundle of "raging hormones," hell-bent on destroying what little decorum we have left in our society. Ask them and they will tell you. Our young students tell us about standing in lines and being passed over by sales clerks in favor of older customers, of being followed by security guards in Wal-Mart, of being told by parents and other adults that their ideas and opinions do not count. It is hard to convince them that their literate acts can make a difference in today's world; it is harder still to ask them to grapple with the host of troubling social issues that students like DeShawn face every day. But that is the task Mary and I set out to tackle last year as I left the university classroom and shifted my role from classroom researcher to fellow teacher.

Making a Difference in the Middle Grades

> Our discussions of standards and curriculum frameworks and outcomes have still not touched seriously upon the matter of our purposes as a society: upon what it means to educate live persons, to empower the young not simply to make a living and contribute to the nation's economic welfare but to live and, along with others, remake their own worlds. (Greene, 1995, p. 170)

Helping our young students to "remake their own worlds" was no mean feat for either of us. It was hard for me—a 30-year veteran teacher—to accept the fact that, although the students seemed to enjoy when I came to class and even complained when I did not, I was not—definitely not—the teacher in charge. When I complained of this fact to Mary, she likened it to ducklings that imprint on the first duck (or person) they see. The students had "imprinted" with Mary for a whole semester before I came in. As much as they liked and trusted me, I was not the adult in charge, and it would take the better part of a semester to change that. I suddenly realized, in living color, how some of my student teachers felt when they had to develop their own teaching identity as a guest in someone else's classroom.

Mary had her own set of issues. For that first fall semester, when I was just researcher in her classroom, she had set up an amazingly comfortable and predictable classroom routine. Her room was a soothing yet evocative play of color, light, and activity. Comfortable furniture was scattered between round work tables. Incandescent light softly brightened the room. There were celebrations of student work all over the place, things to think about, books to choose, opportunities for solitary and collaborative writing, soft music every morning, and a structure of predictability within which students could feel comfortable to be creative. If there is any such thing as the epitome of learner-centered teaching, Mary had captured it. Whereas I had to scream to get their attention, she simply drew her fingers across a wind chime and announced quietly, "opening procedure points begin now."

Each day, the students went to small tables where they wrote the morning's agenda in their notebooks. Whole-class activities were voluntary, within limits. At the beginning of each class, as Mary called the roll, students would choose either "reading/writing workshop" (which meant working quietly around the room on independent projects, going to the library to work on the computers, or finding new books to read), or "literature circle" (usually a teacher-sponsored reading and writing experience).

So why would she want to set off an atomic bomb in the midst of all of this serenity? Why would she want to introduce the divisiveness of issues like racism, intolerance, and social justice into her peaceable classroom? She asked me this many times as that spring semester unfolded and things inevitably fell apart before coming together again.

Our theme for last year was "Making a Difference." This was divided into four subthemes: *Self-knowledge* (We are all products of our life experiences; how do we gain self-knowledge and why is it important?); *Communication* (We communicate most with friends and family; what does it mean to be a good communicator?); *Democracy* (We live in a country that offers us many freedoms; what are the responsibilities of living in a democracy?); and *Legacy* (Each day of our lives we impact the world; what is the global picture and how do we make a difference?).

For the fall semester of 1999, Mary concentrated on the first two subthemes, starting out that first semester fairly close to home. Students read excerpts of books like *Tuesdays with Morrie* (Albom, 2000) and watched a film version of Rodman Philbrick's book *Freak the Mighty* (1993). They explored relationships with friends and family and drafted tentative personal philosophies. As part of an inquiry project, for example, a group of three girls decided to focus on a woman from their church who had pulled herself out of the depths of alcoholism and drug abuse when her daughter was murdered in a drug-related shooting and she suddenly became guardian of her three grandchildren. The girls decided to create a scrapbook of this woman's life and to invite her to our class, supposedly to talk with us about her life. When she arrived, the girls surprised her with flowers and a copy of the scrapbook. After a tearful ceremony, the whole class, including the principal who had dropped in at their invitation, sat around the literature circle and listened with rapt attention as this woman told her story. By the end of that fall, it was time to move into the last two phases of our theme.

From Personal Awareness to Social Action

> [E]ven with our having laid ground rules for [discussing issues], we teachers . . . experience doubt and disillusionment. Knowing that we are responsible for this forum means we reexamine all of our choices. Have we made the most responsible choices in selecting the materials and the pedagogy? As discussion moderators, have we intervened soon enough in volatile discussions? . . . Are our students developmentally ready—even at 16, 17, or 18—to engage in discussions that trigger such anger, sadness, or frustration? And if not now, when? (Dilg, 1999, p. 92)

By January, when I could join Mary full time, we had planned to move into the "social action" phase of our project. This move was not without misgivings on Mary's part. Like the teachers Mary Dilg described, she felt like some of the topics we would be covering—topics like racial prejudice, intolerance, hate crimes, homophobia, and the like—were beyond her expertise and comfort level as an English teacher. They fell into the realm of social studies and, besides that, she thought they would be depressing for her lively group of middle school students.

We spent our first few weeks in January flip-flopping between positions I am not sure either one of actually relished. She would defend her approach based upon personal sharing and individual achievement, whereas I kept trying to steer us into the realm of the political. We each took turns crying over lunch or after school when we had suffered a particularly disappointing day. In a sense, we had both turned into adolescents ourselves.

For the most part, though, it was delightful to share my struggles as a teacher with someone; to have an extra pair of eyes and an extra voice to bail me out; to sit back some days and let Mary be the "bad cop"; to be relatively free (unless Mary went to the rest room) from matters of discipline or final grades. I led, by most teachers' accounts, a charmed life, and I knew it. Our students, and we were prospering.

But something kept nagging at me. The classroom felt almost too safe. Where was the developing social consciousness and the excitement about using reading, writing, and language for social action that we had both envisioned when we had planned our curriculum earlier that summer? Where were the engaging, yet uncomfortable, discussions about race, class, gender, and so on that I had though might happen if we asked students to think about how they could make a difference in the world?

Somewhere in about the third week of the spring semester, a lucky accident turned the corner for us. One of our students brought in a movie called *Cornbread, Earl, and Me* (1975) and begged us to show it. The cover advertised that it was sort of an earlier incarnation of *Boyz N the Hood*.(1991). At first we thought it was far too "seventies" for our students. The actors had Afros and bell bottoms. The film began with a title song called "Cornbread," which sent the students into all kinds of hoots and imitations; but soon they became riveted as the main character, Cornbread, a promising young black athlete, was gunned down accidentally in the street by a group of police who mistook him for a murder suspect. The scenes of the trial that followed, where the three officers (one of them a black man) were acquitted of his death, sobered them for days afterward.

This gave me an idea. I went home the day we finished the film, got on the Internet, and began to download some images of the Rodney King beating, the Los Angeles riots that followed, and the beating of Reginald Denny, the white truck driver who was attacked by a gang of black youths during the riots. We began the next day by asking if our students thought that racism was still alive in America. There were viewpoints all over the map, but the majority of them—white students and students of color alike—seemed to agree that racism was not a daily part of their lives; to most of them, it was something we had dealt with in the past and not really an issue in today's world. I knew though, that these were the students who felt free to talk in the forum of a large class discussion. I wondered about the students who *were not* talking—students like DeShawn, for whom racism had intimately touched their lives.

In her book, *"Why are all the Black Kids Sitting Together in the Cafeteria?" and Other Conversations About Race,* Beverly Daniel Tatum (1997) observes: "Adults, both White and of color, often hesitate to speak to children about racism for fear they will create problems where perhaps none exist, afraid they will make 'colorblind' children unnecessarily color-conscious" (p. xvi). In many ways that morning, I wanted to lull my young students into the mythical colorblindness that Tatum describes. I suppose I should not have been surprised at their denial of racism in contemporary society. As Tatum observes:

> Fifteen years . . . after exhaustive media coverage of events such as the King beating, the Charles Stuart and Susan Smith cases, the O. J. Simpson trial, the appeal to racial prejudices in electoral politics, and the bitter debates about affirmative action and welfare reform, it seems hard to imagine that anyone would still be unaware of the reality of racism in our society. But in fact, in almost every audience I address, there is someone who will suggest that racism is a thing of the past. (p. 3)

That morning, I breathed a worried sigh and placed an image of a burning building in the Los Angeles riots on the overhead projector, asking, "Anybody know what this is?" Most of our students were 4 or 5 years old at the time of the riots; yet, their comments were oddly on target, almost prophetic. They talked of mob violence, of firebombs, of racism. Few thought it was a random act. One student guessed: "I think somebody started it on purpose, uhm, somebody might have thought that in life they were losing, and they have to let it out on other people."

Then we looked at some images of the Rodney King beating. Even though they could not see the police uniforms or a police cruiser, they were quick to figure out what was going on. One of them suggested it might be a "wild police chase." Another thought that maybe "[S]ome guys . . . want to beat up on the other person because he has a different idea or belief." The photos reminded one student of Jonny Gammage, a man from Syracuse who had been stopped by police on a New York highway and was shot to death when they supposedly mistook his cellphone for a gun. Antoine told us that Gammage was his cousin, and things began to hit closer to home. They were not prepared though, when I explained that, even though everything was captured on videotape by a bystander, all four of the officers were acquitted by the primarily white jury. When the case was appealed, only two officers were ever punished, and one of them ended up serving only 2 years of a 3-year sentence.

We talked then about the Los Angeles riots that followed the first acquittal. I explained that Reginald Denny had just happened to be driving his truck through the intersection of Florence and Normandie Avenues when the Los Angeles riots were at their peak. I explained how these young men dragged Denny out of his truck, kicked him in the head, threw concrete blocks and heavy medical equipment that had been looted out of a truck at him, how he suffered permanent brain damage from the blows, and how a helicopter hovered over, filming the entire spectacle. Eventually, I told them, a group of black people from the neighborhood, sickened by the violence they saw on their television sets, ran out of their homes and rescued Denny. Knowing that everything was captured on videotape and that the assailants were black, our students concluded, almost with one voice, that the young men probably received "maximum time." They were stunned when

I explained that in 1993, three defendants were acquitted of the most serious charges in the Denny beating, and a fourth defendant was later sentenced to probation.

The room grew quiet as we all pondered our original question. In light of the film we had just watched, in light of the Rodney King and Reginald Denny incidents, and in light of more recent events so close to our home, including the death of Jonny Gammage, could we still say that racism was not a part of our daily lives?

What followed from that day was a flurry of interest topics like hate, intolerance, racism, and homophobia. I began to download articles from the Internet each night, since the computers in our room were broken. I put them in a big binder and invited students to visit them as they formulated the questions for their next inquiry project. To my delight, I had to replace several articles, as students started to "borrow" them permanently from the file. They became interested in the Matthew Shepard murder and homophobia; the dragging death of James Byrd in Texas; the Columbine massacre; the shooting of a 6-year-old by another 6-year-old; and, of course, the deaths in our own state of Jonny Gammage and Amadeau Diallo at the hands of police.

Our reading and writing began to connect in real ways with the world beyond our classroom. For example, we read Toni Cade Bambara's "The War of the Wall" (2000), a story about two inner-city boys who learned not to judge people by surface appearances or stereotypes. We decided to create our own "wall of hope," plastering our bulletin board with colorful bits of "graffiti" created by our students. The slogans reflected the diversity of our classroom: "I am never the same twice"; "We are all the same underneath our colors"; "Change your view for a day and you will see the world"; "What does not kill us makes us stronger." "I have a dream."

An article by *New York Times* reporter and novelist, Anna Quindlen (2000), called "Homeless" and a companion piece by Sandra Cisneros (2001) called "Bums in the Attic" (2000) later inspired some of our students to volunteer in the local homeless shelter. A story by Gary Paulsen called "Dirk the Protector" (2000) got some of our students thinking about volunteering at the local S.P.C.A. Once, during a talk about intolerance, Tamara, the "gutsiest" 4-foot-tall blonde girl I have ever met, told a tearful story about standing by on a neighborhood street while her friends yelled "faggot" at a lesbian couple with a child who lived next door. In tears, Tamara told us that she vowed never to witness intolerance like that again without stepping in; and she kept that promise more than once that year in the hallways or the cafeteria. When students called each other "retard" or "faggot," they had Tamara to contend with. Brian, an African-American boy, talked about walking down a street and being spat upon by white people in a passing car. Bridgett told about being ignored and later hollered at by the manager of a video arcade just because she and her friends were teenagers.

On the heels of their enthusiasm, we asked them to find a compelling issue for their next inquiry project and explore it through at least one of the following data sources: books, newspapers, magazines, the Internet, documentaries, television newscasts, movies, talk shows, interviews, surveys, and observations. The outcome of this project was a five-page paper and an oral presentation, using one or more of what Mary calls the "smarts," her term for Howard Gardner's eight intelligences (1999). Topics ranged from hate crimes against homosexuals to the influence of popular media on teenagers, violence in a nearby high school, and—my personal favorite—the "Evils of Barbie."

For the last 2 months of the semester, we planned a culminating project. This time, students were asked to investigate an important issue with a group, to keep track of their inquiry in a journal, and to volunteer for at least 10 hours of what we called "community service" or "social justice work." As an aside, we immediately regretted using the term "community service," since some of our students apparently associated it with "doing time" in the juvenile justice system. Nevertheless, we pressed on.

In envisioning the possibilities for this final inquiry, we borrowed from the work of our published colleagues in books and professional journals, explaining that students' final inquiry projects might range anywhere along a continuum from community service to social justice. Realizing the disparate array of terminology in our own professional publications, we outlined an array of choices under the broad umbrella of "social action." For example, within their neighborhoods and community, we suggested that they might pursue "service-learning" (Deans, 2000; Prosser & Levesque, 1997; Schutz & Gere, 1998) or "community service" (Greco, 1992) projects, such as tutoring in community literacy programs or volunteering in local health care agencies, recreational centers, homes for the elderly, or homeless shelters. Beyond this immediate sphere, we suggested that they might explore a variety of "social justice" issues (Allen, 1999; Edelsky, 1996; Lewis, 2001) such as environmental advocacy, animal rights, public health reform, or antidiscrimination policies, among other possibilities. We planned to culminate the year in a "Social Action Fair" where students could display and discuss the results of their projects in the gymnasium in front of parents, teachers, peers, and community members.

Seldom did things go smoothly. There were many moments of discord and angst that year. But over the bumps we went, learning all the way about the complications of moving our literacy curriculum in this direction. On the night of the Social Action Fair, over 300 community members witnessed our students' work. Radio, television, and newspaper reporters covered the story, The event was, by all accounts, an unmitigated success.

Our test scores came in and, by some miracle, our students' real-world literacies "worked" in the world of the standardized test. The eighth-grade students in our school scored higher than those in any other school in upstate New York, when compared on factors of socioeconomic level and other demographics.

Where to? What Next?

> We are not passersby alone, but rather passersby to one another; we are the characters in one another's life narratives, including the narratives of what was and has been, what is, and what is possible. (Mosenthal, 1998, p. 346)

On the June night when the Social Action Fair was finally finished, Mary and I sat in a local restaurant and took inventory of all we had accomplished and all that had fallen by the wayside. For the first time in many weeks, we had a bit of breathing space in which to consider just what roles we had played in each other's "life narratives" and in those of our students. Despite many successes, we realized that our work was not done—as, in a sense, if we are doing our job, I suspect it never will be.

The "stage had been struck" in her classroom—posters taken down, chairs and tables moved to make way for the daily deluge of 170 students making displays and preparing for the event. Our students had done their 10 hours of community service/social action, and then some. They had proudly shared their efforts with the larger community. But in our classroom and in the hallways we continued to hear them calling each other "faggot," "fatty," and "retard." A readers' theater I had tried to put on about racial intolerance was ironically derailed because every rehearsal degenerated into name-calling and pouting and even, I suspect, racism, when students did not get the parts they had hoped for or could not stand the people they were working with. On the day we set up tables in the gymnasium, two students broke into a raging fight and almost destroyed several student displays. Most of them had bought into the grand gesture of the Social Action *fair,* but the ideas of *fair*NESS, tolerance, and an anti-bias classroom still seemed remote from their everyday lives. Along these lines, in his critique of the writing workshop method of teaching, Timothy Lensmire (1994) observes that merely giving students personal choices, opportunities to collaborate with others, and a forum for sharing their personal stories is no guarantee of promoting tolerance and understanding in the classroom. In Lensmire's classroom,

> Peers were a source of support and confidence. They were also sources of conflict and risk. . . . Children evaluated and excluded each other—by gender, by social class, by personality—in ways that echoed some of the worst sorts of divisions and denigrations in our society. (p. 141)

Mary and I realized that evening that the Social Action Fair had been our idea. Although it was largely successful, we were still uncomfortable. Students were required to choose a topic, to do their 10 hours, and to share what they learned in a very public way. Although a great many of them were engaged and intrigued, a few felt co-opted by our agenda. Some never did find a compelling issue of their own and eventually settled on something we suggested, just to complete the assignment. Some opted out altogether.

We also noticed that the vast majority of students chose projects close to home (family or community service projects like babysitting, for instance) and only a very few chose "social justice" issues involving some kind of political or social change. We wanted to see if some students might be interested in moving along that continuum from social action to social justice—from helping out in their neighborhoods and families to making a difference in the larger world. We also realized that they, and we had become a bit burned out by the seriousness of our work together over the last few months. As Carole Edelsky (1999) has observed, we need to learn "how to find sexism, racism, and classism in whatever we're interrogating *without bashing students over the head with it*" (italics in original, p. 154). Early adolescents, and even adults, need a break sometimes. All of us need time to kick back be ourselves, regardless of the social problems that still rage around us.

Back to the Personal

> The unkind voices that surround us are loud and shrill, demanding our thoughtful and truthful attention. All the more reason to listen to the soft breath of friendship and carry our reassuring stories above the din. They are the beacons that help illuminate the moral universe. And we are required, even as is the great blue heron, to capture our prize and fly with it. (Paley, 1999, p. 129)

This fall, we decided to return to what seemed like a safer place, reconsidering the "reassuring stories" of our personal experience against the backdrop of social awareness that we generated last year. In spiraling back to the personal, we have not abandoned the social and political; instead, we are asking our students to consider their responsibilities within a democracy. For the first few weeks of the semester, students have been exploring their unique gifts and special abilities. We look at their varied abilities as a set of "raw materials" they might use within our new theme: "taking a stand." For the past week or so, we have been giving them a chance to do what middle school students love to do best: to show off, to perform, to be special in the eyes of their teachers and classmates. As they share their abilities, we have asked them to consider what they have to give to others in the world and how they might begin to "take a stand," using these abilities.

This year, we plan to negotiate more of the curriculum, giving them a say in the topics and outcome of their work, within a social action or social justice framework. Probably our most important lesson from last year is that although our students live in a democracy, their version of democracy is a very personal one, based on everybody's right to the pursuit of individual happiness and success. Asking them to step away from the personal—not only to consider, but to *act upon* their responsibilities to others in a democracy—was something they were ill-prepared for. These things take time. Thankfully, we are blessed by having these students again this year.

And What About DeShawn?

> How do youth growing up in America's inner cities duck the bullet? How do they construct and pursue alternatives that enrich rather than endanger their lives and provide them with images of productivity? How do young people navigate the tough territories of inner cities to construct a positive identity and a perception of themselves as members of society? (Heath, 1993, p. 38)

A young man of remarkable resilience, DeShawn continues to "duck the bullet" of inner city life that Shirley Brice Heath describes. He has not worked on his draft again, but interestingly, the other day, I walked in and Mary announced,

"DeShawn says he's doing something with you for our class talent show." This came as a surprise to me. But later that morning, he asked me to read his piece aloud to the whole class, as he sat beside me, you could not hear a sound as I shared his words. I believe he was genuinely amazed at his ability to move people in that way. Right now, we do not talk about his language issues. For many students like DeShawn, we must realize that transforming their language into that of the "standard" may be even more threatening than all of the physical violence he has endured. Meanwhile, our students, like the Energizer bunny, are "still writing . . . still reading . . ."

Perhaps this poem by Tamara best captures what we still hope to achieve with all of our young students this year, and in their lives to come:

A Difference

by Tamara W. Simon

The gunshot rings out, followed by an eerie silence more powerful than the bullet.
The blood runs down the black pavement, glistening like a flourescent light.
Another bullet is shot out, louder than the one before.
The two men lay at each other's side, blood highlighting their faces, running down their foreheads and through their brows.
One white, one black, now more equal than ever before.
Equally dead.
Equally cold.
They should have been equal before death.
They should have been able to live in freedom.
It is too late for them.
But it is not too late for us.
Why hate, when you can love?
Why kill, when you can live?
So look beyond skin color.
Look beyond religion.
Reach out to someone. Whether it is common courtesy, or changing a law.
A little love can make a big difference.

I take Tamara's words to heart: "It's too late for them. But it's not too late for us." In the midst of all the pseudo science we read in the popular press about test scores and accountability, in an era where political races are won or lost over sound bytes about making our students more competitive and our schools more effective, we would do well to listen to the individual and collective voices of students like Tamara, DeShawn, and all of the wonderful young people who have touched our lives for the past 2 years. Perhaps with more than a little love, and our unconditional belief in their strength, sensitivity, courage, and insight, they will, indeed, make a difference in their own lives and in the lives of all of us.

References

Albom, M. (2000). *Tuesdays with Morrie: An old man, a young man and life's greatest lesson.* Rockland: Wheeler.

Allen, J. (1999). *Class actions: Social justice in elementary and middle school.* New York: Teachers College Press.

Bambara, T. C. (2000). The war of the wall. *The language of literature, 7th grade* (pp. 107–116). Evanston, IL: McDougal Littell.

Boyz N the Hood. (1991). S. Nicolaides (Producer), & J. Singleton (Director). Columbia Pictures Corporation/US: Columbia Pictures, US.

Cisneros, S. (2001). Bums in the attic. *Language of Literature* (p. 105). Evanston, IL: McDougal, Littell.

Cornbread, Earl and Me. (1975). M. Fink (Producer), & J. Manduke (Director). MGM/Ua Studios: American International Pictures/US.

Cummins, J. (1993). Empowering minority students: A framework for intervention. In L. Weiss & M. Fine (Eds.), *Beyond silenced voices: Class, race and gender in United States Schools* (pp. 101–117). Albany, NY: SUNY Press.

Deans, T. (2000). *Writing partnerships: Service-learning in composition.* Urbana, IL: National Council of Teachers of English.

Delpit, L. (1995). *Other people's children: cultural conflict in the classroom.* New York: New Press.

Dilg, M. (1999). *Race and culture in the classroom: Teaching and learning through multicultural education.* New York: Teachers College Press.

Edelsky, C. (1994). Education for democracy. *Language Arts, 71*(4), 252–257.

Edelsky, C. (1996). *With literacy and justice for all: Rethinking the social in language and education.* New York: Taylor & Francis.

Edelsky, C. (1999). Education for democracy. In J. Allen (Ed.), *Class actions: Teaching for social justice in elementary and middle school* (pp. 147–156). New York: Teachers College Press.

Fecho, B. (1996). Learning from Laura. In Members of the National Writing Project Urban Sites Network, *Cityscapes: Eight views from the urban classroom* (pp. 57–71). Berkeley, CA: National Writing Project.

Finders, M. J. (1998–1999) Raging hormones: Stories of adolescence and implications for teacher preparation. *Journal of Adolescent and Adult Literacy, 42,* 252–63.

Fine, M. (1995). Silencing and literacy. In V. Gadsden & D. Wagner (Eds.), *Literacy among African-American youth: Issues in learning, teaching, and schooling* (pp. 201–222). Cresskill, NJ: Hampton.

Gardner, H. (1999). *Frames of mind: The theory of multiple intelligence.* New York: Basic.

Gee, J. P. (1999). *Social linguistics and literacies: Ideology in discourses.* New York: Taylor & Francis.

Giroux, H. A. 1992). Textual authority and the role of teachers as public intellectuals. In C. M. Hurlburt & S. Totten (Eds.), *Social issues in the English classroom* (pp. 304–321). Urbana, IL: National Council of Teachers of English.

Greene, M. (1995). *Releasing the imagination: Essays on education, the arts, and social change.* San Francisco: Jossey-Bass.

Greco, N. (1992). Critical literacy and community service: Reading and writing the world. *English Journal, 81*(5), 83–85.

Heath, S. B. (1993). Identity and inner-city youth. In S. B. Heath & M. W. McLaughlin (Eds.), *Identity and inner-city youth: Beyond ethnicity and gender* (pp. 1–12). New York: Teachers College Press.

Hynds, S. (1997). *On the brink: Negotiating literature and life in adolescence.* New York: Teachers College Press.

Kotlowitz, A. (1991). *There are no children here: The story of two boys growing up in the other America.* New York: Anchor.

Ladson-Billings, G. (1994). *Dreamkeepers: Successful teachers of African American children.* San Francisco: Jossey-Bass.

Lensmire, T. J. (1994). *When children write: Critical re-visions of the writing workshop.* New York: Teachers College Press.

Lewis, C. (2001). *Literacy practices as social acts: Power, status and cultural norms in the classroom.* Mahwah, NJ: Erlbaum.

Luke, A. (2000). Critical literacy in Australia: A matter of context and standpoint. *Journal of Adolescent and Adult Literacy, 43,* 448–61.

McLaren, P., & Gutierrez, K. (1994). Pedagogies of dissent and transformation: A dialogue about post modernity, social context, and the politics of literacy. *International Journal of Educational Reform, 3,* 327–337.

Mosenthal, P. B. (1998). Reframing the problems of adolescence and adolescent literacy: A dilemma-management perspective. In D. E. Alvermann, K. A. Hinchman, D. W. Moore, S. F. Phelps, D. R. Waff (Eds.), *Reconceptualizing the literacies in adolescents' lives* (pp. 325–352). Mahwah, NJ: Erlbaum.

Noddings, N. (1992). *The challenge to care in schools: An alternative approach to education.* New York: Teachers College Press.

NYC schools chief cited for not acting on evidence of bias/special ed dispute still unsolved. (1998 November). *Houston Chronicle.* Retrieved November 22, 2000, from the World Wide Web: http://proquest.umi.com

O'Connor, S. (1996). *Will my name be shouted out? Reaching inner city students through the power of writing.* New York: Simon & Schuster.

O'Neil, W. (1998). If Ebonics isn't a language, then tell me, what is? (pace James Baldwin, 1979). In T. Perry & L. Delpit (Eds.), *The real Ebonics debate: Power, language, and the education of African-American children* (pp. 38–48). Boston: Beacon.

Paley, V. G. (1999). *The kindness of children.* Cambridge, MA: Harvard University Press.

Paulsen, G. (2000). Dirk the protector (from My life in dog years). *The language of literature, 7th grade* (pp. 143–149). Evanston, IL: McDougal Littell.

Perry, T., & Delpit, L. (1998). *The real Ebonics debate: Power, language, and the education of African-American children.* Boston: Beacon.

Philbrick, R. (1993). *Freak the mighty.* Madison, WI: Turtleback.

Prosser, T. M., & Levesque, J. A. (1997). Supporting literacy through service learning. *Reading Teacher, 5*(1), 32–38.

Quindlen, A. (2000). Homeless. *The language of literature, 7th grade* (pp. 101–104). Evanston, IL: McDougal Littell.

Shakespear, E. (1999). What I'd tell a white gal: What my black male students taught me about race and schooling. In S. W. Freedman, E. R. Simons, J. S. Kalnin, A Casareno, & The M-Class Teams (Eds.), *Inside city schools: Investigating literacy in multicultural classrooms* (pp. 77–88). New York: Teachers College Press/NCTE.

Shannon, P. (1993). Developing democratic voices. *Reading Teacher, 47*(2), 86–94.

Shutz, A., & Gere, A. R. (1998). Service learning in English studies: Rethinking "public" service. *College English, 60,* 129–49.

Smitherman, G. (1998). Black English/Ebonics: What it be like? In T. Perry & L. Delpit (Eds.), *The real Ebonics debate: Power, language, and the education of African-American children* (pp. 29–37). Boston: Beacon.

Tatum, B. D. (1997). *"Why are all the black kids sitting together in the Cafeteria?" and other conversations about race.* New York: Basic.

Teachers and Linking Literacies of Yesterday and Today with Literacies of Tomorrow: The Need for Education That Is Multicultural and Social Reconstructionist

Carl A. Grant
University of Wisconsin–Madison

Before I outline my remarks, let me first acknowledge that I come here not as a scholar in the literacy area, but as a teacher educator and scholar of education that is multicultural and social reconstructionist, with attention to race, class gender, sexuality, ability, and the effects of power. Also, I come here with some personal thoughts about literacies. I believe that literacies are political, social, and cultural. I acknowledge the asymmetries in learning to be literate in multiple ways that are often based upon social, political, and material differences, where some people are prized and rewarded and others are considered lacking in the appropriate cultural capital and denied various privileges (Cherryholmes, 1988). Additionally, I come here as a consumer of the literacies I see in print media, television, movies, the Internet, and exhibits in art and science museums. Finally, I come here as a father and grandfather, and in both of these roles I realize that when I read bed-time stories to my children, Carl and Alicia, and now when I read or tell a story to my grandson, Gavin, I am affected by, and Gavin is affected by, the literacies of yesterday and the inscribed rules and standards that are embodied within them. Furthermore, these rules and standards that Gavin and I are experiencing are conditioning us for the literacies of tomorrow.

As a teacher educator, I have responsibility for preparing teacher candidates and working with experienced teachers who will link literacies of yesterday and today with literacies of tomorrow. Also, as a teacher educator for 25 years, I have gained some insights and understanding of the knowledge, dispositions, and skills that teacher candidates and experienced teachers bring to the linking of literacies. Additionally, as a scholar of education that is multicultural and social reconstructionist (Grant & Sleeter, 1985; Grant, Sleeter, & Anderson, 1986; Sleeter & Grant, 1987), I have some knowledge and understanding of how school policies and procedures, including curriculum and instruction, historically and presently deal with race, class, gender, ability, and sexuality issues. I believe that most educators have an awareness of multicultural issues, and many of them take some form of action to deal with issues of diversity. However, much of the research in this area argues that the level of action that educators take can be described as a prejudice reduction (Banks, 1997) or as human relations (Grant & Sleeter, 1996). In

National Reading Conference Yearbook, 50, pp. 63–81.

other words, the level of action teachers implement in the classroom is one of seeking tolerance, getting along, being respectful, and allowing access to those who differ. Demanding equity for students when access or equality is not enough, disrupting white privilege, eliminating homophobia, and eliminating the pedagogical discourses that are constructed to distinguish and treat urban and rural students differently are levels of action not often pursed in a sustained manner by educators.

One reason I believe that reconstructionist action is not often pursued is because educators are not always mindful of how historically pervasive issues of racism, gender bias, classism, homophobia, and ablism in our society are and how they continue to be reconstructed decade after decade. A discussion of the "linking of literacies of yesterday and today with literacies of tomorrow" offers opportunities for the members of the National Reading Conference (NRC) to discuss such history and reconstruction.

It is therefore as a teacher educator and a student and scholar of education that is multicultural and social reconstructionist that I offer my reflection on teachers "Linking Literacies of Yesterday and Today with Literacies of Tomorrow." I have organized my paper to first discuss the teaching force responsible for linking yesterday's and today's literacies with literacies of tomorrow. Next, I will discuss the pervasiveness of racism, classism, sexism, ablism, and homophobia in literacies of yesterday and today. Finally, I will argue that given the preparedness of teachers and the social construction of yesterday's and today's literacies, the NRC should take action to educate teachers about the race, class, gender, sexuality, and ability asymmetries in literacies and literary practices. The NRC should also educate teachers about how literacies are based upon differences in possessions or characteristics and power is constituted by relationships among those differences.

The Teaching Force Responsible for Linking Yesterday's and Today's Literacies

Who Are They?

The average American public school teacher is a white woman in her early forties, married with children, and with a spouse who is employed (National Education Association, 1992). Using years of teaching experience as a gauge, it can be estimated that in the public school sector, Latino teachers are younger than teachers in all groups other than white, with 48.8% having less than 10 years of experience and only 17.1% with more than 20 years of experience. On the other hand, African-American teachers are older than their counterparts, with 29.4% having less than 10 years of experience and 35.3% with more than 20 years experience. In regard to educational attainment, a greater proportion of African-American, Latino, and Asian or Pacific Islander teachers hold doctorates than white or Native American teachers. A greater percentage of African-American teachers hold master's degrees than any other group. Asian-American teachers lead all groups in education specialist certificates (Snyder & Hoffman, 1995, p. 77).

In 1993 and 1994, the K–12 U.S. teaching force was approximately 2.6 million. Of this number, approximately 13% were teachers of color. Of the K–12 public school teacher work force, 7% of the teachers were African-American, whereas African-American students represent up to 16.1% of all public school students; 4% of the teachers were Latino, as compared to a Latino student population of 12.7%; 1% were Asian/Pacific Islander as compared to 3.6% and fewer than 1% of teachers were Native American, as compared to just over 1% of students. Overall, 87% of public school teachers were white, as compared with 66.1% of public school students (Snyder & Hoffman, 1995, pp. 60, 77).

What Will the Teaching Force Look Like in The Future?

The teaching corps for the foreseeable future will be women—81%, with nearly 90% elementary school teachers, 92% will be white women, and less than 3% will know a language other than English. The number of people of color entering colleges and universities is decreasing with fewer of them entering teaching. Currently, about 9% of teachers are blacks and about 4% are Hispanic, and these figures are projected to hold fairly fast (U.S. Department of Education, 1999, p. 10).

A majority of teacher candidates were born in or after the 1980s. Their background knowledge and personal experiences in multiculturalism are limited (Dilworth, 1990). Also limited is their knowledge of the civil rights movements inspired and led by blacks, women, American Indians, Asian Americans, gays and lesbians, and the wars in Southeast Asia that led to a flow of immigrants from that region. It is not that teacher candidates have not heard about the civil rights movement, but that it comes by and large from a few pages in a social studies text that mainly provide a brief and sterilized account of these movements. Whereas many of these young candidates believe that there are some equity and social justice problems in the United States, they more firmly believe that the "real bad" problems were successfully resolved in the 1960s and 1970s.

Teacher candidates' knowledge and understanding of how and why a Euro-white American-centric education, gender biased toward males, with preferred access to economic opportunities for some groups more so than other groups, continually reproduced over the decades to ensure white superiority and privilege, is limited. Many contend that education in the United States is neutral. It is a prize in which all (or almost all students) have not only equal access in their pursuit, but they have equity in the quality of their pursuit toward an education. When they are assigned to read materials to counter their naiveté, such as Jonathan Kozol's (1991) *Savage Inequalities,* many acknowledge that their faith in the educational enterprise is misplaced. However, this new understanding often loses its impact and fades away when they enter the real world of the school and adhere to the customs and traditions of teaching. Also, this knowledge does not have staying power; its relevance is remote because most teacher candidates want to teach in schools like they attended in towns like their hometowns (Dilworth, 1990). Studies of teachers indicate that many do not desire to work in urban areas. According to an AACTE (1987) report, approximately 80% of the new teaching force grew up in suburban and rural settings and strongly desire to teach in those kinds of environments (see also AACTE, 1988, 1989, 1990; Zempher & Ashburn, 1992). Only 9% report that they would choose to teach in urban or multicultural settings (21st Century, 1991). Teachers most often come from isolated ethnic groups, with professional preparation that does not generally include much direct interaction with different cultures (p. 38).

Teacher Preparation

What is happening in the majority of teacher education institutions as it relates to the multicultural education preparation of teachers? Although the current literature supports the need for excellent teachers to teach children of diverse backgrounds (Haberman, 1987; McCormick, 1990; Stallings, Bossung, & Martin, 1990) and provides some direction on how to train teachers to work with diverse groups of students, few teacher education institutions are reported to take up and implement a full range of course work, field placements, and other experiences that are necessary to provide a quality multicultural teacher education program (Buttery, Haberman, & Houston, 1990; Grant & Secada 1990; Grant & Tate, 1995).

Teacher candidates have spent their freshman and sophomore years in Letters and Science. They have acquired some knowledge and understanding of academic disciplines, but for many those 2 years were mostly about taking their requirements and getting good grades so they would be accepted into the teacher education program. In personal interviews with the author, the candidates report that rarely during their first two years on campus were they asked to construct responses to concepts they were studying based upon their life knowledge and experiences. They were mainly responsible for regurgitating textbook knowledge back to their instructors (Grant, 1990, 1993, 1995, 1998, 1999).

In college, as much through the hidden curriculum as the overt curriculum, teacher candidates are taught the following: that blacks are really the same as white people, except perhaps they are culturally deprived; Asians are the "model minority" (Lee, 1996); education is neutral, with no class base. Additionally, the issues of sexual orientation and ability are often invisible in teacher education programs. Furthermore, few have been taught to work with the students with disabilities who are now included in their classrooms. This is in part because courses in special education are kept separate from courses in "regular education" and content and practice about students with disabilities is not usually infused into traditional education programs.

Teacher candidates accept the present efforts to reform teaching and teacher education as just one more hassle. Some moan and groan because of additional humanities requirements and about how other state mandates have interrupted their course-planning schedule. However, for many there moans and groans are rarely concerned with questioning the social and political nature of the reform effort. They for the most part just want to finish, get hired, get into their own classroom, and teach.

Teacher candidates, at the time of student teaching, often are self-centered (Fuller, 1969). They are mainly concerned about pleasing their cooperating teachers and university supervisors in order to get good letters of recommendation. They become impatient with the training process, especially when asked to learn educational theory. They want management plans and techniques—recipes, lists of do's and don'ts—to help them deal with "those kids" who have difficulty learning and following the codes of the schools. An examination of individual and institutional racism, sexism, classism, and other social problems in the public and hidden curriculum and other aspects of schooling are not areas with which they are eager or comfortable to engage.

Readiness of Teacher Candidates

Some teacher candidates come to schools of education with a degree of uncertainty, seeking to find the "courage to teach" (Palmer, 1998). Many come with very little self-reflection or understanding of "oneself" as this relates to being a member of a helping profession and the systems of reason that inform much of their actions both in and out of school. Many come uninformed about the importance of their biographies to their teaching. Palmer (1998) tells us about the importance of self when he states, "As I teach, I project the condition of my soul onto my students, my subject, and our way of being together" (p. 27). Zeichner and Gore (1990) illuminate this idea when they argue that teachers' biographies and autobiographies provide rich information about the way in which teachers' perspectives are rooted in the variety of personal, financial, religious, political, and cultural experiences they bring to teaching (p. 21). Lisa Delpit (1995), in *Other People's Children,* highlights the importance of self and biography to teaching culturally and racially different students. Delpit states, "One of the most difficult tasks as a human being is communicating meaning across our individual difference, a task confounded immeasurably as we attempt to communicate across social lines, racial lines, cultural lines, or lines of unequal power" (p. 66). Books and articles (Clandenin, 1993; Decker, 1969; Dyson & Genishi, 1994; Paley, 1989; Parkay, 1983) written by white teachers report on how their backgrounds were often a barrier to the education of students of color. Also, Lois Weiner (1993) tells us that a teacher's work can be affected by the socioeconomic class they come from. She believes teacher candidates who are from working-class homes are more susceptible to institutional pressures to conform than teacher candidates from high-status homes for many reasons (p. 121). Weiner continues:

> Unlike their middle class counterparts, many who view teaching as a way station between undergraduate school and the career they will pursue, young, white, working class women are frequently the first members of their families to attend college. Teaching is their foothold out of the working class, and their student teaching introduces them to the milieu in which they will root them-

> selves. (p. 121)

Teachers most often come from isolated ethnic groups with professional preparation that does not generally include much direct interaction with different cultures (p. 38). Mesa-Bains (1993) writes that many teachers have had no sustained contact with individuals of another race prior to entering the inner-city and multicultural classrooms. Not only do they lack familiarity, most are fearful of confronting the issue of race, as well as issues of class, gender, sexual orientation, and ability.

Why Do They Want to Teach?

Teacher candidates want to teach because they love and want to help kids. Collins and Frantz (1993) state that

> studies over the past twenty years have found that nearly seven of every ten teachers decided to become a teacher because of a desire to work with young people, and it is the chief reason cited by six of every ten teachers for staying in the profession. (p. 15)

Douglas Heath (1994), author of *Schools of Hope: Developing Mind and Character in Today's Youth,* asks, "Why do young people choose teaching? For its high salaries? Status? To increase America's international ranking on math achievement tests?" Heath then answers his own question, stating, "Scarcely. They enter and remain in the profession because they care about kids; they are called to help them grow into their full potential-not, as one teacher told me, to become technicians prostituting their hopes to increase students' test scores." Teacher candidates are indeed a unique corps of individuals. They come with the best of intentions. They are inspired to work with and care for individual children. But, are love of kids and good intentions enough?

In Sum

The major point here is that who a teacher is—such as their personhood, education, strengths, anxieties, prejudices, sensitivity, commitment, and background—influences how the teacher learns to teach and finally teaches in the classroom. This is significant for linking literacies of yesterday and today with literacies of tomorrow. The ways that teachers have learned the rules of their own lives and how they reason within these rules of conduct depending on their social status and conditions affects how they conceive of literacies and perceive who has the ability to be literate. To get beyond being a "fish in the water" unable to see or acknowledge the rules and asymmetries that buoy their own ways of being in the world is said by many teacher educators to require a transformation in teachers.

What best practices do we discuss at this NRC conference that can influence such a transformation of the very individuals who have such a strong impact in schools when students learn to be literate? I suggest that teachers must make problematic race, class, gender, sexuality, ability, and the effects of power when linking literacies.

Race, Class, Gender, and Sexuality in Literacies of Yesterday and Today

Literacies, What Are They?

Paraphrasing from a definition of curriculum by Popkewitz (1997), I view literacies as particular historically formed knowledge that inscribe rules and standards that help us to "reason" about the world and our "self" as productive members of that world. The rules "for telling the truth," identifying norms and values in literacies, however, are not only the construction of objects for our scrutiny and observation. Literacies are a disciplining technology that direct how the individual is to act, feel, talk, and "see" the world and "self" and think about others. As such, literacies are a form of social regulation. Gee's (1999) definition of literacy is also significant to this essay. He tells us that literacy is, in a sense, "multiple." Literacy becomes different "literacies" as reading and writing are different and distinctively shaped and transformed inside different sociocultural practices. Additionally, these sociocultural practices always have inherent and value-laden, but often different, implications about what counts as "acceptable" identities, actions, and ways of knowing. They are, in this sense, deeply "political." Furthermore, these practices always fully integrate language, both oral and written, with non-language "stuff," that is with ways of acting, interacting, feeling, valuing, thinking, and believing, as well as with various sorts of nonverbal symbols, sites, tools, objects, and technologies (p. 356).

Literacies, Power, and Asymmetries: Two Examples

Implicit in such an understanding of literacies are the effects of power relationships. Power operates in the asymmetries, in that there are unequal playing fields in which some are qualified and others disqualified from participation. Let me explain by offering two examples, one that takes place in schools and the other at home.

In schools where white European/American literacies are used, and where traditional literary practices are employed, these "asymmetries" are said to be in keeping with the "American way" (Hirsch, 1987; Ravitch, 1991; Schlesinger, 1992). However, this practice and notion of the "American way" is the result of power relationships that grow out of systems of reason that shape the literacies and literary practices that may privilege white male students more so than students of color, white female students, female students of color, and gay and lesbian students.

During Carl and Alicia's childhood, it was difficult to find an assortment of books written by authors of color for children of color. Power operated in the racism that led to white authors receiving many more opportunities to publish their work than authors of color. The systems of reason that guided trade book publishers caused many white authors and many white story lines to be deemed qualified. Many African-American authors and authors of color and many story lines that featured people of color were disqualified from participation and being published. If we consider literature important to the social and academic development of young people, then is it unfair or unreasonable to contend that Carl and Alicia and other children of color may have been affected in some way by the *absence* of literature by authors of color because these authors were disqualified from participation?

Textbooks and the Linking of Yesterday's and Today's Literacies

Teachers work in an educational system that has been and in many ways continues to be racist, sexist, classist, homophobic, and limited in sensitivity toward and inclusion of students with disabilities. The educational system plays a major role in keeping in place the systems of reason that produce race, class, and gender asymmetries; textbooks for decades have served as a primary conduit and advocate. Textbooks have and in many ways still are the constant in communicating the systems of reason that keep in place race, class, gender, sexuality, and ability biases. Hillel Black, author of *The American Schoolbook* (1967), supports this point when he states:

> Of all the artifacts produced by a modern civilization, from the plumbing used by its citizens to the weapons employed by its soldiers, none compares with the schoolbook as a mirror of that civilization's aspirations and failings. Certainly in America, schoolbooks over the decades have embodied most of the nation's beliefs and prejudices. But the textbook is more than just a cultural fossil that will delight and amuse some future anthropologist. As the most important educational tool of the past and (arguably) the present, the textbook is instrumental in molding the attitudes and passions of the young and thus both reflects and shapes the beliefs of the nation itself. Indeed, one may suggest that schoolbooks studied by previous generations have had an influence on the development of the American people that is almost as profound as the achievement of Thomas Jefferson, Franklin Delano Roosevelt, and Henry Ford. (p. 73)

Dewey (1938) also recognized the impact of textbooks on a society when he argued, "Books, especially textbooks, are the chief representative of the lore and wisdom of the past, while teachers are the organs through which pupils are brought into effective connection with the material" (p. 18). Ruth Elson's (1964) *Guardians of Tradition,* a study of the American schoolbooks of the 19th century, is an excellent work for gaining insights into how systems of reason based upon a white male Euro-centric ideology produce race, class, and gender asymmetries that operate both visibly and invisibly in literacies of yesterday and today. It is in these asymmetries that power operates, where white superiority affects what is the content of yesterday's and today's literacies, where maleness is the standard by which we judge success, where students living on the poverty line and in urban areas are not assumed to have cultural capital and are assumed to have learning problems, and also where the less privileged struggle with the privileged to eliminate the asymmetries that hold them in the position in which they are located.

White Superiority and Privilege Dominate Yesterday's and Today's Literacies

Yesterday's Literacies

For decades, teachers have knowingly and unknowingly used text materials that advocate both visibly and invisibly white superiority and privilege. Elson (1964) argues that the 19th-century schoolbooks presented the political, economic, social, cultural, and moral concepts which both created and solidified the American tradition (p. vii) and *that* tradition encourages ways of thinking that are active in today's society. For example, in the arts (e.g., pictures and paintings) and cultural literacies (novels, poems, essays) of yesterday, the social, cultural, and moral superiority of the white race is taken for granted, and very little has changed in these literacies today. An excellent illustration of the asymmetries and white superiority in yesterday's textbooks can be found in the pictures that feature representatives of the races of man. In these illustrations, the white race is always ranked at the top and blacks at the bottom. Sometimes in order to support the idea of white superiority, the picture of the white representative is socially constructed so that the viewer should see the person as upper middle class and wholesomely attractive. To establish the certainty of this idea, sometimes an attractive well-groomed woman (by Western standards) is used (Elson, 1964, pp. 65–66). Whereas pictures of the race of man that blatantly advocated the superiority of the white race through various gimmicks lost their usefulness as an instructional aide, the systems of reason that supports white superiority and privilege has put in place other devices that have remained very much a part of the education of many who teach today. For example, if a teacher received his or her education during the 1960s, they could have taken the Stanford-Binet Intelligence test that discriminated against members of the working class, Southern Europeans, and blacks through the inclusion of derogatory content. The 1960 version asked students to determine "Which is prettier?" and counterposed portraits of non-white people against those of white Anglo-Saxon individuals. The correct choice according to the test makers is the Anglo-Saxon representative in both examples.

Today's Literacies

This idea of "white" as being the more beautiful, *the* standard, has not lost its currency. In fact, its "stocks," unlike stocks in the market today, are secure and steady, which you can witness almost every time you turn on the television or attend the movies. The faces we see in the visual media are very much like the faces we saw in the IQ test. Also, it should be noted that in much of the visual media not only is white seen as "privileges and superior," but particular whites are also seen that way. In other words, not just any white person need apply, unless they have "cover girl looks" or the body of a "hunk." For example, for any one Rosie O'Donnell, Bette Midler, or Roseanne that appear on television or in the movies, I can list 10 Gena Davis, Brooke Shields, and Jessica Parker look-alikes who serve as the standard for much of our cultural, visual literacies.

The mass media in one form or another presents cultural literacies 24 hours each day. Cortés (1995) reminds us that the media disseminate information, images, and ideas concerning race, ethnicity, culture, and foreignness. In doing so they (the mass media) influence the social construction of knowledge about many factors of human diversity such as race, sexual orientation, disability, gender, and class. The media on the whole do very little to consciously disrupt the systems of reason that hold in place the inequities surrounding diversity. Cortés (1995) argues that this critical role of the mass media in the social construction of knowledge has significant implications for the work of teachers. In using the media as a tool to help link the literacies, teachers will have to be mindful that presently the electronic media plays a major role in keeping in place the equity asymmetries. McCarthy's (1998) work illustrates this point. He claims that Hollywood film and television participate in the coordination of the identities of the middle-class inhabitants of the suburbs and the disorganization of the identities of the dwellers of the inner city (p. 31). McCarthy argues that the electronic media play a critical role in the production and channeling of suburban anxieties and retributive morality onto its central target: the depressed inner city (p. 32). He contends that increasingly the underclass or working-class subject is contemporaneously being placed on the outside of the arena of the public sphere and he argues that the middle-class subject of history moves in to occupy and to appropriate the identity of the oppressed: "The center becomes the margin" (p. 37).

McCarthy (1998) refers to how the mainstream news media presents black and Latino America and how "Black and Latino youth appear metonymically" (represented partially and not as complete beings) in the discussion of problems: "kids of violence, kids of welfare moms, car jackers, the kids without fathers, kids of illegal aliens, kids who don't speak 'American.'" The inner city is used as a signifier of danger and the unknown that at the same time narrows the complexity of urban working-class life. You watch network evening news and you can predict when black and Latino bodies will enter and when they will exit. "The overwhelming metaphor of crime and violence saturates the dominant gaze on the inner city" (McCarthy, 1998, p. 39). McCarthy makes an additional point that I believe those liking literacies must consider. He argues that the portrayals of the inner city in films like *Boyz 'n the Hood* and *Falling Down* illustrate that what he calls the "discourse of resentment" not only has powerful rhetorical, or persuasive effects, it also has devastating material effects. Inner-city black school youth are surrounded by this powerful discourse of crime and violence in which they are the constructed other—social objects who grapple with the reality code projected from the popular media culture. Their experience of the reality code is grounded in material practices such as police harassment. Black and Latino youth experience the reality code as a "problem of representation." In other words, they are represented in particular ways by the media and people in society expect these youth to live up to that image portrayed in the media. Thus, this representation affects their access to opportunities and life choices (McCarthy, 1998, p. 42).

Finally, the magazine racks at the check-out counters at most supermarkets teach P/K–12 students monthly the norms and standards in American society.

Additionally, through their selection of content, much of the media says to adults, "herein lies a barometer that you can use to measure your success in life in such areas as sexuality, finances, home, furniture, partner, children and in-laws." This barometer is calibrated by the systems of reason that privilege white, heterosexual, physically normalized males.

The Intersection of Social Markers, Systems of Reason, and Literacies

In order to understand the significance of how power is constituted and how power flows throughout the idea of and discourse about literacies means coming to grips with how race, class, gender, ability, and sexuality are combined to produce oppression that is supported and kept in place by systems of reason that support inequities in all five areas. Three illustrations follow that illuminate this point: Literacies and the American Indians; The Arts and the Linking of Yesterday's and Today's Literacies; and Women in the Literacies.

Literacies and the American Indians

At Thanksgiving, during the elementary and middle grades, teachers teach about American Indians. What has society and schooling taught teachers about the American Indians that has prepared them to link yesterday's and today's literacies with tomorrow's literacies? Are the systems of reason used to inform teachers about the teaching of American Indians overwrought with the legacy of the first Thanksgiving and the wars between whites and Indians during the "settling" of the West?

Yesterdays' literacies featured the American Indians as "noble savages." The "nobleness" of the American Indian is detailed as eloquent, extraordinarily brave, with great hunting abilities, and ability to live off the land. The "savagery" is detailed as treacherous, ignorant, cruel, and morally corrupt (Elson, 1964, p. 72). Battles between American Indians and whites that resulted in the American Indians winning are commonly referred to as massacres. Battles between American Indians and whites that resulted in whites winning are referred to as victories. The systems of reason that informed these ideas about American Indians were constructed upon a love—hate relation that later was manifested in the concept of "Manifest Destiny," where whites reasoned that it was their assign duty and destiny to transform the land on which the Indians lived into town and cities and to build a railway to connect the east and west.

Today's literacies often continue to place the American Indian in the past and hold fast to the ways of thinking from past decades. In some ways the thinking about American Indians has become more negative. Although "savage" is not a word used today to refer to American Indians, also no longer are the American Indians seen as "noble." Additionally, no longer are American Indians' great hunting and fishing skills admired, but instead they are criticized for disrupting the hunting and fishing privileges of white Americans. Furthermore, no longer are the American Indians seen as eloquent spokespersons of their political positions, such as with the League of Iroquois. The Mohawk chief Hiawatha is noted for saying,

> We bind ourselves together by taking hold of each other's hand so firmly and forming a circle so strong that if a tree should fall upon it, it could not shake nor break it, so that our people and grandchildren shall remain in the circle in security, peace and happiness. (Zinn, 1995, p.20)

Instead, American Indians are seen as annoying because of their demand for sovereignty and treaty rights. Furthermore, literacies of yesterday and today about American Indians learned in the homes of some white Americans still have much in common especially in areas where there are debates over fishing rights. In these areas some school-age children stand with their parents and holler epithets at American Indians.

I highlight the view of American Indians in what can be called "literacy practices," or ways that images and symbols of American Indians can be read, in order to show how race intersects with literacies that intersect with what teachers are expected to learn and to teach. How do we teach students to read the symbols and images of groups of people? How do we include this ability to read symbols and images as racist in our conception of literacy? There is no better example of the enactment of racism than the symbols of American Indians that are used for team mascots and logos. How do we teach students and teachers to read and resist such use of these images? Do we include this ability in our definitions of literacy? I think a view of literacies from a perspective of education as multicultural and social reconstructionist can help us to encourage such a conception of literacy and best practices.

The Arts and the Linking of Yesterday's and Today's Literacies

In many teacher education programs, teacher candidates take arts methods courses. These courses are mainly aimed at teaching teacher candidates how to teach art, and do not usually provide a historical critique of the field from a cultural diversity and social justice perspective. So how will teachers deal with linking yesterday's and today's literacies with tomorrow's literacies in the teaching of art?

During the earlier years of the United States when the country was attempting to establish it own national identity, fine art was seen as an important cultural literacy because it was soothing, curative, and inspiring. Park (1963), speaking mainly about the immigrants of the 1900s who were poor and considered to be without cultural capital, argued that the acquisition of cultural literacy that comes with learning the fine arts was essential:

> [O]ur melting-pot of nations must be resolved into a laboratory, the processes of which shall be eliminated and purified, disengaged and recombined. And among the agents to be employed there is no doubt that the fine arts might be one of the most active. They are even now cleansing the city slums as the

> settlement; music schools and elementary courses in drawing and modeling develop, liberating the play-impulse in the mind of those whose lives are set in sordid surroundings. By these beneficent agencies the poor and the rich are brought together, and democracy is so furthered. (p. 1503)

The [fine] arts today are still considered essential to the development of the "total person." Also, the arts today are somewhat more accepting and appreciative of art forms from different cultures and artists from different social groups. In spite of this acceptance and appreciation, Western art forms dominate museums and galleries and signal to people that this is *the* national identity of the United States. A strong link between yesterday's art literacies and today's art literacies continues to be white dominance and privilege. For example, I am a collector of art work, with an interest in the arts by and about people of color, especially African-American art. Wherever I shop for this art, in galleries, museum shops, department stores, most of the time I find these works are in limited quantity, not available, or only available during the duration of a special exhibit.

Let me share two experiences where I personally felt the effects of white dominance and how systems of reason make privilege a natural happening in the lives of whites. During the early part of the 1990s, I visited the National Museum of American Women's Art. After viewing the paintings and other artwork throughout the three-story structure, I discovered none of the art work was about or by a person of color. In order to check the accuracy of my perception, I went to the office of the director of the Museum and inquired if there were any pieces about and by artists of color. I was informed that there was one painting of an African-American woman; however, the frame for the painting was in need of repair. When I asked, "If my daughter had accompanied me to the gallery, what could I tell her about 'why' there was such an omission of women of color?" I was rebuffed and told I was being too sensitive.

Similarly, in 1990 when I visited the Corcoran Gallery of Art in Washington, D.C. to see the exhibit "Facing History: The Black Image in American Art 1710–1940," one of the Museum employees spontaneously commented to me, "We have never had such a large crowd of _____!" and then she caught herself. She was about to say "blacks." I responded by saying, "If you have a product that is of interest to people, one that they can enjoy and relate to, they will come!"

Guy C. McElroy (1990), the curator for the exhibit and author of the catalog for the exhibit, "Facing History: The Black Image in American Art 1710–1940," states:

> The way that America's leading visual artists have portrayed the African American—a slave, servant or member of the middle class, minstrel performer or wartime hero, ridiculous stereotype or forceful leader—form an index that reveals how the majority of American society felt about its black neighbor. Naming is a form of power, and visual images have the persuasive power to identify and define place and personality. (p. 7)

McElroy's statement reflects the effects of systems of reason that lead to power relationships that produce what African Americans would describe as a largely restrictive stereotype of black identity, but would be seen by many others as an honest portrayal of blacks.

Women in the Literacies

Above, I noted that most of the teachers are white females and future teachers will continue to be white women. What have the literacies of yesterday, today, and tomorrow told teachers about the place of women in U.S. cultural history? And, have these literacies had an influence on women and men?

Yesterday's cultural, technology, and art literacies for the most part omitted women as self-asserting and self-fulfilling individuals. Ways of thinking about women in the early 20th century were that they were not physically and mentally fit to use most technologies, such as river boating, herding, rail laying, and blacksmithing. The image of women was one of femininity, not involved with farming or agricultural tools, nor active in industry. School books did not usually claim that women were the intellectual inferiors of men, although they recognized this as a popular opinion: "It is considered by many, by far too many, that woman is often of an inferior order of intellect, of minor capacity, in short, literally, the 'weaker sex' in other senses than a physical one" (Elson, 1964, p. 308).

Also, American females in yesterdays' literacies, except in a few rare cases, were not portrayed as heroines or as great women and citizens. The American women that were raised to heroic status achieved distinction either because they died for love or because they performed great deeds to help their husbands, parents, or children (Elson, p. 310; also see Butterfield, Demos, Grant, Moy, & Perez, 1979). Additionally, although yesterday's literacies present students with stories and pictures that illustrate deeds of virtue, enterprise, courage, generosity, and patriotism, in order to motivate them to copy such noble examples, women were absent (Elson, 1964, p. 186; Butterfield et al., p. 383). Throughout the 19th century continuing well into the 20th century, women in the literacies are regarded as inferior beings whose worth lies only in complete dependence in thought, word, and deed on men. It is important that I point out that I am for the most part discussing views of white women. Women of color were not considered to any extent in the discussion of "women." The systems of reason that produced the gender asymmetries also informed white women that they were superior to women of color. Sojourner Truth's statement at Seneca Falls in 1851 discussing "the rights of women" provocatively and eloquently captures the racism and sexism of the time, a good deal of which continues today. Truth states:

> That man over there says that woman needs to be helped into carriages and lifted over ditches. . . . Nobody ever helped me into carriages, or over mud-puddles or gives me any best place. And ain't I a woman?
>
> Look at my arm! I have ploughed, and planted, and gathered into barns and no man could head me! And ain't I a woman?
>
> I would work as much and eat as much as a man, when I would get it, and bear the lash as well. And ain't I a woman?

> I have borne thirteen children and seen em most all sold off to slavery, and when I cried out with my mother's grief, none but Jesus heard me! And ain't I a woman? (Zinn, 1995, p. 122)

The idea of equality of the sexes in law or in economic and social opportunity was invisible in the literacies featured in the American schoolbook. According to Elson (1964), in the mind of most schoolbook authors the student is male, and being so, he (the student) is encouraged to work hard and follow the examples of great men (p. 302). This notion of the invisible, insignificant woman, it can be argued, plays a significant role in shaping the male attitude on women' rights and career aspirations. For example, women artists such as Mary Cassat were forced because of sexism to leave the United States in order to study their craft. And, in over 30 years of being a frequent flyer, only one time have I flown on a flight where both of the pilots were women; I have yet to fly on a plane flown by a female pilot of color.

The belief that women were second-class citizens was publicly voiced as noted in the poem, "The Future of Women" in an 1871 reader. The poem argues that the lack of women's achievement in the world in the past indicates her proper future:

> What highest prize hath woman won
> In science or in art?
> What mightiest work by women done
> Boast city, field, or mart?
> She hath "no Raphael," Painting saith;
> "No Newton," Learning cries;
> Show us her steamship, her Macbeth,
> Her thought-won victories!

Similarly, In *The Literary Reader for Academies and High Schools*, A. Hall (1850; cited in Elson, 1964) wrote the following:

> Her effect
> Lies not in voting, warring, clerical oil
> But germinating grace, forth-putting virtue.

Women in today's literacies as reported in several evaluation studies of sexism in school textbooks (e.g., Conti & Kimmel, 1993; Reese, 1994; Jones, Kiteutu & Sunderland, 1997; Titus, 1993) indicates some progress in gender equity. However, the overall finding is that much equity work still needs to be conducted. For example, Conti and Kimmel (1993) reported that in the 11 top-selling life span developmental textbooks the amount of information described on events in girls' and women's lives, such as rape and pregnancy, was minimal in all 11 textbooks. Also, information on women of color in today's textbooks are hidden deep in the shadows of gender discourses (e.g., Conti & Kimmel, 1993).

In sum, it can be argued that women—white women—are much more central in the literacies today, but not yet at the center. They are active with many technologies, however, some technologies such as aviation, engineering, and film directing still remain limited in their availability to women.

Conclusion: Literacies and Education That Is Multicultural and Social Reconstructionist

So what is the case that this scholar of multicultural education and teacher education is making to the NRC membership? It is simply that teachers are not prepared to link the literacies of yesterday and today with literacies of tomorrow. Their socialization both in their P/K–college education and in their out of school experiences has not prepared them to undertake this effort. They have not been taught to problematize the literacies of yesterday, today, and tomorrow as they relate to multicultural issues. They have limited or no experience in disrupting the dominant discourses that have historically determined what counts as true, important, or relevant, what gets spoken and read, as well as what remains unsaid and marginalized. And, although teachers should not carry the burden of making visible and disrupting the systems of reason that are responsible for the race, class, gender, sexuality, and ability biases that impact the students they teach, their role and the power they bring to this undertaking should not be underestimated or overlooked. Actions that include more reflective practices are required. Questions that need desperately to be asked include the following: "What is literacy? What does it mean to link literacies, and who is privileged with the way that we link literacies?"

NRC, through its mission, writings, and research, should demand that educators see as problematic pervasive racism, classism, gender bias, homophobia, heterosexism, and ablism when liking literacies of yesterday and today with literacies of tomorrow. This can be accomplished: by using frameworks and practices that lead educators to examine what orders their thinking about literacy; and by using frameworks that lead them to explore the effects of the intersection of race, class, gender, sexuality, ability, and power. These practices can lead educators to construct knowledge that shows how students learn literacies, and learn to be literate, in multiple ways.

In this paper, I have begun to show the multiple ways that literacies might be examined with a brief examination of the ways that American Indians, art, and women are viewed within different literacies. Those participating in NRC can do this same cultural, historical work that can be called "social mooring" (Grant & Wieczorek, 2000; Popkewitz, 1998), remembering to always consider the intersections of multiple factors when considering literacies of yesterday, today, and tomorrow.

Finally, for this scholar of multicultural education when I think about my grandson Gavin (whom I introduced to you at the beginning of this essay) and his friends, who are of color, I am deeply concerned about their life chances. When I discuss with Alicia and Carl the sharing of literacies with Gavin, I tell them to read and explain the literacies using frameworks and practices that will inform Gavin (in a process that relates to his maturity level) about the effects of race, class, gender, sexuality, ability, and power. Also, I tell them to educate Gavin with the knowledge, skill, and attitude so that he will be at "home" in different cultures. As a 5-year-old African-American male child who will probably attend predominantly white schools and be taught literacies by primarily white teaching staffs, and as a young person who lives in a broader society that continues to support systems of reasons that foster inequality and inequities while staunchly claiming major reduction of these biases, he must quickly come to understand how such discourses influences his life chance and opportunities. Equally as important, he must be taught how to resist and disrupt such discourses in literacies and other areas of life without becoming a casualty of the systems of reason that promotes such discourses.

References

American Association of Colleges for Teacher Education. (1987). *RATE I. Teaching teachers: Facts and figures.* Washington, DC: American Association of Colleges for Teacher Education.

American Association of Colleges for Teacher Education. (1988). *RATE II. Teaching teachers: Facts and figures.* Washington, DC: American Association of College for Teacher Education.

American Association of Colleges for Teacher Education. (1989). *RATE III. Teaching teachers: Facts and figures.* Washington, DC.: American Association of College for Teacher Education.

American Association of Colleges for Teacher Education. (1990). *RATE IV. Teaching teachers: Facts and figures.* Washington, DC: American Association of College for Teacher Education.

Banks, J. A. (1997). *Educating citizens in a multicultural society.* New York: Teacher College Press.

Black, H. (1967). *The American schoolbook.* New York: William Morrow.

Butterfield, R., Demos, E. S., Grant, G. W., Moy, P. S., & Perez, A. L. (1979). Multicultural analysis of a popular basal reading series in the International Year of the Child. *Journal of Negro Education, 68,* 382–390.

Buttery, T., Haberman, M., & Houston, R. (1990). *ATE: First annual survey of critical issues in teacher education.* Reston, VA: Association of Teacher Educators.

CherryHolmes, C. H. (1988). *Power and criticism: Poststructural investigations in education.* New York: Teachers College Press.

Clandinin, D. J. (1993). *Learning to teach, teaching to learn: Stories of collaboration in teacher education.* New York: Teacher College Press.

Collins, C., & Frantz, D. (1993). *Teachers talking out of school.* Boston: Little, Brown.

Conti, N. E., & Kimmel, E. B. (1993, March). *Gender and cultural diversity bias in developmental textbooks.* Paper presented at the meeting of the Southeastern Psychological Association, Atlanta, GA.

Cortés, C. E. (1995). Knowledge construction and popular culture: The media as multicultural educator. In J. A. Banks & C. A. McGee Banks (Eds.), *Handbook of research on multicultural education* (pp. 169–183). New York: Macmillan.

Decker, S. (1969). *An empty spoon.* New York: Harper & Row.

Delpit, L., D. (1995). *Other people's children: Cultural conflict in classroom.* New York: New Press.

Dewey, J. (1938b). *Experience and Education.* New York: Macmillan.

Dilworth, M. E. (1990). *Reading between the lines: Teachers and their racial/ethnic culture.* Washington, DC: American Association of Colleges for Teacher Education.

Dyson, A. H., & Genishi, C. (1994). *Cultural diversity in the class room and community.* Urban, IL: National Council of Teachers of English.

Elson, R. M. (1964). *Guardians of tradition: American schoolbooks of the nineteenth century.* Lincoln: University of Nebraska Press.

Fuller, F. (1969). Concerns of teachers: A developmental conceptualization. *American Educational Research Journal 6,* 207–226.

Gee, J. P. (1999). Critical Issues: Reading and the New Literacy Studies: Reframing the National Academy of Sciences Report on Reading. *Journal of Literacy Research, 31,* 355–374.

Grant, C. A. (1990, 1993, 1995, 1998, 1999). *Letters and Science and Teacher Preparation: Interviews with Teacher Candidates.* Unpublished manuscript.

Grant, C. A., & Secada, W. G. (1990). Preparing teachers for diversity. In W. R. Houston (Ed.), *Handbook of research on teacher education* (pp. 403–422). New York: Macmillan.

Grant, C. A., & Sleeter, C. E. (1985). The literature on multicultural education: review and analysis. *Educational Review, 37*(2), 97–118.

Grant, C. A., & Sleeter, C. E. (1996) *Turning on Learning: Five approaches for multicultural teaching plans for race, class, gender, disability.* Englewood Cliffs, NJ: Merrill.

Grant, C.A., Sleeter, C. E., & Anderson, J. E. (1986). The literature on multicultural education: Review and analysis. *Educational Studies, 12*(1), 47–71.

Grant, C. A., & Tate, W. F. (1995). Multicultural education through the lens of the multicultural education research literature. In J. A. Banks & C. A. McGee Banks (Eds.), *Handbook of research on multicultural education* (pp. 145–166). New York: Macmillan.

Grant, C. A., & Wieczorek, K. (2000). Teacher education and knowledge in the knowledge society: The need for social moorings in our multicultural schools. *Teacher College Record, 102,* 913–935.

Haberman, M. (1987). Recruiting and selecting teachers for urban schools. *Urban Diversity Series Number 95.* New York: ERIC Clearing House Urban Education.

Heath, D. (1994). *School of hope: Developing mind and character in today's youth.* San Francisco: Jossey-Bass.

Hirsch, Jr., E. D. (1987). *Cultural literacy: What every American needs to know.* New York: Houghton-Mifflin.

Jones, M. A., Kitetu, C., & Sunderland, J. (1997). Discourse roles, gender and language textbook dialogues: Who learns what from John and Sally? *Gender and Education, 9,* 469–490.

Kozol, J. (1991). *Savage inequalities: Children in America's schools.* New York: Crown.

Lee, S. J. (1996). *Unraveling the "model minority" stereotype: listen to Asian American youth.* New York: Teacher College Press.

McCarthy, C. (1998). *The use of culture and the limits of ethnic affiliation.* New York: Routledge.

McCormick, T. E. (1990). Collaboration works! Preparing teachers for urban realities. *Contemporary Education, 61,* 420–426.

McElroy, G.C. (1990). *Facing history: The Black image in American art 1710–1940.* Washington, DC: Corcoran Gallery of Art.

Mesa-Bains, A. (1993). Introduction. In J. H. Shulman, A. Mesa-Bains (Eds.), *Diversity in the classroom: A Casebook for teachers and teacher educators* (pp. 1–4). Hillsdale, NJ: Research for Better Schools and Erlbaum.

National Education Association. (1992). *Status of the American public school teacher 1990–91.* Washington, DC: Author.

Paley, V. (1989). *White teacher.* Cambridge, MA: Harvard University Press.

Palmer, P. J. (1998). *The Courage to teach: Exploring the inner landscape of a teacher's life.* San Francisco: Jossey-Bass.

Parkay, F. W. (1983). *White teacher, black school: The professional growth of a ghetto teacher.* New York: Praeger.

Park, C. W. (Ed.). (1963). *Fine arts in the Lincoln Library.* Buffalo, NY: Frontier Press.

Popkewitz, T. S. (1997). The production of reason and power: Curriculum history and intellectual traditions. *Journal of Curriculum Studies, 29,* 132.

Popkewitz, T. S. (1998). *Struggling for the soul: The politics of schooling and the construction of the teacher.* New York: Teachers College Press.

Ravitch, D. (1991). A culture in common. *Educational Leadership, 49*(4), 3–11.

Reese, L. (1994). Gender equity and texts. *Social Studies Review, 33*(2), 12–15.

Schlesinger, A. M. (1992). *The disuniting of America.* New York: Norton.

Sleeter, C. E., & Grant, C. A. (1987). An Analysis of Multicultural Education in the United States. *Harvard Educational Review, 57,* 421–444.

Sleeter, C. E. & Grant, C. A. (1987). The literature on multicultural education: Review and analysis. *Harvard Educational Review, 37,* 97–118.

Stallings, J.S., Bossung, J., & Martin, A. (1990). Houston Teaching Academy: Partnership in Developing Teachers. Teaching and Teacher Education, 6, 355–365.

21st Century (1991). *Restructuring the education of teachers.* Reston, VA: Association of Teacher Educators.

Snyder, T. D., & Hoffman, C. M. (1995). *Digest of education statistics 1994.* Washington, DC: National Center for Education Statistics, U.S. Department of Education.

Titus, J. L. (1993). Gender messages in education foundation textbooks. *Journal of Teacher Education, 44,* 38–44.

U.S. Depart,emt of Education, National Center for Education Statistics (1999). *The condition of education 1999.* Washington, DC: U.S. Department of Education.

Weiner, L. (1993). *Preparing teachers for urban schools: Lessons from thirty years of school reform.* New York: Teacher College Press.

Zempher, N., & Ashburn, E. (1992). Countering parochialism in teacher candidates. In M. D. Dilworth (Ed.), *Diversity in teacher education* (pp. 40–62). San Francisco: Jossey-Bass.

Zeichner, K., & Gore, J. (1990). Teacher socialization. In W. R. Houston (Ed.), *Handbook of research on teacher on teacher education* (pp. 329–349). New York: Macmillan.

Zinn, H. (1995). *A people history of the United States: 1492–present.* New York: Harper Perennial.

Bridging Cultures: How Can Inquiries by Outsiders Inform Educational Practice?

Rebecca Barr
National-Louis University

It is becoming common for U.S. educators to participate in educational projects in countries other than the United States. Some pursue opportunities working with literacy programs in Central and South America, in Africa, and in China. Still others contribute as part of the Reading and Writing for Critical Thinking Project in Central Europe and Central Asia (Klooster, Steele, & Bloem, 2001). My particular experience involves working with Pratham, a project supporting the education of poor children from the slum areas of Mumbai, India. I spent 2 months in 1998 working with Pratham preschool and study classes as a Fulbright Scholar. I then returned the following year for a 2-week period. This experience prompts my reflection on the issue of how inquiries by outsiders can inform educational practice in other cultures.

Through our work in other nations, many of us confront major cultural differences. We learn about the ways in which children learn and are taught. We discover how people in other countries think about literacy and how they organize their schools, and have had to come to terms with barriers posed by our not speaking or understanding the language. Trying to find one's way in an unfamiliar culture is a risky and challenging business. Some of the recurring questions I posed were: Should I really be trying to do this? What and how can I learn from it? What might "cultural bridging" consist of and can it be done? How can I contribute through this sort of work? Can any real good result?

I want us to think carefully about questions such as these and the work we are doing in other countries. In trying to tackle these complicated issues, I will use my experiences in Mumbai to illustrate my thinking. I organize my chapter around the following questions: How can we prepare ourselves to live and contribute in another culture? How can we gain access and establish some degree of trust? How should we define the nature of our work? What sorts of records should we keep, and how? What strategies should we use to make sense of our experiences and to test our evolving understandings? How should we share what we learn? What will be the consequences?

Preparing for the Work

In preparing this chapter, I began to realize that scholars do not often discuss the complexities inherent in how we do our work. Certainly there are books on

*National Reading Conference Yearbook, **50**, pp. 82–95.*

methods, in both Education and Anthropology, that give some guidance for fieldwork. But the particulars are stripped away so that it is difficult to gain a sense of the practice. David Riesman (1964) wrote:

> All field workers belong to the club of the initiated and exchange experiences informally, if at time guardedly, although rarely in their publications. But outsiders, including students, cannot share this in-group understanding, and to that extent science as a large cooperative process suffers. (p. xi)

In alluding to Laura Bohannan's anthropological novel, *Return to Laughter*, which she wrote under the pseudonym of Eleanor Smith Bowen (1964), Riesman notes that "She reveals some of the human costs, passions, missteps, frailties, and gaieties that lie behind the often too antiseptic reports of social scientists" (p. x).

I found that *Return to Laughter* was one of my best teachers. It led me to reflect on conflicts that develop in the field between a sense of professional duty and personal friendship: the daily dilemmas of how close to become to certain members of the community; whether we should let our agendas be co-opted and shaped locally; what sort of risks we should take regarding our health. The book vividly reveals how fieldworkers can be caught in local power struggles, can become the pawns of certain groups.

In preparing for work in India, I did several things the year before I left. I read about 25 novels. Even though these books represent the perspective of more affluent Indians who write in English, I gathered glimpses of what life in India might be like. Many stories traced the movement of poor people from ancestral village homes into the promise of urban living and back again. The tenuousness of their crowded lives was clear. I could see that I did not really have a clue about the workings of the caste system. I confronted the ambivalence of Indians toward the British and the remnants of the colonial period. I learned the horrors of the sterilization campaign during the premiership of Indira Ghandi. I particularly loved reading Amitav Ghosh's *Circle of Reason* (1986) and Salman Rushdie's *Midnight's Children* (1980), but I did not understand them until I walked the narrow back streets of Mumbai. The odors, the noise, the colors, the garbage—I had no idea what a protected environment we live in here. Even watching films had not really given me a sense of urban life in the poorest areas.

I read about the educational system. Although I had known about the low literacy rates in India, particularly among women from rural areas, I had not really understood the enormity of the challenge. There are about a billion people in India, with a literacy rate of 58%. This means that about 420 million people are illiterate. If you were to take all the people in the United States and increase it by 50%, this would be the number of illiterate people in India. Programs to address the problem, such as "Operation Blackboard," which sought to bring literacy to 100 million Indian young adults, have failed for a variety of reasons, including insufficient funds. In Mumbai, the population is about 10 million; more than half live in slums. Although the literacy rate in Mumbai is around 85%, it is much lower in the slum areas since many families come from the rural areas.

I also read material that had been developed by Pratham, the organization I would be working with (Chavan, 2000). In December 1994, Pratham was established as a public charitable trust by UNICEF, the Municipal Corporation of Mumbai, and several prominent individuals. Pratham, under the leadership of Madhav Chavan, committed to the ambitious goal of having every child in Mumbai in school by the year 2000 and every child learning. One of my first experiences while riding in from the airport was to see a huge banner across the road that had been put there by Pratham folks to raise the awareness of policy-makers: "Education is not an Option. It is the Future."

I learned about three of Pratham's programs: the Balwadi program involving preschool classes, the Study Classes providing remedial work in schools for third and fourth graders who were lagging behind, and the Bridge Program, which provided a transitional instructional program to bring street children into schools. In this chapter, I focus on the Balwadi preschools. They are similar to Headstart classes—a teacher works with about 20 children each day for about 2½ hours. The growth of the preschool program is astounding. Beginning in 1994–95 with 120 classes, it grew to 1,707 programs in 1997–98 to about 3,000 currently. This means that about 60,000 children are being served. Figure 1 shows the growth in the number of preschool classes from 1994 to 2000. By providing enjoyable preschool experiences, it is expected that children will develop the social and conceptual knowledge that will increase their likelihood of attending primary school and doing well.

This description raised a multitude of questions for me. How was the growth managed and supported? Where were decisions being made and by whom? How were the activities funded? More related to instruction, what did children do in the preschools? Who were the teachers? How were they recruited and trained? Were there any attempts to assure the quality of the children's experiences? So even before I arrived in Mumbai, I was eager to learn more about this program.

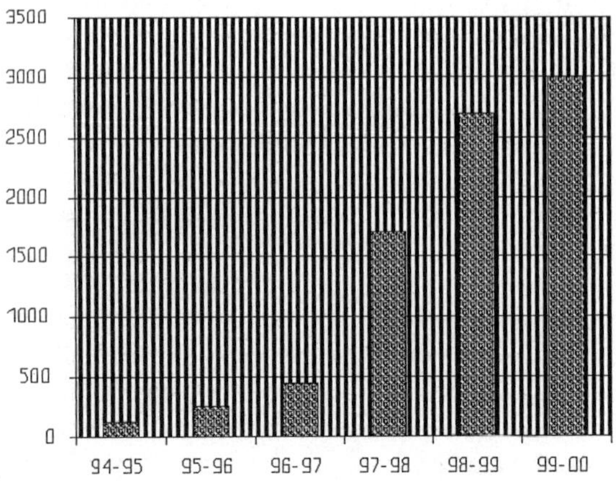

Figure 1. Growth in the number of Balwadi preschool classes from 1994 to 2000.

Gaining Access

I was encouraged to apply for the Fulbright Fellowship by my good friend Rukmini Banerji. We had worked together in Chicago for several years; I had known her from earlier days when she was a doctoral student at the University of Chicago. Ever since she joined Pratham in 1996, we plotted ways of my coming to India. Finally, I was delighted when my Fulbright application was accepted. Since Rukmini was trusted by the Pratham leaders and teachers, gaining access was much easier. Since I was her friend, they accepted me as well.

Yet, some of the trust I felt also developed through the work and problem-solving I shared with them. I spent a lot of time visiting classes and talking with teachers. Rukmini's theory of assimilation was one of immediate and deep immersion. I arrived in Mumbai one evening and the next morning I went with her by train to visit some Balwadi classes. I wrote in my journal:

> We walked through a maze of narrow dirty alleys. The first preschool class we visited was being held in the living area of a one-room home. A small group of children sat on mats playing with blocks and beads that had been given to them by their teacher. She then handed out slates for them to draw pictures with chalk. Some late arriving children, with a younger sibling in tow, joined the group.
>
> To reach the second Balwadi class, we wound our way back through shops, down narrow passages to a second home. I was welcomed in by a poised young woman. In English she had learned in Catholic school, she said she loved teaching. Since her family would not allow her to work outside the home, this gave her something interesting to do and a small income. She brought out some of the materials she had created during the training session, including a matching game. But, the children did not seem to know what to do.

The culture is very different. The poverty is heart wrenching, but there are also riches—parents care deeply about their children, as do members of each community. There were other challenges for me—getting around was difficult because of the competition for limited space. Getting onto a train requires special skill. You may have seen pictures of people hanging out windows and doors of trains—it really is like that. Even though one or two special train cars are set aside for women, to travel at rush hours means you have to be strong and persistent. At other times, traveling by train is not that hard—particularly with the protection of the women's car.

Although we often think about gaining access in terms of others letting us in, most of the major obstacles were within me. Not knowing Hindi or Murati proved to be a huge barrier. Code-switching during conversations was common, so I caught the portion of talk that was in English. Many times in classrooms I was not sure what the nature and purpose of an activity was, even after if was explained to me in English. Though I learned to negotiate the challenges of train transportation with the help of available maps, I was never able to find my way down narrow winding passages stacked with houses to neighborhood Balwadis. Although the destinations were known locally, they were difficult to specify on maps. Tapping into this local knowledge depended on being able to communicate in whatever local language was being spoken.

And language is only the surface manifestation of underlying concepts and experiences that also represented barriers. Only gradually over time did I get glimpses of the very different way Indians think about time, space, and human development. Thinking is not linear. Rukmini would often say to me that she was trying to get the young teachers to think clearly. I was not sure what she meant, but I think it had something to do with both planning and reflection. Was she trying to get them to think more logically and linearly—or was it something else? While caught in the habits of mind of Western thinking, I was also certain that my ways of thinking about problem solving and education limited what I could see. My background clearly influenced how I interpreted what I saw.

Establishing Goals

During my first week working with Pratham people, I started to gain some idea of how things were organized and how decisions were made. Madhav Chavan clearly was the visionary leader of Pratham. But he also attracted and organized a leadership team composed of young "activists."

My friend Rukmini was one of six people who collectively made plans and carried out the work. When I asked Madhav if there was a division of labor among the group, he said it might be that his role was mainly one of envisioning what could be and what needed to be done. But then he said that they all worked together to put the vision in place and support the quality of the programs. Although one person seemed mainly responsible for fiscal matters, and another for research, it became clear that all of the leadership team participated collectively in major activities: surveying neighborhoods to establish need, securing teachers and meeting places, and participating in professional development. They all worked very hard. Rukmini left early in the morning and sometimes did not return until well into the evening. Yet, it was clear to me that the group greatly enjoyed each other's company. And I appreciated being included in their meetings.

The process of establishing goals for my work in Mumbai was twofold. First, I needed to find out what Pratham folks wanted me to do. Second, I needed to think about what my own goals might be. The first was in many ways easier than the second. During my first period of work in 1998, the leadership team asked me to provide a "snap-shot" of what I was seeing and to suggest any ideas I thought they should consider. The assignment seemed straightforward—but it was, after all, a blank check. They gave me permission to struggle to give form to my impressions, and on that basis, discuss what I thought some of their upcoming challenges might be.

Concerning my own goals, Rukmini and I had ongoing conversations about what was really interesting about Pratham. We were intrigued by the fact that in some communities the program worked extremely well and in others required a high level of maintenance. These differences seemed to have less to do with cultural, linguistic, or religious characteristics of the communities, and more to do with the structures and cohesion of the communities. We were also interested in how the lives of the young women who became teachers became transformed; we were interested in giving voice to their stories. The opportunities to become teachers opened up many new learning experiences. At the same time, it had the potential to alienate them from their families as they formed a new network of friends. We were interested in issues of literacy development and whether the preschools were useful for preparing children for first-grade instruction. But though we talked a lot about these goals, we had not made much progress pursuing them because the immediate pressures of project growth and support always seemed to take priority.

Developing Methods for Gathering Data

When I left for Mumbai, I was armed with a camera and a tape recorder. I found that my most useful means of keeping records was in my journal which I carried with me and elaborated each evening. Although I did take pictures, doing so seemed to intrude into the ongoing flow of events. I did not feel comfortable tape-recording conversations since many of the young teachers were shy and struggled with English. My journal was most useful in helping me recall interesting visits and encounters.

I collected many artifacts. I borrowed the English versions of the textbooks being used in the Mumbai Municipal schools. I read reports that had been developed by Pratham people. I studied the tests and the test results from third and fourth graders that had been gathered by Pratham. In a country with almost no formal assessment, these results were extremely useful in trying to think about what was happening to the children of poor people in Mumbai. Affluent folks as well as many from the middle class sent their children to private schools if they could afford to do so. Thus, the public schools were attended mainly by poor children.

In addition, there were a number of descriptive records. Supervisors of the teachers noted characteristics of the classroom programs: the current enrollment, attendance of children, whether a meeting had been held with parents. They also rated the classrooms on cleanliness and displays. They noted the teacher's punctuality, enthusiasm, class management, use of space, rapport with children, teaching methods, use of curricular ideas, as well as the cheerfulness, participation, and cleanliness of children. I poured over these records as another way of learning about the teachers and their supervisors. I found these records to be most useful in understanding the availability of the supervisor to the teacher.

Once I knew that I was going to write some sort of a report, I began to focus on the Balwadi preschool classes and on the Study Classes for children who were achieving far behind their classmates in school. I found that trying to write these reports at an early stage in my fieldwork was useful in letting me know what more I needed to find out and what I needed to think about (Wolcott, 1994).

I realized early on, for example, that the Balwadis I had visited were not from the poorest of poor neighborhoods. Thus, I asked Rukmini to arrange visits to the most challenging communities. These included Balwadis in the illegal slums where living spaces were bounded by canvas, paper, and tin. We visited a community center that had been used for preschool classes but was now locked because of a power struggle among politicians. We saw where a Balwadi, as well as surrounding houses, had been leveled to the ground in attempts to clean up the illegal slums. People were scrounging amidst the debris to locate possessions they had lost. I came face to face with the uncertainty of existence, and the courage that is required to keep living.

Making Sense of Observations and Experiences

My sense-making went hand in hand with my fieldwork. I will focus here on how I tried to gain a sense of how the Balwadi program worked. In many ways the report-writing proved to be a way for me to get my own ideas in order; but it also served to communicate to the leadership team what I was seeing and what I thought was sufficiently important to write about. I organized my report around three questions: (a) How are the teachers recruited? (b) What are the experiences of children in the Balwadis? (c) How are the teachers trained and supported? But additionally, I focused on a fourth area concerning the future of the program.

Teacher Recruitment

The Balwadi Program recruits young women from the community in which the new Balwadis are to be established. Because they are from the same cultural group as the children, they have an "insider's" understanding of the children's culture and home language and can use it as a basis for extending children's language and conceptual experiences.

The Balwadi teacher recruitment process is informal, by word of mouth, based on recommendations from teachers and community members. Young women (ages 18 to 35) who have had a 10th-grade or greater education are sought because it is believed that they will have the interest and energy to relate well to young children and appreciate the importance of joyful learning experiences. The teachers are paid very little, 200 rupees a month (about $5.00), and although parents are asked to pay additional small fees, only some do. Yet, as was true for the teacher who was not allowed by her family to work outside the home, teaching the Balwadi class provided an opportunity for personal growth and a small income.

Children's Experiences

Some of the classrooms I observed were in homes whereas others were in schools or community centers. In most, an attempt was made to decorate the space with interesting pictures. In a few I saw charts listing numbers and the alphabet in the classroom. Most obvious, the children in the classes seemed to be comfortable being with other children in a group and engaging in activities directed by the teacher, in spite of the limited space available. They were learning to listen carefully to their teacher and to respect the needs of other children, as well as to come to class on time and to participate for the 2½-hour period. Children seemed to be engaged; some participated actively, while others watched.

I observed the following sorts of activities: eating snacks, playing with blocks and beads, stringing beads, drawing pictures with crayons on paper, looking at shapes of circles or squares and finding similar shapes in the room, placing bottle caps on a design, listening to the teacher tell a story, singing songs, and looking at pictures, for example, of an elephant and talking about its eyes, ears, tusks, walk, and so on. Judging from the degree to which children were engaged, the most successful activities seemed to be those with a group focus and good teacher questions. These occurred during storytelling and discussion of pictures and shapes. The least successful were those in which a single child participated at a time while the others watched (e.g., putting bottle caps on a design) or ones that were too easy for most children (bead stringing). Eating snacks and preparing to go home seemed to occupy at lot of time. In contrast to what I might see in a Head Start classroom in the United States, there was no storybook reading.

Teachers were patient and encouraging with the children. Children who were shy or worried were treated warmly by the teacher; if a child preferred not to participate in activities, he or she was not forced to do so. The teachers were able to attend to the group as a whole, as well as to the needs of individual children. These young teachers interacted with their children in a confident manner. They were also poised and professional in how they received guests into their classrooms. Those with more than a year's experience showed greater confidence in organizing activities than those with less.

Teacher Training and Professional Support

How have these young women been helped to assume this new identity? The answer seems to lie in the combination of training and the ongoing supervision they receive. Professional training occurs for a 12-day period prior to teaching, and a second 12-day period midyear. A core training team develops expertise and defines activities for training and then instructs a large cadre of trainers, composed of persons from each school zone of Mumbai. These trainers then prepare new Balwadi teachers prior to teaching and midyear. Training consists of some developmental and learning theory, demonstration of instructional activities, and support for teachers to make their own materials. Consideration is being given to the possibility of distributing the second phase of training throughout the first year of teaching at weekly or biweekly intervals.

The program is characterized by a hierarchically organized support structure. Supervisors, responsible for approximately 10 teachers, visit each teacher for a 1½-hour period at least three times a month. Records revealed that many supervisors visited their teachers as many as four or five times a month, but others as little as once a month. During visits, supervisors rated the teachers on various dimension and then discussed the ratings with the teacher. I was surprised to see that there was no organizationally defined overlap in the roles of trainers and supervisors, beyond the requirement that supervisors attend all training sessions in which their teachers are involved.

It also seemed that these young teachers acquire confidence because of the support they receive from members of the community. The best evidence for this was when we tried to locate particular preschools. These young women and the location of their schools were known by community members; they were respected because they were "Balwadi teachers."

Future of Pratham Programs

I asked questions about the future of Pratham's programs. Will Pratham continue to oversee this program 2 years from now? What does Pratham envision 5 years from now? Often when people are extremely busy just keeping a very ambitious program afloat, there is no time to think about the future. One member of the leadership team suggested that Pratham might not exist 5 years from now. He hoped that the Education Department of the Municipal Corporation of Greater Mumbai or some other group would assume responsibility for the program. Another suggested that Pratham as a leadership group might be occupied elsewhere and that local communities would assume responsibility. I was concerned that relatively little thought had been given to the future of the program.

Sharing What I Learned

In fieldwork, as in any interpretive research study, sharing is an ongoing process. Each day as I thought I had learned something, I would share my insights with Rukmini and others. My goal was to produce a "snap-shot" based on what I was learning and to suggest ideas I thought they should consider. I decided to frame this set of ideas as "Challenges for the Future." In this report, I focused on four areas. The first two concerned the quality of the Balwadi program and the experiences of children. The third pertained to the nature of teacher training and support. The final one concerned the future of the Balwadi program.

To my mind, the effectiveness of the program seemed to derive from the combination of (a) teachers who care deeply about children and (b) activities to promote learning. Teachers seemed to be successful in working with families, and children liked coming to the class. These considerations seemed to contribute to children developing understandings about punctuality, regularity, concern for others, and respect for the teacher—all of which would serve them well later in primary school.

Program Quality: Storybook Reading

I also expressed some of my concerns. Given the upcoming experience of being a first grader in a fairly traditional public school class with about 50 other first graders, I was worried that there were so few literacy-related activities. I suggested that storybook reading should become a daily activity. All children love stories. In addition, they need to see print and to begin to understand how print can be used to convey interesting ideas. Obviously this suggestion is based on our experiences in the United States concerning the usefulness of encouraging emergent forms of literacy (Morrow, 1988, 1990; Neuman & Roskos, 1992, 1993; Nielsen, 1993).

Program Quality: Instructional Balance

I expressed concerns about the range of activities that I observed in the classes. The dominating activity was snack time. To encourage a better balance of activities, I suggested that it might be useful to organize activities into three overlapping areas such as (a) communication, including storytelling, book reading, and play acting; (b) physical activities, games, and songs; and (c) creative work such as drawing pictures, making up songs, and making objects. I even recommended that during the 2½-hour class period, there should be time for at least two activities involving communication, one creative activity, and at least one activity that involves songs and physical activity

Teacher Support and Training

As previously mentioned, I was concerned that there seemed to be no organizationally defined overlap in the roles of teacher trainers and supervisors, beyond the requirement that supervisors attend training sessions. Yet, since about half of the supervisors are also members of the training team, an informal relation existed. I suggested that they might want to consider an organizational structure that merges the two roles. Supervisor/trainers could then model various procedures for their teachers both during training and during their class visits, as well as observing how teachers use them. Such linking would likely increase the incorporation of new activities in the classes.

Future of the Balwadi Program

I suggested that when a program seems to be working well and serving the needs of teachers and students, it is not too early to think about its future. Particularly if a transition of some sort is envisioned, it is not too early to anticipate problems that may occur. I suggested that whatever decisions are made about the administration of the program, decentralization of responsibilities and decision making would increase the likelihood that the enterprise could be self-sustaining and that future activities would reflect the values and goals of participants. I argued that it is important to consider issues such as these: How might the recruitment, supervision, and professional development of teachers be decentralized to build a stronger and more autonomous organization? How might the character of the organization be affected if it remains under the purview of Pratham, as opposed to becoming part of the school system, or some other arrangement?

Response to the Report

I completed the report before I left Mumbai. It was familiar to Rukmini, but not to some of the others on the leadership team. Immediately upon returning to Chicago I anxiously reflected on the report. I worried that it would seem to be presumptuous. Who was I to imagine that I—with such a limited understanding of Indian culture—could recommend certain actions and practices? Then I had the opposite fear—What if they took all my suggestions to heart—even those that may well have been inappropriate? At the same time, since I was in constant conversation with Pratham people, the ideas were probably more theirs than mine. In any case, the outcomes are interesting.

The third and fourth suggestions were implemented within several months after I left Mumbai. I suspect that it may have been easier to make changes in the structural arrangements of the organization than in the practice.

The second area pertaining to instructional balance was addressed in several ways. Supervisors modeled appropriate activities in classes. They helped teachers to develop weekly plans listing the activities they selected each day for their students. Perhaps the linking of teacher training and support activities had been useful in encouraging a more appropriate set of activities. My visit back to India in 1999 showed that some teachers were following their plans. These tended to be the teachers who had been teaching in Balwadis for several years. For other teachers with less experience, the planning seemed to be a token activity. I was reminded that the selection of appropriate activities comes from a deeper form of teacher knowledge that develops through practice over time.

Concerning my first suggestion, when I returned to India in 1999, my visits to Balwadi classes showed little change in the inclusion of literacy-related activities. This seemed to be true even though the Pratham supervisors had involved teachers in book-reading activities. Often these books ended up being mounted on the wall.

There are several possible explanations for this. One is that the books available in Hindi and Murati did not seem to be inviting to teachers and children. The pictures in most books are small; many are black-and-white line drawings. Perhaps more important, there tends to be a lot of print on each page. I found a few that had some potential for use, but even these included a lot of print and small pictures.

A second reason may be that changing instructional strategies is generally difficult and takes time. Just as it was the more experienced Balwadi teachers that seemed to be implementing a more balanced set of activities, perhaps the incorporation of book reading also will take time for teachers to gain experience.

Yet there are other possible reasons. I discussed my observations with members of the leadership team. One suggestion was that perhaps the Balwadi teachers did not have much confidence in their own reading and thus would not choose to read aloud.

Madhav Chavan's comments were particularly interesting. He suggested that any oral reading in India is nontraditional. He noted that he had particular difficulty reading a prepared speech. He feels more comfortable speaking extemporaneously and improvising. Indian music is similarly improvised, much like jazz. Thus, in this sense oral reading is nontraditional, whereas storytelling fits well within Indian traditions. Indeed, storytellers feel compelled to change the story rather than standardize it. And such standardizing is what happens to stories as they appear in print.

In a related vein, Brenda and Douglas Louie (in press) suggest that the limited use of storybook reading in Chinese schools derives from historically entrenched views that children's literature is frivolous—fun but not educationally worthy. In other words, they suggest that the absence of children's literature in schools is more than an oversight; it is a choice made on the basis of traditional values.

This, however, is an evolving story. Recently, I received an e-mail from Rukmini that read: "Currently 48 Balwadis have started with the book bag project. Parents are showing considerable interest in the books. In several cases, there have been active reading and demonstration sessions in parent meetings." Parents seem to be interested in their children having the same advantages as those who attend private preschools where storybook reading is common. Thus, it is too soon to know what will occur in this area.

Summary and Reflections

Some may draw the conclusion from this experience that it is inappropriate for researchers working in an unfamiliar culture to make educational suggestions. I suggest otherwise. I believe that some of the most interesting learning occurs by making suggestions and seeing which are taken up or not. Pursuing why a particular response does or does not occur may increase our understanding and may even give rise to new approaches to education, perhaps, for example, in emergent forms of storybook reading.

I grew to respect the potential of this form of research, which is a variant of participant observation or action research. I became able to specify for myself ways in which this research differs from most anthropological field research. My experiences, for example, were quite different from those of Laura Bohannan described in *Return to Laughter* (Bowen, 1964). Her story is that of a single individual searching to understand an unfamiliar culture. In contrast, my fieldwork is much more collaborative. I did not have different agenda from those with whom I was working. Indeed, our common agenda grew out of wanting to improve the life chances of young children. My work also differed from Bohannan's in that she was intent on describing and understanding a culture. In contrast, I along with others were concerned with improving what existed. I worked *with* friends around the work they are doing; the goals are mainly theirs, not mine. The interpretive act was much less a lonely act than it was for Bohannan. I had the opportunity regularly to check my sense-making. My Western pair of eyes noticed many things also seen by the leadership team, with their textured multicultural perspective based in part on their experiences in the West. The ultimate purpose for my being there was also different from Bohannan's. I came to understand my role as a very limited one: I served as the occasion for Pratham leadership to step back from day-to-day operations to ask questions that existed for them in only latent form.

This form of educational inquiry also differs from that of participant observation and action research in that I could not fully engage in activities because of language barriers and I could not formulate new courses of action since I was not the person responsible. My commitments were not long term and did not involve immersion in daily activities for more than a short time period. My role was secondary—part of the supportive cast. Yet, I would argue that the role of being the occasion for reflection is important. The brushing together of two cultures gives rise to questions and ideas about alternative forms of educational support. Indeed, education in the United States might well profit from such scrutiny.

Although my work may or may not have been useful to Pratham, I am certain that it was beneficial to me in a variety of ways. I will describe three of these. First, I believe that learning about the educational issues of another country has enabled me to develop a comparative perspective. From this vantage point, it is easier for me to view educational practice in the United States and to see what is unique and what may be more universal. I am also learning how one's culture, for example, our competitive individualism in the United States, affects our educational practices.

Second, and somewhat related, I have learned strategies and ways of thinking that may help me with my educational work in the United States, particularly in the inner-city schools in Chicago. The ambitious visions and implementation work of Pratham was new to me and differed from the very conservative "scaling up" that we typically practice in the United States. The leadership exemplified a carefully balanced execution of working with the Municipal School System of Mumbai, while at the same time maintaining an independent physical and financial base for their activities. Pressure is brought to bear by demonstrating what can be done—and on a large scale. Finally, their commitment to working with communities is similar to what has been attempted in Chicago, but Pratham takes very seriously the charge of recruiting talent from the local communities and providing the professional development that is needed for growth.

Third, and in a somewhat different realm, this experience has made me think carefully about what I have learned and how these ideas can be represented. The differences between education in our culture and that of other cultures make clear the challenges of communication. Culturally unfamiliar experiences need to be "pictured" in a dynamic fashion. Fortunately, hypermedia technologies make available to scholars a much richer set of possibilities for conveying knowledge of education as it exists in other cultures than is possible within the linear constraints of text. Our methods of communicating about educational practice in the United States often assume a shared culture. As we become more aware of cultural differences within our county, other means beyond linear text become necessary to insure understanding about educational practice. For example, never in the past have I used pictures to show the work that I am doing in Chicago schools even though I now believe that this would have been a useful thing to do. I now think carefully about how this can be done. Clearly, this chapter has provided the occasion for me to think carefully about my work and how inquiries by outsiders can inform educational practice.

References

Bowen, E. S. (1964). *Return to laughter.* Garden City, NY: Doubleday.

Chavan, M. (2000). *Building societal missions for universal pre-school and primary education: The Pratham experience.* Paris: UNESCO–International Institute for Educational Planning.

Ghosh, A. (1986). *The circle of reason.* New York: Viking.

Klooster, D. J., Steele, J. L, & Bloem, P. L. (Eds.). (2001). *Ideas without boundaries: International education reform through Reading and Writing for Critical Thinking.* Newark, DE: International Reading Association.

Louie, B., & Louie, D. (in press). Children's literature in the People's Republic of China: Its purposes and genres. In W. Li, J. S. Gaffney, & J. L. Packard (Eds.). *Chinese Language Acquisition: Theoretical Pedagogical Issues.* New York: Kluwer.

Morrow, L. M. (1988). Young children's responses to one-to-one story readings in school settings. *Reading Research Quarterly, 23,* 89–107.

Morrow, L. M. (1990). Preparing the classroom environment to promote literacy during play. *Early Childhood Research Quarterly, 5,* 537–554.

Neuman, S. B., & Roskos, K. (1992). Literacy objects as cultural tools: Effects on children's literacy behaviors in play. *Reading Research Quarterly, 27,* 202–225.

Neuman, S. B., & Roskos, K. (1993). Access to print for children of poverty: Differential effects of adult mediation and literacy-enriched play settings on environmental and functional print tasks. *American Educational Research Journal, 30,* 96–122.

Nielsen, D. C. (1993). The effects of four models of group interaction with storybooks on the literacy growth of low-achieving kindergarten children. In D. J. Leu & C. K. Kinzer (Eds.), *Examining central issues in literacy research, theory, and practice.* Forty-second yearbook of the National Reading Conference (pp. 279–287). Chicago: National Reading Conference.

Riesman, D. (1964). Foreward. In E. S. Bowen, *Return to laughter.* Garden City, NY: Doubleday.

Rushdie, S. (1980). *Midnight's children.* New York: Penguin.

Wolcott, H. F. (1994). On seeking—and rejecting—validity in qualitative research. In H. F. Wolcott, *Transforming Qualitative Data* (pp. 337–373) Newbury Park, CA: Sage.

Family Literacy and the Mediation of Cultural Models*

Rebecca Rogers
Washington University in St. Louis

June and Vicky Treader taught me that intergenerational literacy is a delicate balance of textual encounters, institutional arrangements, and literate subjectivities. I learned from the Treaders how literate subjectivities are embedded within legacies, transmitted across generations. June Treader is an African-American mother of four children. Her literate life may be defined in relation to "schooled literacy," her own and her children's, and to her identity as a mother. June's belief in the power of literacy over her and her children was seen in her assertion to her adolescent daughter Vicky, "how you gonna get somewhere without readin'?"

In this article, I describe, interpret, and analyze Vicky's literate engagements and the intergenerational transfer of ideologies around schooling and women's work in the analytic space of a family's literacy practices. I specifically ask the following research question: How are values and assumptions pertaining to literacy mediated through family literacy practices?

Theoretical Perspectives

Family literacy practices are more than just ways of using literacy and language in the home. A broad range of studies has documented the following things about the status of literacy in families and communities. First, there is a wide range of literacy practices that exist in families and communities (Barton & Hamilton, 1998; Barton, Hamilton, & Ivanic, 2000; Street, 1995; Taylor & Dorsey-Gaines, 1988). Second, literacy has increasingly been viewed as a social practice that has come to also be seen as a set of processes that shape and are shaped by social institutions (Anderson & Stokes, 1984; Barton & Hamilton, 1998; Cushman, 1998; Silverstein & Urban, 1996; Street, 1995; Wenger, 1998). Third, discussions about family literacy practices often are connected to a set of social debates concerning the differences between Discourses termed as cultural mismatch between the discursive spaces of schools, homes, and communities (Heath, 1983; Moll, Amanti, Neff, & Gonzalez, 1992; Scribner & Cole, 1981). Despite the mis-

*Rebecca Rogers is the recipient of the Outstanding Student Research of the Year Award, 2000.

*National Reading Conference Yearbook, **50**, pp. 96–114.*

alignment between homes and schools, researchers have demonstrated that there is a strong belief and value in the logic of schooling and in schooled literacy, especially with nonmainstream groups (Carger, 1996; Heath, 1983; McCarthey, 2000).

Some researchers have approached the disjunctures between the home and school by documenting the funds of knowledge that exist in the homes and communities of the children in the school and restructuring the curriculum in order to privilege local knowledge (Au, 1981; Ladson-Billings, 1994; McIntyre, Rosebery, & Gonzalez, 2001; Moll & Gonzalez, 1994). Other researchers have turned to Gee's (1996, 1999) framework of primary and secondary Discourses in order to account for this misalignment between Discourses. Central in this framework is the development of the constructs of primary and secondary Discourses and the distinction between acquisition and learning.

Gee distinguishes between d/Discourse and learning and acquisition. Discourse (big D) refers to both language bits as well as the cultural models that are associated with Discourses. Gee (1999) refers to cultural models as "usually a totally or partially unconscious explanatory theory or 'storyline' . . . bits and pieces of which are distributed across different people and in a social group" (p. 45). For instance, there is a university Discourse that includes not only certain language bits particular to academia but also associated ways of thinking, believing, and valuing that are connected with membership in the Discourse of the university. Little d discourse refers to the linguistic elements—the language bits—that are connected with such Discourses. Of course, the linguistic (little d) and the social and cultural models (big D) are constitutive and work together to construct, maintain, and transform interactions. The important thing to keep in mind about Discourse (both big and little d) is that they are social, political, and have histories of participation.

Gee posits that people acquire their primary Discourse within the immediate context of the home and the community. Acquisition implies a preconscious element to understanding the cultural models—the storylines, beliefs, assumptions, and ways of being—that are associated with this Discourse. The construct of acquisition, alongside learning, is important to researching cultural models because it suggests that there is an invisible element to the storylines that people generally pick up unknowingly. The primary/secondary Discourse framework is used to demonstrate that children who do well in school often times have access to schooled literacy, which may include stories read aloud, question-and-answer interactional patterns, multiple experiences with variety of genres of books and texts within the context of their home, or primary Discourse (Purcell-Gates, 1996; Taylor, 1983; Teale, 1986). However, even though children are acquiring ways of being around literacy and texts that are in alignment with school Discourse, they are also learning concepts about print that will help them to negotiate literacy in school. Thus, the distinction between learning and acquisition may not be cleanly relegated to the secondary and primary Discourses.

Similarly, the framework posits that children learn rather than acquire their secondary Discourse. That is, secondary Discourses are often Discourses that children come into contact with prior to acquiring D/discourse within their homes and communities. These might include schools, churches, banks, stores, and other public institutions. However, just as learning occurs during the acquisition process, acquisition similarly occurs within the secondary Discourse. That is, as children learn how to read they also acquire a set of beliefs and values about what counts as reading depending on the types of texts and interactions in the classroom (Luke, 1995; Muspratt, Luke, & Freebody, 1997).

The d/Discourse and learning/acquisition framework holds rich potential for theorizing about children who fail to do well in school. As the literature suggests, there are often differences in language and literacy experiences across primary Discourses. Children who acquire a Discourse in line with the both the explicit and implicit cultural models of schooled literacy are apt to do well in school (Heath, 1983; Neuman & Celano, 2001) . This position has been readily critiqued, most notably by Delpit (1995) who argues that this position is overly deterministic in its positioning of children who do not have access to "codes of power." As a consequence, they are not likely to break into this Discourse. Rather than assuming the Discourses are mutually exclusive, this framework assumes there may be conflicts between Discourses (Gee, 1999; Knobel, 1998; Laraeu, 1989; Valdes, 1996). Further, because the process of acquisition implies the mediation of invisible ways of being with the world that include not only ways of talking but cultural models, it implies that children who have not acquired the school Discourse may have difficulty with the implicit cultural models because the storylines are the most difficult to teach.

In this article, I argue that the boundaries between learning/acquisition and d/Discourse are constantly negotiated. I suggest that both primary and secondary Discourses may also be in *alignment* for children who do fail to do well in school. The process of acquiring a primary Discourse children also acquire cultural models that either (a) support both the explicit and implicit Discourses of the school or (b) support the explicit Discourses of the school (e.g., reading books, doing homework, reinforcing school-types of interactional patterns) but construct and sustain an implicit Discourse that includes the devaluing of language and literacy practices connected with the home and community. The latter scenario offers a way to explain why, despite ample commitment to schooled literacy (Carger, 1996; Purcell-Gates, 1995; Taylor & Dorsey-Gaines, 1988), children and families fail to turn social resources into cultural capital.

In either scenario, two important factors influence the acquisition of cultural models. First, acquisition of cultural models occurs both in primary and secondary Discourses. Second, the framework of Discourses and cultural models needs to account for the acquisition of problematic ideologies—or the emergence of cultural models that will possibly either conflict or align with the secondary Discourse—within the primary Discourse. In this article, I argue that in the process of participating in family literacy practices, participants acquired cultural models that were in alignment, rather than conflict, with the cultural models of the school.

Method

Participants and Research Context

The Treaders—June, Lester, Vicky, Luanne, Shauna, and Evan—are an African-American family living in Sherman Hollows, an inner city in upstate New York. The Treaders receive housing, food, and income assistance. June dropped out of school at the end of ninth grade and returned to school at the local adult literacy center. She was reading at a first-grade level according to the Test of Adult Basic Education when she entered the program. Within 2 years, June was reading at a mid-fourth-grade level. Lester, her husband and father of her four children, has a GED. He was a trained plumber and was a member of the armed services. Vicky, the focal case study participant, is an adolescent girl in sixth grade at the time of the data presented in this paper. Luanne was in third grade, Shauna in preschool, and Evan was 3 months old. The Treaders have a large extended family and social network within the borders of their community. Their community comes together for birthday, holiday, and anniversary parties to share music, food, and stories.

Data Collection and Analysis

Situated within a linguistic anthropological approach to social phenomena (Silverstein & Urban, 1996) and critical discourse studies (Chouliaraki & Fairclough; 1999; Fairclough, 1995; Gee, 1999; Wodak, 1997), the data for this paper represent a thread running through a larger ethnographic research study that describes, interprets, and explains language and literacy practices in the everyday lives of the Treaders across multiple domains (home, school, community) by using complementary methodological approaches of ethnography and discourse analysis (Gee, 1999; LeCompte & Preissle, 1996). Data for the complete project were collected over a 2-year period of time from September 1997 to September 1999. I used methods of participant-observation recorded in fieldnotes; in-depth, semi-structured and informal interviews; and document collection in order to understand the multiple uses of language and literacy.

There were three ongoing phases to the research project. The first phase included documenting the language and literacy practices in the Treaders' home. The second phase involved spending time in the schools of both June and her daughters. I interviewed both June and Vicky's classroom teachers and remedial reading teachers. The third phase involved intensive involvement in the community, interviewing people and observing the language and literacy practices within the Treaders' immediate social network. Data collection included observations twice a week at home and at school with fieldnotes taken during and after the observations. One day of the observations included I assumed the role of a literacy teacher for both June and Vicky, a request June made in exchange for participating in the research. The reading group consisted of four to five adolescents, June, and myself in the dual roles of literacy teacher and researcher. We read and discussed books around themes of social injustice and civil and social rights, and I facilitated critical literacy discussions.

My analysis involved two complementary modes, ethnographic and discourse analytic, both of which were underlined by critical social theory. Using an interpretive method of analysis (Cairney & Ruge, 1998), I developed categories of family literacy practices. Examples of family literacy practices included the presence of schooled literacies, institutional literacies, and personal literacies. With each category I developed ethnographic and discourse-rich vignettes to analyze the vignette itself and the way it was connected to other literacy practices in the Treaders' home. In this stage of analysis, I identified what Fairclough (1995) refers to as "cruces" or moments of conflict in the data. An example of a disjuncture is the differences in representation of literate competency between the school and observations of Vicky in her home and community. In order to explain these conflicts, I used critical discourse analysis to move from description and interpretation of the conflicts to offer an explanation (Chouliaraki & Fairclough, 1999; Fairclough, 1989; Gee, 1999; Luke, 1995; Wodak, 1997).

Critical discourse analysis (CDA) is a discourse analytic framework that combines close attention to linguistic structure (little d, in Gee's Discourse theory) with social theory and analysis (big D, in Gee's Discourse theory). Within a CDA framework, language is ideological, both shaped by and shaping social life. Using CDA, I examined the linguistic properties of texts as well as their social and political dimensions. Following Fairclough's (1995) method of analysis, I attended to three intersecting domains of analysis, (description, interpretation, explanation), as well as three domains of discourse (the local, the institutional, the societal). I went through each of the following levels of analysis. First, I analyzed the texts for the local domain, or the linguistic aspects of texts. I attended to the grammar, turn-taking, modality, pronouns, and tenses used in discourse. The institutional level of analysis is concerned with the process of text production, consumption, and interpretation. It assumes that all oral and written texts have histories and trajectories. The third domain is referred to as the societal level of analysis. This level assumes that cultural models and subject positions are embedded in and constructed by discourse. I coded each of the vignettes, including the ethnographic and linguistic interactions recorded on audiotapes, in terms of local, institutional, and societal domains of discourse. I then looked for patterns both within and across the literacy events. In the analysis for the present paper, I call on the institutional and societal domains of analysis to point to and explain the cultural models that are attached to literacy practices within the context of the Treaders' family literacy practices.[1]

1. I have not included an extended Critical Discourse Analysis within this paper because of the space constraints. Instead, for the purposes here, I combine critical ethnographic analysis with a critical discourse framework in order to point to cultural models that are attached to family literacy practices. However, in doing this, I must acknowledge two of the common critiques of CDA (e.g. Slembrouck, 2001; Widdowson, 1998). The first critique of CDA is that there is often asymmetry between linguistic detail and social theory. That is,

Knowing Vicky

From third to sixth grade, Vicky attended an elementary school within walking distance from the Treaders' house. Prior to that Vicky attended another school, further into the south end of the city, within the same school district. Vicky had an affectionate relationship with her siblings. She enjoyed harassing her younger sisters, as older sisters do, but she also helped them with many things. Part of her relationship with her siblings was connected to literacy and education. Vicky helped her sister Luanne with her homework. Vicky was particularly proud to help Luanne with words she did not know when she was reading. Indeed, when the children got home from school June would tell them to "get their homework done" before they could go outside. On the days when it was raining or they did not have homework, June told the children to "get a book from the library room and read." The Treader children grew up in a household that had a library room started by their mother with a collection of over one hundred children's books housed in a three-shelved red bookcase. June had acquired the books from her adult education center as gifts, and the children had brought books home that the teacher was going to get rid of. In the same room, the children's spelling tests, awards, and certificates for graduating from grade school and for perfect attendance were hung on the paneled walls. June hung her certificates of accomplishment on the living room closet door, including a certificate of parent participation in her daughter's preschool class, a certificate that recognized her work in the school store at the adult learning center, and a photo of her daughter's preschool class.

Vicky's participation as a family member and as the oldest sibling also included watching the younger children when June went to the store or on errands. Vicky would watch the children from the front stoop, just as June did, making sure that they did not go around the corner. When Evan, the youngest of the Treader children, arrived in the late summer of 1998, Vicky acted as a caregiver for him. She often gave him baths, changed his diapers, put him to sleep, fed him, and played with him. June told me that this care-giving was a relief for her because it gave her time to sit outside, play Bingo, or watch TV by herself.

June showed a strong belief in the ability of her children and a dedication to schooled literacy. When she asked me to work with Vicky as a reading tutor, she told me that Vicky needed extra help in reading. June spoke of this extra help not

---

analysts will either privilege social theory and apply the critical discourse framework to the ethnographic data as well as the discourse data in order to illustrate the importance of context. This leads to a second common critique of CDA. CDA is often used out of context, making it difficult to assess where the framework of the researcher ends and the data begins. In the present study, I have situated the critical discourse analysis within 2 years of ethnographic data in order to point to the importance of histories of participation at each level of analysis (local, institutional, societal). Just as ethnographic data strengthens the validity of claims that might be made with a CDA analysis, I argue that the CDA framework may also strengthen the validity of the ethnographic data. In this paper, I have chosen to focus on the institutional and societal domains of analysis because these domains most readily cross through the ethnographic and linguistic data.

as a deficiency but as her daughter's need to have extra practice with reading. Similarly, June stated, "Vicky is smart if she put her head to it. Vicky is really smart, she is. She just need to keep readin'."

When I first met Vicky she was shy but attentive. She seemed to be more of a listener than an initiator of conversations and demonstrated fragility as a literacy learner. When I asked her to tell me about herself as a reader, she told me that she was the "lowest reader in the class" and that she "can't read." When asked how she might teach someone how to read, Vicky responded, "Say the words that are in the book and then just keep readin' and readin'." Vicky had learned from school that literacy meant completing exercises and passively participating in other teacher-driven activities. Whereas she completed her homework assignments, they were not connected to her life outside of school.

Vicky started to attend remedial reading classes in third grade.[2] During the sixth grade, her remedial reading teacher referred to Vicky as "slow," "unable to get her mouth around words," and "reading at a second-grade level." At the end of the sixth grade, she was referred for special education services, and a psychological and academic evaluation was conducted. By the end of the year, Vicky was declared as "multiply disabled" and "speech impaired" by the Committee on Special Education team. Vicky was assigned to a self-contained classroom for her first year in seventh grade in the middle school.

Reading the Social World: Literacy in Conjunction with Local Life

Action Research Project

After reading and discussing the book *Oh Freedom! Kids Talk About the Civil Rights Movement with the People Who Made It Happen* (King & Barrett-Osborne, 1997), Vicky and the other adolescents in the reading group initiated an action research project. *Oh Freedom!* is a book arranged as a set of interviews conducted by adolescents with people who participated in the Civil Rights movement. As a result of our discussions, Vicky and the other adolescents in the reading group became interested in social issues in their own community. They were impressed that other children their age had developed interview questions and interviewed people that were a part of the Civil Rights movement. This interest led them to develop an action research project where they interviewed people in their community to learn more about what "everyday heroes" in their community looked like.

The students went through a number of stages in order to develop the research plan. First, they brainstormed about the people they wanted to interview.

2. In the larger study, I develop the tension between Vicky's competence with literacy in her home and community and her perceived disability within the context of the school. For the purposes of this paper, I briefly mention this tension, pointing to the observations and interviews I conducted in Vicky's school and focus on the mediation of cultural models within the context of family literacy practices that make it possible for the tension between home and school perceptions of ability exist.

Vicky's initial selection of people to interview consisted of their downstairs neighbor, a cousin at the high school, a friend of the family who grew up in the south and "probably knows a lot about racism," the alderman, the barber, and Taquisha, their friend's mother. Then, using the interview questions in the book as a model, they brainstormed the questions they would ask the people they had identified. From here, they set up times to talk with the people. Sometimes these appointments were set up over the phone; other times they walked to the person's apartment to ask for an interview.

Before the "real" interviews, Vicky and her peers conducted mock interviews with various cousins who came over to the Treaders' apartment. The interviews lasted from ½ hour to 2 hours and took place in various apartments in the community. The adolescents took turns asking the questions, and they were all responsible for keeping a written record of what had been said. Sometimes when Vicky interviewed, she listened so intently she forgot to write notes. After the interview, I made sure we had time to write down fieldnotes that were not only a summary of what we had learned but observations and questions that would guide the next interview. During these times, Vicky wrote with stamina and proficiency.

One interview in particular is worth recalling because of Vicky's engagement with the literacy event and her subsequent reflection on her own life. When Vicky interviewed Taquisha, her mother's friend, she told them about her experiences living in the south. Vicky was interested in this subject because Vicky's mother lived for a while in the south and Vicky and her grandmother had taken several trips by bus to the Carolinas to visit relatives. Taquisha described how she had been spit at and how she saw crosses burnt on people's front lawns. This interview led Vicky to think more deeply about the conditions of racism in her community and in her life including the way African-American people were treated in stores and the negative interactions between community members and the police that occurred in her neighborhood.

"She Was Just Goofin' Around": The Pepper Spray Incident

Many of the literacy examples that involved June and Vicky in each domain of their interactions connected with the family. In the following example, Luanne, Vicky's sister, was sprayed in the eye with pepper spray, and Vicky negotiated a newspaper article (see Figure 1), offering a counter interpretation to this event.

When I got to the Treaders' apartment, Luanne complained that her nose and eyes hurt. As June explained the situation to me, she told Luanne to get the paper out of the garbage to show me. June had thrown the newspaper with her daughter's picture, an oxygen mask over her face, in the garbage. As Luanne brought the newspaper into June's room, Vicky intercepted it and went into the living room to look at it. Because of the unbearable heat in the apartment, Vicky and I went to the local air-conditioned library for reading instruction that day. Vicky brought along the paper and asked if she could read it first. I did not introduce the text as I usually did because Vicky was anxious to start reading. Her sister was on the front page of the paper, and she had an alternative interpretation of the situation. Vicky

Pepper spray accident disrupts summer program for kids

[redacted] *Four people are taken to hospital, and girls responsible are dismissed*

By [redacted]
Staff writer

A summer program for kids had to be evacuated Friday when a teenager accidentally discharged pepper spray in the building.

Three children and one adult were treated at [redacted] Medical Center Hospital for exposure to the spray, which can cause burning eyes and breathing problems. The spray, used for self-defense, cannot be legally possessed by minors.

The discharge occurred at 11:10 a.m. at the [redacted] at [redacted]. The program, in its first year, offers 80 [redacted] children ages 5 to 13 a chance to enjoy music, dance, field trips to playgrounds, swimming pools and cultural activities without paying a fee. The children were returning from a visit to the State Museum, and only 14 were there when the spray was discharged.

"I sprayed it by mistake," said a 15-year-old girl who worked as a juvenile counselor there.

A 12-year-old girl said she brought the spray with her to the program, attached to her key chain, and the 15-year-old asked to see it. When the teenager grabbed the small canister, it discharged.

Both girls were dismissed from the program, said [redacted] president of the program named after her father. "They were reprimanded, and they are no longer with us," she said.

Deputy Fire Chief [redacted] said the incident appeared unintentional, and that none of the children suffered serious reactions.

"It was probably just a case of bad judgment," he said.

Beverly Padgett, food service coordinator for the program, said adults there were unaware that the girl was carrying the spray until it discharged. [redacted] said the girl told them afterward her mother had given it to her to protect herself.

A person under age 18 is not legally permitted to carry the spray, and any adult who gives it to a minor can face a misdemeanor criminal charge of endangering the welfare of a child, said [redacted] police officer [redacted]. People also are barred from possessing the spray if they have ever been convicted of a felony or assault in New York state or an equivalent charge in another state.

It can be purchased only at a licensed gun dealer or a pharmacy registered with New York state.

By the time police arrived, the spray could not be found and no one there would say who had discharged it, [redacted] said. The case will be assigned to the department's juvenile bureau.

[redacted] said there are no indications that the spray is commonly carried by juveniles. She could not recall a similar incident.

[redacted] FIREFIGHTER [redacted] helps kids from the [redacted] Friday after an accidental pepper spray discharge.

Figure 1. Pepper Spray newspaper article.

was convinced that Luanne was just "goofin' around" and that "she wanted to go to the hospital for attention" rather than really being hurt by the pepper spray.

I took a running record (Clay, 1993) on Vicky's reading of the newspaper article as she read. The newspaper is written between a fifth- and a sixth-grade level, and Vicky read it at an instructional level. Vicky's background knowledge of what happened with the pepper spray and her interest in the story aided her understanding of it. In addition to reading the text, Vicky asked a number of questions, made personal connections with the text, and added several insights to the article that were not included in the text. For instance, Vicky told me the counselor who sprayed the pepper spray thought the pepper spray was perfume and that is why she sprayed it. She also commented that Nora Porch, the president and owner of the summer school program, had worked with her uncle, Steve, on a community institute and was a nice lady.

Both of these examples highlight the intersections between a family's literacy practices—reading the newspaper, conducting interviews—is intricately connected to social institutions (e.g., the summer school program, the media). Further, analysis of these interactions demonstrates that each of these literacy events involves a history of participation and a process of their subjectivities encoded in texts—or the institutional domain of a critical discourse framework. For instance, Vicky both read the newspaper where her sister's identity had been encoded in texts and offered a counter-interpretation. Or, as Taquisha told of her experiences with racism, Vicky began to think of the ways racism is perpetrated in her community through a range of language and literacy practices.

A number of things might be said about the cultural models—or the societal domain of a critical discourse framework—that Vicky holds about literacy from the two previous examples. First, Vicky was proficient with language and literacy in both of the literacy events—both of which involved processing texts on fifth- and sixth-grade reading levels. Thus, Vicky was not only competent in her home literacy but there was a great deal of alignment with schooled literacy as well. Second, as Vicky interacted with these texts, she demonstrated not only a comprehension of the texts but an emerging critical awareness of literacy as social and political acts (Luke, 1995; Peyton-Young, 2000). She questioned the interpretation of the newspaper, and her interview caused her to see multiple perspectives on racism and to apply them to her everyday life.

The dilemma here is that despite these proficiencies, Vicky does not see these activities as reading and writing. When asked what counts as reading, Vicky answered, "reading fast," "reading hard books," and "figuring out words." Vicky has acquired a cultural model about literacy that suggests literacy is an individual skill, repeated for practice and tested for mastery, rather than engaging with texts for meaningful purposes as she did in these examples. Further, in each of these interactions, literacy is connected to her family. Thus, literacy practices within the context of the home and community are often conducted in relation to family, friends, and close social networks and are primarily, in her household, the work of the women in the household (Mace, 1998; Rockhill, 1995). Although it is an important part of maintaining social relationships in their family, it is neither valued nor recognized by the school or the Treaders.

"Fill Out These Papers": Acquiring Social Relations

Engaging in literacy practices in her family and community, Vicky acquired a set of social relationships and institutional arrangements within the context of family literacy practices. Often, these relationships were invisible and thus sustained the invisibility of the literacy work in which both June and Vicky engaged and did not allow them to see the literacy work they did as legitimate or valuable.

Explaining WIC

"Becky, you like this kind of juice?" June asked me one afternoon as she opened her cupboard and pointed at the surplus of cans of Juicy Juice she received from Women with Infants and Children (WIC) and from the local food pantry. I told her I did. Taz, a friend of Vicky's, saw the juice and commented that he wanted to take a can of the juice home for himself. Vicky, at that point, took ownership over the discussion. First she told Taz he would not bring home any of the juice because he received WIC himself. Then, Vicky explained to me the process of applying for and receiving WIC resources:[3]

Vicky: [to Taz] No, ya'll get them off your own WICS.
Researcher: Where do you get them from?
Vicky: From the store. From Price Chopper off WIC.
June: Yeah you get them off your WIC.
Researcher: What does that mean?
June: Off your WIC check, your WIC check
Vicky: =your WIC check
Researcher: What does it look like?
June: It's just like a piece of paper.
Vicky: [Like a check.
Researcher: And its written on it what you can get?
Vicky: Yeah. Like milk, eggs, juice, peanut butter, dairy.
Researcher: So can I get WIC?
Vicky: No WIC is for babies.
Taz: When you have a baby then you can get WIC
Researcher: Really?
Vicky: You get WIC for yourself and the baby too.
Researcher: Who do you call to get it?
Vicky: She's gonna have a baby to get WIC. [to Taz, laughing] You got to go down to Whitney Young [health center] and fill out the papers. Then once a month you get these checks to use at Price Chopper.

This interaction highlights a number of issues about Vicky's history of practice with these institutions and these texts (institutional domain). First, the relationship between the need to have children and the ability to receive support is clear to Vicky. Second, she knew that Taz and his family also received WIC, and there-

3. Transcription conventions used in extracts—transscriptions reflect the turn-taking structures of the participants and the researcher: = (overlap in talk), [(interruption in talk), / (one-second pause).

fore he would not be able to take any of their supplies home with him. Third, she demonstrated through repetition of what she had seen her mother do that the literacy work of the household, including filling out forms, is women's work. Rockhill's (1995) reminder that, "in addition to the uses of literacy involved in housework, [women] attend to the purchase of goods, as well as the transactions around social services, public utilities, health care and the schooling of children" (p. 167). Vicky learned that June attended to these things and, eventually, so would she.

What is especially problematic about these practices is that Vicky did not recognize this knowledge about texts in her life as part of her literate competence, nor does the school. Instead, as Vicky learned to interact with particular types of literacy practices (e.g., forms), she acquired a set of assumptions, values, ways of interacting with the world that assume her literacy did not count; that she was not literate, and that family literacy practices were women's work. Similar to the other examples, Vicky used language proficiently when she described an event with which she was familiar and comfortable. Vicky explained the process clearly. In addition, Vicky also managed to make a joke at my expense and said, "She's gonna have a baby to get WIC." Kessler-Harris (1990) wrote on the connection between women's work and social consequences:

> [G]ender defines the source of one's identity . . . in the end it serves as both a justification of female behavior and as an explanation of its consequences. . . . It explains the consequences in terms of home attachments and attitudes. And it carries the ring of inevitable repetition since it offers up a picture of female work culture that relies heavily on women's own values to identify acceptable parameters of female behavior. . . . (p. 63)

Observing June and participating in the activities of the home, Vicky learned the "inevitable repetition" and contradictions embedded in literacy as women's work. In the following section I shift the lens first to June and then to Vicky in order to demonstrate how June negotiated a free and reduced lunch form and how Vicky is apprenticed into family literacy practices and the accompanying social roles.

Free and Reduced Lunch Forms

June also negotiated forms in the kitchen as the children were reading at the table. At the beginning of each school year, a free and reduced lunch form gets sent home with the children to be sent back if they qualify for assistance. June brought the paperwork over to the table where I sat with Vicky and showed it to me:

June: . . . Only thing I really need to fill out is this [takes the form and flips through the pages] household, size, what's that? What they mean income ca, chart?

Researcher: [looking at the form] Okay. Household size. Number of people in your house. Is how many?

June: Five.

Researcher: Well let's read this. Okay. Income chart. [I hand the form back to June]
June: The following chart lists income lev-lev-level.
Researcher: Uh-huh.
June: ass, according, according to household size and income level receivin' each year, monthly or weekly if you, if you total in house income is the size, same of less than one amoun' on the income chart below your child can get reduced?
Researcher: Uh-huh.
June: Reduced price meal and maybe eligible to receive free meal.
Researcher: Okay so now you have to, what's your house hold size? How many of you are there?
June: Five.
Researcher: No, there's six of you. Right? Four kids and two adults?
June: You ain't countin' the baby, is you?
Researcher: Well why not?
June: Well six.

As June read this document, Vicky looked over June's shoulder and read the form alongside of June:

Researcher: Okay so if you're six people in your house and you're under that, that means that you are eligible for reduced meals. Okay,
June: So what I put? Just mark six?
Researcher: Yup.

I could tell from the way June gripped the pen tightly, had her white out placed next to the paper, and from the way the pen wavered between putting the "6" on two different lines that she was anxious about filling out the form incorrectly. In this literacy event, June's role as a mother and a literacy student are evoked. In the first set of interactions she was ready to put "5" down for the number in her household. June did not count her newborn, Evan, as a member of the household.

Extending the discussion around the free and reduced lunch form, Vicky and Taz, her cousin, began a discussion about what they had for lunch at school that day. Being at different schools, Vicky and Taz reported different lunch items such as peanut butter and jelly sandwiches, milk, salad, and a brownie. I asked them how they got their lunch. Taz informed me, "I stood in line and they gave me my lunch. I told them my number and I got my lunch." Vicky expanded on this and stated, "he got it for free if his mother signed a paper." They both tell me they have "numbers":

Taz: There's a lunch number.
Vicky: What's your number?
Taz: 485.
Vicky: 485? Mine is 319.
Researcher: So what do you mean? How do you get your lunches?
Taz: You got to tell the person, you got to get your lunch and then you go up to the lady and
Vicky: [they ask you for your number and then they say what's your number and then you tell 'em your number and say if you got

> peanut butter on your tray, ///then they look at your number and if peanut butter not by your number that means you don't got peanut butter so you got to tell your teacher you want peanut butter then you got to get your number. . . . Everybody in my classes got numbers.

Vicky described to me how each year her mother signed a paper so that she could get a number and then get her "free food" just like the one she just filled out. She told me that if "your mother don't sign the paper you got to pay." Vicky showed an awareness of the literacy event of her mother filling out the forms. However, from the above interaction with June filling out the free and reduced lunch form, there is more "work" being done than just "signing the paper" (Rogers, 2000). In order to successfully fill out this form, June had to have knowledge of the financial status of the family (something she takes care of) and of the organization of the school. As shown by the three previous examples, Vicky participated with literacy as a valued and valuable piece of her relationships with her family, but, at the same time, the literacy work involved in these interactions were invisible in two ways. First, she did not see them as literacy. Second, the school did not recognize or build on these as literacy events.

Family Literacy as Apprenticeship

A family's literacy practices provides the context for intergenerational literacy learning as we saw in the WIC example where June and Vicky jointly explain the process of applying for and receiving social services. Rogoff (1995) quotes Lave (1988) as she wrote, "apprentices learn to think, argue, act and interact in increasingly knowledgeable ways with people who do something well, by doing it with them as legitimate, peripheral participants" (p. 2). Aside from reading to learn in early interactions with literacy, Vicky was also acquiring expectations about texts, the consequences of these interactions and about her social roles.

Vicky was being apprenticed into a number of discourses including how literacy is used in her daily life. She learned by observing her mother interact with these forms over time and was then guided through participation as she reminded her mother that she could use the abbreviation when filling out the magnet school form. Finally, Vicky transformed this knowledge of free and reduced lunch forms into a way that made sense to her. That is, the knowledge and social roles connected with each of these literacy events were a part of Vicky's subjectivity as a daughter, a student, and an emerging adolescent. In making this knowledge her own, it was possible to recognize traces of the intergenerational transfer of ideology of women's work entextualized into bureaucratic forms as well as the ways in which these cultural models are acquired (Collins, 1996; Gee, 1999; McElhinny, 1997).

Vicky's development of hypotheses about language and literacy in her home, school, and community depended on the actual literacy events she witnessed, participated in, and interacted with on her own. I have illustrated in this paper that interactions comprising Vicky's "primary" or everyday language and literacy environments were characterized by institutional literacy practices. These literacy practices were (a) women's work and (b) not counted or valued as literacy. Through these practices, Vicky acquired cultural models about what counted as literacy, language and to whom these models counted.

To some extent her subsequent interactions with schooled literacy will depend on how well the instruction she receives in reading and writing is matched to the understanding she has already developed about herself as a literate individuals. The school viewed Vicky as "multiply disabled" and "speech and language impaired," a set of labels that have severe instructional consequences. These literacy practices shape the subsequent interactions and emergence of cultural models that children in these communities will have with literacy in their school worlds. That is, the less they seem themselves as literate in their homes and communities, the less likely they are to perceive themselves as literate within a school community.

Success in school means not only developed concepts about print but also ideological concepts acquired as individuals interact with, learn from, and practice literacy in their homes and community. In the preceding examples, I demonstrated the ideologies—literacy as women's work and their literacy as not counting—attached to Vicky's literate interactions in her home, school, and community. There are several common threads through each of these sets of literacy practices. First, Vicky was apprenticed into these engagements. That is, in each of the interaction she: (a) observed the literacy practice carried out by a more knowledgeable other (i.e., free reduced lunch forms), (b) participated in the social practice in a guided relationship (i.e., interviews, WIC), and (c) carried out the practice independently (i.e., explaining WIC and free and reduced lunch forms). Second, each of these sets of literacy practices involved the use of language and literacy as mediators of sociocultural experiences. That is, Vicky used literacy and language proficiently in authentic and purposeful situations. Third, Vicky had ownership over the interaction. Thus, she had much to contribute, and her contributions exemplified an important point about Vicky as a learner. Vicky was highly successful as she moved from apprenticeship (watching and observing her mother fill out the form), to guided participation (helping her mother with the abbreviation of the middle school), to transformation of how this knowledge played out in her social world.

There are many parallels between June and Vicky's literate lives that enhance the notion of apprenticeship. The transfer and learning from June to Vicky that reading is an individual endeavor and that literacy is woman's work are both ideologies learned through interactions with texts, and they both viewed reading as an individual endeavor and as a value in schooled literacy. Both June and Vicky had fragile literate identities. They did not see themselves as readers and demonstrated profound tensions between their personal and their public literate lives. Second, both June and Vicky demonstrated a local activism with literacy. In their engagements with literacy in their home and community, they portrayed a use of literacy as a sociocultural tool in order to mediate their daily lives. Whereas June engaged in activism through her organization of a petition for a streetlight, Vicky set out to interview "local heroes" in her community. Third, the role of literacy at home, as part of the texture of their lives, seemed to be "invisible." June demonstrated and Vicky learned that literacy is women's work, connected to household tasks and raising children. Connected to their literacy work are the contradictory subject positions that are asked of them as women and as students, that is, their relationship to literacy through schooling and their relationship to literacy through their family (in June's case to her children). The fourth intersecting point in June and Vicky's learning trajectories is that despite their proficiencies, their local literacies go unnoticed and unvalued by the school. June was defined as the "lowest reader in the class" and Vicky, at the end of her sixth-grade year was defined as "multiply disabled" including severe speech and language deficits.

Research into the diversity of literacies has exploded in the past decade—spreading into the technological, the workplace, the family, the community as well as popular culture. This expansion of practice has posed increasing demands on what it means to "be" literate and to "do" literacy. It is simplistic to assume that *more* literacy or the *right* kinds of literacy will lead to a citizenry that is considered better educated. *More* of this cultural capital does not mean that individuals have access to social resources. It is plausible that individuals can have access to such cultural capital and have their attempts at transformation into social resources thwarted. In each of the examples presented (the action research project, the pepper spray incident, WIC and free and reduced lunch forms), Vicky's family literacy practices were connected to institutions other than schools and were connected to the health, safety, and learning of the children in the family. Each of these literacy events involved an entextualization process where identity was encoded through a series of texts. Although Vicky demonstrated proficiency with "reading" these texts, she also demonstrated an awareness of the entextualization process itself and knowledge of the strategies, resources, and practices needed to live in her community. The distinction between primary and secondary Discourses becomes blurry in this case. These points illuminate the intergenerational transfer of a network of practices, including social relations that are acquired as a part of literacy practices.

In line with Gee's (1996) theories of Discourse, Vicky was being apprenticed into a discourse community that was in "alignment" rather than in "conflict." At the same time, she was also acquiring sets of social relationships. There are also histories of participation attached to her interactions with texts and ways of being with the world that are acquired through the apprenticeship model. The alignment between communities of practice provides one potential explanation of how Vicky has acquired problematic ideologies that make it possible for her to believe that her literate competence at home and in her community do not count. An important note to add is that cultural models are not properties of individuals but are mediated across individuals, groups, and social institutions by various discursive means.

This research furthers the discussion on the asymmetry between knowledge systems because it suggests the complexity of cultural models acquired within both local and institutional literacy practices. Further, because individuals have multiple cultural models, some may be in conflict, some in alignment, and others somewhere in between. Framing cultural models as mediated interactions, rather than static entities, reduces the deterministic feel of the Discourse framework. It suggests that continued research into cultural models as they connect to language and literacy practices might recognize that models may be either in conflict or alignment and these degrees of alignment might shift across various discursive contexts. This theoretical framework allows researchers to ask different sets of empirical and theoretical questions, such as: What types of discursive interactions—local, institutional and societal—give rise to particular cultural models? What analytic frameworks allow researchers to understand cultural models? These questions might help us to conceptualize how, as educators and researchers, we can address the asymmetry between knowledge systems and construct productive cultural models across a range of discursive contexts.

Author Note

I would like to thank a number of people for their support, encouragement and feedback on this research. I am indebted to the Treaders who let me into their home and their lives so we might learn more about the complexity of literacy practices in out-of-school contexts. I would also like to thank Peter Johnston, Jim Collins, and Ginny Goatley for their careful reading and thoughtful comments on this research. And finally, thanks go to the anonymous reviewers whose suggestions strengthened this manuscript. Pseudonyms have been used throughout the text for the places and people.

References

Au, K. (1981). Participation structures in a reading lesson with Hawaiian children: Analysis of a culturally appropriate instructional event. *Anthropology and Education Quarterly, 11,* 91-115.

Anderson, A., & Stoakes, S. (1984). Social and Institutional contexts of literacy. In H. Goelman, A. Oberg, & F. Smiths, (Eds.), *Awakening to literacy.* Portsmouth, NH: Heinemann.

Barton, D., & Hamilton, M. (1998). *Local literacies: Reading and writing in one community.* New York: Routledge.

Barton, D., Hamilton, M., & Ivanic, R. (Eds.). (2000). *Situated literacies: Reading and writing in context.* London: Routledge.

Cairney, T., & Ruge, J. (1998). *Community literacy practices and schooling: Towards effective support for students.* University of Western Sydney, Nepean: Department of Employment, Education, Training and Youth Affairs.

Carger, C. (1996). *Of borders and dreams.* New York: Teachers College Press.

Chouliaraki, L., & Fairclough, N. (1999). *Discourse in late modernity. Rethinking Critical Discourse Analysis.* Edinburgh, Scotland: Edinburgh University Press.

Clay, M. M. (1993). *An observation survey of early literacy achievement.* Portsmouth, NH: Heinemann.

Collins, J. (1996). Socialization to text: Structure and contradiction in schooled literacy. In M. Silverstein & G. Urban (Eds.), *Natural histories of discourse* (pp. 203-228). Chicago: University of Chicago Press.

Cushman, E. (1998). *The struggle and the tools: Oral and literate strategies in an inner city community.* Albany, NY: SUNY Press.

Delpit, L. (1995). *Other people's children: Cultural conflict in the classroom.* New York: New Press.

Fairclough, N. (1989). *Language and power.* London: Longman.

Fairclough, N. (1995). *Critical discourse analysis: The critical study of language.* New York: Longman.

Gee, J. (1996). *Social linguistics and literacies: Ideology in discourses.* London: Falmer.

Gee, J. (1999). *An introduction to discourse analysis: Theory and method.* New York: Routledge.

Heath, S. B. (1983). *Ways with words: Language, life and work in community and classrooms.* Cambridge, England: Cambridge University Press.

Kessler-Harris, A. (1990). *A woman's wage: Historical meanings & social consequences.* Lexington: University Press of Kentucky.

King, C., & Barrett-Osborne, L. (1997). *Oh, Freedom! Kids talk about the Civil Rights Movement with the people who made it happen.* New York: Knopf.

Knobel, M. (1998). *Everyday literacies: Students, discourse and social practice.* New York: Peter Lang.

Ladson-Billings, G. (1994). *The dreamkeepers: Successful teachers of African American children.* San Francisco: Jossey-Bass.

Lareau, A. (1989). *Home advantage: Social class and parental involvement in elementary education.* London: Falmer.

Lave, J. (1988). *Cognition in practice: Mind, mathematics and culture in everyday life.* Cambridge, England: Cambridge University Press.

LeCompte, M., & Preissle, J. (1996). *Ethnography and qualitative design in educational research.* San Diego, CA: Academic.

Luke, A. (1995). Texts and discourse in education: An introduction to critical discourse analysis. *Review of Research in Education, 21,* 3-48.

Mace, J. (1998). *Playing with time: Mothers and the meaning of literacy.* London: UCL Press.

McCarthey, S. J. (2000). Home-school connections: A review of the literature. *Journal of Educational Research, 93,* 145-153.

McElhinny, B. (1997). Ideologies of public and private language in sociolinguistics. In. R. Wodak (Ed.), *Gender and discourse* (pp. 106-138). London: Sage.

McIntyre, E., Rosebery, A., & Gonzalez, N. (Eds.). (2001). *Classroom diversity: Connecting curriculum to students' lives.* Portsmouth, NH: Heinemann.

Moll, L. C., Amanti, C., Neff, D., & Gonzalez, N. (1992). Funds of knowledge for teaching: Using a qualitative approach to connect homes and classrooms. *Theory into Practice, 31,* 132-141.

Moll, L., & Gonzalez, N. (1994). Lessons from research with language minority children. *JRB: A Journal of Literacy, 26,* 439-456.

Muspratt, S., Luke, A., & Freebody, P. (1997). *Constructing critical literacies: Teaching and learning textual practice.* Cresskill, NJ: Hampton.

Neuman, S., & Celano, D. (2001). Access to print in low-income and middle-income communities. *Reading Research Quarterly, 3,* 8-27.

Peyton-Young, J. (2000). Boy talk: Critical literacy and masculinities. *Reading Research Quarterly, 35,* 312-337.

Purcell-Gates, V. (1995). *Other people's words: The cycle of low literacy.* Cambridge, MA: Harvard University Press.

Purcell-Gates, V. (1996). Stories, coupons and the TV Guide: Relationships between home literacy experiences and emergent literacy knowledge. *Reading Research Quarterly, 31,* 406-428.

Rockhill, K. (1995). Gender, language and the politics of literacy. In B. Street (Ed.), *Cross-cultural approaches to literacy* (pp. 156-175). Cambridge, England: Cambridge University Press.

Rogers, R. (2000). It's not really writing, it's just answering the questions. *Language Arts, 77,* 428-437.

Rogoff, B. (1995). *Apprenticeship in thinking: Cognitive development in social context.* New York: Oxford University Press.

Scribner, S., & Cole, M. (1981). *The psychology of literacy.* Cambridge, MA: Harvard University Press.

Silverstein, M., & Urban, G. (1996). *Natural Histories of Discourse.* Chicago: University of Chicago Press.

Slembrouck, S. (2001). Explanation, interpretation and critique in the analysis of discourse. *Critique of Anthropology, 21,* 33–58.

Street, B., (Ed.). (1995). *Cross-cultural approaches to literacy.* Cambridge, England: Cambridge University Press.

Taylor, D. (1983). *Family literacy: Young children learning to read and write.* Portsmouth, NH: Heinemann.

Taylor, D. (1990). *Learning denied.* Portsmouth, NH: Heinemann.

Taylor, D., & Dorsey-Gaines, C. (1988). *Growing up literate: Learning from inner city families.* Portsmouth, NH: Heinemann.

Teale, W. (1986). Home background and young children's literacy development. In W. Teale & E. Sulzby (Eds.), *Emergent Literacy: Writing and Reading* (pp. 173-206). Norwood, NJ: Ablex.

Valdes, G. (1996). *Con respecto: Bridging the gap between culturally diverse families and schools.* New York: Teachers College Press.

Wenger, E. (1998). *Communities of practice: Learning, meaning and identity.* Cambridge, ??: Cambridge University Press.

Widdowson, H. G. (1998). The theory and practice of critical discourse analysis. *Applied Linguistics, 19,* 136-151.

Wodak, R. (Ed.). (1997). *Gender and discourse.* London: Sage.

Reading Versus Translating: A Preschool Bilingual's Interpretation of Text

Eurydice Bouchereau Bauer and Kristiina Montero
University of Georgia

According to Barton (1994), "the standard view of reading has been that of a psychological process . . . and it is this view which [some in the field] are stepping beyond" (p. 64). Generally, the field of literacy has seen a shift from a view of learning void of the context to one where the social context is emphasized. Gee (2000) points out the difference by offering us a metaphor of a digital computer versus a computer network. He notes that the digital computer processes information whereas in a network "knowledge and meaning are seen as emerging from social practices or activities in which people, environments, tools, technologies, objects, words, acts, and symbols are all linked to ('networked' with) each other and dynamically interact with and on each other" (p. 184). Central to this perspective is that

> knowledge and intelligence reside not solely in heads, but rather, are distributed across the social practices (including language practices) and the various tools, technologies and semiotic systems that a given "community of practice" uses in order to carry out its characteristic activities. Knowing is a matter of being able to participate centrally in practice and learning is a matter of changing patterns of participation. (Gee, 2000, p. 181)

The move in literacy to address sociocultural issues is also evident in some of the research conducted in the field of bilingualism. Although the psycholinguistics' perspective is still evident in much of the research (e.g., Long, Inagaki, & Ortega, 1998; Pica, 1994), some researchers have examined bilingualism from a sociocultural perspectives (e.g., Brooks & Donato, 1994; DiCamilla & Anton, 1997; Firth & Wagner, 1997) and anthropological perspectives (e.g., Canagarajah, 1993; Harklau, 1994; McKay & Wong, 1996). The focus on the social context for language learning provides a wider lens through which to observe the role of interlocutors (Lanza, 1992), and their shaping influence (Genesee, 1989). What is not always explored is a view of bilingualism that does not use a monolingual perspective as the point of reference for understanding bilinguals. Specifically, in the field of literacy, we need to understand how bilinguals approach emergent biliteracy and how this approach is related to their bilingualism.

According to Cook (1999), our understanding of second-language speakers is limited because of our incessant need to compare their performance to that of native speakers. In doing so, we miss the opportunities to learn about the student's

*National Reading Conference Yearbook, **50**, pp. 115–126.*

multicompetence. Cook (1999) defines multicompetence as a neutral term that describes the speaker's knowledge of both an Ll and L2. From this perspective, "Multicompetent minds that know two languages are qualitatively different from those of the monolingual native speaker." Some of these differences are evident in multicompetent language users' thought processes. Some researchers have shown that bilinguals are less effective at language-related cognitive tasks when compared to monolinguals (Cook, 1997), have memory span in L2 that is less than that of the Ll (such as in lecture situations) (Brown & Hulme, 1992), and do perform slightly below monolinguals in naming objects and marking letters in words (Magiste, 1986). In general, the multicompetent speaker tends to respond more slowly because there is a choice to be made regarding which response to give (Magiste, 1986, p. 118). Other researchers have shown that the process of becoming a multicompetent language user in childhood yields "brain training" opportunities for them—learning other mental skills such as explicit knowledge about their languages. Collectively, these studies have revealed that bilingual children have a keener awareness of language itself and this is tied to their awareness of grammatical properties such as knowing the number of words in a sentence (Galambos & Goldin-Meadows, 1990), and the ability to separate meaning from form (Bialystok, 1986). They also may have an edge in early reading (Yelland, Pollard, & Mercuri, 1993). Although these studies suggest certain positive outcomes from being a bilingual it is not clear how this will impact early reading development.

Few studies have investigated the process of becoming biliterate in young children. Bialystok's (1997) study with 4- and 5-year-old bilingual preschoolers is one of the few metalinguistic studies that directly assess children's knowledge related to beginning reading. She assessed how bilinguals (French-English and Mandarin-English) and English monolinguals responded to a moving word task. In this task, words placed under its corresponding pictures were accidentally moved to a different picture. The bilinguals outperformed the monolinguals and performed equally well in both languages. According to Bialystok (1997), the children's performance reflects their increased understanding of symbolic representation of text.

The awareness of how different symbols are related to text is not limited to simultaneous bilinguals (those who acquired two languages at the same time). Geva, Wade-Wooly, and Shaney (1993) documented the biliteracy development of a group of English-speaking first graders in Canada who were learning Hebrew as a second language. Their study suggests that students can learn to read in two languages at the same time. Their findings also suggest that students may perform certain skills better in one language than in their other language. For example, the children could decode better in Hebrew than in English, which may be a consequence of the fact that Hebrew is more phonetic. This study raises issues related to how students might use the different insights gained from interacting with texts written in different languages.

How metalinguistic knowledge of another language impacts reading performance was directly addressed in the study by Yelland et al. (1993). In this study, the researchers examine the performance of two groups of children (marginal bilinguals and monolinguals) on word awareness and on written word-recognition tasks across the first 2 years of school (K–l). Their results suggest that the marginal bilingual group had an advantage on monolinguals on word awareness tasks. Research in reading has shown a link between metalinguistic awareness and early reading. Specifically, students must move from linguistic knowledge supporting spoken language that is primarily tacit to conscious knowledge—which is metalinguistic awareness (Bryant, MacLean, Bradley, & Crossland, 1990). In this study, the researchers documented gains in the first 6 months of reading for students who received 1 hour of Italian instruction per week during their language arts. Given the fact that the comparison group and the experimental group at the start of the study could not read and were comparable to each other, the researchers concluded there must be a causal relationship between one component of metalinguistic awareness (word awareness) and the development of reading skills. The findings also revealed that both groups performed on the upper range of a written word-recognition task given at the end of first grade. Although both groups did well, direct comparison of their performance indicated that the difference in performance between the marginal bilinguals and the monolinguals was still significant.

All of the studies cited made monolinguals the point for their comparisons. Although this comparison is interesting and important, it is not sufficient to get a full understanding of bilinguals' literacy development and can also be misleading when assessing bilinguals' language competence (Cook, 1999). All of the cited studies compare metalinguistic awareness of bilinguals and monolinguals by focusing on word tasks. Although these studies have implications for early literacy, metalinguistic awareness is only studied as it pertains to words or syntax (i.e., at the micro level of "understanding text" and "being literate"). Global aspects of "literacy" and "understanding text" such as the concept of print, story, summarizing and the metalinguistic awareness supporting these aspects cannot be analyzed, tested or even detected in this way.

This study of one bilingual child offers a vantage point from which to investigate some of these global aspects. Curiously, this vantage point hinges on the bilingualism. In a sense, the second language provides an additional means of contrast that allows detecting the influence of metalinguistic awareness on global aspects of literacy. Current practice when working with bilinguals is to assess them in one or both of their languages individually. Whatever skills they posses as a result of being a bilingual are not often highlighted.

This study uses a "multicompetence-lens" to understand a bilingual who is in a rich literacy environment. Contrary to other metalinguistic studies, this study highlights what she can do because she is a bilingual. Specifically, this study provides a rationale for how bilinguals' multicompetence supports their emerging understanding of text.

Method

Context of the Study

The findings to be reported here are from an ongoing longitudinal study of a bilingual child, Elena, learning English and German from birth. The goal of the research project is to understand the impact of bilingualism on the development of literacy age 2 to 5. Since the age of six months, she was read to daily in both languages. Both parents follow the one-language, one-speaker rule (Ronjat, 1913). Elena's father speaks to her in German and her mother, the researcher, in English. The child has also been cared for by German *au pairs* who address her in German. All of the adults speak to each other in English. In order to support Elena's interest in maintaining her German skills, she visits Germany yearly during the summer.

Although the adults in the home follow the one-language, one-speaker rule, Elena is aware of the fact that the people closest to her are bilinguals or multilinguals. For example, she is aware that her father sometimes speaks to her Haitian maternal grandparents in English and French and her mother speaks to them in English or in French Creole. She has also observed her mother speaking German to her paternal grandparents when visiting in Germany. Clearly, Elena's linguistic and cultural milieu supports the view that the world we live in is diverse.

Data Sources

The findings reported here are from transcripts obtained from the videotaped interactions between Elena and her caregivers. The data were collected during a 5-month period beginning when she was 3 years 7 months and ending when she was 4 years old. Ninety-six books were read to her either before naptime or bed-time. These reading events were videotaped. Generally, English speakers read to her in English and German speakers in German. There were occasions when Elena would initiate a reading of a book that was not in the language of the adult. Since Elena had shown in previous situations that she can identify and label her books as mommy (English) and daddy (German) books with great accuracy, we wanted to examine interactions around these books. Furthermore, given the explorative nature of naturalistic research, we decided to examine not just the events when Elena read to someone in another language, but all other reading interactions around that book. Four books emerged as texts that involved reading within the designated language of the text and reading translations *Miranda und der neue Teddy* (Miranda and her New Teddy) (Thenoir, 1996); *Grope kleine Schwester* (Big Little Sister), (Forslind, 1997), *Jumanji* (Allsburg, 1981), and *Bad Habit* (Berenstain, 1986). All interactions with the four books were transcribed.

Two of the four books were German texts that were read to her by German speakers. On several occasions when her mother was interacting with her, Elena chose to read (in German) to her mother the German texts. When her mother explained that she could not understand all of the text and Elena should read it to her in English, Elena provided her with an abridged English description of the texts. The third text, *Jumanji,* was an English text which Elena retold to her German-speaking *au pair* in German. She used the illustrations to highlight what was happening in the text. The fourth text was *Bad Habit,* one of the stories from the Berenstein Bear series. This story was read to Elena in English by her German *au pair* (after begging for it). The interactions in both English and German around this text were also transcribed.

Data Analysis

A research assistant, a native German speaker who is fluent in English, transcribed the reading events (in both German and English). Additionally, the German transcriptions were translated into English for side-by-side comparisons of the reading events. Analysis occurred at three levels. First, all of the transcripts were coded for Elena's language use, functions, and general style of interaction between the adult reader and listener. Second, Elena's "readings" of the books in both languages were compared to each other and to the book for idea units. Third, her talk during these reading events was analyzed for comments that provided insights on her attempts to interact with the language of print. The data from these analyses were then triangulated.

Results

Three findings emerged from this study: (a) Retellings done in the language of the text are richer, (b) Styles of retellings are linked to metalinguistic awareness, (c) Biliteracy understanding is socially defined. Each will be explored in the following section.

Retellings Done in the Language of Text Are Richer

First, the findings suggest that when this young bilingual attempted to "read" the German texts to her mother in German, she captured the basic story line as well as the descriptive language of the text:

Excerpt #1

E: Mama muß ein - einkaufen, und Miranda darf ein - ein Bär aussuchen. Aber ein—ein heller Bär hat—er lacht neben Miranda. Aber—sie hat desaut (=geschaut), aber die wo—anderen hat so—so ein ander Fell, so ein helles, /hohas/, um, /hohas/ lachen at Miranda. [RETELL]

E: (turns page) Und dann hat Miranda sagt, Mama! Mama! Ich hat den neuen Teddy ausdesucht! Und dann hat Mama, uh, komm und sagt Okay. [RETELL]

E: (turns page) Dann hat sie in de neuen Tüte, und dann wenn, uh, Miranda hat sagt: Ich /wils/ heute de Tüte halten—(Aside) Mom, what's this on here? this needs to get off of this book (tries to remove something from the paper) [RETELL/DIR]

E: Nach hat sie in /Rollstep/ (=Rolltreppe?) und Mama hat desagt, Let's geh Eiskreme essen. [RETELL]
E: (turns page) Dann hat sie e-essen Eiskreme und der Teddy war an Mirandas Soss (=Schoß). [RETELL]
E: (turns page) Dann hat sie—dann hat sie den Teddy em Stück de Eiskreme, dann hat sie in de Mund gekriegt. [RETELL]

English Translation

E: Mommy has to go shopping, and Miranda may pick a bear. But a light-colored bear has—he sits laughing next to Miranda. But—she has looked, but those—the other one has such a different kind of fur, such a light-colored one, /hohas/, um, /hohas/ smiling at Miranda.
E: And then Miranda said, Mommy! Mommy! I chose the new teddy! And then Mom came and said okay.
E: Then she had [it] in the new bag, and then, Miranda said: I /want/ today to hold the bag (Aside)—Mom, what's this on here? this needs to get off of this book (tries to remove something from the paper).
E: Then she has (they were?) on the escalator and Mommy said Let's go eat ice cream.
E: Then she ate ice cream, and the teddy was in her lap.
E: Then she—then she [gave] the teddy a bite of ice cream, then she got (put?) [it] in her mouth.

There was a marked difference when Elena was asked for, or initiated herself a retelling in a language other than the one the text was written in. For example, in the following excerpt it is clear that Elena saw the request to read a German book in English as a qualitatively different endeavor from her reading in German:

Excerpt #2

M: Lena, can you, since my German isn't as good as yours, can you read it to me in English?
E: I can (pause) I can't read it in English very well. [REJECTS REQUEST]
M: You can't read it in English?
E: Um-Um (indicating no) [REJECTS]
M: Can you try to read it in English?
E: (starts to read) The teddy wants de- de- de girl to have a new one, but when the man gived her one . . . [EMERGENT READING]
M: Start from the beginning, so I can get it all.
E: I can't read it in English very well. [REJECTS AGAIN]
M: That's okay, try your best.
E: I can't do it. I can't do it, read it in English. [STRONGER REJECTION]
M: Really?
E: Shakes her head no. [REJECTS]
M: Let's try.
E: I tried. I can't do it mommy. [RES/REJECTS]
M: Can you tell me why you can't do it?
E: Because mommy, [BEGINS EXPLANATION]
M: Uhum
E: Because [BEGINS EXPLANATION]
M: Yeah. Please sit up.
E: Because I can't. When I tried it I couldn't do it. [EXPLAINS]

These differences went beyond her unwillingness to read, something she generally enjoyed doing. In fact, the general style of the reading when Elena "read" the German story in English to her mom was different:

Excerpt #3

E: See, watch. (starts reading) See, the girl try—wants a new teddy, [a new bear. [DIR/RETELL]
E: (gets up) I (need)—I (need) /?/ [DIR]
E: (sits back down) And then her mother wants to her choose one, and she [chose] one—one—from the, one laughed at her. [RETELL]
E: That one right there. (points) [CONF/EXP]
E: And then, and then she chose it, and ma—said ma—and she called her mommy she chose one. [RETELL]
E: So she said—so she said—and this say—she wants to hold the bag. [RETELL]
E: And then she want—and then her mother said: Let's go down and eat some ice cream. [RETELL]

When she attempted to "read" the text in English to her mother, she captured the basic ideas, but her renditions were choppy and had far less descriptive language than the German narration. This same diminished capacity was found when she read *Jumanji* to the *au pair* in German. Elena was less familiar with this text and used the illustrations to describe what might be taking place in the story. It was clear form her body movement (eyes not looking at the text, the speed at which she turned the pages) that she was not "reading" the book.

Styles of Retellings Are Linked to Metalinguistic Awareness

Second, the different styles of retelling are linked to her metalinguistic awareness regarding literacy. That is, she understands that language of text is a stable factor that cannot be easily exchanged. When Elena was asked to share the German texts with her mother in English, their language of communication, Elena resisted and repeatedly said this was not something she could do. She repeatedly told her mother "I can't read it in English." She also told her "I can't do that." Given her oral capabilities in English and the fact that she had done an emergent reading of the text in German, her mother began to wonder where this resistance came from. Elena herself provided some clues. She explained to her mother at the end of an English reading of the German text:

Excerpt #4

E: See, I told you (suggesting she did not "read" the text). I can read it only in German, but I can tell you what it says in English.
M: But you read it to me in English, right?
E: No, I told you what it says.
M: So, you can only read it in German.
E: In German, and I just can tell you in English.

The above exchange seems to be more than a child resisting a request from her mother. She consciously made a distinction between what she perceived to be "reading the text" and "giving a summary of the main ideas."

Literacy Understanding Is Socially Defined

Third, the data suggest that what Elena knows about literacy and the linguistic parameters put around it are tied to her social interactions with different adults. For example, when Elena asked her *au pair* to stop "telling her about the English story" via the illustrations in German and to "read" it instead, suggests that she has a clear understanding of what it means to read. Also, it is clear from the videotapes that when the *au pair* read the English text to Elena [an unusual activity] she did so with less certainty than when she read a German book. Finally, the *au pair* made a point to tell and explain the story in German. Thereby, sending the message that we "read" in the language the text is written in, but I can give you a summary of it in another language. Although unintended, the *au pair* modeled how to translate the ideas from a written text into another language:

Excerpt #5

Au pair: [reading from the book] Well says mama, it's sort of like this path. I've wheeled this barrel over it so many times that It's worn a deep groove right down the middle. And it keeps getting deeper every time I use it. Why it's so deep now that I can't get out of it without a little help.

[*Au pair*'s explanation of the above text] Also des sagt die Mama, wenn die jedesmal zum Garten fährt, mit dem Schubkarren. Da hat sie einen Weg. Und dann sieht man da schon richtig eine Spur von dem Wagen, und des ist genauso weil sie immer die gleiche Spur entlangfährt, und die Erde druckt sich immer dann runter weil die immer viel aufgeladen hat, und dann hat sie eine Spur, und dann wird es immer schwieriger, daß sie da von der Spur wieder rauskommt, da braucht sie Hilfe, und genauso ist es mit dem Fingernägel beißen. Weil sie immer Fingernägel gebissen hat, dann war sie es so schon gewohnt, dann ist es schwierig das aufzuhören. Da braucht sie auch jemanden, der ihr hilft, die Finger gleich wieder einzuwickeln, damit sie immer dran denkt: "Nein, ich darf nicht beißen."

[English Translation] So, that's what the mother says, each time she goes to the garden with the wheel barrel. She has a path for that. And you can already see a groove from the wheel barrel, and that's this way because she always follows the same groove, and the earth is pressed down because she loaded so much onto the wheel barrel, and then she has a groove and it gets ever more difficult to get out of that groove, she needs help for that and that's the same with biting the fingernails. Because she always bit fingernails she was already used to it and then it was difficult to stop. For that she also needs somebody who helps her to rewrap the fingernails immediately so that she always remembers: "No, I may not bite."

Elena did not very often see this sort of translation of text because her readers tended to read text that was written in their language of daily communication with Elena. However, other day-to-day interactions with Elena did reinforce the general concept of "translation." For example, daily she participated in and watched adults take ideas that were first shared orally in German and translate them to English when it was necessary to accommodate an English speaker.

Discussion and Educational Implications

The above findings suggest that Elena is not confused when interacting with print in her two languages. Instead, the data suggest that her experiences with books written in German and English may have provided her with an awareness of how language works in books. From this investigation it is clear that it is important to take a close look at the way bilinguals use language in different contexts.

The findings also suggest that Elena's awareness of her languages and what she can do within a reading context extend beyond epilinguistic (Gombert, 1992) to metalinguistic awareness of text. According to Gombert (1992) epilinguistic activities are

> behaviours manifested from an early age which is related to metalinguistic behaviour but is not (and has never been) consciously monitored by the subject. Such activities in the subject's behaviour are, in fact, explicit manifestations of a functional awareness of the rules of the organization or use of language.

Conversely, metalinguistic activities are activities that involve "reflection on language and its use; the ability [to] intentionally . . . monitor and plan their own methods of linguistic processing (both comprehension and production)" (p. 13).

Elena's unwillingness to "read" a German text to her mother (in English) is likely due to her lack of ability to perform this sort of task. At this stage in her development, reading for Elena is a recreation of the text from memory based on her previous encounters with readers of that text. To ask her to read the same text in another language, that is creating a literary translation, is to ask her to perform something she has little or no experience doing.

However, although Elena resisted reading the German text in English she eventually shared the content with her mother in English. From her attempts, it appears that she defined that task as being qualitatively different from when she "read" in German. Her body language (her fidgeting) and her halting reading pattern (see excerpt #3) deviated from her easy reading pace in German (see excerpt #1). In a sense, what we see is her realization that ideas are language free, and only their representation in writing is tied to a particular language. Each time she attempted to share the content of a book that was written in one language with a speaker of another language, she pulled out the key ideas and conveyed those. Supporting details and intricacies of the literacy make up were often omitted. Indeed, the way pieces of a text are married together is not easily untangled and language specific.

When pressed to provide a literary translation we can see in excerpt #2 her struggle with this task and her admittance of failure. However, this recognition of her limitations is promptly followed by a resolution of the conflict between what she can do and what she is asked to do: "I can read it only in German, but I can tell you in English." This statement and the ones following in excerpt #4 are the strongest indication that her distinction between "reading" and "conveying the main idea" is conscious as well as clear.

Granted this global metalinguistic awareness of text the next issue to be raised is whether it is developmental. During the period under study, Elena took part in translating the "main point" of the story. Previous studies have shown that higher order metalinguistic skills typically develop later in years (e.g., Gombert, 1987). The question that must be posed is whether young bilinguals who are encouraged to explore their languages through appropriate literature in both languages develop these skills earlier. Also, what are the precursors for this type of higher order thinking skills. The importance of investigating these types of questions with young bilinguals may better help educators meet the needs of more students. One of the tasks that young children are asked to complete in school is to distinguish between the details found in the text they read and the main ideas. Young bilinguals may help us understand how this skill is developed. At least in this case study it appears as if challenging Elena, helped (maybe forced) her to recognize her capabilities as well as her limitations and then led her to explore alternative strategies to deal with a literacy challenge.

Certain types of metalinguistic behaviors have been shown to be positively correlated with early reading performance (e.g., Bialystok, 1997; Geva et al., 1993). These studies only highlighted young bilingual children's word-level awareness. This study suggests that immersion in a print rich environment in both languages may also lead to a more complex understanding of the concept of text. Such awareness includes which aspect of text is tied to the language and which is not. This is important because it has implications for the many children who are enrolled in dual immersion programs (Christian, 1996) across the United States and in other countries. That is to say, they too may be developing a qualitatively different sense of language through print interactions across languages and so support their metalinguistic awareness and development in specific ways. Some of the relations hypothesized in this paper should be tested in large sample size studies. This would require the development of an assessment tool for global metalinguistic awareness as described here. The kinds of literacy events analyzed in this paper may provide a basis for the development of such a tool. Additional research is needed to help us better understand what young bilinguals bring to print interactions. To date, we have few studies that address this point.

References

Allsburg, C. V. (1981) *Jumanji.* Boston: Houghton-Mifflin.

Barton, D. (1994). *Literacy: An introduction to the ecology of written language.* Cambridge, MA: Blackwell.

Berenstain, S., & Berenstain, J. (1986). *The Berenstain bears and the bad habit.* New York: Random House.

Bialystok, E. (1986). Children's concept of word. *Journal of Psycholinguistic Research, 15,* 13–22.

Bialystok, E. (1997). Effects of bilingualism and biliteracy on children's emerging concepts of print. *Developmental Psychology, 33,* 429–440.

Brooks, F., & Donato, R. (1994). Vygotskian approaches to understanding foreign language learner discourse during communicative tasks. *Hispanic Modern Language Journal 77,* 262–274.

Brown, G., & Hulme, C. (1992). Cognitive processing and second language processing: The role of short term memory. In R. J. Harris (Ed.), *Cognitive processing in bilinguals* (pp. 105–121). Amsterdam: Elsevier.

Bryant, P., MacLean, M., Bradley, L., & Crossland, J. (1990). Rhyme and alliteration, phoneme detection, and learning to read. *Developmental Psychology, 26,* 429–438.

Canagarajah, A. S. (1993). Critical ethnography of a Sri Lankan classroom: Ambiguities in student opposition to reproduction through ESOL. *TESOL Quarterly, 27,* 601–626.

Christian, D. (1996). Two way immersion education: Students learn through two languages. *Modern Language Journal, 80,* 66–76.

Cook, V. (1997). The consequences of bilingualism for cognitive processing. In A. de Groot & J. F. Kroll (Eds.), *Tutorials in bilinguals: Psycholinguistic perspectives* (pp. 279–300). Mahwah, NJ: Erlbaum.

Cook, V. (1999). Going beyond the native speaker in language teaching. *TESOL Quarterly, 33,* 185–209.

DiCamilla, F. J., & Anton, M. (1997). Repetition in the collaborative discourse of L2 learners: A Vygotskian perspective. *Canadian Modern Language Review, 53,* 609–633.

Firth, A., & Wagner, J. (1997). On discourse, communication, and (some) fundamental concepts in SLA research. *Modern Language Journal, 81,* 285–300.

Forslind, A. (1997). *Kleine grosse Schwester.* Hamburg, Germany: Verlag Friedrich Oetinger.

Galambos, S., & Goldin-Meadows, S. (1990). The effects of learning two languages on metalinguistic awareness. *Cognition, 34,* 1–56.

Gee, J. (2000). NLS: From socially situated to social. In D. Barton, M. Hamilton, & R. Ivanic (Eds.), *Situated literacies: Reading and writing in context* (pp. 180–196). New York: Routledge.

Genesee, F. (1989). Early bilingual development: One language or two? *Journal of Child Language, 16,* 161–179.

Geva, E., Wade-Wooly, L., & Shaney, M. (1993). The concurrent development of spelling and decoding in two different orthographies. *Journal of Reading Behavior, 25,* 383–406.

Gombert, J. E. (1987). Are young children's speech adaptations conscious or automatic? A short theoretical note. *International Journal of Psychology, 22,* 375–382.

Gombert, J. E. (1992). *Metalinguistic Development.* Chicago: University of Chicago Press.

Harklau, L. (1994). Tracking and linguistic minority students: Consequences of ability grouping for second language learners. *Linguistics in Education, 6,* 217–244.

Lanza, E. (1992). Can bilingual two-year olds code-switch. *Journal of Child Language, 19,* 633–658.

Long, M., Inagaki, S., & Ortega, L. (1998). The role of the implicit negative feedback in SLA: Models and recasts in Japanese and Spanish. *Modern Language Journal, 82,* 357–371.

Magiste, E. (1986). Selected issues in second and third language learning. In J. Vaid (Ed.), *Language processing in bilinguals: Psycholinguistic and neurolinguistic perspectives* (pp. 97–122). Hillsdale, NJ: Erlbaum.

McKay, S. L., & Wong, S. C. (1996). Multiple discourses, multiple identities: Investment and agency in second language learning among Chinese adolescent immigrant students. *Harvard Educational Review, 66,* 577—608.

Pica, T. (1994). Research on negotiation: What does it reveal about second language learning conditions, processes, and outcomes? *Language Learning, 44,* 493–527.

Ronjat, J. (1913). *Le développement du langage observé chez un enfant bilingue.* Paris: Champion.

Thenoir, R. (1996). *Miranda und der neue Teddy.* Ravensburg, Germany: Ravensburger Buchverklag.

Yelland, G., Pollard, J., & Mercuri, A. (1993). The metalinguistic benefits of limited contact with a second language. *Applied Psycholinguistics, 14,* 423–444.

The Impact of a Multicultural Young Adult Novel on Intergenerational Dialogue Journal Discussion

Thomas W. Bean
University of Nevada, Las Vegas

Nicole Rigoni
Centennial High School

Five pairs of students read and reacted to Gary Soto's (1997) young adult novel *Buried Onions.* The novel centers on Eddie, a 19-year-old Hispanic character confronting issues of ethnic identity development and survival in Fresno, California. Five at-risk high school students in an urban southwestern community exchanged dialogue journals with five university graduate students enrolled in a required content-area literacy class. A previous multiple case study reported the results for two of the five pairs of students (Bean & Rigoni, 2001). The present research centers on a detailed discussion of three case study profiles of dialogue journal partners representing key differences in their response patterns. This study adds to our understanding of the impact of powerful multicultural literature on students' thinking about ethnic identity issues. In addition, the study suggests ways to scaffold journal responses.

Theoretical Framework

Our work is informed by sociocultural theories and recent studies of reader response showing the reciprocal influences that emerge when diverse groups of students engage in novel discussion (Bean & Rigoni, 2001; Bean, Valerio, & Money Senior, 1999; Finke & Edwards, 1997). In a compelling multicultural young adult novel, the main character's cultural identity is often fluid, multidimensional, and contradictory (McCarthy, 1993). This complexity encourages a consideration of hegemonic power structures, social determinism, and resistance to the status quo (Luke, 2000; McCarthy, 1998).

For example, in an earlier study of intergenerational novel discussion in an advanced high school American literature class and a graduate content-area literacy course, over half of the participants' written e-mail messages about Amy Tan's (1991) *The Kitchen God's Wife* encompassed intertextual and personal interpretive comments aimed at challenging the harsh treatment of women in China during this period (Bean et al., 1999). At times, participants disagreed with each other as they wrestled with gender issues and the main character Winnie's violent

*National Reading Conference Yearbook, **50**, pp. 127–137.*

marriage to Wen Fu in 1940's China. Sociocultural filters including gender, ethnicity, age, and contextual experiences added to the intertextual connections these readers made as they responded to the novel. Spiegel (1998) argued that journal responses encourage student ownership, voice, personal and multiple interpretations, and a move away from superficial responding. Literature should be approached with a critical eye toward personal, social, and cultural dimensions (Rogers, 1997). Providing time for this close reading and interpretive discussion to occur is crucial because intertextual discourse "provides a place where students can begin to see the relationships between the texts of their own lives and the lives of others who are like them as well as different from them" (Rogers, 1997, p. 109). Dialogue journal exchanges help students challenge surface level assumptions, stereotypes, and easy solutions to complex dilemmas.

Intergenerational novel discussion often creates an element of disequilibrium as a result of varying perspectives on events that unfold. These varying perspectives help students to question their assumptions and beliefs (Finke & Edwards, 1997). For example, in *Buried Onions,* Eddie inadvertently causes his employer's Toyota truck to be stolen. Rather than report the truck stolen, Eddie hides out in his apartment, avoiding his job and employer. This ethical dilemma offers students a chance to explore how they might handle this situation, as well as to examine social forces that cause Eddie to avoid the authorities.

The present study involved students in reflecting on the novel's events through the medium of dialogue journals. Other studies show the promise of this response mode, particularly with at-risk students. For example, Miller and Legge (1999) engaged at-risk, 12th graders in reading multicultural novels by Amy Tan and others. Students wrote in daily response journals. Miller and Legge found that at-risk students were less afraid of advancing interpretive comments because they had less experience with responding in traditional ways than other students. In addition, at-risk students found the stories helpful in making sense of their own lives. However, the intergenerational aspect of journaling is not well researched (Spiegel, 1998) and the present study adds to our understanding of its potential in classrooms. Specifically, the present multiple case study sought to describe reader-response patterns that emerged in intergenerational dialogue journal discussion.

Method

Participants

A total of 10 students were involved in the previous multiple case study (Bean & Rigoni, 2001). There were 5 sophomores at Arroyo High School (a pseudonym), and 5 at an urban university of 22,000 students in the Southwest. The 5 high school students included three females and two males. There were three Hispanic students, one African-American student, and one European-American student. All university students in the study were European Americans with three females and two males. Students were paired with same gender partners in order to assure that there would be a positive climate for journaling. Same gender groups tend to provide a comfort zone for engaging in discussion (Anders & Guzzetti, 1996).

In the high school class, students were selected through purposive sampling (LeCompte & Preissle, 1993) with a focus on at-risk students. Arroyo High School is located in a low socioeconomic area with 95% of Arroyo's 2,300-student enrollment classified as low income. The student body is 75% Hispanic with a high percentage of non-English speaking students.

The graduate content literacy course had 29 students enrolled. The 5 students who participated in the study volunteered to do this to fulfill their mid-term project requirement. This group of European-American graduate students were not ethnically diverse. However, they typically taught in schools in an urban southwestern community where ethnic diversity was the norm. Thus, many of the issues dealt with in the novel were very familiar.

The Novel

Participants read a chapter-per-week in Soto's (1997) *Buried Onions.* The novel centers on Eddie, the main character who lives in a Barrio in Fresno, California. Eddie is a 19-year-old community college drop-out, barely surviving by spray painting house numbers on curbs in suburban Fresno neighborhoods. He attempts to avoid gang involvement but is constantly pushed by his family to embrace this lifestyle. His aunt wants him to kill the person she believes murdered his cousin. Eddie experiences racism, poverty, and a constant onslaught of problems before getting on with his life. Soto's lyrical style blends Spanish phrases, gang machismo, and the challenges of establishing one's own identity despite enormous peer and family pressure to do otherwise. Eddie's plight is one that students relate to, and it offers a powerful basis for dialogue journal writing and discussion.

Procedure

Dialogue journals were exchanged once a week and returned the following week with new entries. The study spanned 10 weeks of the semester. Nicole, the Arroyo High teacher, visited class each week to exchange the five dialogue journals from her social studies class with the five students in the university class who were writing to her students. Students wrote to each other in pairs that were maintained throughout the study.

A qualitative, multiple-case-study design was used to collect and code descriptive data (LeCompte & Preissle, 1993). Journals were exchanged once a week for 10 weeks. They were read and reread for emerging patterns, categories, and themes (Strauss & Corbin, 1990) with sentences in the journals comprising the unit of analysis. We met regularly to discuss and confirm our interpretations.

Results

Major Categories

A total of 14 content-analysis categories emerged from our constant comparative analysis. These categories were derived from reading and rereading journal entries with particular attention to sentences as the unit of analysis (see Bean & Rigoni, 2001, for a more detailed description). The 14 categories were examined for overlapping characteristics and reduced to the following 12 reader-response categories and examples: (a) societal conditions ("Those bad neighborhoods are like that."); (b) academic mode (personally detached question-answer dialogue); (c) ethical considerations ("I would have reported the stolen truck."); (d) institutional racism ("The police would assume Eddie stole the truck."); (e) characters alive ("I don't like Norma—it's good Eddie avoided her."); (f) individual resistance ("If I were Eddie, I'd try real hard to be different."); (g) literary evaluation ("I didn't like the ending"); (h) character empathy ("I know how ___ feels."); (i) personal choices ("I would call the police."); (j) interpretive disagreement ("I don't agree that . . ."); (k) artistic interpretation ("This drawing of Eddie shows how he looks . . ."); (l) mutual and peer support ("I really like your ideas . . ."). In considering the descriptive data for the three cases in this study, we report the top three categories by case. We then explore each dialogue journal pair in more detail.

Descriptive data are reported with the high school student first (pseudonyms), in each pair: (a) Salena and Marle (characters alive, ethical considerations, and societal conditions); (b) Jesus and Vince (characters alive, ethical considerations, and literary evaluation); (c) Carmelita and Nancy (mutual support, ethical considerations, and characters alive); (d) Roberto and Nat (academic mode, ethical considerations, and literary evaluation).

Salena and Marle

Salena, a Latina student, wrote to Marle, a European-American teacher in the university class. They both established a strong connection to Eddie.

Characters alive. Salena, at Arroyo High School, visualized Eddie as a real person, trying to cope with a hard life in Fresno:

> I think Eddie is about 5'8" with short black hair. He has a nicely built body with good muscles. He has a peculiar look to him. Like a thug but who is trying to get by. Angel on the other hand is about 6'0" black shaved hair with a dark complexion. He is a little heavy but a lot of it is muscle. In his eyes he has a death defying look.

Later, Marle, writing to Salena, said: "Eddie has a whole new set of worries, these worries are life and death related. If I was him I would be looking to get out of there."

Thus, Eddie was a compelling character facing the challenge of avenging his cousin's murder or trying to find another path. As the novel unfolds, he has few funds, a limited future, and the real possibility of being killed in his own barrio. Both Salena and Marle viewed Eddie as a living person, and they struggled with his ethical dilemmas.

Ethical considerations. Early in the novel, Eddie ignores his aunt's request to avenge his cousin's murder. She attempts to give Eddie a pistol wrapped in some tortillas she leaves at his apartment door. Salena said, "I think Eddie is making the right choice by trying to stay out of trouble with Angel." Marle agreed. "So far he is making some good choices. He needs someone to support him in his choices." A bit farther in the novel, Salena reacts negatively to Eddie's choices:

> At first I thought Eddie was trying to make the right choices, but now his attitude is changing. Ever since his aunt came over with the gun I think there is a lot more pressure for him to try and be good. Now Angel is calling him a sissy. I think he wants to prove to him that he can kill this guy. I don't think he should just go around and find a guy with yellow shoes and accuse him of killing his cousin.

Marle disagrees, saying: "I believe Eddie's conscience will take over and his concern for his self-esteem will kick in." She goes on to describe her life and its differences from Eddie's, largely alluding to societal conditions:

> I have never been in a situation like Eddie's. The pressure I was under as I grew up was directed from my mother, who wanted everything done perfectly. When I grew up there weren't "gangs" as there are today. When I was in high school we were dealing with race riots. I was afraid and other times not. Eddie is struggling with so many pressures from so many directions.

This personalized account from Marle seemed to cause Salena to reciprocate. She offered: "I also believe Eddie's conscience will kick in. I think Mr. Stiles feels kinda violated because he trusted Eddie and Eddie never came back. He said nothing to Mr. Stiles." Salena went on to say:

> My parents don't really put a lot of pressure on me. All they ask is that I be the best I can. My best is good enough for them. I do get pressure sometimes from my peers and it scares me because I want to make the right choices.

Societal conditions. Salena wrote:

> It seems like Eddie had it rough in the past and now he is trying to get by. I think later in the book Angel is going to kill the guy who killed Eddie's cousin and there will be a mix up or a set up and I think Eddie will get blamed for it.

Marle agreed, saying, "I also feel that Eddie has a rough life with not much hope in it. Like you feel that Eddie may get in trouble in relation to his cousin's death."

Overall, Salena and Marle tended to agree with each other's interpretations. For example, they agreed that a constellation of societal conditions made it nearly impossible for Eddie to get ahead. Salena argued: "I also believe that it was a combination of everything that made his attitude change. I feel exactly like you. He was trying to do his best and someone tried to stop it." In addition, Salena viewed the book's title as indicative of Eddie's plight. "I think they called the book

'Buried Onions' because when you cut an onion your eyes burn and you start to cry. In life I think it's the same thing. Life is full of pain and suffering."

Salena and Marle rarely disagreed, mutually arriving at compatible interpretations. They viewed societal forces as overpowering Eddie's efforts at individual resistance. Salena's early views of Eddie as able to overcome all his problems began to slip away as the novel progressed.

Carmelita and Nancy

Carmelita, a Latina student, wrote to Nancy, a European-American inservice teacher in the university class. They established a strong bond of mutual support in their exchanges about the novel.

Mutual support. Nancy, in an early exchange wrote to Carmelita, saying:

> I am glad you thought that Eddie's anger could overwhelm him enough to make him dangerous—but still a good guy. Your story about crashing your parents' car was a good comparison to Eddie's situation. But you had enough insight to know that you would suffer eventually. It might as well be now as later!

In a later exchange, Carmelita begins to echo the style of Nancy's journal entries, saying: "I would like to know what you thought about Eddie when he took the money that his aunt gave him for the dog pound?"

Ethical considerations were carefully considered by Carmelita and Nancy in their dialogues.

Ethical considerations. Carmelita wrote:

> If I were Eddie I would report the stolen truck to Mr. Stiles or the police. Eddie did a mistake by not telling him. The reason I would tell Mr. Stiles that his truck was stolen would be because I knew I was not guilty and had nothing to be afraid of.

Carmelita crashed her parents' car and related this experience to the problem Eddie is experiencing. Nancy shared a similar ethical dilemma with Carmelita:

> Once, at night, I backed my parents car into another car in a parking lot. My dad was a policeman, so I had it pounded into me that I was to leave a note. But the car was covered with dents and I was afraid I would be blamed for causing damage I knew I hadn't done. I never did leave a note, but I hung around so long trying to make the decision that I am surprised someone didn't see me.

Both Carmelita and Nancy related to Eddie as if he were a living person. Their intertextual connections provided links to their lives and experiences whenever they saw parallels with Eddie's struggles.

Characters alive. Carmelita related her own experience with leaving one high school and adjusting to another:

> Last year I went to Silverado High. And then two weeks before school ended we moved to a different zone and my mom said that I had to move from school (Arroyo). I didn't want to go at first but then thought about it you can say that

> I was afraid which I think I was. But now I have lots of friends and it doesn't matter anymore.

Throughout their exchanges, Carmelita reacted to Eddie's loneliness, living in a sweltering apartment with cockroaches as his companions:

> I feel alone once in a while like for example when my sister her dad, my mom and my brother are together I feel alone because their father is not mine. But when I go to my father's house then I feel ok. How about you?

This intertextual link with Eddie held true for Nancy as well:

> Yes—I guess I do feel alone. Not often—but often enough. Particularly when I'm trying to make a decision, and I know what decision I should make; I know what my family and friends think I should do; but it's not what I want to do. I suppose in that sense I identify with Eddie a bit more than I thought!

Carmelita and Nancy's mutually supportive style of dialoging resulted in a number of intertextual connections with Eddie and events in the novel. They looked forward to a sequel to the novel to find out what happened to Eddie after he escaped Fresno by enlisting in the Navy.

Roberto and Nat

Roberto, a Latino student, wrote to Nat, a European-American high school teacher in the inservice class who worked with alternative education students. Their interchanges represented a departure from the other dialogue journal pairs as Nat established a mode of questioning Roberto that resulted in an academic stance in his responses.

Academic mode. Nat's "teacher voice" is apparent in one of the early entries he wrote to Roberto:

> It's good you were able to identify Eddie as the main character because this entire book is about Eddie's feelings and beliefs. What do you think Eddie was feeling when he said to Yellow Shoes, "You like dance, homes?" What do you think was going on in Eddie's head at that moment? (p. 41) Also, I was wondering how you feel about Eddie's character so far? Do you feel that he is trying to better himself everyday or do you feel like Eddie is trapped in his environment and blames everything and everyone around him? It's good to see you are taking an interest in this book. You'll learn more about Eddie's world if you stay on the reading. Looking forward to hearing more of your comments.

At this point in their dialogue, Nat had not revealed how he felt about Eddie's plight in the novel. Roberto seemed to lose track of where he was in the novel, missing some classes and generally regarding having to read the novel as yet another class assignment. At one point, Roberto wrote, "I lost track of where we are at in class so I can't really tell you where I am in the book. Although I can tell you that I think I am in chapter 4 or 5."

As in the other cases, Roberto and Nat considered ethical issues advanced in the novel.

Ethical considerations. Roberto wrote:

> I think that Eddie believes that news about Angel being the killer. Yes. I think more about Eddie keeping the $10. Because if you didn't have any food to eat or money to spent, I think you would do the same. This makes Eddie's character poor. I feel it was not Eddie's fault that Jose was stabbed.

Nat's response to this entry revolved around societal conditions and social determinism. He wrote: "I totally agree with what you said about the environment that Eddie is in."

Literary evaluation. Nat asked Roberto how he felt about the book. "Now that you have read about half the book, I was wondering what do you think about the book? Is this a book you like reading or is this a book you feel like you have to read?"

Roberto responded: "This is a book that I feel that I have to read. I can't relate my life to Eddie's life because I have never been in a situation like his." Indeed, Nat maintained an academic tone in their dialogue journals that did not offer any personal experiences or intertextual connections. This tone was unusual given the mutual support and personal comments evident in other dialogue journal pairs. At various points, Roberto tried to get Nat to venture a personal stance toward the novel. Finally, toward the end of their weekly interchanges, Nat engaged in some personal interpretations and comments about personal choices. Nat wrote: "It seems the one positive thing about Eddie's life is his friend Jose. I wonder where Eddie's sanity would be if Jose wasn't around?"

Roberto wrote:

> I am at the part where coach is pushing him to go to the military. If it was me I would go because like that I would not be around bad influence. How about you? Would you go if you were in Eddie's shoes?

Nat replied:

> I would go to the military if I was in Eddie's place. This is Eddie's way out of this miserable life he lives in. The military may make him a better man. After all, it worked for his best friend. In general though, I would not enlist in the military during my lifetime unless there was a war, then it would be my obligation to serve my country.

Thus, very late in their dialogue journals, Roberto and Nat began to mirror the more personally connected exchanges typical of the other dialogue journal pairs. In the discussion that follows, we point toward future research and implications from the present study.

Discussion

The three cases considered in this study revealed some important variation in their journal-response categories. Although each of the three journal pairs included ethical considerations in their journal interchanges, they differed in other dominant categories: (a) Salena and Marle (characters alive, ethical considerations, societal conditions; (b) Carmelita and Nancy (mutual support, ethical considerations, characters alive); and (c) Roberto and Nat (academic mode, ethical considerations, literary evaluation).

Salena and Marle saw Eddie as a living character, beset by problems and awash in difficult ethical choices. They made intertextual connections with the novel based on their own life experiences and they tended to reinforce each other's interpretive views. Carmelita and Nancy achieved a similar bond in their journal responses. This element of mutual support provided a comfort zone where they related personal experiences and ethical choices from their own lives. For example, Carmelita and Nancy both had accidents with their parent's cars and grappled with decisions they later regretted.

In contrast to these mutually supportive, reciprocal journal pairs, Roberto and Nat framed their dialogues in the familiar ping-pong structure of teacher questioning. This academic mode dominated much of their journaling and, in comparison to other journal pairs, seemed to limit the depth of their interpretive discussions. Finally, toward the end of their writing to each other, they began to make some personal connections with events in the novel that sound more like the dialogues enjoyed by Carmelita, Nancy, Salena, and Marle.

In essence, each of the dialogue journal pairs formed their own social context, and the nature of its parameters influenced the resulting discourse patterns. There is evidence from this study that high school students can establish a productive reader "response development zone" (Moller & Allen, 2000, p. 177). Moller and Allen noted that:

> By reading a variety of culturally diverse literature and discussing personal, societal, and political issues, teachers and students guide each other toward multiple or alternative interpretations of text, self, and the world, creating a new kind of socially connected knowledge. (p. 148)

However, because discourse patterns are heavily influenced by the dialogical dimensions established in a classroom or between dialogue journal pairs, this interpretive ideal may not be realized. If a powerful multicultural young adult novel is to be viewed as worthy of rich interpretive effort, the characters need to be perceived as alive. Otherwise, the novel becomes yet another classroom text to be endured. This was the case for most of the dialogue produced by Roberto and Nat.

In retrospect, it might have been important to scaffold dialogue journal discussion with some examples that modeled seeing characters as real people engaged in tough decisions. For example, excerpts from Carmelita and Nancy's responses could serve to scaffold students' dialogue journal responses. Future studies should explore various forms of dialogue journal literature discussion scaffolding. Moller and Allan (2000) argued that:

> Instruction in a response development zone, mediated by text, teachers, peers, and dialogue, is important for all students. For students who have difficulty with comprehending a text, mediation must help them clarify factual and im-

> plied information without confining them to a singular "expert" determined meaning. (p. 177)

Reader response is a social process that may be enhanced through greater scaffolding. For example, Beach (2000) recommended creating greater specificity in responding through a consideration of activity theory (Engestrom, Miettinen, & Punamaki, 1999). Students, according to this sociocultural theory, learn while engaged in an activity that is motivated by a need to achieve an objective or outcome. Readers may use a variety of tools in responding ranging from print-based tools like dialogue journals, to multimedia tools such as body biographies (Smagorinsky & O'Donnell-Allen, 1998). Characters' actions can then be considered from the standpoint of object-driven activities. Thus, both a greater degree of scaffolding and the tenets of activity theory offer new frames of reference for future studies of reader response to multicultural young adult literature.

References

Anders, P. L., & Guzzetti, B. J. (1996). *Literacy instruction in the content areas.* San Diego, CA: Harcourt Brace.

Beach, R. (2000). Critical issues: Reading and responding to literature at the level of activity. *Journal of Literacy Research, 32,* 237–251.

Bean, T. W., & Rigoni, N. (2001). Exploring the intergenerational dialogue journal discussion of a multicultural young adult novel. *Reading Research Quarterly, 36,* 232–248.

Bean, T. W., Valerio, P. C., & Money Senior, H. (1999). Intertextuality and the e-mail discussion of a multicultural novel in secondary American literature. In T. Shanahan & F. Rodriguez-Brown (Eds.), *National Reading Conference Yearbook, 48* (pp. 376–386). Chicago: National Reading Conference.

Engestrom, Y., Miettinen, R., & Punamaki, R. (Eds.). (1999). *Perspectives on activity theory.* New York: Cambridge University Press.

Finke, J., & Edwards, B. (1997). Teacher education students' insights from intergenerational literature circles. *Journal of Teacher Education, 48,* 367–378.

LeCompte, M. D., & Preissle, J. (1993). *Ethnography and qualitative design in educational research* (2nd ed.). San Diego, CA: Academic.

Luke, A. (2000). Critical literacy in Australia: A matter of context and standpoint. *Journal of Adolescent & Adult Literacy, 43,* 448–461.

McCarthy, C. (1993). After the canon: Knowledge and ideological representation in the multicultural discussion on curriculum reform. In C. McCarthy & W. Crichlow (Eds.), *Race, identity and representation in education* (pp. 289–305). New York: Routledge.

McCarthy, C. (1998). *The uses of culture: Education and the limits of ethnic affiliation.* New York: Routledge.

Miller, S. M., & Legge, S. (1999). Supporting possible worlds: Transforming literature teaching and learning through conversations in the narrative mode. *Research in the Teaching of English, 34,* 10–64.

Moller, K. J., & Allan, J. (2000). Connecting, resisting, and searching for safer places: Student responses to Mildred Taylor's *The Friendship. Journal of Literacy Research, 32,* 145–186.

Rogers, T. (1997). No imagined peaceful place: A story of community, texts, and cultural conversations in one urban high school English classroom. In T. Rogers, & A. O. Soter (Eds.), *Reading across cultures: Teaching literature in a diverse society* (pp. 95–115). New York: Teachers College Press.

Smagorinsky, P., & O'Donnell-Allen, C. (1998). Reading as mediated and mediating action: Composing meaning for literature through multimedia interpretive texts. *Reading Research Quarterly, 33,* 198–227.

Soto, G. (1997). *Buried onions.* San Diego, CA: Harcourt Brace.

Spiegel, D. L. (1998). Reader response patterns and the growth of readers. *Language Arts, 76,* 41–48.

Strauss, A., & Corbin, J. (1990). *Basics of qualitative research: Grounded theory procedures and techniques.* Newbury Park, CA: Sage.

Tan, A. (1991). *The Kitchen God's Wife.* New York: Ivy.

Combining Voices: When Writers Work Together

Ronald E. Benton
University of Texas

Because writing has so frequently been viewed as a solitary activity, writing theorists and teachers have often considered the individual writer as the central focus of writing research and have devoted far less attention to collaborative writing teams. For example, the seminal description of the writing process made famous by Flower and Hayes (1980, 1981, 1984) emphasized the individual writer as monitor and coordinator of overlapping and recurrent cognitive processes of planning, translating (from thought into text), and revision. This cognitive view of the writing process contrasted with an alternative "expressive view" of writing, a perspective concerned more with the feelings, emotions, and motivations of writers (e.g., Cleary, 1991; Elbow, 1981; Rose, 1985). From such a view, the emotional and motivational states of writers were seen as interacting with and even interfering with the cognitive processes of writing, sometimes leading to writer's block or to decreased motivation to engage in a writing activity.

Emphasis on the individual writer began to give way when a "social view" of the writing process emerged, a view in which the writer was seen as embedded in, and a product of, a social environment, and therefore "a constituent of a culture" (Faigley, 1986, p. 535). In this view, human language and writing could only be understood from the perspective of a society, not from an individual's perspective; all writing was seen as a collaborative social act, and all writing contained echoes of many voices from the past (Bakhtin, 1981). Lave and Wenger (1991) used the metaphor of apprenticeship to describe the way a newcomer enters into a community of practice to learn its sociocultural values and to become a legitimate participant. Bruffee (1983, 1984, 1993) framed classroom writing instruction in terms of collaborative learning activities. The "writer's workshop," with classroom peers suggesting revisions or edits, became a common feature in many writing courses. Reither and Vipond (1989) declared that "the case for writing's social dimensions no longer requires arguing," but they also noted that "little substantive change in either course design or classroom practices has come about that can be said to result from this reconsideration of the nature of writing" (p. 855). Thus, after receiving peer responses, a writer would still end up submitting a paper and receiving credit for work as an individual writer.

Renewed interest in collaborative writing emerged from an interest in nonacademic writing in the workplace (e.g., Ede & Lunsford, 1990; Faigley & Miller, 1982; Forman, 1991, 1992; Forman & Katsky, 1986; Odell & Goswami, 1985; Spilka, 1993). "Real-world writing" may be quite different from "school writing," these research-

National Reading Conference Yearbook, 50, pp. 138–149.

ers found, because co-authorship was "especially common in professional and technical occupations" (Faigley & Miller, 1982, p. 567). Ede and Lunsford (1990) suggested that workplace writing fell generally into two patterns: the more common "hierarchical" group, in which one person who had more status directed the writing project, and the "dialogic" group, in which all members had approximately equal control of the decision-making process, though most writing situations were not pure examples of either mode. Ede and Lunsford also noted that contemporary views of authorship have changed from the view of writing as an individual activity to "one that would view texts as contested sites in a complex, situated world of political, cultural, economic, ideological, and other forces" (p. 88).

Syverson (1999) developed the term "ecology of composition" as a unit of analysis for writing situations (p. 2). This idea centers on "the dynamics of interactions among readers, writers, texts, and their environments" (p. xiv) in the sense that writers are situated and co-evolving in a "physical, psychological, social, temporal, and spatial network of relations" (p. 7), including complex interactions with others and with the technological tools available to writers within a particular historical and cultural setting.

This social view of collaborative writing raised several related questions about collaborative writing teams: (a) How is collaborative writing viewed by its participants? (b) How do collaborative writing teams make plans and decide on the division of labor needed to complete the writing task? (c) What advantages or disadvantages do collaborative writing teams report in distributing the writing task? (d) What effects in terms of motivation and emotions do team members experience while writing together? (e) Do collaborative writers ever feel that they are losing their individual writer's voice, and if so, how do they respond? (f) How does the pressure of deadlines affect the collaborative writing process?

Method

Participants

Five experienced writing teams (all having written frequently with the same co-author for at least 5 years), each described in more detail below, agreed to participate in this study conducted in the late 1990s. These teams were obtained through a "snowball sampling" method, that is, through an informal network of professional associates, contacts, and friends that supplied me with the names of people who routinely wrote collaboratively in professional and academic settings. The teams selected for this study typically included only two writers, although several of the teams had occasionally included one or more additional writers for particular projects. Each member described his or her experiences in one-on-one interviews with me. These semistructured interviews were conducted in a large urban area that included computer-related industries, higher education, and the legal profession. The interviews were conducted in the participants' work setting, except in the case of one participant who asked to be interviewed at his home. The teams answered questions about how they typically planned and divided a writing task, how they composed and revised, how they managed conflicts about the writing, and how they produced the final draft, including the effects of deadlines on the writing process. Members of three teams also agreed to brief follow-up interviews.

Data Analysis

An inductive technique based on Strauss and Corbin's (1990) grounded theory approach resulted in preliminary categories and patterns of comments within the written transcripts of the interviews. What emerged from this inductive analysis of the participants' comments was a description of each writer's working relationship with his or her fellow writer, the degree of satisfaction each writer expressed with the collaborative writing process and final written product, a view of each team's typical (and also less typical when deadlines loomed) drafting processes, the writers' sense of having a writer's voice, and the advantages as well as occasional conflicts that resulted from working with another writer. Each team was first treated as a separate case study to reveal as much as possible about the specific relationships, working patterns, and characteristics of the teams. Then, cross-case comparisons were used to find common aspects across the teams.

Results

Case studies revealed different patterns of writers working together. Even though the teams generally had favorable things to say about their collaborative writing experiences, everything was not always rosy for these teams. Conflicts over the writing inevitably arose and had to be managed strategically. Presented below is a brief description of each team.

Team 1

The first team consisted of an attorney, John, and his legal assistant, Brad (all participants are identified by pseudonyms). John generally specialized in civil suits, although he had occasionally handled criminal cases. His assistant, Brad, was the first writer I interviewed for this study. Brad estimated that he and John had written over 100 legal briefs during their 8 years of working together. Their professional relationship was characterized by a sense of mutual respect, and they both mentioned the idea that "two heads are better than one" in legal writing.

One area of interest with this team was the way Brad had learned to imitate John's style and voice while writing. Brad said his ability to write with John's voice reminded him of the way a chameleon can change color:

> I've probably become a much better writer, and it's probably because I've learned to imitate him, because that's my job is to be his writer, so I've learned his voice, and sometimes he can't even tell which parts he wrote and stuff, but that's only because I've learned that from him, so even if I'm doing the writing

> and writing in his voice, then he would still get credit for that. It's a semi-conscious thing. When you see the same corrections over and over again, you think, well, I can save some time and do these before he corrects them and so you automatically pick up certain habits and stuff, but I tend to be a natural chameleon anyway.

Brad said that some of the corrections John would call for were based on knowing the expectations of judges, who would be looking for the main points early in the legal brief:

> He will say . . . we need to cut this down to half size so we can move our argument close [to the beginning] before the judge falls asleep, you know?

When asked if he ever felt he were having to give up his own unique writing voice, Brad laughed and replied, "No, because I never felt like I really had one much."

John said that he and Brad were able to clarify their legal arguments through face-to-face discussions about how to express the ideas in writing:

> I enjoy it [collaborative writing] because the product is better at the end, and often I'm smarter at the end. If there's, that example I gave you earlier of a situation where Brad had . . . an argument that was a good argument but he had expressed it poorly. When we were done with that, I was smarter for having learned the argument, and he was smarter for having learned how to express it better, and so that was a good thing for both of us.

These face-to-face meetings were, in the vast majority of cases, followed by Brad's writing a first draft of the brief and returning it to John for revisions and editing suggestions. Brad said that John would write notes in the margin of the brief and put sticky notes on certain parts of the draft, sometimes calling for a paragraph to be moved or suggesting additions or deletions, as well as marking any edits needed to be made. According to both writers, John had the final say if there were any disagreements about the content of the final draft, because John was the practicing attorney whose name would be on the document once it left the office.

Team 2

The second team (both men, with a third male writer involved in some projects) consisted of a senior products manager (Grady) and his junior engineering staff at a large international company that developed, tested, and manufactured equipment used in the making of computer chips. Based in Japan, with offices all over the world, this company published numerous engineering reports and technical manuals. As the senior writer for an estimated 50 collaborative papers, typically ranging in length from 40 to 400 pages, Grady had worked most often with a particular engineer who had recently left the company and was not available for an interview. Since his previous writing partner's departure, Grady had written collaboratively with several other engineers. Grady said he had 20 years of experience in the computer business.

One idea that Grady emphasized was the importance of early face-to-face meetings in collaborative writing:

> I don't like e-mail to start that kind of process because it's just too slow. I find that it's just not spontaneous enough, and it doesn't generate enough interest, so typically what we do is, we use either another gathering or another opportunity to meet face-to-face.

Grady also said that he would rate videoconferences "at half the efficiency" of face-to-face meetings in planning a writing project, noting that he depended on body language and other subtle indications more easily observed in person:

> The twitch of the eye, that's like, he didn't like that, so then I try to get him to explain to me why he didn't like that. This just makes the whole process, communication process, weaker when you do that [use videoconferencing]. That's probably no different than if you're having a business meeting as opposed to a collaborative writing. . . . It's like, I know you want to tell me something. You're talking into a camera. There's no camaraderie . . . Americans gesture all the time, right? They're almost like Italians. And the Asians will sit very quietly, looking at their tea and writing notes.

Grady also said that a collaborative writing project could help socialize a new engineer into the corporate culture:

> The world is made up of a lot of lone rangers in the engineering world, whereas people in the business world tend to work more, maybe, collectively than people in engineering. We've always had this expression that you put the engineer in the office and you feed him under the door and he puts the product back out under the door. . . . So, I think that the teamwork is probably the one thing that I like best about it . . . the fact that it gives partnership and you build a relationship with an engineer or another colleague.

Grady stated that he did not feel the writing his team produced had a distinctive voice:

> No, there's none. There's not much personality. I put more personality into my personal efforts with these companies more than the others because I'm a Gemini, so I like to split that up between my personality and my profession, but most of our guys don't. They use a lot of third person pronouns, and they don't use enough warmth in the writing.

Grady considered the lack of voice to be related to the expectations of the technical writing's audience, saying that the readers do not expect to find any real voice in most technical writing, but he also said he did not think technical writing necessarily had to be "voiceless," and he even said he thought it was a more recent development in scientific writing in general:

> I think that's a weakness, unfortunately, for us, because we've lost a tremendous ability in the last 100 years in technical writing. You pick up a manuscript from Einstein or from Edison and you find some wonderful prose, even describing the heating aspects of the glass, of the filament on a light bulb. You can find some wonderful, it's eloquent, right? And we write in facts and nouns and verbs.

Grady noted that dividing a writing task was an "elegant" way to get the work done more efficiently. He said that in his experience, writing teams had the advantage of being able to draw upon the combined pool of knowledge and skills of more than one person. The quality of technical papers written collaboratively was almost always better than a technical paper written by one expert individual, he said.

Team 3

The third team consisted of two women who had written together for about 8 years. One writer, Peggy, had worked for 13 years at a privately owned innovative learning academy that for the previous 3 years had been designated as a state-chartered high school for at-risk students. Peggy's position was chief program officer. She wrote curriculum documentation with Beth, the curriculum specialist at the school. Beth had worked at the school for the past 8 years. More than 200 students attended this charter high school, with approximately equal numbers of young men and women. These students were considered to be at risk "socially, economically, and educationally," according to Beth: "Many come to us through the criminal justice or juvenile justice system." Most of this team's collaborative writing consisted of grant proposals and "documenting our innovative programs, educational programs for replication, that sort of thing," Beth said. Peggy estimated that she and Beth had collaborated on about 15 major writing projects. Beth corroborated this number, estimating it to be about two a year for 8 years. This team had also collaborated on numerous shorter written reports, at least two a month for the past 7 years, Peggy said. The program documentation manuals and high school design materials they produced together had to conform to state guidelines, and one of their requirements in writing reports was to find wording that would comply with state-approved standards for high school curricula.

This team demonstrated a strong personal affiliation. They had become friends after meeting on the job, and they had taken a vacation trip together to Italy one summer. Peggy said they had become almost like sisters:

> We're both of an age. We're both Anglo female. We are both into art and literature, and, I mean, there's great similarities. I mean she's a sister essentially. She's the sister I never had, so there's just a, I can say half a sentence and she can complete the thought, and that's the special collaboration.

Their friendship had allowed them to minimize conflicts when writing together, although Beth indicated that they sometimes disagreed:

> No, there were tears on occasion, frustration on occasion, but I think that our, that two things were happening simultaneously. One is that we both had such a high level of respect for each other's skills and talents and that we also on some level were kindred spirits and saw the world through similar lenses, and so, since our perceptions were often very similar, there just wasn't much fodder for disagreement.

Whenever they did have a disagreement about the writing, Beth said, it was usually a minor one about word choice or style:

> Hardly ever, except in choice of expressions. She had certain words that she liked to use frequently, transition phrases—concomitantly, for example—and I

> would just have to rein her in and say, my dear, can we just be a little bit, can we explore a little further in a way to connect the two paragraphs? And sometimes, I would have to be the prosaic part of the partnership and just let her go off on her, as I said, her lyrical tangents and take the wheat and the chaff and throw out the lyricism on occasion as chaff and just keep her wheat.

Peggy also recalled their having occasional disagreements over wording or sentence structure:

> We've hit the wall a couple of times with writer's block. We've reached problems with sentences or word choice where we've had lively debates. Lively! On word choice! And on punctuation! I mean, I'm very fond of the semicolon! What can I tell you? [laughs] I'm serious. You know, you have to be an English major to enjoy this. And then there are times we just sit back and go, wow! Great verb!

One distinctive feature about this team was their drafting process. Their usual method of getting a draft started was to have a face-to-face meeting in which Peggy would talk about what the content of the paper should include, while Beth wrote down in longhand the exact wording of many of Peggy's phrases, even whole sentences that Peggy would compose aloud, as well as the gist of Peggy's ideas. Beth would then take her notes home and construct a first draft that reflected Peggy's ideas and also captured most of Peggy's original wording. After composing this first draft on her home computer, Beth would give the draft to Peggy to read for any suggested changes. Beth noted that their drafting process had clearly defined roles, with Beth being the "pragmatist" and Peggy being the "lyricist":

> I'm generally the one who writes the objectives down. I like to have things in black and white so I can, I see objectives as very much the hub of a wheel and then in the writing process, in the creative process, many spokes are established in that wheel, but to keep us on track, I like to keep coming back to what is the hub? Why are we doing this? Who is our audience? What is our purpose? And, so, I'm pretty much the pragmatic one. I sort of keep us grounded, and Peggy is the visionary, and she sort of engages in flights of fancy, and, you know, being a, I suppose, being a poetry major, she can do that. And my being an education major, I bring it back to where I know it can be of use.

Their usual drafting process sometimes changed when there was an imminent deadline. On those occasions, they composed side-by-side at the computer, according to Beth:

> I mean, there have been times when we've been in terrible deadline crunches. We've been confronted with tasks that were impossible for me to take away and bring back, and Peggy would sit down at the computer, and I'd be over her shoulder, and she'd be typing, typing, typing, and I'd be saying, no, no, no. Delete that line and rephrase it this way. Okay, okay, okay, and then we would work through the document in that fashion, but those were the exceptions rather than the rules, and the documents had to be rather short in order for us to do that effectively.

Both writers had comments about the notion of voice in their collaborative writing. Peggy said, "It's certainly not neutral. I do not write in the passive voice a lot. It's not like a technical manual tone, and Beth is an extremely elegant . . . writer and has a certain flow, and so I can tell our style, and there is a voice there." Beth contrasted their team's writing voice with her own personal writing voice:

> I'm going to just use a metaphor here, it's like a young girl going to her first ball, and if I were to use my voice entirely and not pay attention to the audience, the girl would probably be dressed in, you know, outrageously frilly chiffon and pink taffeta and ribbons, and it would be overmuch, whereas, once I take her to the ball and dress her in the language, collaborative language, she's in a very elegant, conservative but elegant, white satin gown. . . . It's elegant but not flamboyant, and that's a big difference.

Beth added that writing with someone else could diminish the sense of a personal writing voice: "The only caveat I would throw out there is that for me personally, it was always important that I participated in my own personal writing at the same time that I was writing with someone else."

Both women said that writing with a male writer was more difficult than writing with another woman. Peggy said she would have to "pull" information from a male science teacher with whom she sometimes worked, and her usual role of saying sentences aloud while Beth recorded them in longhand was reversed whenever she worked with him, forcing her to take notes and write the first draft herself. Beth said she would prefer not to write with a male author: "Too many distractions!"

Team 4

Team 4 consisted of a male and a female professor who had worked together over a period of 14 years in the same department of a large research university. For about 10 of those years they had written academic journal articles and conference papers together. Ray was the senior member of this team. In commenting on his partner, Brenda, he said, "What happened eventually is that Brenda surpassed what I had done, I mean, which is what you want. Any teacher wants a student to eventually do whatever you could do and then do more." Ray estimated that he and Brenda had written at least 20–30 times together (Brenda estimated 28 papers), with many of the papers they presented at conferences being turned into published journal articles. Ray noted that he and Brenda would divide a project into two related but self-contained papers so that each of them could be the first author on one of the papers, because "if two people are on the same paper, you only get one airfare [travel expense reimbursement from their department], so right then we knew we had two papers."

After dividing the overall project into two papers, they would each write a first draft and give it to the other person for feedback. In a second face-to-face meeting Brenda and Ray would go over the editing and revision suggestions they had made on each other's first draft, and then a second, usually final, draft would be produced for each paper.

Like the women in Team 3, Ray and Brenda sometimes had to alter their usual drafting procedure:

> We'd be under the gun, and it would be a last minute deal, and so we didn't actually have the luxury of . . . doing the back-and-forth, and sometimes we'd actually sit down at the computer, the two of us. Usually I would type, because I'm a better typist than Brenda, and so . . . we would just read sentences aloud, you know, and I'd type in a sentence, you know, and she'd think of some other sentence, and she'd dictate it to me, or then I'd get an idea, and I would just read it out loud as I typed it in, and then we would just sit down, literally, in front of the screen for sometimes hours at a time.

Over the years of writing together, their writing styles had become almost interchangeable, according to Brenda:

> We have almost identical writing styles, and we can just step right in and write for each other. We've done it with turnarounds that have been really short on revisions that come down in our proof pages, and you can't tell who wrote what. And that's because we're very similar in the way in which we approach things.

Ray said that he felt the two of them had merged their individual writing voices into a new collaborative voice:

> She, I think, maybe blended a little bit closer to my style, but that may have also been because I was older. I was her adviser. I was . . . the one who had done work in this area before she had, so I think there was a little bit of, I don't know, a respect or something for me, but I certainly have respect for her, too, but it's just that out of a kind of tradition, she's younger. She was a junior faculty member, a new assistant professor, and I was already a tenured associate professor, or around then I was, and so there was that little status difference, too. I think I also changed. I became more careful and more precise in my use of language. I think I was, had a tendency to be more, uh, sloppy, vague, you know? And a lot of it was Brenda was very much into the precision, making sure that there's no ambiguity about what that word is or what it means, that kind of thing.

Ray also spoke about the problem of receiving credit for collaboratively written academic papers. He noted that single-authored papers are more valued in terms of receiving promotions or in tenure decisions:

> You know, it's really a problem in that the dean will come out in public and . . . say, we have to have a faculty that collaborates. We want inter-disciplinary research. We want people across departments to commingle and work together. We want our faculty to work with the school district. But then, when it comes time to give credit for that collaborative work, that has not been worked out at all. . . . On the one hand, they want you to get involved in collaborative activities, but on the other hand, you can be penalized for it, because the reward system is still geared to single, sole-authorship publication.

Brenda said that she had written less often with Ray once he began to take on more administrative duties in their department. She had more often written with graduate students and other faculty members in recent years, and in an interesting role reversal, she had become the senior writer in a new writing team. Her new role led to an interview with the last writing team.

Team 5

Brenda became the senior member of a writing team when she began to write with Patrick, who had been a graduate student in Brenda's department. Patrick had specialized in the same area in which Brenda taught, and he was recognized for his conceptual knowledge and understanding of advanced mathematical theories. Patrick and Brenda did not have as many years of shared history in their writing together as the other teams in this study did. The two of them had written collaboratively for only about 5 years, with a total of five co-authored papers produced together during that time.

This team had recently completed a project in which the two of them had reached different understandings of what each was supposed to do, and Brenda said they were forced to meet several times over a 2-week period to clarify what each was to do as a deadline was rapidly approaching. Brenda said she felt that it was a "problem" for her "in terms of trying to get it written with somebody who works until the very end. . . . I don't want to read a paper that's so rough I wouldn't send it to anybody, with less than 24 hours to go. That makes me nervous."

Patrick commented on this tension related to the deadline: "Oh, I don't know. It's like any disagreement. You get frustrated, right? A little bit angry, but, you know, it's all temporary." He said the two of them had resolved the conflict by completing the paper on the deadline day and that they would definitely work together again in the future. This team demonstrated the importance of establishing common goals and clearly defined roles when planning a writing project. Although this team is presented in somewhat less detail than the others because of length requirements for this report, it is not an indication that this team was less important than the others. Indeed, this team's working relationship is an interesting work in progress.

Conclusion

This study had several limitations. First, the study depended mainly on self-report data. Second, only two-person teams were interviewed, yet writing teams may be much larger, especially in the world of scientific research. Also, only academic and professional writing teams participated in the study, omitting literary collaborations entirely. Finally, in addition to interviews, actual observation of writing teams at work would have strengthened the study. Despite these limitations, the study provides insights about experienced writing teams in authentic, bounded settings with pragmatic purposes for the writing. The words and voices of the participants themselves help bring the study to life.

Although each team was unique, a cross-case comparison revealed that all of the teams expressed a high degree of satisfaction with the quality of their collaborative writing, with "quality" indicated by the participants' stating that the final documents were more effectively developed than any draft that an individual writer could have written alone. Each team reported that an extra set of eyes helped in revising and editing successive drafts. The teams all reported conflicts, but in each case these writers managed to resolve the conflicts successfully, often because one writer was the "first" author or had a higher status or greater expertise. More than one writer mentioned the need to be open to constructive criticism and to "keep your ego in check" when writing with another person. The writers in this study emphasized the importance of building teamwork and socializing an "apprentice" writer into a professional or academic discourse community through collaborative writing. All of the writing teams depended on early face-to-face meetings to organize and divide the writing tasks, with clear roles and expectations needed to avoid conflicts. Several teams noted that time pressure forced them to change their usual drafting process when a deadline was approaching, with side-by-side composing at the computer required in a time crunch. The teams all reported an awareness of their team's collaborative writing voice, yet none of the writers expressed a sense of losing his or her individual writer's voice when involved in collaborative writing. In fact, writing with another person actually helped the legal assistant on Team 1 to develop an awareness, for the first time, that his writing even had a voice, the result of his consciously imitating the writing style of the attorney with whom he worked. Several of the writers said that being part of a collaborative writing team helped them to stay engaged with the writing task because they could encourage each other and because they did not want to let their partners down.

Future research might examine other issues raised by some of the teams. For example, Beth and Peggy of Team 3 spotlighted the way that gender issues might affect the collaborative writing process, and Ray from Team 4 underscored the problems inherent in receiving credit for tenure and promotions based on academic collaborative writing. Grady (Team 2) emphasized the issue of cross-cultural collaboration in his comments about the Asian engineers. Future studies might also explore the special problems involved in coordinating larger writing teams. As computer technology continues to alter the manner in which we write, more collaborative "distance writing" will likely occur via e-mail and the Internet. Individual writers will continue to work alone, of course, but knowing how group interactions shape writing processes and products could provide valuable insight into the inherently complex nature of collaborative writing. Finally, the affective component of group writing is a rich area of study that has not yet been fully explored.

References

Bakhtin, M. M. (1981). *The dialogic imagination* (C. Emerson, Trans., & M. Holquist, Trans. and Ed.). Austin: University of Texas Press.

Bruffee, K. A. (1983). Writing and reading as collaborative social acts. In J. N. Hayes, P. A. Roth, J. R. Ramsey, & R. D. Foulke (Eds.), *The writer's mind: Writing as a mode of thinking* (pp. 159– 169). Urbana, IL: National Council of Teachers of English.

Bruffee, K. A. (1984). Collaborative learning and the "conversation of mankind." *College English, 46,* 635–652.

Bruffee, K. A. (1993). *Collaborative learning.* Baltimore, MD: Johns Hopkins University Press.

Cleary, L. M. (1991). Affect and cognition in the writing process of eleventh graders: A study of concentration and motivation. *Written Communication, 8,* 473–507.

Ede, L., & Lunsford, A. (1990). *Singular texts/plural authors: Perspectives on collaborative writing.* Carbondale: Southern Illinois University Press.

Elbow, P. (1981). *Writing with power.* New York: Oxford University Press.

Faigley, L. (1986). Competing theories of process: A critique and a proposal. *College English, 48,* 527–542.

Faigley, L., & Miller, T. P. (1982). What we learn from writing on the job. *College English, 44,* 557–569.

Flower, L., & Hayes, R. H. (1980). The dynamics of composing: Making plans and juggling constraints. In L. W. Gregg & E. R. Steinberg (Eds.), *Cognitive processes in writing* (pp. 31–50). Hillsdale, NJ: Erlbaum.

Flower, L., & Hayes, R. H. (1981). A cognitive process theory of writing. *College Composition and Communication, 32,* 365–387.

Flower, L., & Hayes, R. H. (1984). Images, plans, and prose: The representation of meaning in writing. *Written Communication, 1,* 120–160.

Forman, J. (1991). Collaborative business writing: A Burkean perspective for future research. *Journal of Business Communication, 28,* 233–257.

Forman, J. (Ed.). (1992). *New visions of collaborative writing.* Portsmouth, NH: Boynton/Cook.

Forman, J., & Katsky, P. (1986). The group report: A problem in small group or writing processes? *Journal of Business Communication, 23,* 23–35.

Lave, J., & Wenger, E. (1991). *Situated learning: Legitimate peripheral participation.* New York: Cambridge University Press.

Odell, L., & Goswami, D. (Eds.). (1985). *Writing in nonacademic settings.* New York: Guilford.

Reither, J. A., & Vipond, D. (1989). Writing as collaboration. *College English, 51,* 855–867.

Rose, M. (1985). Complexity, rigor, evolving method, and the puzzle of writer's block: Thoughts on composing-process research. In M. Rose (Ed.), *When a writer can't write* (pp. 227–260). New York: Guilford.

Spilka, R. (Ed.). (1993). *Writing in the workplace: New research perspectives.* Carbondale: Southern Illinois University Press.

Strauss, A., & Corbin, J. (1990). *Basics of qualitative research: Grounded theory procedures and techniques.* Newbury Park, CA: Sage.

Syverson, M. A. (1999). *The wealth of reality: An ecology of composition.* Carbondale: Southern Illinois University Press.

Thinking Aloud with Feedback: Implications of a University-School E-mail Dialogue

Kelly Chandler-Olcott
Syracuse University

Lois Pangburn
Mapleton Elementary School

Over the past 20 years, writing has been frequently proposed as a way for prospective and inservice teachers to learn from their own practice. Many teacher preparation programs in literacy education require students to keep journals about their readings, observations, and fieldwork (Graham, Hudson-Ross, Atkins, McWhorter, & Stewart, 1999; Whitmore & Goodman, 1996); a number of well-known schools and districts have placed reflective writing at the center of their reform initiatives (Lester & Onore, 1990; Meier, 1995); and the International Reading Association's Regie Routman Award honors a teacher annually with a $1,000 prize for dedication "to improving teaching and learning through reflective writing about his or her teaching and learning process" (International Reading Association, 2000). In these contexts, writing is clearly seen as a professional development tool.

Recently, as more attention has been paid to the influence of social contexts and relationships on learning, there has likewise been more emphasis on what Fulwiler (1987) calls the "dialogue journal": written exchanges between or among partners, with the expectation of feedback and response. Sometimes, these dialogue journals are kept as a requirement for a class or seminar (Grisham, 1997). In other cases, often during student teaching, they serve to link the university and the field, with both the university supervisor and the mentor teacher responding to teacher candidates' reflections on their internships (Davies, Hogan, & Dalton, 1993; Wallace, 1999). Such partnerships have been shown to encourage inquiry, promote problem solving, and enhance greater communication among program constituents.

Classroom-based inquiry on literacy learning also serves as a context for written dialogue. In some instances, university-based collaborators provide feedback, encouragement, and assistance to K–12 colleagues in the midst of a research project (Isakson & Williams, 1996; Meyer et al., 1998). In others, college teachers pursue journal partnerships with colleagues from other universities. For Lalik and Hinchman (1999), both literacy education professors, e-mail reflections on their teaching provided the primary data source for an investigation of what they called "the inequities that are enacted in literacy discourses." The e-mail

National Reading Conference Yearbook, 50, pp. 150–163.

partnership pursued by MacGillavray and King (1995) helped both authors to "consider the corners of our teaching identities which we typically ignored" (p. 414), as well as to counteract the isolation that many teachers experience.

The project reported here sought to extend these findings about reflective writing in the service of teaching. It differs from previous research, however, because the dialogue journals were exchanged by writers across the traditional university-school divide. One of us (Lois) teaches first grade at Mapleton Elementary in northern Maine, while the other (Kelly) teaches literacy methods at Syracuse University in central New York. Aware of the potential benefits of writing to learn, we decided in August 1999 to initiate a regular e-mail dialogue. We did not begin our exchanges with the intention of conducting a formal inquiry; instead, we hoped to improve and enrich our teaching of two different student populations, using each other as "a critical friend" (Costa & Kallick, 1993). Kelly wrote early on that she saw the project as a way to discuss her teaching with "someone who is doing, every day in a glorious and messy fashion" what she hoped her preservice students could learn to do (E-mail, 8/3/99). Lois perceived the exchange as an opportunity for "thinking aloud with feedback" (E-mail, 8/4/99). We used our entries to recount classes we had taught, consider possibilities for future teaching, and respond to issues raised in the other person's messages.

Six months into the project, we decided to analyze our communication systematically. We were motivated in part because our previous experiences as teacher researchers suggested such analysis would help us learn more from the exchanges but also because we felt that others might benefit from the insights associated with a university-school collaboration that was neither co-teaching nor co-researching in a K–12 classroom. Having saved copies of every message we sent or received from each other, we were able to examine those messages using a retrospective approach that Berthoff (1987) calls "REsearch": not "going out after new 'data' but rather REconsidering what is at hand" (p. 30). The analysis was guided by the following research questions: (a) What does the data captured in our e-mail reveal about our decision-making as teachers in our respective contexts? (b) How does the e-mail partnership itself affect our decision-making in those contexts?

Theoretical Perspectives

The study was grounded in two theoretical frameworks. First, we shared a belief in principles of social constructivism outlined by Boyd and Galda (1997):

> Higher psychological functions such as reading and writing are both social and cultural in nature;
>
> Knowledge is constructed through the interactions among individuals within the social context; and
>
> Learning is fostered through the assistance of more knowledgeable members of the community and culture. (p. 69)

These beliefs caused us to see our students as active agents in their own learning, to value interaction and collaboration within our learning communities, and to perceive our roles as teachers in terms of assisted performance (Rogoff, 1990; Tharp & Gallimore, 1988). In addition, these beliefs caused us to see our e-mail dialogue as a way to construct new knowledge about our literacy teaching through interactions that framed each of us as more knowledgeable in some instances and less knowledgeable in others.

The second source of influence on our work were theories of language articulated by Mikhail Bahktin (1981)—ideas that we began to discuss when Lois responded to an early draft of a paper Kelly wrote about the research group using them as a primary lens (Chandler-Olcott, 2001). Most important to our data analysis was Bakhtin's contention that

> The word in language is half someone else's. It becomes "one's own" only when the speaker populates it with his own intention . . . adapting it to his own semantic and expressive intention. Prior to this moment of appropriation, the word does not exist in a neutral and impersonal language . . . but rather it exists in other people's mouths . . . serving other people's intentions: it is from there that one must take the word, and make it one's own. (quoted in Wertsch, 1991, p. 59)

Bakhtin's conception of dialogicality seemed useful to consider data that was generated through ongoing discussions. Such a lens also helped us to consider influences on our thinking, teaching, and writing beyond our partnership—the other voices contributing to what might otherwise have seemed like a closed conversation between two people.

Methods

Participants and Teaching Contexts

During the year of the project, Lois taught first grade at Mapleton Elementary, while Kelly taught, among other classes, two sections (one in the fall, another in the spring) of a language arts methods course in Syracuse University's elementary education program. When the e-mail partnership began, we had known each other for 4 years through our affiliation with the Mapleton Teacher-Research Group, a schoolwide inquiry collective that Lois co-founded and Kelly facilitated (see Chandler & the Mapleton Teacher-Research Group, 1999, for details). Both of us had kept teaching journals with varying degrees of regularity and commitment in the past. Except for the journal Lois kept between 1997 and 1998—to which Kelly responded monthly, at Lois's invitation—our previous journaling had always been private, meant for no one but ourselves.

Data Sources

The primary data source for our analysis was a set of 99 e-mail messages (230 pages of single-spaced text) that we exchanged between August 1999 and July 2000. Fifty of these messages were written by Lois, 49 by Kelly. Although they were most often sent in an alternating pattern, one sender would sometimes initiate 2 or 3 messages consecutively before the other responded. Additional data, which we used to cross-check some of our conclusions and widen our field of vision about the project, included the following: artifacts from our teaching such as lesson plans, handouts, and assignments; drafts of other writing we were doing at the time of the e-mail exchange; and notes we kept during our data-analysis conversations.

Data Analysis

Although we typically treat data collection and analysis as linked and recursive processes, we chose a different path with this project. We only decided to treat our saved messages as research data in February 2000—six months after we began writing and saving messages. We feared that ongoing analysis might make us too self-conscious about our writing, thereby decreasing the value of the exchanges for our teaching. Consequently, we continued to archive the data without examining it in much detail until the summer of 2000, when the dialogue concluded. At Lois's suggestion, we began our analysis by reading the complete body of messages in one sitting, without taking notes, a decision that helped us to consider the messages as a dialogue unfolding over time rather than a collection of independent writings. After we discussed emerging themes, we engaged in microanalysis (Strauss & Corbin, 1998) of messages from a single month. We used themes that emerged from this fine-grained process to code the rest of the e-mail messages independently, then we met again to collapse and refine our coding system. With each pass through the data, we noted what Spradley (1980) calls "folk terms," words or phrases in our own language that could be used as coding categories, and we kept running lists of "multiple voices," incidents in the data where we were aware of being influenced by others, whether from personal contact or professional reading.

What Does the Data Captured in Our E-mail Messages Reveal About Our Decision-making as Teachers?

Our analysis of the e-mail data suggests two distinct but related patterns in our decision-making. First, despite the differences in our teaching contexts, both of us experienced similar tensions about how to implement constructivist principles in our teaching, particularly how to balance students' interests and desires as learners and our own agendas as teachers. Second, both of us employed the strategy of "looking again," borrowed from our work as teacher-researchers, to help manage the tensions we felt. Each of these themes is discussed below.

Tensions Around Constructivism

During the fall semester, Kelly wrote to Lois about her frustration as she introduced the undergraduates to a curriculum model driven by concepts and generalizations ("Big Ideas"), rather than activities or skills:

> They don't see how it all fits together yet, and I can't blame them. . . . Constructing understandings is so damn much slower than pouring information into their heads, and there are such limits to what they can construct in the field when their host teachers are telling them their Big Ideas have to be about short A or figurative language (the latter being driven by the demands of the fourth-grade [state] test). Eeek. (E-mail, 11/5/99)

In our first coding session, "Eeek," an interjection we had both used at various times, struck us as a potential example of a folk term. Consequently, we reexamined the data with that idea in mind, first for instances where we had used the term literally and then for others that had a similar feel. As we coded, we realized that our "Eeeks" were most often related to situations in our teaching where we perceived some slippage between our methods and the philosophical principles we espoused—what we came to call "tensions around constructivism." Our messages included discussion of what it meant to construct knowledge as a learner, when we first became aware of that term, and how some of our colleagues worked from different theoretical frameworks. Neither of us swerved from our belief in constructivism as a theory about how people learn, but we experienced considerable uncertainty about how to translate that belief system into pedagogy on a daily basis.

Writing instruction in first grade was a source of many of these tensions for Lois, as it brought up questions about where to set the boundaries for student choice and ownership of their work. As she explained, "I'm not excited all the time (big surprise!) about what comes out of Writer's Workshop. The children love it!!! But I fear that they love it because they see it as time when they can do whatever! Is it that I need to change things OR is it that I need to change how I look at what they do??" (E-mail, 11/14/99). The introduction of a new puppet center as one of students' options during literacy block offered Lois an opportunity to consider this question more concretely. "Have I told you about the puppets and the plays (stories, really) that they are writing?" she wrote to Kelly. "No, I just reread my old mail to you and see that I have not. This has been blowing my mind all week!" (E-mail, 10/23/99). Initially, the children handled the new center well, requiring little intervention from Lois. After reading through their writing folders, she noted that some of the reluctant writers in the class produced more text in their scripts than they had during any previous writing activity.

As time passed, though, Lois's weekly observation notes indicated that she needed to adjust her expectations for the puppet center in order to promote more growth for students. Rather than developing stories and fleshing out characters, the children had begun to script shows with the primary purpose of including as many roles as possible—a goal that often left players in their productions with just a single word to say. More than four months after she first mentioned them, Lois discussed the puppets again in an e-mail, writing that she had "changed the puppet center this week. I made a new form that indicates you can use only 2 characters in your play and you are supposed to write a beginning, middle, and end" (E-mail, 3/14/00). Lois reported that they were producing "much better work" and that their fluency and engagement did not seem to be constrained by the change. Not only did this message document an improvement in the puppets' effectiveness as a learning center, but it also documented Lois's greater comfort in providing guidelines to scaffold writing instruction in the classroom.

The tensions reported in our dialogue journal were not always so neatly resolved, however. When one of Kelly's students e-mailed her a draft of a lesson plan that seemed too complicated to teach a simple concept, Kelly agonized over how to frame her criticism. After sending a reply, she forwarded both messages, minus the student's name, to Lois with the following note: "I'm sending you copies of a message I received from a student along with my response. I'd love your read on it—just after I sent it, I found myself doubting what I'd done, wondering whether I'd pushed too hard" (E-mail, 10/6/99). Although Lois wrote back to reassure Kelly that she felt her feedback had been on target and constructive, Kelly continued to wonder whether the student might have learned more from teaching the flawed lesson than from her well-intentioned suggestions.

How much should we intervene, and when? How directive to be? How much authority to take? The e-mail messages show us constantly shifting our positions in response to these questions, worrying, as Kelly put it, that we had "put students on the spot" (E-mail, 9/22/99) or alternatively, that we had missed opportunities to promote growth by underestimating what students "can actually be told and comprehend" (Lois, E-mail, 10/9/99).

"Looking Again"

One strategy we used to manage the tensions we felt around enacting constructivist principles in our classrooms we came to call "looking again," another folk term (Spradley, 1980) from one of our messages. The first example of this language came from an e-mail Kelly wrote to Lois following a workshop activity in the methods class. To help illustrate the concept of emergent literacy for the undergraduate students, Lois sent Kelly a package of drawing and writing samples from the first day of school. After small groups of undergraduates wrote captions for each first grader's work using terminology from their course readings and a lecture, Kelly sent the annotated samples back to Mapleton for Lois to post in the hall near her classroom, where parents could view them during open house. Initially, Kelly was dissatisfied by the undergraduates' work: "I was admittedly a little disappointed by their emphasis on conventions. Many of them got bogged down in left-to-right, letter formation, spelling, etc. and missed some key aspects of meaning construction, illustration development, etc" (E-mail, 9/9/99). Given these trends, Kelly wondered whether she should have provided more instruction and clearer expectations before students began the assignment, but revisiting the data helped her to see it differently: "When I reread their captions by group, not individual (e.g., looked at the three or four done by each small group) and then took some notes about trends I saw . . . I actually felt much better about their quality. I just needed to *look again*" (E-mail, 9/15/99; emphasis added).

Again and again, the e-mail transcripts reveal our "looking again" at data to determine our next moves when we felt tension in our teaching. Sometimes, this process happened in the messages themselves, as the simple act of writing to each other helped us deliberate on our decision-making and come to new conclusions about the meaning of the classroom events we were recounting. Awareness of this feature of the exchanges can be seen in, among others, Kelly's comment about "writing my way out of my panic and fury" (E-mail, 10/26/99) after a bad class, as well as Lois's confession that describing her design of a new spelling center had actually helped her to "figure my motive out for that one!" (E-mail, 11/14/99).

Sometimes, however, the analysis was more systematic and more informed by specific procedures for inquiry we both learned as members of the Mapleton research group. On these occasions, we used teacher-research tools such as rereading, note-taking, charting, and categorizing by theme (Hubbard & Power, 1999) to interrogate data from our classrooms. "Looking again" in these more formal ways helped us to identify instances when students' perspectives differed from our own, and then to determine how to deal with those differences. After portfolio conferences with her first graders, for example, Lois was surprised by how many children wanted to become better at drawing. As she described this trend to Kelly, she included the following aside in parentheses: "now I will have to do some data analysis because, of course, I must see HOW many!" (E-mail, 10/2/99). In the midst of writing the e-mail, she reread her notes to tally the figure then returned to the computer to reflect on what it meant:

> Do I really only value their "writing" when there is penmanship on the page and see their drawings as incidental? It is such hard work to get them up and running as "word producers" that I think I do tend to go that way! If they write a letter or a word or a whole sentence, I celebrate but I was ready to dismiss 13 (I HAD to go look!) mentions of wanting to learn to draw better when asked "What do you want to get better at in writing?" . . . They obviously value drawing a lot more than I do and maybe I should think about honoring that interest. (E-mail, 10/2/99)

As she wrote, Lois resolved to invite a parent who was an accomplished artist to come to class and present some tips on drawing. Data analysis helped her to follow the children's lead in the sense that many proponents of holistic teaching would advocate (Atwell, 1987; Avery, 1993), but it also helped her to identify how she might assist students' performance in this area of interest by providing access to new content and approaches. Through systematic reflection, she devised a way to be more proactive and even authoritative as a teacher even as she negotiated the curriculum with students (Oyler, 1996).

Other instructional moves driven by "looking again" included Kelly's decision to change her approach for whole-class debriefing sessions after keeping track of students' contribution patterns; Lois's inclusion of an explicit spelling station in her literacy centers after analyzing data from student surveys; and Kelly's decision to assemble response groups that were heterogeneous by grade level after coding a set of students' lesson plans by topic. In each case, continued manipulation of classroom data told a different story, and led to a different action on the teacher's part in resolving her tension, than initial impressions did.

How Did the E-mail Partnership Itself Affect Our Decision-Making?

For the purposes of this paper, we have chosen not to analyze electronic mail as the medium for the dialogue, although others have discussed its characteristics as a learning tool (Romeo & Caron, 1999) and as a data-gathering mechanism (Tao, Montgomery, & Pickle, 1997). Instead, we focus here on the content of the messages and the two primary ways the e-mail partnership affected our decision-making in our respective contexts.

Direct Influences

Some of the influences on our teaching were direct and obvious ones. Kelly found that her regular contact with Lois grounded her methods class more thoroughly in the complexities of elementary-school teaching. This "resonance of credibility" (Kelly, E-mail, 8/6/99) was important because Kelly's own teaching experience had been in secondary English, not the elementary grades for which her students sought certification. Kelly frequently quoted examples from Lois's e-mail as she presented new content to students, and she incorporated artifacts from the first graders—writing from science- and social studies-focused centers, for example—into sessions on literacy across the curriculum. Lois also helped Kelly select texts for the course reader and for weekly "Featured Professional Book" e-mails to students.

The partnership had similarly tangible benefits for Lois. She reassessed several of her curriculum topics on the basis of questions Kelly reported asking students as the undergraduates developed thematic units. She made a parent education display outside her classroom with writing samples annotated by Kelly and her class. She also received e-mail feedback from Kelly on a plan for a staff development workshop she led in her district and a unit outline she constructed around Essential Questions, a planning tool Kelly had used frequently in the past.

Indirect Influences

Other effects from the partnership were subtler but just as important. Some of them were difficult to appreciate until we began to analyze the transcripts systematically with a Bakhtinian lens. When we asked Wertsch's (1991) question, "Who is doing the talking here?" about the following data excerpt, we realized that Lois's perspectives were informed—or "interanimated," to use a more Bakhtinian term—by many people's voices, including her colleagues, professional authors, and Kelly. Reflecting on her plans for the first few weeks of school, Lois wrote:

> I am probably going to start the year with my Franklin books again. The children . . . identify so closely with the characters in those books and we get to participate in great conversations about friendship, decision-making, responsi-

> bility, co-operation, and self-concept. This leads to the classroom stuff about community and we build from there. At least that's what we did last year—I know things are always different but that's my overarching plan. Is my overarching theme "community"? What are my essential questions and the generalizations? These are rhetorical questions, by the way, that are in my head, and were NOT in my head last year. Isn't learning fun?? (E-mail, 8/4/99)

Lois's new concerns about generalizations were influenced by her discussion of a book chapter on that topic (Kucer, Silva, & Delgado-Larocco, 1995) with other members of the Mapleton Teacher-Research Group, including Kelly, during the group's annual summer retreat. Her consideration of essential questions (EQs) was informed by participation in district-sponsored staff development, during which grade-level teams had begun to write questions to guide curriculum reform. On several other occasions, she and Kelly had discussed the differences between the district leadership's conception of EQs and what Kelly had learned from involvement with the Coalition of Essential Schools (Sizer, 1992), a secondary education network that uses EQs extensively. Lois's e-mail message offered her the opportunity to explore the potential impact of this information, some of it conflicting, on her practice. Writing to Kelly helped her to test her thinking and take small steps toward integrating the new knowledge with her "overarching plan" from the previous year. The e-mail messages frequently played this role for both of us, serving as what Kelly called "tentative thinking with a safe audience" (E-mail, 8/31/99).

Lois's discussion of "rhetorical questions" in this excerpt also led us to revisit the e-mail data to code the kinds of questions we had asked in our messages. Of the 175 questions in the transcripts, we classified 92 (52.8%) of them as direct, signaling the expectation that the recipient should address them (e.g., "Sooo, how did the staff development day go?"); and 83 (47.2%) as rhetorical, meant more for the writer to ponder than for the recipient to answer (e.g., "Do I see undergrads as often extreme because they are, or because that's what it's easiest to see when there are 37 students in front of you?"). These percentages suggested that the e-mail partnership promoted self-questioning nearly as much as questioning of the other person. The high occurrence of rhetorical questions in certain messages caused us to call them "parallel e-mail," a phrase we coined with reference to "parallel play," an interaction style between toddlers, because, like 2-year-olds who play with separate toys side by side, we often wrote about separate issues in our teaching without expecting—or needing—much problem solving from the other. In these cases, the primary voices with which we dialogued were often our own.

To emphasize that the influence of the partnership on our decision-making was often indirect is not to say that we always ignored each other's presence as we wrote. We often did elicit, and receive, feedback from each other on specific questions. Moreover, numerous entries suggest that our awareness of the other person as recipient kept us reflecting more regularly than we would have if we were writing simply for ourselves. As Kelly explained at the beginning of a message describing her last class, "This is one of those times when having you as my audience is a good thing, as for some reason I'm not feeling motivated to process my teaching but I'll want you to be up-to-speed later in the semester when I have something to vent or celebrate" (E-mail, 1/25/00).

Over time, we also internalized each other's voices. As Lois put it during a data-analysis meeting, "It's as if I hear you talking in my head" (Meeting Notes, 11/27/00). Sentences beginning with "You'll probably think that . . ." and "I know I'm sounding like . . ." indicate our growing ability to anticipate how the other person might respond to a given point. On occasion, we asked ourselves questions within the messages that sounded like questions the other person might ask, as Lois did in this excerpt: "What did I learn today? That the first day is best when it slides along and we don't (meaning ME!) stress too much" (E-mail, 8/31/99). In this way, the dialogue journal helped us serve each other as what Tharp and Gallimore (1988) call "that heard, regulating voice . . . that then becomes the [learner's] self-regulating 'still, small' instructor" (p. 57). This "voice" was present in our minds as we reflected on our teaching, and it continued to be present, even when we were not writing—an indication of the dialogue journal's role in our abilities to self-monitor.

Discussion and Implications for Practice and Research

When we began to reflect on the patterns and themes we saw emerging from our data, our first, half-joking response was that we were not very good teachers. Otherwise, how could we have felt such regular tension about our practice? Why did we not have the voices sorted out in our heads? Why was there not a more clear-cut relationship between theory and practice for us? Whereas we had always entertained these questions, seeing them surface again and again in our e-mail dialogue, where they were crystallized in time, helped us to realize how pervasive they were in our teaching. That the other person, whose work we respected, struggled with similar issues in a different setting pointed out the possibility that experiencing tension might be inextricably tied to teaching well—to be managed on an ongoing basis, not necessarily to be eradicated by refining a particular set of methods.

Eventually, we conceptualized this balance between teacher authority and student initiation, between assisting performance as a teacher and constructing understandings as a learner, as a seesaw. This image appealed to us because it was a constantly dynamic one (no one would choose to play on a seesaw if it stayed stationary!) and because the use of a seesaw required action on the part of both participants—in this case, both teacher and students. It also suggested that the tensions we felt around our roles as constructivist teachers were normal, even predictable, and that they would intensify, then subside, at different times.

Our e-mail dialogue functioned like a seesaw in another way. Analysis of our tensions around constructivism suggested that Lois tended to underestimate what her first graders knew and could do, preventing her from challenging them as much as possible, while Kelly tended to overestimate her undergraduates' experience and knowledge, causing her to frustrate them. Our dialogue with each other helped to curb these tendencies, as the other person's entries presented alternative ways to view the learners in our classes. Because neither of us had direct authority over the other, it was easier to consider the potential shortcomings of our patterns without feeling like our weaknesses had been exposed to someone whose criticism might cost us.

Zeichner (1994) points out that most teacher research is localized, intended to affect only the context in which it is conducted. Whereas we agree that the findings from this study are most germane, and therefore most useful, to us as teachers in particular settings, we do find ourselves repeatedly drawing upon them in our work as a university supervisor (Kelly) and mentor for student teachers (Lois)—roles that transcend the original ones we played when the data were generated. That we have begun to extend these findings to other contexts suggests that others may do so as well. For this reason, we offer the following recommendations for literacy education and research that have their roots in our e-mail dialogue.

Demonstrate Strategies That Promote Teachers' "Looking Again" at Their Practice

Assigning students to write regular reflective entries about their work in the field is a typical practice in numerous education programs (Graham et al., 1999; Whitmore & Goodman, 1996). It appears to be far less common, however, for novice teachers to be shown by experienced ones what such reflective writing might look like, including how fraught with tension it might be. Until 1997, when Lois began sharing her journal with Kelly, neither of us had ever seen an example of reflective writing from a teacher we knew. We learned from each other how such writing might be undertaken to improve our practice. Thus, we advocate that instructors and mentors share excerpts from their own journals to demonstrate the range of possibilities available to writers reflecting on their teaching. In addition, we advocate the explicit teaching of strategies borrowed from teacher researchers (Hubbard & Power, 1999) that are meant to help writers get under the surface of their classrooms and see patterns and relationships across their entire journals that might not have been apparent when each individual entry was written. Instructors can show students how to reread their journals periodically to add marginal commentary about new insights, index recurring ideas, and connect pieces of data to each other. We believe that teachers with access to such strategies will find reflective writing more instructive; perhaps they will be more consistent about engaging in such practices throughout their career.

Research that explores how teacher-writers make sense of these reflective strategies, as well as which ones they adopt, could be very useful for both teacher educators and administrators seeking to promote practitioners' reflection on their decision-making. Studies might consider what sorts of teaching incidents prompt teachers in various K–12 and university contexts to "look again" at their practice, as well as what kinds of action they take as a result of that analysis. Also of interest would be any differences between novice and experienced teachers in their use of such strategies.

Promote Non-Hierarchical Partnerships That Allow for "Parallel Writing"

We are aware of how useful it can be for novice teachers to receive feedback on their work from experts. We have both benefited as learners from instructors' responses to our journals—and we continue to provide that sort of response to our respective students. At the same time, the nature of our own partnership suggests the usefulness of additional kinds of dialogue for teachers learning and refining their craft. Seesaws on the playground work best when the riders weigh about the same amount, allowing both to participate with similar amounts of energy. We believe that reflective journal partnerships may be similar: when participants have different positions in an established hierarchy (e.g., a professor engages in dialogue with a student), then contributions from the writer in a position of power may be construed as authoritative, rather than dialogic, discourse (Bakhtin, 1981). This perception may shut down inquiry and self-questioning, promoting dependence on others' decision-making in ways that dialogue with peers may not. In addition, we see value in journal partnerships where "parallel writing" is valued—where the participants do not always feel the need to help each other solve problems directly.

These complexities could be further investigated by studies that consider the effects of dialogue journals as a professional development tool in different contexts. Research comparing "level" partnerships to more hierarchical ones could illustrate the benefits and limitations of each approach to reflective writing. Additional consideration of the voices that influence such writing might shed light on teachers' writing to learn as a social and cultural practice, not merely an individual one. Any of these lines of inquiry would provide us with additional insight about what it means for teacher-writers to "think aloud with feedback."

References

Atwell, N. (1987). *In the middle: Writing, reading, and learning with adolescents.* Portsmouth, NH: Heinemann/Boynton-Cook.

Avery, C. (1993). *And with a light touch: Learning about reading, writing, and teaching from first graders.* Portsmouth, NH: Heinemann.

Bakhtin, M. (1981). *The dialogic imagination* (C. Emerson & M. Holquist, Eds.). Austin: University of Texas Press.

Berthoff, A. (1987). The teacher as REsearcher. In D. Goswami & P. Stillman (Eds.), *Reclaiming the classroom: Teacher research as an agency of change* (pp. 28–38). Portsmouth, NH: Heinemann.

Boyd, F., & Galda, L. (1997). Lessons taught and lessons learned. In J. Paratore & R. McCormack (Eds.), *Peer talk in the classroom: Learning from research* (pp. 66–87). Newark, DE: International Reading Association.

Chandler, K., & the Mapleton Teacher-Research Group (1999). *Spelling inquiry: How one elementary school caught the mnemonic plague.* York, ME: Stenhouse.

Chandler-Olcott, K. (2001). The spelling symposium: Examining a critical event in the history of a schoolwide teacher-research group. *English Education, 33*(3), 190–213.

Costa, A., & Kallick, B. (1993). Through the lens of a critical friend. *Educational Leadership, 51,* 49–51.

Davies, A., Hogan, P., & Dalton, B. (1993). Journals: The conversations of practice. In J. Clandinin, A. Davies, P. Hogan, & B. Kennard (Eds.), *Learning to teach, teaching to learn: Stories of collaboration in teacher education* (pp. 51–63). New York: Teachers College Press.

Fulwiler, T. (1987). *The journal book.* Portsmouth, NH: Boynton/Cook.

Graham, P., Hudson-Ross, S., Atkins, C., McWhorter, P., & Stewart, J. (1999). *Teacher/mentor: A dialogue for collaborative learning.* New York: Teachers College Press.

Grisham, D. (1997). Electronic literacy learning: Teachers' on-line dialogue journals. In C. Kinzer, K. Hinchman, & D. Leu (Eds.), *Inquiries in literacy theory and practice.* Forty-sixth yearbook of the National Reading Conference (pp. 465–473). Chicago: National Reading Conference.

Hubbard, R. S., & Power, B. M. (1999). *Living the questions: A guide for teacher-researchers.* York, ME: Stenhouse.

International Reading Association. (2000). *Teachers' awards and grants.* Retrieved on December 13, 2000 from http://www.reading.org/about/whatwedo/awards.html.

Isakson, M. B., & Williams, D. D. (1996). Allowing space for not knowing: A dialogue about teachers' journals. In Z. Donoahue, M. A. Van Tassell, & L. Patterson (Eds.), *Research in the classroom: Talk, texts, and inquiry* (pp. 10–35). Newark, DE: International Reading Association.

Kucer, S., Silva, C., & Delgado-Larocco, E. (1995). *Curricular conversations: Themes in multilingual and monolingual classrooms.* York, ME: Stenhouse.

Lalik, R., & Hinchman, K. (1999, April). *Examining the language of our interruptions: A critical discourse analysis of the reflections of two literacy teacher educators.* Paper presented at the meeting of the American Educational Research Association, Montreal, Quebec.

Lester, N. B., & Onore, C. (1990). *Learning change: One school district meets language across the curriculum.* Portsmouth, NH: Boynton/Cook.

MacGillivray, L., & King, J. R. (1995). Inside/out: Talking and questioning our teaching selves through e-mail exchanges. In K. A. Hinchman, D. J. Leu, & C. K. Kinzer (Eds.), *Perspectives on literacy research and practice.* Forty-fourth yearbook of the National Reading Conference (pp. 407–416). Chicago: National Reading Conference.

Meier, D. (1995). *The power of their ideas: Lessons for America from a small school in Harlem.* Boston: Beacon.

Meyer, R. J., Brown, L., DeNino, E., Larson, K., McKenzie, M., Ridder, K., & Zetterman, K. (1998). *Composing a teacher study group: Learning about inquiry in primary classrooms.* Mahwah, NJ: Erlbaum.

Oyler, C. (1996). *Making room for students: Sharing teacher authority in room 104.* New York: Teachers College Press.

Rogoff, B. (1990). *Apprenticeship in thinking: Cognitive development in social context.* New York: Oxford University Press.

Romeo, L., & Caron, T. (1999). Enhancing graduate literacy teaching using electronic dialogue. In T. Shanahan & F. V. Rodriguez-Brown (Eds.), *National Reading Conference Yearbook, 48* (pp. 387–397). Chicago: National Reading Conference.

Sizer, T. (1992). *Horace's school: Redesigning the American high school.* Boston: Houghton-Mifflin.

Spradley, J. (1980). *Participant observation.* New York: Holt, Rinehart & Winston.

Strauss, A., & Corbin, J. (1998). *Basics of qualitative research: Techniques and procedures for developing grounded theory* (2nd ed.). Thousand Oaks, CA: Sage.

Tao, L., Montgomery, T., & Pickle, M. (1997). Content analysis in e-mail research: A methodological review. In C. Kinzer, K. Hinchman, & D. Leu (Eds.), *Inquiries in literacy theory and practice.* Forty-sixth yearbook of the National Reading Conference (pp. 474–482). Chicago: National Reading Conference.

Tharp, R. G., & Gallimore, R. (1988). *Rousing young minds to life: Teaching, learning, and schooling in social context.* New York: Cambridge University Press.

Wallace, J. (1999). The dialogue journal. In P. Graham, S. Hudson-Ross, C. Atkins, P. McWhorter, & J. Stewart (Eds.), *Teacher/mentor: A dialogue for collaborative learning* (pp. 34–45). New York: Teachers College Press.

Wertsch, J. (1991). *Voices of the mind: A sociocultural approach to mediated action.* Cambridge, MA: Harvard University Press.

Whitmore, K., & Goodman, Y. (1996). *Whole language voices in teacher education.* York, ME: Stenhouse.

Zeichner, K. (1994). Personal renewal and social construction through teacher research. In S. Hollingsworth & H. Sockett (Eds.), *Teacher research and educational reform* (pp. 66–84). Chicago: National Society for the Study of Education.

Description, Prescription, or Cultural Reproduction? Rosenblattian Criticism in Reader-Response Research and Teaching

Mark Dressman
University of Illinois at Urbana-Champaign

Joan Webster
University of Alaska, Fairbanks

In this report, we present findings from a continuing series of studies focusing on the theoretical, research, and practical implications of the work of Louise Rosenblatt. In our first study (Dressman & Webster, in press), we comparatively noted and coded each revision in the text of Rosenblatt's most enduring book, *Literature as Exploration,* across its five editions (1938, 1968, 1976, 1983, 1995a). We then related the findings of this analysis to Rosenblatt's other major work, *The Reader, the Text, the Poem* (1978), to studies of her work (e.g., Farrell & Squire, 1990), and to ongoing developments in the field of literary criticism and national/world affairs from the 1930s to the 1990s.

Very briefly, our analysis of revisions over the five editions of *Literature as Exploration* showed a consistent deletion of references to the agency of teachers and authors in the meanings readers take from texts in classroom settings; revision of passages to emphasize the separation of the functions of reading in literature and social science classrooms; and a deletion of any mention of literary texts' historical, cultural, political, and economic meanings for readers. From this evidence, we concluded:

> [O]ur analysis demonstrates a radical shift, over 57 years and five editions, in how [literary] reading is depicted as a social phenomenon within the pages of *Literature as Exploration,* from something that takes place within a sphere of influence that is historically, economically, culturally, and so politically imminent—a sphere conceived as a microcosm, or miniature of the world in its totality—to something that takes place within a sphere of influence that has been reconceived, by the fifth edition, in very local terms, as whatever an autonomous individual reader may choose to take from exchanges of opinion shared among equally autonomous individuals in a (classroom) setting at a given moment. (Dressman & Webster, in press)

We also noted in our analysis that whereas in the first edition of *Literature as Exploration* the ideas advanced were openly prescriptive in their tone—that is, they were presented as ways that teachers should teach and ways readers ought to learn to read—by the fifth edition, the tone of the argumentation was more

National Reading Conference Yearbook, 50, pp. 164–177.

descriptive—that is, ideas were presented to readers less as "good advice" about how to teach literature than as objective facts about how, in fact, literature is read. In Habermasian terms (Habermas, 1985), this communicative shift from normative–evaluative to scientific-objective ways of reasoning (without a corresponding shift in the type of evidence used to warrant one's actions) is a critical event. As Habermas and others (e.g., Carspecken, 1996; Dressman, 1999) have noted, such a shift can lead empirical researchers of social phenomena such as reading to underestimate or completely ignore (and sometimes to deny) the implications of normative, culturally based assumptions in their conceptualization, implementation, and interpretation of empirical social research. In this event, such research and the policies that result from it may not produce new knowledge about the social phenomenon under study but may instead reproduce cultural assumptions and the power relations those assumptions rationalize.

Method of Analysis

One outcome of our first study has been to question the terms by which the field of literacy research and education have engaged Rosenblatt's work. More specifically, we wondered how researchers and essayists who made use of Rosenblatt's work in theirs would themselves conceive of social influences on readers—whether, in their description of readers and settings they would describe the event of literary reading as "a microcosm, or miniature of the world in its totality," or as "whatever an autonomous individual reader may choose to take from exchanges of opinion shared among equally autonomous individuals"—and whether they would take Rosenblatt's "prescriptive description" of literary reading as a given or whether they would challenge its precepts in any way.

We conducted our investigation of these initial questions in five stages. First, we scanned every article in every issue of *English Journal* (*EJ*) and *Research in the Teaching of English* (*RTE*) from 1988 to August 2000 for citations of Rosenblatt's work. Photocopies were made of each article, and each was then read to determine whether Rosenblatt's work played a significant role in an article's conceptualization and/or analysis, or whether the citation was made in passing—that is, without further elaboration or in direct support of arguments within the article.

We must acknowledge here that these two journals do not represent the full range of Rosenblatt's influence or the full range of commentary about her work within the field of literacy education. For example, three recent books on literature education provide critical views of Rosenblatt's work. McCormick (1994) criticized the distinction Rosenblatt's later work makes between literary and nonliterary texts, arguing that "the literary text is no less a product of a particular cultural formation than any other kind of text" and that "like all texts, (literature) is read and interpreted within particular cultural and ideological constraints and enablements" (p. 37). In a broad critique of reader-response pedagogies (many of which claim Rosenblatt as their primary influence), Rabinowitz and Smith (1998) questioned whether the pedagogy described in Rosenblatt's later work met its stated goal of furthering democratic ideals. Finally, Appleman (2000) has noted that emphasizing the "personal" nature of response may not provide teachers or students with the impetus to examine the social nature of their responses, nor can it provide the grounds for reading literary texts that are historically or culturally remote from readers—texts whose full appreciation often requires that readers *put aside* their own frame of reference and attempt to understand points of view from other places and times.

We can find little similar analysis or direct critique within recent journal articles, however. For example, a recent themed issue of *Journal of Literacy Research* (*JLR*) devoted to reader-response research contained one essay by Lewis (2000) that asserted, with little support from or systematic analysis of the actual texts of Rosenblatt's work, that Rosenblatt is frequently misread by researchers and teachers who often overlook the social implications of her work. Two other studies within the same issue of *JLR* acknowledged the influence of Rosenblatt on their work but then quickly also noted: "[W]e have broadened our awareness of the interplay of reader, text, and context through a number of other theoretical perspectives" (Möller & Allen, 2000, p. 147), and that "Rosenblatt's conception of context needs more specificity regarding the various components shaping responding as a social event" (Beach, 2000, p. 238). Our reading of these articles from *JLR*'s recent themed issue suggested to us how conflicted readings of Rosenblatt's work may be. We therefore cannot claim that our analysis of articles taken from two journals presents a comprehensive overview of how the field of literacy research views Rosenblatt's work, but we will argue that as important journals in English education research and secondary English education, they offer a manageable and important sample of the ways in which Rosenblatt has influenced both researchers and practitioners' thinking about reader response.

In the second stage of our analysis, we highlighted each passage within each article in which Rosenblatt's work was mentioned and constructed a brief summary of each article. We then categorized each article found to be significant as either an *essay*—that is, an article whose argumentation was based primarily on theoretical issues that were sometimes supported by brief anecdotal evidence—or as an *empirical report*—that is, a report of evidence collected and analyzed over time and presented in extended detail. In the third stage of the analysis, we noted recurring terms used by Rosenblatt in her work, such as the distinction between *transaction* and *interaction,* and the *aesthetic-efferent continuum.* At the same time, we also noted the ways that these terms were explained and used within different articles within either *RTE* or *EJ*. In the fourth stage of our analysis, we looked for indicators of how broadly or narrowly the author or authors of each article viewed the social environment in which they conducted their research and data analysis. To do this, we returned to each article categorized as an empirical report and tabulated the aspects of participants' identities and backgrounds and the settings of studies that are most often considered to be salient characteristics affecting students' school performance and readers' responses to literature.

In the final stage of our investigation, we compiled data collected in stages two, three, and four to construct a one-page profile for each article in which

Rosenblatt's work was credited as a significant influence. We used these profiles to identify patterns of similarity and difference within articles published in *English Journal* and *Research in the Teaching of English.*

Findings

We found 47 articles in *EJ* and 29 in *RTE* that cited Rosenblatt's work; of these, 13 *EJ* and 18 *RTE* articles made significant use of her views on reader response. Of the 13 *EJ* articles, 4 were categorized as essays, although many included some anecdotal accounts that illustrated their arguments, and 9 were categorized empirical reports, that is, articles that were primarily narrative and that involved some form of systematic data collection and analysis or presentation of participants' writing or transcribed conversation. Of the *RTE* articles, 3 fell into the essay category and contained little or no anecdotal support, whereas 15 articles were empirical reports of systematically designed, conducted, and analyzed research. Of these, 14 involved the study of student readers, and 1 was a study of the practices and beliefs of middle-school language arts teachers.

Table 1 reports characteristics of participants, settings, and outcomes for the 14 *RTE* and 9 *EJ* articles that were empirical reports of students' responses to literary texts. Perhaps the most significant and perplexing finding from this analysis was how little information was presented about the backgrounds of the participating readers in the study. By a wide margin, the largest number of counts in the Participant Identification, Ability Level, Socio-Economic Status, and Gender categories were devoted to the not Mentioned subcategory of each. Only Grade Level was carefully reported in each of the studies that we analyzed. For reports in *EJ,* setting was counted as not Mentioned in 7 of 9 articles, whereas for reports in *RTE* it was named more often: settings in 4 articles were not Mentioned, 4 were counted as Suburban, 3 were Urban, and 2 were University. It should also be noted here that in many, if not most cases, although the identity, ability level, SES, and setting were not specifically stated—and so were counted as not Mentioned—the names of student participants, topics of discussion, and other supporting details of the report clearly implied that the participants were white, of better than average ability, from middle-class (and routinely professional) backgrounds, and that the research was conducted in suburban or relatively affluent settings. Even in cases where, for example, the ethnicity of participants was named as African-American or Latino, the participants so identified were actually only a small minority of participants in the entire study, for instance, 3 of 36 were African-American in one study (Miller & Legge, 1999), and 1 of 16 in another was Latino and bilingual (Earthman, 1992). In fact, of all the empirical reports published in *RTE* and *EJ,* only 2 (McGinley & Kamberelis, 1996; Pagnucci & Abt-Perkins, 1992) made any significant mention of ethnicity as a factor in their design or analysis of their research. Moreover, Mostly Female and Mostly Male categories in our tabulations were reserved for cases in which, within an individual study, one gender predominated by ratios of more than 2:1 (often 3:1 or 4:1). But even in cases where the gender of participants in a given study was coded as Mixed, a majority of

Table 1

Fourteen Empirical Reports in Research in the Teaching of English (RTE) and 9 in English Journal (EJ) by Student Participant Characteristics, Setting, and Outcome

	TE	*EJ*	Total
Participant Identity			
Not Mentioned	10	6	16
White	1	2	3
African-American	2	2	4
Latino	1	0	1
Bilingual	2	0	2
Disabled	1	0	1
Grade Level			
Not Mentioned	0	1	1
Primary (K–2)	2	0	2
Elementary (3–5)	3	0	3
Middle (6–8)	5	2	7
High School (9–12)	4	8	12
Postsecondary	3	2	5
Ability Level			
Not Mentioned	7	7	14
Above Average	4	1	5
Average	1	1	2
Below Average	1	1	2
Socio-Economic Status			
Not Mentioned	6	8	14
Low Income	1	0	1
Middle-Class/Professional	7	2	9
High Income	0	0	0
Gender			
Not Mentioned	8	8	16
Mostly Female	5	3	8
Mostly Male	1	0	1
Setting			
Not Mentioned	4	7	11
Suburban	4	2	6
Urban	3	1	4
Rural	0	0	0
University	2	0	2
Outcome			
Predictable Response to Literature	13	8	24
Unpredictable Response to Literature	1	1	3

Note. One empirical report in *RTE* focused on teacher, not student, participants; it is not included here. Because in some studies, research was conducted in multiple settings, with students in multiple grades, with multiple ethnicities and other characteristics, totals within categories to not "add up" to the number of studies.

participants was female. Finally, although we did not tabulate this finding, we could identify no text used as the central reading in any study in which the protagonist or author was a person of color, except in the McGinley and Kamberelis (1996) study.

On the premise that scholarly research and writing work to advance understanding of a topic through careful and skeptical analysis, we also tried to identify the relationship between the outcome or conclusion of each article and how authors related those findings to Rosenblatt's views on readers' responses to literature. As Table 1 indicates, we found only one empirical report each from *RTE* and *EJ* that challenged any of Rosenblatt's views, although we did find one essay published in *RTE* that raised questions about aspects of Rosenblatt's perspective. In the article published in *EJ,* two teachers in a summer science program found that one student, an African American named Brandon, created a "never-making-sense story," in which he captured both the factual information and emotional involvement of a respiration experiment simultaneously (Pagnucci & Abt-Perkins, 1992). These teachers read Rosenblatt in terms that were congruent with our first study (Dressman & Webster, in press) when they quoted Rosenblatt on the need to help students "to understand the differences between the sciences and the humanities" (Rosenblatt, 1991, p. 60), and then noted that "[c]ontrary to the view Rosenblatt describes, Brandon simultaneously read his experience as both a scientist and a poet. So whereas he explained the mechanics of the experiment, he also wrote about the emotions of the researchers" (p. 56).

The only empirical report in *RTE* that challenged Rosenblatt's views was by Miall and Kuiken (1995), who developed and tested the validity and reliability of a survey instrument, the Literary Response Questionnaire, or LRQ, using 793 college students. They identified two factors, Experiencing and Literal Comprehension, whose characteristics closely resembled those described by Rosenblatt as Aesthetic and Efferent Experience. However, they failed to find any evidence of a *continuum*—that is, any underlying shared features—between Experiencing and Literal Comprehension in their students' responses, and so declared these two to be factorially independent of each other. Moreover, a concern for authorial meaning, which in Rosenblatt's view would indicate an efferent stance toward reading, negatively correlated in their study with Literal Comprehension, another characteristic of what Rosenblatt has described as efferent reading. The only critical essay to challenge Rosenblatt's views was actually a "symposium" of views (Saks, 1995) in which Alan Purves argued that reader-response research had generated "a great deal of heat, but little light" (p. 329). Purves challenged the utility of Rosenblatt's aesthetic-efferent continuum in describing the range of possible stances readers could take. He also charged that much research and writing on the subject was about *prescribing* how readers should read under the guise of *describing* how readers do read, noting that Rosenblatt's work had become a "Procrustean [bed] to the world [it purported] to describe" (p. 331). Respondents to Purves within the same symposium challenged his argument that reader-response research had hit a dead end, but they did not respond directly to either of his other charges, preferring instead to focus on their own research perspectives and on side complaints about the use of jargon.

The remaining 15 articles from *RTE* and 12 from *EJ* fully supported and in many cases illustrated Rosenblattian principles of how readers respond to literature. A number of empirical reports in *RTE* (e.g., Hade, 1988; Hancock, 1993; Whitin, 1996) and *EJ* (e.g., Probst, 1988; Shull, 1989) could accurately be characterized as *simulations* (Baudrillard, 1988; Dressman, 2000) of ideal classroom practices—that is, as idealized depictions that "sanitize" and significantly alter how actual events are perceived. However, in several instances, a closer reading of their findings and arguments could complicate or even contradict the authors' conclusions. For example, one comparative study of the novel *Tess of the D'Urbervilles* and the film version *Tess* urged teachers to have students "perform" the novel and so recreate the world depicted through "imaginative interaction with the text" (Veidemanis, 1988, p. 56). This author also argued that fidelity to Rosenblatt's views implied that "what the teacher happens to think about a given work must never be allowed to color or inhibit the process of discovery in which students are engaged" (p. 56). Yet shortly thereafter, the author stated that "[m]ost high-school students, I have found, benefit from the use of a study guide as well as overview questions that call for an assessment of the novel as a whole" (p. 56)—a guide and overview questions that would, we argue, invariably reflect the directive biases of their (teacher) writer. These, of course, are precisely the kinds of exercises that Rosenblatt has criticized as efferent and damaging to the aesthetic experiences of readers. In another *EJ* article (Pritchard, 1993), the Directed Reading/Thinking Activity (DRTA) was criticized as "efferent" in its focus. Yet the exercises that the author would substitute in its place, in which students would be asked to respond to prereading prompts asking them to predict what would happen in the story, were only slightly variant from the activities of DRTA itself. Later in the article, the author also advised teachers to teach formal, stylistic features to students out of context and prior to reading because "[o]ften with literature, it is the form itself that is baffling to readers, so any keys to formal features that you can provide up front will help" (p. 26). Still later, she provided examples of writing prompts that would elicit aesthetic responses, such as "Describe a typical day in the life of character X before X event happened and after X event happened" (p. 27)—an exercise that, presumably, would require a student to return to the text and efferently collect the facts of that character's daily life. Finally, the author suggested that biographical details about an author were important and should be shared during "post-reading time" (p. 28). These are all, based on our earlier study of Rosenblatt's work, clearly "efferent" activities. In contradiction to Pritchard's criticism of DRTA, however, in a different *EJ* article, Daniel (1996) used response journals as part of her strategy for helping her students to make predictions and support them with evidence from the text: "I encouraged them to 'prove' their reasoning as much as possible by explicitly stating reasons for their predictions, *much the same way as Russell Stauffer (1969) recommends in the Directed Reading/Thinking Activity*" (p. 32; emphasis added).

Such apparent contradictions were also found within and between articles that appeared in *RTE*. Mackey (1997) described aesthetic reading as a "passive" way of "accumulating and synthesizing images" (p. 433), yet the transcripts of her interviews showed readers very actively and, it seemed to us, efferently attending to context clues in order to deduce the definitions of unknown words. Finally, McGinley and Kamberelis (1996) used the aesthetic-efferent distinction to build a case for reading personally and socially relevant literature, but their account of how a teacher's social convictions led her to encourage her African-American students to respond to *Maniac Magee* and other texts in socially active ways would be sanctioned by Rosenblatt's (1995a) admonition that social uses of literary texts undermine the potential for aesthetic response.

Finally, we noted both equations and differences in the use of terminology between articles that were confusing. For example, four *RTE* articles (Galda, 1990; Hade, 1988; Langer, 1990; and Miller & Legge, 1999) equated Bruner's (1986) distinction between narrative and paradigmatic modes of cognition with aesthetic and efferent stances toward text. But whereas three of these also equated Britton's (1970) *spectator* stance with aesthetic and his *participant* stance with efferent reading, the fourth (Miller & Legge, 1999) described Rosenblatt's aesthetic stance as "fully attending to the lived-through experience of the literature as an event in time, a *participatory* approach to pursuing understanding" (p. 30; emphasis added). These and other articles also differed as to whether aesthetic experiences occurred in the moment of reading, or were only produced later, through reflection upon one's experience of the text.

Discussion

We believe the findings we have presented here raise important challenges about the primacy and efficacy of Rosenblattian frames for both the teaching and researching of how readers and texts relate.

First, these findings challenge the utility of Rosenblatt's work as a frame for teachers to use in making sense of their own teaching and their students' learning. This difficulty was particularly evident from teachers' own accounts in *English Journal,* where the biggest problem in literature-based classroom settings often seemed not to be the text-driven, authoritarian pedagogy implied by the new Critics (the foil against whom Rosenblatt is typically placed by university-based authors), but students' inability to read well enough on their own to have what Rosenblatt would term an *aesthetic response* to the text and so engage in literary discussions. We find it ironic that although the blame for this problem was nearly always attributed to the effects of students' prior experiences with efferent ways of reading—that is, answering literal comprehension questions and doing worksheets rather than writing and talking about how they connected to the story—the solutions that they proposed also tended to involve recall of facts, rereading of the text (or of one's own notes written in response) to formulate carefully reasoned positions, and even the use of postreading writing prompts and study guides—all of which also clearly fall within Rosenblatt's definition of efferent reading. From this we suspect that the basic distinctions that the teacher authors of these articles were making in their analyses of the problems they faced when they used the terms aesthetic and efferent did not actually correspond to the way that Rosenblatt would use them, but instead coincided with differences the teachers had observed in their careers between ways of organizing classroom reading that were engaging and effective versus practices that were not. It seemed that these teachers had equated the term "aesthetic reading" with "good teaching," and the term "efferent reading" with "bad teaching." In other words, we are suggesting that Rosenblatt's language (and so perhaps the validation that comes through association with her work), but not her meaning, was appropriated by many of the teacher authors in *EJ* to describe a very real set of conditions in secondary schools today (i.e., the struggle of many students to make basic sense of literary texts) that are never addressed in Rosenblatt's work. Yet we also want to emphasize that we take the contradictions we have noted here not as the inability of teachers to dialogically engage in discussions of practice and theory, but rather as an indication of the inadequacy of the Rosenblattian perspective, and perhaps also of the inadequacy of the theoretical/discursive resources available to them to address the problems that secondary English teachers actually face in their work.

We will also suggest that there is one other problem with Rosenblatt's work as it applies to literature education that authors such as Mark Faust, in articles in both *EJ* (1992) and *RTE* (2000), have alluded to but never openly addressed, and that at least two articles in *EJ* (Probst, 1988; Shull, 1989) have suggested but never examined. This is the extent to which Rosenblatt's concentration on personal response may not encourage readers—or literature educators—to attend to cultural implications of their reading that extend beyond the their own or their immediate peers' concerns within their classroom.

For example, Shull (1989) skillfully interwove quotes from *The Reader, the Text, the Poem* (Rosenblatt, 1978) throughout her account of how she and her class (of apparently all female students) read the novel *Lonesome Dove* (McMurtry, 1986) and then watched the movie version of it on television. Because the high school was located in Texas and *Lonesome Dove* is set largely in Texas, the teacher and the students claimed a strong personal and geographic/cultural connection to the book. They kept response journals throughout their reading and used them to reread and compare their impressions of the book and the movie (an acknowledged efferent practice, but one that was excusable to the author because it led them into deeper aesthetic experiences). Yet we found it surprising, especially considering the apparently all-female gender of the class, that Shull reported no discomfort or questioning on her or the students' parts with the ways that women, American Indians, Mexicans, and almost anyone else not white and male (with the exception of one token African-American cowboy), were depicted in that novel—depictions at least as problematic as that of, say, Jim, in *The Adventures of Huckleberry Finn* (see Arac, 1997). We wondered whether it might not, in fact, be the personal geographic connection, the book's Pulitzer Prize winning status, and Rosenblatt's admonition in the final chapters of *The Reader, the Text, the Poem* against treating literary texts as mere social documents that enabled the treatment and discussion of race, class, and gender with *Lonesome Dove* to pass unexamined. Similarly, Probst (1988) illustrated Rosenblattian principles through an anecdote about how students in an upper middle-class setting responded to a short story in which a young man at an exclusive prep school was caught and expelled for cheating on an exam, although he had been an otherwise exemplary student and had never cheated before. In this case, the students discussed how they would feel if they had been caught and whether it was fair for the young man to be expelled, but they never came to the point of questioning the cultural logic of the examination system itself or the cultural logic of a code of honor that was so unyielding. In the end, their discussion may have reinforced, rather than have caused them to reconsider, tacit beliefs about the fairness of testing and the logic of meritocracy.

These two examples raise important questions, we think, about the ways that a Rosenblattian view of literature education might discourage, or even empower teachers to disregard, a concern for the social and cultural criticism that many literary texts invite, either intentionally or unintentionally. To his credit, we believe, in two articles Faust (1992, 2000) has raised these issues about how an overly personalized and localized response to a literary text can obscure as much for readers as it enables. Yet to fix the problem he identified in both his *EJ* and *RTE* articles, Faust also had to move beyond Rosenblatt to other critics and theorists, such as Bakhtin and Belenky et al. (cited in Faust, 1992), and to a rereading of John Dewey (in Faust, 2000) for the source of his own regenerative response to the issues that Rosenblatt's views raised for him.

A second challenge that we believe our findings raise is about the function of Rosenblatt's work as a theoretical frame for empirical research into the ways that readers and texts relate. Our reading and analysis of empirical reports published in *RTE* and *EJ* from 1988 to August 2000 tend to support Purves's (Saks, 1995) charges that research about readers' response to literature had generated much heat but little light, and that Rosenblatt's frame had become descriptively prescriptive in its focus. Based on previous research that one of us had conducted about the rhetorical project of another teacher practice journal (Dressman, 2000), we were not surprised to find that articles appearing in *EJ* would pay so little attention to setting or to factors of personal identity such as students' ethnicity, social class, or gender; that nearly every narrative was a success story; and that more often than not references to theoretical principles seemed to decorate, rather than engage, events as they were related and their meanings explained. As in the case of that journal, the rhetorical project of most *EJ* articles seemed to be to offer descriptions of literacy education as simulations of good practice (Baudrillard, 1988)—that is, as models of classroom practice whose smoothness and lack of situational complexity would invite readers to imagine themselves to be as successful with a teaching practice as the teachers in the narrative were.

Given Rosenblatt's own dictum that readers bring their background experiences to their reading, and that these experiences have a profound effect on how they read and what meanings they make from a literary text, one would hope to see studies drawing from a wide variety of settings, ethnicities, social classes, and gender combinations, among other varieties of social and cultural difference. It was surprising to see, then, as Table 1 indicates, the same lack of concern with how factors in the backgrounds of participants might influence their response to literature in research articles appearing in *RTE* as in *EJ,* and that the outcomes of research reported in *RTE* were as predictable as the narratives of good practice that appeared in *EJ.*

Conclusion

We will begin our concluding remarks by noting again that we do not claim that the findings from our analysis of two journals are generalizable to all research or discussion about Rosenblatt's work within all journals or other works. However, we do believe that the findings we report here are reliable and valid indications of how Rosenblatt's work is understood and applied within two important journals in the field of literacy education and that they raise important questions about the ways that Rosenblatt's work is applied to literature and literacy education in theory and practice.

The implications both for theory-building and for curriculum development based on a body of research derived from such a narrowly defined a field of participants should not be underestimated. With regard to theoretical issues, although we cannot "prove" this point with the data we gathered in this study, we will note that the only two empirical studies we analyzed for this paper—one in *EJ* (Pagnucci & Abt-Perkins, 1992) and one in *RTE* (McGinley & Kamberelis, 1996)—that challenged Rosenblattian assumptions about the distinctiveness of aesthetic and efferent reading stances were also the only two studies focusing on the reading practices of minorities. This finding hints, we believe, at how significantly diverse and discordant, as opposed to homogeneous and mutually reinforcing, the findings of response to literature research might be were its range of participants and settings much wider.

As for the implications of the articles we have analyzed here for curriculum development and policy-making, again, we have grave doubts about how effectively a curricular approach based on normative findings generated from a body of readers who are mainly white, suburban, middle to upper middle class, of above-average reading ability, and mostly female might apply to schools located in urban or rural areas with large multicultural, working-class populations, or in vocational-technical programs with mostly male students, or in settings where students lack proficiency in reading or writing. Decades of research into the relationship of marginalized students with the pedagogical practices of an educational force that is predominately white, suburban, and middle to upper middle class in its perspective have repeatedly shown that their differing cultural practices can have significant consequences for how students receive and respond to—and how teachers apply—even the most well-reasoned and well-intentioned of curricular approaches (e.g., Delpit, 1988; Heath, 1983; Jordan, 1985; McCarthey, 1994). The findings of these studies show repeatedly that when one dominant cultural group seeks to apply practices deemed successful for itself on others, the result is most often not the reproduction of the dominant group's success but misunderstanding, resistance, and/or failure. We make this argument here not to suggest that students of all cultural groups would not benefit from reading literature or that all students do not have a right to respond to powerful, creative, generative texts in ways that are sensible to them, but rather that the details of such experiences—for example, what counts as a *literary* text, the circumstances in which reading and response take place, and the stances that readers take as they read and respond—are likely to be very different from the culturally and historically grounded details of the literary experience as they implicitly function in research and practice articles grounded in the work of Louise Rosenblatt.

References

Articles in *Research in the Teaching of English*

Earthman, E. A. (1992). Creating the virtual work: Readers' processes in understanding literary texts. *Research in the Teaching of English, 26,* 351–384.

Eeds, M., & Wells, D. (1989). Grand conversations: An exploration of meaning construction in literature study groups. *Research in the Teaching of English, 23,* 4–29.

Faust, M. (2000). Reconstructing familiar metaphors: John Dewey and Louise Rosenblatt on literary art as experience. *Research in the Teaching of English, 35,* 9–34.

Galda, L. (1990). A longitudinal study of the spectator stance as a function of age and genre. *Research in the Teaching of English, 24,* 261–278.

Hade, D. D. (1988). Children, stories, and narrative transformations. *Research in the Teaching of English, 22,* 310–325.

Hancock, M. R. (1993). Exploring the meaning-making process through the content of literature response journals: A case study investigation. *Research in the Teaching of English, 27,* 335–368.

Hansson, G. (1992). Readers responding—and then? *Research in the Teaching of English, 26,* 136–148.

Hynds, S. (1989). Bringing life to literature and literature to life: Social constructs and contexts of four adolescent readers. *Research in the Teaching of English, 23,* 30–61.

Langer, J. A. (1990). The process of understanding: Reading for literary and informative purposes. *Research in the Teaching of English, 24,* 229–260.

Mackey, M. (1997). Good-enough reading; Momentum and accuracy in the reading of complex fiction. *Research in the Teaching of English, 31,* 428–458.

McGinley, W., & Kamberelis, G. (1996). *Maniac Magee* and *Ragtime Tumpie:* Children negotiating self and world through reading and writing. *Research in the Teaching of English, 30,* 75–113.

Miall, D. S., & Kuiken, D. (1995). Aspects of literary response: A new questionnaire. *Research in the Teaching of English, 29,* 37–58.

Miller, S. M., & Legge, S. (1999). Supporting possible worlds: Transforming literature teaching and learning through conversations in the narrative mode. *Research in the Teaching of English, 34,* 10–64.

Saks, A. L. (Ed.). (1995). Viewpoints: A symposium on the usefulness of literacy research. *Research in the Teaching of English, 29,* 326–348.

Smolkin, L. B. (1997). Dealing with dialogue: Fifth graders' responses to reading a play. *Research in the Teaching of English, 31,* 240–266.

Whitin, P. E. (1996). Exploring visual response to literature. *Research in the Teaching of English, 30,* 114–140.

Williams, C. L., & McLean, M. M. (1997). Young deaf children's response to picture book reading in a preschool setting. *Research in the Teaching of English, 31,* 337–366.

Zancanella, D. (1991). Teachers reading/readers teaching: Five teachers' personal approaches to literature and their teaching of literature. *Research in the Teaching of English, 25,* 5–32.

Articles in *English Journal*

Auciello, J. (2000). Chronicle of a battle foretold: Curriculum and social change. *English Journal, 90*(3), 89–96.

Daniel, P. L. (1996). Inducting an eighth grader into the literacy club. *English Journal, 85*(3), 32–35.

Faust, M. A. (1992). Ways of reading and "the use of force." *English Journal, 81*(7), 44–49.

Glasgow, J. N. (1999). Recognizing students' multiple intelligences in cross-age buddy journals. *English Journal, 88*(6), 88–96.

Matthews, R., & Chandler, R. (1998). Using reader response to teach *Beloved* in a high school American Studies classroom. *English Journal, 88*(2), 85–92.

Pagnucci, G., & Abt-Perkins, D. (1992). The never-making-sense story: Reassessing the value of narrative. *English Journal, 81*(8), 54–58.

Petersen, S. A. (1999). A love affair with American literature. *English Journal, 89*(2), 40–47.

Pritchard, R. J. (1993). Developing writing prompts for reading response and analysis. *English Journal, 82*(3), 24–32.

Probst, R. E. (1988). Dialogue with a text. *English Journal, 77*(1), 32–38.

Schaars, M. J. (1988). Teaching *My Antonia,* with guidance from Rosenblatt. *English Journal, 77*(1), 54–58.

Shull, E. M. (1989). *The Reader, the Text, the Poem*—and the film. *English Journal, 78*(8), 53–57.

Smagorinsky, P. (1995). Multiple intelligences in the English class: An overview. *English Journal, 84*(8), 19–26.

Veidemanis, G. V. (1988). *Tess of the D'Urbervilles:* What the film left out. *English Journal, 77*(7), 53–57.

Other References

Appleman, D. (2000). *Critical encounters in high school English: Teaching literary theory to adolescents.* New York: Teachers College Press

Arac, J. (1997). *Huckleberry Finn as idol and target: The functions of criticism in our time.* Madison: University of Wisconsin Press.

Baudrillard, J. (1988). M. Poster (Ed.), *Jean Baudrillard: Selected writings.* Stanford, CA: Stanford University Press.

Beach, R. (2000). Critical issues: Reading and responding to literature at the level of activity. *Journal of Literacy Research, 33,* 237–251.

Britton, J. (1970). *Language and learning.* London: Allen Lane, Penguin.

Bruner, J. (1986). *Actual minds, possible worlds.* Cambridge, MA: Harvard University Press.

Carspecken, P. F. (1996). *Critical ethnography in educational research: A theoretical and practical guide.* New York: Routledge.

Delpit, L. (1988). The silenced dialogue: Power and pedagogy in educating other people's children. *Harvard Educational Review, 58,* 280–298.

Dressman, M. (1999). On the use and misuse of research evidence: Decoding two states' reading initiatives. *Reading Research Quarterly, 34,* 258–285.

Dressman, M. (2000). Theory *into* practice? Reading against the grain of good practice narratives. *Language Arts, 78,* 50–59.

Dressman, M., & Webster, J. P. (in press). Retracing Rosenblatt: A textual archaeology. *Research in the Teaching of English.*

Farrell, E. J., & Squire, J. R. (1990). *Transactions with literature: A fifty-year perspective: For Louise Rosenblatt.* Urbana, IL: National Council of Teachers of English.

Habermas, J. (1985). *The theory of communicative action, Vol. 1: Reason and the rationalization of society.* (T. McCarthy, Trans.). Boston: Beacon.

Heath, S. B. (1983). *Ways with words.* Cambridge, England: Cambridge University Press.

Jordan, C. (1985). Translating culture: From ethnographic information to educational program. *Anthropology and Education Quarterly, 16,* 105–123.

Lewis, C. (2000). Critical issues: Limits of identification: Personal, pleasurable, and critical in reader response. *Journal of Literacy Research, 33,* 253–266.

McCarthey, S. J. (1994). Authors, text, and talk: The internalization of dialogue from social interaction during writing. *Reading Research Quarterly, 29,* 200–231.

McCormick, K. (1994). *The culture of reading and the teaching of English.* Manchester, England: Manchester University Press.

McMurtry, L. (1986). *Lonesome Dove.* New York: Simon & Schuster.

Möller, K. J., & Allen, J. B. (2000). Connecting, resisting, and searching for safer places: Students respond to Mildred Taylor's *The Friendship. Journal of Literacy Research, 33,* 145–186.

Rabinowitz, P. J., & Smith, M. W. (1998). *Authorizing readers: Resistance and respect in the teaching of literature.* New York: Teachers College Press.

Rosenblatt, L. M. (1938). *Literature as exploration* (1st ed.). New York: Appleton-Century.

Rosenblatt, L. M. (1968). *Literature as exploration* (2nd ed.). New York: Noble & Noble.

Rosenblatt, L. M. (1976). *Literature as exploration* (3rd ed.). New York: Noble & Noble.

Rosenblatt, L. M. (1978). *The reader, the text, the poem: The transactional theory of the literary work.* Carbondale: Southern Illinois University Press.

Rosenblatt, L. M. (1983). *Literature as exploration* (4th ed.). New York: Modern Language Association.

Rosenblatt, L. M. (1995a). *Literature as exploration* (5th ed.). New York: Modern Language Association.

Money Talks: The Power of Government, Business, National, and Philanthropic Groups in Literacy Education

Jacqueline Edmondson
Pennsylvania State University

Kimberly McCollum-Clark
Millersville State University

Susan Pitcher
Bloomsburg Area School District

Patrick Shannon
Pennsylvania State University

In many states, and indeed nationally, efforts to open classroom doors to particular business influences are gaining force. In this study, we offer a brief overview of neoliberalism and four specific examples of its effect on literacy education: (a) university entry into the marketing of ideas, (b) corporate philanthropy brokerage of consensus in the English language arts, (c) the economy of assessment for school district assessments, and (d) federal funding for research agendas.

Social Context: A Brief Overview of Neoliberalism

Neoliberalism, the dominant political ideology in the Western world during the last two decades, is based on the notion that people's freedom and prosperity are best left to the marketplace (Chomsky, 1999; Harvey, 2000; McChesney, 1999). Advocates of neoliberalism suggest that all facets of public and private life are better served by the pursuit of corporate and personal profits than they are by planning or substantial entitlements of social services (e.g., housing, income, food, health care) (Taylor & Webber, 1997). They point to the demise of the Soviet Union and the boom in the U.S. economy for a decade as supporting evidence for this proposition. Accordingly, governments seek to establish the best conditions for profit-making in market competition by peeling away the burden of taxation, environmental impact regulation, and antitrust legislation in order to keep more money in the hands of businesses (Friedman, 1999). This is the logic behind the North American Free Trade Agreement (NAFTA) and the General Agreement on

National Reading Conference Yearbook, 50, pp. 178–188.

Tariffs and Trade (GATT), the ending of welfare, as we know it, and the deregulation of airlines, banks, and telecommunications (Greider, 1997). Beyond the national level, neoliberalism is the driving force of the International Monetary Fund (IMF) and the World Bank.

Because of neoliberalism, we live in a time when sociologist Max Weber's prediction is nearly complete—capitalism has rationalized both our public and private lives. As Marshall Berman (1999) puts it, "The crucial reality is the need to sell your labor to capital in order to live, the need to carve up your personality for sale—to look at yourself in the mirror and think, 'What have I got that I can sell?'" (p. 262). We are now understood socially as simply the sum of our human capital in others' efforts to make profits (Chomsky, 1996). We see this in the downsizing of profitable sections of businesses because they do not make enough profits, the reduction of social services at every level of government, or even the high school kid who rents his head as advertising space by cutting his hair accordingly. One consequence of rationalization is that all business, all social organizations, and all individuals must compete in the marketplace in order to "live."

Theoretically, the neoliberal pressures of rationalization and markets reduce the flow of public money into universities', professional organizations', schools', and research budgets, forcing each to compensate with funding from other sources (Heilbronner, 1995). This, in turn, increases the power of capital over the activity in these institutions as university faculty members, school personnel, and researchers must look in the metaphoric mirror and ask, "What have I got that I can sell?"

This study begins our examination of how money talks in English language arts in the United States. We adopt a critical approach (Siegel & Fernandez, 2000) to investigate the policies, contracts, and opportunities that present themselves in four prominent contexts surrounding literacy researchers and teachers. Our study is critical because we reject naturalism (the assumption that research represents unmediated reality), rationality (the assumption that research is the result of science and logic), neutrality (the assumption that research is not reflective of any particular interests), and individualism (the assumption that research affects individuals without regard for their membership in particular groups) (Popkewitz, 1990). As critical researchers, we rely on several types of knowledge: facts, the interpretation of those facts, normative and philosophical arguments, and causal relationships (Schneider & Ingram, 1997). We hope to expand the notion of literacy research in terms of what constitutes relevant facts, which values are important to consider, and how much validity there is to competing arguments. This research, then, does not seek to establish universal or objective truth, but to facilitate discussions inside and outside the literacy education community.

Method

We conducted intrinsic case studies (Stake, 1995) in four specific contexts: in a university, in professional organizations, in state policy, and in federal research funding. As such, we focused primarily on explaining and conveying the complexity of each case. Our central goal was to describe ways in which market forces were growing in influence. We began our investigations with the assumption that each case represented a social construction (Lemert, 1997; Mills, 1997), meaning each had a specific history, including social interactions that crossed many different groups, and each had direct connections to political and economic structures that were negotiated at particular times and places.

Data sources included interviews with key individuals, documents, secondary accounts, and artifacts. Data were triangulated to ensure trustworthiness of findings (Miles & Huberman, 1994). No statement is based on single sources. Our initial coding was primarily descriptive, followed by interpretive coding that connected our initial findings to broader semantic fields, such as neoliberalism and capitalism (Barthes, 1967). Although case studies are limited because the results may not be generalizable to other situations, it is hoped that those who read this study can make naturalistic generalizations (Stake & Trumbull, 1982) based on our use of thick descriptions (Geertz, 1973).

Findings

Following is a brief summary of four cases, each of which demonstrate different aspects of the market's influence in literacy research and education.

Money Talks at Pennsylvania State University

The encroachment of market forces and pressure to become entrepreneurs come from three sources at this time: pressure to obtain grants, attention to sources of capital in hiring, and finding new markets for instructional products. Faculty in colleges of education are under increasing pressure to win grants and bring outside operating expenses to their respective campuses. New reward systems for faculty revolve around bringing funds from sources other than the state or tuition. At Pennsylvania State University, this pressure takes three forms. First, central administration officials have sold their football scoreboard and students to the Pepsi Company in exchange for $14 million in order to build a convocation/concert/sports center. Other contracts have been signed with Nike (sports uniforms and equipment), ATT (telecommunications), MBNA (student IDs which double as debit cards), Barnes and Noble (textbooks), and Microsoft (Internet server). Each of these contracts limits faculty, staff, and student options.

Second, pressure to increase revenues has complicated hiring practices. At Penn State, corporations have sponsored chairs and professorships. For example, DuPont endowed a chair in Chemistry, KPMG Peat Marwick funded a chair in the Accounting program, and Murata supported a professorship in the Materials Research department. Corporate representatives served on the hiring committees for each of these posts. A new complication in hiring has emerged in social sciences and professional schools in order to position universities to capture more grant money. At Penn State, two new hires in reading education and research have been tied directly to the closeness of fit between the candidate's research agendas and the federal government's call for proposals for educational research.

Third, courses for credit on the World Wide Web are expected to increase university revenue. More than an attempt to use the latest technology effectively, these courses are offered to significantly increase course enrollments from students who would not ordinarily attend campus. At Penn State, the Early Childhood Education major has been closely scrutinized concerning their continued value given the mission of the college and university. Their enrollments are down and their faculty members have not generated significant grant awards. As a first step in evaluating whether or not to continue the program on the main campus, administrators have encouraged the ECE faculty to offer their course on the web. Their first offering will be a family literacy course. This would enable faculty to demonstrate that they are in accord with the outreach parts of the college mission as well as to show ability to tap new markets. On the web, they will compete with HeinemannU and UNext.com for "clients."

According to Aronowitz (2000), Press and Washburn (2000), and Slaughter and Leslie (1997), Pennsylvania State University is not the only campus experiencing these pressures. The desire for faculty to create surplus value (Smith, 1776/1991) stems from the encroachment of commercial concerns into more and more aspects of our lives. Until recently, universities, particularly large publicly funded ones, successfully resisted corporate advances into arts, humanities, social sciences, and some professional schools. At Penn State, the dean of the College of Education explained that outside sponsors are necessary because the Pennsylvania legislature has reduced its portion of budget funding from 40% during the 1980s to just under 17% in 2000—a trend commonplace in many states across the country. "We must accommodate this decline," the dean explained. "Penn State must generate more of its own funds. We'll never sacrifice our standards or the University's mission. You won't see banners all over campus. But you have to understand. This is now a way of life. It's not a question of good, bad or indifferent—it's the way it is."

The dean's fatalism about inevitability of neoliberalism on campus raises questions about the ability of universities and individual faculty to conduct research apart from commercial considerations. It has placed considerable pressure on the Language and Literacy Education faculty to carry this weight. As David Pearson (1990) noted in his introduction to Marilyn Adam's *Beginning to Read,* the influence of capital is real. In order to continue funding the Center for the Study of Reading, they were required to conduct research on phonics—"We knew we could not ignore these issues" (p. v).

Money Talks for IRA/NCTE Standards

The agendas of professional organizations can likewise be influenced by money. This point is evident in the National Council of Teacher's of English

(NCTE) involvement in developing standards for the English language arts. The origins of the standards movement in English language arts can be traced to four

Table 1

Goals of Groups Influencing Standards

Business Advocacy Groups

Assert the need to standardize and rationalize educational structures, based on business' desired template for workers in the "global economy" and technological changes ahead

Create national conversation about educational reform framed by the role of education and human capital in economic revitalization

Examples: Business Roundtable, Business–Higher Education Forum, Committee for Economic Development, Twentieth Century Fund

Liberal Philanthropy

Advance a "planned articulation of people" (Lagemann, 1987) through standardization of educational structures

Advance notions of a more complete "meritocracy" in which those who "deserve" more, get more

Involvement belies the liberal belief that life can be improved by rational organization (i.e., technical solutions to complex problems with intricate social and political ramifications)

Examples: Carnegie Corporation of New York, Carnegie Foundation for Advancement of Teaching

Conservative Philanthropy

Exert conservative values on social, political, economic policy

Relieve the state of the burden of publicly funded schooling (the "last bastion of the welfare state")

Promote free-market ideas and solutions

Reassert a monolithic cultural mandate of authority and stability in a time of difference and "chaos"

Examples: Educational Excellence Network, Empower America, Heritage Institute, Thomas Fordham

Quasi-Governmental Groups

Employ networks of advocacy and funding from other three groups to cobble together policy recommendations, legislation

Maintain their own influence within key debates

Examples: National Governor's Association, Education Commission of States, Educational Leaders' Council specific, complex groups—including business advocacy, liberal philanthropic, conservative philanthropic, and think tanks (see Table 1). These groups' seemingly divergent agendas came together to "broker" a formal consensus on a national level about the need and structure of education reform.

Each group enacted a series of moves to position (Hall, 1997) the minds of American citizens. In its early stages, their victories were primarily discursive. They successfully established the commonplace discourse about what should count in schooling and what should be done to achieve the same. In the early 1980s, the discourse around "excellence" drowned out concerns over equity, and later, any opponent of the movement was said not to have "high standards" or want to improve education for students. The standards discourse created "patterns of communication that hid the social relations and power" implicit in them (Popkewitz, 1991, p. 129). This unavoidable juggernaut of standards discourse was created through the technologies of influence (Lagemann, 1987), or what Joel Spring (1992) calls "ideological management."

Ultimately, this ideological management led to NCTE's, the International Reading Association's (IRA), and the Center for the Study of Reading's (CSR) decision to participate in the standards movement (although CSR eventually withdrew when it had to ante up some of its own money). From 1990 to 1995, NCTE officials introduced a period of intense activism on behalf of the vision of NCTE-sponsored standards, which stood in bold relief from NCTE's more traditional role as a service organization to the "teacher-scholars" of English (McCollum-Clark, 1995). In its activist role, NCTE officials intended to "take over" the momentum of the standards movement for their own progressive vision of the discipline.

Through their action, these professional organizations legitimated the standards movement with their participation. Even after the federal government withdrew funding in 1994, NCTE and IRA were dogged in their insistence on standards as the best vehicle for their reform efforts. This case demonstrates that consensus about schooling, brokered in part by business and philanthropic groups, led these professional organizations to compete to be players in the standards arena on business' terms, and to likewise compete for funding. In the end they were played by the market.

Money Talks for School Districts

In 1995, Pennsylvania's newly elected Republican Governor Tom Ridge began to phase out outcome-based education. Although the state's K–12 assessment (the Pennsylvania System of State Assessment, or PSSA) continued to cite the National Assessment of Educational Progress' (NAEP) definition of reading as an interactive process, the language in the assessment handbooks for teachers began to reflect levels of achievement standards. By 1998, in compliance with the 1994 Title I Reauthorization Act, the PSSA was aligned with the Pennsylvania Academic Standards for Language Arts, and school districts began to compete for state money awarded for high test scores. This competition for funding means that schools must now operate on the state's terms. Further, because Pennsylvania emphasizes test scores, money is involved in two ways: (a) tests come from private influences and (b) schools must look for programs to raise test scores.

Private organizations have had much influence on the development and implementation of assessments, including the NAEP (Vinovskis, 1998). Private companies are contracted for assistance in test development and administration services. For example, the Educational Testing Service (ETS) develops assessments, scores students' responses, and analyzes and reports subsequent data. ETS further contracts with NCS (National Computer Systems) to print, distribute, scan, and score student assessments, and AIR (American Institute of Research) to develop background questionnaires. WESTAT, an independent commercial testing company, secures school samples, collects data, trains assessment personnel, and manages field operations.

As schools work to improve their test scores, private corporations market programs, curriculum, and textbooks that are aligned with tests. As one example, Harcourt General, a mega-corporation resulting from mergers and acquisitions that have included but are not limited to the General Cinema Company and Harcourt Brace Jovanovich, generated $2.14 billion in revenues from education products, services, and testing in 1999. Its mission follows:

> Harcourt General, through its wholly owned subsidiary, Harcourt, Inc., is a broadband learning company that is a major participant in the growing global markets for education, assessment, training and professional information. Broadband describes our strategy focusing resources on four key points along the lifelong learner spectrum, and creating, marketing and distributing our high quality, value-added content to those markets. Harcourt, Inc. has organized its businesses into four strategic groups targeting specific customer sets: K–12 Education, Higher Education, Corporate and Professional Services and the Worldwide Scientific, Technical and Medical Group. (home page for Harcourt, www.harcourtgeneral.com)

Harcourt publishes the Standford 9, the Otis-Lennon School Ability Test, the News Standards Reference Exams, and the Metropolitan Early Childhood Assessment Program, among others. Meanwhile, Harcourt owns publishing companies including Holt, Rinehart & Winston, Academic Press, and Steck Vaughn, and it operates several assessment corporations, including Assessment Systems, Incorporated. Keeping in step with the globalization of learning, it also owns Netg, a global e-learning company.

Whereas educational policy-making often seems to be located publicly within state legislatures, private corporations set and maintain the parameters. The link between state and national educational policy-making becomes even more complicated as financial contributions from businesses and foundations wield an underlying power and control over educational policy-making.

Money Talks Through the Sandia Report

On September 24, 1991, an exclusive audience, including then Deputy Secretary of Education David T. Kearns and then Assistant Secretary for the Office of

Educational Research and Improvement Diane Ravitch, listened as representatives from the Sandia Laboratories, a federally funded research center in New Mexico, presented a report at a meeting in Washington D.C. The report, prepared as part of the Energy Department's Education Initiative, suggested that the perception of a systemwide education crisis gaining momentum through *A Nation At Risk* and other corresponding reports both overstated and misstated the problem (Miller, 1991a). Rather than supporting the Bush administration's reform agenda, the Sandia report indicated the crisis mentality which shaped those reforms was misguided and did not focus on actual circumstances facing educators (Stedman, 1994). Researchers pointed out that, contrary to popular belief, test scores in the country had been relatively stable for more than two decades and some areas had actually improved as the United States remained a worldwide leader in high school and college graduation rates (Stedman, 1994). Further, the Sandia report noted that since the 1960s, public education served children who in previous generations would have been excluded from schools (Rothman, 1991) and, due to this trend, it called for more assistance for racial and ethnic groups who continued to "lag behind" (Stedman, 1994, p. 144).

Reaction to the report was swift and volatile. According to congressional sources, Mr. Kearns and other administration officials "reacted angrily" during the meeting, and Diane Ravitch proceeded to give interviews and make public appearances "in which she angrily attacked the report" (Miller, 1991b). Meanwhile, Robert Huelskamp, one of the authors, announced that his continued involvement in the "educational arena" was, in his management's opinion, not in the best interest of Sandia (Miller, 1992).

More than a year later, the report remained unpublished, leaving some openly questioning whether the Bush administration suppressed it because of obvious conflicts with the administration's views (Miller, 1992). During that same year, it was also written that Sandia researchers "reported being berated and even threatened with loss of funding by Administration officials." Peggy Dufour, the chief education advisor to then Secretary of Energy James T. Watkins, responded to these accusations by acknowledging that researchers were "chastised" by officials for "circulating their findings before the report had been reviewed by experts and revised." She concluded, "They have chosen to play this out in a political arena, and when you do that, the gloves come off" (Miller, 1991a). For Sandia, this meant retreating from research in the educational arena or facing a loss of grant monies. Three years later, *Project Censored* ranked the Sandia report third on its list of top 25 most censored stories (Apple, 1995).

Today, the gloves still seem to be off for researchers who do not support the government's position. As one recent example, Dr. Joanne Yatvin, the one member who voiced dissent from the National Reading Panel, has publicly discussed her criticism of the report. Because of her concerns about both the process and product of the Panel's work, Yatvin has sacrificed her job as an elementary school principal in Oregon, and currently she is the only panel member who receives no financial support for travel to professional conferences to discuss her role in the report.

Discussion

Robert McChesney (1999) writes of neoliberalism:

> Neoliberalism is the defining political economic paradigm of our time—it refers to the policies and processes whereby a relative handful of private interests are permitted to control as much as possible of social life in order to maximize their personal profit. (p. 1)

That private interests influence literacy education agendas is evident across these four cases. In particular, we can see how universities are vulnerable to particular research agendas and money-making endeavors as demands for external funding increase. In addition, we see how professional organizations for English and language arts educators can be seduced by the market. Through the allocation of funds based on test scores, we see how school districts compete with one another with new bottom lines. And finally, we see how literacy education, research, and assessment are influenced by the support (or not) of funds that forward specific ideological positions. Given the influence of capital in literacy education and research, we are left to wonder how our conversations might be otherwise if research funding in literacy education truly supported and generated a free market of ideas where researchers were encouraged to open their doors to contribute to a rich and diverse conversation about literacy.

Based on our research, we suggest three ways to monitor the influence of money talks in the literacy field: (a) ask who is involved, (b) question consensus, and (c) examine research requests for proposals.

Attend to Who Is Involved a Small Group of Like-Minded People

Close attention to the players in education literacy and policy reveals that few are involved in tangled webs of participation as they cross groups and positions. For example, Marc Tucker, a former Carnegie Corporation of New York (CCNY) grantee, has worked at various times as the executive director of the Carnegie Forum on Education and the Economy, as the director of the National Center on Education and the Economy, and as a founding partner of the New Standards Project. Meanwhile, he testifies regularly to Congress and the National Governor's Association, has participated in National Governor's Association Education Summits, and has worked with the National Council of Education Standards and Testing. President Bill Clinton also appointed Tucker to the National Skills Standards board. This crossing in and among groups is not unique to Tucker. Indeed, a few others have wielded similar influence. Keeping an eye on individual participants and their past and present connections can help us to see why certain ideas circulate so regularly in policy decisions of literacy education.

Attend to Consensus-Building

Careful attention to the ways in which consensus is brokered—by whom and for whom—demonstrates aspects of how money talks in literacy education. Recent consensus-building in literacy research and education has included the National Reading Panel's Report *Teaching Children to Read,* the National Research Council's *Preventing Reading Difficulties,* the Brookings Institute's Forum on Reading and Math, and the 1999 Education Summit in Palisades, New York. Consensus-building is a social construction, complete with social interactions and direct connections to political and economic structures (Lemert, 1997). These constructions, negotiated at particular times and places through various individuals and groups, make some issues and solutions appear to be more or less viable. The process of consensus-building can be better understood by asking questions such as: Why are particular individuals or groups involved? How are issues framed? What values are implicit in the brokering of consensus? How are diversity of ideas, values, and interactions accommodated? Although these are not the only questions to consider, their answers should begin to unravel the influence of money on consensus-building events.

Carefully Read Requests for Proposals

A careful reading of requests for proposals (RFPs) from the U.S. Department of Education, which provides 75% of the funding for educational research (Olson, 1999), and other funding agencies provides important insight into the ways in which money will be attached to research agendas. The criteria outlined in these RFPs foreshadow the conference agendas and journal publications that are sure to follow. For example, perusal of recent literacy conference programs evidences the ambitious work of the Center for the Improvement of Early Reading Achievement (CIERA). This group has worked seemingly tirelessly on early literacy issues—a primary emphasis of the U.S. Department of Education throughout Bill Clinton's second term as president. The group begins with Clinton's premise that all children should read well and independently by the end of the third grade, and focuses their research accordingly. Much research money has been directed toward these early literacy endeavors.

Money talks in and around many aspects and at all levels of literacy research and education. More often than not, it inveigles compliance with particular economic and political agendas. Our hope is that studying money's influence will assist educators in becoming more savvy political players who can understand not only how markets influence and narrow literacy education and research, but also how we might think and work differently.

References

Apple, M. (1995). What's news. *The review of education/pedagogy/cultural studies, 17,* 207–216.

Aronowitz, S. (2000). *The knowledge factory.* Boston: Beacon.

Barthes, R. (1967). *The elements of semiology.* London: Cape.

Berman, M. (1999). *Adventures in Marxism.* New York: Verso.

Chomsky, N. (1996). *Class warfare.* Monroe, ME: Common Courage.

Chomsky, N. (1999). *Profit over people.* New York: Seven Stories.

Friedman, M. (1999). *Free market economics: Commanding heights.* Princeton, NJ: Films for the Humanities and Sciences.

Geertz, C. (1973). *The interpretation of cultures.* New York: Basic.

Greider, W. (1997). *One world, ready or not.* New York: Touchstone.

Hall, S. (1997). *Representations.* London: Sage.

Harvey, D. (2000). *Spaces of hope.* Berkeley: University of California Press.

Heilbronner, R. (1995). *Visions of the future.* New York: Oxford University Press.

Lagemann, E. C. (1987). *Private power for public good: A history of the Carnegie Foundation for the Advancement of Teaching.* Chicago: University of Chicago Press.

Lemert, C. (1997). *Social things.* Oxford: Rowan & Littlefield.

McChesney, R. (1999). Introduction. In Chomsky, N. *Profit over people.* New York: Seven Stories.

McCollum-Clark, K. (1995). National Council of Teachers of English, Corporate Philanthropy, and National Education Standards: Challenging the ideologies of English education reform. An unpublished dissertation, The Pennsylvania State University.

Miles, M., & Huberman, A. (1994). *Qualitative data analysis* (2nd ed.). London: Sage.

Miller, J. (1991a). Congress weighing proposal to rein in E.D. research unit. *Education Week.* [On-line] Available: http://www.edweek.org.

Miller, J. (1991b). Report questioning "crisis" in education triggers an uproar. *Education Week.* [On-line] Available: http://www.edweek.org/ ew/1991/06crisis.h11.

Miller, B. (1992). Energy department lab's education report still on hold. *Education Week.* [On-line] Available: http://www.edweek.org.

Mills, S. (1997). *Discourse.* London: Routledge.

Olson, L. (1999). NRC seeks new agenda for research. *Education Week.* [On-line] Available: http://www.edweek.org.

Pearson, P. D. (1990). Foreword: How I came to know about *Beginning to Read.* In Adams, M. (1990). *Beginning to Read* (pp. v–viii). Washington DC: U.S. Department of Education.

Popkewitz, T. (1990). Whose future, whose past: Notes on critical theory and methodology. In E. Guba (Ed). *The paradigm dialogue.* (pp. 46–66). Newbury Park, CA: Sage.

Popkewitz, T. (1991). *A political sociology of educational reform: Power/knowledge in teaching, teacher education, and research.* New York: Teachers College Press.

Press, E., & Washburn, J. (2000, March). The kept university. *Atlantic Monthly,* 39–54.

Rothman, R. (1991). Revisionists take aim at gloomy view of schools much more progress needed, critics assert. *Education Week.* [On-line] Available: http://www.edweek.org/ew/1991/11view.h11.

Schneider, A., & Ingram, H. (1997). *Policy design for democracy.* Lawrence: University Press of Kansas.

Siegel, M., & Fernandez, S. (2000). Critical approaches. In M. Kamil, P. D. Pearson, & R. Barr (Eds.), *Handbook of reading research* (Vol. 3, pp. 141–152). Mahwah, NJ: Erlbaum.

Slaughter, S., & Leslie, L. (1997). *Academic capitalism: Politics, policies, and the entrepreneurial university.* Baltimore, MD: Johns Hopkins University Press.

Smith, A. (1776/1991). *The wealth of nations.* New York: Prometheus.

Spring, J. (1992). *Images of American life: A history of ideological management in schools, movies, radios, and television.* Albany: State University of New York Press.

Stake, R. (1995). *The art of case study research.* London: Sage.

Stake, R., & Trumbull, D. (1982). Naturalistic generalizations. *Review Journal of Philosophy and Social Science, 7,* 1–12.

Stedman, L. (1994). The Sandia report and U.S. achievement: An assessment. *Journal of Education Research, 87*(3), 133–146.

Taylor, W., & Webber, A. (1997). *Going global.* New York: Penguin.

Vinovskis, M. A. (1998). *Overseeing our nation's report card.* Washington DC: National Assessment Governing Board.

Why Class Size Matters: An Investigation of Teacher, Administrator, and Parent Perceptions

Douglas Fisher, Diane Lapp, James Flood,
Nancy Frey, and Kelly Moore
San Diego State University

School districts throughout the United States continually attempt to meet the challenge of educating culturally and linguistically diverse students who come to school with a range of prior literacy experiences. One response to this challenge has been class size reduction. To many school personnel, smaller class size promises to increase student-teacher interactions, reduce teacher stress and burnout, allow for greater individualized instruction, and provide increased flexibility for teaming and planning (e.g., Betts & Shkolnik, 1999; Finn & Achilles, 1990). To many administrators, smaller class size promises to reduce teachers' responsibilities for record-keeping, thus allowing increased time for teaching and fewer discipline problems resulting in trips to the office (Boyd-Zaharias, 1999; Lapp et al., 1999; Zahorik, 1999). At the same time, however, smaller class size requires considerable investment especially in terms of the number of teachers required and the physical space to locate these additional classrooms.

Interestingly, the research evidence is less than conclusive. It seems that the effects of class size reduction are strongest for primary-grade students (Educational Research Service, 1980); for students who were struggling to learn to read (Stasz & Stecher, 2000); and for students at risk for school failure (Slavin & Madden, 1987). However, others have argued that government funds should be prioritized for teacher induction (Moir & Gless, 2001) or technology (Milken Exchange on Education Technology, 1998) rather than class size reduction.

The debate regarding ideal class size has been ongoing for years (Hanushek, 1999; Rivera-Batiz & Marti, 1995). Although there has been some research on this subject (e.g., Allen, Brannon, & Sims, 1999; Nyhan & Alkadry, 1999), it is limited. In fact, an ERIC search on the topic of "class size reduction" between 1996 and 2000, resulted in 54 articles, only 6 of which were data-driven studies (five were published in a special issue of *Educational Evaluation and Policy Analysis*). Thus, conclusive answers are difficult to obtain. Even in the absence of totally conclusive data, board members and administrators argue that class size reduction is a worthwhile expenditure (Black, 1999; Chollet, 1998). Interestingly, the bulk of the research on class size reduction has focused on the outcomes of class size reduction rather than the reasons that reduced class size mattered (Boyd-Zaharias, 1999; Nyhan & Alkadry, 1999). In fact, Nye, Hedges, and Konstantopoulos (2000) believe that "it is not yet clear *how* small classes lead to

*National Reading Conference Yearbook, **50**, pp. 189–199.*

higher achievement. Understanding the mechanism could lead to more effective ways to implement class size reductions and improve their effectiveness" (p. 150).

Despite the lack of research evidence favoring smaller classes, during the 1996–97 school year the state of California spent over $1 billion to reduce the size of classes in Grades K–3. Since then, school districts in California have been lowering class size in these grades in an attempt to enable teachers to meet the challenge of educating increasingly diverse students. Unfortunately, as McRobbie (1996) pointed out, the urgency of the legislation that resulted in class size reduction in California did not allow for an increase in the number of credential teachers, facilities planning, or professional development for existing teachers. In other words, districts received funds to hire teachers and some limited funds for facilities (typically portable classrooms). Funds were not identified for universities or school districts to increase the pool of qualified teachers nor to provide educational opportunities for inservice teachers.

Thus the purpose of the present study was to gain insights about the dynamics of class size reduction. More specifically, this study was designed to examine teacher, administrator, and parent beliefs explaining the achievement gains in small classes.

Method

Participants and Procedures

Teacher survey. A survey was administered to 240 classroom teachers, Grades K–3, who had been teaching at least 4 years. The rationale for the 4-year requirement was based on the fact that the California reduced class size to 20 students in Grades K–3 occurred during the 1996–97 school year. We wanted to ensure that all teacher participants had at least 1 year of experience teaching a larger class (30–38 students). Surveys were administered during a regularly scheduled staff meeting, and teachers were asked to return the survey to the principal's secretary who would then forward the whole set to the researchers. A total of 203 surveys (85%) were returned.

Of these 203 teachers, 94% were female, 76% were white, 12% were Latino/Hispanic, 7% were African-American, 5% were Asian-Pacific Islander, and 1% identified as other. Their years of experience ranged from 4 to 31, with an average of 11.4. All 203 teachers worked in 1 of 10 elementary schools in an urban community in Southern California. Each of these 10 schools reflected the urban community in which they existed. No school had fewer than 25% of its student body identified as "limited English proficient" or fewer than 36% of its student body eligible for free lunch. The schools ranged in size from 945 students to 1,440 students.

Teacher interviews and observations. Thirty teachers were randomly selected for interviews and classroom observations from those who returned surveys. The interviews were scheduled during lunch or after school. Each of the randomly selected teachers agreed to participate in the interview. Additionally, each of the 30 randomly selected teachers agreed to a classroom observation. The observations, which were conducted by at least two of the researchers during the language arts morning block, were not scheduled in advance with the teacher.

Parent questionnaire. Each of the 30 teachers who participated in interviews and observations were provided with 10 parent questionnaires (see Figure 1). Teachers were asked to distribute these to 10 parents who they believed had opinions to share about class size. It was suggested that teachers send the questionnaire home in a homework packet. A total of 140 (47%) were returned.

Administrator interviews. Four principals were randomly selected from the ten participating schools. Each of the four principals agreed to be interviewed. Interviews were conducted by at least two of the researchers in the principal's office during the school day.

Instruments

Teacher survey. The teacher survey contained nine items in addition to a request for demographic data (see Figure 2). Participants were asked to respond to several questions regarding various aspects of class size reduction. The first question required participants to decide if they believed that class size reduction positively affected what happened in their classroom. If a yes response was given,

Class Size Reduction
Parent Survey

1. Have you seen benefit from reduced class size? YES NO
2. What are the positive effects of reduced class size?
3. What do you believe most helps your child become a better reader?
4. Please indicate your belief for each of the following statements.

Statement	Strongly Disagree	Disagree	Not Sure	Agree	Strongly Agree
Reducing class size is the best way to increase student achievement					
Reducing class size is better than receiving more instructional materials					
Reducing class size is better than receiving additional computers in the classroom					
Reducing class size is better than having teacher aides					

Figure 1

the participant was asked a series of open-ended questions such as: "How do you know that positive consequences occurred?" or "How has reduced class size impacted your instruction?" A total of four open-ended questions comprised this section of the survey. The last section of the survey consisted of four likert-type questions that focused on the effectiveness of using funding allocations for class size reduction rather than on computers, paraprofessionals, or other instructional materials as a means to promote improvement in student achievement.

Teacher interviews and observations. The teacher interviews focused on the reasons that teachers believe that class size reduction is effective in increasing student achievement. The opening question was used to confirm that the participant believed that class size reduction was effective. The second question was "Why do you believe this expenditure has been effective?" The final interview question was "How has your teaching changed as a result of class size reduction."

Class Size Reduction
Teacher Survey

Gender: _______ Ethnicity: __________ Years Teaching: _______

1. Has class size reduction positively affected your classroom? YES NO

If yes, answer questions 2–5:

2. How do you know that positive consequences occurred because of class size reduction?
3. How has class size reduction changed your teaching?
4. What would you tell a colleague about the difference between the 1995–96 school year and now?
5. What can you do now with 20 students that you couldn't do before with more than 20?
6. Please indicate your belief for each of the following statements.

Statement	Strongly Disagree	Disagree	Not Sure	Agree	Strongly Agree
Reducing class size is the best way to increase student achievement					
Reducing class size is better than receiving more instructional materials					
Reducing class size is better than receiving additional computers in the classroom					
Reducing class size is better than having teacher aides					

Figure 2

The observations were used as confirmatory evidence that the teachers were, in fact, implementing instruction as they reported via the survey and the interview. We were interested in how teachers used time for literacy instruction and how they interacted with students in the class. The observations were unannounced and occurred during the time in which literacy instruction occurred. Fieldnote forms (LeCompte & Preissle, 1993) were used to create a record of classroom events and conversations. To ensure consistency and interrater reliability, teachers were always observed by at least two of the researchers. All researchers have experience with ethnographic and qualitative research. Classroom observations typically lasted between 45 and 65 minutes.

Parent questionnaire. The parent questionnaire consisted of a yes/no question about the benefits of reduced class size, an open-ended question about the positive effects of reduced class size, and four likert-type questions focused on class size reduction compared with other uses of funds to improve student achievement such as computers, paraprofessionals, or instructional materials. Similar to the teacher survey, parents were asked to list factors that they believed increased the literacy performance of their children.

Administrator interviews. Administrator interviews also focused on the reasons that class size seemed to be effective in increasing student achievement. The interviews lasted between 35 and 60 minutes. A series of open-ended questions were used to elicit administrator's beliefs about the benefits of class size reduction.

Data Analysis

Survey responses were quantified to determine frequency of responses made by teachers and parents regarding the effects of class size reduction. Data from the surveys were used for measures of central tendency and to create frequency tables. Observational data were categorized using a constant comparative method (Bogdan & Biklen, 1992). As interviews and observations were completed in groups of five, researchers independently reviewed the observation notes and then met to talk about findings. Thus, after every five interviews or observations, we compared the current data set with our previously established coding categories and either added this new data to the existing categories or revised the categories (LeCompte & Preissle, 1993). The researchers agreed on the final categories and representative quotes. Each of these categories was named and quotes that typified the category were identified. Discussion of each continued until consensus was reached. In addition, direct quotes were obtained from the surveys, interviews, and observations.

Limitations

Several potential limitations exist in this study. First, this study was designed to examine teacher, administrator, and parent beliefs explaining the achievement gains in small classes. We did not collect achievement data to confirm these achievement gains given that we were most interested in the possible explanations for findings that have been documented elsewhere (e.g., Finn & Achilles, 1990). Second, to ensure privacy and participation, we allowed the classroom teachers to identify the parents who received surveys. To control for this, we provided each teacher with 10 surveys (at least 50% of the class) and had a response rate of 47%. Finally, this study relies on survey research which creates a self-report bias. To control for this, we added interviews and classroom observations in an attempt to verify the survey findings.

Findings

Support for class size reduction was consistent across participants. When asked if they believed that reduced class size positively affected what happens in the classroom, 100% of the teachers, 100% of the administrators, and 90% of the parents responded "yes." When asked how they knew that positive consequences had occurred as a result of class size reduction, teachers in this study identified a number of ways they knew. In rank order (with the frequency of occurrence) teachers reported: improved academic scores on formal assessments (38%), observations and anecdotal records (31%), instructional assessments that were teacher-made (28%), parent feedback (25%), student behavior (22%), running records (22%), journal writing (19%), student productivity (16%), and a collection of others (16%) including "no one cried," the "report cards are better," and "intuition."

When the administrators were asked the same question in the interviews, all four of them reported that their school's achievement data had increased over the past few years, especially at the second- and third-grade levels. This "bubble" as one of them put it, represented students who had been in classes of 20 or fewer since kindergarten. Three of the administrators reported that in addition to the academic achievement data increases there had been a significant decrease in the number of students sent to the principal's office for discipline. One of the administrators reported a 35% decrease in referrals in 2 years. Another administrator said, "Teachers have significantly more time to individualize instruction—even our special education referrals are down."

The data on the positive effects of class size reduction were fairly consistent across participants. Teachers reported (in rank order, with the frequency of occurrence): time to individualize instruction (78%), time to observe students and meet individual needs (41%), time to design and administer assessments related to instruction (40%), less time spent on discipline problems (34%), time to develop relationships with students (28%), and time to focus on professional development activities (20%). As one of the teachers said in the interview, "I now have three hours to teach reading and language arts. I used to have just over one hour. With fewer students and more time, I really can meet all of their needs for the first time in my fifteen year career."

The survey data from the teachers were consistent with that of the parents and administrators. The parents reported (in rank order, with the frequency of occurrence) that the benefits of class size reduction involved four factors: more one-to-one time with students (67%), better parent-teacher communication (55%), the belief that the child was safer at school (27%), and teachers seemed more relaxed (12%). The administrator interviews focused on similar ideas. As one of the administrators said:

> I've been an administrator for 13 years. I've never seen so much individual attention. Every time I walk into a class, I see teachers working with small groups of students or working with one particular student. That just wasn't possible with the class sizes we used to have.

Another administrator suggested that the individualized instruction also provided students "an opportunity to learn. They have to focus when they know that the teacher is right there to help or re-direct. Teachers have time to do the things that they know need to be done."

The classroom observations supported the survey and interview data in terms of individualized instruction. In 27 of the 30 classes that we visited, teachers used small-group guided reading as their instructional strategy during some point of the visit. One first-grade teacher who was observed asked students to read aloud from a narrative text while she listened. After all four students at the table had finished reading the book three times, she initiated a conversation that encouraged text to text and text to self connections. She then began a mini-lesson on the rime *–op* and invited students to create new words with this spelling pattern. After discussion of the meanings of the words, they were added to their personal dictionaries.

A third-grade teacher was observed guiding students through the reading of an informational science text. Each student had a concept map next to the book that was used to record information from the text. When this group finished, the teacher asked students to retell the information to a partner while he listened. Then each member of the group was asked to write a summary of the information and to create a visual that could be shared.

The three teachers who were not observed in small-group instruction were reading aloud to whole classes of kindergartners during the initial part of their observations. Each teacher paused to ask questions during their read-aloud. The questions ranged from noticing textual information to making intertextual connections with other books the class had read, to predicting what might happen next in the book. When the read-aloud was over, the students in these classes returned to their desks to write in their journals. Following the individual journal writing, all three teachers began interactive writing with the whole class. Although these were all whole-class activities, there were some opportunities for students to receive individual feedback from the teacher.

When asked about the priority of class size reduction compared with other ways to spend funds, there were some differences between teachers and parents (see Table 1). Although parents and teachers were generally supported class size reduction and believed that it was the best way to improve student achievement, teachers were more likely to value materials and computers whereas parents val-

Table 1

Educational Funding Priorities

Item	Parent *M** (*SD*)	Parent Responses Per Question	Teacher *M* (*SD*) *N*=23	Teacher Responses Per Question	t-test Value (Statistical Significance)
Reducing class size is the best way to increase student achievement	4.1 (1.8)	140	4.3 (1.3)	203	-1.19 Not Significant
Reducing class size is better than receiving more instructional materials	4.3 (.8)	138	3.1 (.6)	203	15.86 *p*<.05 Significant
Reducing class size is better than receiving additional computers in the classroom	4.4 (.4)	138	3.4 (1.2)	203	9.50 *p*<.05 Significant
Reducing class size is better than having teacher aides	3.1 (1.6)	138	2.7 (2.1)	203	1.9 Not Significant

*On a scale of 1 to 5, 1=Strongly Disagree to 5=Strongly Agree.

ued instructional aides. For example, teachers were fairly evenly split on the issue of materials versus reduced class size (*M*=3.1). Interestingly, parents agreed with the statement, even more strongly than teachers, that reduced class size is better than more instructional materials.

Teachers were also asked how class size reduction had impacted upon their instruction. While the previous question provides some insight into the instructional changes that teachers implemented as a result of class size reduction, their responses to this survey question reinforced the reasons why class size reduction seems to improve student achievement. Teacher responses are presented in rank order with the frequency of occurrence in parentheses. The impact that class size reduction had on instruction included: increased time to individualize instruction (44%), increased small-group instruction (38%), enrichment or learning centers in place (34%), in depth coverage of curriculum topics (22%), increased conference time with students (19%), more time to observe students (18%), more time for oral sharing or oral reading (18%), and more group interactions (16%). Individualized instruction was again the most important difference that resulted from class size reduction.

Several instructional methods such as the use of learning centers and conference times that were not previously mentioned were identified in this question. During classroom observations, students in 25 of the 27 classrooms in which guided reading occurred were at learning centers. The center activities included word processing, listening to books on tape, silent reading, and working with words. Students in the two additional classrooms were engaged in individual phonics-related seatwork while the teacher conducted guided-reading groups.

Results of the teacher and administrator interviews also suggest that instructional changes had occurred as a result of class size reduction. One administrator commented on the instruction he was observing by saying, "Teachers matter and what they do matters most. I see great teaching since we have implemented CSR!" Another administrator reported that "The staff development combined with the lower class sizes has allowed us to meet our accountability targets for the first time in 12 years." A third-grade teacher said:

> I never could manage groups before. Can you imagine 34 kids trying to work in groups of four? That would be 8 or 9 group activities that I'd have to plan. Where would I find the time or the space in my classroom? Now I have 5 group activities and one of these groups is with me during the literacy block. Smaller class size gives me a chance to individualize my teaching by grouping students who have similar strengths or needs. I have time to really observe them and then plan appropriate instruction for them.

Discussion

These findings provide evidence that teachers, administrators, and parents are responding favorably to class size reduction. Although parents and teachers opinions differed about the use of funding for computers and instructional materials, it was clear from these data that class size reduction was overwhelmingly supported (100% by teachers, 100% by administrators, and 90% by parents). Most teachers, parents, and administrators reported that the most important outcome of class size reduction was that it promoted more individualized attention for students. Teachers and administrators also reported that class size reduction resulted in fewer discipline and classroom management concerns, thus allowing students the opportunity to learn. It is also clear from these data that student achievement requires more than just reduced class size. The participants suggested that when teachers have time to observe the strengths and needs of their students and then plan related instruction, literacy growth occurs.

Teachers in this study reported significant changes in their teaching as a result of class size reduction. Consistent with the findings of Baumann, Hoffman, Duffy-Hester, and Ro (2000), teachers today devote considerable time to reading and language arts instruction. Teachers in this study reported spending between two and one-half to three hours of instruction teaching reading and language arts per day because they had fewer students to instruct and manage. Unlike the Baumann et al. (2000) study, we found that teachers frequently implemented flexible grouping patterns during their language arts instruction. Teachers and administrators reported using and observing individualized instruction, small-group instruction especially for guided reading and learning centers. Our observations confirmed these reports.

The findings from this study suggest that class size reduction has allowed teachers to implement the instructional repertoire that they have always known works best. Whereas we acknowledge that class size reduction alone is not sufficient to improve student achievement, study participants identified the reasons that they believe class size reduction results in positive student growth. Their reasons suggest an increase in teacher time that can be used to: (a) talk with family members; (b) link assessment to instruction and conference with students; (c) individualize instruction; (d) focus on reading, writing, and oral language development; (e) use technology; and (f) grow as a professional.

The findings from this study also raised a concern for us. Without significant parental and taxpayer support for class size reduction, the next recession could result in returns to larger groupings of students. Whereas the parents in this study were supportive of class size reductions and noted changes in their child's education as a result, there were questions about priorities. And whereas we should not have to pit computers and instructional materials against class size, the realities are such that many states and districts must make these decisions. We caution policy-makers to ensure that parents and community members are educated about the benefits of class size should fiscal resources diminish.

References

Allen, A., Brannon, P., & Sims, L. (1999). Class size influences on student performance, attitudes, and behavior: How big is too big? *MAHE Journal, 22,* 28–47.

Baumann, J. F., Hoffman, J. V., Duffy-Hester, A. M., & Ro, J. M. (2000). The first r yesterday and today: U.S. elementary reading instruction practices reported by teachers and administrators. *Reading Research Quarterly, 35,* 338–377.

Betts, J. R., & Shkolnik, J. L. (1999). The behavioral effects of variations in class size: The case of math teachers. *Educational Evaluation and Policy Analysis, 21,* 193–213.

Black, S. (1999). Less is more. *American School Board Journal, 186*(2), 38–41.

Bogdan, R. C., & Biklen, S. K. (1992). *Qualitative research for education* (2nd ed.). Needham Heights, MA: Allyn & Bacon.

Boyd-Zaharias, J. (1999). Project STAR: The story of the Tennessee class-size study. *American Educator, 23*(2), 30–36.

Chollet, P. (1998). From boardroom to classroom. *American School Board Journal, 185*(9), 42–43.

Educational Research Service. (1980). *Class size research: A critique of recent meta-analysis.* Arlington, VA: Author.

Finn, J. D., & Achilles, C. M. (1990). Answers and questions about class size: A statewide experiment. *American Educational Research Journal, 27,* 557–577.

Hanushek, E. A. (1999). Some findings from an independent investigation of the Tennessee STAR experiment and from other investigations of class size effects. *Educational Evaluation and Policy Analysis, 21,* 143–163.

Lapp, D., Flood, J., Fisher, D., Geiss, R., Goss, K., LeTourneau, M. (1999). First grade teachers' reflections of reduced class size. *California Reader, 32*(2), 26–27.

LeCompte, M. D., & Preissle, J. (1993). *Ethnography and qualitative design in educational research* (2nd ed.). San Diego, CA: Academic.

McRobbie, J. (1996). *Focus on California's class-size reduction: Smaller classes aim to launch early literacy.* San Francisco: WestEd.

Milken Exchange on Education Technology. (1998). *Preparing our young people for a changing world: Policymakers, business leaders and the public speak out on the role of education technology in America's classrooms.* Los Angeles: Milken Family Foundation National Education Conference.

Moir, E., & Gless, J. (2001). Quality induction: An investment in teachers. *Teacher Education Quarterly, 28*(1), 109–114.

Nye, B., Hedges, L. V., & Konstantopoulos, S. (2000). The effects of small classes on academic achievement: The results of the Tennessee class size experiment. *American Educational Research Journal, 37,* 123–151.

Nyhan, R. C., & Alkadry, M. G. (1999). The impact of school resources on student achievement test scores. *Journal of Education Finance, 25,* 211–228.

Odden, A. (1990). Class size and student achievement: Research-based policy alternatives. *Educational Evaluation and Policy Analysis, 12,* 213–227.

Rivera-Batiz, F. L., & Marti, L. (1995). *A school system at risk: A study of the consequences of overcrowding in New York City Public Schools* (Institute for Urban and Minority Education Research Report No. 95-1). New York: Columbia University.

Slavin, R. E., & Madden, N. A. (1987). *Effective classroom programs for students at risk* (Report No. 19). Baltimore: MD: Johns Hopkins University, Center for Research on Elementary and Middle Schools.

Stasz, C., & Stecher, B. M. (2000). Teaching mathematics and language arts in reduced size and non-reduced size classrooms. *Educational Evaluation and Policy Analysis, 22,* 313–329.

Zahorik, J. A. (1999). Reducing class size leads to individualized instruction. *Educational Leadership, 57*(1), 50–53.

Teaching as Persuasion: Approaching Classroom Discourse as Refutational Text

Helenrose Fives, Patricia A. Alexander, and Michelle M. Buehl
University of Maryland

What is it teachers actually do? One obvious response to this probe is "teach." But what does "to teach" actually mean? Is teaching a process of knowledge transmission, opportunities for knowledge construction, scaffolding, or a combination of such roles? What is the goal of the teaching enterprise? These are questions with which we have been grappling of late. In response to this reflection, we and others have forwarded a new metaphor for teaching—teaching as a persuasive process—that varies from transmission, scaffolding, or constructive models (Alexander, Fives, Buehl, & Mulhern, 2000; Murphy, 1998). The persuasive metaphor, which holds written and verbal discourse at its heart, challenges the notions of teacher as dispenser of knowledge or as creator of learning environments and probes the motivations behind teachers' actions in classrooms. It suggests that a fundamental goal of teaching is to change students' thinking and explore their beliefs with regard to topics under study (Fives & Alexander, in press). As method, it seeks to transform the traditional classroom lesson into a form of refutational text by presenting two-sides of an argument or two views of an issue and then specifically refuting one of these two views (Hynd, 1999). For this study, the refutational text dealt with moral reasoning.

Theoretical Framework

Persuasion, as discussed in the psychological literature, is not focused on manipulating individuals' beliefs (Cooper, 1932). Rather, the focus is on "convincing individuals to look more deeply at some concept or subject" (Alexander et al., 2000). Within this framework, reason and emotion are used to bring about change in another's behaviors, judgments, or understandings (Murphy, 1998). When such changes occur, the individual is said to be persuaded (Miller, 1980). Thus, in classrooms, as teachers employ various strategies and techniques to educate students, to promote their mental processing, and to stimulate their construction of understandings, teachers are utilizing principles of persuasion. For example, when a teacher begins to teach his or her class that the world is round, the intent is for students to understand, accept the premise, and hopefully become interested in the idea. When queried, many young children will state that "yes the world is round" but will, when probed, reveal that they do not necessarily believe this to be true (Vosniadou, 1994). Similarly, when taught about the Law of Falling

National Reading Conference Yearbook, 50, pp. 200–212.

Objects, teachers want their students not only to learn the law but to accept it as accurate (Hynd, 1998). Yet, this could not be achieved until students truly question their existing beliefs or naive conceptions.

Premises of Teaching as Persuasion

Four premises rooted in the nature of teacher-student interactions frame teaching as persuasion. First, teaching as persuasion recognizes that all learners, individually and socially, form unique interpretations of what they see or hear (Chambliss, 1995; Dole & Sinatra, 1998). Thus, each student in a classroom will form his or her own interpretations of the message, unique from the conceptions of the messenger or from others.

Second, the persuasive metaphor assumes that students' knowledge, interests, and beliefs may only be weakly influenced by compelling evidence (Chinn & Brewer, 1993; Vosniadou, 1994). Changing knowledge, interest, and beliefs is a difficult challenge. Often, individuals do not want to enter into the change process or their beliefs are so intertwined with how they view the world that changing them is not always a possibility.

Third, teaching as persuasion presumes that the quality of the message is a significant determiner of whether or how individuals are persuaded (Guzzetti & Hynd, 1998; Murphy, 1998). Specifically, individuals are more likely to be persuaded when the message is perceived to be authoritative and believable, utilizes logical arguments, provides ample evidence, and makes appropriate appeals to emotion and personal experiences (Chambliss, 1995; Guzzetti & Hynd, 1998; Murphy, 1998).

Finally, the persuasive model calls on teachers to become active in the process of their students' learning through the creation of lesson activities, selection of materials, modeling of strategies, and the provision of clear explanations that resonate with the students, unearths their existing base of knowledge and belief, and challenges their ideas. Lesson planning and class activities should promote social and individual reflection on arguments or evidence underlying a topic (Hynd, Alvermann, & Qian, 1997). Moreover, teachers should utilize quality refutational texts as effective tools to present alternative perspectives and counter arguments, which enhance discussion and challenge students' naive conceptions (Hynd, 1998).

Teachers should also model reflective and analytic techniques for students, since such abilities cannot be taken for granted (Chambliss, 1995). Additionally, teachers should employ sourcing techniques to increase intertextual examination and questioning of authors' positions as a means of fostering deep reflection of underlying concepts (VanSledright, 1998; VanSledright & Frankes, 1998). Specifically, sourcing techniques involve a search for site information (e.g., author or publishing organization), an identification of author's purpose, and an analysis of author/editorial bias in the work. Thus, these techniques are useful in ascertaining the credibility of the author, the validity of the information presented, and the perspectives from which explanations or interpretations of events arise. Finally, teachers should show their students that there are multiple sources of credible information to be found. The teacher and textbooks are only two of such sources (Chambliss, 1995).

Research Questions

The purpose of this research was to investigate the role of persuasion in the classroom. A recent study by Alexander and colleagues (2000) demonstrated that a lesson structured on the principles of persuasion had significant effects on middle-school students' knowledge, level of interest, and beliefs related to the domain of science. The present study extends this line of inquiry by investigating the potential effects of the persuasive teaching metaphor on undergraduate students studying moral reasoning. Undergraduate students come to the learning environment with substantial background knowledge, prior experiences, areas of interests, and deeply held beliefs. Thus, these students may be more adept than middle school students at engaging in discussions, argumentation, and written discourse. On the other hand, the beliefs held by these students, given their age and experience, may be more thoroughly entrenched than those of younger students.

We approached this research with three questions. First, we sought to discern if undergraduate students exhibit changes in their knowledge, interests, and beliefs with regard to the topic of moral reasoning following a persuasive lesson. Second, we asked whether students taught via a persuasive lesson manifest different levels of knowledge, interest, or beliefs from students taught in more traditional ways. Finally, we explored whether students react differently to lessons presented in persuasive rather than in traditional ways. Specifically, we wanted to determine whether students' reactions to the lesson differed as a result of presentation mode with respect to their levels of belief, interest, and/or understanding.

Method

Participants

Ninety students enrolled in four undergraduate human development courses at a large, land grant university in the mid-Atlantic region of the United States participated in this study. Eighty percent were female, a gender pattern common for these courses. The participants represented a variety of ethnic backgrounds. Specifically, 67% were European-American, 19% African-American, 7% Asian, 4% Hispanic, 2% Native American, and 1% Other.

The students represented a variety of academic majors and had varying amounts of exposure to the field of human development in general. Moral reasoning, which served as the content of the persuasive lesson, was a topic in the curriculum for all classes. Students received extra course credit for participating in this research. This study required that students be present for two consecutive class periods to be included in the final analysis. From the three classes, 20 students missed one or both of those class periods, and their data were thereby excluded. Based on instructor information, these 20 students did not differ markedly in general ability, gender, or ethnicity for the 90 students present for the two class periods.

Conditions and Procedures

We established three conditions for the students participating in the study. For the first condition, persuasion-regular instructor (P-RI), students (n=29) received the persuasive lesson from their current instructor, the first author. Students (n=31) in the second condition, persuasion-guest instructor (P-GI), received the persuasive lesson from the first author who was a guest speaker in the class. The third condition, control-regular instructor (C-RI), consisted of 30 students from two classes taught by their regular instructors.

To ensure that these conditions were comparable at pre-lesson, we assessed students' pre-lesson levels of knowledge, interest, and beliefs by condition (i.e., P-RI, P-GI, and C-RI). Specifically, a MANOVA was conducted on the pre-lesson data. The pre-lesson measures described in the subsequent section were the dependent variables. No significant differences existed by teacher condition [$F(10, 1666)=1.736, p=.077$].

Students in the C-RI classes received a lesson on moral reasoning from their current instructors, who used their normal pedagogical styles. The first author observed in these classes during lesson delivery. Both instructors utilized a traditional lecture format; the instructor was the center of attention in the class and the dispenser of information. The content, verbally presented, paralleled the course texts (Beck, 1999; Sigelman, 1999). First, the work of Piaget was discussed, and then Kohlberg's additions and changes were added. This presentation was followed by a criticism of Kohlberg's theory as framed by Carol Gilligan. The lecture ended with a criticism of Gilligan's work. Throughout these lessons the instructors asked questions of the class but maintained control of the content through lecturing.

Measures

Five measures were used to assess students' knowledge, interest, and beliefs with regard to moral reasoning. Four of these measures were administered the class period before the lesson was given. These measures were re-administered immediately after the lesson, along with the lesson reaction measure.

Demonstrated knowledge. The demonstrated knowledge measure was used to assess student levels of knowledge pertaining to moral reasoning at pre- and post-lesson. This measure consisted of two parts, an open-ended component and an objective component. The open-ended component consisted of five items addressing Lawrence Kohlberg, Carol Gilligan, moral development, moral reasoning, and diversity. Students were asked to "jot down words, phrases, and sentences that show what you know about each of these terms."

We scored this component using a 4-point rubric applied in other studies. This rubric focuses on the accuracy and quantity of the information given (e.g., Murphy & Alexander, 2000). A response earned a zero if no correct information was provided and a 1 if a response contained limited (i.e., less than 3 ideas) information that was only partially correct. Similarly, a score of 2 was awarded responses with limited but fully correct information, and a 3 was given for more elaborate (i.e., 3 or more ideas) partially correct responses. Finally, a response was rated a 4 if the information was both elaborate and fully correct. Thus, the maximum score for this portion of the demonstrated knowledge test was 20 points.

The following are examples of responses to the item "Carol Gilligan" that received scores of 1 and 4, respectively:

> Challenged Kohlberg; No research has supported claim yet. (Score=1)
>
> Criticized Kohlberg for being gender biased, did her own research, said women have a morality of caring, men of justice. (Score=4)

Two of the co-authors were trained to use the scoring rubric. After training, they jointly scored 12% of all student responses. The interrater agreement (i.e., proportion of correct responses over the total responses) was .96. For those items with disagreements, the rating was discussed. The two raters scored the remainder of the open-ended questions independently.

The second part of the demonstrated knowledge measure was an objective component. This component contained seven multiple-choice items and six matching items, for a maximum score of 13 points. These items assessed students' levels of knowledge about moral development, such as Kohlberg's stages and the meaning of morality. As seen in the example below, each multiple-choice item had four response options, with correct responses scored as 1 and incorrect responses scored as 0:

> All of the following are considered to be a basic component of morality *except:* (a) an affective component, *(b) a social component, (c) a cognitive component, and (d) a behavioral component.

The matching section consisted of six quotations from U.S. congressional debates on a resolution supporting the administration's policy on Iraq's invasion of Kuwait (Shapiro, 1995). Students were asked to "Read the quotations and indicate the stage of Kohlberg's theory demonstrated." Each correctly identified quotation was rated 1 and incorrect responses earned a score of 0:

> *Arguments against U.S. Involvement: "We shouldn't consider war . . ."*
> "Because we don't want to appear too militaristic . . ."
> Answer: "good boy" or "good girl" morality (Stage 3)

The entire demonstrated knowledge measure, both open-ended and objective components, had a Cronbach's alpha of .37 at pre-lesson and .54 at post-lesson. This low pre-lesson coefficient was indicative of student's relative lack of explicit knowledge about moral development.

Perceived knowledge. We also included a measure of perceived knowledge. That is, we asked students to rate how much they felt they knew about the content of the lesson. The items were identical to the statements used in the open-ended section of the demonstrated knowledge component. For these five items, students were asked to "... indicate how much you think you know by placing an X on the appropriate point on the line." Students' rated their knowledge level on a 10-segment scale running from *relatively nothing to a great deal* (see Figure 1). The Cronbach's alpha for the perceived knowledge measure was .76 at pre-lesson and .65 at post-lesson (maximum score=50).

Interest. A self-report measure of interest was also administered. Students again used a 10-segment scale, ranging from *not very interested* to *very interested.* We asked students to respond to the five statements used in the open-ended demonstrated knowledge component and the perceived knowledge measure. The Cronbach's alphas for this test (maximum score=50) was .82 and .84 at pre- and post-lesson, respectively.

Beliefs. To unearth students' beliefs, we administered an eight-item belief measure. This 10-segment scale ranged from *strongly disagree* to *strongly agree,* and required students to rate their stance with regard to statements related to issues about moral reasoning. These statements explored students' views about diversity of moral reasoning (i.e., "Moral reasoning is different for males and females." and "Different cultures have different bases for moral reasoning."), its nature (i.e., "Moral reasoning is not the same as morality."), its importance (i.e., "It is important to recognized the moral reasoning behind decisions."), its form (i.e., "There are clear and distinct stages of moral reasoning."), and its manifestation (i.e., "Individuals who demonstrate higher levels of moral reasoning make decisions that are distinctly different from individuals who reason at lower levels."). Negative items were reverse scored. This measure had a maximum score of 80.

Lesson reactions. Our final measure assessed students' response to the lessons presented them. Our objective was to determine whether students' responses were associated with the teaching condition they received. Thus, the six-item measure asked students to rate the lesson in terms of whether a balanced perspective was offered, if the information presented was believable, whether the lesson was easy to understand, if the student was emotionally moved during the lesson, if the student found the lesson to be interesting, and the degree to which the

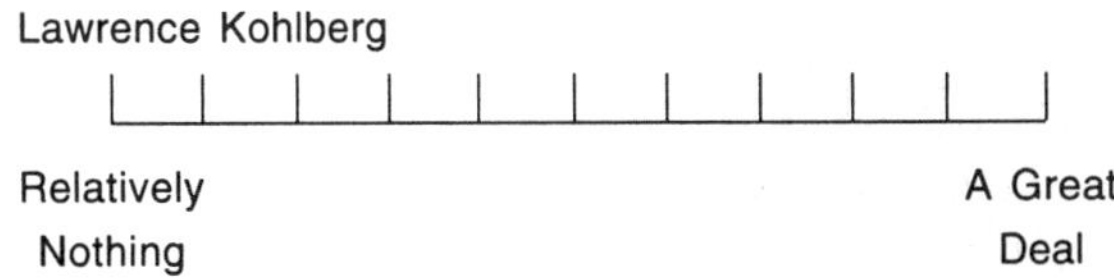

Figure 1

materials were helpful and informative. Students rated these items using a 10-segment scale that ran from *strongly disagree* to *strongly agree.* The Cronbach's alpha for this measure was .76 (maximum score=60).

Persuasive Activities

All students in the study received a lesson on moral reasoning during the next class following their completion of the initial knowledge, interest, and beliefs measures. The first author (hereafter referred to as the instructor) conducted the lesson for the persuasion-regular instructor (P-RI) and persuasion-guest instructor (P-GI) conditions. The lesson took place during one 75-minute class session and was conducted during the first 60 minutes of class. The length of the lesson was dictated by the time allotted to this topic in the course curricula. The post-lesson measures were completed during the final 15 minutes of the class session. The lesson centered on the meaning of moral reasoning and how it has been studied in the research literature. The goal of the persuasive lesson was to present the information in a manner consistent with refutational text, or debate, in which multiple explanations were offered, refuted, and restated.

The lesson opened with a class brainstorming activity, directed by the instructor, in which students responded to the question "Morality, what is it?" Student responses were recorded on an overhead sheet and these comments were used to segue to the identification of the three generally agreed upon components of morality (affective, cognitive, and behavioral). Students were then introduced to Piaget and Kohlberg's theories of moral reasoning. These theories were outlined and explained in terms of where these theorists started, how they researched their theories, and the findings of their research. Specific attention was place on Kohlberg's stage theory and the meaning of each of the stages of moral reasoning that he identified.

Students were then given an opportunity to apply Kohlberg's stages. The students' were divided into groups of three or four, and each group was given a children's book that features several characters. The students were asked to identify the main characters, assess their stage of moral development, and provide evidence from the story to substantiate their determination. Following this activity, the students as a large group discussed the difficulty in assigning stages of moral reasoning using Kohlberg's scale. At this time other criticisms and problems with Kohlberg's theory were brought up and discussed.

The class was then introduced to the work of Carol Gilligan, including her criticisms of Kohlberg's theory, and the development of her stage theory of moral reasoning. Students were also presented with a description of Gilligan's research techniques and the findings of her work. The work of Gilligan was then opened to criticism. The resulting class discussion criticizing the work of Gilligan was directed by the instructor toward a reassessment of Kohlberg's research techniques and findings. At this point, some of the criticisms of Kohlberg's theory generated by Gilligan were addressed. Thus, Kohlberg's theory was, in a sense, able to refute the criticisms raised earlier in the class.

The class was then asked to identify the difference between moral reasoning and moral development. Specifically, students were given an opportunity to delineate the distinction between morality and the decision-making processes of moral reasoning. Students discussed the distinction between societal standards or "moral action" and moral reasoning, the decision-making process. The class ended with a few final issues raised to the class for future discussion and reflection. Students were asked, "What is the real difference? Do men and women think differently? Do people of different cultures and backgrounds have different cognitive abilities? Or, is it a matter of value and interpretation?"

Results and Discussion

Pre-instruction to Post-instruction Differences

We first examined data to determine what, if any, changes occurred in students' knowledge, interest, and beliefs across all conditions following instruction. Towards this end, we performed a repeated measure MANOVA, with time (pretest and posttest) as the repeated measure, and perceived knowledge, demonstrated knowledge (objective and open-ended), interest, and beliefs as the dependent variables. The MANOVA was statistically significant for time [$F(5, 85)=122.67$, $p<.001$]. Univariate analyses revealed significant changes in perceived knowledge, demonstrated knowledge, beliefs, and interest [$Fs(1, 89)\geq18.01$, $ps<.001$, $MSes<24.48$] as a result of participating in the lessons.

Condition Comparisons

Using the post-lesson data, we compared student responses across the three teacher conditions. We conducted a MANOVA by condition with demonstrated knowledge (objective and open-ended), perceived knowledge, interest, and beliefs as the dependent variables. Significant group effects were found at the multivariate level [$F(10, 166)=5.16$, $p<.001$]. Specifically, group differences were identified for objective demonstrated knowledge [$F(2, 87)=14.64, p<.001, MSe=4.51$] and beliefs [$F(2, 87)=3.89, p<.05, MSe=55.53$].

Students in the P-GI group demonstrated significantly higher levels of demonstrated objective knowledge ($M=8.84$; $SD=1.61$) than students in the P-RI ($M=7.52$; $SD=2.69$) or in the control (C-RI) classes, ($M=5.90$; $SD=1.45$). Students in the P-RI condition also scored significantly higher on the objective component of the demonstrated knowledge measure than students in the control condition at posttest. This pattern suggests that the persuasive lessons provided students with an opportunity to develop a greater knowledge base with regard to moral reasoning than did the control conditions.

However, students who received the persuasive lesson from a guest instructor (P-GI) demonstrated stronger beliefs at post-lesson (*M*=54.97; *SD*=8.78) than students in the persuasive-regular instructor (P-RI) class (*M*=99.67; *SD*=6.45; see Table 1). This suggests that the novelty/familiarity of the instructor may have an affect on the persuasiveness of a lesson.

Lesson Reactions

Lastly, we investigated the relationship between lesson reactions and instructional condition. When we conducted a MANOVA by teacher condition for the individual lesson reaction items (see Table 2), there were significant group difference [$F(12, 16)=2.74, p<.01$]. Univariates indicated a significant main effect

Table 1

Pre-lesson and Post-lesson Means (and Standard Deviations) for Total, Objective, and Open-ended Demonstrated Knowledge, Perceived Knowledge, Interest, Beliefs, and Lesson Reactions

	Condition: Pre-Lesson			Condition: Post-Lesson		
	P-RI (*n*=29) *M* (*SD*)	P-GI (*n*=31) *M* (*SD*)	C-RI (*n*=30) *M* (*SD*)	P-RI (*n*=29) *M* (*SD*)	P-GI (*n*=31) *M* (*SD*)	C-RI (*n*=30) *M* (*SD*)
Variable						
Demonstrated Knowledge (max=33)						
	12.17 (4.27)	12.25 (3.73)	11.20 (4.41)	21.07 (4.61)	21.81 (3.49)	20.20 (4.44)
Objective (max=13)						
	3.48 (1.18)	4.26 (1.83)	4.37 (2.41)	7.52_b (2.69)	8.84_a (1.61)	5.90_c** (1.95)
Open-ended (max=20)						
	8.70 (3.86)	7.97 (3.48)	6.83 (3.01)	13.55 (3.31)	12.97 (3.21)	14.30 (3.25)
Perceived Knowledge (max=50)						
	20.69 (5.51)	17.97 (5.90)	20.30 (5.25)	32.31 (5.89)	35.23 (6.05)	34.80 (6.94)
Interest (max=50)						
	24.45 (8.03)	23.71 (8.00)	26.03 (9.68)	34.00 (7.90)	32.74 (8.70)	36.03 (7.44)
Beliefs (max=80)						
	48.12 (6.02)	49.84 (6.07)	49.17 (6.70)	49.67_b (6.45)	54.97_a (8.78)	52.13* (6.83)
Lesson Reactions (max=60)						
	—	—	—	43.83 (7.55)	45.61 (7.94)	42.53 (7.19)

Note. Subscripts indicate significant differences.
*$p<.05$. **$p<.001$.

Table 2

Means (and Standard Deviations) for Lesson Reaction Items by Condition

	Condition		
	P-RI (n=29) M (SD)	P-GI (n=31) M (SD)	C-RI (n=30) M (SD)
1. The lesson presented a balanced perspective on the topic.	7.59 (2.11)	8.58 (1.41)	8.00 (1.73)
2. I found the information believable.	7.79 (1.78)	8.52 (1.31)	8.30 (1.64)
3. The lesson was easy to understand.	8.66 (1.59)	8.77 (1.69)	8.77 (1.33)
4. I was moved, emotionally during the lesson.	3.55 (2.13)	4.13 (2.29)	3.88 (2.27)
5. The lesson was interesting.	7.97 (1.57)	7.58 (2.09)	7.62 (1.93)
6. The materials used were helpful and informative.	8.28 $(1.60)_a$	8.03 $(1.66)_a$	6.40 $(2.07)_b$*

Note. Subscripts indicate significant differences.
*p<.001.

for item 6: "The materials used were helpful and informative" [F(2, 87)=31.07, p<.001, MSe=3.68]. Students in both persuasive groups responded significantly higher to this item (M=8.28, SD=1.60 and M=8.03, SD=1.66, respectively) than students in the control classes (M=6.40, SD=2.07).

Conclusions and Implications

In this study, we explored the effectiveness of a teaching as persuasion metaphor (Alexander et al., 2000; Murphy, 1998). Our findings demonstrate that this metaphor is applicable to undergraduate students, specifically with regard to changes in their beliefs and demonstrated knowledge. However, several limitations of this work should be noted. First, due to the time allotted to this content in the curriculum, we were only able to devote 60 minutes to the topic. Thus, presenting a large amount of information and providing ample time for discussion and reflection was a challenge. More time for interaction would have allowed greater opportunity for students to delve into the issues and to reflect on the challenges that emerging arguments presented to their current beliefs. Certainly a longer exposure to persuasive teaching would enable us to assess better the underlying assumptions of this approach and would therefore allow for even stronger outcomes than those reported here.

Second, we were not able to assess the long-term effects of the persuasive lesson. That is, we measured belief change only one time, immediately after the lesson was presented. It would be of interest to know whether or not these changes held and altered broader-based beliefs and moral reasoning. It is unrealistic to assume that we have done anymore in this investigation than explore the effects of persuasive teaching on deep-seated beliefs

A third limitation of the study that we must also acknowledge is that the presentation of moral development in textbooks and in the control classrooms is often cast as two-sided refutation. That is, this topic is commonly framed as a contrast between well-known theories. One argument or conception is explicated, usually Piaget and Kohlberg's work, then Gilligan's theory is offered as a counterpoint. This fact may have attenuated the effects we would expect for a persuasive teaching approach. Therefore, alternative topics should be investigated for use with persuasive teaching. Evidence suggests that the strength of a persuasive approach may best be revealed when this model is applied to less debated or seemingly less contentious topics (Alexander et al., 2000). Topics, like Galileo's verification of a helio-centric solar system, which are often taught as facts to be memorized, may be more interesting opportunities to explore persuasive effects.

Finally, this study suggests that the teacher-student relationship may have been an important consideration in determining the impact of persuasive teaching. Specifically, the students in the P-RI class may have been accustomed to the persuasive teaching approach generally used by their instructor. Further, the students in the guest instructor condition may have attributed particular expertise in the area of moral development to the guest instructor. Because multiple instructors taught the control and persuasive lessons, unique characteristics of the instructors (e.g., enthusiasm, knowledge of the topic, interest in the material) may have also influenced differences in the students' responses. Thus, in further work, within-classroom differences should also be examined.

Despite the limitations, the current research informs both the research and teaching communities on the implementation and effectiveness of teaching as persuasion. For one it offers additional support for this orientation to teaching. That is, we documented positive outcomes for our undergraduates studying moral reasoning via a persuasive approach, as we did for middle-school students studying Galileo and his scientific discoveries (Alexander et al., 2000). In both studies, students participating in lessons framed as persuasive discourse demonstrated significant increases in their knowledge, as well as changes in their beliefs, over students taught in more traditional ways.

However, these findings lead us to a new question: Is there a threshold level at which a persuasive teaching model is viable? There is reason to wonder whether this model would work successfully with elementary-age children. As this teaching approach relies heavily on students' ability to formulate and analyze verbal and written arguments related to their existing knowledge and established beliefs; this method may not be effective with young students.

Finally, this study demonstrates that persuasion can be used to create single lessons that impact students' beliefs and knowledge. Therefore, the expansion of the persuasive teaching model to entire units or course of study should also be explored. This expansion could take shape through the selection of materials, structure of the course or unit, and through continued use of persuasion to guide individual lessons. For example, instructors can formulate controversial questions and use these as the structure of the course. These key questions would focus class discourse and reflection on the materials. Lastly, the continued use of persuasive lessons across a semester may enable students to achieve deeper understandings of the content and enriched interest and beliefs.

Viewing teaching as persuasion provides us with a new approach to the craft of education. The strength of this metaphor rests in the questioning of central concepts and the consideration of multiple perspectives through oral and written discourse cast as refutational text. Through this approach, the classroom ceases to be either student or teacher centered; instead the communication between these parties around the content is the focus of the learning environment. Teachers are urged to select materials, activities, and assessments that promote student reflection, challenge existing beliefs, and increase student interest in the material. Additionally, students are expected to challenge the texts, investigate the evidence, assess the findings presented, engage in verbal and written discussion with their peers and teachers, and to develop their own beliefs based on a systematic study of the information. Thus, this approach equips students with the skills and strategies they need to succeed in and out of the classroom.

References

Alexander, P. A., Fives, H., Buehl, M. M., & Mulhern, J. (2000, April). *Teaching as persuasion: Case in point.* Paper presented at the meeting of the American Educational Research Association, New Orleans, LA.

Beck, L. A. (1999). *Infants and children: Prenatal through middle childhood* (3rd ed.). Needham Heights, MA: Allyn & Bacon.

Chambliss, M. J. (1995). Text cues and strategies successful readers use to construct the gist of lengthy written arguments. *Reading Research Quarterly, 30,* 778–807.

Chinn, C. A., & Brewer, W. F. (1993). The role of anomalous data in knowledge acquisition: A theoretical framework and implications for science instruction. *Review of Research, 63*(1), 1–49.

Cooper, L. (1932). *The rhetoric of Aristotle.* New York: Appleton-Century.

Dole, J. A., & Sinatra, G. M. (1998). Reconceptualizing change in cognitive construction of knowledge. *Educational Psychologist, 33,* 109–128.

Fives, H., & Alexander, P. A. (in press). Teaching as persuasion: Case in point. *Theory Into Practice.*

Guzzetti, B., & Hynd, C. (Eds.). (1998). *Theoretical perspectives on conceptual change: Multiple ways to understand knowing and learning in a complex world.* Mahwah, NJ: Erlbaum.

Hynd, C. (1998). Conceptual change in a high school physics class. In B. Guzzetti & C. Hynd (Eds.), *Theoretical perspectives on conceptual change: Multiple ways to understand knowing and learning in a complex world* (pp. 27–36). Mahwah, NJ: Erlbaum.

Hynd, C. R. (1999, April). *Refutational text and the change process.* Paper presented at the meeting of the American Educational Association, Montreal.

Hynd, C., Alvermann, D., & Qian, G. (1997). Preservice elementary school teachers' conceptual change about projectile motion: Refutation text, demonstration, affective factors, and relevance. *Science Education, 81,* 1–27.

Miller, G. R. (1980). On being persuaded: Some basic distinctions. In M. E. Roloff & G. R. Miller (Eds.), *Persuasion: New directions in theory and research* (pp. 11–28). Beverly Hills, CA: Sage.

Murphy, P. K. (1998). *Toward a multifaceted model of persuasion: Exploring textual and learner interactions.* Unpublished doctoral dissertation. University of Maryland, College Park.

Murphy, P. K., & Alexander, P. A. (2000). *Persuasion as a dynamic, multidimensional process: A viewfinder for individual and intraindividual differences.* Manuscript submitted for publication.

Shapiro, H. K. (1995). Dr. Kohlberg goes to Washington: Using congressional debates to teach moral development. *Teaching of Psychology, 22,* 245–247.

Sigelman, C. K. (1999). *Life-span human development* (3rd ed.). Pacific Grove, CA: Brooks/Cole.

VanSledright, B. A. (1998). On the importance of historical positionality to thinking about and teaching history. *International Journal of Social Education.*

VanSledright, B.A., & Frankes, L. (1998). Literature's place in learning history and science. In C. Hynd (Ed.), *Learning from text: Views across conceptual domains* (pp. 117–138). Hillsdale, NJ: Erlbaum.

Vosniadou, S. (1994). Capturing and modeling the process of conceptual change. *Learning and Instruction, 4,* 45–69.

Conversations Before Writing During Reading Recovery Lessons: Negotiation or Tug of War?

Susan King Fullerton and Diane E. DeFord
Ohio State University

Of the one-to-one interventions found to be effective in reducing the number of children failing to read and write (Adams, 1990; Allington & Walmsley, 1995), Reading Recovery is one of the most effective (Wasik & Slavin, 1993). But what happens within these one-to-one interactions that makes Reading Recovery effective? How do the interactions between teacher and student promote the development of literacy? What can we learn from these interactions to inform instruction in Reading Recovery and other one-to-one instructional settings?

This study is part of a larger investigation that responds to a need expressed in the literature (Pinnell, Lyons, DeFord, Bryk, & Seltzer, 1994; Wilkinson & Silliman, 2000) for more detailed analyses of teacher-student interactions, providing insights into what effective teachers do and say to teach the lowest achieving students how to read and write. Earlier research by DeFord (1994) and Hobsbaum, Peters, and Sylva (1996), as well as our pilot research, suggest that the writing portion of Reading Recovery lessons is quite rich in teacher-child interactions. Building upon these previous studies, we set out to learn more about the interactions during the initial conversation that leads to the written message.

Such instructional conversations are central to sociocultural and social constructivist theories of learning. Language is one of the primary tools used (Luria, 1979; Vygotsky, 1986) as learners interact with and construct knowledge (Bakhtin, 1986; Vygotsky, 1978), yet there is limited research that analyzes the language used by teachers in scaffolded instruction (Wilkinson & Silliman, 2000). Scaffolding refers to conversation and activity that support learning processes (Cazden, 1988; Clay & Cazden, 1990). Clay and Cazden (1990) suggest that Reading Recovery, an early intervention program for at-risk first graders, "as a whole is such a scaffold." In year-long training, teachers learn that each 30-minute lesson is situated and carried forth as a teaching-learning interaction. The teacher and child work in tandem, while the teacher, as the more knowledgeable other, scaffolds instruction (Rogoff, 1990; Wood, Bruner, & Ross, 1976). Based on observations of the child's needs and growth, instructional moves and careful teaching decisions support the development of a strategic, self-improving system in reading and writing, enabling the child to eventually perform within the average range and benefit from classroom instruction (Clay, 1993b.)

*National Reading Conference Yearbook, **50**, pp. 213–227.*

Within the writing portion of the lesson, the learner and teacher converse, negotiating a topic that provides ownership as well as powerful learning opportunities for the child. Students talk and think about topics that motivate them, drawing and building upon prior knowledge and experiences. Dyson's (1983, 1999) investigations of preschool and early school learners' writing has provided insights into the oral language processes that children use as they develop proficiency in written language. One characterization of this use of oral language is the way that young writers transcribe their oral messages into written language (Dyson, 1983) or what Britton, Burgess, Martin, McLeod, and Rosen (1975) characterized as "written down speech" (p. 11). Therefore, "talk, in its representational (and interactional) functions" (Dyson, 1983, p. 2) is the "recruiting area" (Britton, 1970, p. 29) for writing. Thus, this "talk written down" may serve as a starting point when conferring with emergent writers in classrooms and in Reading Recovery. Through scaffolded interactions with the teacher, the child comes to understand that they can generate a message and use what they know to represent their spoken message in written form. Yet, in Reading Recovery, there are aspects of the conversation that may differ from writing conferences as the teacher provides support during the construction of the message. Most children make the transition from verbal interactions into written interactions within the instructional context provided within classroom settings (DeFord, 1994). However, the children who come into Reading Recovery may not make this transition without a stronger scaffold. In the short time that the Reading Recovery teacher works with the child, she is helping to build reciprocal understandings across reading and writing. "Reading and writing are not separate in the child's learning, nor do they develop sequentially. Instead, the two processes are mutually supportive and are intimately related to oral language" (Sulzby & Teale, 1985).

Classroom research has shown that teachers conferring with emergent writers give attention to helping the child form a simple idea or message to write, knowing that the child will reread the message as part of an inner processing system (Clay, 2001; Sowers, 1985; Sulzby & Teale, 1985). In Reading Recovery, the teacher's assistance in helping the child reread and "remember" their message is essential. Clay (1982) suggests that "when the learner is a novice with only tentative strategies for responding correctly he needs more sources of error detection" (p. 209). Thus, early on in the program, the child's written message echoes the child's oral message. This enables the child to monitor the text since it is memorable and familiar (the child's oral language written down). Initially the message consists of one sentence, gradually two or three sentences, or the continuation of a message or "story" written over several sessions if the child chooses. Most children can only write their name or perhaps, at best two or three words when he or she enters the program. So teacher support is needed. For whatever reason, these students have not made literacy progress comparable to their peers. In order to support the child to achieve accelerated literacy growth, the teacher works alongside the child, helping to develop the notion that ideas and language can be represented in writing.

Language, text (oral and written), and the discourse patterns that characterize these literacy co-constructions between teacher and child influence and impact each other (Denzin, 1978). The teacher's role is essential. The child appropriates the language of the more knowledgeable other at first, and eventually uses this language internally. This enables the child to "plan, guide and monitor his behavior from within and flexibly according to changing circumstances" (Diaz, Neal, & Amaya-Williams, 1990, p. 130). The teacher carefully observes the child to determine how knowledge of language is changing. Thus, over time, the child's knowledge of oral and written language begins to correspond to the teacher's language. With appropriate levels of scaffolding the teacher guides the child toward independence. With additional competency, the scaffolding decreases, and by the end of a child's program, the child is facile in representing their ideas in more complex ways as they write. The child no longer needs the teacher to scaffold and prompt to use what he or she knows; the child's strategies are self-extending.

A case study design (Merriam, 1998; Stake, 1995) was used to examine student and teacher interactions before writing. The case studies of two experienced Reading Recovery teachers and their students provided a frame in which to examine socially shared cognition (Damon, 1991). We felt this would offer ways to better understand the nature of complex interactions that influence student growth in writing. The questions that guided our study were: (a) What is the nature of the interactions between the teacher and child before writing? (b) How do the interactions change in relation to the child's writing development?

Method

Participants

Two effective Reading Recovery teachers and one student (per teacher) from a large urban school district participated in this study. Each teacher was deemed effective based upon the recommendation of the school district's teacher leader. Consequently, these teachers were more likely to have a second round of children complete a full program in Reading Recovery. The first participant, Stella, was a veteran Reading Recovery teacher, having had more than 10 years of experience in this role. Stella worked half the day in Reading Recovery and during the remainder of the day, she worked as a resource teacher, teaching small groups of children. The second participant, Nancy, had been trained as a Reading Recovery teacher the previous year, so the year of the study was her field year in Reading Recovery. Nancy was a first-grade teacher during the other portion of her day. Nancy and Stella worked in the same elementary school. Both teachers and their students were Caucasian. The two students, Marcy and Jan, were considered at risk at the beginning of the year but were not selected for Reading Recovery until midyear; they were, in Reading Recovery terms, "second round" students.

Data Collection

Samples were collected for each case study separately using the dimension of people, context, and time (Hammerly & Atkinson, 1983). The first dimension is the teacher-and-child dyad, with each teacher and her respective student representing a case (Stella with Jan, Nancy with Marcy). We focused on the conversations between each teacher and child before writing within daily lessons in Reading Recovery. The focus for this analysis was the interactions and discourse structures co-created during the negotiation of the written message. In the majority of lessons, once the sentence is negotiated, it remains the same throughout the process of getting the message on paper. The teacher serves to "remind" the child about the intended sentence until he or she can take over that function. The dimension of time spans the entire period of the child's work in Reading Recovery but differs for each of the students. Stella's student, Jan, was reading within the average range of her peers in 10 weeks. Nancy's student, Marcy, did so in 16 weeks.

A collective case study (Stake, 1995) was conducted after the analysis of each case. This preliminary study is part of a larger, long-term research effort to study teacher-child interactions during Reading Recovery lessons using a series of case studies. Multiple data-collection methods included audiotaping and subsequent transcription, interviewing, and document analysis. Data collection began during the first week of lessons within each child's program and continued until the program ended.

Lesson audiotaping. Audiotaping of each lesson began on the first day's lesson and continued until program completion. Audiotapes were transcribed for 5 consecutive days of lessons at three points: beginning, mid-point, and end of the program. Although 15 lessons were transcribed for each case, only 12 lessons of Stella and Jan's lessons included writing, so only these 12 were analyzed, as compared to 15 for Nancy and her student, Marcy.

Interviewing. Teacher interviews and child interviews were conducted at the beginning and end of the program; interviews were not transcribed.

Artifact/Document analysis. All Reading Recovery records were collected and photocopied for each of the teachers and students. These records included information about books read, teacher's notes on writing, the final written products of students, and teacher's lesson plans/records. The student's daily writing work was photocopied, and the child's entry and exit tests and scores of *The Observation Survey* (Clay, 1993a) were also collected.

Data Analysis

During the first cycle of analysis, tentative themes, patterns, and categories were generated (Patton, 1990) using all data sources. After each collection cycle (program beginning, mid-point, and end), the process of uncovering themes and patterns and establishing categories was continued. Discourse analysis was conducted at both a "micro" and "macro" level (Riggenbach, 1999). Analysis at a micro level involved coding each move (the first and subsequent language utterances by either the child or teacher). The codes indicated who was speaking, the type of response (such as a question) and the function or purpose of the response. The most common moves/responses were categorized and are presented in Table 1, along with examples from the lessons.

Table 1

Categories of Teacher-Child Talk

Teacher initiates an idea (TI) "So, we can write about your Mom getting a new car today."	*Teacher prompts the child to initiate* (TPI) "Tell me about . . ."
Teacher questions to help child initiate an idea (TQI) "Okay, how are we going to start this story?"	*Teacher initiates an expansion* (TIX) [Teacher repeats child's statement: I am going to be in a program.] "Oh, you'll get to sing on that stage. That will be so much fun."
Teacher questions to help child expand (TIX) "Okay, what would you say about Caitlin?"	*Teacher paraphrases story* (TPar) [Child stated: "My grandma rode in it and she picked us up. . . ."] "My grandma took me to school in it today."
Teacher repeats story (or idea thus far) (TRe) [Child says, "We went to see giraffes, zebras, ducks."] "Okay, we went . . ."	*Teacher accepts expansion* (TAX) Child states: "And she had high heels on too."] "Okay, and she had high heels on too."
Teacher clarifies story (TCS) or *Teacher questions for clarification* (TQC) "Let me make sure I've got all this. I played for one hour. . . ." "Is that what you want to write in your story today . . . I heard you say, I went to listen to my Backstreet Boys CD."	*Teacher redirects idea or topic* (TRT) [Initially they had discussed the child's ponytails, but then the teacher shifted the topic.] "How'd you like the concert this morning? Would you like to play any of those instruments or sing in the choir?"
Teacher limits expansion (TLX) "Well, we already wrote about going to the zoo on the bus."	*Child initiates an idea* (CI) "I have a loose tooth, and I'm trying to pull it out."
Child initiates an expansion (CIX) "And then I went to sleep."	*Child redirects idea or topic* (CRT) "New story."

At a macro level, the moves/responses (discussed above) were considered as a unit or a cycle of interaction. Each cycle of interaction was delineated by topic initiation and expansion focusing on a single idea. In some lessons, only one topic was initiated and subsequently accepted within the conversational exchanges. This resulted in only one interaction cycle. However, it was also possible for more than one interaction cycle to occur. For example, an initial topic could be suggested by the teacher or child and be coded as the first interaction cycle. The topic (and conversation) might then be redirected by either of the participants, resulting in a second interaction cycle. Again, these interactions were examined. Additionally, for each cycle, the person initiating the topic and redirecting the topic or focus of the conversation and the number of moves was determined.

Findings

The Nature of Interactions

We began our analysis by coding the responses of each teacher and child (a micro-level analysis) within each case. Eventually, as we stepped back from the data and viewed it from a different perspective (a macro-level analysis), we gained several critical insights. The importance of looking at the data from a "wide angle lens" was valued even more when we looked across both cases and compared them. Therefore, we will discuss the findings at a macro level first, discussing the interactions within and across cases. We will then discuss individual teacher and child responses (micro level), in light of the previous findings related to interaction cycles.

Cycles of interaction in topic selection. The analysis and the first teacher interview indicated that Marcy, the student working with the less experienced teacher, Nancy, responded in a more passive manner. The teacher indicated that encouragement and stronger scaffolding was needed in early lessons to support her writing. Thus, in early lessons, the teacher made approximately two thirds of the conversational moves. Gradually, as the teacher and child worked together, the child began to take a more active role. The following is an example of how Nancy, the teacher (T) accepted Marcy, the child's (C) topic, then supported her through questioning, paraphrasing, or repeating the child's response:

T: Did you like the kids that were singing . . .
C: I saw Mrs. K. She was pretty.
T: Yeah. Uh-Hmmm.
C: That's what I want to write.
T: You want to write about Mrs. K being pretty? And can we say what she was doing?
C: She was moving her hips like this.
T: She *was* moving her hips wasn't she? When she was getting the kids ready to sing. Okay, so what would you like to say? Mrs. K . . .
C: shook her hips.

T: Mrs. K shook her hips. Okay.
C: And she was pretty.
T: And she was pretty. At the program?
C: Umm-hmm.
T: Okay.
C: She had high heels on too.
T: Whoa! Mrs. K shook her hips . . .

This example is representative of the interactions of this teacher and child. There was an equal level of teacher and child talk across the lessons. From the beginning, Nancy's interactions with Marcy suggested a less directive stance, one of negotiation. Within almost all lessons, Nancy supported the initiation of the topic by referring back to the previous day's topic. The child accepted the initial teacher suggested topic in 6 of 8 such lessons (75% of the 8 lessons, 40% of the total 15). The average number of moves within these 6 lessons was 8.5. Similarly, in the first 4 lessons analyzed, the story was generated in 8, 6, 9, and 10 moves, respectively. In these cases there seemed to be a 50–50 teacher/child acceptance or renegotiation of topic. Within 9 of the lessons, however, there were multiple interaction cycles. In these lessons, when the child took a more active stance of redirecting or accepting the initiation or expansion of the topic (60% of the time for the 15 lessons analyzed), the number of topics discussed increased to two or three topics, increasing the number of moves to a mean of 14.1. Even when redirection occurred, or the number of moves increased, the overall pattern of interactions was one of collaboration. For example, in these instances, the teacher did not counter the child's suggestion; rather, she supported the child in refining or expanding the idea. As a result, the child's ability to focus on a topic and further develop or elaborate upon that topic was enhanced. In early lessons, Nancy questioned or initiated (by modeling) a possible topic based on the previous day's story, or the child made a comment, and the teacher began to scaffold by asking an initial question that built upon the child's response. The most common types of responses will be discussed within the next section.

The overall pattern of interactions with Nancy and Marcy was clearly different from the pattern that we found in the interactions of Stella, the veteran teacher, and Jan. We noted during interviews that Jan was a very talkative child who often needed to be reminded of the task at hand. In an interview, Stella indicated that she found it difficult at times to guide Jan, to help maintain a focus. Stella indicated that it was the same in the first-grade classroom. The concern about Jan's ability to attend and stay "focused" appeared to strongly impact their interactions. Even in instances when Jan was clearly engaged and becoming more capable and independent, Stella seemed to "micro-manage" the content of the stories and Jan's behavior. As a result, there was, at times, an underlying struggle for control of what would be written as indicated in the following lesson transcript:

T: Now yesterday,
T/C: we wrote a story about art!
T: Go ahead.
C: [reading previous day's story] Tuesday today [self-correction in reading]

I have art. I made a picture about flowers.

C: Today I would write about fishing [the child read the book *Father Bear Goes Fishing* earlier in the lesson].

T: You know yesterday when we wrote about this story, about your art thing, you wanted to write more about what you did with this picture about—

C: Give it to my mom!

T: Do you want to put that in today's story. Well, then how . . .

C: I gave it to my mom.

T: What did you give to your mom?

C: A gift.

T: Okay. I—

C: We could put gift in there.

T: We could. We could put the word gift in there. Okay, how are we gonna do that? I—

C: got

T: What'd you do with it? I—

C: got a picture for my mom. She liked it.

T: Okay, yesterday you wrote about making the picture and today we're gonna write about what you did.

C: And she liked it.

T: Okay, so let's think about this. You know, you keep talking but we've gotta get a story here. You took that picture with that flower home and today we're gonna write about what you did when you got it home. Let's think about this. What did you do? I—

C: I gave it to my mom and she liked it. You know what we could write next?

T: We're not thinking about tomorrow. Listen to what you said. I gave it to my mom. Now you said you wanted to use the word gift. Could we use it right here? I gave it to my mom.

C: For a gift.

T: Oh, that's marvelous. Let me get that down. I gave it to my mom for a gift. And then what did you say about how she felt about it?

C: She—

T: She—

C: liked it.

T: Okay.

C: She hanged it on the wall.

T: How nice! Okay.

In examining Stella and Jan's interactions, we found that within six of the writing lessons, the teacher established the topic, and it was accepted and responded to by the child. (The mean number of moves was 9.8). However, in the other six lessons analyzed, the interactions were characterized metaphorically as a "tug of war." Within these interactions, the number of moves substantially increased (mean=23.2), indicating a great deal more teacher talk to establish a topic. Within four of the lessons analyzed, the child was the one to initiate the topic; each time, the teacher contested the topic. In the other instances, (two of six), the teacher initiated and the child contested.

These "tug of war" interactions were a result of the teacher's attempts to redirect the topic to connect with the previous day's topic. Commonly, the child rejected this attempt. Even when the child initiated a topic, the teacher still attempted to focus on the previous day's idea, as in the example provided. Within these interactions, the teacher seemed unaware of or at least did not acknowledge, the child's attempt to connect the text just read, *Father Bear Goes Fishing,* to her own prior knowledge and experiences. Through the idea, "Today I would write about fishing," the child conveyed the ability to make text-to-text connections, a desirable goal that indicated the level of the learner's thinking and independence. Unfortunately, the teacher did not encourage such responses. Instead, in these instances, what resulted was a frame clash with the child perceived as hard to focus and the teacher's goals at odds with the child's responses, interests, and independence.

In contrast to the interactions of Nancy and Marcy, this "tug of war" limited the opportunity to initiate, refine, or even reject a topic for a more interesting or desirable one. Although we did not evaluate the quality and growth of writing in this study, such difficulty in selecting a topic potentially could limit the child's growth or independence in writing. Fortunately, near the end of the child's program, analysis of the interaction patterns suggested that Stella and Jan developed a more collaborative stance.

The number of moves/responses. At a more micro level of analysis, we quantified the number of conversational moves or responses made by each participant and categorized them by type. As might be predicted, the number of verbal moves was greater for the teachers than for the students. Because Stella chose not to include writing in three of the last 5 lessons, in this case, 12 lessons were analyzed. The mean number of teacher moves was 10.75 for Stella (within 12 lessons) as compared to 8.6 for Nancy (within 15 lessons). In terms of student talk, it is interesting to note that although Jan was characterized as talkative and active, and Marcy more passive, the amount of talk for the children was not very different. In 12 lessons, Jan's moves totaled 105 (mean=8.75 responses) compared to 93 moves for Marcy across 15 lessons (mean=6.2).

However, as the discussion in the previous section suggests, the amount of talk within each lesson varied a great deal. The number of teacher-and-child moves across the 12 lessons with Stella and Jan ranged from 3 to 38 (mean=12) as compared to a range of 3 to 39 (mean=14) in Nancy and Marcy's 15 lessons. Again, the amount of talk, or the number of moves, was not very different in the two dyads. Yet, quantifying the amount of talk does not adequately represent the nature of the talk and the scaffolding that were discussed in the previous section.

The type of moves/responses. The analysis of "moves" in this study characterized the speaker's purposes or intent indicating a variety of functions for the teacher or child's utterances: (a) initiating an idea or topic; (b) responding (through expression of interest or *backchanneling*—a way to indicate to the speaker that he or she maintains the "floor"; (c) redirecting the conversation; (d) questioning (for generation of an idea, for elaboration or expansion of an idea, for clarification); (e) repeating or "echoing" an idea; (f) paraphrasing an idea; (g) accepting an idea initiated or expanded.

The results discussed here focus on the categories that were most representative of the teacher or child's talk. As might be predicted, the most consistent category that came from the teachers was questioning. Questions functioned in different ways. They functioned to initiate a topic (from the child) in 14% of Stella's conversational overall moves as compared to 15.8% for Nancy. Questions also functioned to encourage the child to expand upon an idea or topic. This type of questioning represented 12% of both Stella and Nancy's talk. Only once was any type of question offered by either child, when Jan asked for clarification regarding the teacher's previous response. In relation to percentage of responses, the only category that emerged as frequently as questions was the repeating of the child's idea or topic. For both teachers, this response represented 12% of the moves. However, this repetition of the idea seemed to serve several purposes. Often the teacher served to *remember* the child's idea, supporting them as they wrote or as they expanded an idea. In such scaffolding, the teacher's language functioned as a *place-holder*. This helped the child hold their idea in memory, or allowed them to further expand upon their idea. Less frequently, the teacher seemed to repeat as a way to help the child clarify.

In many instances, we found that repetition functioned to show the teacher was listening, signaling acceptance of the composition. Other times, the teachers' language functioned similar to backchanneling (see Riggenbach, 1999). Examples include comments such as "yeah," "okay," and "uh-hmm." The role of such responses is to indicate to the speaker that they can continue with their talk, affirming that the speaker has an audience. We suggest that the use of such language might be worthy of further investigation in Reading Recovery lessons. Although we did not code or quantify such instances of backchanneling, they were evident in the talk of both teachers, but seemed to be more varied and frequent in Nancy's talk. In interactions with Jan, Stella's frequent use of "okay," seemed to affirm Jan's idea, but it seldom served as a way of signaling to Jan that she had "the floor." Both the teacher's voice and the rapidity with which "okay" was immediately followed by a question or comment indicated teacher control of the conversation. Such simple responses from Nancy as "yeah" and "uh-hmm," often followed by pauses, served as an impetus for elaboration and expansion. These verbal indicators, signaling that the teacher was in the role of listener and the child was in the role of speaker, gave more control to the child resulting in elaboration of an idea from Marcy. This also resulted in more ownership of the topic from Marcy and a conversational style of negotiation.

Although the teachers seldom initiated a topic by stating directly what the student should write, both attempted to influence the topic or direction of the conversation by starting with a requisite rereading of the previous day's story and following up with questions. This seems unnecessary when considering each child's capabilities in initiating or expanding upon ideas. Both initiating (19% of all moves) and expanding (20%) were strongly representative of Jan's conversational moves. Although Marcy was less likely to initiate an idea first, she took control of the conversation by responding to the teacher's question or prompt for initiation (22.5%) and elaborating or expanding upon ideas (33% of the moves).

During Reading Recovery lessons, Clay's design (1993b) suggests that the child's interests and experiences should be the focus in terms of topic selection; the child should have "ownership" of the topic. The task of the teacher is to support this topic generation and to scaffold the child's selection so they compose an interesting and productive story (allowing for new learning for the child). Initially there may be a need to model to provide support for topic selection and composition, but gradually the teacher must relinquish most of the control of the task and turn it over to the child (Clay & Cazden, 1990). Most Reading Recovery teachers arrive at this, but for some it takes longer to adjust their teaching to be attuned to the importance of scaffolding as a *temporary* framework for construction. In the cases of both teachers, it seemed difficult for each to relinquish control even though there was strong evidence that the children were becoming increasingly capable and independent.

Changes in Teacher-child Interactions Across the Child's Program

The most consistent interactions within and across both cases related to the initial attempts to establish a topic. Both teachers attempted to direct topic selection and expansion of the idea to varying degrees, most commonly using questions. Although neither teacher tended to initiate a topic "up front," through both subtle and less subtle interactions, each teacher attempted to focus the conversation by relating back to the previous day's story. This did not always serve the purpose intended.

Another strong commonality in both cases was how the topics related to school events and experiences. In referring back to the previous day's topic, there was the potential for the teachers to increase the child's "accessibility" (Clay & Cazden, 1990), for learning by accessing prior knowledge. These conversations served as reference points to previous writing as well as previous conversations during the walk to the classroom. As a result, these reference points had the potential to serve as "rehearsal" mechanisms. Topic selection served the same function. By writing about school life, the writing became more personal and accessible. On the other hand, the focusing of topic selection within such a narrow range seemed to constrain the child's options. Although their approaches differed, each student began to reject topics suggested by the teacher. Perhaps they had tired of writing within such a narrow range of topics or had become more confident in their ability to self-select. Either way, the more narrow focus of topics decreased the opportunities for assisting students in generating a variety of topics for writing, potentially affecting opportunities for transfer of such skills in their classrooms.

As the students became more skilled in procedural knowledge and in using genre knowledge, in this case, in selecting and developing topics, the number of teacher moves or interactions within a lesson decreased. We might also hypothesize that as a student gained confidence in her skills, she might provide an increased number of responses. Hobsbaum, Peters, and Sylva (1996) found a decrease in teacher talk and increase in student action in the findings of their study focusing on the talk as the message was written. Although our study focused on the conversation *before* the writing of the message, we expected comparable findings in relation to the teacher's relinquishing of conversational control, resulting in fewer teacher moves. However, as pointed out in relation to our first research question, the range of moves in lessons was quite varied as we looked across each case. We also determined little change in relation to the types of responses or the interactions, especially in relation to the teachers, and only one clear consistency in the number of moves. In the case of Stella and Jan, at the end of the program, the overall number of moves for the last two lessons did decrease (n=8, n=7, respectively) with a more equal level of talk. Since Stella did not include writing across the other three of the final five lessons, it is difficult to determine if this represented a change in the level of scaffolding. Analysis of the interactions across Stella's lessons did not suggest clear changes; however, she did allow the student to have more ownership of the topic, represented both in the tone of the conversation as well as in more equal sharing of the talk. Whether Stella actually recognized Jan's increasing level of independence is unclear.

It is also interesting to note that the greatest number of interactions between Nancy and Marcy occurred within the final lesson. Unfortunately, there was not an opportunity to have the participants reflect on specific lessons, but the nature of the interactions suggests that Marcy's level of engagement was not high. (We wondered if the child was aware that this was her last lesson.) Nancy's talk increased as she attempted to encourage Marcy to elaborate or expand her idea.

Basically, our findings indicate that the types of responses provided by the teachers across days were similar, and except in the earliest lessons, we could not determine any consistent changes in the type of talk as lessons progressed. Likewise, the level of scaffolding used by the teachers to support the development of a topic remained fairly consistent across lessons at the beginning, midpoint, and end of lessons that were analyzed, indicating limited evidence of change across lessons in both cases.

In relation to our findings, it is important to note that this study focused on only one portion of the Reading Recovery lesson. Analysis of other lesson components is needed to determine if the types of interactions and levels of scaffolding we observed in the conversation before writing are similar in other parts of the lesson. Also, further examination of the data may be needed to determine whether more subtle changes in the conversational interactions might be present; however, our analysis suggests that each teacher's initial perceptions of their student's abilities and behavior (as indicated in interviews) may have influenced the conversational interactions before writing. Although we agree with the teacher's initial characterizations of each child's responses and behavior (Jan as more assertive and Marcy more passive), as their program progressed, it seemed that students had made substantial gains in a number of areas. For instance, we found examples of increased procedural knowledge (e.g., Jan's comment, "We could put that in our story"), genre knowledge in making a connection to the story read (e.g., "Today I would write about fishing"), as well as increased independence in selecting a topic (e.g., "No, I don't want to write about that; I want to write about

. . ." Both students also demonstrated increased reading and writing ability as indicated by teacher records and students' exit scores on *The Observation Survey* (Clay, 1993a). In fact, both students completed their program reading within the average range of their classmates. Yet, to different degrees, in relation to the conversations before writing, the teachers had difficulty adjusting and relinquishing levels of scaffolding, making on the spot decisions about their use of talk. Thus, in these writing conversations, the knowledge and independence that was gradually achieved by these students was not capitalized upon consistently.

Discussion

This study responded to a need for examination of teacher-child interactions in Reading Recovery and other one-to-one tutorial settings. Interactions between teachers and students in Reading Recovery settings were suggested as an important factor in student success (Pinnell et al., 1994). Our goal was to characterize the interactions of two Reading Recovery teachers and their students, examining the nature and types of interactions before writing and to determine how these interactions changed.

In examining the cycle or pattern of interactions, we characterized the nature of the conversation between one of the dyads, Stella, the teacher, and Jan, the student, as resembling a "tug of war." In many of their interactions, the teacher and child seemed to be wrestling for control of the conversation, especially in relation to topic choice. In the other case, the teacher, Nancy and the child, Marcy developed a negotiated conversation. Although both teachers consistently began the conversation by requiring the child to reread their previous day's story in an attempt to connect the present day's topic, Nancy allowed her student to redirect the conversation and reject the teacher's initial focus. In contrast, Stella tended to hold steadfast to her initial intent.

As these characterizations indicate, the nature of the conversations differed in these two cases. This was determined through a macro analysis of teacher-child moves during the conversation. It is important to note that coding and quantifying the types of responses/moves (micro) seemed to suggest a different story. There were no strong differences in the types of responses by participants. Levels of talk were similar for both teachers, suggesting that the teachers controlled more of the talk, and thereby, the interactions and topic selection. Instead, in the case of Nancy and Marcy, as indicated through the macro analysis of their cycles of interaction, control of the conversation and topic was negotiated whereas the overall pattern of interactions for Stella and Jan suggested a vying for control. This point illustrates the importance of looking at interactions from many perspectives. Clearly, looking at these interactions from a single lens does not adequately capture the nature of the interactions.

We suggest that many types of studies of teacher-child interactions in one-to-one settings are needed, but that case studies are an important part of building a foundation of research, providing in-depth study of complex phenomena. In relation to Reading Recovery, there is limited research examining teacher-child interactions within the various components, as well as in-depth analysis of interactions throughout the lesson and across a child's program. For us, this study raises many new questions, and we echo the need expressed by others to develop a foundation of research that focuses on closer examination of multiple factors that influence teacher-child interactions in one-to-one literacy settings.

References

Adams, M. J. (1990). *Beginning to read: Thinking and learning about print.* Cambridge, MA: MIT Press.

Allington, R. L., & Walmsley, S. A. (1995). *No quick fix: Rethinking literacy programs in America's elementary schools.* New York: Teachers College Press.

Bakhtin, M. M. (1986). *Speech genres and other late essays* (C. Emerson & M. Holquist, Eds.; V. W. McGee, Trans.). Austin: University of Texas Press.

Britton, J. (1970). The student's writing. In E. Evertts (Ed.), *Explorations in children's writing.* Urbana, IL: National Council of Teachers of English.

Britton, J., Burgess, T., Martin, N. McLeod, A., & Rosen, H. (1975). *The development of writing abilities.* London: Macmillan.

Cazden, C. (1988). *Classroom discourse: The language of teaching and learning.* Portsmouth, NH: Heinemann.

Clay, M. M. (1982). *Observing young readers.* Portsmouth, NH: Heinemann.

Clay, M. M. (1993a). *An observation survey of early literacy achievement.* Portsmouth, NH: Heinemann.

Clay, M. M. (1993b). *Reading Recovery: A guidebook for teachers in training.* Portsmouth, NH: Heinemann.

Clay, M. M. (2001). *Change over time in children's literacy development.* Portsmouth, NH: Heinemann.

Clay, M. M., & Cazden, C. (1990). A Vygotskian interpretation of Reading Recovery. In L. Moll (Ed.), *Vygotsky and education* (pp. 206–222). New York: Cambridge University Press.

Damon, W. (1991). Problems of direction in socially shared cognition. In L. R. Resnick, J. M. Levine, & S. D. Teasley (Eds.), *Perspectives on socially shared cognition* (pp. 384–397). Washington, DC: American Psychological Association.

DeFord, D. E. (1994). Early writing: Teachers and children in Reading Recovery. *Literacy, Teaching, and Learning, 1,* 32–56.

Denzin, N. (1978). *The research act: A theoretical introduction to sociological methods.* New York: McGraw-Hill.

Diaz, R., Neal, C., & Amaya-Williams, M. (1990). The social origins of self-regulation. In L.C. Moll (Ed.), *Vygotsky and education* (pp. 127–154). New York: Cambridge University Press.

Dyson, A. H. (1983). The role of oral language in early writing processes. *Research in the Teaching of English, 17,* 1–30.

Dyson, A. H. (1999). Writing (Dallas) Cowboys: A dialogic perspective on the "What did I write?" question. In J. Gaffney & B. Askew (Eds.), *Stirring the waters: The influence of Marie Clay* (pp. 113–127). Portsmouth, NH: Heinemann.

Hammerly, M., & Atkinson, P. (1983). *Ethnographic principles in practice.* New York: Travistock.

Hobsbaum, A., Peters, S., & Sylva, K. (1996). Scaffolding in Reading Recovery. *Oxford Review of Education, 22,* 17–35.

Luria, A. (1979). *The making of mind.* Cambridge, MA: Harvard University Press.

Merriam, S. B. (1998). *Qualitative research and case study applications in education.* San Francisco: Jossey-Bass.

Patton, M. Q. (1990). *Qualitative evaluation and research methods.* New York: Sage.

Pinnell, G. S., Lyons, C., DeFord, D. E., Bryk, A., & Seltzer, M. (1994). Comparing instructional models for the literacy education of high-risk first graders. *Reading Research Quarterly, 29,* 8–39.

Riggenbach, H. (1999). *Discourse analysis in the language classroom.* Ann Arbor: University of Michigan Press.

Rogoff, B. (1990). *Apprenticeship in thinking: Cognitive development in social context.* New York: Oxford University Press.

Stake, R. E. (1995). *The art of case study research.* Thousand Oaks, CA: Sage.

Sowers, S. (1985). Learning to write in a workshop: A study in grades one through four. In M. Farr (Ed.), *Advances in writing research, volume one: Children's early writing development* (pp. 297–342). Norwood, NJ: Ablex.

Sulzby, E., & Teale, W. H. (1985). Writing development in early childhood. *Educational Horizons, 64,* 8–12.

Vygotsky, L. (1978). *Mind in society: The development of higher psychological processes.* Cambridge, MA: Harvard University Press.

Vygotsky, L. (1986). *Thought and language.* Cambridge, MA: MIT Press.

Wasik, B. A., & Slavin, R. E. (1993). Preventing early reading failure with one-to-one tutoring: A review of five programs. *Reading Research Quarterly, 28,* 178–201.

Wilkinson, L. C., & Silliman, E. R. (2000). Classroom language and literacy learning. In M. L. Kamil, P. B. Mosenthal, P. D. Pearson, & R. Barr (Eds.), *Handbook of Reading Research* (Vol. 3, pp. 337–360). Mahwah, NJ: Erlbaum.

Wood, D., Bruner, J., & Ross, G. (1976). The role of tutoring in problem-solving. *Journal of Child Psychology, 17,* 89–100.

A Theoretical Discussion of Young Bilingual Children's Reading (Preschool-Grade 3)

Georgia Earnest García
University of Illinois at Urbana-Champaign

Currently 9.9 million children in the United States live in homes in which a language other than English is spoken (Anstrom, 1996). Yet, relatively few researchers have investigated how young U.S. bilingual children, from preschool to the third-grade level, interact with and process texts (August & Hakuta, 1997; García, 2000). In this paper, I draw on U.S. and international research findings to discuss the reading acquisition of young children who are in the process of acquiring two languages or who have acquired two languages, simultaneously or sequentially, regardless of the instructional setting. When I refer to bilingual children's reading, I am referring to children's exposure to print in two languages to various degrees at home and in school.

My purpose is threefold: (a) to briefly identify similarities and differences in the reading processes of young bilingual and monolingual children, (b) to raise theoretical questions about bilingual reading that still need to be investigated, and (c) to explore the implications of the following quote by Brisk and Harrington (2000):

> Bilinguals do not function as two monolinguals shutting off one language while using the other, but as an integrated individual with two active languages affecting each other and serving as efficient resources for communication. (p. 7)

Comparison to Monolingual Readers

Many of the same underlying processes that characterize the reading of monolingual children also appear to characterize the reading of bilingual children. There is evidence that children's emergent understanding of print as demonstrated by their use of invented spellings appears to be universal (Tolchinsky, 1998). Phonological awareness and word recognition also appear to be key characteristics of young monolingual and bilingual children's reading (Bernhardt, 2000; Chiappe & Siegal, 1999; Comeau, Cormier, Grandmaison, & Lacroix, 1999). Oral miscue analyses have revealed that young bilingual readers use the same types of hypothesis testing procedures and language cues (graphophonemic, syntactic, semantic, discourse) as young monolingual readers (Huddleson, 1981). Vocabulary (Fitzgerald & Noblit, 2000), background knowledge (Delgado-Gaitán, 1989; Droop & Verhoeven, 1998), and syntactic knowledge (Chiape & Siegal, 1999; Droop &

National Reading Conference Yearbook, **50**, *pp. 228–237.*

Verhoeven, 1998) seem to be key factors that affect both monolingual and bilingual children's reading performance and comprehension. Finally, a sociocultural perspective (Moll, 1990; Wertsch, 1985), one that explains how children acquire and internalize the reading process, seems applicable to both monolingual and bilingual children (John-Steiner, Panofsky, & Smith, 1994; Lantolf & Appel, 1994; Willet, 1995).

Nevertheless, there are differences in how these processes are operationalized and demonstrated by bilinguals attributable to the process of learning to read in a second language or in two languages simultaneously, the different language structures that bilingual students encounter, and the varied sociocultural and instructional contexts they experience. For example, Geva, Yaghoub-Zadeh, and Schuster (2000) speculated that the processes that underlie bilingual and monolingual children's word recognition are similar but not identical. They reported that phonological awareness and rapid letter-naming significantly predicted the English word identification of young monolingual and bilingual children, who were receiving English reading instruction, although the role that each of the variables played in accounting for individual differences varied between the two groups. The bilingual children's performance on the rapid letter-naming task appeared to play less of a role in their English word recognition than their phonological awareness. Chiape and Siegal (1999) found that monolingual (English-speaking) and bilingual (Punjabi-English) children, who were receiving reading instruction in English, performed equally well on word-recognition and phonological processing tasks in English, but the bilingual children's performance on a cloze syntactic task in English was significantly lower. The effects of these performance differences on bilingual children's reading development and comprehension are topics that merit further investigation.

Variation in performance according to differences in the structures of the two languages also occurs. Comeau et al. (1999) compared the phonological processing and word-decoding performance in French and English of English-speaking students enrolled in French immersion classrooms for Grades 1, 3, and 5. They reported that there was a strong relationship between phonological awareness and word-decoding in French for Grades 1, 3, and 5, but that after Grade 3, this relationship diminished in importance for English. They speculated that the difference in strength of relationship could be due to "factors that maintain the relevance of the associations between graphemes and phonemes in French" (p. 41), and/or to differences in how the students were taught to read in each language. Researchers who have investigated the invented spelling of Spanish-speaking students have noted that these children initially emphasize vowels and syllables (Ferreiro & Teberosky, 1979; Tolchinksy, 1998) rather than consonants and onset rhymes, which tend to characterize the early reading instruction of English-speaking students. How bilingual children who are exposed to instruction in both languages resolve such differences is not known, but deserves to be studied.

Differences in sociocultural contexts also may affect how bilingual children interact with text and the types of processes or strategies that they demonstrate while reading in each of their languages. Moll, Estrada, Diaz, and Lopes (1980) reported that Spanish-English bilingual students demonstrated comprehension strategies during their Spanish reading instruction but grapho-phonemic strategies during their English reading instruction because the English-speaking teacher was unaware of what they could do in Spanish reading and emphasized phonics and decoding instruction.

Unique Factors that Characterize Bilingual Readers

When young bilingual children's reactions to print and reading are examined across their languages, then at least four issues emerge that differentiate monolingual from bilingual readers. A review of these issues can be used to address Brisk and Harrington's (2000) contention that bilingual individuals interactively use or draw on their two languages while reading.

Enhanced Metalinguistic Awareness

A number of researchers have reported that bilingual children younger than age 6 outperform their monolingual counterparts on metalinguistic awareness tasks related to reading (García, Jiménez, & Pearson, 1998). Metalinguistic awareness tasks assess children's ability to play with, talk about, analyze, or make judgements about language. The data show that very young bilingual children, compared to monolingual children, have a more sophisticated understanding of the referential nature of words (e.g., the length of a word does not reflect the size of the referent, as in mosquito versus ox, Göncz & Kodzopelijic, 1991). Compared to monolingual children, bilingual children also seem to have a heightened sense of grammatical acceptability, as demonstrated in Galambos and Goldin-Meadow's (1990) research with young Spanish-English bilingual children in El Salvador. They reported that the bilingual children not only outperformed monolingual Spanish speakers on sentence grammaticality tests in Spanish, but also performed as well as monolingual English speakers on English grammaticality tests in English, the children's second language. Bialystok's (1997) research with French-English and Mandarin-English bilingual preschoolers in Canada not only demonstrated that the two groups of bilingual children outperformed their monolingual English-speaking counterparts on a moving word task, in which a word placed under its corresponding picture was accidentally moved to a different picture, but that they also did this equally well in both languages. She interpreted this finding as indicating cross-linguistic transfer of metalinguistic awareness.

The metalinguistic data suggest that very young bilingual children are not shutting off one language while using the other, but appear to have developed a heightened awareness of language due to their oral experiences and exposure to print in both languages. As Bruck and Genesee (1995) explained, bilingualism seems to provide bilingual children with a type of "contrastive linguistics instruction which leads [them] to compare and analyze the structural aspects of language in more advanced ways than monolinguals" (p. 308). To what extent all bilingual children develop this metalinguistic awareness and how it can be channeled to enhance their biliteracy development are two questions that still need to be addressed.

Biliteracy Development

In the United States, we have paid very little attention to the potential for biliteracy, or concurrent literacy, development of young bilingual children. Whether bilingual children become confused when they are exposed to print in two languages may depend on how and when they are taught or exposed to print in two languages, their age, their emergent literacy development in at least one language, and motivational factors. If bilingual individuals merely function as two monolinguals when they read in each of their languages, as stated in the beginning half of the Brisk and Harrington (2000) quote, then we would expect interference and confusion to occur when young bilingual children are given concurrent literacy instruction.

Bauer's (2000) longitudinal study of her U.S. bilingual (German-English) daughter's responses to storybook reading in German and English showed that even at the age of 2 the child was not confused when she was read to in two languages. In a household in which the one parent–one language rule tended to predominate, she primarily used German to respond to texts read in German, and English to respond to texts read in English. However, her occasional use of code-mixing and code-switching to discuss realistic fiction indicated that she was reacting as a bilingual individual, transferring information across languages, when she used her other language to discuss the text according to the person or social context being discussed.

In contrast, Bialystok's (1997) metalinguistic comparative study of bilingual (French-English and Mandarin-English) and monolingual children (English speakers) in Canada suggests that very young bilingual children who encounter radically different languages may initially and temporarily become confused. However, once they resolve their confusion, they appear to increase their metalinguistic awareness and outperform all the other groups. In her study, the 5-year-old Mandarin-English bilingual children outperformed the 4-year-old Mandarin-English bilingual children, the French-English bilingual children (4- and 5-year-olds), and the English monolingual children (4- and 5-year-olds) on a task that required them to match words with their phonological representations when conflicting pictures of the words' representation were included (e.g., dandelion and bus). She interpreted the performance differences between the 4- and 5-year-old Mandarin-English bilinguals as being developmental and transitory.

Geva, Wade-Wooly, and Shaney (1993) found that English-speaking, first-grade children in Canada who were learning Hebrew as a second language were not confused when they were given explicit spelling and decoding instruction in their two languages: English, their native language, and Hebrew, their second language. When they compared the children's literacy development in first and second grades, they discovered that the children's spelling and decoding performances in Hebrew and English were not parallel but had varied according to the structure of the respective language.

Language loss issues often have been cited as a reason not to pursue concurrent literacy instruction (Crawford, 1997). Hornberger (1992) analyzed the complex role that family, community, and societal support plays in bilingual children's motivation for biliteracy development. Although not all of the conditions identified by Hornberger were in place for the biliteracy development of the children in the research by Geva and her colleagues (Geva et al., 1993; Geva & Wade-Wooley, 1998; Geva et al., 2000) and in the Bauer (2000) study, family and community support of the respective languages were present. In the studies by Geva and colleagues, the children were not simultaneous bilinguals as in the Bauer study, but sequential bilinguals. They had received kindergarten instruction in English and were acquiring Hebrew at the same time that they were learning to read and write it. Because English was the language of society, they were in no danger of losing it. The children's families valued highly the learning of Hebrew for religious and cultural purposes. Bauer's daughter lived in the United States, where English is dominant, and spent each summer in Germany. In addition to her father, who spoke German, she also was taken care of during the day by a German-speaking *au pair.* Thus, both German and English were valued by her family, and she had authentic opportunities to use them both.

With the presence of dual-immersion programs in the United States, we now have an opportunity to investigate how well young bilingual children respond to literacy instruction in two languages. Investigation of this topic needs to document not only young children's acquisition of literacy in two languages, but also the types of instruction and exposure to print that they have received in their two languages, as well as motivational and sociocultural issues.

Cross-Linguistic Transfer of Knowledge, Strategies, and Skills

An underlying assumption of bilingual education, and one that is in line with Brisk and Harrington's (2000) contention, is that bilingual individuals can transfer specific knowledge and skills acquired while reading in one language to reading in a second language. Cummins's (1986) interdependence hypothesis usually is cited as the theoretical basis for this assumption. According to Cummins, once bilingual students have developed a literate base in one language, they should be able to transfer knowledge and skills gained while reading in that language to reading in a second language, as long as they are adequately exposed to the second language and motivated to acquire it.

In support of Cummins's (1986) hypothesis, and Brisk and Harrington's quote, a number of researchers in the United States and other countries have reported correlations between young bilingual students' reading test performance in their first and second languages (García, Pearson, & Jiménez, 1994). In research with Turkish first and second graders in the Netherlands, whose initial reading instruction varied by language (Dutch vs. Turkish), Verhoeven (1994) found evidence for bi-directional transfer. The students' reading performance in one language was predicted by their reading performance in the other language, according to which language they had first learned to read.

Other researchers have reported that bilingual children's phonological awareness in one language is a strong predictor of phonological and word-recognition performance in the other language (Cisero & Royer, 1995; Comeau et al., 1999; Durgunoğlu, Nagy, & Hancin-Bhatt, 1993). Durgunoğlu and colleagues found that Spanish-speaking first graders in the United States were able to use their Spanish phonological awareness to decode English-like pseudo words without receiving formal instruction in English or first developing their oral English proficiency. They reported that the students' level of Spanish phonological awareness and Spanish word recognition significantly predicted their English word recognition and pseudo word recognition, indicating cross-linguistic transfer. Comeau and colleagues tested the transfer of phonological awareness and word-decoding of English-speaking students in Grades 1, 3, and 5 in French Immersion programs in Canada. They found that the children's phonological awareness in French was as strongly related to their word-decoding in French as their phonological awareness in English was related to their word-decoding in English. They interpreted their findings as demonstrating bi-directional cross-linguistic transfer across the children's two languages.

Both Durgunoğlu et al. (1993) and Comeau et al. (1998) warned that their findings imply a general underlying metalinguistic or metacognitive competency rather than language-specific skills. Their interpretation clearly is in concert with Brisk and Harrington's (2000) argument that "bilinguals do not shut off one language while using the other . . ." (p. 7). According to Geva et al. (2000), what transfers is

> the child's growing understanding that words can be divided into constituents that can be manipulated in various ways through deletion, transposition, and reassembly. This awareness does not have to be learned separately in each language. . . . (p. 7)

Topics that require further investigation include the age, the conditions, and the extent to which young bilingual children are conscious of cross-linguistic transfer and can skillfully and purposefully transfer knowledge and skills from reading in one language to another. García (1998) reported that the reading profiles for Spanish-English bilingual fourth graders, who were strong readers in Spanish, were similar in their two languages, implying cross-linguistic transfer. However, in a study with middle-school bilingual students (Jiménez, García, & Pearson, 1996) reported that only the successful readers had a unitary view of reading across their two languages, and made conscious use of knowledge and strategies acquired while reading in one language to read in the other language. The less successful bilingual readers thought that they had to keep the two languages separate or they would become confused.

Second-Language Oral Proficiency and First-Language Literacy

Oral language development is a major issue in monolingual reading and a controversial issue for bilingual students' reading. Educators in the United States often ask how much oral English do bilingual students need before they can be exited from a bilingual classroom to an all-English classroom. However, a number of researchers (e.g., Durgunoğlu et al., 1993; Verhoeven, 1994; Geva et al., 1993) have reported that phonological awareness and word-recognition skills in the first language are stronger predictors of bilingual children's beginning reading in either language compared to their oral proficiency. This finding could be due to the fact that there is wide variation in the reading performance of young children who have attained a relatively high oral-proficiency level in either language, and, as a result, first-language literacy becomes the deciding factor.

Nevertheless, the important and predictive role of first-language literacy also is substantiated by research with adults (Bernhardt, 2000) and by a comparative analysis of immigrant children's academic performance in the United States (Collier & Thomas, 1989). Collier and Thomas reported that non-English-speaking immigrant children did best in American schools when they arrived in the United States at ages 8 and 9, with already developed literacy skills in their native languages, as compared to younger children who arrived at ages 5 and 6 without native-language literacy skills. These findings support Cummins's (1986) contention that academic proficiency in one language, not oral language skills, is what characterizes bilingual individuals' effective transfer of skills and knowledge from one language to the other. Effective cross-linguistic transfer is a cornerstone of the Brisk and Harrington (2000) quote.

Whether continued development of the students' first-language literacy (beyond the primary grades), in addition to second-language literacy, enhances bilingual students' overall literacy development is another question that merits further consideration. In an evaluation of late-exit transitional bilingual education instruction for Spanish-English bilinguals in the United States, Ramirez, Yuen, and Ramey (1991) reported that the projected growth curves in English reading were significantly higher for those students who received 40% of their instruction in Spanish from fourth through sixth grade than for those who received less than 40% of their instruction in Spanish.

Implications

In a quest for a theory that can explain how young bilingual children interact with and process text, we need to understand more about the following issues: (a) the unique factors that characterize bilingual reading, (b) how the underlying processes that appear to characterize both monolingual and bilingual reading not only are operationalized in specific languages but also are affected by bilingualism, second-language acquisition, and varied sociocultural contexts; (c) how bilingual students' simultaneous or successive acquisition of literacy in their two languages affects their biliteracy development; and (d) how additive and subtractive bilingual settings (societal, school, home, community) affect bilingual students' motivation to develop their biliteracy.

Brisk and Harrington's (2000) argument that bilingual individuals are not simply two monolinguals functioning separately, but individuals who can use their two languages interactively was supported by findings on four interrelated factors: young bilingual children's enhanced metalinguistic awareness, their biliteracy development, demonstration of cross-linguistic transfer, and the predictive role of first-language literacy. Although Brisk and Harrington's quote may be applicable to bilingual children who are effective readers, it does not necessarily apply to the reading of all bilingual children. We need to know more about what characterizes the effective and ineffective reading of bilingual children, and the roles that instruction and motivation play.

Because many second-language children enrolled in second-language settings may be exposed to print in another language at home, it is important to include these children in this type of research, as well as children who receive concurrent or sequential classroom instruction in two languages. Research on biliteracy needs to examine how the children make sense out of print in both of their languages and how they use knowledge of literacy in one language to approach another, even when only one language is emphasized at school. At the same time, it is equally important to take into account how the different sociocultural and instructional contexts affect the types of processes and text interactions that the children demonstrate.

References

Anstrom, K. (1996). Defining the limited-English-proficient population. *Directions in Language and Education, 1*(9) (Summer). Washington, DC: National Clearinghouse for Bilingual Education.

August, D., & Hakuta, K. (Eds.). (1997). *Improving schooling for language-minority children: A research agenda.* Washington, DC: National Academy Press.

Bauer, E. B. (2000). Code-switching during shared and independent reading: Lessons learned from a preschooler. *Research in the Teaching of English, 35,* 101–131.

Bernhardt, E. B. (2000). Second-language reading as a case study of reading scholarship in the 20th century. In M. L. Kamil, P. B. Mosenthal, P. D. Pearson, & R. Barr (Eds.), *Handbook of reading research* (Vol. 3, pp. 791–811). Mahwah, NJ: Erlbaum.

Bialystok, E. (1997). Effects of bilingualism and biliteracy on children's emerging concepts of print. *Developmental Psychology, 33,* 429–440.

Brisk, M. E., & Harrington, M. M. (2000). *Literacy and bilingualism: A handbook for all teachers.* Mahwah, NJ: Erlbaum.

Bruck, M., & Genesee, F. (1995). Phonological awareness in young second language learners. *Child Language, 22,* 307–324.

Chiappe, P., & Siegel, L. S. (1999). Phonological awareness and reading acquisition in English and Punjabi-speaking Canadian children. *Journal of Educational Psychology, 91,* 20–28.

Cisero, C. A., & Royer, J. M. (1995). The development of cross-language transfer of phonological awareness. *Contemporary Educational Psychology, 20,* 273–303.

Collier, V. P., & Thomas, W. P. (1989). How quickly can immigrants become proficient in school English? *Journal of Educational Issues of Language Minority Students, 16,* 187–212.

Comeau, L., Cormier, P., Grandmaison, E., & Lacroix, D. (1999). A longitudinal study of phonological processing skills in children learning to read in a second language. *Journal of Educational Psychology, 91,* 29–43.

Crawford, J. (1997). *Best evidence: Research foundations of the Bilingual Education Act.* Washington, DC: National Clearinghouse for Bilingual Education.

Cummins, J. (1986). Empowering minority students: A framework for intervention. *Harvard Educational Review, 56,* 18–36.

Delgado-Gaitán, C. (1989). Classroom literacy activity for Spanish-speaking students. *Linguistics and Education, 1,* 285–297.

Droop, M., & Verhoeven, L. (1998). Background knowledge, linguistic complexity, and second-language reading comprehension. *Journal of Literacy Research, 30,* 253–271.

Durgunoğlu, A., Nagy, W. E., & Hancin-Bhatt, B. J. (1993). Cross-language transfer of phonological awareness. *Journal of Educational Psychology, 85,* 453–465.

Ferreiro, E., & Teberosky, A. (1979). *Los sistemas de escritura en el desarrollo del niño* [English literacy before schooling]. Mexico: Siglo XXI.

Fitzgerald, J., & Noblit, G. (2000). Balance in the making: Learning to read in an ethnically diverse first-grade classroom. *Journal of Educational Psychology, 92,* 3–22.

Galambos, S. J., & Goldin-Meadow, S. (1990). The effects of learning two languages on levels of metalinguistic awareness. *Cognition, 34,* 1–56.

García, G. E. (1998). Mexican-American bilingual students' metacognitive reading strategies: What's transferred, unique, problematic? *National Reading Conference Yearbook, 47,* pp. 253–263.

García, G. E. (2000). Bilingual children's reading. In M. Kamil, P. B. Rosenthal, P. D. Pearson, & R. Barr (Eds.), *Handbook of reading research* (Vol. 3, pp. 813–834). Mahwah, NJ: Erlbaum.

García, G. E., Jiménez, R. T., & Pearson, P. D. (1998). Metacognition, childhood bilingualism, and reading. In D. J. Hacker, J. Dunlosky, & A. C. Graesser (Eds.), *Metacognition in educational theory and practice* (pp. 193–219). Mahwau, NJ: Erlbaum.

García, G. E., Pearson, P. D., & Jiménez, R. T. (1994). *The at-risk situation: A synthesis of reading research (Special Report).* Champaign: Center for the Study of Reading, University of Illinois.

Geva, E., & Wade-Wooley, L. (1998). Component processes in becoming English-Hebrew biliterate. In A. Y. Durgunoğlu, & L. Verhoeven (Eds.), *Literacy development in a multilingual context: Cross-cultural perspectives* (pp. 85–110). Mahwah, NJ: Erlbaum.

Geva, E., Wade-Woolley, L., & Shany, M. (1993). The concurrent development of spelling and decoding in two different orthographies. *Journal of Reading Behavior, 25,* 383–406.

Geva, E., Yaghoub-Zadeh, & Schuster, B. (2000). Understanding individual differences in word recognition skills of ESL children. *Annals of Dyslexia, 50,* 3–34.

Göncz, L., & Kodzopeljic, J. (1991) Exposure to two languages in the preschool period: Metalinguistic development and the acquisition of reading. *Journal of Multilingual and Multicultural Development, 12,* 137–163.

Hornberger, N. H. (1992). Biliteracy contexts, continua, and contrasts: Policy and curriculum for Cambodian and Puerto Rican students in Philadelphia. *Education and Urban Society, 24,* 196–211.

Huddleson, S. (Ed.) (1981). *Learning to read in different languages.* Papers in Applied Linguistics: Linguistics and Literacy Series: 1. Washington, DC: Center for Applied Linguistics.

Jiménez, R. T., García, G. E., & Pearson, P. D. (1996). The reading strategies of bilingual Latina/o students who are successful English readers: Opportunities and obstacles. *Reading Research Quarterly, 31,* 90–112.

John-Steiner, V., Panofsky, C. P., & Smith, L. W. (1994). Introduction. In V. John-Steiner, C. P. Panofsky, & L. W. Smith (Eds.), *Sociocultural approaches to language and literacy: An interactionist perspective* (pp. 1–33). New York: Cambridge University Press.

Lantolf, J. P., & Appel, G. (1994). Theoretical framework: An introduction to Vygotskian approaches to second language research. In J. P. Lantolf, & G. Appel (Eds.), *Vygotskian approaches to second language research* (pp. 1–32). Norwood, NJ: Ablex.

Moll, L. (Ed). (1990). *Vygotsky and education: Instructional implications and applications of sociohistorical psychology.* New York: Cambridge University Press.

Moll, L. C., Estrada, E., Diaz, E., & Lopes, L. M. (1980). The organization of bilingual lessons: Implications for schooling. *The Quarterly Newsletter of the Laboratory of Comparative Human Cognition, 2,* 53–58.

Ramirez, J. D., Yuen, S. D., & Ramey, D. R. (1991). *Executive summary: Final report: Longitudinal study of structured English immersion strategy, early-exit and late-exit transitional bilingual education programs for language minority children.* San Mateo, CA: Aguirre International.

Tolchinsky, L. (1998). Early writing acquisition in Catalan and Israeli communities. In A. Y. Durgunoğlu & L. Verhoeven (Eds.), *Literacy development in a multilingual context: Cross-cultural perspectives* (pp. 267–288). Mahwah, NJ: Erlbaum.

Verhoeven, L. T. (1994). Transfer in bilingual development: The linguistic interdependence hypothesis revisited. *Language Learning, 44,* 381–415.

Wertsch, J. (1985). *Vygotsky and the social formation of mind.* Cambridge, MA: Harvard University Press.

Willet, J. (1995). Becoming first graders in L2: An ethnographic study of L2 socialization. *TESOL Quarterly, 29,* 473–503.

"She Can Read Them by Herself!": Parents and Teachers Respond to a Kindergarten School-Home Literacy Project

Sharan A. Gibson and Patricia L. Scharer
Ohio State University

Literacy scholars have consistently documented the positive relationship between early experiences with books and learning to read (Snow, Burns, & Griffin, 1998; Whitehurst et al., 1994) as well as the importance of home support and book reading practice (Yaden, Rowe, & MacGillivray, 2000). Access to books and other reading material in homes with preschool children often varies resulting in students entering school with a wide range of familiarity with reading and writing (Feitelson & Goldstein, 1986). Some publishers have responded to the need to provide large quantities of early reading texts by developing inexpensive, consumable, easy-to-read series of books that children keep at home and which are suitable for distribution at school.

In this study, we analyze and describe the range of uses and depth of experiences which occurred during the distribution of KEEP Books® in both the home and school environments of kindergarten students in 27 classrooms across three large, urban school districts. In conjunction with the distribution of approximately 37,000 copies of KEEP Book titles to the 633 kindergarten students participating in this project, we analyzed interviews and questionnaires from participating parents and teachers regarding the use of KEEP Books in home and school settings. This data allowed us to identify parents' and teachers' perceptions of the key characteristics of the KEEP Books as well as those contexts for using KEEP Books which contributed positively to family involvement with their children's literacy learning, to early student experiences with print, and to students' confidence and willingness to read.

It is clear that creating access to books and other reading materials for families is essential for early literacy learning, as is providing parents with opportunities to interact with children around texts (McCarthey, 2000). Research on programs such as Books Aloud has documented significant changes in literacy achievement when young children have increased access to books (Neuman, 1999). Morrow (1989) found storybook reading, even just once a week, to be more effective than traditional readiness activities. Baker, Sonnenschein, Serpell, Fernandez-Fein, and Scher (1994) report that there are at least 10 common core characteristics of home environments associated with positive reading outcomes, including the guidance and encouragement of reading by parents, conversation with parents,

*National Reading Conference Yearbook, **50**, pp. 238–247.*

ready availability of books for children, and ample space and opportunities for children to read.

Henderson (1987) states unequivocally that the evidence is beyond dispute: "When parents are involved, children do better in school" (p. 1). Children's literacy development grows out of their experiences including the views and attitudes that they encounter within family literacy activities. Through active reading and writing, early literacy learners take on the important semiotic, functional, and linguistic principles which will serve as a foundation to all later literacy learning (Goodman, 1984).

However, the nature and quality of children's early experiences with print, rather than just the quantity of access to books, also contributes to student learning (McCarthey, 2000). Sattes (1985) emphasizes that the impact on student achievement is most evident when parents view their involvement as meaningful and of direct benefit to their children. In order to fully optimize the positive effects of home-school partnerships, educators need to understand the bi-directional nature of home reading engagement:

> That is, many studies focus on how parental behaviors affect the child without considering that children's behaviors may affect the behaviors of their parents. We believe that the influences on development are bi-directional: Parents behave in a manner that impacts on children's behavior, which in turn impacts on the parents' future behavior. (Sonnenschein, Brody, & Munsterman, 1996, p. 8)

In order to more fully conceptualize these relationships, this study presents those key characteristics of the KEEP Books which teachers, parents and students identified as important to the ease and confidence with which most students were both willing to engage with the texts and able to do so independently and successfully. Two broad themes emerged through the analysis of participants' responses: factors which made the KEEP Books truly easy to read for even very beginning readers and factors leading to students' sense of ownership of the books themselves and thus, perhaps, of their own literacy learning.

Method

Participants and Materials

This study was conducted during the 1999–00 school year in 27 kindergarten classrooms within three large urban school districts in the Midwest. The project provided over 48 individual KEEP Books (approximately 1 title each week across the school year) to 633 kindergarten students in addition to classroom copies and 8 enlarged versions of the titles for classroom use. In each classroom, the 24 teachers participating in the study received training and support for introducing KEEP Books as they worked with either the whole class or with small groups of children during guided reading instruction. Then, each child took each book home to keep and read to family members. The project also provided each child with a special container to store the KEEP Books in at home, along with a pad of paper and a marker for writing or drawing activities related to the KEEP Books.

KEEP Books are designed to be appealing and engaging to primary-grade students, and provide opportunities for extended, supported, and independent practice using a wide range of effective beginning reading strategies. The themes of these books include nursery rhymes, folktales, and songs, as well as simple caption books and texts including early sight vocabulary and/or phonetic elements. They are small paperback books with colorful covers and illustrated with black-and-white line drawings. KEEP Book texts are written by experts in early literacy instruction and are purposely inexpensive in order to facilitate the ability of schools to provide many of these books across the year for each student to keep and read multiple times in both home and school contexts.

Each of the schools participating in this project are located within urban, public school districts with a high percentage of students qualifying for free or reduced price lunch. The schools also participate in a multiyear, K–2 staff development project, the Literacy Collaborative, designed to accelerate student literacy learning (Williams, Scharer, & Pinnell, 2001). A Literacy Coordinator at each school receives intensive training and provides staff development courses and on-site coaching for the school's K–2 teachers. All instructional staff at each school receive training in the use of a literacy framework (Fountas & Pinnell, 1996), a conceptual tool to help teachers of young children create, organize, and use a curriculum that supports effective literacy development from the beginnings of schooling. Underlying theories regarding student learning are linked to classroom instructional practices through teacher training in systematic observations of students and using this knowledge to inform instruction on an ongoing basis. The framework requires student engagement in every aspect of reading and writing so that they can build connected knowledge through authentic experiences in using these powerful tools. The development of school-home partnerships in literacy learning is crucial to the success of this literacy framework, and is centered on the KEEP Books.

Measures

Data collected to study the reported uses of KEEP Books in school and home settings included parent questionnaires, teacher questionnaires, and parent interviews. Each parent was contacted and given three options: agreeing to their child's participation in the study, completing a questionnaire and/or participating in an interview. Of the 266 parents who agreed to complete a questionnaire for this study, 81% returned a completed questionnaire in spring, 2000. On this questionnaire, parents were asked to describe the ways children and other family members used the KEEP Books at home, the amount of time their child read the KEEP Books each week and with whom, and how both the parent and the child felt about the KEEP Books.

Through questionnaires, all participating teachers (n=24) documented how they introduced KEEP Books to students and their parents, how they used KEEP Books during the year, the degree of usefulness of KEEP Books, student and parent responses to the books, and factors associated with successful reading of the books. Teachers also noted if any children experienced difficulty reading the KEEP Books.

Additionally, 30 parents (selected from those parents agreeing to participate in an interview and from across the 24 schools) were interviewed by telephone in May and June 2000. Interview data were entered into the computer during each interview in order to ensure accuracy of the recording of parents' comments about the ways their child used KEEP Books, their child's responses to the books, and the ways KEEP Books affected their child as a reader. Parents were also asked if they had any suggestions regarding KEEP Books.

In order to examine and describe the general patterns of student literacy achievement, a sample of students (*n*=48) was selected with a range of Fall Letter Identification (LID) scores from the 24 schools and three districts participating in the project. These students were tested in both September 1999 and April or May 2000 using LID and in April or May 2000 using Hearing and Recording Sounds in Words (HRSW), Concepts about Print (Clay, 1993), and an investigator-created Word Test. The Word Test (WT) consisted of 20 high-frequency words presented to students in isolation, and was developed through a content analysis of the 48 KEEP Book titles distributed to all students in the project.

Analysis

The coding and analysis of the questionnaire and interview data was initially guided by a limited number of a priori codes of interest derived from the researchers' review of literature and such research questions as the contexts of uses of the KEEP Books and parent, child and teacher reactions. Using cross-case analysis, answers were grouped together for common themes and perspectives on central issues across all respondents (Patton, 1990). The researchers carried out on going, recursive and inductive analyses based upon grounded theory (e.g., Glaser & Strauss, 1967; Ryan & Bernard, 2000). The themes identified within the study emerged through multiple, line-by-line readings of the data, with attention given to the processes, actions, assumptions and consequences of the uses of and responses to KEEP Books reported on by parents and teachers. The researchers specifically analyzed the data for the respondents' own, explicit statements of links between KEEP Book characteristics or contexts of use and student responses. This analysis process was facilitated by a computer program (QSR NUD·IST, 1997).

Results

Patterns of Achievement

The mean score for the sample of students tested (*n*=48) on LID (54 total possible points) was 24.3 in fall 1999 (*SD*=19.46) and 48.6 in April or May 2000 (*SD*=9.28). The April or May 2000 mean scores for this sample of students were 15.8 on Concepts about Print (24 total possible points, *SD*=3.31), 24.8 on HRSW (37 total possible points, *SD*=11.05) and 12.6 on the WT (20 total possible points,

SD=6.49). This achievement test data, while not conclusive, points to a general pattern of early literacy learning. A score of 13 on the WT, for example, would indicate an end-of-year kindergarten student who could typically read the following words in isolation: a, I, the, and, to, at, we, see, on, is, can, go, me. A student who scored 16 on CAP would typically have demonstrated accurate left-to-right directionality and one-to-one word-matching.

Patterns of Implementation at School

In their questionnaires, all 24 teachers responded that the KEEP Books were a positive addition to their kindergarten literacy programs. On a scale from 1 (not useful) to 6 (very useful), the mean response from teachers in this project was 5.9, with 88% choosing #6. A typical teacher comment on the questionnaire was: "Our children don't have access to many books at home and we lose many of the books we allow them to take from the room. The KEEP Books are a perfect solution to both problems." Teachers reported that the KEEP Books were used within a variety of whole class, small group, and independent classroom literacy activities. Typical uses included: shared reading, guided reading, buddy reading, Writer's Workshop, teacher read aloud, big books and charts, free reading, homework, free choice activity, and ABC centers. Teachers also reported that the KEEP Books became a classroom resource for such activities as the building up of, and referencing to, word walls, as a resource for specific sight words or context words, learning nursery rhymes, vocabulary or concepts, and as resources for classroom themes or units of study.

Patterns of Implementation at Home

Contexts of use and responses to the KEEP Books. A large majority of parents (91% of those who returned questionnaires or were interviewed) responded that the KEEP Books were a positive experience for their children. Overall, parents reported that the KEEP Books were read by their child anywhere from 0 to 120 minutes per week. Only four parents reported that their child did not read the books at all, with two of these stating that their child preferred to read library books. A number of parents commented, particularly through the interviews, that they were not actually sure how much time their child spent reading the KEEP Books due to the amount of self-initiated, independent reading that occurred: "She'll go and line up her baby dolls and read them by herself" (Parent interview, 6/1/00).

It was very clear from all of the parent questionnaire and interview responses that children were reading the KEEP Books within a community of parents, siblings, cousins, grandparents, friends, and neighbors. A typical parent comment was:

> If I'm in the middle of doing something, I'll say, you can read, I'll work. You sit right beside me. So she sits beside me and reads, holds the book out to show me the pictures, and goes on to the next page. When she first got them anybody that

> came in the house had to sit down and listen to her read. You know, a salesperson coming to the door, she'd make them sit down. (Parent interview, 6/1/00)

Parents reported that their child read the KEEP Books on car trips, at restaurants or doctor's offices, during dinner preparation, at the baby sitter's, while playing school, at bedtime or even bath time. One parent stated that their child had "decorated one to give us a present" (Parent questionnaire).

The concerns listed by 9% of parents included a mismatch between the book and their child's ability as a reader (too easy), overly familiar reading material (nursery rhymes), story lines with limited appeal to boys, and simplistic story lines. Out of this group of parents (those with any negative comment(s) at all regarding the usefulness or format of the KEEP Books) only one response did not also include positive comments. One parent, for example, stated that her son did not particularly like the story lines of the KEEP Books and would have preferred more stories about animals or sports. The same parent also stated: "I thought they were very worthwhile. They were simple, but he really liked the fact that they were his, that he knew he had them for himself" (Parent interview, 6/27/00).

Early success with school-type literacy activities. Parents identified a number of crucial characteristics of the KEEP Books, which they felt enabled and sustained their child's engagement with the materials, including both the ease of independent reading and a strong sense of individual ownership of each book:

> It is nice to have something they feel "ownership" over. She can "master" the books easy since they are not HARD reading and easy to hold, etc. She likes that. They are an excellent literacy incentive—especially for young school children who might not have resources or opportunities for library books or owning their own. (Parent questionnaire)

The degree to which these early literacy materials very quickly became both independently accessible to individual children and personally owned by the children themselves was specifically linked by parents and teachers to an increase in the amount of time children read and reread both the KEEP Books themselves and other reading materials as well. One parent wrote: "These books motivate my daughter to read other 'Big' books" (Parent questionnaire). Parents commented frequently that, because of the ease with which their child could read the books independently, they developed a high degree of both confidence and willingness to practice: "Great idea! This helped my daughter's self-confidence, to know she can already read a whole book by herself" (Parent questionnaire).

Many parents commented explicitly on specific characteristics of the KEEP Books which they felt created an easy, confidence building reading experience for their child with the most frequently cited characteristic being their short length. Parents stated explicitly that this allowed for their child's sustained attention across a whole book. This quick, independent reading of a whole book was emphasized by many parents as being of strong importance for their child's reading success. Other characteristics leading to the ease of independent reading listed by parents included the small, non threatening and convenient size of the KEEP Books, the use of nursery rhymes and storylines which were familiar to their child as well as the use of decodable words and the repetition of sight vocabulary within each title. Without specific prompting, many parents explicitly connected the text characteristics of the KEEP Books to their child's lack of frustration while reading and willingness to attempt to read independently.

It seems clear from the narratives presented by nearly all parents responding to this study that the KEEP Books became texts that their child could read and reread across multiple contexts. Both the ease with which their child could read each KEEP Book and the sense that these were theirs to keep, read and organize created situations in which children did not necessarily require parent demands or permission in order to practice reading.

Due to the highly scaffolded and very easy nature of the KEEP Books, in addition to each child's sense of ownership, the KEEP Books appear to have connected beginning literacy learners to successful early involvement with school-type literacy activities. A number of parents commented that the KEEP Books provided opportunities for them to participate in their child's new skill learning as well as for one-on-one quality time together with their child: "I take great pride in watching my daughter learn each day, and be able to share it with her father and I" (Parent questionnaire).

The importance of each child's ownership of the KEEP Books was very evident throughout the responses of parents. The KEEP Books are deliberately designed so that children write their name in the book and color the pictures. And, once each title is sent home with students, the books become their own personal property. Parents commented specifically that writing their name, coloring the pictures, and having a special container to organize the KEEP Book titles in across the year made the KEEP Books both more personal and more important to each child. Parents specifically linked this sense of ownership to children's willingness to read and reread the books frequently.

Engagement with reading skills. Unprompted, virtually every parent responding to the questionnaires or interviews (94%) stated that the KEEP Books provided opportunities for their child to practice specific reading skills. Parents listed a wide variety of skills they observed their child learning from the KEEP Books, including one-to-one pointing, story telling, nursery rhymes, and coloring within the lines. Learning words, however, was the most commonly mentioned skill. Parents frequently stated that their child was learning "the little words" that were repeated throughout the KEEP Books as well as using the KEEP Books as a resource for writing those words:

> She has copied some of the books word for word or will just use some of the books to write words from the story. I think this comes from school. They use journals. She'll write the words she should know by the end of the year. She has a list. (Parent interview, 6/1/00)

In fact, a number of parents specifically linked the child's sense of ownership of the books to a sense of ownership of skills learning as well. A parent stated, for example, that the books "are his to learn from" (Parent questionnaire).

Parents also included comments that indicated that they were concerned with their child's progress over time as a reader: "My son read all the books out loud the other day. It was a pleasure to see how far he has come since the beginning of school" (Parent questionnaire). Parents also frequently compared the reading progress of their kindergarten child with that of older siblings who had not had KEEP Books during their own kindergarten year:

> He definitely learned a lot. My other daughter, my other sibling, is twelve and she was not able to do what he could do in kindergarten when she was in first grade. She was difficult, with sight words. He's a year ahead of schedule than my daughter was. I even worked more then with my daughter, and he can even recognize words. I know it helped a great deal. (Parent interview, 6/15/00)

The parents and teachers responding to this study, then, felt that the KEEP Books were a very positive component of each child's literacy program. Their comments indicate that the use of the KEEP Books typically led to successful, independent and multiple readings of whole texts within a wide literacy community. Parents identified key characteristics of the KEEP Books, which they felt enabled their child's engagement with the texts and learning of specific reading skills, including the accessibility, easiness and personal ownership of the books.

Discussion

The results from this study suggest that kindergarten school-home literacy projects do not necessarily need to be of a complex nature in order to be successful. Baker et al. (1996) ask: "What would a genuine partnership between families and teachers look like if the teacher were not trying to teach or 'train' the parents, but simply to engage them in a literacy triangle with the teacher and child" (pp. 30-31)? This study has identified several key characteristics of early literacy texts, reported by teachers and parents, which can enable and encourage both beginning readers and their families to form partnerships with teachers in support of strong early literacy learning. These key characteristics may be of great help to educators as they select and purchase early literacy materials from the large array of currently available published materials.

The ease with which students were able to engage in both shared and independent readings of the KEEP Books at home appears to have created bi-directional effects, with children willing and able to read and parents then able to interact with their child's growing abilities and thus provide support and encouragement for further growth.

An abundant supply of storybooks can have a strong impact on children's language growth, provided that teachers ensure that the children interact productively with the books on a daily basis:

> In many reading programs elsewhere, the control of learning is taken almost completely out of children's (and teachers') hands. Children get too little time to try things out for themselves, to solve their reading problems in real contexts,

> and to make mistakes and correct them. (Elley, Cutting, Mangubhai, & Hugo, 1996, p. 2)

Clay (1998) believes that children's early awareness of the complex variety of important components of early literacy learning "arises out of many successful performances or acts, as a result of which children become aware of what works" (p. 46). Parents and teachers in this study reported that the short-length, small-size, familiar storylines, and repeated sight vocabulary in the KEEP Books supported children's engagement in successful literacy performances. This, in turn, appears to have created contexts in which children and their parents could interact around each child's emerging understandings.

Purcell-Gates (1996) found that low-SES parents may view the onset of formal literacy instruction as the appropriate time to begin or increase their own involvement with their children's literacy learning:

> The issue is not, thus, getting them ready to learn, but rather creating literacy environments within which the learning that they already do on an ongoing basis includes the different emergent literacy concepts needed for school success. (p. 427)

According to the teachers and parents in this study, easy-to-read, personally owned, inexpensive early literacy texts can be a key component of early literacy learning at school as well as in the establishment of home-school literacy partnerships. At this point, however, a variety of factors supporting the literacy development of kindergartners are inextricably linked and the specific contribution of materials such as KEEP Books to achievement remains unclear. Future research looking more closely at the achievement of kindergarten students over time might provide additional insight into the specific contribution of such school-home partnerships to literacy learning as well as answer such remaining questions as: What are the best ways to introduce such books in school settings? What are the best ways to match books with children? and, What is the relationship between these books and parent-child reading experiences using quality children's literature? Future research on school-home literacy projects that respond to these questions will make an important contribution to our current understanding of early literacy learning.

References

Baker, L., Allen, J. Shockley, B., Pellegrini, A. D., Galda, L., & Stahl, S. (1996). Connecting school and home: Constructing partnerships to foster reading development. In L. Baker, P. Afflerbach, & D. Reinking (Eds.), *Developing engaged readers in school and home communities* (pp. 21–41). Mahwah, NJ: Erlbaum.

Baker, L., Sonnenschein, S., Serpell, R., Fernandez-Fein, S., & Scher, D. (1994). *Contexts of emergent literacy: Everyday home experiences of urban pre-kindergarten children* (Research Report No. 24). Athens: National Reading Research Center, University of Georgia.

Clay, M. M. (1993). *An observation survey of early literacy achievement.* Portsmouth, NH: Heinemann.

Clay, M. M. (1998). Literacy awareness: From acts to awareness. In M. M. Clay, *By different paths to common outcomes* (pp. 41–84). York, ME: Stenhouse.

Elley, W. , Cutting, B., Mangubhai, F., & Hugo, C. (1996, March). *Lifting literacy levels with story books: Evidence from the South Pacific, Singapore, Sri Lanka, and South Africa.* Paper presented at the World Conference on Literacy, Philadelphia, PA.

Feitelson, D., & Goldstein, A. (1986). Patterns of book ownership and reading to young children in Israeli school-oriented and non-school-oriented families. *Reading Teacher, 39,* 924–930.

Fountas, I. C., & Pinnell, G. S. (1996). *Guided reading: Good first teaching for all children.* Portsmouth, NH: Heinemann.

Glaser, B. G., & Strauss, A. L. (1967). *The discovery of grounded theory: Strategies for qualitative research.* Chicago: Aldine.

Goodman, Y. (1984). The development of initial literacy. In H. Goelman, A. A. Oberg, & F. Smith (Eds.), *Awakening to Literacy* (pp. 102–109). Portsmouth, NH: Heinemann.

Henderson, A. (1987). *The evidence continues to grow: Parent involvement improves student achievement.* Columbia, MD: National Committee for Citizens in Education.

McCarthey, S. J. (2000). Home-school connections: A review of the literature. *Journal of Educational Research, 93*(3), 145–153.

Morrow, L. M. (1989). The effect of small group story reading on children's questions and comments. In S. McCormick & J. Zutell (Eds.), *Cognitive and social perspectives for literacy research and instruction.* Thirty-eighth yearbook of the National Reading Conference (pp. 77–86). Chicago: National Reading Conference.

Neuman, S. (1999). Books make a difference: A study of access to literacy. *Reading Research Quarterly, 34,* 286–311.

Patton, M. Q. (1990). *Qualitative evaluation and research methods* (2nd ed.). Newbury Park, CA: Sage.

Purcell-Gates, V. (1996). Stories, coupons, and the TV Guide: Relationships between home literacy experiences and emergent literacy knowledge. *Reading Research Quarterly, 31,* 406–428.

QSR NUD·IST [Computer software]. (1997). Thousand Oaks, CA: Scolari.

Ryan, G. W., & Bernard, H. R. (2000). Data management and analysis methods. In N. K. Denzin & Y. S. Lincoln (Eds.), *Handbook of qualitative research* (2nd ed., pp. 769–802). Thousand Oaks, CA: Sage.

Sattes, B. (1985). *Parent involvement: A review of the literature* (Occasional Paper No. 21). Charleston, WV: Appalachia Educational Laboratory.

Snow, C. E., Burns, M. S., & Griffin, P. (Eds.). (1998). *Preventing reading difficulties in young children.* Washington, DC.: National Academy Press.

Sonnenschein, S., Brody, G., & Munsterman, K. (1996). The influence of family beliefs and practices on children's early reading development. In L. Baker, P. Afflerbach, & D. Reinking (Eds.), *Developing engaged readers in school and home communities* (pp. 3–20). Mahwah, NJ: Erlbaum.

Whitehurst, G. J., Epstein, J., Angell, A., Payne, A., Crone, D., & Fischel, J. (1994). Outcomes of an emergent intervention in Head Start. *Journal of Educational Psychology, 86,* 542–555.

Williams, E. J., Scharer, P. L., & Pinnell, G. S. (2001). *Literacy collaborative 2000 research report.* Columbus: Ohio State University.

Yaden, D. B., Rowe, D. W., & MacGillivray, L. (2000). Emergent literacy: A matter (polyphony) of perspectives. In M. L. Kamil, P. B. Mosenthal, P. D. Pearson, & R. Barr (Eds.), *Handbook of Reading Research* (Vol. 2, pp. 425–454). Mahwah, NJ: Erlbaum.

Media Literacies: Varied But Distinguishable

Margaret C. Hagood
University of Georgia

In the fall 2000, the U.S. Department of Education and the National Endowment for the Arts allocated nearly $1 million to schools for the implementation of media literacy education. Richard Riley (2000), the U.S. Secretary of Education, stated:

> Parents, educators, and kids themselves need to be concerned with and careful about what young people see on TV, in movies, and in video games. Anything we can do to help them critically analyze the wide spectrum of media messages that they are exposed to each day will help them make wiser decisions and lessen the chances that they will consider violence an acceptable way to solve problems. (www.arts.gov/endownew/news00/edliteracy1.html)

Media literacy is an important component of literacy education. However, just as Riley believes that "anything we can do" in the way of developing youths' "critical analysis" of media will affect the decisions they make in their daily lives, I think it is equally important for researchers and teachers to critically analyze how we will assist youth in such analyses. As educators and researchers, we must reflect upon our own definitions of media literacy to understand the kinds of critical analysis given credence in media literacy instruction. The purpose of this paper is to examine the multiplicity of meanings for the term "media literacy," particularly as those meanings intersect with various understandings of popular culture, and to examine those meanings in relation to media literacy instruction. A discussion of approaches to media literacy instruction based upon adults' conceptions of adolescents' interests in contemporary popular culture texts seems apropos as popular culture is intricately twined with media and infused within media literacy instruction.

Like media literacy, popular culture is a contested term with multiple meanings. In an uncomplicated way, popular culture is defined matter-of-factly as a culture that appeals to many people (Fiske, 1995; Storey, 1998). This definition conveys a quantitative basis for defining how large-scale manufacturing inundates consumers' lives and influences which texts are available for consumption. This description, however, does not acknowledge the relevancy consumers attribute to popular culture, nor does it address everyday cultural practices consumers create from texts considered popular culture. Others have examined popular culture from consumer perspectives, emphasizing the audiences' uses of texts. For example, Willis (1977) described popular culture as "the very material of our daily lives, the bricks and mortar of our most commonplace understanding"

*National Reading Conference Yearbook, **50**, pp. 248–261.*

(p. 185). He argued that we better understand people's constructions of the world when we study how people use popular culture in daily contexts. Turner (1996), a fellow British cultural theorist, reiterated this claim, stating that popular culture "is a site where the construction of everyday life may be examined" (p. 6). Just as numbers indicate how production plays a part in determining what gets dubbed popular culture, audiences' pleasures in and uses of texts influence how they consume and create their own meaning from texts.

Because popular culture is ingrained in media and is a term that conjures up varying feelings, it is useful to illustrate approaches to media literacy based on differing perceptions of popular culture. In the following pages, using recent scholarship in media studies and cultural studies, approaches to media literacy are traced as they intersect with definitions of popular culture as mass culture, folk culture, and everyday culture. Examinations of these approaches to media literacy using a popular culture text help illustrate that media literacy is not a singular entity at all, but is multiply situated, such that differing perceptions of the term popular culture its production and consumption yield differing media literacies and differing media literate readers. Before discussing these approaches to media literacy, introductions to the popular culture texts of interest and to the context of the illustration are necessary. Meet the *Hot Boys:* Lil' Wayne, B.G., Young Turk, and Juvenile (see Figure 1).

This foursome rap group from New Orleans, Louisiana, meets the quantitative criteria to be considered a popular culture text. Rapping about life in Magnolia, a subsidized housing community in New Orleans, they have, through album

Figure 1. Guerilla Warfare (*Hot Boys,* 1999).

sales alone, impacted the literacy habits of many U.S. youth. Each is a member of their recording studio's, Cashmoney Records, "Millionaires Club," having sold over 2 million albums as solo artists with titles such as *Tha Block is Hot* (Lil' Wayne, 1999), *Chopper City in the Ghetto* (B.G., 1999), and *400 Degreez* (Juvenile, 1998). *Guerilla Warfare* (*Hot Boys,* 1999), the most recent group album, sold over 400,000 copies in the Southern United States during the first month of its release. Furthermore, this rap group has received wide media coverage, having videos played on music television channels, songs aired on the radio, and articles written about them in national music magazines. Images of the *Hot Boys* and two excerpts about them will be used to illustrate how approaches to media literacy differ dependent upon adults' conceptions of popular culture and how youth engage with and use popular culture texts.

This example about adolescents' uses of the *Hot Boys* as a popular culture text is drawn from a study about adolescents' after-school uses of popular media texts in a public library (Alvermann et al., 2000). Three groups of 10 to 12 African-American and European-American middle and high schoolers met once a week for 1½ hours over 15 weeks with three adult facilitators (of which I was one) and partook in media related activities, one of which included media literacy instruction the adults created using popular culture texts of interest to the adolescents.

To get to know the youth and their popular culture interests, we observed the Internet web sites most frequented and attended to their music preferences during weekly meetings. The *Hot Boys* often came up in conversations among the adolescents and was particularly liked by the girls. As the youths talked in small groups or worked on computers, they often sang *Hot Boys'* songs and used language from the songs as points of reference for themselves. Knowing nothing about this group, I searched for material on the *Hot Boys* to engage the adolescents in a media literacy discussion. Looking in various popular magazines, I came across this picture of the group in *The Source* (October 1999), a music rag specializing in rap (see Figure 2).

During three separate meetings with the three groups of adolescents, I used this image to initiate a textual analysis of media's portrayal of the *Hot Boys* in the picture. Noting the large rings, watches, and medallions, the wad of cash held in one rapper's hand, and the cell phone, I tried to elicit an analysis of representation (Hall, 1997), calling attention to the materiality and signification the items portrayed in the picture. Without trying to encumber the discussion with technical language, I began with questions such as "How are the *Hot Boys* portrayed in this picture?" in order to call attention to the structural and semiotic signifiers of the text and to develop an understanding that media producers used specific techniques and icons to depict the *Hot Boys* in specific ways.

The girls commented freely, noting first the objects in the picture, "They have cell phones, watches, and rings," and "They have money." Pushing them further, I asked them what these objects represented in the picture. Their comments were brief and seemingly abrupt. "They're rich," "They tight," "They bling, bling!," "They're fine," "Money!," and "They ballin'," were a few of the responses given. I then attempted to get them to articulate and justify how they knew and why they felt these rappers represented attractiveness and wealth. Several argued from examining the image that the stances the rappers assumed connoted success because they were "muggin'," which, as they explained, was a way of showing off expensive wares. The adolescents noted that the accessories featured in the picture portrayed the *Hot Boys* as thriving rap artists.

Following the image analysis, the adolescents read two short excerpts from an article entitled "Boyz at War," from the Vibe web site:

> *Excerpt 1:* The *Hot Boys* compared themselves to NWA saying, "NWA ain't change their style, they ain't go commercial. They just kept it all the way street and all the way ghetto and that's what you gonna hear from Cash Money. We respect them to the fullest cause they ain't care. But you know how *The Beatles* was? That's how the *Hot Boys* are gonna be." (www.vibe.com)

Figure 2. Image of the *Hot Boys* (*The Source,* October 1999).

> *Excerpt 2:* Although part of the rap game for Cash Money and the *Hot Boys* means continuing to ice-out the bezels on their Rolleys, keeping the Moet Chandon, Cristal and the Hennessey flowin' and fattenin' their wads of cash, the camaraderie that exists between the respective members of the group and label goes beyond studio time. Cash Money Records and the *Hot Boys* consider themselves family. (www.vibe.com)

After reading these excerpts, we discussed again how the article portrayed the *Hot Boys* using particular statements the adolescents found interesting. Unlike the previous text that focused on the production of the *Hot Boys'* image, the adolescents seemed more agreeable about discussing their own views of the *Hot Boys* based on their reading. Their responses combined their analyses of both the image and print-based texts and addressed how the rappers simultaneously incorporated divergent images of themselves. The girls explained that the *Hot Boys* maintained multiple images of success, which included a homeboy ghetto image while embracing a wealthy image of fame. They elaborated, saying that the *Hot Boys* understood the struggle of becoming prominent rappers, and as one girl explained, "they want to go back to the ghetto where their lives were before." Also, acknowledging the differences between the rappers' "ghetto lives" and the lives outside of Magnolia that their popularity had afforded them, one girl commented, "People didn't talk to them before. Now they talk to them because they have money."

Central to the adolescents' analyses and commentaries were connections between the rappers past and present images as depicted in the excerpts they read. "They are thugged out. They came from nothing. They don't forget where they came from," expressed one girl. And, another girl quickly added, "they're thuggin'." Like muggin', I was unfamiliar with the term "thuggin'" and inquired about it. Thuggin', the girls defined, is looking tough while muggin' about their prosperity. They said, "Because they have money, they're mugging."

Having observed the adolescents' interest in the *Hot Boys* over several weeks' meetings, I tried to link our discussion to the way that they used the *Hot Boys* in their everyday lives. I noted that some of the adolescents emulated the *Hot Boys,* using similar language and wearing similar clothing and accessories. For example, by physical appearances alone, the adolescents read each other and commented on each other's attire, often remarking "bling, bling" when someone donned a new set of bangle bracelets, a sparkly ring, or an initialed pendant necklace. And it was common to hear the girls singing a unique version of the *Hot Boys'* hit "I need a hot girl," changing the words to "I need a hot boy." Using parts of the *Hot Boys* to create their own meaning was not only confined to girls' practices. Several boys created pseudonyms in their friendship groups and referred to themselves as Lil' someone, like Lil' Wayne of the *Hot Boys.* One of the boys had also formed a rap group with some friends, and a couple of the boys wore braided hairstyles similar to pictures of Lil' Wayne. It was curious seeing these seamless connections between the *Hot Boys* and the adolescents' everyday literacy practices.

When discussing the song "I need a hot girl," I told them that I felt uncomfortable printing and sharing the lyrics with them. Although I knew they were familiar with the song, I nevertheless did not want to share in print the overt lyrics that I thought might be problematic in the group. Most of the adolescents immediately understood my uncertainty because, in their words, "there is explicit content," "parents might think that they will have a bad influence," and from "the way the boys and girls are" in the music video. Although a couple of boys stated they did not like nor did they listen to the *Hot Boys* because they disagreed with the sexually explicit content, the lyrics' profanity, and the portrayal of women, most of them nonchalantly claimed that these factors did not bother them at all. In fact, most of the girls and boys disagreed vehemently with me, rationalizing that the lyrics were not offensive to them because "adolescents hear curse words all the time."

I also told them that I felt uneasy sharing the lyrics because I found the song degrading to women. My critique of the song as a statement about the objectification of women began a discussion about gender and class related to our perceptions of the *Hot Boys* texts. As before, the girls disagreed with me, stating that they liked the song and explaining that the lyrics spoke of one kind of woman. As one girl said, "They are talking about freaks, hookers. I don't want to be a hooker or a freak." Others said, "I like the song. It doesn't bother me," and "They're not talking about me." In defense of their answers, another girl chimed in, "Those girls [the ones depicted in the song] are different" in that "they give it up." And, one girl explained the difference like this, "They [the *Hot Boys*] are talking about women from the ghetto who like to act like that."

In the end, two girls bolstered the other girls' analyses of the text as related to their own lives and disputed my interpretation of and discomfort about the text, "I need a hot girl." One girl thought I might not like the text because as she said, "You might think they [the *Hot Boys*] have a bad attitude." Another girl reasoned that because this rap group sings about the problems and pleasures of living in the ghetto I might potentially be hesitant about the *Hot Boys* in general. She said, "Not to be mean, but you probably don't listen to this. You're not from the ghetto." In short, these girls thought that I would not or could not understand the text because I did not seem to understand the cultural significance of the music in their lives.

Approaches to Media Literacy Based on Perceptions of Popular Culture

Approaches to media literacy vary according to perceptions of popular culture. Specifically, these approaches vary according to perceptions of media and audiences' control of knowledge and power related to pleasures derived from production and consumption of popular culture texts. In the following sections, an analysis of the previous discussion illustrates how definitions of popular culture and of pleasures created from popular culture texts shape the kinds of approaches adults take toward media literacy instruction when working with youth.

Popular Culture as Mass Culture

Popular culture is sometimes referred to as *mass culture.* Described in this way, popular culture is distinguished from so-called high culture of the elite and recognized as culture produced for the masses, associating it with ordinary life and that of alleged uncivilized or less civilized culture. As a culture *for the people,* mass popular culture is often assumed to be a monolithic site of textual production, powerful enough to demand and to ensure that consumers read and extract meaning from texts in similar ways (Storey, 1998). A transmission model of popular culture as mass culture acknowledges only the power of media to determine the meaning of texts and the culture industry to be the sole proprietor of messages implicit in texts. As part of mass culture, media that produce popular culture are ultimately negative influences that seek to legitimate knowledge and information that lack moral seriousness. This perception stems from theorists such as Horkheimer and Adorno (1976) of the Frankfurt School who critiqued mass culture and asserted that the culture industry socializes people in common ways by exposing them to mindless drivel. Audiences are perceived as insatiable and nondiscriminatory because their interpretations of and pleasures in popular culture texts seem always in agreement with ideologies presented in the text.

Reflecting upon the brief depiction of the adolescents' encounter with a textual analysis of the *Hot Boys* image, I might assume that this popular culture text is solely a creation of mass culture. Following Adorno and Horkheimer's argument (1993), the media as the "culture industry" mass-generate texts such as the *Hot Boys* in order to push particular perceptions of culture onto audiences. Those who equate popular culture with mass culture and with mass consumption often speculate that popular culture texts add little to aesthetic and refined values and turn people into passive recipients, accepting wholly the culture industry's ideologically charged media messages.

In keeping with the theory of popular culture as mass culture, it certainly seemed that the adolescents' textual analyses were in agreement with the messages I read/received in/from the images. They looked at the images and recognized that the jewelry, money, and clothing all represented wealth and status. Several girls described the *Hot Boys* as "fine" and liked how the media presented them. Furthermore, the adolescents described the *Hot Boys* as thugs in the picture, muggin' about their stardom. In short, from a structural and semiotic analysis, the adolescents recognized the semiotic codes and read the icons and techniques the media used to portray the rappers as wealthy. The focus was not one of readers' pleasures in the text; rather, it was in determining how the media portrayed pleasures to draw the audience into accepting the text on the semiotic terms presented.

Often critics of adolescents' pleasures in popular culture feel that youth resign themselves to passive acceptance of identities and ideologies offered by the media and attribute social decline and decay to youth's pleasure in passive engagement of leisure activities (Gordon, Underwood, Wiengarten, & Figueroa, 1999). To combat the passively and negatively perceived effects associated with exposure to and consumption of mass culture, some media literacy approaches create media literacy instruction emphasizing textual analyses and critique using a semiotic approach that silences readers' pleasures. Such an approach is often characterized as "the process of accessing, critically analyzing media messages, and creating messages using media tools" (Hobbs, 1996).

Textual analyses within media studies emphasize the deconstruction of the genre, narrative, and image structure in the text in order to assist audiences in scrutinizing and identifying ideologies promoted from those structures and in learning how to resist particular ideologies in their everyday lives (Lusted, 1991). Using semiology, the study of signs, the main focus of the study of popular culture as mass culture is in determining the meaning produced from the signs in the text. The analysis assumes the media's power to produce meaning in the sign is greater than audiences' power to create their own meaning and pleasures from the sign that is applicable to their own lives. Therefore, a semiotic approach to media literacy based on media studies aims to teach readers to become active and resistant participants in the process of media infiltration of mass culture rather than to act as passive recipients subservient to the images communicated to them from the media (Brown, 1998; Du Gay, 1997).

Though the adolescents capably analyzed the structure of the visual text of the *Hot Boys* and connected it to their readings of the print-based text, they liked and valued the images of the rappers as muggin' thugs. They viewed the *Hot Boys* texts as high status and elite culture. From a semiotic analysis of media production of text, the adolescents' pleasures in the texts were not discussed, validated, or problematized when examining the text as a form of mass culture. In keeping with a conception of popular culture as mass culture, knowledge and experience that readers bring to the text are less important than teaching about the intended messages in the text. As illustrated in the discussion of the *Hot Boys,* textual analyses that view popular culture as a monolithic mass culture often ignore both the pleasures that readers create from their engagement of the text and the ways audiences use the text in their everyday lives.

Popular Culture as Folk Culture

Unlike the top-down model of mass culture that views popular culture as a product of the culture industry in producing meaning for people, a *folk culture* perspective of popular culture celebrates a bottom-up popular culture *of the people* (Storey, 1998). This stance toward popular culture began in British Cultural Studies research in the 1960s as a response to critiques of earlier research that characterized working class people as cultural dupes of mass culture. Researchers showed that those characterized as working class created their own meaning of popular culture texts that was often in opposition to the dominant reading of the text (e.g., Frith, 1983; Walkerdine, 1997). Folk culture perspectives of popular culture, therefore, acknowledge class divisions between readings of popular and high culture, emphasize meanings audiences create from texts, and focus on audiences' uses of texts based on class understandings (e.g., Jenkins, 1992; Willis, 1977). Meaning, therefore, lies not in intended messages set forth by text producers but in the audience's interaction with and uses of the text—in their production of text consumption. Audiences' everyday practices, which resist monolithic understandings of popular culture texts, are vital to a folk culture view of popular culture (Fiske, 1989a, 1989b; Sardar & Van Loon, 1998).

Examining the discussion about the *Hot Boys* as folk culture rather than as mass culture highlights different aspects of meanings in an approach to media literacy instruction. When the adolescents explained the uses of the terms muggin' and thuggin' related to the *Hot Boys* texts, they exemplified a view of popular culture as folk culture. As they elaborated on their understanding of the texts, they articulated the importance of the multiple images the *Hot Boys* portrayed, giving credibility to both images of the ghetto from which they came and of the stardom they achieved. They read the *Hot Boys* texts as celebratory in that the *Hot Boys* had no intentions, like other bands had, of selling out but rather planned to keep their street image while gaining popularity equivalent to *The Beatles.* Upon further analysis, this juxtaposition between the *Hot Boys* and *The Beatles,* the former retaining an image of "poor kids gone rich" whereas the latter succumbed to image reinvention from rough-looking working class adolescents to clean cut mop tops during their early career to gain popularity (McKeen, 1990), is also a form of folk cultural critique of the success of white male icons in popular culture.

By the adolescents' very recognition of the *Hot Boys'* emphatic efforts to keep their ghetto image and of their pleasures in emulating that image in their own lives, the adolescents' reading and interpretation of the *Hot Boys* subvert and critique the system that defines the rules of success. When they flaunt their success by wearing expensive clothing and jewelry that "bling, bling," the adolescents who described themselves as being from the ghetto and who identified with the *Hot Boys* redefine images of the ghetto and of success, giving them reasons for muggin'.

In this example, the text meaning and textual pleasures ascribed by the adolescents as the audience result from the social and cultural appropriation of the text to their own lives. So, contrary to the critiques that the culture industry controls all power and forces particular readings on audiences that produce negative effects, popular culture as folk culture views audiences as those who hold power. Audiences use pleasure in texts to assert their power to actively produce their own meanings.

Rather than condemning popular culture as the downfall of youth, those working in media literacy and who view popular culture as folk culture acknowledge youth's pleasure in texts as celebratory and connected to their understanding of the world through social and cultural contexts. Instead of teaching from a top down model of production control, they study how youth construct meaning for themselves through the transformation of texts and practices set forth by the culture industry (Fiske, 1989a, 1989b). From a folk cultural perspective of popular culture, media literacy approaches examine groups' readings of texts and legitimate the pleasures and uses created from engagement of the text.

Popular Culture as Everyday Culture

Popular culture conceptualized as *everyday culture* is concerned with the study of the culture of everyday life. Those who espouse this perspective reject definitions of popular culture as characterizations of mass and folk culture. They rebuff the term *mass culture* because it perpetuates the high/low culture binary concerned only with media's power and with audience's lack of knowledge and passive consumption of texts (cf. Bourdieu, 1984). They reject also the term *folk culture* as it discounts media's power to disseminate textual interpretations and focuses predominantly on audience production of meaning (cf. de Certeau, 1984). Proponents of popular culture as everyday culture attend to the power and knowledge held by both producers and consumers of media and to meaning making and uptake of pleasures in texts as important aspects of study in media literacy (e.g., Buckingham, 1998; Luke, 1997; McRobbie, 1992; Tobin, 2000).

Whereas media studies often constructs popular culture as mass culture and is more interested in analysis of textual production, cultural studies focuses on readers' everyday culture and social uptake of texts. The study of popular culture as everyday culture that incorporates both media and cultural studies focuses on the power in discourse that surrounds the dissemination (production) of and uses (consumption) of texts (Buckingham & Sefton-Green, 1994). Examining popular culture as everyday culture that incorporates both media studies and cultural studies pushes against structuralist approaches of determination, which often ignore pleasures and subsumes all meaning making into the study of the production of static images lacking a context of textual uses (Johnson, 1987). Such an approach is also skeptical of valorizing subcultural uses of media texts often associated with folk cultural views of popular culture.

Revisiting the discussion about the *Hot Boys* from a perspective of popular culture as everyday culture and attending to the adolescents' pleasures created from the text shows a different kind of media literacy instruction. The adolescents' comments involving their pleasures in the *Hot Boys* combines components of media literacy that connect understandings of both production and consumption in three specific ways. First, the adolescents' discussion clearly revealed that they understood that texts are produced for various audiences with various pleasures in mind. When they attributed my distaste of the song "I need a hot girl" to profanity, to explicit content, and to the rationale that "parents might think that they will have a bad influence" and then explained that these aspects were not problematic to them, their comments showed, at least tacitly, that they understood that media produce images that appeal to different audiences. In this case, they indicated that their own youth culture highly enjoyed this sort of media production and representation.

Second, the girls' comments that I would not understand the lyrics because I was an adult and because I was not from the ghetto demonstrates that they believed that media portrayals often invite some readers to engage with texts using particular production techniques that appeal to various people while excluding others. Third, by the girls' contrasts between the hot girls depicted in the songs and themselves, they displayed that they understood the discourse of the song and the persona of the hot girl created in the song. Though they liked the song and often parodied it in their actions with one another, they were quick to point out that the representation of a hot girl in the text is not the same sort of hot girl they desired to be themselves. The adolescents' pleasures in the text also illustrate that as consumers they created meaning for themselves pertinent to their own lives and to their everyday culture. By enjoying the song, "I need a hot girl" but also by separating themselves from the kind of girl they thought was portrayed in the text, they developed their own reading of being a hot girl. Many of the girls did not take up or confess to an affinity of the image of a hot girl about whom the *Hot Boys* sang.

Unlike the previous conceptions of media literacy that looked at popular culture as mass culture and as folk culture, an implementation of media literacy that views popular culture as everyday culture incorporates both pleasures and critiques in discussions of media literacy. This sort of media literacy instruction that combines both media and cultural studies considers what Lewis and Jhally (1998) call a "contextual approach," or what Hall (1997) calls the "discursive approach." Such an approach attends to the social, cultural, political, and historical factors that surround media-constructed texts and to readers' constructed meanings of those texts. Those who view popular culture in this way acknowledge that audiences shape and are shaped by texts and incorporate this perspective into media literacy activities.

Recognizing the polysemic nature of popular culture texts in everyday culture means that readers may render different interpretations and derive conflicting pleasures from texts. This complicates discussions, allowing for more in-depth and perhaps conflicting understanding of the conditions that affect the perspectives we hold about our pleasures. Aware that audiences consume and create meaning from engagement with texts, Walkerdine (1997) explained that audiences' meaning making of texts is neither wholly resistant nor fully duped, but rather individual and group uses of texts reflect a bit of both. Thus, audiences may at times look like cultural dupes who passively accept ideologies presented in texts, whereas at other times produce novel readings from popular culture texts (Buckingham, 1998). By highlighting audiences' negotiation of consumption and production of popular culture texts, media literacy educators and researchers interested in the adolescents' meaning making of media production and consumption teach and study both media's power to control cultural markets and products and audiences' power to value certain texts and to create meaning from texts that may or may not seem in agreement with the produced meaning.

Media Literacy and Pleasure

Researchers and teachers of media literacy often think that when adolescents resist adult interpretations of popular culture they are merely naive, resistant to adults' readings, or experiencing false consciousness. Buckingham (1993) spoke to the issue of pleasures and media literacy. He said:

> in demonstrating our ability to distinguish between truly critical perspectives and those which are (by implication) merely uncritical, we are making a powerful claim for our own authority. And if we are critical, those who do not share our views are either merely ignorant and misguided or actively engaged in an attempt to obscure the truth. (p. 142)

When attributing adolescents' understandings of popular culture to these factors, we, as researchers and teachers, ultimately place popular culture into the category of mass culture. In developing media literacies, we need to contemplate our definitions of popular culture and how youth make sense of popular culture texts as part of media in their lives. If popular culture entices readers to engage texts to understand our worlds in critical and uncritical ways, then perhaps media literacy instruction should be focused upon exploring not only media's production of texts but also readers' pleasures in their own production of meaning.

Returning to the earlier observation that substantial monies have been granted to school districts around the United States for media literacy education, it behooves us as researchers and educators to be mindful of our perceptions of popular culture texts. Upon the awarding of grants for media literacy education in schools in the United States, Arts Endowment Chairman Bill Ivey (2000) stated:

> With the pervasiveness of media in the lives of our young people, it becomes ever more imperative that they are able to interpret the *messages they receive* [emphasis added]. If our children don't learn to shape images, images will shape them. (www.arts.gov/endownews/news00/edliteracy1.html>)

The pervasive nature of media in our lives warrants media literacy instruction, but I think it dangerous to assume that readers are solely acted upon and only receive messages without actively consuming, shaping, and producing their own meaning from texts. When media literacies instruction is constructed in this way, it becomes viewed in a myopic manner and textual analysis of mass culture becomes the norm for a media studies curriculum. Within media literacies instruction, I believe, however, that it is equally imperative that adults strive to understand youths' investments in pleasures created from media texts. Teaching and learning as multifaceted components of media literacies instruction would include not only understanding popular culture as mass culture and of textual and structural analyses within media studies, but also folk and everyday culture interpretations of popular culture, which incorporate observations of and discussions about audiences' pleasures in and uses of texts connected to cultural studies and to youth culture. It is in this complicated mix of how popular culture is produced and consumed by both media and audiences that media literacies instruction addresses its aim to develop more critical readers of media texts.

References

Adorno, T. W., & Horkheimer, M. (1993). The culture industry: Enlightenment as mass deception. In S. During (Ed.), *The cultural studies reader* (2nd ed.) (pp. 31–41). London: Routledge.

Alvermann, D., Hagood, M., Heron, A., Hughes, P., Williams, K., & Yoon, J. (2000). *After-school media clubs for reluctant adolescent readers* (Grant #199900278—Final Report to Spencer Foundation).

B.G. (1999). *Chopper city in the ghetto.* [CD]. New York: Cashmoney Records.

Brown, J. A. (1998). Media literacy perspectives. *Journal of Communication, 48,* 44–57.

Bourdieu, P. (1984). *Distinction: A social critique of the judgement of taste* (R. Nice, Trans.). Cambridge, MA: Harvard University Press. (Original work published in 1979)

Buckingham, D. (1993). Young people and the media. In D. Buckingham (Ed.), *Reading audiences* (p. 1–23). Manchester, England: Manchester University Press.

Buckingham, D. (1998). Introduction: Fantasies of empowerment? Radical pedagogy and popular culture. In D. Buckingham (Ed.), *Teaching popular culture: Beyond radical pedagogy* (pp. 1–17). London: UCL Press.

Buckingham, D., & Sefton-Green, J. (1994). *Cultural studies goes to school: Reading and teaching popular media.* London: Taylor & Francis.

de Certeau, M. (1984). *The practice of everyday life.* Berkeley: University of California Press.

Du Gay, P. (Ed.). (1997). *Production of culture/Cultures of production.* London: Sage/The Open University.

Fiske, J. (1989a). *Reading popular culture.* Boston: Unwin Hyman.

Fiske, J. (1989b). *Understanding popular culture.* Boston: Unwin Hyman.

Fiske, J. (1995). Popular culture. In F. Lentricchia & T. McLauglin (Eds.), *Terms for literary study* (pp. 321–335). Chicago: University of Chicago Press.

Frith, S. (1983). *Sound effects: Youth, leisure, and the politics of rock.* London: Constable.

Gordon, D., Underwood, A., Wiengarten, T., & Figueroa, A. (1999, May 10). The secret life of teens. *Newsweek,* pp. 45–50.

Hall, S. (1997). The work of representation. In S. Hall (Ed.), *Representation: Cultural representations and signifying practices* (pp. 13-64). London: Sage.

Hobbs, R. (1996). Media literacy, media activism. *Telemedium: The Journal of Media Literacy, 42,* 57–72.

Horkheimer, M., & Adorno. T. W. (1976). *Dialectics of enlightenment.* (J. Cumming, Trans.). New York: Herder & Herder.

Hot Boys (1999). *Guerilla warfare* [CD]. New York: Cashmoney Records.

Ivey, B. (2000, October 4). *Riley and Ivey announce nearly $1 million in media literacy grants.* National Endowment for the Arts. <http://www.arts.gov/endownews/news00/edliteracy1.htm>

Jenkins, H. (1992). "Strangers no more, we sing": Filking and the social construction of the science fiction fan community. In L. A. Lewis (Ed.), *The adoring audience: Fan culture and popular media* (pp. 208–236). New York: Routledge.

Johnson, R. (1987). What is cultural studies anyway? *Social Text, 16,* 38–80.

Juvenile (1998). *400 Degreez* [CD]. New York: Cashmoney Records.

Lewis, J., & Jhally, S. (1998). The struggle over media literacy. *Journal of Communication, 48,* 109–121.

Lil' Wayne (1999). *Tha block is hot* [CD]. New York: Cashmoney Records.

Luke, C. (1997). Media literacy and cultural studies. In S. Muspratt, A. Luke, & P. Freebody (Eds.), *Constructing critical literacies* (pp. 19–50). Cresskill, NJ: Hampton.

Lusted, D. (1991). Introduction. In D. Lusted (Ed.), *The media studies book* (pp. 12–38). London: Routledge.

McKeen, W. (1990). *The Beatles: A bio-bibliography.* New York: Greenwood.

McRobbie, A. (1992). Post-Marxism and cultural studies: A post-script. In L. Grossberg, C. Nelson, & P. Treichler (Eds.), *Cultural studies* (pp. 719–730). New York: Routledge.

Riley, R. (2000, October 4). *Riley and Ivey announce nearly $1 million in media literacy grants.* National Endowment for the Arts. <http://www.arts.gov/endownews/news00/edliteracy1.html>

Sardar, Z., & Van Loon, B. (1998). *Introducing cultural studies.* New York: Totem.

The Source. (October, 1999).

Storey, J. (1996). *Cultural studies and the study of popular culture.* Athens: University of Georgia Press.

Storey, J. (1998). *An introduction to cultural theory and popular culture* (2nd ed.). Athens: University of Georgia Press.

Tobin, J. J. (2000). *Good guys don't wear hats: Children's talk about the media.* New York: Teachers College Press.

Turner, G. (1996). *British cultural studies: An introduction* (2nd ed.). London: Routledge.

Walkerdine, V. (1997). *Daddy's girl: Young girls and popular culture.* Cambridge, MA: Harvard University Press.

Willis, P. (1977). *Learning to labour.* New York: Columbia University Press.

Features of Excellence of Reading Teacher Preparation Programs

Janis Harmon, Wanda Hedrick, Miriam Martinez, Bertha Perez, and Susan Keehn
University of Texas at San Antonio

Joyce C. Fine
Florida International University

Deborah Eldridge
Hunter College

Amy Seely Flint
Indiana University

Denise M. Littleton and Mona Bryant-Shanklin
Norfolk State University

Rachelle Loven
University of Sioux Falls

Lori Assaf and Misty Sailors
University of Texas at Austin

As American school achievement has come under increased scrutiny in recent years, there have been accompanying calls for reform of teacher preparation programs. Despite compelling evidence to the contrary (Berliner & Biddle, 1995), there continues to be public outcry regarding the declining performance of American children, especially in the area of reading achievement. In spite of these questionable claims, attacks on reading preparation programs have been especially harsh (e.g., Moats, 1999).

Yet Pearson (2000) has questioned the assumption that current approaches to teacher education are ineffective. Citing the work of a variety of researchers, Pearson observed that: (a) fully prepared and certified teachers are better rated and more successful with students than teachers who lack either subject matter or teaching knowledge, (b) students taught by fully certified teachers score higher on a variety of reading measures than do students taught by non-certified teachers, and (c) the largest share of variation in achievement by state on the National Assessment of Educational Progress (NAEP) is explained by the percentage of well-qualified teachers in a state (those with full certification and a major in the field they teach).

Teacher certification programs do appear to have a positive impact. Nonetheless, there is a paucity of research on reading teacher education. Anders, Hoffman, and Duffy (2000) have observed that the topic has not received high priority within the reading research community. There has been an increase in teacher

National Reading Conference Yearbook, 50, pp. 262–274.

education research in recent years, but this research has focused on topics such as journaling in field experiences, inquiry stance, technology queries, cooperative planning, and other topics related to the context of the teaching environment (Anders et al., 2000). There are few studies in the existing research literature that assume a *programmatic* perspective. The American Association of Colleges for Teacher Education (AACTE) has published a series of case studies of seven outstanding teacher preparation programs. Darling-Hammond (2000) identified a number of common characteristics across these programs: (a) a common vision of good teaching that guides faculty, (b) well-defined standards of performance that serve as a basis for evaluating teacher candidates, (c) well-grounded and broad-based curricula, (d) extended and carefully designed field experiences, (e) strong relationships between university-based and school-based faculty, and (f) attention to ensuring that learning is applied to real problems of practice. Despite the importance of these case studies, the research community has not focused on what effective *reading* teacher preparation programs at the preservice level look like. Hoffman and Pearson (2000) have called for investigations of the features of successful reading teacher preparation programs, their "characteristics, coursework patterns, course content, instruction, internship experiences, and enrollments in reading education courses" (p. 41). The purpose of this study was to identify the features of 4-year undergraduate reading preparation programs that lead to excellence in beginning teachers' reading instruction.

Method

This qualitative investigation focused on the eight reading preparation programs that are participants in the International Reading Association's Commission on Excellence in Elementary Teacher Preparation for Reading Instruction.

Participants

The Commission on Excellence in Elementary Teacher Preparation for Reading Instruction is engaged in a 3-year research effort to study excellence in 4-year undergraduate teacher preparation programs in reading. Through a competitive application process, a panel of reading educators selected eight sites they judged to have outstanding 4-year preparation programs. The panel, consisting of John Guthrie, David Pearson, Dorothy Strickland, and Carol Santa, based their selections on criteria that included: (a) special attention to reading in the program, (b) focus on service to minority populations, (c) history of research and development, (d) faculty active in teacher education research, (e) track record of success in preparing teachers, (f) commitment to field-based practices, and (g) collaboration with schools.

No program was expected to meet all the criteria, and the goal was to obtain a representation of diverse programs. The selected universities are: Florida International University (Miami, FL), Hunter College (New York, NY), Indiana University (Bloomington and Indianapolis, IN), Norfolk State University (Norfolk, VA), University of Nevada, Reno (Reno, NV), University of Texas at Austin (Austin, TX), University of Texas at San Antonio (San Antonio, TX), University of Sioux Falls (Sioux Falls, SD). We refer to the sites collectively as Sites of Excellence in Reading Teacher Preparation (SERTE). While the Commission is conducting a series of studies related to reading teacher preparation, this article focuses on only one of the investigations, the Features of Excellence Study.

Procedures

Faculties at each of the eight sites were asked to identify the features of their programs that lead to excellence in beginning teachers' reading instruction. Each individual site then prepared a draft document presenting the identified features and narrative descriptions of each feature. Sites shared their drafts with the other Commission sites, and the Commission agreed upon a common format for site documents. After drafts were revised using this common format, the Commission then examined the eight program documents using constant comparative methods to identify eight common features that lead to excellence (Glaser & Strauss, 1967; Strauss & Corbin, 1990). Commission members prepared a short description of each feature. Each site then provided a narrative description of the implementation of each feature in their teacher education program. Following this, the Commission completed a final "Features of Excellence Report" that states and explains each feature and provides concrete examples of implementation.

Findings

In this section we present the eight features of excellence identified in the investigation followed by a concise explanation of each feature and selected examples from the SERTE sites. The eight features of excellence are:

1. Programs are based on clearly articulated institutional missions that reflect a sense of who we are and who we want to become (Mission).
2. Faculty has a clear vision of how the mission is instantiated in the teacher education program (Vision).
3. Based upon current research and professional standards, programs deliver broad-based content to best meet the need of diverse students (Content).
4. Faculty and school personnel model the student-centered learning they expect their students to use in teaching children (Personalized Teaching).
5. Carefully supervised apprenticeship experiences are critical features of the teacher preparation programs (Apprenticeship).
6. Programs foster the professional identity of preservice teachers and teacher educators within and across a variety of communities (Community).
7. A discriminating admissions/entry/exit continuum of procedures for maintaining standards and academic accountability, both supportive of diverse candidates and aimed at producing quality reading teachers, insures that teachers

are knowledgeable, have the necessary skills, and are able to teach reading effectively (Standards).

8. Faculties strive to maintain the integrity and quality of the literacy program while working within the limited resources and constraints imposed by schools, the university, and the state (Autonomy).

Mission

A clearly articulated mission guides the teacher preparation programs at the eight Sites of Excellence in Reading Teaching. Based upon its history and context, each institution has a mission statement that provides the framework for the cohesive goals of its teacher preparation program. Consequently, the programs across the SERTE sites reflect a sense of identity and purpose.

In cross-site analyses to determine how institutional mission statements are reflected in reading teacher preparation programs, common elements emerged: (a) careful planning of literacy coursework and field experiences based upon established standards, (b) experiences to enable preservice teachers to meet the needs of children in diverse communities, and (c) experiences to encourage inquiry and reflective teaching.

At Norfolk State University, a historically black university, the institution's mission is supported by the School of Education's aim to prepare caring, competent, cooperative, and creative teachers. Literacy coursework and sequential field experiences are based upon standards of the National Council for Accreditation of Teacher Education (NCATE), the International Reading Association (IRA), the Virginia Department of Education, and the Norfolk State University's School of Education (School of Education Committee at Norfolk State University, 1990, 1996). Student volunteerism and participation in the Reading Partners' Clinic provide additional opportunities for prospective teachers to meet the needs of diverse students, to become reflective practitioners, to develop skills in caring, cooperation, and creativity, and to become catalysts for child advocacy and change.

At Florida International University, an urban, multicultural institution, the mission of the College of Education particularly reflects the feature of diversity in line with established standards. Its mission is to prepare professionals who have the knowledge of sound theory and practice, as well as the ability and disposition to facilitate learning in diverse settings. Throughout the curriculum, performance-based instruction and assessment are used to document effectiveness based on the standards of the Teachers of English to Speakers of Other Languages (TESOL), NCATE, IRA, and the state of Florida. Similarly, the remaining SERTE sites have programs that support their respective institutional mission statements.

Vision

SERTE faculties are committed to a vision of preparing effective reading teachers and identified vision as a powerful engine driving teacher education reading programs toward excellence and long range success. SERTE faculties think of themselves as lifelong learners who have a broad range of expertise and who work hard to foster effective reading teachers. Vision and a commitment to the vision help to insure the effective preparation of teachers for all children. The following critical components emerged in the analysis of this feature of excellence:

Faculties impart their visions through program continuity. For example, Hunter College faculty members have taught and supervised undergraduates for an average of 10 years. The length and breadth of faculty involvement in this New York City undergraduate teacher preparation program has resulted in a School of Education that is committed to, respectful of, and sensitive to the challenges and issues involved in undergraduate teacher preparation.

The vision involves concern for individual students. At the University of Texas at San Antonio (UTSA), the faculty's concern for individuals is apparent in the scheduling of courses. The cycle of reading specialization courses offered each semester typically results in groups of students moving together through the program. As a result, students form strong relationships and support groups with peers in a fashion similar to cohorts. The University of Texas at Austin maintains the care for the individual through a formal cohort structure. Teaching assistants, school-based faculty, and university faculty work as a team with cohort groups limited to 22 students. This organization results in a program that is responsive to student needs. In addition, most students complete their internship and student teaching with the same teacher.

The integration of research, theory, and practice is integral to the visions of SERTE programs. The University of Sioux Falls faculty has a reputation for balancing current reading research with a realistic view of reading instruction practices. This integration of theory and practice assists preservice teachers in applying their newly learned teaching theories in actual classroom situations while providing sufficient theoretical support for changing classroom instruction beyond the status quo.

SERTE faculty members are guided by their visions for effective teacher preparation. These visions are well developed and serve as a driving force in university curriculum decision making, faculty hiring practices, and relationships with school-based cooperating teachers and teacher preparation students.

Content

Research links success in teaching with the amount of declarative, procedural, and conditional knowledge possessed by the beginning teacher (Pearson, 2000). The eight SERTE programs have paid particular attention to the content of their reading preparation programs. Each SERTE program provides content that gives preservice teachers the knowledge and skills they need to succeed in classrooms serving America's increasingly diverse population.

Program content in SERTE sites is broad-based and enables preservice teachers to acquire critical knowledge and skills necessary to teach reading successfully. The programs offer content that includes theoretical foundations that help prospective teachers develop a congruent set of principles and practices for effective teaching. In addition, the content focuses on sound instructional methods, practices, and strategies derived from both theory and research. Finally, assessment for evaluating students' literacy progress is addressed in program content. SERTE programs have been (and continue to be) involved in ongoing analyses of their program content in response to both internal and external forces.

Faculty knowledge of current literacy theory and research shapes program content. Drawing on faculty expertise in the literacy development of learners from diverse backgrounds, faculty at the University of Texas at San Antonio developed a course, entitled *Language, Literacy, and Culture,* in which students explore issues related to the literacy needs of English language learners, bilingual students, and students with dialectical differences.

Faculty experience with public education influences program content. At the University of Texas at San Antonio, one course, *Introduction to Reading Problems,* moved to a field-based setting in the inner city so that preservice teachers would acquire skill in diagnosing student needs and planning instruction to meet those needs.

Feedback from program participants guides program content. Based on feedback from students, UTSA faculty members realized a need to help students learn to apply knowledge of phonemic awareness and phonics. The faculty created a new required course that directly addresses these topics and others pertinent to early literacy learning.

Program content is examined in light of current professional standards for teacher preparation articulated by professional organizations. For example, the University of Nevada, Reno, as part of their NCATE accreditation study, examined their program content using the International Reading Association's (1998) *Standards for Reading Professionals.* Likewise, Florida International University shaped the content of its program through the use of Teachers of English as a Second Language (TESOL) standards.

Program content is affected by state accountability systems for teacher preparation. Both Texas SERTE sites identified key competencies that preservice teachers must demonstrate on the Examination for the Certification of Educators in Texas (ExCET) and infused these competencies into their courses.

State curricula for school children influences program content. For example, the Texas Essential Knowledge and Skills (TEKS) emphasizes phonemic awareness. In response to this, at the University of Texas at San Antonio, students become familiar with and administer a specific state assessment tool entitled the Texas Primary Reading Inventory (Texas Education Agency, n.d.).

At SERTE sites, multiple forces, both internal and external, encourage ongoing revision of program content to create more knowledgeable and competent teachers of reading. This process results in program content that is broad based and supportive of the decision making that graduates must do in their own classrooms.

Personalized Teaching

Within the SERTE programs, faculty model the critical elements and conditions required of personalized teaching, so that preservice teachers in turn can model them with their own students. Such personalized teaching includes attention to the individual student, scaffolding of learning, and the creation of a caring context for learning.

Faculty support learners as individuals both inside and outside of class. Across SERTE sites there are some accommodations that address special needs of students, including small class sizes, offering course sections at varied times, personal and professional counseling, and assistance in placements. The University of Indiana at Bloomington offers three program options so that prospective teachers may match their own interests and needs with a program. One program is designed as a cohort with a focus on democracy, diversity, and social justice. Another program offers extensive field placements, and the third program follows a more traditional model.

Faculty scaffold learning and create experiences to challenge simplistic views of literacy learning and teaching. Instructors encourage preservice educators to move beyond the safety of their current knowledge to explore more theoretically grounded literacy processes. This movement is supported in whole class or small group discussion, reflective writing, and modeling and guidance as preservice teachers work with students. At the University of Nevada, Reno, the course in which preservice teachers tutor struggling readers is one in which a considerable amount of scaffolding takes place.

Literacy faculty create environments where students feel a sense of community. At the University of Indiana at Bloomington and the University of Texas at Austin, cohort members stay together over multiple semesters of study. Within the learning community, preservice teachers use the support of others to explore challenging ideas. Faculty also build-in time for talk and reflection on preservice teachers' evolving beliefs related to literacy learning. Thus, preservice students in reading education in SERTE programs benefit from personalized teaching, caring learning communities, and scaffolded instruction.

Apprenticeship

Carefully supervised field experiences were identified as a critical feature in each of the eight SERTE programs. However, as we studied this feature in greater depth, we discovered that it was not simply the presence of school-based experiences in learning and teaching that constituted excellence. SERTE programs exemplified components of apprenticeship in their provision of authentic experiences for preservice teachers over extended periods of time in collaboration with master teachers.

Apprenticeships are characterized by extended experiences. In New York City, the Hunter College program maximizes opportunities to place preservice teachers in contact with public school students and teachers early and often. This is done by pairing each of the undergraduate methods and foundations courses with one-credit field experiences.

Apprenticeships contain authentic activities. The University of Nevada, Reno program provides authentic opportunities through its Early Learning Center, a regular, multi-age, first- through third-grade classroom housed in the university's College of Education and through its Center for Learning and Literacy that coordinates tutoring experiences linked to literacy coursework in assessment.

Apprenticeships occur in social contexts. Hunter students take advantage of the full range of diversity that New York City schools offer in terms of grade levels, school philosophies, student populations, and teaching styles. A full-time Director of Clinical Field Placements coordinates and diversifies field experiences by placing students in classrooms that do not duplicate previous assignments.

Modeling, coaching, fading, and an increase in independence characterize apprenticeships. Field experiences at Norfolk State University are sequenced and enable students to move through stages of increased responsibility for classroom instruction or other professional roles in schools. Additionally, each of these sequenced field experiences is designed to highlight the particular concepts, skills, attitudes, or competencies that complement the corresponding coursework.

Learning in an apprenticeship occurs over time. The reflective quality of field experiences at Hunter College is supported by faculty that teach both the courses offered on campus and supervise in the field. Ongoing reflection is encouraged through in-class discussions, the utilization of field placement examples to illustrate theoretical concepts, the creation of portfolios or the use of journals, and regular feedback during multiple observations, written evaluations, and post-observation conferences.

Apprenticeships enculturate. Most of the cooperating classroom teachers for the University of Sioux Falls have been involved with the university on an ongoing basis. A critical characteristic for the University of Sioux Falls is that of a "welcoming" teacher who has made a place for the teacher candidate in his or her classroom including the teacher candidate's participation in open-house activities and parent conferences.

SERTE programs demonstrate the basic components of quality apprenticeships in the early, sequential, purposeful, and diverse placements of students with master teachers. Additionally, quality apprenticeships involve opportunities for students to dialogue about, reflect upon, and negotiate the meaning of their experiences. Such opportunities complement field experiences and build within SERTE program graduates the repertoires that high quality literacy teaching demands.

Community

One critical feature of excellence in the SERTE programs is the construction of a positive learning community, similar to what is advocated for elementary and secondary classrooms. This feature of community reaches deeper than making new friends or finding colleagues who are supportive. Development of community is potentially transformative in helping students achieve the identity of teacher.

The feature of community and how it can influence teacher development is grounded in several theories that help to explain the importance of community as a necessary feature of teacher preparation programs. Bruner (1990) explored the development of personal identity within the family. He asserted that these experiences are internalized as narratives and become the fabric of a developing identity. Similarly, preservice teachers' experiences with peers and mentor teachers impact their developing identities as teachers. Gee's (1990) notions of "discourse communities" help to explain "teacher identity." Gee argues that every individual has a primary discourse community, usually the family. As the individual matures and moves outside the familiar, new discourse communities are encountered and entered. Teaching, like law, medicine, and the military, is considered one of the basic social discourse communities in society. Learning this discourse is a large part of what preservice teachers do in a preparation program. As they acquire this discourse, the identity of *teacher* takes root. Finally, as students learn the "speech genres" of teaching (Bakhtin, 1986), they further develop their teacher identity within the familiar social context of this learning community. Teacher preparation programs can provide the aspiring teacher with a safe context, or community, in which to explore and acquire this discourse.

The SERTE programs work in clear ways to actively encourage the creation of a learning community that is centered on teaching as an identity. Listed below are specific ways in which this community feature is nurtured:

Programs provide both a place and space for the learning community. One reading specialization cohort at the University of Texas at Austin is currently based in a public school serving a low-income area of the city. The majority of classes, as well as the tutoring experiences, are held in this school. Students and professors become part of the larger school community.

Preservice teachers are given opportunities to engage in community study. A course called "Community Literacy" at the University of Texas at Austin encourages students to understand and appreciate the meanings of literacy in the low-income communities surrounding the home-base school. The students tutor in adult literacy and family literacy programs, engage in a semester long study of community literacy, and conduct home visits with the students they tutor.

Preservice teachers become part of teacher networks. The students at the University of Texas at Austin are placed for a year-long observation and student teaching experiences. This year-long experience is with classroom teachers who have been carefully selected based on their exceptional qualities as models and mentors. Because these teachers have worked with the program for a number of years, they have become an integral part of the community.

Preservice teachers participate in virtual networks. The University of Texas at Austin supports an electronic communication network called TeachNet. The system offers a virtual space for the creation of a community that extends into the first year of teaching. In a similar fashion, at the University of Texas at San Antonio, as part of their organized coursework, students frequently communicate with peers and instructors in e-mail discussion groups.

Community building experiences are a critical part of the SERTE programs. These collaborative efforts provide students with a sense of community within and beyond teacher education programs and strengthen their identities as teachers.

Standards

To be accountable, teacher educators must meet two important goals for the profession (Holmes Group, 1986). One is to prepare teachers who are capable and the other is to increase the number of minority teachers. To insure both quality and equity of opportunity, the eight SERTE programs have designed continuums of admissions and exit standards along with other supportive structures for diverse students.

SERTE programs have initiated a variety of strategies to accomplish these goals. Some programs have raised academic and performance standards by articulating goals and objectives and setting high standards for achievement. Other programs have created recruitment plans and flexible schedules to make their programs more congruent with nontraditional students' needs. Educators also systematically monitor program results as a basis for continuous improvement. Measures to support students found across sites include the following:

Multiple measures are used for admission. For example, students at Florida International University must have a 2.5 GPA and must pass a state test on academic skills after completing their first 2 years as an undergraduate. They must submit SAT or EACT standardized scores. Florida International University also has a committee that reviews applications of underrepresented candidates who have not met program requirements. This committee judges the applicant's records, strengths, and demonstrated commitment to elementary education.

Program faculty members monitor student progress to insure quality. For example, at Florida International University faculty members evaluate portfolios that students maintain as they progress through the program. Occasionally, monitoring may include referring students to support services for academic or personal guidance.

SERTE programs use alternative class schedules and field experiences to meet the needs of nontraditional students. At Florida International University, classes are offered at various times to accommodate students who are employed full-time or who have young children. In consideration of students' life demands, field experiences at the University of Texas at San Antonio are offered during the day in the schools and at the university-based clinic in the evenings.

High standards for program completion are maintained. At Florida International University, exit criteria include documenting performance on state standardized exams, accomplished practices, successful performance in student teaching, and a final GPA of at least 2.5.

The SERTE programs constantly consider the goal of providing excellent training of teachers of reading. This goal is coupled with a second and equally critical goal of being inclusive of a more diverse population of teacher candidates.

Autonomy

Autonomy—the act of being self-governed and having self-directed freedoms—plays an important role in the eight SERTE programs. Faculty at these sites demonstrate a commitment to best meet the needs of their students. In many cases, this commitment is reflected in their autonomous actions and decisions regarding instruction, field experiences, standards, and budget.

The research literature on autonomy is based in the work of teacher reform and teacher empowerment. Efforts to engage in teacher reform include careful reconsideration of what teachers know and learn about curriculum design and instructional methodology (Popkewitz, 1985). These informed decisions are based on knowledge of school organization and structures, as well as the social and political contexts of the classrooms. Dewey (1933) addressed teacher autonomy and decision-making when he sought to empower teachers with a greater understanding of the complexities of teaching through inquiry and experimental learning opportunities. One avenue teachers pursue is to assume an inquiry stance. This mindset is important as faculty and students make informed decisions regarding the instructional practices in classrooms.

Responding to a variety of constraints and mandates (e.g., budget, limited personnel, licensing/credentialing requirements), the eight SERTE sites have extended beyond the university structures to provide meaningful programs in literacy education in the following ways:

SERTE programs with large student enrollment meet the accompanying challenges in creative ways. Large student enrollment is an issue at Indiana University, Florida International University, the University of Texas at Austin, and the University of Texas at San Antonio. To encourage cohesiveness among the faculty and adjunct faculty (retired professors, classroom teachers, and graduate students), regularly scheduled conversations and meetings are held to discuss courses, readings, and other issues related to reading teacher preparation.

SERTE programs have developed innovative structures to best meet students' needs. Implementing innovative reading programs, encouraging additional courses, and working in cohort structures demonstrate some of the ways in which

SERTE faculty members make autonomous decisions. With minimal internal support, the reading faculty at the University of Texas at San Antonio launched a literacy center at the downtown campus to provide additional opportunities for preservice teachers to work with inner city children. At Florida International University, the faculty successfully petitioned the state legislature to allow the university to increase the number of literacy courses required for graduation. Indiana University (IUPUI–Indianapolis) and the University of Texas at Austin have cohort options available for students, encouraging them to build professional relationships between and among colleagues, faculty, and teachers.

SERTE programs create innovative structures to build professional relationships with students. For example, the cohort structures at Indiana University and the University of Texas at Austin provide faculty with more flexibility in how content is presented. This is similar to the way that elementary school teachers teach in multi-age or looping configurations. Cohort faculty who work with students for an extended period of time (in this case three to four semesters) demonstrate a greater level of autonomy in how theory, materials, and pedagogical practices are presented and implemented. This structure contributes to empowerment because faculty members are not as constrained by time, as in traditional one semester courses.

Faculty at the eight sites demonstrated autonomy in establishing meaningful structures and in making decisions. Such models appear to positively influence the ways in which beginning teachers respond to children as individual learners (Goyne, Padgett, Rowicka, & Triplett, 1999; Melenyzer, 1990).

Discussion

Preparing future teachers with the knowledge and skills to successfully teach reading to an increasingly diverse population is one of the most crucial tasks that teacher preparation programs face. While this analysis of the eight SERTE programs identified common features in outstanding reading preparation programs, the analysis also suggests that the task of building an outstanding program is complex and requires the commitment and collaboration of faculty members. Faculty members must begin their program building efforts by defining their mission and clearly articulating a vision to guide program building efforts. To ensure success, faculty members must examine the content of their programs so that students acquire the broad-based knowledge—both theoretical and practical—that they will need to teach reading. Further, to ensure that students internalize this knowledge, faculty must model the elements of personalized teaching and engage students in apprenticeships in the field. Faculty must build community within their programs while simultaneously ensuring high standards for future teachers. To achieve these ends, faculty members must frequently act autonomously and creatively.

The features identified in this investigation do not offer a formula for the successful preparation of reading teachers. In fact, we discovered that the eight features played out in a variety of ways across the sites. Thus, thoughtful attention to the way in which each feature might be best implemented within a particular context appears to be important in building outstanding reading preparation programs.

Author Note

We would like to acknowledge the contributions of Commission members J. V. Hoffman, B. Maloch, S. Templeton, and D. Barone.

References

Abrahams, J. (1995). *The mission statement book.* Berkeley, CA: Ten Speed.

Anders, P. L., Hoffman, J. V., & Duffy, G. G. (2000). Teaching teachers to teach reading: Paradigm shifts, persistent problems, and challenges. In M. L. Kamil, P. B. Mosenthal, P. D. Pearson, & R. Barr (Eds.), *Handbook of reading research* (Vol. 3, pp. 719–743). Mahwah, NJ: Erlbaum.

Bakhtin, M. M. (1986). *Speech genres and other late essays.* Austin: University of Texas Press.

Berliner, D. C., & Biddle, B. J. (1995). *The manufactured crisis: Myths, fraud, and the attack on America's public schools.* Reading, MA: Addison-Wesley.

Bruner, J. (1990). *Acts of meaning.* Cambridge, MA: Harvard University Press.

Darling-Hammond, L. (Ed.). (2000). *Studies of excellence in teacher education: Preparation in the undergraduate years.* Washington, DC: American Association of Colleges of Teacher Education.

Dewey, J. (1933). *How we think.* Lexington, MA: Heath.

Gee, J.P. (1990). *Social linguistics and literacies: Ideologies in discourses.* London: Farmer.

Glaser, B. G., & Strauss, A. L. (1967). *The discovery of grounded theory: Strategies for qualitative research.* Chicago: Aldine.

Goyne, J., Padgett, D., Rowicki, M., & Triplett, T. (1999). *The journey to teacher empowerment.* (ERIC Document Reproduction Service No. ED 434 384)

Hoffman, J., & Pearson, P. D. (2000). Reading teacher education in the next millennium: "What your grandmother's teacher didn't know that you granddaughter's teacher should." *Reading Research Quarterly, 35,* 28–44.

Holmes Group. (1986). *Tomorrow's teachers.* East Lansing, MI: Author.

International Reading Association. (1998). *Standards for reading professionals.* Newark, DE: Author.

Melenyzer, B. (1990, November). *Teacher Empowerment: The Discourse, Meanings and Social Actions of Teachers.* Paper presented at the meeting of the National Council of States on Inservice Education, Orlando, FL.

Moats, L. C. (1999). *Teaching reading is rocket science: What expert teachers of reading should know and be able to do.* Washington, DC: American Federation of Teachers.

Pearson, P. D. (2000). *Learning to teach reading: Setting the research agenda.* Paper presented at the meeting of the International Reading Association, Indianapolis, IN.

Popkewitz, T. (1985). *Curriculum studies, knowledge and interest: Problems and paradoxes.* ((ERIC Document Reproduction Service No. ED 267 478)

School of Education Committee at Norfolk State University. (1990, 1996). *The knowledge base for professional education.* Unpublished institutional reports for the National Council for Accreditation of Teacher Education.

Strauss, A., & Corbin, J. (1990). *Basics of qualitative research.* Newbury Park, CA: Sage.

Texas Education Agency. (n.d.). *Texas Primary Reading Inventory.* Austin, TX: Author.

Professional Development Programs in Reading: A National Survey of District Directors

Marie Tejero Hughes
University of Illinois at Chicago

Michele Mits Cash, Janette Klingner, and Suzette Ahwee
University of Miami

Well-prepared teachers are critical to students' success in learning to read, yet many new teachers begin their careers without knowing how to help all students become proficient readers (Snow, Burns, & Griffin, 1998). Teaching reading is complex and requires: (a) a sophisticated understanding of how students learn to read, (b) knowledge of the difficulties experienced by some students and how to provide support, and (c) the ability to implement a variety of multilevel instructional practices (National Reading Panel, 2000). It is not realistic to expect that prospective teachers would acquire these competencies during their teacher preparation programs—it can take years to develop the necessary skills and expertise. As life-long learners, teachers must always be honing their teaching abilities. School districts around the country have responded to the need for teachers to continue their professional growth by providing a wide range of professional development programs.

Quality professional development in reading is relevant to teachers' and students' needs (Anderson, 1997). Teachers who receive high-quality professional training which is directly focused on their classroom curriculum and instruction are more likely to use instructional practices that are associated with higher reading achievement than those who do not (Darling-Hammond, 2000; Joyce & Showers, 1995). Moreover, effective reading programs that meet the needs of struggling readers are lead by teachers who integrate effective reading interventions into their curriculum (Broaddus & Bloodgood, 1999). For teachers to deliver high-quality instruction, they must be provided with "sufficient opportunities to access and use high-quality instructional strategies" (p. 24). Continuing professional development allows teachers to stay abreast of best reading practices (American Federation of Teachers, 1999).

The test of the success of a professional development program is whether students benefit from the reading instruction delivered by the teacher as an outcome of the program. In general, results indicate that quality professional development can produce higher reading achievement (Anders, Hoffman, & Duffy, 2000). Yet the effects that professional development programs have on teachers and students vary widely because of differences in program content, structure

National Reading Conference Yearbook, ***50***, *pp. 275–286.*

and format of the experience, and the context in which new practices are implemented (Guskey, 2000; National Staff Development Council, 1994, 1995a, 1995b). Also, it is difficult to make simple causal inferences about the relationships between professional development programs and improvements in student learning because typically there are many intervening variables (Guskey, 1997; Guskey & Sparks, 1996). However, we do know enough to conclude that quality professional development programs (e.g., providing intensive levels of support, opportunities for reflection) are more likely to have a greater impact than those that do not (Anders et al., 2000). We also know that ineffective programs are much more common than effective ones.

Most professional development programs do not result in change in teachers' reading instruction, and therefore do not enhance students' reading achievement. Few teachers experience long-term quality professional development programs that have the potential to promote significant and lasting change (Porter, Garet, Desimone, Yoon, & Birman, 2000). Typical professional development programs are "one shot" sessions that lack substantive, research-based content and the systematic follow-up necessary for sustainability (Snow et al., 1998). These professional development activities are linear or "top-down" in approach with participants listening to the latest ideas regarding teaching and learning from "experts" (Abbott, Walton, Tapia, & Greenwood, 1999; Hawley & Valli, 1998; National Joint Committee on Learning Disabilities, 2000). Little consideration is given to what teachers already know or believe, and seldom are teachers observed following the professional development to determine if they are implementing the practices presented (Hoffman, 1996).

Although the duration and intensity of many professional development programs have increased during the past couple of decades (Joyce & Showers, 1995), high-quality, long-term professional development programs are still uncommon. Yet we have learned a great deal about what "works" (Darling-Hammond, 1995; Hawley & Valli, 1998). The salient characteristics of effective models are: (a) intensive and extensive levels of support (Anders & Evens, 1994), (b) monitoring and coaching (Moore, 1991), (c) teacher reflection (Bos & Anders, 1994), (d) ongoing conversations and dialogue (Combs, 1994), (e) voluntary participation (El-Dinary & Schuder, 1993), (f) help assimilating new information into existing belief structures (Malouf & Schiller, 1995), and (g) collaboration among different role groups (Short & Kauffman, 1992). Furthermore, professional development programs that do not rely solely on a small group of volunteer teachers, but rather encompass the entire faculty of the school, have higher rates of teacher implementation (Joyce & Shower, 1995).

High-quality professional development programs allow teachers the opportunity to develop and change their teaching over time rather than just "try out" what they have learned. The purpose of professional development should not just be on "training" teachers on the specific reading practices, but rather on educating teachers to become more strategic and reflective in their application of practices (Anders et al., 2000). Teachers are able to directly relate the new practices they are learning to the everyday realities they experience in their classrooms (Cuban, 1988). With ongoing support, they are able to successfully integrate new practices into their instructional repertoire. After all, teachers taking ownership of their learning should be the goal of every professional development program (Finch, 1999).

In response to the need for better-prepared teachers, professional development programs in the area of reading have accordingly and recently increased (Anderson, 1997). It is not uncommon to see a list of professional development opportunities posted on faculty bulletin boards across the nation. Most states and districts have no clear answer as to how much is actually spent on these professional development programs, but estimates are usually between 3% and 5% of school districts' budgets and between 1% and 3% of state spending for public education (Corcoran, 1995). In most cases it is the local school districts that provide the majority of the funding related to professional development programs. Expenditures vary from district to district but can include personnel costs associated with planning and delivering the workshops, supervising and evaluating personnel, providing substitute coverage, opening schools extra days per year, and paying for teacher stipends (Corcoran, 1995). Administrators spend valuable budget money on professional development and usually without questioning whether teachers and students are benefiting significantly from their efforts (Robb, 2000). Measuring this impact over the long term is critical, because even when teacher change has occurred, sustaining such changes are challenging for teachers due to school constraints and pressures (Duffy, Roehler, & Putnam, 1987). However, little is known about the procedures school districts follow when designing professional development activities or their methods for determining implementation and accountability.

The purpose of this study was to describe the professional development programs of school districts across the nation. Specifically, we sought to determine what professional development programs were being offered to elementary and special education teachers in the area of reading in their districts as reported by directors of reading/language arts and special education. We were interested in determining the content, structure, and context of the programs, as well as the districts' methods of assessing accountability. We focused on how these facets of professional development assist teachers in implementing and sustaining effective reading practices.

Method

Participants

Surveys were mailed to 294 randomly selected school districts as well as to the 20 largest school districts in the United States (n=314). Participants were selected using the information available from the National Center for Educational Statistics. In all states two districts from each metropolitan status (rural, suburban, urban) were randomly selected to receive the survey. States with less than two districts in any category had an alternate district randomly selected to maintain a six district per state ratio. If states had less than six districts in total, all of the districts were used in the sample. For each selected school district one survey was sent to the program director of elementary-level reading/language arts and one to the program director of special education, the total *N* consisted of 628 mailed surveys. These directors were requested to complete the survey or pass it on to a colleague they felt was better able to provide the information we were seeking. A total of 292 surveys were returned (46%), 149 from the reading/language arts subsample and 143 from the special education subsample. The directors represented 225 of the 314 school districts sampled.

Measures

Survey. A National Survey of Professional Development Practices in Reading for Elementary School Educators was mailed to selected participants. The survey was a 19-item questionnaire centered around three themes related to professional development programs: program content, program structure, and post-program accountability. The research literature on professional development in reading, as well as the literature on reading instruction, served as a guide as to which programs and concepts to include on the survey (e.g., Hoffman & Pearson, 2000; Snow et al., 1998).

The first question on the survey asked the respondent to identify their professional role in organizing professional development programs for their district. Four questions covered the first theme of content and sought information regarding what was offered in professional development programs. Specifically, what types of programs and or concepts were offered; what factors were important to decision makers when choosing content; and whether or not they felt that the professional development programs were providing their teachers with the tools they needed to be successful in the classroom. The second theme, program structure, consisted of seven questions that were developed to elicit information regarding program structure and included information about types of incentives offered to teachers for attending professional development programs; who generally conducts programs; and what is the format of the program. For the third theme, post-program accountability, there were six questions that focused on teacher responsibility following participation in a professional development program and addressed issues such as what percentage of teachers in the district attended at least one professional development program; to what extent they implement and sustain what they learn, and how implementation is monitored if at all. The final question on the survey asked if the respondent would be willing to participate in a follow-up telephone interview.

Procedures

The survey was mailed to all 314 selected school districts with a #2 pencil (for ease of completion) and a postage-paid return envelope. Participants were requested to complete and return the survey within two weeks of receiving it in the mail. As an incentive to increase the response rate, the participants were offered an opportunity to win a $100 gift certificate upon return of the completed survey. After the first mailing a second mailing was sent to those school districts that had yet to respond. A 46% response rate was achieved at the end of 6 weeks.

Data Analysis

The survey data was analyzed using the SPSS statistical software package to generate frequencies and descriptive information. Nonparametric analysis was used to determine statistical significance between comparative participant groups on appropriate survey questions.

Results

Directors were asked to provide information about the professional development conducted in their district. The findings of the study are grouped into the three themes surveyed, content of professional development, structure of professional development, and accountability. After examining the responses of both the special education and reading language arts groups no significant difference between groups on any item was found. To further explore this issue, a data set containing only districts in which both the special education and reading language arts directors (n=73) responded was analyzed for differences. No significant differences were found in this subset of data. Therefore, answers for both groups of directors (reading and special education) have been merged and percentages indicate the total number of respondents who provided information. Because several of the survey questions offered the respondents the opportunity to check multiple items, the percentages calculated on some items is greater than 100%.

To determine if reading and special education directors believed that teachers were prepared to teach reading, they were asked if the professional development in their district provided teachers with the tools and knowledge they needed to prepare students to meet the established criteria of their state and district. Fifty-three percent of the respondents perceived that the professional development offered in their district prepared teachers moderately well in meeting this need with 28% indicating that the professional development programs did very well. On the other hand, about 8% thought that the professional development did not prepare the teachers, whereas the remaining directors did not state their opinion.

Content of Professional Development

The directors were asked to identify the professional development topics presented in their district during the past school year (see Table 1). Frequently mentioned workshops focused on providing instruction on implementing specific packaged reading programs. Sixty-five percent of the directors indicated that pack-

Table 1

Most Common Professional Development Topics and Selection Factors

	Percentages
Topics	
Specific reading programs	65
Specific reading practices	64
General reading strategies	58
Instructional techniques and methods	57
Phonological awareness	46
Reading comprehension	40
Emergent reading	31
Remedial reading	29
Factors	
Fits school district's philosophy	82
Expected to increase test scores	81
Research-based	81
Teachers request	75
Professional experience	56

aged programs, typified by Reading Recovery or Success for All, were the most common topics presented. Specific reading practices like Making Words (Cunningham & Cunningham, 1992) or Collaborative Strategic Reading (Klingner & Vaughn, 1996) constituted the second most common topic with 64% of the directors selecting this. Besides providing professional development on specific programs or practices, 58% of districts provided inservices that focused on teaching teachers a variety of general reading strategies. Over half the directors (57%) also indicated that workshops geared to developing the teacher's instructional skills were provided. This type of professional development covered a wide range of topics including computer-based instruction, using multicultural literature, and collaborative learning. Directors were also asked to rate how important certain factors were in influencing their selection of professional development topics offered in their district (see Table 1). Three factors were rated as very important or important by at least 80% of the directors. The district's reading philosophy played a major role in determining what topics were presented at workshops. In addition, directors indicated that they considered the impact the practice potentially had to increase students' reading test scores. Directors also strongly felt that information presented to teachers should be research based. In turn, the national popularity of the topic and whether the program was prepackaged and ready to use were not factors frequently reported by directors as influencing their decision.

Structure of Professional Development

Teacher participation in district sponsored inservice programs was almost evenly split between voluntary (53%) and required (47%) participation. However, most of the districts (88%) provided incentives for teachers attending workshops. The most frequently cited incentive was providing the teachers with credit for attending professional development that could be used toward state recertification (66%). Directors also stated that teachers were provided with release time (59%) to attend professional development programs during the workday and/or were given a stipend (43%) upon completion of the workshop. Other incentives such as mileage reimbursement (31%), classroom resources (26%), and salary increases (17%) were provided by several of the districts.

Our survey indicated that districts offered workshops in a variety of formats. The most frequent formats for inservices across the country were 1-day workshops (70%) or half-day workshops (64%), although multiday workshops (55%) and workshops with follow-up support (45%) were also used. Lengthier and more individualized professional development programs were not as common, however it is interesting to note that about a quarter of the directors indicated that the district offered them. Presenters at workshops were usually outside consultants hired by the schools (84%) or school district personnel (80%). School-level administrators and lead teachers (59%) also regularly lead professional development workshops. Directors indicated that publishers and developers of the reading program or practice presented at inservices 45% of the time.

Directors were asked to describe the kinds of resources and support most frequently provided to teachers during and after the professional development program (see Table 2). The most common resources provided to teachers during the workshops were handouts about the presentation (64%) and supplemental materials (51%) such as charts and activities related to the topic. After attending the professional development teachers were provided with minimum support in most cases. The most frequent support available to teachers was the contact information (63%) of a person who could answer their questions. More extensive support such as in class observations to provide feedback, support groups, additional training, and mentors were provided in less than a third of the districts.

Accountability

When directors were asked if there was a mechanism in place for collecting data on implementation and sustainability of practices presented at professional development programs only 50% replied with an affirmative response. Therefore our report on findings regarding the extent to which teachers integrated practices, and who was responsible for determining the extent of implementation and effectiveness of strategies on student outcomes is limited to the 145 directors whose districts collected these types of data.

District directors reported that in their opinion teachers who attend professional development programs tended to integrate practices presented to them completely into their daily instruction about 8% of the time; partial integration occurred approximately 69% of the time; and only 1% did not implement at least part of what they learned. Eighteen percent of directors reported that they were

Table 2

Resources and Support Provided to Teachers

	Percentages
During the Professional Development	
Handouts	64
Supplemental materials	51
Books	47
Internet resources	37
Videos	47
Mentors	19
Other	10
After the Professional Development	
Contact person	63
In class observations	33
Teacher support groups	30
Advance training	21
Mentors	21
Post-program meeting	15
None are available	14
Other	11

unable to answer the question. For those teachers who did integrate all or part of the practices learned at workshops information regarding their sustainability of the practice or program was not available in 61% of the cases. Of the remaining responses 7% felt that practices learned were not sustained beyond 12 weeks, 17% felt that 3 months to 1 year was the total extent of sustainability and another 14% felt that practices were sustained for more than 1 year.

Teacher implementation of the strategies acquired through professional development was primarily assessed and determined by teacher's self-report (73%) and by the school principal (70%). Other mechanisms for determining implementation included another teacher's observation (33%) of the practice being implemented and by student feedback (22%). Directors were asked to identify how the districts determine the effectiveness of practices. Effectiveness was principally determined by reviewing the students' results on standardized achievement tests (89%), although in most cases no direct link to the professional development program was available. The principals' (79%) and teachers' self-reports (72%) were also important determinants of effectiveness of the practice. Other sources for determining the effectiveness of a practice or program included curriculum based assessment (67%) and observations by other teachers (36%). However, 20% of the directors reported that the data for effectiveness of practices was not available.

Discussion

The responses from district directors of reading/language arts and special education have provided us with a snapshot of the content, structure, and accountability of professional development opportunities in reading. Ongoing professional development is critical for teachers to meet the challenges of a growing and diverse number of students (Hoffman & Pearson, 2000). Unfortunately, professional development programs are often inadequate to prepare teachers to meet the challenges of teaching all students to read (Snow et al., 1998). However, if we want to obtain instructional improvement in reading, educators and community leaders need to acknowledge that teacher education is the key (Darling-Hammond, 1997).

Our nationwide survey of directors revealed that there is still much improvement needed in preparing teachers to meet the reading needs of all their students. However, school districts often lack the infrastructure and knowledge of what works to implement effective professional development. To translate needed reforms into practice, schools and districts need information and guidance on the characteristics and conditions that can help them provide high-quality professional development.

Across the country, one-shot professional development experiences continue to be the most common form of delivering information to teachers. About half the school districts did provide some multiday workshops and follow-up, although this usually took the form of "call if you have questions." Encouragingly, a small percentage of the districts did provide their teachers with more extensive professional development that went beyond the "sit and get" format. If teachers are to gain the most benefit from professional development, districts need to reexam their professional development delivery methods. Programs need to provide for transfer of training, practice, feedback, reflection, and full support and reinforcement for the use of skills in natural settings (Hoffman & Pearson, 2000). Besides incorporating the principles of high-quality professional development programs (e.g., support, reflection, collaboration) into their current programs (Anders et al., 2000), school districts should also consider alternative approaches to preparing teachers to teach reading. There have been notable examples of professional development efforts, which have moved away from the workshop format and have achieved a positive impact (Anders et al., 2000). The use of teacher or action research (Gray-Schlegel & Matanzo, 1993), portfolio development (Kieffer & Faust, 1994), reflective journals (Botel, Ripley, & Barnes, 1993), and book clubs (Flood, Lapp, Ranck-Buhr, & Moore, 1995) have all shown to have assisted teachers in gaining new knowledge and practices, although further study on impact on student achievement is warranted.

Although most administrators state that it is important to supervise teachers to see if they are implementing the ideas and concepts of the professional development (Thompson & Cooley, 1986), about half the school districts surveyed did not have a means of determining implementation. Directors who did monitor teacher implementation for the most part relied on teacher or principal self-report and/or principal observations. Directors reported that they perceived that the majority of the teachers implemented some aspect of the information they were presented with, but were unable to provide solid evidence beyond self-report. This finding confirms that most professional development programs focus on measuring teachers' satisfaction with the professional development or changes in teachers' attitudes, but that few measure the change in teachers' practice and degree of implementation (Killion, 1998). Furthermore, most professional development efforts do not demonstrate evidence of their impact on student performance (Killion, 1998). Although it is difficult to create and carry out an evaluation that links staff development and student achievement, the monitoring of teacher progress following professional development insures that activities are beneficial in terms of improving teacher skills and student achievement.

References

Abbott, M., Walton, C., Tapia, Y., & Greenwood, C. R. (1999). Research to practice: A "blueprint" for closing the gap in local schools. *Exceptional Children, 65,* 339–352.

American Federation of Teachers. (1999, June). *Teaching reading is rocket science: What expert teachers of reading should know and be able to do* (Item No. 372). Washington, DC: Author.

Anders, P. L., & Evens, K. S. (1994). Relationship between teachers' beliefs and their instructional practice in reading. In R. Garner & P. Alexander (Eds.), *Beliefs about text and instruction with text* (pp. 137–154). Hillsdale, NJ: Erlbaum.

Anders, P. L., Hoffman, J. V., & Duffy, G. G. (2000). Teaching teachers to teach reading: Paradigm shifts, persistent problems, and challenges. In M. Kamil, P. B. Mosenthal, P. D. Pearson, & R. Barr (Eds.), *Handbook of Reading research* (Vol. 3, pp. 719–742). Mahwah, NJ: Erlbaum.

Anderson, N. A. (1997). Improving reading inservice. *Kansas Journal of Reading, 7*(1), 37–39.

Bos, C. S., & Anders, P. L. (1994). The study of student change. In V. Richardson (Ed.), *Teacher change and the staff development process: A case in reading instruction* (pp. 181–198). New York: Teachers College Press.

Botel, M., Ripley, P. M., & Barnes, L. A. (1993). A case study of an implementation of the "new literacy" paradigm. *Journal of Research in Reading, 16,* 112–127.

Broaddus, K., & Bloodgood, J. W. (1999). We're supposed to already know how to teach reading: Teacher change to support struggling readers. *Reading Research Quarterly, 34,* 426–450.

Combs, M. (1994). Implementing a holistic reading series in first grade: Experiences with a conversation group. *Reading Horizons, 34*(3), 196–207.

Corcoran, T. B. (1995, June). *Helping teachers teach well: Transforming professional development* [On-line]. Available: http://www.ed.gov/pubs/CPRE/t61/

Cuban, L. (1988). A fundamental puzzle of school reform. *Phi Delta Kappan. 69,* 341–344.

Cunningham, P. M., & Cunningham, J. W. (1992). Making words: Enhancing the invented spelling-decoding connection. *Reading Teacher, 46,* 106–115.

Darling-Hammond, L. (1995). Changing conceptions of teaching and teacher development. *Teacher Education Quarterly, 22*(4), 9–26.

Darling-Hammond, L. (1997). *Doing what matters most: Investing in quality teaching.* New York: National Commission on Teaching and America's Future.

Darling-Hammond, L. (2000). Teacher quality and student achievement: A review of state policy evidence. *Education Policy Analysis Archives, 8*(1), [On-line]. Available: http://epaa.asu.edu/epaa/v8n1/

Duffy, G. G., Roehler, L. R., & Putnam, J. (1987). Purring the teacher in control: Basal reading textbooks and instructional decision making. *Elementary School Journal, 87,* 357–366.

El-Dinary, P. B., & Schuder, T. (1993). Seven teachers' acceptance of transactional strategies instruction during their first year using it. *Elementary School Journal, 94,* 207–219.

Finch, C. (1999). Using professional development to meet teachers' changing needs: What we have learned. *Centerpoint, 2*(1), 1–14.

Flood, J., Lapp, D., Ranck-Buhr, W., & Moore, J. (1995). What happens when teachers get together to talk about books? Gaining a multicultural perspective from literature. *Reading Teacher, 48,* 720–723.

Gray-Schlegel, M. A., & Matanzoa, J. B. (1993). Action research: Classroom teachers' perceptions of its impact on the teaching of reading. In T. B. Rasinski & N. P. Padak (Eds.), *Inquiries in Literacy Learning and Instruction* (pp. 135–142). Pittsburgh, KS: College Reading Association.

Guskey, T. R. (1997). Research needs to link professional development and student learning. *Journal of Staff Development, 18*(2), 36–40.

Guskey, T. R. (2000). *Evaluating Professional Development.* Thousand Oaks: Corwin.

Guskey, T. R., & Sparks, D. (1996). Exploring the relationship between staff development and improvements in student learning. *Journal of Staff Development, 17*(4), 34–38.

Hawley, W. D., & Valli, L. (1998). *Guide to the National Partnership for Excellence and Accountability in Teaching (NPEAT)* (Report No. EDO-SP-97-5). Washington, DC: Office of Educational Research and Improvement (ED). (ERIC Document Reproduction Service No. ED 426 056)

Hoffman, J. V. (1996). Teacher and school effects in learning to read. In R. Barr, M. Kamil, P. B. Mosenthal, & P. D. Pearson (Eds.), *Handbook of Reading research* (Vol. 2, pp. 911–950). Mahwah, NJ: Erlbaum.

Hoffman, J. V., & Pearson, P. D. (2000). Reading teacher education in the next millennium: What your grandmother's teacher didn't know that your granddaughter's teacher should. *Reading Research Quarterly, 35,* 28–35.

Joyce, B., & Showers, B. (1995). *Student achievement through staff development: Fundamentals of school renewal* (2nd ed.). White Plains, New York: Longman.

Kieffer, R. D., & Faust, M. A. (1994). Portfolio process and teacher change: Elementary, middle, and secondary teachers reflect on their initial experiences with portfolio evaluation. In C. K. Kinzer & D. J. Leu (Eds.), *Multidimensional aspects of literacy research, theory, and practice.* Forty-fourth yearbook of the National Reading Conference (pp. 82–88). Chicago: National Reading Conference.

Killion, J. (1998). Scaling the elusive summit. *Journal of Staff Development 19*(4), 12–16.

Klingner, J. L., & Vaughn, S. (1996). Reciprocal teaching of reading comprehension strategies for students with learning disabilities who use English as a second language. *Elementary School Journal, 96,* 275–293.

Malouf, D. B., & Schiller, E. P. (1995). Practice and research in special education. *Exceptional Children, 61,* 414–424.

Moore, M. (1991). Reflective teaching and learning through the use of learning logs. *Journal of Reading Education, 17,* 35–49.

National Joint Committee on Learning Disabilities. (2000). Professional development for teachers. *Learning Disability Quarterly, 23,* 2–6.

National Reading Panel. (2000). *Teaching children to read: An evidence-based assessment of the scientific research literature on reading and its implications for reading instruction* [On-line]. Available: http://www.nichd.nih.gov/publications/nrp/smallbook.pdf

National Staff Development Council. (1994). *Standards for staff development: Middle level edition.* Oxford, OH: Author.

National Staff Development Council. (1995a). *Standards for staff development: Elementary school edition.* Oxford, OH: Author.

National Staff Development Council. (1995b). *Standards for staff development: High school edition.* Oxford, OH: Author.

Porter, A. C., Garet, M. S., Desimone, L., Yoon, K. S., & Birman, B. F. (2000). *Does professional development change teaching practice? Results from a three year study* (Report No. 2000-04). Washington, DC: U.S. Department of Education.

Robb, L. (2000). *Redefining staff development: A collaborative model for teachers and administrators.* Portsmouth, NH: Heinemann.

Short, K. G., & Kauffman, G. P. (1992). Hearing students' voices: The role of reflection in learning. *Teachers Networking: The Whole Language Newsletter, 11*(3), 1–6.

Snow, C. E., Burns, M. S., & Griffin, P. (Eds.). (1998). *Preventing reading difficulties in young children.* Washington, DC: National Academy Press.

Thompson, J. C., & Cooley, V. E. (1986). A national study of outstanding staff development programs. *Educational Horizons, 64,* 94–98.

Young Readers' Academy: Opportunities for Conversations About Literacy Teaching and Learning

Carole Janisch and Amma Akrofi
Texas Tech University

An ever-increasing focus of legislators, policy-makers, researchers, and educators alike is on the reading achievement of elementary school learners. National initiatives (e.g., America Reads Challenge) and state initiatives (e.g., Texas Primary Reading Initiative) have focused attention on the importance of helping children become proficient readers. At the same time—and more specifically—the major issue uppermost in the minds of many reading educators is "how best to teach [reading]" (International Reading Association, 1998). However, researchers in reading teacher education argue that teaching is more than identifying "best practices" (Anders, Hoffman, & Duffy, 2000). What has been overlooked is how teachers learn to implement teaching methods, how they come to acquire knowledge as opposed to strategies and methods used to cause increased student learning. Historically, teacher education has emphasized what teachers should learn in course work or the idea that research-based effective practices, properly used, ensured student learning. The question not addressed relates to how teachers acquired the aforementioned knowledge, how they learn to implement new methods and to accomplish the teaching of reading. More recently, researchers (e.g., Alvermann, 1990; Barr, in press; Russell & Korthagen, 1995) have turned attention to how teachers learn and how that learning is enacted in their professional responsibility. Indeed, Alvermann (1990) has noted what she calls "inquiry-oriented" teacher education that is concerned with how teachers "acquire knowledge of complex reading instructional strategies and what beliefs, or implicit theories of teaching they use to guide their reading instruction" (p. 689). This study examines the question of how we help inservice teachers and preservice teachers develop understandings about theory and practice related to literacy education and what avenues are available to accomplish that goal. Conversations among the participants in the context of a university course and an elementary school setting has the potential to be an avenue. One opportunity to engage in conversations about literacy teaching and learning occurred with a university and public school collaborative project.

Young Readers' Academy (YRA), a year-long funded literacy project, was situated at a large urban elementary school site. The project originated with a twofold purpose: offer supplemental reading instruction to primary grade children and offer inservice teachers an opportunity to further develop their understandings about literacy teaching and learning through a university graduate course.

*National Reading Conference Yearbook, **50**, pp. 287–299.*

University involvement centered around the literacy course and the joint participation of preservice teachers and inservice teachers. Although the course is typically open only to graduate level preservice teachers, the inservice teachers in the YRA project enrolled also. Therefore, the two groups of teachers paired together to carry out the project components: after school tutoring for children, professional development experiences for inservice teachers, and elementary school classroom experiences for preservice teachers. The purpose of this study was to examine conversations that occurred as the participants came together and to note the understandings that developed in conjunction with the project.

Theoretical Framework

Researchers are beginning to examine how preservice teachers develop their knowledge particularly as it pertains to struggling readers (e.g., Mallette & Smith, 1997; Nierstheimer, Hopkins, Dillon, & Schmitt, 1998; Roskos & Walker, 1993, 1994). Some researchers have examined the effects of methods courses on preservice teachers' knowledge and confidence in their abilities to teach reading (e.g., Risko, Peter, & McAllister, 1996). Others have included inservice teachers in their research. Collaborative projects carried out in classroom settings and involving both classroom teachers and university faculty members can promote understandings about students' literacy development (e.g., El-Dinary, Pressley, & Schuder, 1992; Huling-Austin & O'Bryan-Garland, 1992). Finally, the role of parents in the promotion of children's literacy development and supporting efforts for classroom instruction has been considered (Purcell-Gates, 1996). This study explored understandings developed by inservice teachers and preservice teachers as they paired together for work in the classroom and school and as both groups participated together in the same university literacy course.

The social constructivist perspective (Vygotsky, 1978) suggests that concepts and meanings are socially and culturally embedded. The concept of school/classroom discussion originates from Vygotsky's (1978) idea of socially meaningful activity, which posits that individuals know and learn because of their interactions with others. He stated that the functions of voluntary attention, logical memory, and formation of concepts develop first on the interpsychological level (*between* individuals) and then on the intrapsychological level (*inside* individuals). "All the higher functions originate as actual relations between human individuals" (Vygotsky, 1978, p. 57). Vygotsky's (1978) notion of collaboration or cooperation in developing understandings is generally applied to group work by school-age children. Jennings and Di (1996), for instance, believe that emphases in kindergarten and primary classrooms on interactions between teachers and children, children and other adults, and among children themselves force children to think as well as communicate their thinking to each other, leading to "co-knowledge" (Leontiev, 1981, p. 56). Almasi (1996) differentiates between passive discussion in which students recite uninteresting and personally meaningless answers to teachers' questions, and one in which participants actively engage in "a dialogic conversation with one another" (Almasi, 1996, p. 2). Eeds and Wells (1989) refer to passive discussion as the "inquisition mode" (p. 4) and suggest it be replaced with "grand conversations" (p. 4) in which students and teachers work collaboratively to disclose, confirm, and extend each other's interpretations and create richer understandings of texts for all participants. This view of discussion supposes deliberation, reasoning out, talking over, considering pros and cons, and exchanging points of view about a subject in order to arrive at a conclusion acceptable to all (*The Merriam Webster Thesaurus*, 1991).

Although Vygotsky's ideas are generally viewed as germane to children, Sternberg (1987) suggested that Vygotsky's (1978) concept applies equally well to adults' processes and expressions of thought, and also to their expression of critical thinking. In workshops on staff development, Sternberg (1987) found that administrators, teachers, and university faculty place an undue focus on ownership and the promotion of individual ideas, resulting in a lower quality of output in critical thinking. He argued, therefore, that discussion and a "healthy group mentality" result in "the very best possible collective product" (p. 459), and recommended that teachers, especially, learn discussion and critical thinking skills so they can better pass them on to their students. Griffith and Laframboise's (1997) study on case-based instruction also confirms the value of discussion, in this instance by teachers in a graduate course on literacy. They found that the "interaction of a set of discussion structures" (p. 18), that is, humor, consultation, negotiation, and summarization contributed to the teachers' ability to think and learn.

The YRA offered opportunities for discussion among many individuals including parents, teachers, university students, and children. Discussions among course participants occurred during the scheduled meetings times, the tutoring preparations, the collaborative classroom experiences, and continued on in casual talk in the school corridors.

Background of the Study

The elementary school site and the university are located in the same mid-sized southwestern city. The elementary school serves K–6 students and was targeted for the YRA funding because the school is located in the lowest SES area of the city (98% of the children are considered economically disadvantaged). The school population of 564 students living in the immediate neighborhood is comprised of 14% African-American, 75% Hispanic, and 10% Anglo. These demographics also reflect a population of struggling readers whose parents are not always a presence in the day-to-day school activities of their children nor always able to provide home support for their children's literacy development. YRA was viewed as a means to provide intervention for children who were identified by their teachers and school testing measures as struggling readers. Although not the central focus of this report, a parent component of the YRA was intended to assist parents with ways they could take a role in promoting their children's literacy development and provide a venue for encouraging parents to visit the school and converse with teachers about the work of the classroom.

The intent of the YRA was to furnish students in first, second, and third grades with additional help to improve their reading and writing. To that end, the project provided classroom teachers with a stipend for serving as after school tutors for selected children and tuition for a university course that focused on literacy teaching and learning. Through the course activities, teachers could enhance their understandings about the reading process and reading instruction. Although the project began in the fall semester with the initiation of the parent component and pre-kindergarten and kindergarten lab sessions, the tutoring sessions and the university involvement began at the beginning of the spring semester in early January.

The semester-long graduate course is typically taken by students who are seeking a reading specialization or a master's degree in the language and literacy education program. The course offers these preservice teachers an opportunity to extend their literacy understandings, to apply these understandings in a classroom setting, and to provide a forum for subsequent discussions and reflections on the classroom experiences. Because YRA inservice teachers and preservice teachers (at the post-baccalaureate level) were enrolled, the course became a forum for everyone to gather and reflect on the classroom experiences, the tutorial sessions, and growing understandings about literacy teaching and learning. The class met once a week for about two hours. These weekly meetings were held after school and at the elementary school site. The meetings included discussions of assigned readings that related to topics such as reading comprehension, strategy development, guided reading, assessment of reading, literacy center development, and book selection. All course participants were assigned weekly papers that included a summary of and reaction to the classroom experiences of that week. The meetings also provided a forum for discussing issues or concerns relative to the classroom teaching and the tutorial sessions. An additional requirement of the course was the videotaping of a segment of classroom instruction. Preservice and inservice teachers collaborated on the taping of a segment, and either or both individuals were filmed. The tapes were shared at course meetings and preservice and inservice teachers had the opportunity to elaborate on the instruction as recorded. Additionally, all individuals participated in a critique of the lesson and raised questions.

University students were assigned to the teachers in the YRA project and spent one entire morning a week with them in their classrooms. In collaboration with the inservice teacher, the university student completed a variety of instructional activities, for example, teaching guided reading lessons to small groups of children. Through the lessons and in discussion with the inservice teacher, preservice teachers developed their ability to assess and understand the literacy needs of individual children. While in the classrooms, the university students teachers taught whole-class lessons and assisted individual students with teacher-assigned tasks.

The preservice teachers and the inservice teachers worked with small groups of children in the after school tutorial setting. On Mondays and Wednesdays, each of the inservice and preservice teachers met with two to four children who were enrolled in the YRA. Students in the YRA were nominated by their classroom teachers, and 66 children in Grades 1 through 3 joined the project with parental approval. The project coordinator at the school reported the following about the selection of children:

> Students that we know are really, really low and we know can't be helped in this program, we don't identify. We picked the kids that we know will benefit from this program, but we know for sure that we didn't pick the high students.

In most all cases, the children were from the classrooms of participating teachers. Inservice and preservice teachers conferred about the tutorial activities which typically represented an extension and elaboration of the classroom instruction.

The parent component was administered by the school's project coordinator who also served as the school/home liaison. During these monthly meetings geared for parents of children enrolled in YRA, school staff and faculty provided parents with information and materials to promote their children's literacy development. For example, book selection for read alouds at home was the topic for one session.

Method

Nine classroom teachers and nine university students participated in the course and paired together for working in the classroom and the tutorial setting. The inservice teachers, all females (seven Anglo and two Hispanic), volunteered for the project. All held bachelor's degrees and eight had 5 or fewer years of teaching experience. One of the eight had a master's degree and one had taken previous graduate courses. The ninth had taught 6 years. The preservice teachers (university students) were all females and had completed the prerequisite of a minimum of 15 hours in the language and literacy education program. In five cases the students were seeking master's degrees and this was one of their final courses in the program. As a professor in the language and literacy education program, I taught the course, and as a researcher I teamed with a doctoral student who assisted with data collection and data analysis.

Data Collection

To answer the research questions ("Who engaged in literacy conversations?" and "How can the conversations be characterized?"), data collection procedures included interviews, questionnaires, and fieldnotes. Eight of the nine inservice teachers were individually interviewed at the end of the semester. One teacher was not available for an interview. Through a series of open-ended questions, teachers were asked the following: what was your role in the YRA, what was most significant about the experience and least significant, what was most beneficial and least beneficial, what were gains for the participants—students, preservice teachers, and yourselves, and what concerns remained about the teaching of reading. The interviews, approximately an hour in length, were tape-recorded and all tapes were transcribed.

The nine preservice teachers completed an open-ended questionnaire at the end of the semester. They indicated their understandings through the same series of prompts as used in the interviews. The first author took fieldnotes during the visits to classrooms and the after-school tutoring sessions. From these notes retrospective summaries were written. The second author attended the literacy course sessions (and the parent meetings). Her observations and fieldnotes were the source of additional data for the second set of retrospective summaries also written by the first author and following the course sessions.

Data Analysis

Data were analyzed using the constant comparative method of content analysis (see Strauss, 1987). Both authors read all the interview transcripts and highlighted the instances of teachers reporting conversations they had engaged in about literacy instruction and children's literacy development. For example, one teacher said, "I learned from talking with Susan [a pseudonym] that the book has a good chapter on prompts [for guided reading]." Understandings gained from sources other than conversations, for example, "I learned from reading that book. . . ." were not included in the analysis. The same procedures were used for analyzing the questionnaires.

All highlighted portions of the transcripts and questionnaires were reread by both authors and coded separately for (a) conversational participants and (b) content or topic of the conversation. All differences were resolved through discussion. The following categories of conversational groupings emerged from the data: inservice teacher with preservice teacher, inservice teacher with inservice teacher, inservice teacher with inservice teacher/preservice teacher, inservice teacher with children, inservice teacher with parents, and parents with children.

The data were further analyzed to identify the literacy understandings. Two categories, related to the content of the conversations, emerged from the data: gains and outcomes. The gains represented more immediate understandings and those contextualized in the classroom settings. For example, in the inservice teacher with inservice teacher/preservice teacher grouping, a conversation centered on specific prompts and improved prompts to be given to students during guided reading instruction as a means for promoting strategy development (e.g., "Try that again and think what would make sense," a prompt that helps support the reader's use of all sources of information). The outcomes represented something more long-term, more general, and often more attitudinal or dispositional in nature. For example, in an inservice with preservice conversational grouping, the inservice teacher noted she became a better teacher and a better trainer of teachers as a result of the inservice teacher's classroom observations and subsequent comments about what had taken place.

In addition to the transcripts and questionnaires, supplementary data from the researcher's fieldnotes and subsequent retrospective summaries were analyzed. Supplementary data were juxtaposed with data from the interviews and questionnaires to aid in extending interpretations.

Results and Discussion

The teachers reported that they were talking more with each other outside of class, and we noted the talk among all the project participants, not only in the class sessions but on subsequent days as we spent time in the school on our visits to the classrooms and the tutorial settings. Conversations were occurring spontaneously and informally as teachers, university students, and university personnel came together in the university course, the school classrooms, and the school hallways. Conversations were also taking place between classroom teachers and parents as the latter joined the parent component of the project, attended the meetings, and paid visits to the classrooms of their children enrolled in YRA. The following sections highlight the two main groups of participants and describe the conversational groupings along with the characteristics of the conversations.

Inservice Teachers

All eight inservice teachers mentioned conversations between themselves and the preservice teachers; the majority of the reported conversations occurred between inservice teachers and preservice teachers. The following example is typical of the conversations that promoted understandings. The inservice teacher learned something new about read alouds which represented gains for her; the ideas were immediately applicable to her classroom practices:

> It was good to have her input on [read alouds]. Because you know every year that you go through, there's going to be something that's new and improved in education. She shared a lot of reading aloud things with me . . . it's been [directly] beneficial to me.

At the same time the inservice teacher reported long term outcomes in the form of collegiality, professional development, and open-mindedness which epitomized "group mentality" as noted by Sternberg (1987):

> It's been a while since I had read something in an article . . . just some of the things that [the preservice teacher] brought up really made me go back and think. Yes, we did talk about that in college. Yes, I do remember something like that. But you know there are a lot of things that we do at college that don't really help us out that much in a classroom, not to hurt you . . . but [her presence] was good because it helped me relate with another colleague. . . . She knew something about reading and going through the classes she's taking now that I hadn't

> thought about in a while, or that I hadn't even heard about. . . . It teaches you to be able to go and talk to someone in your grade level or at another school.

Four inservice teachers reported conversations involving themselves and other inservice teachers. One teacher noted the immediate gains from the video tapes shown in the course meetings and the critiques offered by peers; they illustrated practices of her peers and ones she could think about further and implement in her classroom. She also noted outcomes of the project in terms of professional development. Ideas at a practical level as well as issues were part of the conversations:

> I did a guided reading lesson [for the video taping] and other teachers did read alouds. Just getting to see all of that and talking about the different cues you give children as they're reading and being aware of what you need to say to get them to focus on meaning. That was a good thing that really helped me. It improved my reading lessons. . . . I thought [the project] was good. We [also] discussed a lot of the [practical concerns and issues] that were really pertinent in my room.

Yet another inservice teacher reported her immediate gains in learning about administering running records as a means for assessing children's reading achievement. The class became a starting place for conversations that continued on after class and led to understandings that might not otherwise have occurred. Professional development outcomes are implicit in conversations such as these taking place between inservice teachers:

> After class I would walk down to Ms. Perez's (pseudonym) room and spend more time there [talking]. And since I'm already there, I'd just stay longer, and she taught me more about how to do those running records.

Three inservice teachers mentioned conversations occurring between themselves and other inservice teachers as well as preservice teachers. One teacher's comment exemplifies the promotion of literacy understandings derived from her work with a preservice teacher who was just beginning to build her understandings about teaching reading. The teacher gained specific information about how to provide her children with immediate help in reading comprehension and at the same time became aware of the benefits of a reciprocal exchange of ideas, a long-term outcome:

> [The preservice teacher] wasn't really into [teaching] reading so she would ask me questions, and we'd be talking and it would get me into thinking. Well, I would say, "I really don't know much about that [either], so let's learn together." As a result, we were helping and giving support to those readers.

An additional outcome for this same teacher was an awareness of broader views about productive teaching practices that cannot be acquired from readings but can result from conversations:

> If I wasn't in the project, then I wouldn't have gained all the knowledge from the other teachers or from the other students in that class. And it would have just been me going from the book. The university class gave me more of a different, a wider view of everyone's approach to teaching. It helped to give us new

> information, new insights that we probably wouldn't get because most of us just have our college textbooks up on our shelves [to rely on].

Four inservice teachers reported conversations that involved teachers with children and parents with children. One teacher reported that she and the children were reading and talking about a variety of books during the tutoring sessions, and gains for children were evident not only in the fact they had passed the statewide achievement test, but their growing self-confidence, an outcome, was noted:

> My kids just love reading. You talk to them now [and they love reading]. We wrote a letter to the fourth grade teachers, and that's what they said, I love reading. That is really neat because usually they [the children] don't say that. . . . Their confidence [was apparent] just looking at them during the classroom time when they would help each other.

Another teacher noted conversations she was having with parents. Parents told her about interactions with their children in connection with home literacy activities. Ability of parents and children to work together on literacy tasks was an immediate gain and attitude changes in children were identified outcomes:

> He [my child] comes home now and he wants to read to me. He picks up the paper and finds words. With the magnetic letters he's making up new words for me. This was something he didn't do before.

In a casual conversation documented in the researcher's fieldnotes and retrospective summaries, a teacher indicated that the YRA parent meetings brought parents to school, and those meetings represented a "neutral" setting as opposed to the often unfriendly atmosphere of a required conference with a principal or teacher about disciplinary matters. She further stated that parents told her, in effect, as long as they were in the building, they would just stop by and visit.

The parent component was a viable part of the project, and parents were present during school hours. However, only the inservice teachers reported conversations involving parents and children. This may be explained by the teachers' awareness of the goal to help children achieve in reading, which was at the forefront of their thinking, while preservice teachers were more concerned with developing their own understandings about reading instruction per se.

The conversational topics as reported by the inservice teachers predominately centered around procedures, activities, and concrete ideas, for example, how to do guided reading and read alouds. The researcher's fieldnotes and retrospective summaries indicated similar topics were considered during course meeting times. Questions such as "what is a good activity to include in the classroom centers?" were asked by inservice teachers whereas preservice teachers asked more abstract questions such as, "How do I connect reading and writing and relate both to a topic or theme?" In only one instance did the conversations involving inservice teachers include a topic of a more abstract nature: developing patience with struggling readers and appropriate pacing of the instruction offered to them. The predominance of topics of a practical nature might suggest that inservice teachers, who are held immediately accountable for students' gains in reading achievement, may tend to consider ways to expedite the process. Although the inservice teachers relied more on the talk accompanying the collegial relationships—including those formed with the other teachers and the university students—than did the preservice teachers, one semester is a short period of time to see evidence of extensive conversations of a more complex nature.

Preservice Teachers

Three of the nine preservice teachers mentioned conversations as an important means for promoting literacy understandings. Typical examples did not allude to immediate gains but outcomes were apparent:

> The most helpful was the time I spent just quizzing the classroom teacher about things I observed in her classroom day to day. Then I better understood what was the purpose and benefit of the different activities. There is so much that the textbook cannot explain that this experience did in so many ways.

A second preservice teacher noted an outcome. In writing the following, she implied the reciprocity of the conversations in promoting her understandings:

> I worked with a teacher who was very flexible, valued my input, and was willing to explain her techniques. I haven't worked at this grade level, and I learned a lot about teaching second grade from my teacher.

In the writing of the third preservice teacher, a specific topic was not discernible, but the complexities of teaching reading as mentioned early in this paper were looming in her mind:

> The actual classroom experiences that [the first author] and I discussed were helpful. Not everything works for the same child, and you can never give up on trying new ways to teach. There is no set pattern for teaching reading.

As compared to the inservice teachers, fewer preservice teachers noted the benefits of conversation on the questionnaires. However, they did note the move from *talking* in university course work about helping children achieve in reading to the beneficial aspects of *working* with children in the classroom. A typical example of preservice teachers' comments included the following:

> So many times in my classes I am told how to teach, but actually being able to work with the students and having to make the decisions of what to do next was a very good experience for me. It allowed me to see how all of the things I have been taught in my classes work with actual students.

It is puzzling that so few preservice teachers wrote little about the value of conversations and other social interactions with inservice teachers. There could be several explanations for this. First, data were collected differently from inservice and preservice teachers. The questionnaires distributed to preservice teachers did not allow us to probe further about literacy understandings examined and developed through the project. Moreover, identifying conversations in teacher self-reports has limitations. Second, the three preservice teachers who mentioned the importance of conversations may have had different experiences with their cooperating teachers than the others. We do know of one instance where the paired participants worked together as professionals in the classroom, but they were not always comfortable in an open and ongoing exchange of ideas. Third, preservice teachers often want, more than anything else, to work with children. They are anxious to begin teaching, rather than listening to more information. Perhaps preservice teachers with little actual experience working with children are not to the point where they can reflect on their teaching practices, which is often the essence of conversations. The complexities of teaching reading and the questions about day-to-day procedures of teaching reading may become apparent as classroom teaching experience increases. Conversations and the importance of a "group mentality" to build understandings at any level may take on greater importance with increased classroom teaching experience, which appears to have been the situation in this study. Until then, novice teachers of reading may need to take their understandings to the practical setting and test out the implementation for themselves. As noted by two of the preservice teachers, the "experience explains" and one needs to see how things "work with actual students."

Conclusion

The project was an avenue to accomplish the goal of helping inservice and preservice teachers advance their understandings about literacy teaching and learning. It presented opportunities for conversations, albeit viewed differently by the two main groups of participants, that would not otherwise have been available. Individuals know and learn because of their interactions with each other (Vygotsky, 1987), and certainly the project had the potential to promote a "healthy group mentality" and "the very best collective product" (Sternberg, 1987). It represented one effort after helping all address the complexities of teaching reading. Many individuals, including teachers, university graduate students, university faculty, parents, and children, were able to join conversations advanced by the project and the talk which engendered literacy understandings.

Struggling readers were provided instruction in the classroom and their teachers had the will and new-found skills to not only see that children were accommodated in the classroom, but these teacher qualities carried over into the support further offered in the tutoring sessions (see Duffy-Hester, 1999). We believe the YRA project and the conversations carried out the admonition: "We need to instill the confidence, knowledge, and will in preservice teachers and practicing teachers to teach struggling readers" (Duffy-Hester, 1999, p. 492).

Although 55 of the 66 children made significant gains in reading achievement as indicated in the end-of-the year reading achievement tests, Allington (1991) suggested that markers for success in reading go beyond test scores. One classroom teacher noted the children's response and the popularity of the tutoring sessions connected to the YRA:

> It's like when you call it tutoring they know it's like you're having trouble. It's like oh no, no, this is not tutoring. This is the Young Readers' Academy. This is taking these kids that are doing all of [these extra activities] and then everybody was wanting to come. It was like, oh sorry [not everyone can come].

A second teacher noted the following about gains made by one of the participating children:

> During tutoring everybody got their chance, and [the child] felt comfortable with the few she was in there with. She did make mistakes, and the other ones made mistakes. It really wasn't a big deal [for her], but in the classroom she's really intimidated by the other kids.

The common concern of how to promote reading teacher education and help children with their literacy development remains uppermost in the minds of educators and practitioners. The project afforded all participants an opportunity to develop their literacy understandings through conversations: raising questions about the instructional activities and practices carried out with the children, sharing assessment and interpretations of children's reading behaviors, and exchanging insights about the teaching of reading. Time needs to be made available for inservice and preservice teachers to discuss and construct understandings about teaching reading and children's reading development.

References

Allington, R. L. (1991). Effective literacy instruction for at-risk children. In M. Knapp & P. Shields (Eds.), *Better schooling for the children of poverty: Alternatives to conventional wisdom* (pp. 9–30). Berkeley, CA: McCutchan.

Almasi, J. F. (1996). A new view of discussion. In Linda B. Gambrell & Janice F. Almasi (Eds.), *Lively discussion! Fostering engaged reading.* Newark, DE: International Reading Association.

Alvermann, D. E. (1990). Reading teacher education. In R. W. Houston, M. Haberman, & J. Sikula (Eds.), *Handbook of research on teacher education* (pp. 687–704). New York: Macmillan.

Anders, P. L., Hoffman, J. V., & Duffy, G. G. (2000). Teaching teachers to teach reading: Paradigm shifts, persistent problems, and challenges. In M. L. Kamil, P. B. Mosenthal, P. D. Pearson, & R. Barr (Eds.), *Handbook of reading research* (Vol. 3, pp. 719–742). Mahwah, NJ: Erlbaum.

Barr, R. (in press). Research on the teaching of reading. In V. Richardson (Ed.), *Handbook of research on teaching* (4th ed.). Washington, DC: American Educational Research Association.

Duffy-Hester, A. M. (1999). Teaching struggling readers in elementary school classrooms: A review of classroom reading programs and principles for instruction. *Reading Teacher, 52,* 480–495.

Eeds, M., & Wells, D. (1989). Grand conversations: An exploration of meaning construction in literature study groups. *Research in the Teaching of English, 23,* 4–29.

El-Dinary, P. B., Pressley, M., & Schuder, T. (1992). Teachers learning transactional strategies instruction. In C. K. Kinzer & D. L. Leu (Eds.), *Literacy research, theory, and practice: Views from many perspectives.* Forty-first yearbook of the National Reading Conference (pp. 453–462). Chicago: National Reading Conference.

Griffith, P. L., & Laframboise, K. (1997). The structures and patterns of case method talk: What our students taught us. *Action in Teacher Education, 18,* 10–22.

Huling-Austin, L., & O'Bryan-Garland, S. (1992). Increasing faculty involvement with the public schools. *Action in Teacher Education, 9,* 41–48.

International Reading Association (1998). Making a difference. *Reading Today, 17,* 1, 24.

Jennings, C. M., & Di, X. (1996). Collaborative learning and thinking: The Vygotskian approach. In Lisbeth Dixon-Krauss (Ed.), *Vygotsky in the classroom: Mediated literacy instruction and assessment* (pp. 77–91). New York: Longman.

Leontiev, A. N. (1981). The problem of activity in psychology. In J. V. Wertsch (Ed.), *The concept of activity in Soviet psychology* (pp. 37–71). Armonk, NY: Sharpe.

Mallette, M. H., & Smith, M. M. (1997, December). *How do preservice teachers construct meanings of reading difficulties? A cross-case analysis.* Paper presented at the meeting of the National Reading Conference, Scottsdale, AZ.

The Merriam Webster Thesaurus (1991). Springfield, MA: Merriam-Webster.

Neierstheimer, S. L., Hopkins, C. J., Dillon, D. R., & Schmitt, M. C. (1997, December). *Identifying and confronting preservice teachers' beliefs about children experiencing difficulty learning to read.* Paper presented at the meeting of the National Reading Conference, Scottsdale, AZ.

Purcell-Gates, V (1996). Stories, coupons, and the TV guide: Relationships between home literacy experiences and emergent literacy knowledge. *Reading Research Quarterly, 31,* 406–428.

Risko, V. J., Peter, J. A., & McAllister, D. (996). Preservice teachers' pathways to providing literacy instruction. In E. G. Stutevant & W. M. Linek (Eds.), *Growing literacy.* The eighteenth yearbook of the College Reading Association (pp. 104–119). Texas A&M University, Commerce: College Reading Association.

Roskos, K., & Walker, B. (1993). An analysis of preservice teachers' pedagogical concepts in the teaching of problem readers. In D. J. Leu & C. K. Kinzer (Eds.), *Examining central issues in literacy research theory, and practice.* Forty-second yearbook of the National Reading Conference (pp. 325–334). Chicago: National Reading Conference.

Roskos, K., & Walker, B. (1994). Preservice teachers' epistemology in the teaching of problem readers. In C. K. Kinzer & D. J. Leu (Eds.), *Multidimensional aspects of literacy research, theory, and practice.* Forty-third yearbook of the National Reading Conference (pp. 418–428). Chicago: National Reading Conference.

Russell, T., & Korthagen, F. (Eds.) (1995). *Teachers who teach teachers: Reflections on teacher education.* Washington, DC: Falmer.

Sternberg, R. J. (1987). Teaching critical thinking: Eight easy ways to fail before you begin. *Phi Delta Kappan, 68,* 456–459.

Strauss, A. L. (1987). *Qualitative analysis for social scientists.* New York: Cambridge University Press.

Vygotsky, L. S. (1978). *Mind in society.* Cambridge, MA: Harvard University Press.

Preservice Reading Teachers' Self-Awareness of Past Learning and Development as Motivation for Continued Learning

Diane S. Kaplan
Texas A&M University, College Station

Discussion continues about how best to provide opportunities in teacher preparation programs for preservice teachers to obtain a fundamental knowledge base of subject matter (Tillema & Knol, 1997); practical experiences for applying, questioning, and reconstructing that knowledge base; and opportunities for self-reflection and self-evaluation to help increase both feelings of self-efficacy and awareness of the need for continued learning and inquiry. The reflection and inquiry referred to in this study involves both preservice and classroom teachers in serious questioning and ongoing reexamination of (a) their process for pedagogical goal development, including their generation of rationales and supporting evidence for developing and modifying those goals; (b) the results of their attempts to use their teaching goals as a basis for their classroom teaching; (c) the sufficiency or insufficiency of their knowledge, skills, and abilities for developing pedagogical goals and for implementing them in schools and classrooms; and (d) their ability to identify the type and location of resources they need for improving their ability to develop, implement, and revise their teaching goals.

Although researchers and teacher educators debate what abilities, skills, competencies, and stances need to be emphasized in a teacher education program, they do not often ask the students themselves to identify what they think is important to learn to become effective teachers (Engstrom & Schwaab, 1984; Gilberts & Lignugaris-Kraft, 1997; Standerford, 1996). Likewise, during the course of their teacher preparation program, including both their classroom reading instruction courses and their field-based reading internships, preservice teachers are not consistently asked what they feel they have adequately learned and what they feel they still need to learn to become effective and reflective teachers. Asking preservice teachers at each stage of their teacher education program to consider what they would need to learn to become effective teachers could benefit them not only by encouraging them to engage in the act of reflection on all aspects of their development as teachers (their values, goals, performance, and needs), but also by recognizing their developing autonomy as they continue to become more responsible for their own learning. Responding to these specific types of questions throughout their teacher education program could be impor-

*National Reading Conference Yearbook, **50**, pp. 300–310.*

tant for preservice teachers in their development of reflection as a natural and productive activity. Being asked these questions could also be important for increasing their sense of autonomy, which in turn could contribute to their motivation for continued learning (Ryan & Deci, 2000) as they come to perceive themselves as powerful enough to use their self-motivated learning in their classrooms and in their own professional development.

The role of self-awareness of knowledge acquisition/deficiency as motivation for continuing learning and inquiry was the focus of this study. The students' perceived need to pursue further knowledge about literacy pedagogy after completion of a 24-hour teacher education program in teaching reading was predicted as a function of perceived importance of the knowledge to becoming an effective reading teacher and perceived prior experience with the subject matter. I also predicted that these relationships could be affected by students' knowledge acquisition in their final classroom reading methods course and by their experiences in their field-based reading practicum. The research questions guiding the study were as follows: (a) To what extent were preservice reading teachers' perceptions about their continued need to learn more about select literacy pedagogy topics related to their pre-course motivation to learn about the topics and to their perceptions of the importance of these topics, their pre-course knowledge of the topics, and their immediate learning about them in their current reading methods course? and (b) To what extent were preservice reading teachers' perceptions about their continued need to learn more about select literacy pedagogy topics related to their experiences in their field-based reading practicum classroom?

In this investigation, I examined whether it was their valuing of the knowledge (Wigfield & Eccles, 2000), their past exposure to it, their felt need to learn about it, their most recent learning, or some combination of these factors, that would most affect the preservice teachers' perceived need for continued learning. In line with the underlying assumptions of achievement goal theory that goals are "cognitive representations of what individuals are trying to accomplish" (Pintrich, 2000, p. 96) and, therefore, consciously accessible to the individual, I used self-report measures of student values and goals.

The fundamental questions addressed were about the motivation for continued learning exhibited by preservice teachers at the onset and at the end of a semester during which they were beginning to make a transition in perspective from that of a university student to that of a classroom teacher as they responded to the requirements of both a university reading methods course and a reading practicum in a public school classroom. During this transition semester, I expected that some students might begin to experience shifts in motivational orientation, perhaps from a performance to a mastery orientation (Dweck & Leggett, 1988). In addition, these preservice teachers may experience this transition semester as a period of relative disequilibrium, during which they may feel uncertain about their preparedness for their field experiences and they may have their preconceptions about teaching challenged by actual classroom experiences. Thus, I wondered whether a developing sense of or need for self-efficacy (Zimmerman, 2000) would affect the preservice teachers' perceptions of their continued need to learn about the teaching of reading, as defined by the literacy goals initially presented to them.

Method

Participants

For this study I examined responses from students in a reading education program that had as its capstone semester a reading practicum in a local public school. Participants were 166 undergraduate preservice teachers with reading education as their teaching emphasis who participated in one or both testing sessions (pretest and posttest) and who were enrolled in the final semester or next to final semester of their reading education sequence some time during 1997–2000. In terms of demographics, the participants were typically white (94%) women (97%) with some variation in hometown backgrounds, including students from urban, suburban, and rural communities. Prior to this final semester of reading courses, they typically had taken 18 hours in reading instruction that included children's literature, language and reading, language arts, and literacy acquisition by culturally diverse learner, as well as survey courses in general reading concepts and in reading assessment. Students in the spring of 2000, however, had only taken 12 hours of reading instruction prior to the semester of their reading practicum.

Setting

During this semester of their reading emphasis program, the students were enrolled in a reading methods course and a field-based reading practicum. The methods course, which met for three hours each week, was designed to provide theoretically informed and practical methods for teaching and assessing reading in a wide variety of settings. For the field-based reading practicum, each student was assigned to a mentor teacher in a local public school, in addition to attending weekly 1-hour seminars during which students shared and obtained help with their classroom experiences. For 10 weeks, the reading interns went to their field-based classroom during reading instruction 4 days each week for 1 hour per day. After 1 week of observing, the interns were required to spend at least part of each day interacting with students by teaching a lesson, helping students with center activities, reading to them, or listening to them read. Assignments for the practicum included the construction and teaching of a 5-day thematic unit and the keeping of a weekly journal in which students recorded their lesson plans and their weekly reflections in response to classroom experiences.

Three assignments from the methods class were integrated with this field experience: (a) writing a paper on how the ideas from the text *Literacy Instruction in Multicultural Settings* (Au, 1993) applied or did not apply to their practicum classroom, (b) administering comprehension assessment procedures to their students and discussing the benefits and drawbacks of those procedures, and (c) adapting reading strategies from *Reading Strategies and Practices* (Tierney & Readence, 2000) for use in their classrooms.

Measurement

On the first day of class and again at the end of the semester, students evaluated each of 23 course objectives (a full copy of these may be obtained from the author). The 23 objectives could be grouped into the following topics: (a) important concepts related to literacy development and the best ways for fostering that development; (b) integration of these concepts into the teaching of strategies for improving reading instruction; (c) learning of specific strategies and methods for teaching and assessing reading in the classroom; (d) learning about the relationship between student differences and reading instruction; (e) learning to use a wide variety of assessment procedures and activities, including both objective and qualitative/holistic assessment, as well as self-assessment and reflection; and (f) the importance and integration of the affective dimension into the teaching of reading.

On the first day of class, each student was asked to respond to three questions for each course objective. The first question asked:

> For helping an education student learn how to be a proficient reading teacher, how important would you say this objective is? (very important, somewhat important, not very important) (*Perceived Importance Scale*)

The second question asked:

> In terms of your previous courses, how much information has already been presented to you on this topic? (a considerable amount, a moderate amount, very little, or none) (*Perceived Previous Learning Scale*)

The third question asked:

> In terms of your current instructional needs, how much more do you think you need to learn about this topic in order to perform well as a teacher in a reading classroom? (a considerable amount, a moderate amount, very little, or none) (*Pre-Course Motivation Scale*)

At the end of the semester, the students were asked to respond to two questions for each objective. The first asked:

> In looking back at the content of Reading 360 this semester, how much information was provided to you on this topic? (a considerable amount, a moderate amount, very little, or none) (*Perceived Learning Scale*)

The second question asked:

> How much more do you think you still need to learn about this topic in order to perform well as a teacher in a reading classroom? (a considerable amount, a moderate amount, very little, or none) (*Perception of Need for Continued Learning Scale*)

Students also were asked to evaluate the reading internship on a number of dimensions, including whether they thought it was helpful to take the methods course and the internship at the same time and whether they thought their reading coursework had adequately prepared them to teach reading in the classroom. They were also asked to rate the level of benefit (high, medium, or low) each assignment in the reading internship afforded them. Grades earned in both reading courses were also available to include in analysis.

Construction of Scales

To recap, data were organized into five general scales consisting of student responses to the five questions asked about each of the 23 objectives presented. The first three scales were based on the students' responses to pretest questions about the importance of each objective, the amount of information presented on each topic in other courses, and the additional learning needed on each topic to perform well as a classroom teacher. The posttest scales were based on the students' responses to questions on each topic concerning the amount they had learned during the semester and the amount they still felt they needed to learn to perform well in the classroom. On four of the scales, participants responded to a 4-point scale, and on the importance scale, they responded to a 3-point scale. Students' scores were calculated by simply adding up the scores for all 23 items on each scale. Scores on the importance scale could range between 23 and 69, and scores on the other scales between 23 and 92. Reliability tests of the scales indicated respectable alphas, ranging from .86 to .95.

For one missing response on any given scale, the student's mean score on the other 22 items of the scale was substituted for the missing data point. A student's scale score was not computed if more than one item was missing. Also, because there were students who missed taking either test, there were between 11 and 40 missing cases depending on the analysis.

Analysis

Ordinary Least Squares (OLS) regression was used to analyze the relationship between students' perception of previous exposure to a reading instruction topic and their self-described perceived need to learn more about that topic both prior to and after their field-based reading internship and their reading methods course. It was hypothesized that students' motivation to learn more about select literacy topics at both the beginning and the end of the semester would be directly related to their perception of the importance of the topic and inversely related to their self-report of previous exposure to that topic.

Results

Summary Statistics

Means and standard deviations for the five scales are presented in Table 1. A comparison of means for the equivalent pretest and posttest scales (the two perceived learning scales and two perceived need for more learning scales) indicated significant differences ($p<.001$), with scores increasing on the perceived learning scales and decreasing on the perceived need for more learning scales.

Results from Regression Analyses

The results obtained in the first regression equation (see Table 2) provided evidence of a statistically significant direct relationship ($\beta=.262$) between pre-course perceived need to learn and the perceived need for continued learning after the course is over, and a statistically significant inverse relationship ($\beta=-.208$) between perceived learning during the course and perceived need for continued learning at the end of the course. These relationships were found even

Table 1

Means (M) and Standard Deviations (SD) for the Pretest and Posttest Survey Scales

Scale	Reliability α	Possible Range	*N*	*M*	*SD*
At Pretest					
Perceived Importance	.86	23–69	157	65.14	4.47
Perceived Previous Learning	.88	23–92	158	66.07	8.45
Pre-Course Motivation	.92	23–92	156	75.26	9.92
At Posttest					
Perceived learning	.91	23–92	146	75.68	9.46
Perception of Need for Continued Learning	.95	23–92	146	58.68	12.65

Table 2

Ordinary Least Squares Regression Coefficients for Variables Affecting End-of-Course Perception of Need for Continued Learning (N=135)

	B	SE B	β
Perceived Learning	-0.281*	0.118	-0.208*
Pre-course Motivation	0.336**	0.120	0.262**
Perceived Importance	0.272	0.258	0.093
Perceived Previous Learning	0.127	0.132	0.087
Reading Methods Grade	-0.118	0.179	-0.055
Constant	39.527	25.036	
R^2	0.095		
Adjusted R^2	0.060		

*$p<.05$. **$p<.01$.

when controlling for the effects of the students' perceiving or not perceiving the items as important, the effects of the perceived previous learning related to these items, and the students' grades in their reading methods course. The results seemed to indicate that a predisposition to feeling the need to know more about a topic was related to a continued perception of needing to learn more about the topic even when taking into consideration the negative relationship between perceived new learning on a topic and the need to learn more about that topic.

To explore the nature of the two independent variables significantly related to the perceived need for continued learning, an attempt was made to determine which other variables were significantly related to each of these variables. Results obtained in the second regression equation (see Table 3) provided evidence of a significant positive relationship between a pre-course perception of the need to learn about reading pedagogy and the perceived importance of the learning to becoming a proficient reading teacher (β=.277), and a significant inverse relationship between a pre-course motivation to learn and the students' perception of having learned the material in an earlier course (β=-.346). These results seemed to indicate that the perception of importance was provided by the scale at the original time of administration and had an effect on the students' motivation to learn at that time. Subsequently, the students' motivation to continue learning might have been more affected by the students' original learning motivation that might have translated into action during the course than by the more abstract act of valuing or judging the learning that was provided by students' scores on the importance scale.

Results from the third regression equation (see Table 4) provided evidence of significant direct effects of pre-course motivation to learn (β=.231), prior learning related to topics in the current curriculum (β=.219), and perception of the benefits of keeping a journal during the semester-long reading practicum (β=.219) on perceived learning during the course. Here, students' perceived learning during the semester in the reading methods course seemed to be directly related to beginning motivation, prior learning about reading, and a willingness to use and find

Table 3

Ordinary Least Squares Regression Coefficients for Variables Affecting Pre-Course Motivation to Learn (N=155)

	B	SE B	β
Perceived Importance	0.652***	0.174	0.277***
Perceived Previous Learning	-0.402***	0.086	-0.346***
Constant	59.100***	12.226	
R^2	0.178		
Adjusted R^2	0.167		

****p*<.001.

Table 4

Ordinary Least Squares Regression Coefficients for Variables Affecting End-of Course Student Learning Measure (N=126)

	B	SE B	β
Pre-course Motivation	0.200**	0.077	0.231**
Perceived Previous Learning	0.226*	0.091	0.219*
Perception of Journal as Beneficial	2.819*	1.099	0.219*
Constant	40.493 ***	9.372	
R^2	0.141		
Adjusted R^2	0.120		

*$p<.05$. ** $p<.01$. ***$p<.001$.

benefit in a major ongoing assignment used to record and reflect upon the field experience in the classroom.

Overall, these results seemed to indicate that the motivation to learn about a topic continued to stimulate the perceived need for further learning, whereas previous learning on a topic tended to increase current learning about the topic and at the same time current learning seemed to decrease the perceived need for further learning.

Discussion

This research was grounded in the belief that by providing students with a "university class and an elementary lab experience taught simultaneously, [teacher education programs can influence] many preservice teachers to become investigators of thinking and action" (Boyd, Boll, Brawner, & Villaume, 1998, p. 69). If the goal of teacher education programs is to provide opportunities for students to become reflective practitioners and decision-makers (Morine-Dershime, 1989), we as researchers need to be developing ways of measuring the degree to which this is happening and the factors most important to helping students develop "an understanding of the need for ongoing professional inquiry" (p. 68). It has been suggested that one way to encourage students to perceive a need for continued learning and inquiry is to put them into situations (like the field-based classroom) that promote some feelings of disequilibrium. It would seem important for us to determine how to help our students recognize the benefit of those feelings of disequilibrium as a basis for generating questions, creating new modes of thinking and problem-solving, and developing coordinated avenues of inquiry about the reading curriculum, the reading classroom, and the application of reading instruction to meet the needs of individual children.

The results of this study were intriguing in that they seemed to reveal two countervailing forces on the question of whether preservice teachers would feel the need to pursue further learning on topics that had recently been stressed in a reading methods course taken concurrently with a reading practicum. On the one hand, previous motivation to learn about select reading topics seemed to increase the perceived need for further learning. On the other hand, increased learning during the course about the topics seemed to have a tendency to decrease the perceived need for further learning on those topics. This relationship was evident for the full 23-item scales, and preliminary results indicated it was also found for select subsets of items.

Although these results seemed to indicate that the more students felt that they had learned about a topic the less they felt a need to learn more about it, the results could also be interpreted to mean that the less the students felt they had learned about a topic they valued, the more they perceived a need for additional learning. Both explanations fit the results of a negative relationship between course emphasis and perceived need for future learning. Examined specifically in terms of individual objectives the nature of this inverse relationship could be an interesting future research focus.

What also still needs to be more fully examined is the role of the field-based experience in increasing or decreasing the pre-course motivation to gain more of an understanding of what it takes to be a successful reading teacher and to be able to apply that understanding to the classroom. Because these students were called upon to teach a variety of types of lessons in actual reading classrooms, it seemed that by the end of the semester they would perceive how much they still needed to learn about teaching in general, about teaching reading in particular, and about meeting the literacy developmental needs of a widely varied student population. It had seemed likely that students striving for a greater sense of self-efficacy related to teaching reading or moving in perspective from a performance to a mastery orientation would be more focused by the end of the semester than at the beginning of the semester on increasing their learning about various aspects of literacy pedagogy.

Based on the data from this study, this did not seem to have happened with respect to the students' full-scale responses to the 23 literacy pedagogy goals presented. One question for further study might be whether or not there were specific objectives that remained or became areas of perceived need for further learning because they were connected to the students' practicum experiences. In fact, the two objectives that individually received the highest average scores in perceived need for additional learning, one in classroom management and the other in providing instruction for students with special needs, seemed to fit this description.

Based on the current study, however, most of the data obtained from the students' field experience surveys did not seem to be related to their perceived need for further learning about the topics covered in their reading methods class. The only relationship between a field experience variable and any of the general scales was the significant positive relationship found between the students' perception of current course learning and their positive evaluation of the journal keeping process in their practicum. This relationship made sense in that both variables seemed to reflect a student's overall level of academic engagement and commitment. However, the question remained as to why there did not seem to be a carryover in this academic engagement to a perceived need to pursue a broader and deeper understanding of teaching reading in a future university class or field experience. It may have taken the explicit inclusion of questions asking the students to judge the degree to which their development in teaching in their field experience was related to the fulfilling of those objectives in their methods class to have evaluated more accurately the influence of the internship on their perception of the need for continued learning in those areas.

Some adjusting of the scales might also have been needed as the instrument design might have led students to feel that it would be natural to say they needed little additional learning if they had learned "a lot" about a given topic. In the future it would be interesting to study whether scaffolding type questions could be added to items that students indicate they have learned a considerable amount about to see whether they would want to pursue more specifically described learning in those areas. In keeping with the original focus of this research, it would be ideal to ask the students to construct and specify the questions to be pursued and the new knowledge to be obtained based on these initial topics and on concerns that they have generated during their methods class and their field experience.

This study has implications for determining ways to help preservice teachers become reflective and inquiring professionals, something that Zeichner (1996) indicated is an essential function of the practicum experience when he stated, "Unless the practicum helps to teach prospective teachers to begin to take control of their own professional development and to learn how to continue learning, it is miseducative, . . ." (p. 217). First, it may indicate the need for university teacher educators to connect and help their students to connect more explicitly the theoretical and practical information taught in a reading methods class with the instructional decisions the students make in their reading practicum. Second, it makes clear that teacher educators need to be careful in their presentation of materials insofar that they do not act as if they are providing students with most of what they need to know about teaching reading. Last, and most important, it reveals the importance of listening to students concerning their perceived needs for additional learning as these will be the areas that are most likely to engage them in problem-solving, serious study, and deliberate action. Indeed these could be the areas that will be most opportune for stimulating student reflection and for demonstrating its value.

References

Au, K. H. (1993). *Literacy instruction in multicultural settings.* Fort Worth, TX: Harcourt Brace Jovanovich.

Boyd, P. C., Boll, M., Brawner, L., & Villaume, S. K. (1998). Becoming reflective professionals: An exploration of preservice teachers' struggles as they translate language and literacy theory into practice. *Action in Teacher Education, 19,* 61–75.

Dweck, C. S., & Leggett, E. L. (1988). A social-cognitive approach to motivation and personality. *Psychological Review, 95,* 256–273.

Engstrom, D. A., & Schwaab, K. E. (1984). Views of the importance and learnability of selected teacher competencies. *Teacher Educator, 20,* 19–25.

Gilberts, G. H., & Lignugaris-Kraft, B. (1997). Classroom management and instruction competencies for preparing elementary and special education teachers. *Teaching and Teacher Education, 13,* 597–609.

Morine-Dershime, G. (1989). Preservice teachers' conceptions of content and pedagogy: Measuring growth in reflective, pedagogical decision-making. *Journal of Teacher Education, 40,* 46–52.

Pintrich, P. R. (2000). An achievement goal theory perspective on issues in motivation terminology, theory, and research. *Contemporary Educational Psychology, 25,* 92–104.

Ryan, R. M., & Deci, E. L. (2000). Intrinsic and extrinsic motivations: Classic definitions and new directions. *Contemporary Educational Psychology, 25,* 54–67.

Standerford, N. S. (1996). Teacher research at the preservice level: Developing a stance toward knowledge, agency, and collaboration. *Journal of Reading Education, 21,* 30–43.

Tierney, R. J., & Readence, J. E. (2000). *Reading strategies and practices: A compendium* (5th ed.). Boston: Allyn & Bacon.

Tillema, H. H., & Knol, W. E. (1997). Promoting student teacher learning through conceptual change or direct instruction. *Teaching and Teacher Education, 13,* 579–595.

Wigfield, A., & Eccles, J. S. (2000). Expectancy-value theory of achievement motivation. *Contemporary Educational Psychology, 25,* 68–81.

Zeichner, K. (1996). Designing educative practicum experiences for prospective teachers. In K. Zeichner, S. Melnick, & M. L. Gomez (Eds.), *Currents of reform in preservice teacher education* (pp. 215–234). New York: Teachers College Press.

Zimmerman, B. J. (2000). Self-efficacy: An essential motive to learn. *Contemporary Educational Psychology, 25,* 82–91.

Examining Two Preservice Teachers' Practices for Promoting Culturally Responsive Literacy in the Middle Grades

Janine A. Kaste
College of Staten Island, CUNY

Teacher education programs today face the challenge of preparing teachers for the diversity of students in classrooms today. One challenge is that a majority of teachers and teacher candidates today are white and middle-class, having lived and learned in a mainstream middle-class culture with little exposure to the differences their students bring (Delpit, 1995; Ladson-Billings, 1994; Reyes, 1992). In addition, standardized curricula, instructional practices, and assessment measures continue to predominate as a means to run school systems in efficient ways, with little regard to differences among learners (Darling-Hammond, 1993). Consequently, students of diverse backgrounds, particularly children of color, from low-income families, and with a home language other than standard American English, continue to be more likely to experience difficulties learning literacy (Au, 1998; Reyes, 1992). Difficulties in school literacy achievement present a serious problem, since literacy is necessary for success in pursuing all other subjects (Boyer, 1996). Furthermore, the literacy demands of our society have increased from writing one's name to comprehending, synthesizing, and evaluating complex texts (Bruer, 1994; Resnick, 1987).

In response to the challenge of educating our diverse learners, a number of researchers have documented alternative instructional approaches for literacy learning that have been successful with diverse groups of children (Au, 1998; Heath, 1983; Lee, 1995; Moll, 1994; Purcell-Gates, 1995; Reyes, 1992). These studies describe teaching that attended to the diverse needs and experiences of the learners by mediating learning experiences for students. Scaffolds, attentive to students' cultures and abilities, supported students to achieve new literacy skills and behaviors. Such support gradually transferred the responsibility of new knowledge from teacher to students (Greenfield, 1984).

Attending to a social constructivist orientation, these studies embraced an expanded notion of literacy to respect individual backgrounds and provide many opportunities for reading and writing as well as reasoning, articulating, and applying knowledge for meaningful purposes and contexts. This approach also recognizes the importance of acquiring multiple literacy practices as dependent on understanding the behaviors for different discourse communities (Gee, 1991; Langer, 1991). Au (1998) asserts that efforts to close the literacy achievement gap of diverse learners necessitate a *diverse* social constructivist orientation. She

National Reading Conference Yearbook, ***50,*** *pp. 311–322.*

identifies seven elements prevalent in the research on school literacy achievement that are inclusive for all learners. These elements serve both to value and extend students' literacy within their own cultures while teaching the necessary skills and support for learning literacy to succeed in the larger society. Students in the classrooms described in these studies exhibited a sense of ownership of the learning both in the content and process. Connections to their lives outside of school were deliberate in topic and in interaction patterns. The instructional materials used were authentic and inclusive of multiple perspectives. In addition, explicit instruction met students' abilities to support their literacy achievement, engaging learners as independent and critical thinkers and communicators.

Examination of the literature on teacher education reveals little attention to promoting school literacy learning beyond mainstream practices, particularly at the middle and secondary levels where preparation is focused primarily on the teaching of the content of academic disciplines. Some studies have examined preservice teachers' beliefs on diversity as they participate in courses on diversity awareness (Fry & McKinney, 1997; LaFramboise & Griffith, 1997; Olmedo, 1997). Fewer studies have investigated the types of literacy strategies preservice teachers use when teaching in the content areas during their field experiences (Bean, 1997) and the kinds of culturally responsive practices they exhibit in their lessons during student teaching (Duesterberg, 1998; Rodriquez & Sjostrom, 1995). This study focused on preservice teachers' practices in promoting literacy in content area instruction that is responsive to all learners.

Method

Background

This research study occurred during the field experiences of two preservice teachers in the middle grades who identified themselves as wanting to be culturally responsive and to attend to literacy in their content area teaching. I examined these preservice teachers' practice for literacy and cultural responsiveness and the role that reflection played on their subsequent instruction.

The literature on successful practices for literacy learning among diverse student populations informed this inquiry. I used Au's (1998) conceptual framework of diverse social constructivism to promote school literacy learning among diverse populations to analyze the data for literacy practices that were culturally responsive to learners. The six elements I focused on were (a) the goal of instruction, (b) the role of the home language, (c) instructional materials, (d) classroom management and interaction with students, (e) relationship to the community, and (f) instructional methods. In addition, I examined the preservice teachers' instruction for inclusion of scaffolds for literacy learning. I defined literacy learning as those experiences that promote the active engagement of making meaning from text, creating meaning with text, or both. These experiences included the ability to create oral texts through instructional conversations (Tharp & Gallimore, 1988) and literate thinking (Langer, 1991). During student teaching, I used the preliminary findings from my ongoing analysis of the data to focus debriefing sessions on the preservice teachers' instructional challenges.

Participants and Contexts

The two preservice teachers studied, Shonsi, an African-American female, and Lynn, a white female, were enrolled in a middle-grade teacher preparation program at an urban university in the Southeast. They had participated in a required course on diversity which I taught. The course included readings and discussions about diversity with respect to their own awareness and that of students in urban schools, including a 3-week observational practicum in an urban middle school. Assignments included an autobiography, reflective journals, a self-selected project, and completion of a diversity plan for their field experiences and future teaching. Shonsi and Lynn were among nine preservice teachers who responded to an invitation to participate in the study. I selected them as study participants; their coursework (i.e., autobiography, journals, research project, and diversity plan) indicated that they were both committed to culturally responsive teaching.

The context for the first teaching practicum was a metropolitan area middle school with approximately 1,300 students for Grades 6–8. The student population was diverse with respect to race, language, and socioeconomic status, and represented over 30 different languages and countries. Both preservice teachers participated in this setting for 7 weeks and were required to teach in all of the content areas. Shonsi and Lynn participated in two different settings for their 15 weeks of student teaching. Shonsi's setting was a metropolitan school serving approximately 675 students in Grades 7 and 8. The student population was diverse, representing about 40% each African-American and white, and about 20% of Hispanic and Asian ethnicity. Socioeconomic status ranged from low income to middle class. In this setting, Shonsi taught seventh-grade mathematics, reading, and social studies. Lynn's school was also in the metropolitan area, serving 1,000 students. The student population represented 54 different countries and 21 languages; socioeconomic status ranged from low to middle class. In the classes Lynn was observed, about 25% of her students were Latino. Lynn taught eighth-grade mathematics exclusively in this setting.

Data Collection

Data sources included: (a) fieldnotes and videotapes of observed lessons, (b) audio tapes of the debriefing sessions with the preservice teachers, (c) lesson plans and other instructional artifacts, (d) fieldnotes of informal interviews and course artifacts from the preservice teachers' diversity course, and (e) copies of the preservice teachers' field journals. The journals were required program assignments. In the practicum, preservice teachers were required to log their daily experiences and reflect on one critical teaching incident per week. The field supervisor of the first experience responded to these journals weekly. The student teaching journal was a similar assignment; however, the supervising teacher for their second experience did not provide ongoing feedback.

I played the role of a participant observer which allowed me to support Shonsi and Lynn through our reflective debriefing sessions. I played no role in their field evaluations. Each week, I observed a minimum of one lesson and held at least one debriefing session with each preservice teacher over the course of two semesters. These formal debriefing sessions focused on three guiding questions. After we reviewed the previous lesson's transcripts I began each session by asking their perspective on (a) how they implemented literacy scaffolds, (b) how they were culturally responsive to their students, and (c) what influenced their planning and teaching. My ongoing analysis of the data was used to focus the preservice teachers' attention to neglected areas and consider future practice.

Data Analysis

Data analysis was ongoing and guided according to naturalistic procedures to ensure rigor (Lincoln & Guba, 1985). I analyzed the data for the first six elements in Au's (1998) conceptual framework of diverse social constructivism. I also examined the data for the preservice teachers' instructional scaffolding attempts through constant-comparative analysis (Glaser & Strauss, 1967). This analysis revealed patterns with respect to the role that preservice teachers played (i.e., modeling, supporting), the focus of the scaffolds (i.e., content, literacy processes,), and the duration of these incidents.

I executed all of my analysis with the word processor and hard copies of my raw data. I established tables by case for each guiding question to organize the appropriate data to determine patterns. The data were coded by sources to triangulate the findings. Once patterns were established, I consulted my peer debriefer to conduct an audit. My analysis continued with a second look at the raw data to ensure credibility within the context of the lessons. I found a few additional incidents in this second examination that were neglected prior to the refined patterns. These new incidents were also audited by the debriefer and reexamined in the raw data.

Results

Lynn

Lynn often voiced her goal to become "a great teacher." She epitomized the exemplary preservice teacher who followed all requirements and consistently took initiative. For example, during my first field visit, Lynn had already met with the cooperating teachers and mapped out her teaching and observation schedule for the semester. Lynn expressed an interest in working with diverse students, particularly Latino populations. Throughout our time together she grappled with her limited experience and knowledge of students with diverse backgrounds as a result of her monocultural upbringing. The data revealed a consistent tension between Lynn's actual practice, what she perceived others to expect of her teaching, and what she believed her teaching should be.

Culturally responsive literacy in practice. Examining Lynn's practice with Au's (1998) framework and for literacy scaffolds revealed that Lynn's greatest strength was *instructional methods* by modeling skills (averaging four scaffolding incidents per lesson); however her attention to other elements was sporadic and often missing (averaging only one per lesson). For example, during a review lesson on graphs, Lynn modeled how to construct a semantic web and thought aloud as to how to use the web to study for the upcoming exam.

Lynn: What did we say a bar graph does? What do you compare?
Student: Quantities.
Lynn: You can compare quantities, so if I was using this as a study tool, which I hope you will, I'll write myself a little definition that a bar graph compares quantities. This is a great way to organize your thoughts when you have a lot of information.

Consistently, Lynn made deliberate attempts at scaffolding new learning through modeling. These attempts, however, seldom provided students the opportunity to exercise the skill or behavior independently. In a lesson on understanding and distinguishing the different mathematical properties (i.e., distributive, associative), Lynn guided students in making connections to derivatives of words they knew in more familiar contexts. Her support in this scaffolding remained very structured and allowed for minimal student construction. As with most of her teaching, her questioning followed an Initiate-Response-Evaluation pattern (Mehan, 1979).

Her consistent attention to explicit teaching provided little or no attention to the *goal of instruction,* defined as establishing student ownership so that literacy learning is personally meaningful and useful. For example, in a lesson on child labor during the Industrial Revolution, Lynn integrated a variety of texts as a way to build students' schema on child labor both past and present. She utilized a collection of sources that she displayed in the front of the room, including nonfiction books, the novel *Oliver Twist,* and a magazine issue that addressed students taking action to raise awareness about notable companies who are supporting child laborers today. Missing however, was an opportunity for students to explore these texts. Lynn read aloud and commented on all the examples, asking students occasional close-ended questions. Consequently, *classroom management and interaction with students* also received little to no attention in her teaching since her approach placed students in a primarily passive role.

Lynn also found *role of home language* challenging. In both of Lynn's experiences, Lynn encountered Latino ESL students, a particular challenge during her student-teaching setting in which one class contained six Latino males. These boys were situated together by the cooperating teacher so that the more proficient speakers could translate for the Limited English Proficient students. Lynn knew of the prevalent Latino population in area schools and had focused her diversity project in this area. During the practicum and beginning of student teaching, however, Lynn made no deliberate effort to support these students during instruction. She often expressed concern in "doing more damage than good" or "infringing" during our debriefing sessions. In a written reflection she wrote:

> For the most part, ESL students are mainstreamed into the math classes since math is supposed to be the "international language." However, I have watched our ESL students struggle day after day. No real modifications are made to accommodate them. . . . I am not even sure I would know where to begin.

In the student-teaching setting, Lynn worked in a school whose district emphasized high stakes accountability. As a result, Lynn implemented little beyond the school texts and gave little attention to *instructional materials* that were reflective of multiple perspectives, including those representative of the student population. Although her instructional examples would reflect common experiences to her students, little integration of community issues and funds of knowledge were used, also limiting her use of *relationship to the community.* Lynn knew little about her students' lives outside of school. Aside from drawing conclusions from driving around the neighborhood and consulting her cooperating teacher, when asked what she knew about her students she responded, "That's hard to say. Because of the discipline plan, I really don't hear a lot of chatter going on."

Reflection on practice. During Lynn's student-teaching experience, we focused on providing more student ownership in her lessons, particularly with respect to practicing literacy behaviors. Lynn did move toward more student involvement. For example, during a unit on graphs and statistics, she involved students in collecting and graphing their own data and used examples such as their music preferences. Students also worked at their own pace during one lesson in the computer lab, and for the first time deliberate attention was given to her second language learners as Lynn sat with two Latino boys to support their understanding of the assignment. Toward the end of the experience, as pressure to cover curriculum for the exam became paramount, Lynn returned to a teacher-directed approach to cover the material. At our final debriefing, after viewing her last taped lesson, Lynn reflected from the eyes of her students and proposed what she would like to do instead:

> It was so much me—so much me! I said, "Good Lord, I am boring myself to death!" I think I would take a completely different approach to that entire unit. I would make it to where—assign a group a topic—you take line graphs, you take this and give them a day or so to look at it, work with it, play with it, then have the students teach it. Or maybe do centers where they travel around the room and look at the different points rather than standing up there and droning on and on and on. I definitely will approach it where there is much more of them doing rather than me talking.

Shonsi

Shonsi often spoke of the importance of knowing children to teach them. As a product of growing up in a predominantly African-American community in the city, she valued the support and involvement from her teachers, staff, neighbors, and family and credited their motivating support for her school success. During her experience, Shonsi's culturally responsive practice and attention to literacy fluctuated according to her depth of content knowledge and the degree of mentoring she received.

Culturally responsive literacy in practice. An analysis of Shonsi's practice for literacy learning scaffolds and for elements from Au's (1998) framework revealed that Shonsi's student-centered approach attended frequently to many elements, yet the absence of explicit guidance yielded few incidents of scaffolding. In addition, when Shonsi's content area knowledge was limited, she attended less to culturally responsive elements and more to a traditional teaching stance.

Throughout her planning and instruction, Shonsi deliberately attended to the *goal of instruction* as she made learning meaningful and purposeful to the students. For example, a lesson on note taking during a reading lesson centered on the reading for the students' science class. She designed this lesson based on her observations of the students' struggles in this class, "I know the students were having trouble. I listen to the students a lot and hear them say, 'Oh no I hate that class. He gives me a test every day.'" To connect reading and writing in another lesson, she had students create news articles on one of their personal reading choices. In mathematics, she often created tasks that involved them in applying concepts in real ways, such as using negative integers during a lesson on credit card purchasing. On other occasions she allowed students to design their own mathematical word problems. These instructional situations also attended to *classroom management and interaction with students* as she established opportunities for student collaboration. During her first field experience, which involved a cohesive team of predominantly African-American teachers, I watched Shonsi adopt the consistent interaction patterns enforced by each team member. These patterns included expecting students to "stand up and be heard." On other occasions, she used call and response to reinforce concepts they were learning about, as in this science lesson:

> Shonsi: So mixtures can be separated, but compounds cannot. What did I say?
> Class: (In strong voices) Mixtures can be separated, but compounds cannot!

Her lessons also attended to *relationship to the community.* Students' ownership in designing word problems and choosing their own writing topics allowed students to draw upon their worlds outside of school. Shonsi also integrated community knowledge into her instruction. In her lesson on negative integers as applied to credit card spending, Shonsi was sensitive to include items and community stores that reflected the socioeconomic levels of the students. She also spent the introduction of the lesson having students share knowledge of earning paychecks, as seen with their own parents. Shonsi tuned in to her students' lives in and out of school, and used this knowledge in her teaching. Throughout our debriefings, she prefaced her decision making with comments such as "I talked to the students . . ." and "I hear them say . . ."

Elements that appeared less frequently included *role of home language* and *instructional materials.* Shonsi's contexts involved little contact with ESL students. Although she interacted with students who used their home discourses, there was no deliberate attention to validating their use of a home language within their school tasks. Like Lynn, Shonsi used the required texts for instruction with little supplemental materials. The exceptions were materials she made for mathematics, the use of magazine advertisements during a lesson on propaganda, and using *Every Day Heroes* by Beth Johnson, a collection of stories about everyday people from diverse backgrounds who overcame insurmountable odds.

Shonsi found *instructional methods* most challenging. Her instructional scaffolds were often too brief (averaging less than one per lesson), and, in contrast to Lynn, she would transfer the responsibility over to students too quickly. For example, during the lesson on note-taking through concept maps, Shonsi gave one brief example, then assigned students to create their own concept maps, given specific pages in their science texts. As a result, the students exhibited much difficulty in completing the task. In addition, an absence of assignment expectations often resulted in superficial products, as exhibited in the students' cooperative social studies projects and their mathematical word problem constructions.

Reflection on practice. Consequently, our attention during the latter part of the study focused more on Shonsi's implementation of deliberate literacy scaffolds and Au's (1998) element of instructional methods. This process involved more than our debriefing sessions, but also my presence during her lesson planning. For example, when Shonsi acquired social studies, she began teaching by modeling the cooperating teacher's method of reading the text aloud while giving notes. Shonsi's comments during one lesson, "Who can tell me what we just read? If you were paying attention, what you read was what we just recorded in our notes," clearly indicated that students were neither attending to notes nor text. Later, my participation in her planning often resulted in Shonsi trying to implement my suggestions without full understanding. My ongoing analysis kept me in check to return to a support role that kept Shonsi in charge. Shonsi evolved from modeling the cooperating teacher, then adopting my suggestions, to adapting her own style, as she became comfortable with the content and thought more about her scaffolding practices. As a result, she returned to attending more to culturally responsive elements.

During the last social studies lesson on Indian removal in the southeast, Shonsi had students consider what it would be like if strangers suddenly kicked them out of their own neighborhoods. As students thought about the text through the perspectives of the Indians and settlers, they began to question the actions of those involved and of their portrayal in the text. For the first time, students discussed the text:

Student: The Indians keep losing more land?
Shonsi: That's right. Remember, King George took the Creek Indian land. That's why we had the Oconee War.

Student: The Indians are lazy. They are giving up their land too easily.
Shonsi: You really think that? Open your books to page 190. (She reads) "Bad feelings between the Creek and the settlers grew during the late 1700s. Pioneers kept pushing into Creek lands along the Oconee River. Tribes led by Chief Alexander McGillivray sent warriors against some of the pioneer settlements. The Indians burned houses, stole horses and cattle, and killed or captured over two hundred settlers. [The] colonists got some men together and told them to kill on sight any Creek who were not members of friendly tribes. . . ." They are fighting back, but how is that worded?
Student: It sounds like they are the bad ones.
Shonsi: (Rereads part: told them to kill on sight any Creek—)
Student: I would get friends with them then—Pow!
Shonsi: Now listen to what they promise the Indians. (Shonsi continues to read about the meeting between McGillivray and Washington, which leads to another treaty where the Indians give up more land and the settlers promise to stay out of the land west of the river).
Student: Another promise they won't keep.

Shonsi's innate kidwatching ability contributed to her high attention to student ownership during the lessons. Another influence on her practice was the degree of content knowledge she had. Lessons outside of her math major also showed less attention to scaffolding and culturally responsive practice. She commented on this during her first experience after teaching a science lesson on elements and compounds, "Science is not my strong subject, so I was feeling a little shaky—trying to stay close to the text book. I didn't want the kids to pick up on it." Another influencing factor was mentorship. During her practicum field experience, Shonsi participated with a cohesive and supportive team and a university supervisor who was visible and provided continual feedback during observations, conferences, and on their weekly journals. In contrast, her mentoring teachers during her student teaching experience were less overt in their support and the university supervisor visited infrequently. For example, in the practicum experience I observed her cooperating science teacher reviewing the lesson with her prior to the class and supporting her when needed during the lesson. In contrast, although I noted the social studies teacher sitting in on her lessons during student teaching, he provided no support during the lesson. When I inquired if he was giving her feedback, Shonsi replied, "Just to keep my notes shorter and to use a big enough font." This contrast also influenced my greater involvement, particularly in those lessons I mentored her planning.

Our debriefing experiences focused predominately on Shonsi's degree of content knowledge, her use of scaffolds in lessons, and her acute sense of knowing who her students were as individuals. At the end of the experience, when asked about what she had learned, she began, "I need to know my information before I get up there. I need to be more knowledgeable and that may mean that I need to resort to other sources." She concluded with her philosophy about students and the importance of catching herself when losing this focus. She spoke of this with conviction, "There are always ways to motivate students and make connections."

Discussion

Shonsi and Lynn shared a determination for wanting to be culturally responsive and for attending to literacy in their teaching. Au's (1998) framework for improving the school literacy learning of students of diverse backgrounds served as a useful tool for examining Lynn's and Shonsi's practice with respect to the research. In particular, sharing my ongoing analysis with the students on their use of scaffolds and culturally responsive practice also promoted more deliberate attention to those areas missing in previous lessons. As Au states herself, "the greater challenge is not in proposing frameworks but in bringing about changes in schools that will close the literacy achievement gap" (p. 316). This study represents one means for addressing the gap by attending to culturally responsive teaching more deliberately during the field experience. This however, is only one piece. The constraints of the school context faced by Shonsi and Lynn limited its effectiveness. For example, rigid standards and accountability that emphasized curriculum coverage impeded Lynn's ability to include student ownership as pressure to complete a unit for an upcoming test held precedence. Shonsi's varying mentorship in the field showed how positive models supported her growth in content knowledge and responsive practice, whereas lack of models resulted in the absence of culturally responsive elements and meaningful instruction.

In practice, Lynn's and Shonsi's scaffolds to promote literacy learning were beginning attempts. Patterns emerged that reflected the types of literacy promoted and the kinds of support provided; however, there was little to indicate deliberate use of scaffolds to promote independent learning. Lynn's teacher-directed approach demonstrated literacy behaviors, but limited opportunities and scaffolds to support student independence. Although Shonsi included learner-centered activities that involved students, absent were scaffolds to promote meaningful engagement in these tasks.

More deliberate attention to scaffolded instruction needs to be included in teacher preparation programs. Beyond theory, examples of scaffolded learning should be demonstrated and supported by teacher education faculty within the context of understanding the discourse practices of particular disciplines. Studies are needed that address the use of scaffolding in teacher education programs for literacy learning at the middle/secondary level with respect to both our coursework and field mentoring. These programs may require literacy educators to support faculty from content area disciplines.

Those elements most challenging for Shonsi and Lynn included the *role of home language, relation to the community,* and *instructional materials.* These are elements that lacked full attention in Shonsi and Lynn's preparation. Application of Au's (1998) framework in analyzing program courses can shift attention to culturally responsive pedagogy beyond incorporating diversity terminology in course objectives. For example, how are we preparing our preservice teachers to articulate and demonstrate how to accommodate language diversity and draw upon community funds of knowledge to promote content literacy learning?

This study also calls for more attention to responsive mentoring from both the university and the schools. Au's (1998) framework can be applied to build a mentoring program that addresses these issues. Another recommendation is to involve peer collaboration. Lynn could learn from Shonsi's attention to ownership in lessons and her insightful kid watching observations. Conversely, Shonsi could have benefited from Lynn's ability to plan carefully and implement structured scaffolds for literacy learning. Field experiences that allow preservice teachers to support each other in practice may help support their development of new practices not used by the cooperating teachers. This approach would also foster collaborative teaching and support structures.

Responsive teacher preparation also needs to move preservice teachers beyond learning of best practices to develop their own philosophies of effective teaching (Cochran-Smith & Lytle, 1993). My work with Shonsi exemplifies the need for a constructivist focus. Shonsi's lessons were most effective during those debriefing sessions when she chose ideas that were meaningful to her. As in Lynn's case, more studies are needed to examine ways to promote responsive practice and meaningful accountability.

This study examined what preservice teachers do; however, studies that include the voices of students are needed. Particularly, in studying preservice teachers in practice do we see evidence of student literacy achievement when instruction includes culturally responsive elements and scaffolds for literacy? How do we know when students take ownership? Additionally, how can we, as teacher educators, implement culturally responsive pedagogy to accommodate preservice teachers' unique strengths and needs, and foster their ownership as reflective practitioners?

References

Au, K. H. (1998). Social constructivism and the school literacy learning of students of diverse backgrounds. *Journal of Literacy Research 30,* 297–319.

Bean, T. W. (1997). Preservice teachers' selection and use of content area literacy strategies. *Journal of Educational Research, 90,* 154–163.

Boyer, E. L. (1996). Literacy and learning. In M. F. Graves, P. Van Den Broek, & B. M. Taylor (Eds.), *The first R: Every child's right to read* (pp. 1–12). New York: International Reading Association and Teachers College Press.

Bruer, J. T. (1994). *Schools for thought.* Cambridge, MA: MIT Press.

Cochran-Smith, M., & Lytle, S. L. (1993). *Inside outside: Teacher research and knowledge.* New York: Teachers College Press.

Darling-Hammond, L. (1993). Reframing the school reform agenda: Developing capacity for school transformation. *Phi Delta Kappan, 74,* 753–761.

Delpit, L. (1995). *Other people's children: Cultural conflict in the classroom.* New York: New Press.

Duesterberg, L. M. (1998). Rethinking culture in the pedagogy and practices of preservice teachers. *Teaching and Teacher Education, 14,* 497–512.

Fry, P., & McKinney, L. (1997). A qualitative study of preservice teachers' early field experiences in an urban, culturally different school. *Urban Education, 32,* 184–201.

Gee, P. (1991). What is literacy? In C. Mitchell & K. Weiler (Eds.), *Rewriting literacy: Culture and the discourse of the other* (pp. 3–11). Westport, CT: Bergin & Garvey.

Glaser, B., & Strauss, A. (1967). *The discovery of grounded theory.* New York: Aldine.

Greenfield, P.M. (1984). A theory of the teacher in the learning activities of everyday life. In B. Rogoff & J. Lave (Eds.), *Everyday cognition: Its development in social context* (pp. 117–138). Cambridge, MA: Harvard University Press.

Heath, S. B. (1983). *Ways with words.* New York: Cambridge University Press.

Ladson-Billings, G. (1994). *The dreamkeepers: Successful teaching for African American students.* San Francisco: Jossey-Bass.

LaFramboise, K., & Griffith, P. (1997). Using literature cases to examine diversity issues with preservice teachers. *Teaching and Teacher Education, 13,* 369–382.

Langer, J. A. (1991). Literacy and schooling: a sociocognitive perspective. In E. H. Hiebert (Ed.), *Literacy for a diverse society* (pp. 9–27). New York: Teachers College Press.

Lee, C. D. (1995). A culturally based cognitive apprenticeship: Teaching African American high school students skills in literary interpretation. *Reading Research Quarterly, 30,* 608–630.

Lincoln, Y. S., & Guba, E. G. (1985). *Naturalistic inquiry.* Newbury Park, CA: Sage.

Mehan, H. (1979). *Learning lessons: Social organizations in the classroom.* Cambridge, MA: Harvard University Press.

Moll, L. (1994). Literacy research in community and classrooms: A sociocultural approach. In R. B. Ruddell, M. R. Ruddell, & H. Singer (Eds.), *Theoretical models and processes of reading* (pp. 179–207). Newark, DE: International Reading Association.

Olmedo, I. M. (1997). Challenging old assumptions: Preparing teachers for inner city schools. *Teaching and Teacher Education, 13,* 245–258.

Purcell-Gates, V. (1995). *Other people's words: The cycle of low literacy.* Cambridge, MA: Harvard University Press.

Resnick, L. B. (1987). *Education and learning to think.* Washington, DC: National Academy Press.

Reyes, M. de la Luz (1992). Challenging venerable assumptions: Literacy instruction for linguistically different students. *Harvard Educational Review, 62,* 427–446.

Rodriguez, Y. E., & Sjostrom, B. R. (1995). Culturally responsive teacher preparation evident in classroom approaches to cultural diversity: A novice and an experienced teacher. *Journal of Teacher Education, 46,* 304–311.

Tharp, R. G., & Gallimore, R. (1988). *Rousing minds to life: Teaching, learning, and schooling in social context.* Cambridge, England: Cambridge University Press.

A Study of the Impact of a Reading-Specialization Program on First-Year Teachers

Susan Keehn, Janis Harmon, Wanda Hedrick, Miriam Martinez, and Bertha Perez
University of Texas at San Antonio

The need for more extensive research in teacher education has become increasingly imperative in light of restructuring efforts and recurring demands for improvement of teacher-preparation programs. National reports (Holmes Group, 1995; National Commission on Teaching and America's Future, 1996), calling for reform in teacher education programs, underscore the importance of this line of research. The reading research community also identifies teacher preparation as an important topic of investigation (Cassidy & Cassidy, 2000). In spite of these reports and earlier Holmes Group reports (1986, 1990), however, there is a dearth of research addressing how teachers should be taught to teach reading (Anders, Hoffman, & Duffy, 2000; Hoffman & Pearson, 2000).

Reviewing the research on teacher preparation in general, Pearson (2000a) concludes that fully prepared and certified teachers are more successful with students than teachers who lack either subject matter or teaching knowledge. Moreover, teachers admitted with less than full preparation are less satisfied with their training and have greater difficulties planning curriculum, managing the classroom, diagnosing students' learning needs, and adapting their instruction (Pearson, 2000b). Thus, Pearson's findings affirm the value of effective teacher-preparation programs. Yet research designed to define the specific aspects of these preparation programs that lead to effective literacy instruction is nonexistent.

Examining research specifically related to teacher preparation in reading, Anders et al. (2000) note that early studies focused largely on "translation of theory into practice" (p. 721) rather than examining the effectiveness of the preparation programs themselves. The studies that did investigate programs focused on topics such as teacher attitudes about their preparation programs (Furr, 1965; Smith, Otto, & Harty, 1970) and the value of field experiences (Britton, 1975). Other studies (e.g., Noe, 1994) examined the influence of undergraduate programs on teachers' theoretical orientations and classroom practices. Anders et al. (2000) and Hoffman and Pearson (2000) call for research to study the effectiveness of preparation programs in reading and to follow preservice teachers into the early teaching years. The current investigation examined the effectiveness of one teacher-preparation program in reading, addressing the following questions: (a) Do beginning teachers with reading specializations differ in reading knowledge

*National Reading Conference Yearbook, **50**, pp. 323–332.*

and knowledge of practice from beginning teachers without reading specializations? (b) If these groups do differ, in what ways do they differ?

Method

Subjects

The subjects were 26 first-year teachers, all graduates of the University of Texas at San Antonio (UTSA). Teachers in one of the two groups (13 subjects) had selected reading as their area of academic specialization in their preparation program (reading group). Teachers in the second group (13 subjects) had specialized in various other academic areas (comparison group). Teachers in both the reading group and the comparison group were randomly selected, resulting in variations in ethnicity, age, academic record, and grade-level assignments.

Description of reading courses taken by all subjects. Two reading courses are required for all UTSA students who seek elementary certification. *Introduction to Developmental Reading* offers basic knowledge about the reading process, literacy acquisition, instruction in word identification, assessment, and a focus on teaching reading to diverse populations. In the *Introduction to Content Area Reading* course, students develop an understanding of the reading needs of upper elementary/middle school students. The course focuses on strategies for teaching comprehension, vocabulary, and thinking skills in the content areas. The two-course sequence provides an overview of literacy learning across the grades.

Description of content of courses taken by reading-specialization group. In addition to the required introductory reading courses, reading-specialization students take an additional 18 semester hours of reading courses. The four required specialization courses include (a) introduction to reading problems, (b) reading comprehension, (c) relationships between reading and writing, and (d) children's and adolescent literature. Reading-specialization students also select two electives from the following courses: (a) early literacy learning; (b) assessment practices in reading; (c) language, literacy, and culture; (d) oral language and reading; (e) social psychology of literacy; and (f) reading and studying as a cognitive process.

All reading courses at UTSA include the objective of developing students' awareness of issues of diversity and inclusion. In reading courses, students learn to adjust and modify instruction to meet the diverse needs of learners. Content includes:

1. Incorporation of children's home language into literacy lessons;
2. Knowledge about first- and second-language development;
3. Exploration of children's literature that reflects the diverse learners' experiences;

4. Selection of appropriate materials and instructional strategies to meet diverse needs; and
5. Knowledge of issues affecting diverse learners such as tracking, ability grouping, and biases in assessment instruments and practice.

Finally, identification of strengths and weaknesses of readers is incorporated into both course content and field experiences. In addition to a course specifically devoted to formal and informal assessments, specific types of literacy assessments are addressed in various reading courses so that students learn to administer multiple assessments and interpret the results to develop worthwhile instructional procedures as they work with children. Students explore the relationship between assessment and instruction in light of what teachers know about learners, the situated context in which reading and writing occur, and the resulting interactions between learner and context. The underlying thread in all discussion of assessment tools is a continual reference to issues of appropriateness for culturally, linguistically, and economically diverse students.

Description of field experiences of reading-specialization group. Field experiences are integrated into courses within the reading-specialization program to help students connect what they learn in their course work to what they see happening in schools. This balance between literacy theory and practice provides students with a basis for instructional decision-making, ensuring that students have the opportunity to connect theory to practice. Field experiences are designed so that students work with children at different levels of literacy development, in different contexts (one-on-one, small groups, whole group) and in a variety of settings. Field experiences are based in schools, as well as at the University's downtown literacy center, offering one-on-one tutorials for San Antonio's inner-city population. A student who pursues a reading specialization at UTSA engages in an additional 55 hours of fieldwork specifically related to literacy. In contrast, students who are not in the reading specialization engage in 5 hours of literacy fieldwork.

In sum, content offered through the UTSA reading specialization includes: (a) theoretical foundations that help prospective teachers develop a congruent set of principles and practices for effective teaching; (b) sound instructional methods, practices, and strategies derived from both theory and empirical research; and (c) a variety of assessment and evaluation methods for evaluating students' literacy progress.

Procedures

Two groups of first-year teachers, the reading group and the comparison group, were interviewed regarding their students, their teaching experiences, and their literacy practices. Both groups of teachers were interviewed before school began in August, at midyear in January, and near the end of the school year in April. Each interview included the following prompts/questions:

1. Describe your students' progress in reading.
2. Describe how you teach reading.
3. How does that [the way you teach reading] compare to the way reading is taught in your school?
4. How does your teaching of reading compare to what you learned in your preparation program?

All of the teachers were interviewed by one of the five authors. Participants were free to express their points of view without concern for censorship or offense because none of the interviewers was the teacher's supervisor or evaluator.

The interviews were transcribed and analyzed by constant comparison methods. The authors read the transcriptions for both the reading and the comparison groups to identify thematic strands. The thematic strands that emerged, such as grouping policies or integration of the language arts, became the categories for coding the data. The transcriptions were reread and coded using these categories to identify similarities and differences among informants (Lincoln & Guba, 1985). Team members read through the coded transcripts and thematic categories, meeting regularly throughout the study as a form of peer debriefing (Erlandson, Harris, Skipper, & Allen, 1993).

Word counts were made of the responses given by participants in both the reading group and the comparison group. The number of words was totaled for each group.

Findings

The authors analyzed responses to each of the prompts and questions in the teacher interviews conducted at midyear of the participants' first teaching year. Findings are described below by question.

Describe your students' progress in reading. More comparison-group participants responded at a general level in evaluating student progress. For example, one comparison participant described student progress by saying, "They're coming along." More reading-group participants discussed the particular reading levels of individual students. For example, one reading participant responded, "Most of the class is between a preprimer 1 and a preprimer 3." Another said, "There are three students in my fourth-grade class who are reading at an early second-grade level."

Five of the reading participants talked of assessment, compared to one in the comparison group who made mention of the state assessment instrument. Only the reading-group participants mentioned particular reading-assessment instruments by name. For example, one reading-group teacher said, "For comprehension, I have been using the Jerry Johns' Basic Reading Inventory."

There were no differences between the two groups in the number of comments addressing areas of strengths and weaknesses. More comparison participants, however, discussed their students' growth in terms of reading motivation than the reading-group participants. For example, one comparison teacher responded, "Some of them have gone from despising reading to now I can't get them to put their books down." Table 1 summarizes the responses of all subjects by categories.

Describe how you teach reading. In response to the prompt, "Describe how you teach reading," seven reading participants described their particular programs compared to two comparison participants, both of whom identified the programs by name rather than described them. Reading participants talked at greater length about the programs they were implementing, as exemplified by the response of this reading-group teacher:

> It's a scripted type of program. It's teaching them spelling patterns to look for in words so that when they get stuck on words they will be able to try and find something that they know and build on that.

Reading-group participants clearly articulated the organization of their reading programs, some even reflecting on organization over time instead of just daily lessons. Comparison-group teachers did not describe specific organizational structures, but rather talked in general terms. For example, one comparison-group participant responded:

> Well, in kindergarten we do letters of the week and I just try to base all my lessons on the letter of the week. . . . Kindergarten teachers have pretty much a set theme, like ocean is for the letter "O." That way it kind of gives us an idea if we want to do it or we can find our own.

In contrast, reading-group teachers responded with specific information about classroom organization for reading instruction, such as this response from a reading-specialization teacher:

> I do small-group reading and while I'm doing reading there are three rotating groups. One does centers, one does seatwork, and the other group is with me. . . . I have a library center where they can just go and sit and read books. . . . I

Table 1

Categories of Responses to Prompt: Describe Your Student's Progress in Reading

Gives Descriptive Category	Gives Global Evaluation of Progress	Identifies Reading Levels of Students	Identifies Particular Reading Assessment Instrument	Identifies Global Areas of Strength or Weakness	Identifies Particular Areas of Strength or Weakness	Discusses Growth in Motivation to Read
Reading Group	3	8	5	1	4	3
Comparison Group	7	3	1	2	4	5

> have a computer and they either do the Kidworks or Kidpix. At the beginning of the week for all groups, we introduce vocabulary, talk about whatever the book is going to be about. . . . We read the book for fluency first and then we will discuss the book. Then we will go back and read for comprehension . . . and they have a test at the end.

Almost equal numbers of comparison and reading participants responded to this prompt by identifying the materials they used in their program. Slightly more reading participants than comparison participants responded to the prompt by describing the focus of instruction, such as spelling patterns, fluency, and vocabulary.

In describing how they teach reading, five reading participants talked about the way they integrated the language arts, whereas none of the comparison participants mentioned integration. For example, one reading-group teacher responded, "Our language arts program is a really strong one, so usually I connect the phonics with the spelling words with the reading words. I interweave them and they use those [words] throughout the week."

Many participants from both reading and comparison groups responded to the prompt by identifying and describing instructional activities. For example, one reading participant said, "They have been doing a lot of writing, a lot of reading of their own poetry, and authored poetry. They have been doing some collaborative reading and writing. They have been doing some presentations, some dramatics."

Seven reading participants responded to the prompt by discussing grouping or the needs of their students, whereas only one comparison participant responded in this manner. As an example, a reading-group participant explained:

> I use a lot of rubrics, trying to figure out if each one has different needs, so sometimes one group may be focusing on phonics, another group may be focusing on story details. And even within my one group, I may have two students who may be doing something different from the others.

Table 2 summarizes the categories that emerged from the responses of all subjects and provides the numbers of responses in each category by group.

Table 2

Categories of Responses to Prompt: Describe How You Teach Reading

Descriptive Category	Describe Focus of Instruction	Discusses Integration of Language Arts	Describes Instructional Activity	Discusses Grouping/ Student Needs	Mentions Specific Program	Describes Classroom Organization	Identifies Materials Used in Program
Reading Group	7	5	11	7	7	8	7
Comparison Group	4	0	9	1	2	3	5

How does that compare to the way reading is taught in your school? Table 3 groups responses provided by all subjects and provides the numbers of responses by group. Generally, most participants felt that the way they taught reading was comparable to the way it was taught in their schools. Nonetheless, some articulated notable differences, as in the following comment from a reading-group teacher: "It's a lot different, and I've taken a little bit of heat from it because the other fifth-grade teacher is a very traditional teacher." Another reading-group participant commented, "I'm seen a little bit as a wild child. I approach it differently. I actually try to have meaningful activities and then pick out the little pieces that I need to work on with the students."

How does your teaching of reading compare to what you have learned in your preparation program? Table 4 summarizes the categories that emerged from the responses of all subjects and provides the numbers of responses by group. Comparison-group teachers acknowledged that the way they were teaching literacy differed from what they had been taught in their reading courses, but they seemed to feel powerless to change the situation. For example, one comparison-group teacher responded:

> It's nothing like what I learned. Anyone could teach this reading program because it's written in the book. . . . The program's laid out. We just feed the activities to them, and they know what they do Monday through Friday. I don't feel that I teach them reading skills at all.

Table 3

Categories of Responses to Question: How Does the Way You Teach Reading Compare to the Way Reading Is Taught in Your School?

	Same	Different	Not Sure
Reading Group	8	5	0
Comparison Group	9	2	2

Table 4

Categories of Responses to Question: How Does the Way You Teach Reading Compare to What You Learned in Your Preparation Program?

Descriptive Categories	Unrelated to Preparation	Quite Consistent with Preparation	Striving to Implement More of What Was Learned in Preparation Program
Reading Group	3	6	4
Comparison Group	8	5	0

Another comparison-group member said:

> My preparation at UTSA does not correlate with the program being taught at this school. . . . For the TAAS [Texas Assessment of Academic Skills] test, strategies are pushed on the kids, but it's very cumbersome. It's continuous and very repetitious and boring to me and to the kids.

In contrast, teachers with reading specialization talked about making adjustments to teach the way they have learned to value. One reading-group teacher responded:

> I'm trying to pull in the things that I learned in my reading classes. For instance, for *The Giver* (Lowry, 1993) I had my students do journal responses and they enjoyed them. Then I had them create a front page of a newspaper.

Other reading-specialization participants referred to aspects of literacy instruction they still wanted to incorporate, as evidenced by this reading teacher's response: "It looked great in the [university] reading program, and I want to get it that way." Another reading teacher said, "I don't feel like I do a fraction of what I was taught in my reading courses yet."

Word counts

Participants in the two groups differed in the quantity of their responses, as measured by word counts. The responses provided by subjects in the reading group contained more than twice the number of words as the responses given by subjects in the comparison group. For example, when asked to describe their reading programs, teachers in the comparison group averaged 83.6 words per response. To the same prompt, teachers in the reading group averaged 248.1 words per response.

Discussion

Although the data were limited to self-reported information, responses of members of the two groups revealed differences. These differences were evident in both the quantity and quality of their responses. The courses and field experiences in the reading-specialization program appeared to provide first-year teachers with a rich knowledge base for making thoughtful and appropriate instructional decisions. The findings provide ample evidence to suggest that reading-specialization students acquired a rich knowledge base about reading instruction as evidenced by their ability to articulate actual application in their classrooms. Further evidence is provided by the fact that the reading-specialization teachers had much more to say about their reading instruction. The very general nature of many of the responses made by the comparison teachers reflects their more limited knowledge about reading.

The teachers who graduated with a reading specialization also appeared to be more aware of their students as individual learners and were familiar with specific assessment tools that enable them to gain insight into learners. On the other hand, comparison participants gauged progress in reading primarily in terms of student motivation. Moreover, the reading-specialization participants described specific strategies that they were implementing to support learning. Whereas both groups described their instructional activities, the comparison teachers were less likely to discuss the purpose of the activities.

Although obviously not at the level of master teachers, these beginning teachers who specialized in reading demonstrated competencies that were not evident in the comparison group. They appeared better able to talk about reading instruction at a programmatic level, discussing a variety of components for effective reading instruction. In particular, the data revealed that reading-specialization participants recognized the importance of integrating the language arts instruction and addressing the needs of individual students. Those reading-specialization teachers who perceived a need to modify the existing school programs appeared to have the self-confidence to do so. This confidence may have been the result of a broad knowledge base that had been internalized through the fieldwork they did in their preparation program. Some of these reading participants also articulated additional innovations they hoped to implement, indicative of a broader vision of what good reading instruction can be. In contrast, comparison teachers appeared to be more accepting of the status quo. Even those comparison-group teachers who recognized the inadequacies of their school's reading program did not perceive themselves as capable of making changes.

Implications

Duffy and Hoffman (1999) argue that the outstanding teacher of reading is one who "thoughtfully and analytically integrates various programs, materials, and methods as the situation demands" (p. 11). The findings of this study suggest that a strong knowledge base, combined with multiple field experiences, supports new teachers on the path toward becoming thoughtful and analytical decision-makers in the classroom. Our data suggest that when new teachers are well prepared, they make decisions about reading instruction based on the needs of their students, even when they find themselves under pressure to conform to the existing school practices. This study adds to an understanding of what makes teacher-preparation programs in reading effective. The findings suggest that colleges of education must move beyond the one or two courses in literacy instruction that are typically required in teacher-preparation programs. Instead, the findings support the value of in-depth opportunities to explore reading theory, knowledge, and instruction and to apply this learning in real-life classroom settings. Our data suggest that a broad based reading-specialization program that provides preservice teachers with ample opportunities to internalize knowledge through field experiences has the potential to prepare outstanding reading teachers.

References

Anders, P. L., Hoffman, J. V., & Duffy, G. G. (2000). Teaching teachers to teach reading: Paradigm shifts, persistent problems, and challenges. In M. L. Kamil, P. B. Mosenthal, P. D. Pearson, & R. Barr (Eds.), *Handbook of reading research* (Vol. 3, pp. 719–742). Mahwah, NJ: Erlbaum.

Britton, J. (1975). Assessing preservice reading methods courses. *Reading Improvement, 10,* 29–32.

Cassidy, J., & Cassidy, D. (December, 2000). What's hot. *Reading Today, 18,* 3. Newark, DE: International Reading Association.

Duffy, G. G., & Hoffman, J. V. (1999). In pursuit of an illusion: The flawed search for a perfect method. *Reading Teacher, 53,* 28–44.

Erlandson, D. E., Harris, E. L., Skipper, B. L., & Allen, S. D. (1993). *Doing naturalistic inquiry.* Newbury Park, CA: Sage.

Furr, O. R. (1965). The effectiveness of a college course in the teaching of reading. In J. A. Figurel (Ed.), *Reading and Inquiry, Proceedings of the International Reading Association* (pp. 370–372). Newark, DE: International Reading Association.

Hoffman, J. V., & Pearson, P. D. (2000). Reading teacher education in the next millennium: What your grandmother's teacher didn't know that your granddaughter's teacher should. *Reading Research Quarterly, 35,* 28–44.

Holmes Group. (1986). *Tomorrow's teachers.* East Lansing, MI: Author.

Holmes Group. (1990). *Tomorrow's schools: Principles for the design of professional development schools.* East Lansing, MI: Author.

Holmes Group. (1995). *Tomorrow's schools of education: A report of the Holmes Group.* East Lansing, MI: Author.

Lincoln, Y. S., & Guba, E. G.(1985). *Naturalistic inquiry.* Beverly Hills, CA: Sage.

Lowry, L. (1993). *The Giver.* Boston: Houghton-Mifflin.

National Commission on Teaching and America's Future. (1996). *What matters most: Teaching for America's future.* New York: Author.

Noe, K. (1994). Effectiveness of an integrated methods curriculum: Will beginning teachers teach as we have taught them? *Journal of Reading Education, 19,* 45–49.

Pearson, P. D. (2000a, April). *Learning to teach reading: Setting the research agenda.* Paper presented at the Reading Research 2000 Conference of the International Reading Association, Indianapolis, IN.

Pearson, P. D. (2000b). *Learning to teach reading: Setting the research agenda.* Online. May 24, 2000. http://ed-web3.educ.msu/pearson/ppoint/TE_IRA/sld001.html

Smith, R. J., Otto, W., & Harty, K. (1970). Elementary teachers' preferences for preservice and in-service training in the teaching of reading. *Journal of Educational Research, 63,* 445–449.

A Framework for Conceptualizing and Evaluating the Contributions of Written Language Activity in Oral Language Development for ESL Students

Youb Kim, Karen L. Lowenstein, and P. David Pearson
CIERA/Michigan State University

Meredith McLellan
Spartan Village Elementary School

Popular views of English as a Second Language (ESL) programs suggest a limited role for English language reading in educating young ESL students. Although they champion ESL students' first-language reading, they come with a proposal that English reading instruction should not be introduced until ESL students are orally proficient (Mills, Cowen, & Guess, 1977; Snow, Burns, & Griffins, 1998; Wong-Fillmore & Valadez, 1986). When the importance of the sociocultural milieu of ESL learning is considered, however, reading and writing may look different in classrooms in which it involves usage of all language modes (Cummins, 1986; Snow, 1992). In such learning contexts, reading can play a more extensive role in teaching ESL children. Based on data gathered in a year-long empirical study during the 1999–2000 school year, we argue that ESL reading instruction and activities can contribute to the development of English oral skills for at least those ESL students who had already acquired literacy skills and, more important, some mastery over the written language register, in their native languages.

When researchers and educators take as a given that oral language is the basis of language development (Ticknor, 1833; Vietor, 1905, as cited in McLaughlin, 1978), ESL reading is likely to take a secondary role in ESL learning. Two corollary assumptions seem to follow. The first corollary states that ESL learning recapitulates native language acquisition (McLaughlin, 1978). The second states that reading comprehension and writing are cognitively and linguistically more demanding than speaking and listening; thus reading (and perhaps writing) cannot be introduced as initial linguistic input (Mills et al., 1977; Wong-Fillmore & Valadez, 1986). In our study, we used data gathered from a year of empirical work in ESL classrooms to raise questions about these assumptions regarding the role that written language should play in ESL students' oral language acquisition. In order to situate our study, we briefly trace the historical precedents of the overarching assumption and its corollaries, along with the problems entailed by each.

The overarching assumption that oral language is the basis of all language development has a long history that dates back to Montaigne, Locke, and Wilhelm

National Reading Conference Yearbook, **50**, *pp. 333–345.*

Vietor in the 1700s and continues to the 1900s (McLaughlin, 1978; also note Chomsky, 1965). More recently, the direct method (e.g., Berlitz) and the audio-lingual method have popularized this view. The result is widespread language instruction based squarely on the oral primacy assumption; reading and writing are relegated to secondary skills that can easily be acquired once oral competence is in place (McLaughlin, 1978). This oral-primacy view, however, has been questioned from time to time by researchers (e.g., Goodman, Goodman, & Flores, 1978; Olson, 1996; Weber, 1970) who have proposed that writing is not simply a secondary representation of speech but has its own register and sociolinguistic functions.

The first corollary assumption, that the processes of ESL learning recapitulate developmental sequences of native language acquisition, can be traced back to scholars who favored the audio-lingual method in the 1950s and 1960s. The audio-lingual method appealed to the new breed of psycholinguists "because it paralleled the natural way in which children learned their first language" (McLaughlin, 1978, p. 136). This view of ESL learning was also supported by proponents of communicative competence in the field of second-language teaching (e.g., Savignon, 1972) and by many linguists writing in the 1970s (McLaughlin, 1978; Snow, 1992). Although the first-language recapitulation view acknowledges the natural, creative, and active processes of second-language learning, when carried to its logical extreme, it can lead to a lock-step instructional approach whereby cognitively challenging tasks must await the mastery of easier tasks. The paradox entailed by this assumption is this: if students are never faced with cognitive challenges, such as reading and writing or semantic categorization, they are not likely to mobilize and expand problem-solving skills necessary for ESL learning.

A second corollary assumption of language learning postulates that reading comprehension (and perhaps writing) are cognitively and linguistically more demanding than speaking and listening; therefore reading (and writing) should not be a part of initial language input for ESL learners (Mills et al., 1977; Wong-Fillmore & Valadez, 1986). An example of the "oral-before-written" phenomenon comes from the work of Snow and her colleagues. They found that certain oral language structures (e.g., formal definitions of words), because they carry a syntax that is more similar to written language as it might be encountered in school than it is to everyday oral language, predict later success in school literacy tasks (Snow, Cancino, Gonzalez, & Shriberg, 1987; Snow, Tabors, Nicholson, & Kurland, 1995). Although the "oral-before-written" assumption has currently gained a foothold in the national policy discussion (e.g., Snow et al., 1998), it has been continuously challenged over several decades by many researchers, such as Anderson and Roit (1996), Elley (1991; Elley & Mangubhai, 1983), Goodman et al., (1979), Hudelson (1984), Saville-Troike (1984), and Seda and Abramson (1990). These authors have argued for parallel synergies between English oral and written language development, suggesting that ESL learners can read and write without developing fully proficient English oral language, and that English reading and writing can facilitate English oral language development (e.g., Fitzgerald, 1995; Garcia, 2000; Weber, 1991).

In trying to sort out the issues and controversies entailed in the arguments surrounding these assumptions, all of which suggest potentially important contributions of written language activities, we developed a framework for conceptualizing the complex relationship between written and oral language development for ESL students, or more accurately, for the particular set of ESL students in our study. Our framework details a set of plausible contributions of English written language activities to English oral language development. Some of the contributions are transparent and direct; others are more subtle and indirect. The framework was only partially specified before we began our research. Indeed most of the categories emerged from our empirical work, in which we tried to answer one single and central research question: What role, if any, should English reading (and writing) instruction play in the development of English oral language? To answer this question, we shadowed one fifth-grade and one second-grade ESL learner in their ESL and general classrooms for an entire school year. We also used data from our observations of four additional second-grade students who were part of another study.

The scarcity of research on the written-oral relationship, dramatically documented by Weber in both the 1970s and the 1990s, makes work like ours all the more important. Only a handful of empirical efforts has been mounted focused specifically on ESL learners. For example, in her research synthesis, Fitzgerald (1995) cited only four research studies (i.e., Lara, 1991; Saville-Troike, 1984; Snow, 1991; Tragar & Wong, 1984, all cited in Fitzgerald, 1995) that addressed the relationship between written and oral language in K–12 ESL learning. Thus, our framework is potentially vital because it adds to such a scant knowledge base.

We hoped that our framework, though specific to the context and the students in our work, would prove useful in informing ESL literacy research and teaching practice. An important question to be addressed was whether literacy (instantiated as school-based reading and writing activities) could be used as a route to language learning, and if so, under what circumstances and with what consequences (August & Hakuta, 1997). We want to acknowledge at the outset that our framework illustrates specific examples of English learning processes of two successful ESL learners *within* an integrated language arts program in which reading and writing were an integral part of ESL and general classroom instruction. Whether the same findings would emerge from a classroom setting in which compartmentalized skill instruction prevailed is a question we did not address directly but to which we will return in the conclusion.

Method

School Context

The research site was a public school located in mid Michigan with a population of 240 K–5 students. At the time of our work, the majority of the students were children of international graduate students or visiting scholars in the neighboring university, and represented over 20 different languages and cultures. Among ESL students, who constituted approximately 80% of the student population in the school, 27% possessed such limited English skills that they needed additional ESL support. To accommodate such a high percentage of ESL students' diverse cultural and linguistic needs, two ESL teachers coordinated and implemented a pull-out ESL program to complement the accommodations of the regular classroom teachers. The students in our study worked with one of the two ESL teachers throughout the year of our research.

The ESL Program

The ESL program at the school was tailored for K–5 students who spoke no or limited English. ESL instruction took place in small groups outside of the general classroom. During the remainder of the day, the ESL students were mainstreamed in the general classrooms. The main emphasis of the program was to provide a supportive atmosphere that encouraged second-language learning within an integrated language arts program in which oral and written language were viewed and implemented as natural complements to each other. Children worked on oral and written expression and comprehension until they were able to function at grade level in the general classroom. Students were helped to learn content knowledge and to make connections among subject areas, to develop feelings of empowerment in English, to increase strategic reasoning for problem-solving, and to form appropriate constructs for authoring, reading, and learning to converse. During the process, the ESL teacher worked closely with the classroom teacher so that language learning would "flow seamlessly from one setting to the other."

Focus Students

Our framework was developed primarily from the observational notes gathered while we shadowed two focal students. Our selection criteria included student age, English language proficiency, length of residence in the United States, and native language background. We chose students from the same native language background (Korean) as one of our researchers in order to facilitate interviews with both students and their families. Finally, we chose one primary (Grade 2) female and one intermediate (Grade 5) male student who had recently arrived in the United States with well-developed literacy skills in their native language. We observed them in their ESL and regular classrooms on a weekly basis throughout the academic year. Data from these two students helped us to construct a picture of how they used reading and writing to develop their oral skills in English. We were able to develop a framework that describes clear connections between written language activities and oral proficiency. As mentioned earlier, we also used data from our observations of four students in another second-grade classroom, but mainly to corroborate our emerging hypotheses rather than generate new ones. The bulk of our insights came from our close work with the two focus students, Yonsu and Sungie.

Yonsu was a second-grade female student from Korea. She had lived in the United States for 1 year with her family accompanying her father who had come as a visiting professional to the university nearby. Before Yonsu came to the United States, she had attended a public elementary school for 1 year and acquired full literacy skills in her native language. Yonsu had mostly Korean playmates outside of school and spoke Korean with her friends and family. Her parents encouraged her to read and write regularly at home, and she kept a home journal throughout the year. Entries in her journal were written in Korean in the beginning and gradually included English writing as the year progressed. Sungie, the other focus student, was a fifth-grade student from Korea who had lived in the United States for 1 year with his family. Unlike Yonsu's parents, Sungie's parents used a variety of strategies to foster English language acquisition. They encouraged him to speak in English with them and his sister, and they encouraged him to watch English television programs. In addition, his parents asked him to give 3-minute speeches in English at home and in return, they compensated him monetarily for his work.

Data Collection and Analysis

In developing our framework, we used data collected in both the ESL and regular classrooms from three sources: (a) weekly ESL and regular class observations, which we recorded through fieldnotes, audiotapes, and videotapes; (b) student work samples; and (c) student oral language samples. In particular, the classroom observations required deliberate planning with the teachers. Where possible, we consulted with the teachers about their upcoming lesson plans and observed lessons in which there was a high likelihood of written-oral connections.

In order to measure student progress in English language learning and the effectiveness of ESL instruction for these students, we also collected assessment information from standardized (i.e., Woodcock-Muñoz Language Survey, Woodcock & Munoz-Sandoval, 1993; Peabody Picture Vocabulary Test, Dunn & Dunn, 1997; and Bilingual Syntax Measure, Burt, Dulay, & Hernandez, 1976) and informal ESL assessments (i.e., Qualitative Reading Inventories, Leslie & Caldwell, 1995; English oral and written vocabulary tests). Assessment results showed positive gains in English oral and written language development for both students. For example, the Woodcock-Muñoz test showed that Yonsu's oral English improved from *very limited to limited* (level 2–3) in November, to the *fluent* level (level 4) in May. Her reading and writing progressed from *very limited to limited* (level 2–3), to *fluent to advanced* (level 5) between November and May. Sungie also made progress based on the same test during the same period although his gains were more modest than Yonsu's. His oral English was initially *limited to fluent* (level 3–4) in November and became *fluent* (level 4) in May. His written English improved from *fluent* (level 4) to *fluent to advanced* (level 4–5). We cross-validated these standardized measures against informal samples gathered from both classrooms throughout the study; our assessment of progress from these samples mirrored the results from the standardized assessments.

In analyzing our data, we used a constant comparative method and analytic induction (Glaser & Strauss, 1967). We reviewed students' oral and written language production, identified segments that seemed to illustrate written to oral connections, shared our candidate segments with one another, and generated analytic categories that captured the essence of each example. We also used self-contained triangulation (Fetterman, 1984), a process that we realized through ongoing weekly data analysis conversations among ourselves as a research team. This process helped us generate, revise, and refine our framework for analyzing the functions of reading and writing in ESL oral language development.

Results

Framework

In its current iteration, our framework consists of four categories: (a) materiality, (b) close inspection, (c) discussion crutch, and (d) rehearsal. These four categories describe the contributions of English written language activities to English oral language development for two focal and four additional ESL students in our study.

Materiality

When students make language *material,* they enact one of the most important functions of written language, to connect language to its base in the everyday world. There are several ways in which this occurs in classrooms: (a) writing to label an object (e.g., labeling objects in a classroom), (b) writing to describe a picture (e.g., picture word cards or sentences describing pictures), (c) writing to prompt speech (e.g., seeing and saying the word), and (d) combinations of the above.

Vocabulary acquisition exemplifies the process of making language material. For Yonsu, her teachers' use of word sheets or word banks that involved pictures and matching English words helped her learn basic English vocabulary. Words from the ESL classroom included objects available in children's everyday lives such as shapes, body parts, and playground items. Pictures helped Yonsu use her knowledge of objects in her native language to understand the meanings of matching English words. As she read the words in her word sheets and word banks repeatedly to the ESL teacher and peers in school and to her parents at home, she began to understand meanings of individual words without assistance of pictures. Thus, written language helped her acquire English vocabulary. Based on the Peabody Picture Vocabulary Test–form 3B, she made substantial progress moving from an age equivalence of 3 years 2 months in receptive vocabulary in November, to an age equivalent of 5 years by the end of May.

The process of making language material seemed to work at a different level for Sungie, possibly because, as an older student, his vocabulary needed to go beyond one-to-one correspondence between word and object. In his case, the use of novels, worksheets, and short texts facilitated his vocabulary acquisition by enabling him and his teachers to represent and talk about objects and ideas that were not physically present in the classroom. One clear case from our observations demonstrated the appearance of a new word in a written text that Sungie first read and later used orally. The word "musket" first appeared in a novel that Sungie was reading with his general class, and it later appeared in Sungie's own extemporaneous use of the word in conversation. Sungie first encountered the word "musket" on April 17 when he and his classmates discussed the definition of the word in the mainstream class. The word appeared later on that same day in the ESL class while discussing the same text, as indicated in our fieldnotes:

> Sungie (S) is in ESL class discussing the *War Comes to Willy Freeman* text. One of the researchers (K) interrupts to ask Sungie if he knows what a musket and a bayonet are. His teacher (T) asks him where he learned this word, and Sungie shares that this was being discussed in his mainstream classroom.
>
> K: Do you know what a musket is?
> S: A gun.
> K: And a bayonet?
> S: There's some knife on the gun.
> T: How do you know that?
> S: We were talking about that in class.

A few weeks later, we observed the word in Sungie's natural speech when the students were discussing the same text in an ESL class conversation on May 11:

> Student C and Sungie summarize what has happened most recently in their reading of the novel. Student C explains that Captain Ivers retrieves his gun. Sungie adds to Student C's summary that Captain Ivers specifically has a musket.
>
> C: That night Willy was somewhere and Captain Ivers came to house and get gun.
> S: Yeah, musket.

This incident shows how written language first introduced the object "musket" that Sungie and his teachers discussed, thus contributing to Sungie's acquisition of the word.

Close Inspection

This category refers to using written language to highlight specific aspects of language use (oral or written), making language "stand still" so that it can be inspected closely, carefully, and deliberately. This is what Olson (1996) called the metalinguistic advantage of written language, and he claimed that this advantage facilitates meta-awareness of both oral and written language, what is typically labeled linguistic analysis. According to Olson, it is this metalinguistic feature of written language that accounts for the many differences in cognitive reflection that differentiate literate to preliterate societies. Examples of this category also include using written language to study phenomena such as past tense markers, morphological elements, and phonemic awareness.

The function of making language stand still was evident in two examples from Yonsu. She used written language to help her remember how to pronounce English words. In November, Yonsu rewrote a title of her weekly spelling list, "Spelling words for the week of November 8th," using Korean phonetic system so that she could be sure to pronounce and hear the words correctly. By writing the title and the date in Korean (the orthography in which she was already competent), she made the English pronunciation of the title "stand still" so that she could pronounce the words in the title. In this interesting application of cross-orthographic transfer, she essentially used a more well-developed orthographic system (the Korean alphabet) to do the job (i.e., assist in the oral production task) that English orthography would later do.

Books made language stand still and helped Yonsu acquire a vowel sound during reading. In late April, she participated in a guided pair-group reading activity with the regular classroom teacher. When faced with an unknown word, "Elvira," the name of a main character, she skipped reading it. The teacher then pronounced it for her. As the word reappeared several times in the text, she gradually approximated its conventional pronunciation. Because the book made the word stand still, the teacher was able to notice that Yonsu had skipped the word and to model how to pronounce it. Written language provided Yonsu with opportunities to practice the word repeatedly and learn to pronounce it.

We also observed close inspection of language with our auxiliary group of four intermediate-level ESL second-grade students. In one incident, the second-grade teacher implemented a written language activity to offer explicit instruction on the forms and functions of past tense. She used chart paper with three columns to delineate past, present progressive, and base words with example sentences for each. Then she explained what the past tense meant. After the teacher's explanation, students individually found base words and wrote the past tense for each word. Interestingly, in the ESL class the following week (October 18), students were given an opportunity to describe their weekend experiences orally. While students took turns and explained what they did, the ESL teacher occasionally chimed in to highlight the forms and functions of the past tense. Hojun, a student from the second-grade classroom used the lesson he had learned from "making language stand still" while he described his weekend activity:

Hojun: I played computer.
Meredith: Why did I say played?
Hojun: Because you did it . . . like yesterday.

We found that the most common examples of close inspection of language focused on usage, such as verb forms or inflections. Typically teachers wrote the forms of instruction on chart paper or the chalkboard, as they directed students' attention to the appropriate contrast (e.g., make vs. made, dog vs. dogs).

Discussion Crutch

The discussion crutch category was prompted by Sungie's intentional use of written language as a scaffold to facilitate participation in routine oral language activities in school contexts, such as class discussions. The mainstream teacher in Sungie's fifth-grade classroom expected each student to contribute orally to class discussions. Written language seemed to assist Sungie in fulfilling this expectation and through his own writing, Sungie was able to participate orally in whole-class discussions. From his reading of textbooks, novels, and other print materials used in the classroom, Sungie created what turned out to serve as written scripts, or discussion crutches, from which he literally read when he volunteered to talk in class. These texts mediated his participation in class throughout the school year. Perhaps his written preparation of texts gave him confidence to know that he would be able to contribute a worthwhile answer to the class discussions.

During our weekly observations of the general class, we found Sungie's voluntary whole-class participation to be almost always mediated by written texts that he had created. Sungie did not volunteer to speak in whole-class discussion (with only one exception in our fieldnotes) without having had a chance to work things out beforehand in writing. His written language artifacts included advanced organizers, homework assignments, or warm-up written activities before a whole-class discussion. Moreover, his whole-class oral participation was his reading of the exact words and sentences that he had constructed in the preceding written activity. In general class lessons that relied upon extemporaneous oral conversation from the class, we did not observe Sungie participating unless he had written work from which he could share. In short, without a written text that he created, Sungie did not volunteer to talk. In situations when ESL students might not feel comfortable about their ability to engage in "decontexualized" academic discourse (i.e., when shared background knowledge with the interlocutor is minimal and use of conversational devices is eschewed, Snow et al., 1987), they may resort to written language as a crutch.

Rehearsal

Rehearsal bears a strong resemblance to discussion crutch; it refers to using written language to practice emerging English skills, in much the same way as a person would rehearse for a play. The rehearsal can be either overt, as in rehearsing for participating in a reader's theater reading, or covert, as when a student uses a journal as a way of practicing or rehearsing a specific language pattern for later use in an informal conversational setting. Unlike discussion crutch, however, covert rehearsal focuses on the process of repeated practice of one or more language forms over an extended period of time; in this way, repeated practice contributes to the development of both written and oral English proficiency. Covert rehearsal also differs from the discussion crutch category because the purpose of rehearsing a language form is for personal reflection rather than immediate public sharing, and the rehearsal process is not likely to be available to researchers; it was serendipitous that we found Yonsu's home journal. Nonetheless, it is clear that written language activity, albeit private in character, allowed her to practice her emerging oral language skills.

The following example suggests the process by which writing helped Yonsu acquire a specific sentence structure "I went to" and produce it orally in the ESL class. After Yonsu's ESL class discussed places students had visited during the Christmas break, she copied what the teacher had written on the chalkboard in her journal on January 16. She wrote the title in Korean and the rest in English:

> *Places where my friends went* (italicized parts are written in Korean)
> Han said, "I went to Niagara Fall."
> Kyle said, "I went to Canada."
> Andy said, "I went to Seoul."
> Aluba said, "I went to Chicago."
> Elina said, "I went to New York."
> Wally said, "I went to *Caesar* Land."
> Wook said, "I went to Washington D.C."

Practicing these sentences through writing in her home journal helped her acquire the sentence structure. She seemed to have understood that names of places could come after the preposition "to." Her understanding of this sentence structure enabled her to use the sentence again in February when she wrote about her family trip to a local YMCA swimming pool. She wrote in English, "Today my family went to swimming pool. (no father)." In this sentence, she changed the subject and the place after the preposition appropriately.

The form "I went to" that she had rehearsed repeatedly in her home journal seemed to have become readily available for oral language production and enabled her to answer in a complete sentence on February 22. When the ESL teacher asked the students to share their experiences during the weekend, Yonsu answered, "I went to Frankenmuth" after the teacher's second prompting:

> Meredith (looking at Yonsu): Did you do something for the weekend?
> Yonsu gives no answer.
> Meredith (with a smile): Can you tell me one thing?
> Yonsu (in a soft voice): Franken . . .
> Meredith: You went to Pokemon? I am sorry?
> Yonsu: I went to Frankenmuth.

Producing this complete sentence was a definite accomplishment. Her earlier productions during this critical period typically consisted of one word sentences, and her use of more complete English sentences increased dramatically after the writing incident just reported. Although we would not want to argue for a strict causal connection, we would certainly claim that this written language activity made a contribution to her oral language proficiency.

Conclusions

Our framework, drawn largely from two case studies, is an attempt to conceptualize and evaluate the contributions of written language to oral language development for ESL students. The four categories in our framework describe the functions of English reading and writing in oral language development of the ESL students in our sample, both for Yonsu and Sungie and for the four students in our other study (Pearson et al., 2000). Whether these categories will generalize to other learning situations and classroom contexts remains to be seen.

As we consider our framework for future research and practical classroom use, a few issues merit special consideration. First, the categories in our framework (and, we suspect, almost any conceivable framework that might be developed) are not mutually exclusive. For any given example of written language transfer, we could have attached more than one category label. For example, Yonsu's rehearsal involved the process of close inspection by writing sentences down to highlight English syntactic structures in addition to her silent rehearsal of the language form, "I went to." We chose for the purposes of analysis to emphasize the most salient category label to a given example. We could have just as easily assigned it to more than one category or to a primary and a secondary category. Future analyses should consider, or perhaps even privilege, the overlapping nature of the categories.

Second, researchers must address issues of classroom contexts in designing ESL research. The classrooms in which our data were collected offered integrated language arts program in which oral and written language activities were conceptualized and implemented as natural complements to each other. The ESL instruction focused on the meaning and function of English rather than its formal, structural aspects; form truly did follow function. The ESL teacher's instruction on English language structure was contextualized through reading and writing from the beginning. Whether our results would have been replicated in a more conventional literacy program, with distinct time slots or, as we have seen recently in California and other regions, scripts for reading, writing, and oral language, is an interesting question for future research. At the very least researchers should consider classroom contexts in studying the relationship between oral and written language in ESL learning.

Third, participants in our study consisted of students who had already acquired substantial literacy expertise in their native language. Our students all had the benefit of having acquired the "written language" register in literacy rich environments in their homes and schools in Korea. Thus, we acknowledge limitations in generalizing our framework to the overall ESL student population other than those from literate, educated backgrounds. Having developed categories that explain the contributions of written language to oral language development for these students, it is our hope to consider how the framework might be adapted to explain the oral and written language development of struggling ESL readers, especially those who may come from low income homes in which first language literacy skills are likely to be less fully developed.

Fourth, we hope that the framework we developed, along with the opportunistic methodology employed (e.g., planned weekly visits with immediate follow-up of observed instances of written to oral transfer), will contribute to the much needed research on this important relationship between written and oral language for ESL learners. In this regard, we need to point out that we could have chosen to investigate this issue experimentally rather than descriptively; that is, we could have created an experimental task in which we guaranteed particular sorts of written language exposures and then conducted immediate and delayed post tests in order to evaluate the impact of written language on oral language development. Indeed we considered just such an approach. In the final analysis we settled on our "look and wait" approach for a host of reasons, the most important being that we felt that credibility among ESL teachers would be compromised by the low authenticity of the materials and tasks in an experimental approach. Although our more naturalistic approach is expensive in terms of observer time and probably underestimates the range of possible written-oral connections, it has the virtue of focusing on links that really did occur in everyday classroom contexts rather than those that might be created through the pre-planned manipulation of specific language tasks.

Much remains to be done on this important issue. Both ESL teachers and regular classroom teachers have important questions about policy and practice that can only be answered by careful research that is simultaneously grounded in our best theoretical knowledge about second-language learning and in the realities of classroom practice.

References

Anderson, V., & Roit, M. (1996). Linking reading comprehension instruction to language development for language-minority students. *Elementary School Journal, 96,* 295–309.

August, D., & Hakuta, K. (Eds.). (1997). *Improving schooling for language-minority children: A research agenda.* Washington, DC: National Academy Press.

Burt, M. K., Dulay, H. C., & Hernández, E. (1976). *Bilingual syntax measure.* San Antonio, TX: Harcourt Brace Jovanovich.

Chomsky, N. (1965). *Aspects of the theory of syntax.* Cambridge, MA: MIT Press.

Cummins, J. (1986). Empowering minority students: A framework for intervention. *Harvard Educational Review, 58,* 280–298.

Dunn, L. M., & Dunn, L. M. (1997). *Peabody Picture Vocabulary Test* (3rd ed.). Circle Pines, MN: American Guidance Service.

Elley, W. B. (1991). Acquiring literacy in a second language: The effect of book-based programs. *Language Learning, 41,* 375–411.

Elley, W. B., & Mangubhai, F. (1983). The impact of reading in second language learning. *Reading Research Quarterly, 14,* 53–67.

Fetterman, D. M. (1984). *Ethnography in educational evaluation.* Beverly Hills, CA: Sage.

Fitzgerald, J. (1995). English-as-a-second-language learners' cognitive reading processes: A review of research in the United States. *Review of Educational Research, 65,* 145–190.

Garcia, G. E. (2000). Bilingual children's reading. In M. L. Kamil, P. B. Mosenthal, & P. D. Pearson (Eds.), *The handbook of reading research* (Vol. 3, pp. 813–834). Mahwah, NJ: Erlbaum.

Glaser, B. G., & Strauss, A. L. (1967). *The discovery of grounded theory: Strategies for qualitative research.* Chicago: Aldine.

Goodman, K., Goodman, Y., & Flores, B. (1978). *Reading in the bilingual classroom: Literacy and biliteracy.* Rosslyn, VA: Clearing House for Bilingual Education.

Hudelson, S. (1984). Kan Yu Ret an Rayt en Igles: Children become literate in English as a second language. *TESOL Quarterly, 18,* 221–238.

Lara, S. M. (1991). Code switching and reading achievement of first-grade bilingual students. *Dissertation Abstracts International, 52*(01), 99A.

Leslie, L., & Caldwell, J. (1995). *Qualitative reading inventory.* New York: HarperCollins.

McLaughlin, B. (1978). *Second language acquisition in childhood.* Hillsdale, NJ: Erlbaum.

Mills, F., Cowen, A., & Guess, W. (1977). *Bilingual-bicultural education in the classroom.* Oklahoma City: Oklahoma State Department of Education. (ERIC Document Reproduction Service No. ED 146 794)

Olson, D. R. (1996). *The world on paper: The conceptual and cognitive implications of writing and reading.* Cambridge, England: Cambridge University Press.

Pearson, P. D., Kim, Y., Lowenstein-Damico, K., McLellan, M., McPherson, A., & Roehler, L. (2000, December). *The function of written language in oral language development for ESL students.* Paper presented at the meeting of the National Reading Conference, Scottsdale, AZ.

Savignon, S. J. (1972). *Communicative competence: An experiment in foreign-language teaching.* Philadelphia, PA: Center for Curriculum Development.

Saville-Troike, M. (1984). What really matters in second language learning for academic achievement. *TESOL Quarterly, 18,* 199–219.

Seda, I., & Abramson, S. (1990). English writing development of young, linguistically different learners. *Early Childhood Research Quarterly, 5,* 379–391.

Snow, C. E. (1992). Perspectives on second-language development: Implications for bilingual education. *Educational Researcher, 21,* 16–19.

Snow, C. E., Burns, S., & Griffins, P. (Eds.). (1998). *Preventing reading difficulties in young children.* Washington, DC: National Academy Press.

Snow, C. E., Cancino, H., Gonzalez, P., & Shriberg, E. (1987). *Second language learners' formal definitions: An oral language correlate of school literacy* (Report No. CLERA-75). Los Angeles: Center for Language Education and Research. (ERIC Document Reproduction Service No. ED 287 307)

Snow, C. E., Tabors, P. O., Nicholson, P. A., & Kurland, B. F. (1995). SHELL: Oral language and early literacy skills in kindergarten and first-grade children. *Journal of Research in Childhood Education, 10,* 37–48.

Ticknor, G. (1833). *Lecture on the best methods of teaching the living languages.* Boston: Carter, Hendee.

Tragar, B., & Wong, B. K. (1984). The relationship between native and second language reading comprehension and second language oral ability. In C. Rivera (Ed.), *Placement procedures in bilingual education: Education and policy issues* (pp. 152–164). Clevedon, England: Multilingual Matters.

Vietor, W. (1905). *Der Sprachunterricht muss umkehren.* Leipzig: Barth.

Weber, R. M. (1970). *Linguistics and reading.* Washington, DC: Center for Applied Linguistics. (ERIC Document Reproduction Service No. ED 043 852)

Weber, R. (1991). Linguistic diversity and reading in American society. In R. Barr, M. L. Kamil, P. Mosenthal, & P. D. Pearson (Eds.), *The handbook of reading research* (Vol. 2, pp. 97–119). New York: Longman.

Wong-Fillmore, L., & Valadez, C. (1986). Teaching bilingual learners. In M. C. Wittrock (Ed.), *The handbook of research on teaching* (3rd ed, pp. 648–685). New York: Macmillan.

Woodcock, R. W., & Muñoz-Sandoval, A. F. (1993). *Woodcock-Muñoz Language Survey.* Itasca, IL: Riverside.

Transcript Analysis Project (TAP): An Opportunity for Student Teachers to Engage in Practical Inquiry into Classroom Discussion

Linda Kucan
Appalachian State University

> Before doing the present research, I thought that a discussion consisted of students providing answers to the questions that the teacher proposed. And to be honest, I thought I had led several discussions based on that criteria. However, I have come to realize that all I was doing was quizzing the students on information that they could find in the textbook. . . .
>
> I reiterate the importance of exposing students in the education department to the experience of leading a discussion themselves and analyzing their own transcripts in order for them to find out what they are doing or not doing to promote student thinking (Steven Norman, Student Teacher).

The impetus for the present study came from a former student whose senior project involved videotaping, transcribing, and analyzing three social studies discussions (Norman, 1998). Based on my student's experience and advice, this study was designed to investigate preservice teachers' analyses of their own discussion transcripts as a way to engage them in constructing an understanding of classroom discussion and of themselves as discussion facilitators and participants. Transcript analysis is presented as an example of practical inquiry as described by Richardson (1994).

Classroom discussion as a context for the collaborative construction of meaning has been an important area of literacy research (e.g., Cazden, 1988; Heath, 1983; Wells, 1986), and discourse analysis has been an important tool for researchers in this area (e.g., Green, 1983; Hicks, 1995; Luke, 1995). Discourse analysis has provided information not only about the kinds of thinking students can demonstrate during a discussion but also about the ways that thinking can be elicited and encouraged (e.g., Mercer, 1993), or repressed and discouraged (e.g., Thorne, 1986), by teachers and other students in the context of a discussion.

The literacy discussion literature is growing, making available detailed descriptions of the kinds of talking, thinking, and learning that teachers and students do during discussions (e.g., Beck, McKeown, Hamilton, & Kucan, 1997; Donoahue, Van Tassell, & Patterson, 1996; Gambrell & Almasi, 1996; Goldenberg, 1992; McKeown, Beck, Hamilton, & Kucan, 1999; McMahon & Raphael, 1997; Paratore & McCormack, 1997). These descriptions are often provided in the form of transcript excerpts with related analyses. Such descriptions can provide ex-

National Reading Conference Yearbook, *50*, pp. 346–355.

amples and models of productive and less productive meaning-making discussions and ways to analyze discussion dynamics.

Engaging with the ideas and examples in texts that describe and analyze discussions can become a context for practicing teachers' focused reflection. For preservice teachers, however, information about the discussions of others gained through reading or even viewing videotapes or observing in classrooms may have limited impact. Not only do preservice teachers lack experiences to relate to examples, they also may be intimidated by the expertise demonstrated in the examples.

Another option for supporting preservice teachers in developing understanding of and expertise in facilitating discussion is to engage them in what Richardson (1994) calls practical inquiry. "Practical inquiry is conducted by practitioners to help them understand their contexts, practices, and, in the case of teachers, their students. The outcome of the inquiry may be a change in practice, or it may be an enhanced understanding" (p. 7). Richardson uses a definition of inquiry proposed by Clift, Veal, Johnson, and Holland (1990) as "a deliberate attempt to collect data systematically that can offer insight into professional practice" (p. 54).

Although practical inquiry focuses on professional practice, it also offers a conceptual framework to support the efforts of preservice teachers to engage in inquiry and reflection. In describing experiences in teacher education programs that foster intellectual growth, Rogers (1985) posited a number of characteristics including opportunities to: (a) engage in genuine inquiry, (b) communicate ideas and experience, and (c) reflect. Rogers also emphasized the importance of classroom experiences for preservice teachers, suggesting that the time spent in school placements can be not only a time for teaching but also a time to inquire and reflect upon teaching.

The student teaching experience is an occasion when preservice teachers can pose genuine questions and collect data related to those questions. Moreover, the process of analyzing the data and communicating their findings to others can provide a context for preservice teachers to engage in focused reflection and an opportunity to gain insight into their developing practice. Such insight can be difficult to obtain when invitations to reflect are underspecified.

In the present study, an assignment, the Transcript Analysis Project (TAP), was developed to engage student teachers in practical inquiry. TAP was designed to provide student teachers with support and opportunity to inquire into their own developing practice in facilitating discussion through planning a text-based discussion, taping and transcribing it, analyzing it, and then describing and interpreting their findings.

Methods and Data Sources

The Transcript Analysis Project involved 12 elementary education majors from a small liberal arts college in West Virginia who were taking a methods course during their 14-week student teaching placement. All students agreed to participate in this investigation by making their projects available for analysis and interpretation.

TAP was made up of three phases: (a) learning about discussion, (b) planning and audiotaping two discussions, and (c) analyzing and reflecting on the discussions. The first phase of TAP took place before student teaching began. In this phase, student teachers met for class sessions in which they read and talked about Questioning the Author (QtA) (Beck et al., 1997), an approach in which discussion is used as the context for engaging students in constructing meaning from text as they read it. Questioning the Author was selected because it is described in written materials that are accessible to preservice teachers and that offer well-defined terms to describe teacher questions and responses to student comments during discussion. The approach can also be used with large or small groups, a feature that offered flexibility to accommodate the variety of school placements to which student teachers were assigned.

Teachers who use QtA initiate discussion through open-ended questions and respond to student comments using a variety of follow-ups. Some examples of open-ended questions are: What's going on here? What do we know so far? How does this connect with what we read earlier? Some examples of follow-ups, or responses to student comments, include: marking, or repeating student responses to emphasize their importance and relevance; turning back, or asking students to elaborate or clarify their responses; and revoicing, or rephrasing student comments in order to make them more coherent and understandable.

During the first phase, the student teachers also had an opportunity to view a videotape of a QtA teacher and his students during a social studies discussion. They read a transcript of the videotaped discussion and learned how codes were developed to analyze the teacher's questions and comments.

The second phase of TAP took place while the student teachers were teaching in their field placements. In this phase, student teachers planned two text-based discussions of approximately 15 minutes in length and then audiotaped the discussions. The discussions could be based on texts that were being used in the classroom, such as a section of a social studies textbook or another content-area text, or a story from a literature anthology. Alternatively, student teachers could bring in copies of a magazine or newspaper article, or a section from a tradebook. Based on the texts they chose, the student teachers had to indicate learning goals for the discussion; that is, what understandings they hoped students would build as a result of participating in the discussion. They also had to make a copy of the text and mark where they would stop during reading to ask questions and what questions they planned to ask.

Because the TAP assignment was to be completed during student teaching, there were a number of variables affecting the discussions that had to be accommodated. The student teachers were placed in classrooms from second through eighth grades to teach one or more of the traditional elementary subjects including language arts, social studies, mathematics, and science. Student teachers who were qualifying for specific learning disabilities certification were placed in special education settings for one of their placements. The student teachers had the option of having their discussions with a whole class or a small group within the class. They could meet with the same group of students for both discussions, or they could meet with two different groups.

In the third phase of the project, student teachers transcribed the two 15-minute text-based discussions they had conducted with the students in their placements. Then, they analyzed the transcripts by paying attention to three things: (a) amount of teacher talk and student talk, (b) kinds of initiating questions, and (c) kinds of follow-ups.

To analyze the amount of teacher and student talk, the student teachers had to compute percentages based on their count of the number of lines in the transcript spoken by the teacher (themselves) and by the students. To analyze the kinds of initiating questions they used, the student teachers had to develop a code and use it to categorize each initiating question they posed during the discussion. They also had to develop a code and apply it to the instances of follow-ups to student responses they used throughout the discussion. After analyzing their transcripts for both discussions, the student teachers had to display the results of their analyses using graphs. Finally, after analyzing and displaying their data, the student teachers had to reflect on the two discussions by commenting on differences and similarities between them and by describing what they had learned about discussion from completing the project.

The tasks in the TAP assignment were deliberately specified and sequenced to engage and support the student teachers in inquiry and reflection. First, the student teachers were asked to think about who was doing most of the talking in their discussions by calculating the ratio of teacher-to-student talk. Second, they were asked to consider the kinds of talk they were using by developing codes to describe it. The codes for the initiating questions described the kinds of thinking they were asking students to do during the discussion. The codes for follow-ups described how they responded to the thinking that their students revealed. Third, student teachers were asked to summarize their findings in order to create a graphic display. Fourth, they were invited to compare their two discussions and to reflect on what they had learned about discussion by completing the TAP assignment. The student teachers were also encouraged to meet with the investigator, their teacher, twice: first to discuss plans for discussing the texts they had chosen, and second to discuss plans for analyzing their transcripts.

The two data sources for the present study included the discussion analyses and the reflections of the student teachers. These sources were analyzed to discover evidence for the possible outcomes of practical inquiry: "enhanced understanding" (Richardson, 1994, p. 7) and "insight into professional practice" (Clift et al., 1990, p. 54).

Analyses and Results

The TAP assignment was intended to provide ways for student teachers to learn how to think and talk about discussion. Their discussion analyses and written reflections were the main sources of evidence for this learning.

Discussion Analyses

After transcribing their discussions, the student teachers analyzed their discussions by developing coding categories to describe their initiating questions and follow-ups. The coding categories were meant to identify the kinds of thinking the initiating questions were designed to elicit from students and to categorize the different ways the student teachers had responded to student comments.

The student teachers submitted a description of the coding categories they used and the coded transcripts. Each transcript was examined by the investigator and the coding categories used by the student teachers were noted. Table 1 summarizes the kinds of questions student teachers said they were asking during their two discussions. As the table shows, there were a limited number of question types employed. The five types of initiating questions used by more than half of the student teachers included asking students to (a) retrieve information from the text, and (b) explain, (c) connect or compare, (d) describe, and (e) summarize text information.

The transcripts of the student teachers' discussions were examined a second time to identify the kinds of follow-ups they had used to respond to their students' comments. Table 2 shows the kinds of follow-ups the student teachers said they used during their discussions. As the table shows, more than half of the student teachers responded to their students by asking for more information, turning back, and rephrasing or revoicing what students had said.

The student teachers' analyses of the kinds of questions and follow-ups they had used during their discussions were important sources of information for them as they reflected on their discussions. In their discussion reflections, all 12 student teachers referred to the kinds of questions they had used and related specific kinds of questions to students and to student responses.

Table 1

Kinds of Initiating Questions Used by Student Teachers

Kinds of Initiating Questions (What Students Were Asked to Do with Text Ideas)	Number of Student Teachers Who Used This Kind of Initiating Question/Total Number of Student Teachers
Retrieve Information/Check Understanding	12/12
Explain	12/12
Connect/Compare	10/12
Describe	8/12
Summarize	7/12
Predict	1/12

Table 2

Kinds of Follow-Ups Used by Student Teachers

Kinds of Follow-Ups (What Student Teachers Did in Response to Student Comments)	Number of Student Teachers Who Used This Kind of Follow-Ups/Total Number of Student Teachers
Turn Back: ask students to elaborate or clarify initial comments, or turn back to find specific text information to support an answer	9/12
Revoice: rephrase student comments to make them more coherent and understandable	7/12
Model: provide a model response or provide a model of how to think about the text	4/12
Mark/Repeat: emphasize the importance and relevance of a student comment	4/12
Annotate: provide information not provided in the text	1/12

Discussion Reflections

The student teachers' written reflections were analyzed by identifying comments that provided evidence of developing understanding and insight into discussion. The student teachers' comments were described by the investigator in general terms. For example, the following sentences from one student teacher's reflection were marked with the notation "amount of student talk related to student interest":

> The students seemed very interested in the story. I think this caused them to talk about the story thoroughly.

The following reflection excerpt provides another example. These sentences were annotated as "kinds of questions and student responses":

> I asked many retrieving questions. . . . The students did not really elaborate on their answers because they read them straight from the book.

A review of the annotations revealed that most of the student teachers' comments could be organized into two general categories representing specific kinds of developing understanding and insight. These categories were: (a) the relationship between kinds of questions and student responses during discussions and (b) factors influencing the quality of discussion.

All 12 student teachers included comments in their reflections about the different kinds of questions they used and the relationship between the kinds of questions they posed and the ways students responded. For example, one student teacher wrote:

> Specific questions helped me to attain the goal of getting the students to talk more. I totally got rid of retrieval questions and replaced mainly with follow-ups. I think that by forming follow-up questions based on student responses to other questions the students get more involved in the lesson. The retrieval questions gave little to the discussion as a whole.

Another student teacher explained why she decided to use retrieving information questions:

> I tried to stay away from the retrieving information questions in the second discussion but this did not work because I felt that the students were not understanding the material and I wanted to check for understanding.

These comments suggest that the student teachers who wrote them were developing an understanding of the kinds of decisions involved in posing questions during a discussion. They were aware that specific kinds of questions could influence student participation and developing understanding.

Another student teacher summed up the differences between his two discussions by noting how student responses related to the kinds of questions he asked:

> The students were much more involved in my second discussion. I would speak and then four or [more] student[s] would then go ahead and voice their opinion. . . . My first discussion was a ping pong match. I would ask a question and then the students would respond and it would go on like this for the whole discussion. . . . In my first discussion I . . . was asking them to turn back to the story. . . . In my second discussion I asked [students to] explain. . . .

In the example below, another student teacher commented on the overall pattern he saw in his discussions:

> I saw that my discussion technique has a pattern. . . . In particular, I used the question type of turning back [turning back to students the responsibility for thinking things through] and explaining [requesting students to explain their ideas] over 20 percent of the time in both discussions to draw the students into a thinking mode. I wanted students to go beyond the text and try to think.

Half of the student teachers provided comments in their reports about factors that they believed influenced the quality of a discussion. These factors included: time of year, age and academic ability of students, student experience with discussion, student interest in the text being discussed, students' prior knowledge about and the complexity of the material being discussed, and student-to-student responses. For example, the following comments from a student teacher describe her reasoning about the differences in two discussions about sections from the same book:

> The sections in our history books can be the reason for most of the differences in the two discussions. The first part that we read was one in which the students can relate to because it was a subject they have a lot of prior knowledge in, remedies for colds. Also they know what is done for the problems now and can make definite opinions on the information.
>
> The second section was a little more dry and complex than the first. This

> required different types of questions and more explanation and talking on my part. It also took a lot longer for the students to thoroughly discuss it because the material was difficult. This section was about roads and the development of land transportation, not something students are going to find enjoyable.

Another student teacher analyzed her discussions in terms of her experience in leading discussions and her students' experiences in participating in discussions:

> First, the discussion was just the beginning of me starting these techniques with the students. Normally, the students just answer the questions asked of them and they move on. Students were not encouraged to agree or disagree with each other so when asked to do this, the students were a bit nervous. The students in the first placement did speak more than the students in the second for a good reason. The fourth-grade class was so advanced that they all wanted to speak and get the correct answer.
>
> In the second placement I did my second discussion and it was quite different from the first. . . . In this class, I have a BD [behavior disorder] student, MI [mentally impaired] students, a bipolar student, and dyslexic students. . . . These students are also below level and because of their [lack of] confidence they do not answer many open ended questions. . . .

Asking the student teachers to compare their two discussions seemed to provide a useful framework for them to identify variables that might have contributed to similarities and differences. The cumulative list of variables that the student teachers generated was thoughtful and comprehensive. It suggests that the student teachers were becoming more aware of the complexities of planning and facilitating a text-based discussion.

Discussion

Current interest in language and teaching has its roots in sociocultural as well as linguistic perspectives. If language is one of the most important tools for thinking as Vygotsky (1986) suggests, and if classrooms are discourse communities in which both teachers and students are involved in constructing negotiated meanings and identities (e.g., Green, 1983), then it follows that teaching can be viewed as largely a linguistic enterprise. It also follows that those who are learning to teach need opportunities to become aware of effective ways to use language. They also need opportunities to analyze their own language use to discover how effective it is in eliciting and supporting student thinking.

Dewey (1916/1996) maintained that "Without initiation into the scientific spirit one is not in possession of the best tools which humanity has so far devised for effectively directed reflection" (p. 189). The TAP assignment was designed to introduce student teachers to the basic tools of discourse analysis and to provide a meaningful context for them to use those tools to inquire and reflect on their developing practice with text-based discussion.

Although the student teachers seemed very interested and motivated to analyze their discussions, there were several difficulties they had to face in order to do so. They were frustrated by the transcription process. It took a long time to do, and it was tedious. Many student teachers seemed to expend so much time and effort on transcribing their discussions that they were less than energized when it was time to analyze the transcripts. The coding process was also difficult for the student teachers, and there was no opportunity provided for students to work with their teacher or peers to establish reliability. Student teaching can be a busy and stressful time for student teachers. During the day, they are teaching; during the night, they are focusing on their day-to-day lesson plans and classroom management challenges.

It is important to acknowledge, however, that teachers must also deal with multiple demands on their time, attention, and effort when they engage in inquiry and reflection on their own practice and when they attempt to share their findings with others (e. g., Cochran-Smith & Lytle, 1999; Freedman, Simons, Kalnin, Casareno, & the M-Class Teams, 1999). If a goal of teacher education programs is to prepare preservice teachers for thoughtful, reflective teaching through projects and assignments such as TAP (Houston & Warner, 2000; Winitzky & Arends, 1991), then such challenges need to be addressed.

Grossman (1990) suggests that "As teacher educators and researchers of teacher education, we need more detailed descriptions of both what teacher educators teach and how they teach it" (p. 115). This study provides some information about a specific assignment that seemed to provide a context and a level of support that allowed student teachers to engage in practical inquiry about discussion and to achieve the enhanced understanding Richardson (1994) suggested would result from such effort. The student teachers' analyses and reflections suggest that the student teachers were developing understandings about general and specific aspects of discussion. The TAP assignment seemed to provide a level of specificity and structure that supported student teachers' progress toward productive inquiry and reflection. As one student teacher commented:

> The two lessons looked at here are excellent examples of my work in progress. ... This project really opened my eyes to what was happening in my classroom.

References

Beck, I. L., McKeown, M. G., Hamilton, R. L, & Kucan, L. (1997). *Questioning the Author: An approach for enhancing student engagement with text.* Newark, DE: International Reading Association.

Cazden, C. B. (1988). *Classroom discourse: The language of teaching and learning.* Portsmouth, NH: Heinemann.

Clift, R., Veal, M. L., Johnson, M., & Holland, P. (1990). The restructuring of teacher education through collaborative action research. *Journal of Teacher Education, 41*(2), 104–118.

Cochran-Smith, M., & Lytle, S. L. (1999). The teacher research movement: A decade later. *Educational Researcher, 28*(7), 15–25.

Dewey, J. (1916/1966). *Democracy and education: An introduction to the philosophy of education.* New York: Macmillan.

Donoahue, Z., Van Tassell, M. A., & Patterson, L. (Eds.). (1996). *Research in the classroom: Talk, texts, and inquiry.* Newark, DE: International Reading Association.

Freedman, S. W., Simons, E. R., Kalnin, J. S., Casareno, A., & the M-class teams. (1999). *Inside city schools: Investigating literacy in multicultural classrooms.* New York: Teachers College Press.

Gambrell, L. B., & Almasi, J. F. (Eds.). (1996). *Lively discussions! Fostering engaged reading.* Newark, DE: International Reading Association.

Goldenberg, C. (1992). Instructional conversations: Promoting comprehension through discussion. *Reading Teacher, 46,* 316–326.

Green, J. L. (1983). Research on teaching as a linguistic process: State of the art. In E. W. Gordon (Ed.), *Review of research in education* (Vol. 10, pp. 151–252). Washington, DC: American Educational Research Association.

Grossman, P. L. (1990). *The making of a teacher: Teacher knowledge and teacher education.* New York: Teachers College Press.

Heath, S. B., (1983). *Ways with words: Language, life, and work in communities and classrooms.* New York: Cambridge University Press.

Hicks, D. (1995). Discourse, learning, and teaching. In M. W. Apple (Ed.), *Review of research in education* (Vol. 21, pp. 49–95). Washington, DC: American Educational Research Association.

Houston, W. R., & Warner, A. R. (2000). Inquiry and reflection: Twin needs for improved teacher education. In D. J. McIntyre & D. M. Byrd (Eds.), *Research on effective models for teacher education* (pp. 72–77). Thousand Oaks, CA: Corwin.

Luke, A. (1995). Text and discourse in education: An introduction to critical discourse analysis. In M. W. Apple (Ed.), *Review of research in education* (Vol. 21, pp. 3–48). Washington, DC: American Educational Research Association.

McKeown, M. G., Beck, I. L., Hamilton, R. L., & Kucan, L. (1999). *"Questioning the Author" accessibles: Easy-access resources for classroom challenges.* Bothell, WA: Wright Group.

McMahon, S. I., & Raphael, T. E. (Eds.). (1997). *The Book Club connection: Literacy learning and classroom talk.* Newark, DE: International Reading Association.

Mercer, N. (1993). Culture, context, and the construction of knowledge in the classroom. In P. Light & G. Butterworth (Eds.), *Context and cognition: Ways of learning and knowing* (pp. 28–46). Hillsdale, NJ: Erlbaum.

Norman, S. (1998). *Classroom discussion: What's all the talk about?* Unpublished senior project, Bethany College, Bethany, WV.

Paratore, J. R., & McCormack, R. L. (1997). *Peer talk in the classroom: Learning from research.* Newark, DE: International Reading Association.

Richardson, V. (1994). Conducting research on practice. *Educational Researcher, 23*(5), 5–10.

Rogers, V. (1985). Ways of knowing: Their meaning for teacher education. In E. Eisner (Ed.), *Learning and teaching the ways of knowing: Eighty-fourth yearbook of the National Society for the Study of Education* (pp. 250–264). Chicago: University of Chicago Press.

Thorne, B. (1986). Girls and boys together . . . but mostly apart: Gender arrangements in elementary schools. In W. W. Hartup & Z. Rubin (Eds.), *Relationships and development* (pp. 167–184). Hillsdale, NJ: Erlbaum.

Vygotsky, L. (1986). *Thought and language* (A. Kozulin, Ed. & Trans.). Cambridge, MA: MIT Press.

Wells, G. (1986). *The meaning makers.* Portsmouth, NH: Heinemann.

Winitzky, N., & Arends, R. (1991). Translating research into practice: The effects of various forms of training and clinical experience on preservice teachers' knowledge, skill, and reflectiveness. *Journal of Teacher Education, 42*(1), 52–65.

Commonplace Books, Commonplace Practices: Uncovering the Bones of a Complex Pedagogy

Linda Laidlaw
York University

> The artifact of my first commonplace book leaves only the evidence of what occurred, the remains of a set of practices and relations, lingering like the bones of some creature who has moved into history. It becomes something other than it was before, a site of memory, a tracing of time and space. And yet, these are not only the bones of my story, the voices of others linger in the spaces between the lines, as a kind of invisible flesh.
>
> my commonplace book

In the above excerpt, written several years ago in a *commonplace book* I kept as an interpretive research tool, I began to consider a relationship among bones, writing, and pedagogy. The commonplace book, though it might appear somewhat like a journal, functions rather differently. It is an interpretive structure that focuses on "the complex relations that collect because of its material presence" (Sumara, 1996b). I examine the folder which contains this collection of writings—it exists as a material "thing"—but the softened corners of the pages, the scribbled additions and sticky notes represent more than what appears in a superficial inspection. This writing marks a specific location in time and space, reaching into memories, recording a particular set of relations. My commonplace book is a site of ongoing interpretation, coming to life in new ways each time I return to it. As Canadian poet Anne Michaels (1999) writes, "The past is a long bone" (p. 18)—my writing seems an embodiment of the bones of a recent past, also linked to the bones of other texts in a complex and intricate relation.

The imagery of bones that I first engaged within my commonplace book writing has also led me to rethink the importance of metaphor for pedagogy. A problem for contemporary literacy teaching and research is the deeply pervasive influence of modernist metaphors and their effects on perceptions; actions; and structures of teaching, learning, and research. What possibilities might alternative metaphors offer for rethinking and reframing curriculum forms? How might different images encourage the development of more complex structures for literacy education? How might commonplace book structures and practices embody such alternative metaphors? These questions have led to an exploration and examination of the metaphors and literacy practices that I advance in this article.

I begin with an introduction to the concept and structure of the commonplace book as a complex, intertextual, and nonlinear site for teaching and learning. Next,

*National Reading Conference Yearbook, **50**, pp. 356–366.*

I examine the influence of metaphors in framing educational understanding and pedagogy, contrasting the metaphor offered by the imagery of bones with more familiar modernist metaphors. Finally, I explore how the metaphor of bones might offer possibilities for developing notions of the commonplace book as a complex, nonlinear site for interpretation.

Commonplace Books

In *The Bone Keeper*, a picture book by Megan McDonald (1999), a tale is told of a Bone Woman, an ancient gatherer, hunter, and Keeper of the Bones. This old one searches and sifts through the sand, collecting the scattered bits of "lonely bone," piecing them together to form something new and mysterious, a ghost creature of sorts. There are rumors, too, of her powers:

> Some say she has three heads,
> past, present, and future.
> Some say she carries the snake,
> walks with the wild hare.
> Some say Bone Woman brings the dead back to life. (n.p.)

This fictional text reminds us that there are some objects, some structures, like the bones in the story, that hold a kind of history, a memory of past patterns and relations and that might yet "come to life" when gathered and shaped to invent something new. With a little digging and rearranging, something living might be uncovered, as the Bone Woman discovers. Commonplace books and the practices linked to them might be understood, similarly, as a kind of "bones," representing a complex approach to literacy (and literary) teaching and learning.

The commonplace book is an unusual sort of text, a structure which locates multiple layers of interpretation, history, memory, artifacts of experience, and rituals of reading, writing, and response. However, the commonplace book is different from a simple scrapbook collection or a reflective journal or chronological diary. It is not a mere assembly of items or continuing stream of narrative, but instead, the interrelations among the collected texts, writings, objects, and narratives are key to this structure. The commonplace book presents a moving form rather than a static one, becoming a site for ongoing interpretation, continuing conversation, and a place where the writer (or the reader, or listener) might reflect on past, current, and projected experiences in new ways (Laidlaw & Sumara, 2000; Sumara, 1996a, 1996b).

Recently, I wrote in my commonplace book, after rereading some of my previous excerpts:

> This odd and rather jumbled collection—mostly bunches of paper attached together—is my commonplace book, one I began several years ago. It's a little strange to look through this folder now, to reread the old entries. Some of what I have written surprises me, looking at it now. . . .
>
> my commonplace book

It is interesting, and a little odd, I must confess, to rediscover myself in between the pages of my commonplace book, to revisit familiar texts and the former classmates, colleagues, and students that weave in and out of my interpretations. It seems I am always reading a new text each time I return to these pages, each time I add another layer of interpretation. This text seems to shift and alter in my readings and rereadings; new bones uncovered each time I return.

My experience is not unlike the descriptions of the use of a commonplace book found in Michael Ondaatje's (1992) novel, *The English Patient.* The main character, the English patient, has a commonplace book that he has kept with him during his travels, "a copy of *The Histories* by Herodotus that he has added to, cutting and gluing in pages from other books or writing in his own observations—so they are all cradled within the text of Herodotus" (p. 16). Within this layered text, the English patient has included "other fragments—maps, diary entries, writings in many languages, paragraphs out of other books" (p. 96), and even glued in a piece of a fern.

Over the course of the novel, the English patient's commonplace book becomes a focal point for the relations among the characters as the others attempt to uncover his identity, which has been obscured after he was burned (to the bone, in some places) in the aftermath of a fiery crash. His commonplace book is a site of memory as well as possibility. The reading of his text, for both the English patient and the other characters in the novel, assists in the understandings and interpretations of the past, the present, and the imagined future, as the novel unfolds.

Both the English patient's use of his commonplace book and my own experiences with such texts offer nonlinear structures for reading and writing. The present is framed in relation to the past; one moment in the text may be linked to other moments or other texts. There is a careful weaving of interconnections, interpretations, and reinterpretations. It is not surprising, then, that such recursive structures can be difficult to describe within the typical linear language and metaphors common to pedagogy. Though it can be tempting to reduce descriptions to one-size-fits-all frames or descriptions that provide a simple "step by step" sequence of procedures, none of these is quite adequate for representing the interpretive complexity of commonplace book structures.

The Influence of Metaphors

Within the field of education, the frames and structures for teaching and learning have been traditionally shaped by the metaphors and images of modernism. Cartesian understandings of how knowledge is acquired have profoundly influenced how products, processes, and practices have been conceived, described, and imagined within educational settings. Several examples of these modernist conceptions are: the linear acquisition of knowledge and skills, a separation of knowledge from knower, and "shapes" of curriculum structured by Euclidean geometric forms. As Lakoff and Johnson (1999) observe, metaphors are pervasive within human existence, structuring our reasoning, experience, and language. We are not immune from the power of metaphor in education—it is knitted through all educational experience, including how pedagogy is structured and enacted, as well as embedded in the ways research narratives and activities are described and organized.

Though much of the time metaphors are used unconsciously and automatically (Lakoff & Johnson, 1999), changing metaphors and frames for understanding and experience can invite similar shifts in practices and ways of knowing. According to Rorty (1989), "to change how we talk is to change what . . . we are" (p. 20). In education, this might mean that to change the language and metaphors used to describe practices, structures and events is also to change what we *do*. As William Doll (1993) suggests, "Metaphors are generative; they help us to see what we don't see" (p. 169); they alter the ways in which perception is framed, and influence subsequent actions.

One modernist image that is familiar to education is the idea of "mind as a container," where knowledge is understood to be an object that might fill the mind's void and as something to be gained, owned, banked, or manufactured (Davis, Sumara, & Luce-Kapler, 2000; Sfard, 1998). Sfard (1998) labels this image the "acquisition" metaphor because of its focus on acquiring knowledge, and notes that the underlying assumption of this frame is the notion of learners as undeveloped or otherwise lacking in some way. She observes that this metaphor has influenced both skill-based pedagogy and constructivist perspectives. Davis and Sumara (2000) observe, as well, that modern curriculum has also been organized by the metaphors and shapes of Euclidean geometry—the lines, boxes and grid-like forms that have tended to dominate curriculum structures.

In recent years, however, alternative frames for understanding emerging from theories of complexity have begun to offer flexible, nonlinear, and dynamic alternatives to the lines, squares, and boxes along which curriculum has been traditionally organized. Complex approaches challenge the separations and dualisms typical of modernist thought, as well as having in common a number of beliefs and sensibilities. For example, complexity places emphasis on patterns of interaction, on relation and reciprocity, stressing the importance of context and the collective "ecology" of events and experience (Capra, 1996; Cohen & Stewart, 1994; Waldrop, 1992). Emerging from developments in science and mathematics, theories of complexity continue to be taken up in new areas of inquiry and examined and applied in areas such as economics, organizational systems, and education, to name only a few domains in which complexity theories have been used (Briggs & Peat, 1999; Davis & Sumara, 1997). As well as providing alternatives for understanding basic structures (e.g., in the alternative models offered by complexity in areas such as physics, biology, and mathematics), complexity offers new language and metaphors that stand in contrast to those of modernist science and modernist models of research and pedagogy.

One example of an alternative frame and metaphor that complexity offers is the irregular and recursive geometric form of the *fractal*. A fractal shape is one where "characteristic patterns are found repeatedly at descending scales so that their parts, at any scale, are similar in shape to the whole" (Capra, 1996, p. 138).

Many examples of fractal shapes can be found in nature: a small branch of a cauliflower is like a whole cauliflower in miniature, and trees and ferns often exhibit fractal structures. Fractal patterns are also found in many structures within the human body, including arteries and blood vessels, neurons, and the branching of bronchi in the lungs. Within the structure of bones, a fractal pattern is also present, where tree-like branchings of fibers tangle together in a kind of multiply dimensioned form (Richardson & Gillespy, n.d.). This arrangement is what gives bones their strength and ability to heal and grow. Within bones and other fractally shaped forms, the smaller "parts" do not become simplified or reduced; instead each tiny branch of a fractal form reveals a high degree of complexity. The smaller structures and the larger ones are understood as interrelated rather than being regarded as separate forms.

Such images, of fractals and the example of bones, offer complex frames and possibilities as metaphors for teaching and learning. It is true, however, that the notion of the fractal is not yet familiar to most educators or researchers. Most of us, though, have at least a passing knowledge of bones—our own or those we have observed or studied in other circumstances. As such, I present the image of bones as illustrating a nonlinear metaphor that might be used to consider or structure notions of teaching, learning, within literacy education. What possibilities might exist for teaching and learning within the marrow and interstices of bones?

Bone Readings

Although "bones" seem simple and familiar on first consideration, when examined more carefully, they are revealed as intricate and multidimensional. Unlike the linear "building/edifice" metaphors often used in describing curriculum ("foundations," "building blocks of knowledge," "steps to learning," "the basics"), or the other modernist metaphors I have previously discussed, bones provide an image of complex, living structures, connective tissue made of layers of living cells, existing within a system of reciprocal bodily interactions.

I have had some recent personal experience with the complex intricacy of bones. After experiencing back pain for several months, assorted medical "readings of the bones" determined that my discomfort resulted from a tiny bit of extra bone that had developed between two vertebrae. In a kind of feedback cycle, the small piece of bone irritated nerves, which in turn, caused muscles to react, resulting in a complex branching of response and involvement of other bodily systems, including in this weave, a subjective response to pain and a change in patterns and habits of daily experience. A tiny change in the bones of my body created multiple reverberations and patterns of response.

It is likely, too, that this tiny bony growth occurred as a reaction to a complex array of events including some sort of injury combined with habits of living an academic life (e.g., regularly slinging a heavy book bag over a shoulder and spending hours at a keyboard and computer screen). My bones have responded to events and experiences in my life, and in turn, influence my own living system in complex ways. As I have discovered, bones are not inert and unchanging "parts" of the body, unrelated to everything else—they may influence one's entire experience, even if the change is as subtle as a small growth of cells.

Bones are also unique in being aspects of ourselves (and other mammals) that tend to be more permanent than our other tissues. Bones remain when their inhabitants are gone, and can be both living and also not living, part of the biology and anthropology of bodies. As well, they are also points of entry into the realm of history and archeology. This varied existence seems rather like pedagogy and its artifacts. In the moment of teaching and learning, objects, structures and processes become a part of a living tissue of interaction and relation, and where seemingly small acts, decisions, and changes in structure create complex shifts and an intricate web of response. Yet, the processes and events of teaching and learning eventually result in more permanent items or artifacts. Long after the moment of pedagogy has passed, it is also possible to examine the objects, records, and memories of such events to interpret or reinterpret experiences of teaching and learning. Something remains, like my commonplace book, for example. As I suggest in the excerpt at the beginning of this article, the text of my commonplace book has been transformed with the passage of time, changed into something other than it was before, collecting layers of history and memory within its form.

"*Writing Down the Bones*"

The commonplace book is a flexible structure that may be used for a variety of purposes with a wide range of learners. I have used a commonplace book as a research tool and a method for collecting data, as well as incorporating this structure in my teaching. Though here I examine commonplace book practices and products in terms of both interpretive reading and writing pedagogy, it is also an interpretive structure that may be used more specifically for focusing, collecting, and interpreting engagements with particular literary texts (Sumara, 2000).

Commonplace books and the practices associated with them provide a nonlinear framework for writing (and reading), interpretation, and inquiry, yet also provide the tangible "bones" or frame for teaching and learning while defying the more prescriptive tendencies of more commonly used writing structures (Sumara, 1996b). The commonplace book becomes an evolving collection where writing, narrative, and other representations are gathered and juxtaposed. It provides a nonlinear framework where the "parts" are interrelated with the "whole." Though in a group or classroom setting each individual will create his or her own commonplace book and will experience commonplace practices in a unique manner, the structures belonging to the individual will also be joined to the collective structures and experiences of the group.

The material structure of the commonplace book may be embodied in a number of different forms. It may be "contained" in the form of a book or a three ring binder, gathered in a collection of folders, or set up as files on a computer. As well, it may be located around and within a literary text where interpretations are gathered on sticky notes, in margin spaces, or attached small booklets. I have expanded one commonplace book (which I am using as a research structure) into a shelf that consists of a number of folders and containers that collect a number of artifacts and other "memory objects." There are infinite possibilities for the embodiment of the commonplace book—but most significant is that it provides a "backbone" of juxtaposed texts and interrelated resymbolizations, interpretations and reinterpretations.

Reading and writing (and rereading and rewriting) are essential to the creation of a commonplace book. I provide students with some specific guidelines regarding these readings and writings, believing "liberating constraints" to be helpful in provoking new ideas or relationships among ideas and texts. The term "liberating constraints" refers to a creation of a balance between "enough organization to orient students' actions and sufficient openness to allow for the varieties of experience, ability, and interest that are represented in any classroom" (Davis et al., 2000, p. 87). Students are frequently asked to engage in writing practices such as "timed writings," as outlined in Natalie Goldberg's (1986) *Writing Down the Bones,* or the use of poetry structures (see Kowit, 1995, for a number of helpful examples). Additionally, students also use their commonplace books to gather their responses to texts, record experiences, and engage in autobiographical writing. Eventually, when students are required to provide more formal kinds of responses, they can draw upon the commonplace book as a resource that they reread and reinterpret, uncovering the "bones" that will appear in new configurations, such as essays, course papers, or theses. In my own prior experiences with using commonplace books and engaging in the "tissue" of practices in which they were embedded, I also discovered many of the consistent obsessions, recurring questions, and observations that eventually led to later research or inquiry. (A series of graduate seminars offered by Dr. Dennis Sumara, at Simon Fraser University, provided an introduction to commonplace books. Further description of some of this work may be found in Alvermann and Hruby's [2000] research study on mentorship, in which our cohort group participated.)

The texts students are asked to read are also important in relation to the commonplace book. As well as the nonliterary course texts with which students are asked to engage in more "efferent" readings, where attention is focused upon analysis of ideas (Rosenblatt, 1994), it is also helpful to select a number of literary texts that might lend themselves to more "aesthetic" readings—including novels, short fictions and poetry. Texts that invite interpretive response and conversation, those that, as Eco (1994) describes, cause readers to linger "in the fictional woods" offer interesting pedagogical possibilities when read in juxtaposition with commonplace book practices. Such literary texts allow students to attend differently to reading (and to their reflective writing) and provide spaces and gaps necessary for more complex juxtapositions and interpretations. As Iser (1993) acknowledges, such fictions can invite "boundary-crossings" that modify consciousness, where "the fictive simultaneously disrupts and doubles the referential world" (p. xiv).

Central to practices surrounding the commonplace book is the reading aloud of student texts. Perhaps this is part of "the mystery of the bones" (McDonald, 1999), the way in which the "thing between" invents itself, becoming something that gathers and connects individual student histories and narratives into a collective one:

> The students are preparing to read a page, a few paragraphs from the commonplace books. There's a small rustle as paper is retrieved, and the scrape of chairs as everyone settles in to listen. Then comes the focussed quiet, like the hush in a theatre. Sometimes it seems we even forget to breathe as we listen to the narratives of educational experience, the traces of memories, texts, histories, and theories. Words, phrases, bubble up from below the surface. . . .
>
> my commonplace book

This "oral-aural" ritual, as Mary Doll (1995) describes such reading aloud events, is where we might find the bones of our own histories, and the connecting joints of shared relation. It is the place where fragments of time are uncovered, moments linking us back to the ancient world of the storyteller that lurks within, the buried history of oral memory, from childhood or perhaps something even more cellular, from time before memory. Reading aloud both performs and transforms. As most of us of a certain age have experienced through the childhood literacy practice of "round-robin" reading, reading aloud always becomes a sort of performance. We know we must rehearse, we prepare in advance by reading our words aloud, at home. These oral readings link us in a unity normally disrupted by the ways in which writing and print are used in the modern world, where individuals usually read and write privately (Ong, 1982), or engage in separate, parallel conversations with a teacher or instructor. Reading aloud creates a kind of sacred dimension—listening to classmates read is an "out of the ordinary" experience. Afterward, all are joined in a new collective, linked together by these small oral texts, building the slow bones of an interpretive community, where memories of others' texts intersect present and future writings and readings.

It is important to engage in such oral readings at the beginning of group experiences and to continue them regularly. Each time we meet as a class, students are required to bring with them a brief excerpt from their commonplace book to be read orally. Their readings might include several "interesting bits" or the reading aloud of a suggested writing activity or précis of a required reading. During these readings aloud, students follow some general expectations that enhance the context for collective listening and the sharing of writing. Students are asked not to comment or respond to one another's shared reading (or to their own), but instead, each reading flows into the next. This practice has several implications. First, because there are few interruptions, the readings create an unbroken text and might be considered as a multilayered "whole." As well, this unbroken reading practice means there are no debates or discussions about ideas in the moment of the sharing—diverse views can remain in juxtaposition, existing as a larger collective text rather than as disconnected individual texts. I have noticed repeatedly that, as the shared readings and the ongoing writings continue, groups of diverse individuals are able to find points of intersection, incorporating and interpreting notions shared by their peers. As the shared readings/writings continue, students usually begin to endow the experience with elements of ritual, viewing these oral reading practices as occurring in a dimension outside of the more usual space of curriculum:

> We meet in the early evenings, leaving behind the rain of a bleak winter night. We've come for the class. But. It's no longer just for the class, now we come for something else, something we cannot quite explain, something that seems to have happened because of the commonplace books. These bits of paper—notebooks, manila folders, computer printed pages (we have our own preferences and particularities for the forms and structures we use)—are the bones at the middle of this experience, connecting the tissues of our diverse histories, backgrounds, and life experiences, intersecting the practices and the rituals that bring us together every week. Like Natalie Goldberg's book, *Writing Down the Bones,* it seems that we've written down some bones of our own. I've kept those bones, as we all did, long after the course had ended, passed into memory.
>
> my commonplace book

As students begin to share longer interpretive papers developed from their commonplace books and the layers of writing and response evolving from the process of listening to others' oral readings, they can be invited to take a moment to write to one another, in a small note responding to each person's shared oral reading. Rather than being congratulatory or evaluative, these small writings should respond to ideas presented in the shared texts. These notes often become a part of each student's commonplace book, additional artifacts of memory and experience. As courses (or larger projects) are concluded, students are invited to bring copies of their interpretation papers or projects to give to one another. In experiencing these practices myself as a graduate student and using them both as a classroom teacher and as a course instructor, I know that these collections of notes, individual student writing, and the writings of the other class members are often returned to, reread, and reinterpreted long after a particular course (or school year) has ended. The material artifacts of students' commonplace books and interconnected materials may become the "sacred bones" of memory, sites of future rereadings and reinterpretations.

As many have suggested (McLuhan 1996; Olson 1994; Ong 1982), the use of writing and texts involves ongoing interpretation. Written texts are full of gaps, never able to fully represent speech or thought. As Iser (2000) indicates, literary experiences always involve a kind of translation, creating a liminal space between a text and one's reading (or writing) of it. What is important, then, is what takes place in this "in between" of reading and writing, in the aesthetic transformation necessary for literary experience or engagements in other art practices (Gadamer, 1999). In the creation and oral sharing of commonplace books, pedagogical experience also must become aesthetic experience, the place where the bony structures of reading and writing practices become fleshed with collective experience. A kind of life is breathed into the long lines of words, the bits of paper. Like the Bone Woman's creature, these also stretch and spring to life, no longer just a collection of scattered bits and pieces:

> They say
> if you listen to the desert
> if you listen,
> you may hear
> a laughing,
> a chanting,
> a singing. (McDonald, 1999, n.p.)

The nip of fall is in the air and I have a craving for a bowl of steamy soup. The real kind, something that hints of my peasant ancestors. Perhaps my tongue still remembers. . . . I leave in search of materials—soup bones are not so easy to come by these days, when it's easy to choose a can from the wall of soup in the grocery store. I find my bones wrapped and frozen, for $1.27, beef bones so large I can barely submerge them in the soup pot. I add the ingredients required for a flavorful stock, and a little vinegar, and set the burner for a long, slow simmer. It takes time to make a good soup, for the bones to release their magic.

In the beginning, things seem less than appealing—a collection of separate ingredients combined loosely together, a few bones, some water and vinegar, a collection of spices and other "soup bits." I am never quite sure at the beginning that this collection will become soup, but, in the slow cooking, bone and liquid are transformed. Later, I remove the bones when I find that they have released their marrow and flavorful essences. They are hot and fragrant, changed by their immersion, bearing the traces of soup making, a clinging bit of celery leaf, a peppercorn or two embedded in the hollows. These bones have transformed water into something else, into the stock ready for future nourishment.

This practice of soup making reminds me of teaching. It is always something more than a simple combining of particular "ingredients"; the bones of pedagogy have the possibility to transform their context, to alter and be altered by the subtle and complex layering of learners, histories, identities, and practices. As teachers or instructors, like soup-makers, or even "Bone Keepers," we create something new from the bones of our work; something that might remain long after the moment of pedagogy has passed into history.

References

Alvermann, D. E., & Hruby, G. G. (2000). Mentoring and reporting research: A concern for aesthetics. *Reading Research Quarterly, 35,* 46–63.

Briggs, J., & Peat, F. D. (1999). *Seven lessons of chaos: Timeless wisdom from the science of change.* New York: HarperCollins.

Capra, F. (1996). *The web of life.* New York: Anchor.

Cohen, J., & Stewart, I. (1994). *The collapse of chaos: Discovering simplicity in a complex world.* New York: Penguin.

Davis, B., & Sumara, D. (1997). Cognition, complexity, and teacher education. *Harvard Educational Review, 67,* 105–125.

Davis, B., & Sumara, D. (2000). Curriculum forms: On the assumed shapes of knowing and knowledge. *Journal of Curriculum Studies, 3,* 821–845.

Davis, B., Sumara, D., & Luce-Kapler, R. (2000). *Engaging minds: Learning and teaching in a complex world.* Mahwah, NJ: Erlbaum.

Doll, M. (1995). *To the lighthouse and back: Writings on teaching and living.* New York: Peter Lang.

Doll, W. E. (1993). *A post-modern perspective on curriculum.* New York: Teachers College Press.

Eco, U. (1994). *Six walks in the fictional woods.* Cambridge, MA: Harvard University Press.

Gadamer, H-G. (1999). *Truth and method* (2nd ed.). New York: Continuum.

Goldberg, N. (1986). *Writing down the bones: Freeing the writer within.* Boston: Shambhala.

Iser, W. (1993). *The fictive and the imaginary: Charting literary anthropology.* Baltimore, MD: Johns Hopkins University Press.

Kowit, S. (1995). *In the palm of your hand: The poet's portable workshop.* Gardiner, ME: Tilbury House.

Laidlaw, L., & Sumara, D. (2000). Transforming pedagogical time. *JCT: Journal of Curriculum Theorizing, 16,* 9–22.

Lakoff, G., & Johnson, M. (1999). *Philosophy in the flesh.* New York: Basic.

McDonald, M. (1999). *The bone keeper.* New York: DK Publishing.

McLuhan, M. (1996). *Understanding media: The extensions of man.* Cambridge, MA: MIT Press. (Original work published 1964)

Michaels, A. (1999). *Skin divers.* Toronto: McLelland & Stewart.

Olson, D. R. (1994). *The world on paper: The conceptual and cognitive implications of writing and reading.* New York: Cambridge University Press.

Ondaatje, M. (1992). *The English patient.* Toronto: McClelland & Stewart.

Ong, W. J. (1982). *Orality and literacy: The technologizing of the world.* London: Routledge.

Richardson, M. L., & Gillespy, T. (n.d.). Fractal analysis of trabecular bone, Seattle Washington: University of Washington, Department of Radiology. [On-line]. Available: www.rad.washington.edu/exhibits/fractal.html.

Rorty, R. (1989). *Contingency, irony, and solidarity.* Cambridge, England: Cambridge University Press.

Rosenblatt, L. M. (1994). *The reader, the text, the poem: The transactional theory of the literary work.* Carbondale: Southern Illinois University Press. (Original work published 1978)

Sfard, A. (1998). "On two metaphors for learning and the dangers of choosing just one." *Educational Researcher, 27,* 4–13.

Sumara, D. (1996a). *Private readings in public: Schooling the literary imagination.* New York: Peter Lang.

Sumara, D. (1996b). Using commonplace books in curriculum studies. *JCT: Journal of Curriculum Theorizing, 12,* 45–48.

Sumara, D. (2000). Researching complexity. *Journal of Literacy Research, 32,* 267–281.

Waldrop, M. M. (1992). *Complexity: The emerging science at the edge of order and chaos.* New York: Simon & Schuster.

Preparing White Preservice Teachers for Urban Classrooms: Growth in a Philadelphia-Based Literacy Practicum

Althier Lazar
West Chester University

Literacy educators are challenged to prepare a largely white population of future teachers to serve a growing population of poor children of color. How to help these future teachers develop the sensitivity, knowledge, and desire to serve these children is one of the most critical questions facing educators today (Hoffman & Pearson, 2000). The need to address diversity issues within literacy education courses raises new questions about how to structure curricula to maximize preservice teacher growth (Xu, 2000). In this paper, I share my experiences helping preservice teachers begin the process of learning about children, caregivers, and classrooms within an urban African-American community. I argue that much more needs to be done to understand these growth processes to prepare teachers to serve children in particular cultural communities.

Related Literature Review

Nurturing culturally sensitive teachers for urban and low-income communities requires fundamental changes in teacher preparation curricula, including: (a) infusion of diversity issues across the teacher preparation curriculum, (b) close, supportive inquiry-based mentoring by professors and successful cooperating teachers, and (c) immersion experiences in racially/culturally diverse field-settings (Gomez, 1993; Haberman, 1996). Evidence suggests that integrating diversity studies and experiences in only one or two courses does not produce culturally sensitive teachers. Wiggins and Follo (1999), for example, found their efforts to explicitly address diversity issues in one field-based urban practicum produced more confident preservice teachers. However, many continued to underestimate children's abilities and convey doubts about teaching in urban schools. Preservice teachers' perspectives toward others are difficult to change (Gomez, 1993), supporting a more intensive weaving of diversity studies throughout the teacher preparation curriculum, including literacy education. Three themes dominate diversity-oriented courses in preservice teacher programs: cultural identity (Helms, 1990; Howard, 1999; Tatum, 1999) the sociology of achievement (Avery & Walker, 1993) and cultural congruence (Au & Kawakami, 1991; Ladson-Billings, 1994).

One hypothesis is that teachers misperceive children's literacy potential because they are unaware of the many social arrangements that privilege whites and

*National Reading Conference Yearbook, **50**, pp. 367–381.*

penalize other racial groups. Accesses to quality public schools, well-stocked libraries, or neighborhood bookstores are privileges. As Howard (1999) states, "it is important to ask ourselves as white educators how our own social positionality and history of dominance might be implicated in the disproportionate distribution of privilege and penalty in contemporary educational systems" (p. 34). To explore preservice teachers' developing understanding of privilege and social positioning, I draw primarily from Helms's first phase of white identity development, "the abandonment of racism." In the "contact" stage, little attention is paid to one's racial group membership and prejudices about others are often denied. When white privilege is realized in the "disintegration" stage, many whites simultaneously acknowledge their own culpability in contributing to a system that advantages them and disadvantages others. Feelings of discomfort, guilt, and conflict often surface here. Personal relationships with people of color allow whites to see first-hand the effects of racist system. Some whites turn these feelings into action by challenging racial jokes or pointing out signs of racial discrimination (Tatum, 1999). Another characteristic of identity growth may include repressing guilt and redirecting anger toward people of color in what Helms calls the "reintegration" stage. In this stage, whites do not see how they can change to make the system work more equitably for people of color; rather they expect people of color to change.

Depending on one's orientation, commitment to learning more about identity development, and opportunities to learn, one can abandon this phase and move toward a positive white identity. This phase includes learning more about one's own identity, learning about others, and ultimately being actively engage in anti-racist activity (see Helms, 1990, for a detailed description of white identity development). Helm's description of the stages of white racial identity is a helpful guide for looking at preservice teacher change; actual growth is not so linear or predictable (Howard, 1999). Helping preservice teachers become familiar with the significance of whiteness has been achieved by constructing courses that include a combination of immersion experiences, course readings, discussions, and reflective writing activities (Bollin, 1997).

Growth in identity development is dependent on a simultaneous examination of the outside world. Preservice teachers have a vague understanding that inequality is perpetuated in schools (Avery & Walker, 1993). Avery and Walker found that preservice teachers have very simplistic explanations for low literacy achievement among children of color. Academic disparities between white and black children are attributed to the presumed values of the ethnic culture, and preservice teachers are less apt to acknowledge context-specific factors such as schooling, or the sociohistorical or political factors that impact literacy achievement. Growth is observed when preservice teachers link their school-based explorations with inquiries about race and culture (Cochran-Smith, 1995).

The third theme of diversity education draws from ethnographic research on cultural compatibility between schools and homes. It addresses what teachers can do to integrate knowledge of families, communities, and culture into the curriculum and everyday teaching practices, and bring the literacies of schooling into homes (Au & Kawakami, 1991). Some teachers, by virtue of their close ties with the community outside of school, have acquired the attitudes and knowledge to be successful teachers in specific communities (Ladson-Billings, 1994). It follows that teacher educators could guide preservice teachers toward this ideal in a number of ways by helping them (a) communicate with parents and construct literacy events around family stories (Edwards, Pleasants, & Franklin, 1999); (b) use culturally relevant literature in literacy teaching and staging critical discussions of this literature (Wolf, 2000); and (c) explore language, its history and social significance, and use of Standard forms when situations warrant it (Perry & Delpit, 1998). Growth is observed as preservice teachers begin to understand and use information about home language, communication patterns, and social customs of children and their families to create relevant learning opportunities for children.

I hypothesized that weaving these principles of diversity into a literacy practicum course would help preservice teachers confront preconceptions about children, families, and schools in the urban community, and begin to see themselves as successful teachers of these children.

Method

Context of the Study

West Chester University is a state supported university located about 25 miles west of Philadelphia. During the fall semester, 2000, I acted as participant-observer to explore the impact of my field-based literacy course that explicitly addressed white identity development, sociocultural explanations of literacy achievement, and culturally conscious literacy teaching. The 6-hour per week practicum included seminar and teaching time scheduled each Tuesday and Thursday morning during the 13 weeks of the semester.

Twelve female and one male preservice teacher agreed to participate in the study. Three were raised in urban communities, and the others grew up in suburban and rural parts of Pennsylvania and New Jersey. All were senior-level students, having taken most of their prerequisite professional courses, including two literacy education courses and a course in children's literature.

As part of the practicum, students worked with children in a Philadelphia public elementary school, which primarily serves African-American children in Grades K–4. All children qualified for the school-subsidized meal program. Interns' cooperating teachers participated in the second year of a 3-year Reading Specialist Certification program at West Chester University.

Course Experiences

1. Interns participated in 25 hours of on-campus seminar discussions about literacy development, assessment, and teaching. Principles of cultural congruence, developmental fit, balanced literacy instruction, strategy use, and self-reflection were stressed. I encouraged preservice teachers to select literature

reflecting African-American themes and experiences and demonstrated ways of helping children respond critically to this literature. I also demonstrated how to draw from children's lives to create purposeful reading and writing events at school.

2. Interns tutored one child for 1 hour each day throughout the semester. They were shown how to assess children using interviews, running records with retellings, writing and spelling samples. Tutorial time was devoted to authentic reading and writing events and analytic word study activities. Interns completed teaching records that included literacy tasks with children, a rationale for these tasks, anecdotal notes, and a reflection of the teaching process.

3. Interns were asked to initiate communicate with caregivers by sending home open-ended questions about the child's attitude and interest and literacy behaviors. Interns who did not receive written responses back from parents were asked to contact caregivers by telephone.

4. Each preservice teacher co-taught with a peer and a cooperating teacher in a regular classroom for 6 weeks. Instruction included shared reading, guided reading, literature response, word study, and writer's workshop. During this time, preservice teachers observed the ways particular children interacted with the classroom setting (teacher/peer discourse, instruction, materials).

5. Students participated in an on-line discussion with me weekly, responding to open-ended questions about diversity issues. Figure 1 lists the articles and the major topics addressed in these articles.

Data Sources and Analysis

Data for this study came from five sets of sources, including: (a) surveys given before and after the course, (b) written responses to open-ended questions, (c) written communication between preservice teachers and parents, (d) fieldnotes of conversations in my office and teaching/discussion activity, and (e) reflective teaching records. These data collection procedures were followed:

1. Preservice teachers responded to surveys before and after the course (a modified version of Cultural Diversity Awareness Inventory [Henry, 1985]). Using a 4-point Likert scale (strongly agree, agree, disagree, strongly disagree), preservice teachers responded to statements addressing their affiliations with people in diverse communities, their beliefs about children's literacy and language abilities, children's caregivers' level of literacy support at home, teachers' instruction in urban classrooms, racial identity, race relations and the significance of race in teaching, and their interest and feelings of confidence in teaching in urban classrooms.

2. Preservice teachers responded to the following at weeks 1 and 7: (a) How would you describe your interest and confidence in teaching literacy in urban classrooms? (b) How would you describe your cultural identity? (c) What factors do you think contribute to the literacy achievement of the children you teach in the practicum? and (d) How would you describe your efforts to teach in culturally relevant ways?

3. Parents' written notes and preservice teachers' notes about parental input indicated that the nature and frequency of communication between parents and preservice teachers.

4. Fieldnotes included preservice teachers' questions and comments during seminars and office hours and interns' teaching activities in the field.

5. Teaching records reflected the degree to which preservice teachers actually used culturally relevant literature, incorporated home/family stories in literacy events, and applied knowledge about dialect in teaching literacy lessons.

These data were analyzed in two phases, guided by the procedures for qualitative data analysis described by Erickson (1990) and Bogdan and Biklen (1998). Phase one involved examining each set of data sources separately. First, I calculated the percentages of preservice teachers who either "agreed" or "disagreed" with pre- and post-survey statements, noting changes in their responses. I analyzed the other resources by reading and rereading the materials in each set and making analytic notes about emerging themes and patterns in the categories "interest in urban teaching," "confidence in urban teaching," "white identity devel-

Authors/Titles	*Major Themes Addressed*
McIntosh, P. (1989). *White Privilege: Unpacking the Invisible Knapsack.*	• White Privilege • Privilege as Unearned Advantage • Racism as a System of Dominance
Tatum, B. (1999). *Why Are All the Black Kids Sitting Together in the Cafeteria?*	• Prejudice vs. Racism • Domination and Subordination • White Identity Development
Ladson-Billings, G. (1994). *The Dreamkeepers: Successful Teachers of African American Children.*	• Segregation & Schooling • Teacher Attitudes & Behaviors • Culturally Relevant Teaching • Conceptions of Knowledge • Culturally Relevant Teaching

Bennett, C. (1999). *Conflicting Themes of Assimilation and Pluralism Among African Americans.*	• African American History
	  • Enslavement
	  • Emancipation, Sharecropping
	  • Northern Migration
	  • Solidarity, Civil Rights

Perry, T. & Delpit, L. (1998). *The Real Ebonics Debate: Power, Language and the Education of African American Children.*	• Ebonics Debate Defined • Language and Identity • Teacher Attitudes Toward Ebonics • Dialect and Reading/Writing • Definitions/Patterns of Ebonics • Myths & Realities of Ebonics • Classroom Practices
Nieto, S. (2000). *Toward an Understanding of School Achievement.*	• Deficit Theories • Economic/Social Reproduction • Cultural Incompatibilities Theory • Resistance Theory

Figure 1. Articles and themes from course readings.

opment," "understanding literacy achievement," and "culturally relevant teaching." Students' perceptions of their own growth in each category were ranked using ordinal scales "low-moderate-high." Explanations of growth for each category were subcoded.

Phase two involved comparing data to achieve triangulation. I looked for common themes between survey responses, written responses to open-ended questions, and my own fieldnotes. Changes in interns' attitudes and understandings, according to the categories listed above, were noted for each of the thirteen interns. I also noted similarities and differences between interns in the ways they responded to the course, until I found key linkages (Erickson, 1990) between particular interns based on their background experiences and future plans. Analysis of the linkages between interns in each group continued until I found that interns in one group differed from interns in the other group in at least two categories and some interns differed in at least six categories. Instances of atypicality, where an intern differed from other group members, were also noted.

To show the impact of the course, I first provide evidence of growth for all students. I then present findings about the diversity within the group and how key differences between interns played a role in interns' interpretation of and engagement in the course.

Results

Patterns of Responses to the Practicum

Understanding children and caregivers. Survey data reveal conflicting accounts of preservice teacher growth in this area of realizing children's literacy potential. Nearly all preservice teachers agreed that children in their practicum had the potential to read well on pre- and post-surveys, so growth in realizing children's literacy potential could not be derived from these statements. Pre-surveys showed that 69% of interns believed *children's capacity to learn* impeded their literacy success; post-surveys revealed that 46% of interns continued to agree with this statement. Thus, one-third of those interns who questioned the children's innate capacity to learning prior to the study changed their belief. Yet, the response to this survey question indicates that nearly half of the interns continued to believe children's capacity to learn hindered literacy success. Interestingly, many of these interns' anecdotal notes detailed their student's growth during tutorials. The evidence suggests that some interns' prejudgments about children's innate capacity were clearly entrenched and difficult to change. Twelve of the 13 interns wrote that environmental factors (across home and school contexts) explained children's below grade-level performance, leaving me to infer their views that children would perform at grade level if these environments supported literacy growth.

The surveys showed robust growth among interns in their understanding of Ebonics (46% to 92%), their understanding of the history of Ebonics (31% to 85%), and, most significantly, their positive feelings toward Ebonics (15% to 77%).

Students' awareness about the history and usage of Ebonics related directly to reading and responding to the chapters in *The Real Ebonics Debate*. However, other evidence indicates that these new understandings were superficial. Survey data indicate that only 23% of preservice teachers believed that Ebonics had a grammatical structure, despite exposure to research describing the grammatical consistencies in the language and their own observations of the regularities in the ways children used language. I knew from past experiences that preservice teachers frequently misinterpret the word "grammatical" to mean "correct" or "Standard English" rather than understanding "grammatical" as a way of describing consistencies in the ways members of a community use language in terms of pronunciation, syntax, vocabulary and prosody. My attempts to make this distinction clear during through a seminar discussion and discussion board communication proved unsuccessful, suggesting continued misunderstanding of Ebonics and quite possibly reflecting prejudices about the language.

Five interns received written feedback from parents, another three communicated with parents via the telephone, and one intern met with a parent at school. The remaining four interns were unable to contact parents; these interns speculated in writing that parents who were unavailable for communication would be less apt to support their children's literacy growth at home. Although some of the feedback supplied by parents did not indicate active parental support in the area of literacy, parents' attempts to communicate to preservice teachers left many feeling that parents cared about their children's education. Surveys showed a change in interns' beliefs about parents' ability to support their children's literacy development (38% to 69%) and act as resources for helping teachers to understand children (38% to 77%). Written responses nevertheless showed a near split of six students attributing literacy failure to parents' lack of involvement (among other environmental factors) and seven interns attributing literacy failure to factors unrelated to parenting.

Survey responses indicated that many interns believed they acquired understandings about African-American history and culture (38% to 62%). However, I noted definite gaps in interns' knowledge of history and its cultural significance. As an example, fieldnotes from one class discussion indicate interns' reluctance to contribute to discussions of post-slavery history. Slavery and civil rights were the only two issues brought up by interns during a class discussion on African-American history. Other significant aspects of African-American history were not cited by interns, such as the social conditions during reconstruction, consequences of northern migration, and legalized segregation in the South. If these events were not understood, I wondered if interns could understand the views, patterns of living, language and communication, or behaviors of many African Americans.

However, about 75% of the interns claimed they had become more familiar with literature that mirrored the themes, images, and stories of people who lived in the community. Teaching records show that about half of the interns addressed the themes that reflect certain aspects of African-American culture. Examples included: the importance of family and extended family, solidarity with the community, the emphasis on education, and the struggle to overcome prejudice and adversity. The range and depth of interns' understanding about culture was not systematically studied.

Instruction and culturally relevant teaching. Survey responses show an increase in the numbers of preservice teachers who felt they could be successful teachers in the community (69% to 85%). More dramatic gains were noted in the percentages of preservice teachers who felt comfortable assessing children's literacy needs (15% to 100%), providing individualized literacy lessons for the children they tutored (62% to 100%), integrating information about children's lives and culture into literacy lessons (46% to 85%) and teaching literacy skills in the context of real reading and writing events (77% to 100%). My own fieldnotes confirm preservice teachers' increasing ability to (a) adapt their lessons to the out-of-school experiences of students, (b) use ongoing assessments and anecdotal notes to refine instruction according to children's abilities, and (c) incorporate culturally responsive literature into literacy lessons. About 70% of interns consistently used literature written and illustrated by African Americans; the remaining interns used this literature periodically. Almost all of these interns claimed they felt comfortable leading critical discussions of this literature. However, I only observed once such discussion, and interns' teaching records did not support this claim. My own observations suggest preservice teachers felt "safer" engaging children in literature response discussions that included personal responses, predictions, and discussions of story elements; only a few preservice teachers planned literacy discussions aimed at building children's social consciousness. All 13 preservice teachers revealed moderately high confidence in tutoring children at the sixth week according to their written responses.

White identity development. All but four students began the course without having previously explored their own cultural identities, nor had they described themselves according to their race, connected whiteness with privilege, or thought about the significance of race in literacy teaching. Surveys indicated that some interns increased their awareness that race should matter to teachers (23% to 62%). By week 7, all students developed awareness of their own whiteness and its significance, and about half of the students indicated in writing they were struggling with this new knowledge. Two of these students came to my office to discuss difficulties in trying to communicate their knowledge about white privilege to relatives at home.

Five interns believed they were in the process of seeking a positive white identity and would like to find out more about their own and others' culture. I remained skeptical about this kind of growth for two of these students, given that each indicated on post-survey questions that race should not be a factor in teaching. This view is inconsistent with recognizing that race does matter and that inequalities based on race continue to affect schooling and educational achievement. Also, since movement toward a positive white identity requires time, rigorous interrogation of one's cultural identity, and a commitment to learning about others (Tatum, 1999), one would not expect growth from a state of unexamined whiteness to a state of achieving a positive white identity in a span of 13 weeks.

Attributing Literacy Achievement to Schools. At the beginning of the semester, interns attributed literacy failure primarily to a lack of home support. Home influences accounted for 54% of the attributes mentioned by interns. Thirty percent of the mentions implicated schools, 11% implicated society, and 5% of the mentions addressed children's low motivation. By week 7, perceptions about the relative influences of school and home changed dramatically: school influences accounted for 70% of the total number of attributes and home influences accounted for 14%. Most interns believed crowded classrooms, low expectations of students, and limited funds were barriers to literacy achievement. The number of societal and child influences remained the same.

My fieldnotes shed some light on the reasons for interns' new realizations about the relative impact of schooling and home influences. As previously mentioned, nine interns successfully contacted parents by this time and these interns believed parents were interested in supporting children's literacy. At the same time, interns raised several concerns about the school system during our seminar discussions. Interns realized children struggled to read based on grade expectations. They voiced concerns about the crowded conditions within classrooms and doubted that classroom teachers could give children intensive support. These observations were confirmed when I learned that two of the classrooms contained 40 children during the first 3 weeks of school because of hiring difficulties. Some interns criticized the district's promotion policy, which led to questions about how children could possibly catch up without extra help. Interns were also struck by the fact that the school did not have a reading specialist or a librarian.

After the sixth week of the practicum, interns spent more time in the classrooms and observed cooperating teachers who seemed dedicated to teaching. I explained that district funded their cooperating teachers' education through West Chester's graduate program in reading. Interns discovered that each classroom contained a full range of leveled book sets and trade books (secured through the University-School District partnership and the school's adoption of the 100 Book Challenge program). Preservice teachers were struck by how well teachers organized literacy events for so many children. However, interns did not spend enough time observing how these teachers met children's individual literacy needs. Although interns collaborated with their cooperating teachers to plan literacy lessons, there was little time left during the busy morning literacy block to talk with cooperating teachers. Cooperating teachers often gave up their preparation periods to fill in for another teacher's absence (substitute teachers were rare).

By the end of the semester, interns concluded that inequalities existed in public education, yet most did not relate the shortcomings of the school and district to the broader social landscape that shaped these inequalities. Racism did not surface as a factor influencing these inequalities, despite our seminar and discussion board responses to articles that addressed these topics. Only two preservice teachers cited "historical hardships" as a cause of literacy failure and survey results showed a decrease in the numbers of interns who agreed that racism negatively affects the quality of schooling for children (85% to 62%). These data suggest most preservice teachers attributed literacy achievement to the immediate school environment, rather than the school as a part of multiple sociohistorical, sociocultural influences.

Diversity among preservice teachers. In this section, I contrast the nine preservice teachers who reported increased interest in urban teaching during the literacy practicum with those who showed a lack of interest in urban literacy teaching despite their growth in some knowledge and skill areas. Of students in the "high interest" group, three had been raised in an urban environment, and five had participated in a prior field-based course in which they studied diversity issues in conjunction with participating in an after-school tutoring program in the homes of Latino children. The exception is one student who had very little contact with people of color or engagement in diversity studies, yet indicated an increased interest in urban literacy teaching. One intern in the "low interest" group became increasingly disillusioned with the idea of urban teaching as the semester evolved. Of significance, members of this "low interest" group had few direct prior experiences with diversity.

Six of the eight interns whose interest in urban literacy teaching increased during the course wrote they wanted to provide a service to this community through teaching. Five of these students reported the satisfaction of having developed personal relationships with children, two wrote about enjoying the challenges inherent in urban teaching, and two wrote about the vitality of the city and looked forward to living in Philadelphia after graduation.

In contrast, the four interns whose interest in urban teaching was low or decreased during the semester tended to focus on the unsupportive schooling conditions they believed interfered with literacy learning, including crowded classrooms, a lack of materials, technology, and support services for struggling readers. The tendency for this group to focus on the limitations of urban schooling is also reflected in the number of times these limitations were mentioned; this group averaged three per person, whereas the interns in the "high interest" group averaged two mentions. Moreover, students with low interest in urban teaching had greater concerns about their own ability to confront these conditions. One intern wrote, "I would not be able to handle the responsibility of teaching thirty kids how to read," reflecting her insecurity about taking on this challenge. Two of these interns wrote about their uneasiness in the school setting and one claimed she was "disheartened by the experience of seeing children in this environment." A key difference between those who did and those who did not wish to teach in urban classrooms was the first group's ability to derive satisfaction from knowing and serving children despite recognizing some of the limitations of teaching in this school setting.

Interns in both groups indicated similar levels of agreement in using culturally relevant literature, using information from the child's life to construct literacy lessons, and allowing Ebonics-related miscues that preserve text meaning. Interns in both groups indicated they occasionally helped children write using Standard English, and only a few interns in the "high interest" group used suggestions from book *The Real Ebonics Debate* to teach children about code-switching. Most interns in the two groups did not address issues of race and culture.

At this point, I will highlight specific intern characteristics that track best with their level of interest in urban teaching. These are exemplified by comparing two interns with strong interest (Amy and Alison) to those who showed low interest in urban teaching (Jenn and Julie).

1. *Diversity background:* Amy and Alison were raised in racially diverse communities and maintained friendships with people of color throughout their lives. Alison had the experience of tutoring Latino children in a previous course where she also studied about white identity development. Julie and Jenn did not grow up in racially diverse communities, maintain relationships with people of color, or participate in practical experiences in diverse communities.

2. *White identity development:* Amy and Alison reported growth in white identity development to the point where they believed they were seeking a positive white identity by examining their own and others' cultural values. Alison also claimed to be involved in anti-racist activities at the university. Julie and Jenn acknowledged the realities of white privilege and racism, and they believed they were still in the process of abandoning racist beliefs. As Jenn stated, "I have some feelings resembling the reintegration stage, but they do not consume me." One of her statements, however, showed she was beyond reintegration: "I felt that if these families wanted to get out of this type of life, they could, if they worked hard enough. Only through personal reflection and class discussion did I realize that it's not that easy."

3. *Out-of-school affiliations:* Survey and written reports indicate Amy and Alison were comfortable relating to caregivers, felt comfortable relating to members of the black community, and felt comfortable being in the community. Julie and Jenn disagreed with these statements.

4. *Culturally relevant teaching:* Amy and Alison integrated children's lives and culture into literacy lessons, used culturally relevant literature, and discussed issues of race and culture in literature discussions. In contrast, Julie and Jenn seldomly used culturally relevant literature and did not consider other principles of cultural congruence in their planning or implementation.

5. *Beliefs about language:* Amy and Alison felt positive about children's language, avoided correcting dialect-related miscues (that preserved text meaning), discussed code-switching with children during writing activities, and believed children spoke grammatically. Julie reported that she allowed for dialect-related miscue, but had strong negative views about children's language. She and Jenn both doubted that Ebonics has a grammatical structure.

6. *Affect:* Amy and Alison showed greater personal attachment to the children and to teaching. Amy stated, "This experience has given me a deep passion to teach these children. I want to be there to celebrate and live all of the experiences with them." Alison's comment expresses this most poignantly: "I genuinely care for these kids. I want them to succeed, be happy, grow into strong men and

women, help their families and neighborhoods, and change the world. I can see and feel what amazing, beautiful things each one of them is capable of doing if people just give them some time, love, and guidance." Jenn and Julie, presented a more detached perspective of children and teaching, as is reflected in Jenn's comment: "I feel as though I wanted to relate to these children as much as possible in order to ensure that they were comfortable with learning." Although Julie described that she was "elated" with the performance of her students after one successful lesson, she felt unable to relate to the children and members of the community: "I feel as though I would not be one hundred percent comfortable teaching in a community like this mostly because I feel as though I can't relate to the children or the community."

Although Amy and Alison displayed some characteristics that are associated with successful teaching in this community, they struggled at times with teaching in the regular classroom. Amy complained about being disorganized in her planning and I observed that she occasionally omitted key details and reflections in her teaching records. Alison said she had difficulty adopting an authoritative stance when teaching and felt children sometimes took advantage of her "niceness," a view that was confirmed in my fieldnotes. Both Julie and Jenn were highly organized and detailed in their planning. My fieldnotes indicate Jenn was especially successful in engaging children in literacy events.

Among the two pairs of students, Jenn and Alison differed most in the way they approached their own future needs in serving African-American children. According to Jenn: "To be a successful literacy teacher of African-American students, I would need to extend myself to learn more about the children, their community, and their history." Alison's future plan shows much greater specificity:

> There are so many things I need to work on to be a successful teacher. I need to understand African-American culture at a deeper level so I can tie learning into students' lives. I need to research better strategies that allow kids to code switch between Standard English and Ebonics when necessary. I need to develop an arsenal of fantastic and meaningful culturally relevant books and materials that I can use to build lessons. I need to continue working toward my positive white identity so I will never blame my students and their parents, pity them, or be ashamed in front of them. I also need to learn more about teaching literacy. I am confident I will meet all of these goals and find many new ones to strive for.

Alison's desire to serve the children and her capacity to reflect at this level may help her adjust her teaching style to one where she can feel more comfortable about securing children's attention and respect. Jenn will need to specify strategies for growth in this area irrespective of her plans to teach in a suburban district. Not only is she likely to have children of color in her suburban classroom and will need to consider their needs when teaching, but she will also need to help white children learn about people of color.

The results of this study can be summarized as follows:

1. All preservice teachers recognized their own privileged status; however,
2. Variations in identity growth existed.

3. All interns recognized the negative factors of urban schooling; however,
4. Only some interns saw themselves able to confront the challenges of teaching.
5. All interns applied some culturally responsive principles and practices; however,
6. Interns varied in their ways of applying these principles to literacy teaching.
7. Prior experiences with diversity were common to seven out of the eight interns whose interest in urban teaching increased.
8. Five of these eight interns experienced diversity at the University through a previous education course involving tutoring Latino children in children's homes and studying diversity issues.
9. Explicit study of diversity issues guided field-based inquiries.

Conclusions and Implications

These findings highlight the complexities of preparing preservice teachers for diversity. They are consistent with other findings showing the impact of preservice teachers' prior experiences on constructing diversity issues, perceiving children, and applying instructional knowledge (Xu, 2000). The devotion some interns showed to pursuing urban teaching jobs and recognizing how they could grow to be better teachers in these communities challenges the view that European Americans may not the best candidates for teaching in urban communities (Haberman, 1996). On the other hand, some preservice teachers' persistent assumptions about children's literacy abilities and language, and their own lingering insecurities about teaching in urban schools, leave me cautious about the potential of this course, or any 6-credit course, to prepare interns for urban teaching. This study shows some perceptions are firmly entrenched, requiring novel approaches to preparing teachers for diversity.

Integrating diversity studies and immersion experiences into literacy education curricula are two critical components of a reform agenda. As Howard (1999) states:

> White multicultural awareness must be mediated through actual engagement with "the other." Authentic engagement with the reality of those whose stories are significantly different from our own can allow us to transcend, to some degree, the limits of social positionality and help us see dominance in a clearer light. (p. 36)

He argues that white teachers cannot fully know or experience the struggles of students of color, but preservice teachers can be placed in environments in which the stories and experiences of others can be acknowledged and shared. This process of knowing others must coincide with acknowledging privilege and interrogating assumptions of dominance.

Practical integration of diversity and literacy studies requires several modifications in curricula. Close mentorship of college supervisors is essential to monitor how interns are making sense of this material, emphasizing the need for small group seminars for practical courses. Misperceptions about children's literacy potential require thoughtful reflection and discussions of children's growth and the circumstances that affect growth. Lingering concerns about large class size and limited staffing need to be addressed by structuring time for interns to work alongside cooperating teachers who successfully organize learning events, differentiate instruction, collaborate with colleagues, and reform teaching. Ongoing misconceptions about Ebonics require more time observing and recording the consistencies in children's language use and learning about the sociopolitical place of language in this society, indicating an inquiry-oriented curriculum. Uncertainties about the community warrant more meaningful contact with those outside of the school through creative immersion experiences. The findings also support the need to help white interns understand the history and culture of particular groups of people and how this knowledge can be used to understand others and reform literacy teaching.

Structuring teacher preparation curricula around pluralistic models is challenging since the present curriculum draws primarily from a psychological base emphasizing universal patterns of child development rather than relationships between thought, language, and culture in specific communities (Haberman, 1996). Educational psychology, not cultural anthropology, has been the core of the teacher education program. Literacy educators would need to collaborate with colleagues across departments and schools to reconceptualize teacher education around learning about children and schooling within particular cultural communities. Research to understand how diversity-oriented curricula impacts preservice teachers and their future students will be required to support these changes in teacher preparation.

References

Avery P., & Walker, C. (1993). Prospective teachers' perceptions of ethnic and gender differences in academic achievement. *Journal of Teacher Education, 44,* 27–37.

Au, K. H., & Kawakami, A. J. (1991) Culture and ownership: Schooling of minority students. *Childhood Education, 67,* 280–284.

Bennett, C. (1999). *Comprehensive multicultural education.* Boston, MA: Allyn & Bacon.

Bogdan, R. C., & Biklen, S. K. (1998). *Qualitative research for education: An introduction to theory and methods.* Boston, MA: Allyn & Bacon.

Bollin, G. (1997). Multicultural tutoring: An experiential community service approach to preparing preservice teachers for diversity. *Educational Forum, 61,* 68–76.

Cochran-Smith, M. (1995). Uncertain allies: Understanding the boundaries of race and teaching. *Harvard Educational Review, 65,* 541–570.

Edwards, P. A., Pleasants, H. M., & Franklin, S. H. (1999). *A path to follow: Learning to listen to parents.* Portsmouth, NH: Heinemann.

Erickson, F. (1990). *Qualitative methods.* New York: Macmillan.

Gomez, M. L. (1993). Prospective teachers' perspectives on teaching diverse children: A review with implications for teacher education and practice. *Journal of Negro Education, 62,* 459–473.

Haberman, M. (1996). Selecting and preparing culturally competent teachers for urban schools. In J. Sikula (Ed.), *Handbook of research on teacher education* (pp. 747–760). New York: Simon & Schuster.

Helms, J. (1990). *Black and white racial identity: Theory, research and practice.* Westport, CT: Greenwood.

Henry, G. (1985). *Cultural Diversity Awareness Inventory.* Hampton, VA: Hampton University Press

Hoffman, J., & Pearson, P. D. (2000). Reading teacher education in the next millennium: What your grandmother's teacher didn't know that your granddaughter's teacher should. *Reading Research Quarterly, 35,* 28–45.

Howard, G. (1999). *We can't teach what we don't know: White teachers, multiracial schools.* New York: Teachers College Press.

Ladson-Billings, G. (1994). *The dreamkeepers: Successful teachers of African American children.* San Francisco, CA: Jossey-Bass.

McIntosh, P. (1989). White privilege: Unpacking the invisible knapsack. *Peace and Freedom, 49,* 10–12.

Perry, T., & Delpit, L. (1998). *The real ebonics debate: Power, language and the education of African-American children.* Boston: Beacon.

Tatum, B. (1999). *Why are all the black kids sitting together in the cafeteria?* New York: Basic.

Wiggins, R. A., & Follo, E. J. (1999). Development of knowledge, attitudes, and commitment to teach diverse populations. *Journal of Teacher Education, 50,* 94–105.

Wolf, S. (2000, December). *"Only connect!" Cross cultural connections in the literacy engagement of a preservice teacher and the child who taught her.* Paper presented at the meeting of the National Reading Conference: Scottsdale, AZ.

Xu, S. H. (2000). Preservice teachers in a literacy methods course consider issues of diversity. *Journal of Literacy Research, 32,* 505–531.

Making Teacher Education Critical

Christine H. Leland
Indiana University, Indianapolis

Jerome C. Harste
Indiana University, Bloomington

Cynthia A. Jackson
Indiana University, Indianapolis

Omaia Youssef
Ains Shams University, Cairo

Many veteran and prospective teachers say that they are not interested in political issues. Some conclude that they chose a career in education because they saw it as a field far removed from politics. We wondered whether this might be due, in part, to the fact that the political nature of education is typically not highlighted in most teacher education programs. A number of critical theorists (e.g., Luke & Freebody, 1997; Macedo & Bartolome, 1999; Shannon, 1998) and critical educators (e.g., Altwerger & Saavedra, 1999; Cochran-Smith, 2001; Edelsky, 1994) have argued that this needs to be changed. All of these theorists and educators insist that in addition to providing information about learning theory and teaching methods, teacher educators should also be providing learning opportunities that will help future teachers understand the political dimensions of education.

As teacher educators who have spent most of our professional careers investigating literacy development more specifically, we were interested in exploring how we might begin to help our students understand how education and politics are inextricably joined. We wondered how we could use the time in a teacher education program to build their awareness that "education is politics" (Shor & Pari, 2000) and that all schools are political places whether or not we want to admit it. As literacy educators, we have been interested in discovering ways to help our students develop an understanding that "systems of domination are part of reading and writing, part of classroom interaction, part of texts of all kinds" (Edelsky, 1994, p. 255) and that literacy can be a tool for asking questions about what is unfair and, ultimately, for bringing about societal change (Freire & Macedo, 1987; Luke, 1995). The hypothesis we have been testing over the past 5 years suggests that how teacher educators design their programs can make a big difference in whether or not prospective teachers attain a critical perspective.

*National Reading Conference Yearbook, **50**, pp. 382–393.*

Researchers have found little evidence of critical thought (in the sense of addressing moral and ethical concerns) on the part of teacher education students (e.g., Hatton & Smith, 1994; McLaughlin & Hanifin, 1994). In a study that examined all of the articles in *Language Arts* and *The Reading Teacher* from 1993 through 1995 for the purpose of identifying trends and issues in literacy education, Swafford, Chapman, Rhodes, and Kallus (1996) found that "Issues related to encouraging students to ask important questions about their 'places' in society and then providing them with the means to do something to change their positions were rarely discussed" (p. 442). We suspect that the lack of attention to critical issues might be directly related to the generic "reflections" that teacher education students are frequently asked to submit as evidence of their learning. Although students are often asked to make personal connections and examine alternative perspectives in their reflections, they are not usually encouraged to address issues of social justice in the sense described by Edelsky (1994).

Background

This study spans two phases of research and documents our ongoing efforts to evaluate and reform our own approach to teacher education. Specifically, we worked with two cohorts of teacher education students (interns) over a 2-year period for each group. When we started out with the first group (Cohort 1), we wished to determine whether issues of equity and justice would emerge from their own reflections on educational issues and observations of classroom life, or whether we needed to make a more deliberate effort to call students' attention to them. Our findings from the first phase (Leland, Harste, & Youssef, 1997) set the agenda for the second phase and led to a number of modifications to our program for students in the second group (Cohort 2). This paper reports the findings for phase 2 of the project.

Through an arrangement with the university, the first two authors were assigned to work with each of the cohorts over four semesters, teaching all of the education courses (not just the ones dealing with reading and language) and supervising all of the field experiences and student teaching. All classes and field activities took place in one of two public elementary schools where university faculty and teachers worked together to plan and implement the program. Both of these schools had strong connections with the local university and were designated as Professional Development Schools. Both schools were located in an urban area and had a high percentage of African-American students (80%–90%).

An ongoing assignment for the interns in both groups was to keep a reflective journal and make an entry for each day they were at the school. In framing the journal assignment, we encouraged the interns to use topics like "What's on my mind?" or "What's new?" as a focus for their entries. We discouraged the catalogue approach of "Here's what I did today," and instead invited them to examine issues from multiple perspectives, to identify and reflect on anomalies, and to hypothesize mini-inquiries that might help them to answer some of their own questions. We advised the interns to listen carefully to the children's voices and to let those voices lead their instructional efforts and help to focus their reflections at the end of the day. We did not ask them to examine events from the specific perspective of critical literacy or to concentrate on issues of equity and social justice.

In phase 1 of the project, we analyzed and coded 1,450 entries from cohort 1 and concluded that this particular group showed more instances of critical thinking than what the literature suggested about other groups studied in the past. However, we did not find evidence that they were poised at the end of the program "to take pedagogically liberating action" (Leland, Harste, & Youssef, 1997).

Findings from phase 1 led to program modifications for Cohort 2, and to another set of data collected and coded in the same way. In the second phase of the study, we collected and analyzed 80 entries (40 from Cohort 1 and 40 from Cohort 2). These samples included 4 entries from each of 10 randomly selected interns in each cohort who had turned in complete sets of journal entries. Entries were collected at a similar date in the program sequence for both groups: the first entry in October and the first entry in February for each of the 2 years students were in the program. For 10 randomly selected members of Cohort 1, we analyzed the first entry for October 1995, February 1996, October 1996, and February 1997. For 10 randomly selected members of Cohort 2, we analyzed the first entry for October 1997, February 1998, October 1998, and February 1999.) The second phase of the project also included documenting and analyzing differences in the instruction that was provided for the two groups.

Method

Data sources include the two instructors' curricular planning and reflections on the role that critical literacy played in the curriculum for the 2 groups and 80 journal entries (4 entries × 10 students × 2 groups).

Analysis of Instruction

Instruction for the two groups differed in four major ways: (a) general approach, (b) choice of children's books shared, (c) assigned readings, and (d) specific curricular engagements. Our general approach with Cohort 1 was to discuss critical topics (like power and equity) when they came up in normal conversation, but not to introduce these topics as part of our curriculum. With the second group, however, we attempted to be more articulate about critical issues. We talked about them in various contexts and used examples that built off of critical issues whenever we could. For example, while both groups were introduced to the idea of creating curricular invitations (Short, Harste, & Burke, 1996), different samples were used with the two groups. Several of the sample invitations developed for Cohort 2 were overtly critical in terms of their focus. For example, we asked interns to think about topics like how Barbie dolls influence young girls, how Happy Meal toys from McDonald's position children as consumers, and the roles that teachers and students play in books like *Lily's Purple Plastic Purse* (Henkes, 1996) and *Dear Mr. Blueberry* (James, 1991).

We also introduced interns in both cohorts to different children's books. While we simply shared many examples of what we considered good children's literature with Cohort 1, we introduced the interns in Cohort 2 to a text set of children's books that specifically focused on topics related to power and equity. Many of these books addressed difficult social issues like racism, gender discrimination, and ageism (Leland, Harste, Ociepka, Lewison, & Vasquez, 1999). Examples of books in this text set include *White Wash* (Shange, 1997), *White Socks Only* (Coleman, 1996), and *Sister Anne's Hands* (Lorbiecki, 1998). These three picture books deal with instances of overt racial discrimination. Another book in this set, *Voices in the Park* (Browne, 1998), focuses on the issue of socioeconomic stereotyping. Although many interns initially judged these books as "not nice" and "not appropriate for children," others thought that the issues they addressed were not very different from what these urban children experienced on a daily basis. As a curricular piece, we extended an invitation for students in Cohort 2 to conduct one of their required mini-inquiries around the question of what happened when they introduced one or more of these books to children. The interns who chose to engage in this project (about half of the group) discovered that children were very interested in these books and were more likely to listen attentively (and cause fewer discipline problems) when these books were being explored.

We assigned some different course readings to the two groups as well. While everyone in Cohort 1 read *Reading Denied* (Taylor, 1991), this book was one choice from a larger group of books for Cohort 2. While students in Cohort 1 read *The Struggle to Continue* (Shannon, 1990), interns in Cohort 2 read *text, lies & video tape* (Shannon, 1995), *Affirming Diversity: The Sociopolitical Context of Multicultural Education* (Nieto, 1996), *On Reading* (Goodman, 1996) and *The Right to Learn* (Darling-Hammond, 1995).

Finally, students in Cohort 2 experienced several new curricular engagements that were created to help them develop a more critical stance. During their first semester in the program, interns took part in an activity that focused on the role of gender in children's literature. They examined a number of children's books and documented the different roles given to male and female characters. They were then asked to analyze which roles had more power and whether these roles were more often assigned to male or female characters.

During their second semester, interns in Cohort 2 were asked to collaborate with children in their field experience classroom to plan and implement a social action project that would "make the world a better place" in some way. One intern worked with kindergartners to write letters to elderly people in nursing homes. Another intern worked with his class to write to the Mayor's office on several occasions about an illegal betting operation that was housed across the street from the school. Although no cause and effect relationship can be inferred, it is significant to note that this house was boarded up and sold by the end of the school year.

A third new engagement added for Cohort 2 was a "learner project" that required interns to study someone who had not been well served by schools in general. We saw this a way to encourage interns to begin to problematize schooling in an institutional sense and to critique aspects of schooling that they had previously taken for granted.

A new experience added to the program for Cohort 2 was a weekly "Town Meeting" led by interns. This allowed students to bring up any issue that they wanted the entire group of interns and instructors to address in a public forum. Though we sometimes regretted this addition (since it tended to make us more vulnerable), we think it made a difference in terms of challenging traditional ideas about teacher control and allowing more voices to be heard.

Coding of Journal Entries

The 80 journal entries were coded according to Van Manen's (1977) evaluative framework. This model is frequently referenced in the literature dealing with levels of reflection (e.g. Cutler, Cook, & Young, 1989; Gore & Zeichner, 1991; Pultorak, 1993). Van Manen's first level, "Technical," is used to categorize reflections which focus on means rather than ends. At this level individuals are concerned with the technical application of educational knowledge and of basic curriculum principles for the purpose of attaining a given end. The end itself is not examined. At the second level, "Interpretive," the focus is on an interpretive understanding of the nature of educational experience, and of making practical choices. Teachers consider competing educational goals and how contexts influence teaching. At the third level, "Moral," the focus is on the worth of knowledge and "the social conditions necessary for raising the questions of worthwhileness in the first place" (Van Manen, 1977, p. 227). Teachers look critically at the ethical basis for what happens in the classroom. They judge educational goals, experiences and activities against the criteria of justice and equity.

We used Van Manen's third level ("Moral"), with its focus on equity and justice, as the criterion for selecting critical entries. Critical thought units were identified as sections of text consisting of one or more sentences that addressed a topic within what we judged as Van Manen's "Moral" level. Entries which were thought to contain one or more critical thought units were first identified and then further analyzed. Of the 1,450 entries from Cohort 1 that were reviewed in phase 1 of the study, 180 (12.41%) met the criterion for being considered critical. In phase 2, the 40 samples from Cohort 1 yielded 25 critical thought units and the 40 samples from Cohort 2 yielded 73 critical thought units. All entries nominated for this category by one of the raters/authors were reviewed by the others; inter rater reliability among the raters was 80%, with total agreement after discussion.

As we read through the journal entries that met Van Manen's criterion of "Moral" (or what we called critical), we identified three categories: (a) Instruction, (b) Culture of Schooling, and (c) Larger Social Forces (see Figure 1). Whereas all of these entries addressed some aspect of fairness, the three categories helped us to sort out the various contexts of critique. Category one, Instruction, focused on

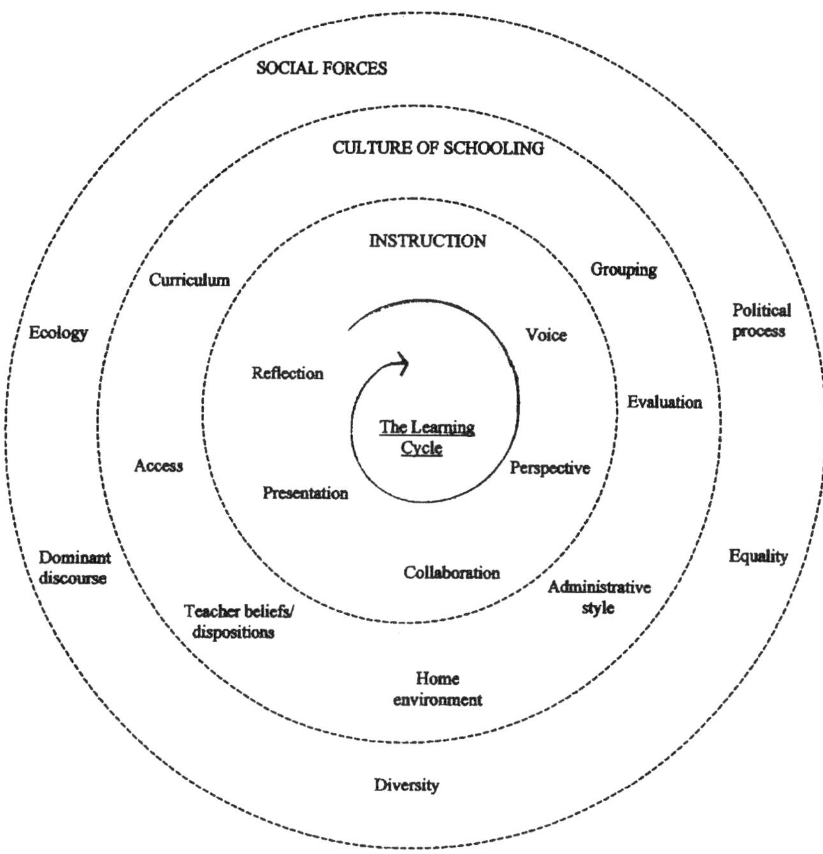

Figure 1. Categories and topics of critical journal entries.

the learning cycle (Short, Harste, & Burke, 1996) and how the interns judged students' opportunities to engage in the various processes of this cycle. Entries in this category addressed the importance of honoring learners' voices, encouraging collaboration and engaging in reflection. Entries in category two, the Culture of Schooling, addressed issues of equity at the institutional level and focused on topics like grouping, administrative style and evaluation. Finally, entries in category three, Larger Social Forces, looked beyond classroom instruction and the institution and focused on broader societal issues.

Category one: Instruction. Journal entries in this category generally related to instructional matters and clustered around topics involving issues of fairness in the learning process. In each instance, students implicitly or explicitly challenged the underlying assumptions or forces at work that kept what they saw as better instruction from taking place. Entries talked about the importance of encouraging students to develop their own voices, take ownership of the learning process, make use of multiple sign systems, collaborate with others, share what was learned, and reflect on experience, as shown in the following examples:

> I took my small group out to the hall and we read two ghost stories. I know, maybe not "fine" literature, but that was what they wanted to read. (Karen, Cohort 2, 10-2-97)
>
> Because the end products are not graded they have total control over their work and don't have to worry about fulfilling an assignment. (Elizabeth, Cohort 2, 2-2-99)

These entries called attention to the importance of student voice in instruction and the unfairness of denying this voice. Karen confirmed the need for children to have choice in what they read; Elizabeth spoke to the importance of maintaining student ownership.

Other examples in the category of instruction addressed the issue of collaboration and document interns' discoveries of its role in learning:

> Brittany, Robyn and I were collaborating together and each of us helped one another and got some great ideas in the process. The ideas I had were pretty good, but it was the little extra things that Robyn and Brittany suggested that made me like my invitations even better. (Ryan, Cohort 1, 10-11-96)
>
> I did learn today from my club after watching the boys tell the story, that the kids respond well to each other. They will probably do good [sic] teaching each other dance steps rather than Brad and I working so hard. (Ann, Cohort 2, 10-2-97)

Category two: The culture of schooling. Journal entries in this category reflected upon the "invisible center" (Ferguson, 1990) of schooling; how assumptions about grouping, evaluation, and the nature of children were taken for granted and built into the system, often beyond open discussion or consciousness. For example, one intern commented: "I feel that a program suited for the best students is also good enough for the average ones" (Vickie, Cohort 2, 2-2-99). This entry spoke to the common practice of separating gifted children from their (non-gifted) peers and subsequently providing them with a richer curriculum. The student challenged the fairness of a common practice in many schools. Other entries in this category addressed the dual pressures of teaching to the test and being scrutinized by administrators who are driven by test scores:

> I feel constrained to "cover curriculum" in a way that I didn't last semester . . . I am supposed to give them a test—it hardly seems fair to hold students accountable for information if I'm not directly presenting that information to them. Another factor is knowing that someone (the Vice-Principal) is looking over my lesson plans. (Jennifer, Cohort 2, 2-2-99)

Another example showed how a teacher's disposition can help her to understand that her influence has the potential to go far beyond the classroom. In describing her interactions with a single child, the intern spoke about the impact that access to schooling can have:

> I hoped over the past couple of weeks and the few positive experiences that she has been able to have that she will continue to pick up books and read them and that this will make a difference in her life. (Julie, Cohort 2, 2-3-98)

Entries in this category all addressed issues that go beyond classroom instruction, yet still are very much part of the context (or culture) of schooling.

Category three: Larger social forces. Entries in this category addressed social forces that encompass educational issues but go even further in terms of challenging the fairness of dominant discourses. One intern reacted to a math teacher who argued that it was his job to weed out students:

> We look at how much education a person has, and equate that with what kind of job is suitable for that person. Elementary school is something that everyone has a right to, and if at that level we're letting people slide through the system, or not making sure that everyone is learning, then we are weeding out people. (Mandee, Cohort 2, 2-3-98)

Another intern used her struggle to develop an understanding of stereotyping as a vehicle for critiquing one of the course texts:

> Shannon espouses the perspective that all those of European descent (European Americans) consider themselves culture-free and "normal," while seeing others as culture-laden and "abnormal." I found such a generalization disturbing, as it occurred to me that such a view is just as stereotypical as the anti-diverse view with which European Americans are being labeled. Vicki, Cohort 2, 2-3-98)

Whether one agrees with Vicki's interpretation of the text or not, it appears that she was attempting to make sense of larger social issues within the dominant social discourses that frame the discussion.

Findings

Figure 2 shows the distribution of critical journal entries by type across the two cohorts. These data suggest that there was a difference between the amount and type of critical journal entries made by the groups, with instructional entries dominating in Cohort 1 (64%) and entries relating to either instruction or the culture of schooling dominating in Cohort 2 (45% and 48%). There was an increase across the groups in the overall number of critical entries, with students in the second group becoming increasingly aware and critical of the invisible forces that operate on meaning making in schools. Students in Cohort 2 were three times more likely to write from a critical perspective than were students in Cohort 1. In the 80 samples we reviewed, the number of thought units coded as "critical" increased from 25 for Cohort 1 to 73 for Cohort 2. The average number of critical entries written by individual interns rose from 2.5 for Cohort 1 to 7.3 for Cohort 2, with a gain of 4.8. The distribution of critical entries across the two groups suggests that the interns in these groups were concerned with different issues. Of the 25 critical references made by the 10 interns in Cohort 1, 16 related to instruction, 8 related to the culture of schooling and 1 related to social forces. Of the 73 critical

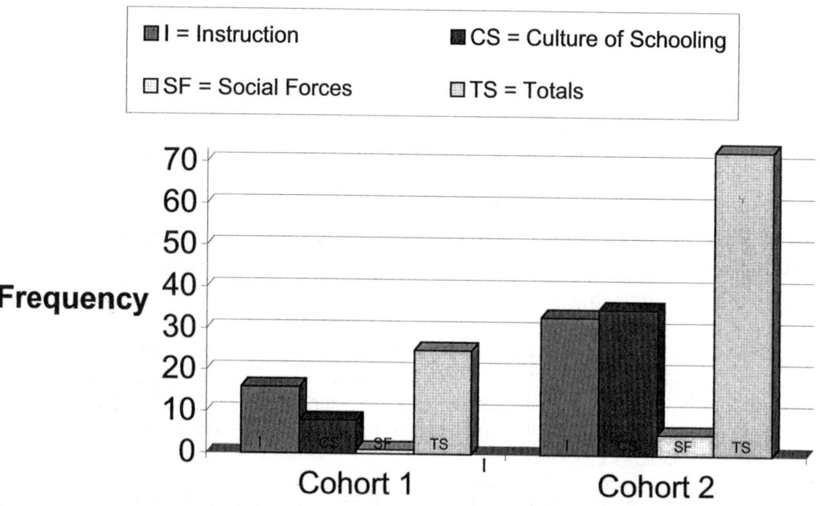

Figure 2. Distribution of critical journal entries by semester and type.

references made by the 10 interns in Cohort 2, 33 entries related to instruction, 35 related to the culture of schooling, and 5 related to larger social forces.

Discussion

Our findings prompt us to ask why Cohort 2 showed more instances of critical thinking than Cohort 1, and why the vast majority of these instances related to instruction and/or the culture of schooling rather than to larger social issues. Although several components of our program might well have influenced the development of a critical perspective in our students, we provide three of several hypotheses that merit further investigation.

Students Learn What We Teach

Given the fact that most of the instances of critique focused on issues of schooling and instruction, one might rightfully conclude that despite our efforts to support a critical perspective more generally, we were more effective at some levels than others. Although research repeatedly shows that children learn what their teachers teach (Harste, 1989), one does not necessarily think of this finding as being applicable at the college level. However, in retrospect, this finding makes sense given the focus of our teacher education program. Moving from a holistic language pedagogy to a critical literacy perspective necessitates a shift in thinking. According to Edelsky (1991), whole-language educators have put "theory (framework, perspective, belief) in the foreground," but have kept their "political light under a bushel" (p. 36). In our belief, it is not that whole-language educators never talk about political issues with their students; it is more that it is not a top priority most of the time. So, although we encouraged the students in Cohort 1 to be critical in terms of challenging the dominant theories of teaching and learning, we did not overtly encourage them to be critical in the broader societal sense.

The Inquiry Model of Curriculum Does not Take Us Far Enough Without a Critical Perspective

Because of our beliefs about how children acquire literacy, we front-loaded our curriculum with issues from the whole-language paradigm: inquiry (Short, Harste, & Burke, 1996), kidwatching (Goodman, 1978), and the importance of induction into the "literacy club" (Smith, 1988). Both cohorts began the first semester of their 2-year program by reading *Creating Classrooms for Authors and Inquirers* (Short, Harste, & Burke, 1996). This text focuses on instructional matters, specifically how the "authoring cycle" can be conceptualized as a framework for teaching. Many of the entries coded as instructional in both cohorts reflected a concern for students having voice and ownership, two issues emphasized in this book. But the fact that students in Cohort 1 seemed less able to move beyond this narrower category into the ones that focused on broader issues suggests that the addition of the critical curricular components for Cohort 2 made a difference.

Building a Political Consciousness Takes Time

Although it is disappointing that there were not more instances of social critique, it may be that looking at the categories of responses hierarchically ("category 3 is better than category 1") is not warranted. If we see critical literacy as a perspective, then we might reasonably expect that teachers who take on this perspective will eventually develop the ability to move flexibly between and among categories. That being said, however, we also have to report that there were some interns in Cohort 2 who did not appear to move beyond instructional concerns (category 1) during their 2 years in the program. Whereas these students were bothered by what they perceived as poor instruction, they tended to resist the idea that education is political. One student decided that she did not wish to spend anymore time in urban schools and transferred out of our program so that she could student teach in the suburbs. Although most of our students did come to see teaching as a politically charged undertaking, a few did not. These individuals might benefit from continuing to engage in conversations about critical issues during their first years of teaching.

Recommendations for the Future

Currently there is a need to problematize both education in general and teacher education more specifically in terms of critical literacy, situated cognition and identity theory in order to understand the complexities involved in each endeavor. If we want teachers who can engage children in conversations about difficult social issues, then we need to begin these conversations in our teacher education classes. Whereas at one level we know that teachers cannot provide experiences for children which they have not yet had themselves, at another level we now understand that knowledge is built up from contextualized instances of experience in situations where identities are socially negotiated and enacted. Significantly, these insights can help us begin to build a much-needed model of education based on diversity and difference.

Because how teachers define literacy makes a big difference in the kinds of literate behaviors they value, a critical definition of literacy raises the ante in terms of what we teach undergraduate students during their stay in our teacher education programs. To be literate is not only to be cognizant of the "invisible center" that operates on our individual meaning making, but to know how to position ourselves to make a difference. Given these insights, we as teacher educators need to think carefully about what we can do to help our students achieve a greater measure of critical literacy. Planning for the future, we now know that we will be much more overt in encouraging our students to adopt a critical perspective. Whereas it is important that students ask themselves, "Who benefits from the position I have taken?" as well as "Who loses?" it is equally important that prospective teachers figure out how to make a difference and then study the moral and ethical effects of their action through inquiry. Such inquiry can support the kind of "teaching against the grain" (Cochran-Smith, 2001) that ultimately makes a difference in the lives of teachers and children.

References

Altwerger, B., & Saavedra, E. (1999). Foreword. In C. Edelsky (Ed.), *Making justice our project: Teachers working toward critical whole language practice* (pp. vii–xii). Urbana, IL: National Council of Teachers of English.

Browne, A. (1998). *Voices in the park.* New York: Dorling Kindersley.

Cochran-Smith, M. (2001). Learning to teach against the (new) grain. *Journal of Teacher Education, 52,* 3–4.

Coleman, E. (1996). *White socks only.* Morton Grove, IL: Albert Whitman.

Cutler, B., Cook. P., & Young, J. (1989, February). *The empowerment of preservice teachers through reflective teaching.* Paper presented at the meeting of the Association of Teacher Educators, St. Louis, MO.

Darling-Hammond, L. (1995). *The right to learn: A blueprint for creating schools that work.* San Francisco: Jossey-Bass.

Edelsky, C. (1991). Reading history. *Review of Education, 14,* 31–40.

Edelsky, C. (1994). Education for democracy. *Language Arts, 71,* 252–257.

Ferguson, R. (1990). Introduction: Invisible center. In R. Ferguson, M. Grever, T. Minh-ha, & C. West (Eds.), *Out there: Marginalization and contemporary cultures.* Cambridge, MA: MIT Press.

Freire, P., & Macedo, D. (1987). *Literacy: Reading the word and the world.* South Hadley, MA: Bergin & Garvey.

Goodman, K. S. (1996). *On reading.* Portsmouth, NH: Heinemann.

Goodman, Y. M. (1978, June). Kid watching: An alternative to testing. *National Elementary Principal, 57,* 41–45.

Gore, J., & Zeichner, K. (1991). Action research and reflective teaching in preservice teacher education: A case study from the United States. *Teaching and Teacher Education, 7,* 119–136.

Harste, J. (1989). *New policy guidelines for reading.* Urbana, IL: National Council of Teachers of English.

Hatton, N., & Smith, D. (1994). *Facilitating reflection: Issues and research.* (ERIC Document Reproduction Service No. ED 375-110)

Henkes, K. (1996). *Lilly's purple plastic purse.* New York: Greenwillow.

James, S. (1991). *Dear Mr. Blueberry.* New York: Aladdin.

Leland, C., Harste, J., Ociepka, A., Lewison, M., & Vasquez, V. (1999,September). Exploring critical literacy: You can hear a pin drop. *Language Arts, 77*(1), 70–77.

Leland, C., Harste, J., & Youssef, Y. (1997). Teacher education and critical literacy. In C. Kinzer, K. Hinchman, & D. Leu (Eds.), *Inquiries in literacy theory and practice.* Forty-sixth yearbook of the National Reading Conference (pp. 385–396). Chicago: National Reading Conference.

Lorbiecki, M. (1998). *Sister Anne's hands.* New York: Dial.

Luke, A. (1995). When basic skills and information processing just aren't enough: Rethinking reading in new times. *Teachers College Record, 97,* 95–115.

Luke, A., & Freebody, P. (1997). Shaping the social practices of reading. In S. Muspratt, A. Luke, & P. Freebody (Eds.), *Constructing critical literacies* (pp. 185–225). Cresskill, NJ: Hampton.

Macedo, D., & Bartolome, L. (1999). *Dancing with bigotry: Beyond the politics of tolerance.* New York: St. Martin's.

McLaughlin, D., & Hanifin, P. (1994, July). *Empowering the novice: Promoting reflection in preservice teacher education.* Paper presented at the Conference of the Australian Teacher Education Association, Brisbane, Queensland (ERIC Document Reproduction Service No. ED 375 096).

Nieto, S. (1996). *Affirming diversity: The sociopolitical context of multicultural education.* White Plains, NY: Longman.

Pultorak, E. (1993). Facilitating reflective thought in novice teachers. *Journal of Teacher Education, 44,* 288–295.

Shange, N. (1997). *White wash.* New York: Walker.

Shannon, P. (1990). *The struggle to continue: Progressive reading instruction in the United States.* Portsmouth, NH: Heinemann.

Shannon, P. (1995). *text, lies & video tape.* Portsmouth, NH: Heinemann.

Shannon, P. (1998). *Reading poverty.* Portsmouth, NH: Heinemann.

Shor,I., & Pari, C. (Eds.). (2000). *Education is politics: Critical teaching across differences, postsecondary.* Portsmouth, NH: Heinemann.

Short, K., Harste, J., & Burke, C. (1996). *Creating classrooms for authors and inquirers.* Portsmouth, NH: Heinemann.

Smith, F. (1988). *Joining the literacy club: Further essays into education.* Portsmouth, NH: Heinemann.

Swafford, J., Chapman, V., Rhodes, R., & Kallus, M. (1996). A literature analysis of trends in literacy education. In D. J. Leu, C. K., Kinzer, & K. A. Hinchman, (Eds.), *Literacies for the 21st century: Research and practice.* Forty-fifth yearbook of the National Reading Conference (pp. 437–446). Chicago: National Reading Conference.

Taylor, D. (1991). *Learning denied.* Portsmouth, NH: Heinemann.

Van Manen, M. (1977). Linking ways of knowing with ways of being practical. *Curriculum Inquiry, 6,* 205–228.

Using the Triple Transfer Lesson Plan to Guide Teachers' Reflection: What Are the Effects on Client Growth?

Debra Bayles Martin
San Diego State University

Several important classes in our Reading Master's program occur at the Community Reading Center, where graduate students assess clients' literacy development and provide one-on-one tutoring. Tutors are credentialed teachers with 1–20 years in the classroom. Many have completed advanced training in administration or programs such as Reading Recovery. Surprisingly, most students approach the tutoring course as if they were novice teachers. During the past 3 years, I have sought to understand why students approach the course in this manner, how they reflect on their learning during the course, and how that reflection might be enhanced to support an increased sense of efficacy among the graduate students.

I am also concerned about Center clients. Ranging in age from 6 to 30 years, our clients entrust us with 2 hours a week for 13 weeks, hoping to grow in literacy competence. The challenges of helping the graduate students and the clients make discernible progress during one semester are often daunting, especially given the history of literacy failure common to our clients. This paper will report key data from a 3-year study focused on supporting teacher reflection while addressing client literacy growth.

Study Perspectives

"Learning" is often described as involving two aspects: experience and one's reflection upon that experience. The idea that "you really don't understand what you know until you begin to examine it" (Whitford, Schlechty, & Shelor, 1987, p. 164) is widely accepted in teacher education. Beginning with Schon's (1983) work on the reflective practitioner, teacher education literature has often called for teachers to reflect upon their teaching to enhance professional development (cf. Ash, 1993; Vogt & Au, 1995).

Although the notion of reflection as a problem-solving approach leading to deliberate action is compelling, the idea is not without its vagaries: Is all reflection of the same value? Are there times when reflection is more useful than others? Does one "learn" to reflect? What is most useful to reflect upon? Another question involves the directionality of reflection: Must reflection always involve look-

*National Reading Conference Yearbook, **50**, pp. 394–408.*

ing back upon past instruction, or may it, as Noordhoff and Kleinfeld (1988) suggest, also include the ability to look forward and spin out potential consequences of one's actions, and thus evaluate instructional decisions *prior* to interaction with students? Such questions precipitated this 3-year study.

First Year Findings

Context

During the study's first year, Center tutors used an adaptation of Don Holdaway's (1984) Lesson Plan Guide. Holdaway's original five steps were maintained (Tune-In, Old Favorites, Learning About Language, New Story, Independent Reading/Writing), and a sixth step was added to encourage reflection after the tutoring session. Prior to tutoring, tutors completed the first five steps of the lesson plan and handed plans to the course instructor for written feedback. Plans were returned to tutors before each tutoring session. Feedback included suggestions for refining activities to better meet specific client needs. Immediately after teaching, tutors completed the reflection section of the lesson plan and returned the entire plan to the instructor for further feedback. Tutors also submitted plans for the next session at this time, allowing the instructor to discern possible connections between current and future sessions. Throughout the course, instructor feedback included questions designed to prompt reflection, such as: "Why did you choose this activity?" "Why do you think this went well?" and "Will you use this activity again?—Why?"

Because the first year of the study was designed to investigate reflection and its role in instructor effectiveness, reflection was discussed during the seminar portion of the tutoring course, but not taught directly. Rather, study participants were simply encouraged to reflect upon lesson activities, objectives, and interactions and consider those reflections in their plans.

Client Growth for Study Year 1

Client growth was determined through a pre- and post-test format. Two months before entering the Community Reading Center for tutoring, potential clients completed an assessment battery administered by graduate students enrolled in a literacy assessment course. Scores on these assessments were then compared with assessments given during the last week of tutoring the following semester. For the purposes of this report, students are identified by ethnicity, age, gender, and assigned grade level at school (see Table 1). While other assessments were administered (depending upon client characteristics), the Slosson (SIT-R) scores (Slosson, 1991) and results of the Classroom Assessment of Reading Processes (CARP) informal reading inventory (Swearingen & Allen, 1997) are included here because they were common to almost all clients. It is important to note that the SIT-R was interpreted only as an indicator of verbal experience with concepts common to traditional schooling, and not as an I.Q. measure. CARP scores are designated by the test authors as independent reading levels (unless noted oth-

Table 1

SDSU Community Reading Center Client Progress 1997–1998, Study Year 1

ID	Eth	Age[a]	Grade	Gender	Slosson	Pre IRI	Post IRI	IRI Gain
1	His	6.0	1	M	86	*	**	NA
2	Cau	7.5	2	F	104	PP	Gr 3.5	3.5
3	Cau	7.6	2	M	99	PP	Gr 1	1
4	His	8.2	3	M	110	Gr 1	Gr 2	1
5	AA	8.8	3	M	93	PP	Gr 2	2
6	Cau	8.9	3	M	130	Gr 1	Gr 3[b]	2
7	Cau	9.0	3	M	119	Gr 1	Gr 3[b]	2
8	AA	9.11	5	F	95	Gr 2	Gr 3	1
9	AA	10.1	5	F	109	PP	Gr 3	3
10	Cau	10.1	5	M	115	Gr 4	Gr 4[c]	0
11	AA	10.7	6	F	94	Gr 4	Gr 5.5	1.5
12	AA	11.5	6	F	90	Gr 2	Gr 3	1
13	Cau	11.8	6	F	91	Gr 4	Gr 6[b]	2
14	Cau	12.0	6	F	71	Gr 3	Gr 2	-1
15	Cau	12.2	6	F	98	Gr 3	Gr 5	2
16	Cau	12.3	7	F	114	Gr 5	Gr 6	1
17	Cau	12.7	7	F	102	Gr 2	Gr 5	3
18	AA	14.9	9	M	51	Gr 1	Gr 1	0
19	Cau	16.7	11	M	102	Gr 5	Gr 6	1
Averages		10.5	5		99	2.1	3.6	1.4
SD		2.7			17.6	1.7	1.7	1.1

[a]Given in years and months (e.g., 6.0=6 years 0 months).
[b]At grade level.
[c]Client was upset by a home problem on day of posttesting, scores do not likely reflect actual reading growth.
*Identified 20 letters and no sounds. **Identified 26 letters and their sounds.

erwise). Because all assessments were administered by graduate students (under the supervision of a course instructor), the reported scores should be viewed only as rough indicators of client growth.

Tutor Reflections

Grounded theory analysis of tutor reflections in Year 1 offered somewhat surprising and discouraging results (Bayles Martin, LaMaster, & Vinge, 1999). Overall, tutors reflected on a surface level, simply reporting sessions. Reflection remained minimal even amidst instructor requests for more detail. Further, tutors rarely linked one lesson plan with the next, except to repeat particular activities for a time (e.g., using the same Tune-In activity for several sessions). Tutors also altered routines suddenly, without explanation.

The fact that tutors' writings tended more toward reporting than what we viewed as reflection highlighted the need to adopt an operational definition of reflection to guide tutors' planning and reflection efforts during Years 2 and 3. The operational definition of reflection for this study was drawn from Noordhoff and Kleinfeld (1988) and included five components.

Operational Definition of Reflection: Five Aspects

Reflection begins as one *names and frames a situational issue or problem* worthy of consideration. During Study Year 1, tutors labeled activities their clients enjoyed as "successful," but rarely engaged in deeper consideration about WHY something went well, if it should be used again, or if it truly supported a client's literacy growth. Interventions that did not result in positive client/teacher affect were generally dropped from future tutoring sessions with little or no analysis. Whereas we agreed with Cinnamond and Zimpher (1988) that dissonance between tutor expectations and actual session events was a natural place for reflection to occur, it appeared that our tutors avoided writing about negative events, thus circumventing deeper processing of their causes. This avoidance suggested that tutors might benefit from being required to address all aspects of a lesson.

Appraising the worth of goals is the second step in reflection. During Study Year 1, tutors often implemented an intervention technique immediately after it was introduced in class, regardless of client needs. This suggested a conflict between helping the client and becoming a Reading Specialist familiar with a number of intervention strategies. Sometimes it appeared that tutors "tested" techniques on clients merely for the practice—but without actually identifying this as their goal. Although such experimentation may be defensible, I was concerned that tutors seemed unaware of multiple and/or competing goals for their actions.

Another concern was helping tutors select the most useful intervention for a given client. Our clients arrive with a number of reading and writing challenges, and determining where to begin intervention can be overwhelming even for an experienced clinician. Incorporating a simple checklist into the lesson planning process seemed a reasonable way to help tutors consider more balanced approaches to their tutoring plans.

The third operational aspect of reflection requires *sorting of images and selecting strategies* to address them. Once a tutor selects a reflection issue and develops possible interpretations for it, it is time to determine the most plausible frame and select an appropriate strategy to address it. I found it necessary in Years 2 and 3 to spend a fair amount of class time reminding tutors that their first interpretation of a child's literacy challenge might not be the only or even the most plausible explanation.

For example, one tutor determined that her client did not like writing because she routinely laid her head on the table whenever a writing task was introduced. The tutor undertook several motivational activities to increase the client's willingness to write, all to no avail. As class members considered other possible frames for this behavior, they suggested that the client could be tired, hungry, or have vision problems. When the tutor checked with the client's mother, she discovered that the child had been fitted with glasses but did not wear them. Her apparently negative affect was attributable not so much to disliking writing as being unable to see what was written. Seeking alternative explanations for client (and tutor) behavior consistently challenged tutors; they tended to interpret unexpected or undesired behaviors as negative and avoided wrestling with these areas. This avoidance behavior highlighted the necessity of creating a safe and emotionally supportive environment where tutors could take the risks of dealing with potentially painful ideas.

The fourth operational aspect of reflection involves *spinning out consequences of the selected strategy.* Year 1 study data were most bleak in this area. As noted above, tutors often chose an intervention strategy without articulating selection criteria or expectations. When asked what they would do during the session if the strategy proved ineffective, they remained mute. Tutors seemed to succumb to "strategy worship," believing that any strategy presented in class was robust enough to address the needs of any or all clients. This sense of the all-powerful strategy suggested a need for tutors to assume greater evaluative control over their teaching choices.

Finally, the fifth operational aspect of reflection is *re-viewing and revising.* Year 1 data suggested that tutors reviewed their sessions at a cursory level ("It went well"), and there was little data suggesting planful strategy revision. Indeed, electronic bids to re-view strategies and events generally went unanswered, as did those written on tutors' lesson plans (Bayles Martin et al., 1999). Further, the notion of revising a plan during teaching was relatively rare—tutors generally made a plan and stuck with it, or abandoned it in its entirety—but they rarely altered a plan during a session to meet various contingencies as they arose.

Changes for Study Years 2 and 3

As I reflected on Year 1 findings with colleagues and with students who had just completed the course, two specific changes were indicated for Years 2 and 3. The first involved greater support in lesson planning. During Year 1 of the study, I selected Holdaway's (1984) frame specifically because it was open-ended and would thus honor what I viewed as my students' extensive backgrounds in lesson planning. I had feared that too directive a frame would offend these practicing teachers. To my surprise, students were vocal in their desire for greater support in lesson planning—noting the overload they felt in trying to learn a number of literacy interventions as well as place them in a logical and useful sequence for a particular client.

The second change arose from the dearth of apparent reflection data in Year 1 of the study. Because I believed that tutors were reflecting more deeply about their teaching than was apparent through lesson plans, e-mails, and other written efforts analyzed, I wondered if perhaps I had failed to structure data sources to capture this thinking. I decided that I needed to take a more directive role as course instructor and require students to deal with all aspects of their lessons rather than only those they self-selected.

The Triple Transfer Lesson Plan as a Reflection and Tutoring Aid

To address these issues, I devised the Triple Transfer Lesson Plan (TTLP) for Study Years 2 and 3 (Bayles Martin, 2000, 2001). Like most lesson planning guides, the TTLP includes a component for reflecting after a lesson is taught. What is unique in its design, however, is the provision for reflection *before* teaching—asking tutors to spin out possible consequences of their instructional decisions and plan for possible contingencies *prior* to entering a tutoring session. A second unique feature is the inclusion of a transmediation activity (Siegel, 1983, cited in Reutzel & Cooter, 1992) in every tutoring session to help students gain flexibility with new literacy concepts (Bayles Martin, 2000). A third unique feature is the specific scripting of a lesson goal that is explicitly shared with Center clients in a number of ways throughout the lesson (Bayles Martin, 2000, 2001).

The TTLP was piloted with a group of graduate students in 1999 and used again in 2000. In the next sections, the TTLP will be described, client growth data from Years 2 and 3 of the study will be presented, and preliminary observations regarding teacher reflection using the TTLP will be discussed.

Briefly described, the TTLP helps tutors plan a 1-hour tutoring session comprised of six specific activities. To avoid planning ruts (e.g., selecting the same opening activity for every session because another one does not come easily to mind), the form includes a number of prompts, listing instructional strategies tutors already know or which will be presented in course readings and meetings (the first page of the two-page TTLP appears in Figure 1). Once a strategy is selected, a specific instructional objective and method of measurement is determined. Again, the lesson plan provides structured prompts for these areas. The tutor next plans for three contingencies that may occur during each lesson activity: (a) what to do if the client encounters difficulty, (b) what to do if the client is successful (e.g., the activity fails to challenge the client), and (c) what to do if the client appears neutral (e.g., it is difficult to tell from the client's response whether the activity is suited to the client's needs).

The second part of the TTLP involves a structured response grid which requires tutors to reflect on each activity in specific categories: (a) how the client responded to the activity and why that may have occurred, (b) whether the instructional objective was met and how that is determined, and (c) whether the planned contingencies were of use during the lesson (see Figure 2). The tutor also determines whether he or she would use the same approach or a similar activity in the next lesson and why. Tutors are encouraged to note how they feel about each activity and examine the source(s) of those feelings. They are also encouraged to note ideas that occur during a session on the plan as they teach or immediately after the lesson is over.

Triple Transfer Lesson Planning Guide (TTLP)
Debra Bayles Martin, Ph.D., 2000

Date: ________ Clinician: ____________ Client: ____________ Client's Grade: ______ Room No. & Time: 4:00 p.m. 5:00 p.m.

Today's Instructional Goal (in one sentence):

Activity 1: Warm-Up (Plan 1-2 activities, one of which is lesson-related and clearly connects to the most recent session.) (Time: 5-10 minutes)

Activity Description and Materials	Activity Goal	Contingencies
List the name of the selection/game on the lines provided. If your choice is not here, write it in. ☐ Chant, read, sing favorite poem, song, jingle… ☐ Add motions or musical accompaniment to a reading ☐ Act out a short story/poem with puppets or other materials ☐ Read together an "Old Favorite" selected by the client ☐ Dictate or take dictation of fun jingle, rhyme, poem, riddle… ☐ Alter a familiar text to create a new piece ☐ Play a language game such as Scrabble, Boggle, etc. ☐ Alternate Activity: ________ What we'll read/play: ________	We are doing this activity because/to ________ How will you know you've reached your goal? ________	What will you do if your: Client encounters difficulty? ________ Client is successful? ________ Client's response is neutral? ________

Activity 2: Modeling (Demonstrate what fluent reading/writing look and feel like and why each is enjoyable.) (Time: 10 minutes)

Activity Description and Materials	Activity Goal	Contingencies
Circle your choice. If it is not featured below, write it in. ☐ Read aloud to client to model fluent reading ☐ Neurological Impress ☐ Choral Reading ☐ Take dictation from the client (as in LEA) ☐ "Share the pen" with the client ☐ Listen to a commercial recording with/without a text ☐ Computer software (list) ________ ☐ Other: ________ What we'll read/write: ________	We are doing this activity because/to ________ How will you know you've reached your goal? ________	What will you do if your: Client encounters difficulty? ________ Client is successful? ________ Client's response is neutral? ________

Activity 3: Explicit Skill/Strategy Transfer [Work from a whole text to a part (skill/strategy) and back to the whole. This experience should help your client see a way to be a better reader or writer.] (Time: 10 minutes)

Activity Description and Materials	Activity Goal	Contingencies
Mark the strategy area with an X and describe specifically on the lines below. ☐ Word Recognition (Sight, Context, Phonics, Structural Analysis, Reference Materials) ☐ Vocabulary Development (Listening, Speaking, Reading, Writing) ☐ Narrative Comprehension (Before, During, After, Sharing Literature) ☐ Expository Comprehension (Before, During, After, Strategies) ☐ Writing Specific Strategy: ________ What we'll read/write: ________	We are doing this activity because/to ________ How will you know you've reached your goal? ________	What will you do if your: Client encounters difficulty? ________ Client is successful? ________ Client's response is neutral? ________

Figure 1. Triple Transfer Lesson Planning Guide (Activities 1–3)

Triple Transfer Lesson Plan REFLECTION Guide: Spring 2000

- ☐ **We achieved today's Instructional Goal.**
- ☐ **We did not achieve today's Instructional Goal.**

Date: ________ Clinician: ______________________________ Client: ____________________

Activity 1: Warm-Up

Reflections on Activity Selection	Reflections on Activity Goal	Reflections on Contingencies
The activity selection was: ☐ Right on ☐ Close ☐ Neutral ☐ A little off ☐ Way off ☐ The activity was great, but my client was ________ ☐ Other: ________ ☐ I'll use this activity next time because ________ ________ ☐ I'm going to use a different activity next time because ____ ________	I think this goal was met/not met because: My measure of this goal was ________ because ________ ________ ________ ________	My contingency plan was: ☐ Successful because ________ ________ ☐ Neutral because ________ ________ ☐ Not useful because ________ ________

Activity 2: Modeling

Reflections on Activity Selection	Reflections on Activity Goal	Reflections on Contingencies
The activity selection was: ☐ Right on ☐ Close ☐ Neutral ☐ A little off ☐ Way off ☐ The activity was great, but my client was ________ ☐ Other: ________ ☐ I'll use this activity next time because ________ ________ ☐ I'm going to use a different activity next time because ____ ________	I think this goal was met/not met because: My measure of this goal was ________ because ________ ________ ________ ________	My contingency plan was: ☐ Successful because ________ ________ ☐ Neutral because ________ ________ ☐ Not useful because ________ ________

Activity 3: Explicit Skill/Strategy Instruction

Reflections on Activity Selection	Reflections on Activity Goal	Reflections on Contingencies
The activity selection was: ☐ Right on ☐ Close ☐ Neutral ☐ A little off ☐ Way off ☐ The activity was great, but my client was ________ ☐ Other: ________ ☐ I'll use this activity next time because ________ ________ ☐ I'm going to use a different activity next time because ____ ________	I think this goal was met/not met because: My measure of this goal was ________ because ________ ________ ________ ________	My contingency plan was: ☐ Successful because ________ ________ ☐ Neutral because ________ ________ ☐ Not useful because ________ ________

Figure 2. Reflection Guide for Triple Transfer Lesson Plan (Activities 1–3)

Methods and Data Sources for Study Years 2 and 3

During both 1999 and 2000, my graduate assistants and I provided direct instruction in using the TTLP and helped participants complete lesson plans in small groups and individually. All graduate assistants completed the tutoring course the year prior to assisting. The 1999 assistant did not use the TTLP during her tutoring course (as it had not yet been developed), but she did use it a semester later when she tutored students for another course. All TTLP instruction focused on three issues: (a) how to look back to each activity of a just-taught lesson and evaluate its effectiveness, (b) how to look forward to the next lesson and spin out possible consequences of an instructional decision and thereby determine on-line contingencies for teaching, and (c) how to consider experience with the TTLP in settings beyond the Reading Center (i.e., their own classrooms).

Data sources included copies of all TTLP forms completed by each tutor as well as fieldnotes taken by the course instructor and graduate assistants. Fieldnotes included tutoring observations, as well as experiences with tutors as they completed TTLPs in class. The course instructor and graduate assistants regularly observed tutors' actual instruction to document instructional effectiveness and adherence to lesson plans. As in Study Year 1, client pre- and post-tests provided evidence of tutors' instructional effectiveness. Tutors each completed 24–26 1-hour tutoring sessions with their assigned client during the study period. Fourteen tutors were followed in Study Year 2, and 23 tutors informed Year 3.

Data Analysis and Results

Client growth data for Study Years 2 and 3 were tabulated in the same manner as for Study Year 1. These data were then examined using the SPSS statistics program for personal computers (Windows Standard Version 7.5.1, 1996) to determine whether significant differences existed between client growth in Years 2 and 3 as compared with Year 1. Tables 2 and 3 outline the basic descriptive data for client growth. The third edition of the Bader Reading and Language Inventory (Bader, 1998) was used during the second and third year of the study for pre- and post-test reading measures.

In contrast to Study Year 1, average client gains in Study Year 2 were almost one grade level greater (1.2 compared to 2.1). Because tutors knew a new lesson plan format was being used in Study Year 2, a second year of TTLP implementation was undertaken to address a possible Hawthorne effect. Client growth was similar in Study Year 3, averaging 2.3 grade levels.

To determine whether groups differed across study years, comparisons were completed for Study Years 1, 2, and 3 by age, ethnicity, gender, verbal language experience (as represented by SIT-R scores) and informal reading inventory pretest scores using the SPSS General Linear Models procedure. No significant differences were found among groups on any of these measures.

Analysis of the informal reading inventory posttest scores by study year yielded a significant difference for both grade (p=.000) and study year (p=.040).

Table 2

SDSU Community Reading Center Client Progress 1998–1999, Study Year 2

ID	Eth	Age[a]	Grade	Gender	Slosson	Pre IRI	Post IRI	IRI Gain
1	AA	7.1	2	M	91	Gr 1	Gr 3[b]	2
2	His	9.1	3	F	77	*	Gr 2 (Ind)	3
3	Cau	9.1	4	M	NA	Gr 1	Gr 3	2
4	Cau	9.2	3	M	100	Gr 2	Gr 4[b]	2
5	Cau	9.6	3	M	86	*	Gr 1	2
6	Cau	9.6	4	M	99	Gr 2	Gr 4[b]	2
7	AA	9.8	4	M	93	Gr 2	Gr 4[b]	2
8	Cau	10.0	4	M	93	Gr 3	Gr 3	0
9	Cau	10.5	5	M	116	Gr 4	Gr 6[b]	2
10	Cau	11.1	5	M	93	Gr 3	Gr 5[b]	2
11	His	12.2	7	F	92	Gr 5	Gr 7[b]	2
12	Cau	13.0	7	F	81	Gr 4	Gr 6	2
13	Cau	16.11	11	M	64	Gr 4	Gr 7	3
14	Cau	28.7	12	M	105	Gr 8	Gr 12[b]	4
Averages		11.9	5		92	2.8		2.1
SD		5.4			13	2.2		.9

Note. Grade levels are given at the instructional level unless indicated otherwise (Fr = frustrational).
[a]Given in years and months (e.g., 6.0=6 years 0 months).
[b]At or above grade level.
*Scored below PP.

The interaction between grade and study year was not significant (p=.185). Scheffe post hoc comparisons indicated that informal reading inventory posttest scores for Year 1 differed significantly from those for Year 2 (p=.035) and from Year 3 (p=.012), whereas scores from Years 2 and 3 did not differ significantly (p=.99).

Because there was a change in assessment instruments between Year 1 and 2 (from CARP to Bader), an analysis of gains on the informal reading inventories was completed. The Year 1 assessment ranked students at their independent reading levels, while the assessment for Years 2 and 3 ranked students at their instructional reading levels. This could have resulted in higher pretest scores associated with students in Year 1 and lower pretest scores in Years 2–3. Use of gain scores rather than posttest scores helps address this problem. A General Linear Models procedure analyzing gain scores by study year approached significance at the p=.06 level (see Table 4). A post hoc comparison (Scheffe) indicated that gain scores for Study Year 1 and 3 differed at a level of p=.08, whereas Study Years 1 and 2 did not differ significantly (p=.20). Although client growth scores failed to reach significance at the .05 level, the differences were extremely close to significance, especially given the small sample size. Further, the effect size (delta) for mean differences between Year 1 and Year 2 was 0.563 and 0.713

Table 3

SDSU Community Reading Center Client Progress 1999–2000, Study Year 3

ID	Eth	Age[a]	Grade	Gender	Slosson	Pre IRI	Post IRI	IRI Gain
1	Hisp	6.5	1	F	97	*	PP	.5
2	Cau	6.11	2	M	120	PP	Gr 3 (Ind)[b]	3.5
3	Cau	7.9	2	F	126	P	Gr 1	1
4	AA	8.5	3	M	98	Gr 2	Gr 4 (Ind)[b]	2.5
5	Other	8.6	3	M	107	Gr 3	Gr 4.5[b]	1.5
6	AA	8.8	3	F	98	Gr 1	Gr 4[b]	3
7	Cau	8.10	3	F	98	P	4*	4
8	AA	8.10	3	M	108	Gr 2	Gr 3 (Ind)[b]	1.5
9	Hisp	8.11	3	F	109	Gr 3 (Ind)	Gr 5[b]	1.5
10	Hisp	9.3	3	M	97	Gr 2 (Ind)	Gr 4 (Ind)[b]	2
11	Cau	10.1	4	M	119	Gr 5	Gr 7[b]	2
12	Hisp	10.6	5	F	75	Gr 4	Gr 5 (Ind)[b]	1.5
13	Cau	10.9	5	F	109	Gr 4	Gr 5 (Ind)[b]	1.5
14	Cau	11.2	5	M	93	Gr 3	Gr 4	1
15	Cau	11.4	6	M	83	Gr 3	Gr 4 (Ind)	1.5
16	AA	11.6	6	M	107	P	Gr 3	2.5
17	AA	12.4	7	F	84	Gr 4	Gr 5	1
18	Phil	12.4	7	F	97	Gr 4 (Ind)	Gr 8 (Ind)[b]	4.5
19	Cau	12.4	7	M	NA	Gr 4	Gr 8[b]	4
20	Cau	12.7	7	F	NA	Gr 5	Gr 8[b]	3
21	Other	13.5	8	M	90	Gr 4	Gr 8 (Ind)[b]	4.5
22	Cau	14.6	8	F	75	NA	NA	NA
23	Cau	18	12	M	64	NA	NA	NA
Averages		10.5	5		98	2.6	4.9	2.3
SD		2.8				1.7	2.2	1.2

Note. Grade levels are given at the instructional level unless indicated otherwise (Ind=independent, Fr=frustrational).
[a]Given in years and months (e.g., 6.0=6 years, 0 months).
[b]At or above grade level.
*Scored below PP.

between Year 1 and Year 3. Effect sizes of .5 are generally considered meaningful with respect to educational interventions.

Discussion of Client Growth and Preliminary Analysis of Reflection Data

The TTLP was designed to support client literacy growth through enhanced teacher reflection. Client gain scores for Study Years 2 and 3 are encouraging and suggest that further research with the TTLP is warranted—at least as related to client literacy growth. The next step for the larger study will involve detailing the role of the TTLP in enhancing teacher reflection. A confounding variable in this

Table 4

Tests of Between-Subjects Effects for Informal Reading Inventory Posttest by Study Year and Grade Level

Source	Type III Sum of Squares	*df*	Mean Square	*F*	Sig.	Eta Squared
Grade	163.614	10	16.361	10.241	.000*	.762
Study Year	11.440	2	5.720	3.580	.040*	.183
Grade by Study Year	19.604	8	2.450	1.534	.185	.277
Error	51.124	32	1.598			
Corrected Total	265.679	52				

$^{*}p \leq .05$.

study will likely be the fact that the TTLP was designed to address both client growth and teacher reflection. While the TTLP apparently meets the goal of addressing client growth, it may be difficult to determine exactly how that occurs. Should further analysis indicate that the TTLP is also successful in enhancing teacher reflection, questions arise as to whether client growth increases because of greater teacher reflection, the specificity and order of outlined activities in the plan, or perhaps a combination of the two. Although all teacher reflection data are not yet analyzed, some initial analysis has been completed and may offer preliminary insights into at least part of this complex question.

A grounded theory approach was used to survey the effects of the TTLP on teacher reflection and efficacy (Strauss & Corbin, 1990). Lesson plans were selected for a purposive sample of six tutors from Study Years 2 and 3 whose clients showed the greatest gains, the greatest reversals, or no gain. Upon completion of initial scanning for themes, informal interviews regarding the TTLP and its effects were conducted with these teachers to verify emerging themes. Although a grounded theory analysis will be completed on all TTLP forms and accompanying field notes during the next year and reported at a later date, four basic findings emerged. These were: (a) the value of greater lesson planning structure and support for new clinicians, (b) the difficulty of determining objective measurement criteria for lesson activities, (c) the challenges and rewards of learning to reflect forward and plan for contingencies, and (d) the developmental nature of reflection.

Lesson Planning: Structure and Support

When the TTLP was first introduced in Study Year 2, tutors appeared to appreciate its structure, and tended to utilize a greater variety of teaching strategies than their Year 1 peers. The structure of the TTLP provided prompts and supported tutors in drawing upon course materials to enhance and individualize their lesson plans. Tutors often commented on the check-off format, saying, "I think I'll try _____ this time—I had forgotten about that."

Difficulty in Determining Objective Measurements

Although tutors readily completed TTLP sections requiring an activity choice and its accompanying instructional objective, they had difficulty articulating how they would know if an objective was met. Early lesson plans contained vague measurement notions (e.g., "She'll write paying attention to sounds"). Although class members were vocal about writing behavioral objectives during preservice programs, they also confided that they rarely determined lesson success by objective criteria after student teaching. The fact that study teachers often judged lesson success by perceived student affect appears to be an issue that can and should be addressed in clinical settings. My sense as course instructor is that over time, many, but not all tutors grasped the fact that client growth should not be judged solely on perceived student affect. I look forward to further data analysis in this area to determine when and how evidence for this insight appears on each tutor's TTLP forms.

Challenges of Reflecting Forward and Planning for Contingencies

Although determining how to judge achievement of lesson objectives was difficult for most tutors, the contingency section of the TTLP was even more challenging. The idea of planning contingencies for a successful activity was especially confusing. "What do you mean?" tutors would ask. "Isn't student success the whole point of our lessons?" During both years, it took 3 to 6 weeks for most tutors to understand that an "easy" activity might be focused beneath a client's zone of proximal development. Although occasional "easy" activities may help build client confidence and motivation, a consistent diet of such activities may not appropriately challenge the client, therefore limiting the benefits of the tutoring period.

Tutors also found it difficult to plan for the "neutral" contingency. The idea behind this contingency is that many interpretations are possible when a student fails to engage in an activity. Perhaps the activity appears too easy and the client, offended, fails to engage. This is often observed with teenage clients reading far below expected grade level. In contrast, a planned activity may appear too difficult to a client who lacks confidence, or who regularly invokes behaviors of learned helplessness to avoid revealing a perceived lack of skill. Sometimes clients may not understand what is desired, and withhold participation pending more information. Any of these eventualities (and others) can block the effectiveness of an activity.

Planning ways to address some of these possibilities ahead of time allows a tutor to be better prepared (thus increasing a sense of efficacy and decreasing anxiety) and also increases the chance that the teacher will alter the activity online to achieve its goal. It is my sense that the growing ability among tutors to alter a session "on-line" rather than to wait for the next meeting was an important factor in maximizing client success at the Center. Interactions with tutors from Study Years 2 and 3 suggest that as tutors gained facility in planning for all three contingencies, their sense of efficacy as literacy tutors grew. They entered tutoring sessions feeling fully prepared, and often saw their ability to successfully and planfully alter an activity *during* the lesson as a mark of growing expertise.

Reflection as Developmental

Preliminary data analysis of TTLP forms supports the notion that reflection may be developmental (Bayles Martin et al., 1999; Stahlhut & Hawkes, 1997). Further, the ability to reflect forward and spin out consequences of future instructional plans seems to appear after a tutor develops facility with reflecting on past lessons.

Future Directions

Taken together with data from the first year of this study (Bayles Martin et al., 1999), findings from Study Years 2 and 3 suggest that both novice and veteran teachers experience significant anxiety when asked to teach in a new setting such as a Reading Center. Working with a structured lesson plan such as the TTLP and learning to create contingency plans prior to tutoring sessions resulted in increased client literacy growth. Preliminary data analysis also suggests that using the TTLP enabled teachers to feel more prepared for "the unexpected"—thus decreasing teacher anxiety and increasing personal efficacy.

Future data analysis from this and related studies should focus on how teachers develop specific contingency planning and reflection skills and how these skills impact instructional plans and delivery. Further testing of lesson plan formats (such as the TTLP) which require that teachers not only look back at their practice, but also look forward to spin out instructional contingencies in specific, explicit ways appears warranted. This testing could include plans with a different order of activities or with alternate activities, etc. Systematic variations would enable researchers to determine the most important aspects of lesson planning and teacher reflection for clinical settings. Finally, provision should be made to check for transferability of clinical experience to other settings. Retrospective interviews are planned with participants in this study to determine the extent to which aspects of the tutoring course influence day-to-day teaching at other sites. Other such connections across sites and over time should also be investigated to determine how reflection, as operationally defined here, affects teachers who embrace its tenets.

References

Ash, T. (1993). *Reflective teaching, What am I doing? Why am I doing it this way?* Instructional Strategies Series No. 11. Saskatchewan: The Saskatchewan Instructional Development and Research Unit and The Saskatchewan Professional Development Unit. (ERIC Document Reproduction Service No. ED 360 309)

Bader, L. A. (1998). *Bader reading and language inventory* (3rd ed.). Upper Saddle River, NJ: Merrill.

Bayles Martin, D. (2000, May). *Successful literacy intervention for learners of all ages:*

Planning for triple transfer and closure using the Triple Transfer Lesson Plan (TTLP). Paper presented at the meeting of the International Reading Association, Indianapolis, IN.

Bayles Martin, D. (2001). *Triple transfer and closure: Successful literacy intervention for learners of all ages.* Manuscript in preparation.

Bayles Martin, D., LaMaster, K., & Vinge, S. (1999). An exploration of guided reflection using interdisciplinary intervention and electronic expression. In T. Shanahan and F. Rodriguez-Brown (Eds.), *National Reading Conference Yearbook, 48* (pp. 398–411). Chicago: National Reading Conference.

Cinnamond, J., & Zimpher, N. (1988). Reflectivity as a function of community: An analysis of teacher socialization and the reflective process. In H. C. Waxman, H. J. Freiberg, J. C. Vaughan, & M. Weil (Eds.), *Images of reflection in teacher education* (pp. 16–17). Reston, VA: Association of Teacher Educators.

Holdaway, D. (1984). *Stability and change in literacy learning.* Portsmouth, NH: Heinemann.

Noordhoff. K., & Kleinfeld, J. (1988). Rethinking the rhetoric of "reflective inquiry" in teacher education programs. In H. C. Waxman, H. J. Freiberg, J. C. Vaughan, & M. Weil (Eds.), *Images of reflection in teacher education* (pp. 27–29). Reston, VA: Association of Teacher Educators.

Reutzel, D. R., & Cooter, R. B., Jr. (1992). *Teaching children to read from basals to books.* New York: Merrill.

Schon, D. A. (1983). *The reflective practitioner.* New York: Basic.

Slosson, R. L. (1991). *Slosson intelligence test SIT-R.* Aurora, NY: Slosson.

Stahlhut, R. G., & Hawkes, R. R. (1997, February). *An examination of reflective thinking through a study of written journals, telecommunications, and personal conferences.* Paper presented at the meeting of the Association for Teacher Educators, Washington, D.C.

Strauss, A., & Corbin, J. (1990). *Basics of qualitative research.* Newbury Park, CA: Sage.

Swearingen, R., & Allen, D. (1997). *Classroom assessment of reading processes (CARP).* Boston: Houghton-Mifflin.

Vogt, L. A., & Au, K. H. P. (1995). The role of teachers' guided reflection in effective positive program change. *Bilingual Research Journal, 19,* 101–120.

Whitford, B., Schlechty, P., & Shelor, L. (1987). Sustaining action research through collaboration: Inquiries for invention. *Peabody Journal of Education, 64,* 151–169.

A Review of Research on Children's Responses to Literature

Miriam G. Martinez
University of Texas at San Antonio

Nancy L. Roser
University of Texas at Austin

Only in the final quarter of the twentieth century did researchers begin to grapple, to any significant extent, with the ways in which children (rather than older readers) respond to literary texts (Martinez & Roser, 1991). In this paper, we synthesize this now-burgeoning strand of research on children's responses to literature. Based on a review of more than 100 investigations conducted between 1978 and 2000, we report: (a) changes in perspective on what constitutes response, (b) the increasingly diverse methodologies and approaches used to investigate children's literary meaning-making, and (c) key findings that have emerged from the research.

Approach

To produce this review, we selected Arthur Applebee's (1978) and Janet Hickman's (1979, 1981) seminal studies as the launch point for research directed toward understanding children's literary thinking. To locate potentially relevant research, we surveyed the tables of content of major language/literacy journals published in the United States for the subsequent 20-year period (including *Research in the Teaching of English, Reading Research Quarterly, Language Arts, Journal of Literacy Research,* and others). Next, we used the bibliographies of the located studies, reports, and essays to locate other potentially relevant published works. We limited our review to studies with subjects no older than middle schoolers

To create an initial description of the research, we read quickly to record for each piece its: (a) purpose/hypotheses, (b) description of subjects, (c) context, (d) methodology, and (e) significant findings. We then reread the studies to identify those works that seemed to ask significant questions and appeared to have been systematic in their approaches to addressing those questions.

Like Purves and Beach (1972) who produced their comprehensive review of research on responses to literature almost 30 years ago, we were faced with two major problems: The first was finding some way of classifying the studies being examined; the second was weighing the merits of those studies. Following the

National Reading Conference Yearbook, ***50,*** *pp. 409–418.*

lead of Purves and Beach, we sorted the located set of studies using a classification system based on the studies themselves rather than on a preordained formulation. For examples, many reports addressed the nature of children's responses in particular contexts, the roles of the participants in literature discussion, or the organization of instruction to support children's responses.

As noted above, we gauged the contribution of any study from the importance of the question being considered—the conception of a worthwhile problem—rather than solely from the sophistication of the analyses. Because many of the studies summarized in this review were reported in the pages of journals intended for curriculum *implementers,* the studies often moved quickly from the evidence to the findings, so that the analysis of the data was often the least visible part of the report. We did not discount such studies intended primarily for a teacher audience; neither did we permit only one or two such studies to shape a category of evidence. Rather, as we restacked, we attempted to identify major themes, findings, and the state of knowledge based upon a preponderance of evidence necessary to make summative claims.

Results

Changes in Perspective on What Constitutes Response

From its beginnings in the late 1970s, research on children's responses to literature addressed the question of *how* children respond, a question researchers have continued to address. However, the perspectives from which the question has been addressed have changed dramatically. Much of the early research on children's responses to literature was shaped by a developmental focus as researchers sought to describe differences in how children talk about literature at different age levels (e.g., Applebee, 1978; Cullinan, Harwood, & Galda, 1983). For example, the category system Applebee (1978) developed to describe children's responses reflected a Piagetian perspective.

However, as literary response theory captured more attention in educational circles in the last decades of the twentieth century (Iser, 1980; Rosenblatt, 1938/1976, 1978), the earlier developmental perspective has been largely superseded. Researchers have increasingly drawn on their understanding of the literary response process to describe children's literary meaning-making. In contrast to earlier work, the category systems devised by later researchers reflected an understanding of reading as an aesthetic experience. For example, McGee (1992), building on the work of Garrison and Hynds (1991) and Eeds and Wells (1989), described her category system as representing "a continuum of responses from attention to evocation of readers' experiences and emotions to attention to the text" (p. 179). Similarly, Hancock (1993) developed a category system that reflected theoretical beliefs about the nature of the literary transaction; she identified three ways of approaching literary texts: Immersion, Self-Involvement, and Detachment.

Increased understanding of the social nature of learning has also influenced response research. Stemming from the influence of Vygotsky (1978) and others who consider the vital role that social development plays in shaping and clarifying language and thought, response researchers argued that the deepest levels of literary understanding are made possible though social interaction, or what Fish (1980) calls "interpretive communities." Working with these broader visions of response, researchers moved beyond merely describing children's literary meaning-making to "consider[ing] the purposes underlying various response types" (Beach & Hynds, 1991, p. 480) as well as attempting to understand how contexts and cultures nurture and support responses (Bloome & Bailey, 1992). The grounding of research in response theory and social constructivism has resulted in a more detailed picture of children's transactions with literature.

Changes in Methodologies and Approaches

Published research over the past two decades has also reflected increasingly diverse ways of investigating responses. As more researchers have focused on the nature of children's literary meaning-making, they have chosen diverse methodologies—from interview studies (e.g., Lehr, 1988) to case studies (e.g., McGill-Franzen & Lanford, 1994; McMahon, Pardo, & Raphael, 1991) to ethnographies (e.g., Hickman, 1981; McGinley & Kamberelis, 1996). Recently, researchers such as Almasi (1995) have undertaken more complex combinations of methodologies toward understanding how groups undertake literary meaning-making.

From a variety of inductive techniques for data analysis have come a number of different response classification schemes (e.g., Leal, 1992; McGee, 1992; Martinez, Roser, Hoffman, & Battle, 1992). This diversity of categorization systems makes the compilation of evidence across studies challenging. For example, we found ourselves pondering whether differences in findings across studies reflected actual differences in children's responses or simply ways of defining and labeling categories.

In addition, researchers have employed more innovative instructional strategies both to evoke and support responses in classrooms (e.g., Hancock, 1993; Kelly, 1990; Raphael & McMahon, 1994; Wollman-Bonilla & Werchadlo, 1995). Some of these strategies include free response journals, planned response prompts, discussion groups, selected text sets, and the study of literature through units (among others).

Finally, recent studies have inspected the responses of diverse groups of children—including prereaders, children learning English as their second language, handicapped children, and struggling readers involved in the process of response; researchers have looked at gender differences, and at the effects of culture on response (e.g., Cochran-Smith, 1984; Enciso, 1994; Evans, 1997; Goatley, Brock, & Raphael, 1995; Liaw, 1995; McGill-Franzen & Lanford, 1994; Morrow, 1988; Rice, 2000; Smith, 1995; Williams & McLean, 1997; Wollman-Bonilla, 1994). Changes in methodology, innovative analysis, and instructional interventions have contributed to a broadened view of the child as responder.

Summary of Research

From our review of over 100 studies of children's responses to literature, two key characteristics of children's responses to literature seemed to emerge: (a) children demonstrate a rich repertoire of responses that include both text-centered and reader-centered responses, and (b) children's responses are best nurtured in social contexts. In addition, we identified three characteristics of instruction that nurture children's responses: (a) teachers can shape children's responses through the organization of literature study, (b) children's responses during literature discussion are best nurtured when teachers and students assume different roles, and (c) a variety of instructional tools have been found to sustain children's responses.

Children respond in varied and distinct ways. Across studies, children seem to respond to literature in both text-centered and reader-centered ways. Text-centered responses—reflected in children's engagement in story worlds (Martinez and Roser, 1994)—have been shown to be active and dynamic, as children question, make predictions, interpret, and analyze as they read (Hancock, 1993; Sipe, 1998). Further, and in contrast to the work of earlier investigators (Applebee, 1979; Cullinan, Harwood, & Galda, 1983) who found that children respond to literature primarily at literal levels, more recent researchers have found even young children are able to analyze and make inferences about many facets of stories. For example, Lehr (1988) and McGee (1992) found that young children show sensitivity to story themes when the stories themselves are appropriate to the children's levels of understanding. Similarly, the young children in Sipe's (1998) study were able to analyze illustrations, narrative elements, the relationship between reality and fiction, and the language of stories. Children's text-focused responses also include their attention to the story as a crafted object (Kelly, 1990; Roser et al., 2000; Smolkin, 1995; Wollman-Bonilla, 1989). Children are especially likely to focus on the artistry of literature in contexts in which their attention is directed toward features of author and illustrator craft (Bloem & Manna, 1999; Kiefer, 1988; Madura, 1995).

Although text-centered responses constitute an important part of children's response repertoire, researchers have documented more reader-centered responses (e.g., Farest & Miller, 1993; Martinez et al., 1992; Raphael et al., 1992; Short, 1992; Sipe, 1998; Wollman-Bonilla, 1989). In these studies, children build bridges between their personal experiences and the literature they read, making what Cochran-Smith (1984) has termed "life-to-text" connections and Hickman (1981) has described as "personal associations." Other researchers, too, have shown that children become personally involved with characters as they vicariously step into roles and make judgments about how they would feel if they found themselves in a character's situation (Hancock, 1993; Wollman-Bonilla & Werchadlo, 1995). Children's personal experiences include their familiarity with other texts, helping to explain the intertextual connections they make when responding to literature (Farest & Miller, 1993; Short, 1992; Sipe, 1998). Investigations of children's responses also indicate that cultural experiences can be important in shaping response (Sims, 1983; Smith, 1995). And conversely, McGinley and Kamberelis (1996) found that the children in their investigation used literature as a lens through which they could better understand their own personal experiences and their world.

Not surprisingly, research characterizing the nature of children's responses has shown that children respond differently across age levels (Applebee, 1978; Hickman, 1981; Lehr, 1988; Many, 1991; Martincz & Roser, 1994). Yet, it is not clear the extent to which these differences reflect the influence of factors such as instructional context rather than developmental constraints. Like others, Lehr (1988) found that her subjects' previous experience with literature was a predictor of their ability to respond at higher levels. Further, researchers such as Galda (1982), Hancock (1993), McGinley and Kamberelis (1996), and Sipe, (1998) identified distinctive styles of response that point to the individual rather than the developmentally predetermined nature of children's transactions with literature.

Literary understanding is social in nature. Although there has been testimony to the need for children to work together in literature circles, book clubs, and discussion groups, there is not a great deal of evidence as to "how" children work together, or clear documentation of the effects of their thought and talk on one another. Nevertheless, some researchers have described what children actually do or accomplish collectively as they talk about literature in groups. Eeds and Wells (1989), for example, identified a number of ways in which children and teachers worked together as members of literature discussion groups: First, participants relied upon one another as they constructed meanings, even changing as they encountered different perspectives. Second, participants deepened their own understanding by sharing personal stories, which in turn shaped the text's significance for others. Third, participants engaged in a group inquiry process by predicting, confirming, and disconfirming; and finally, they engaged in collectively critiquing stories. In a similar fashion, the fourth graders in Almasi's (1995) investigation worked together to resolve their questions and confusions during literature discussion.

The organization of literature study shapes response. The instructional approach to literature study and the use of particular frameworks have also been found to positively affect children's responses (Many & Wiseman, 1992; O'Flahavan, 1989; Raphael & McMahon, 1994; Roser, Hoffman, & Farest, 1990; Wiseman, Many, & Altieri, 1992). For example, Raphael and McMahon (1994) designed literacy instruction with book clubs in which students engaged in reading, writing, "community share," and instruction. O'Flahavan (1989) designed an instructional framework he called "Conversational Discussion Groups" which allowed teachers to gradually relinquish their social and interpretive authority over discussions.

A related strand of response research has focused on the way in which unit approaches to the study of literature influence response. In her study of children's literary responses in literature-rich classrooms, Hickman (1981) found that children were most likely to make explicit connections among pieces of literature when the selections were part of literature study. Roser et al., (1990) provided books organized into literature units (focusing on author-, theme-, topic-, or genre-related works) and reported significant changes in children's range of literary connections. Short (1992), too, found that children made varied intertextual connections when she introduced children to text sets. Bloem and Manna (1999) organized instruction around an author study, and found that their second- and fourth-grade subjects responded aesthetically in rich and diverse ways. Although instructional frameworks have differed in their particular features, effective ones appear to reflect an instructional plan, often allow children to choose the books they read, and to read books in their entirety. In addition, regular "meetings" for talk about books, and opportunities to take the lead in sharing thoughts about stories are associated with effectiveness.

Roles in book discussion groups vary. A burgeoning strand of the research in the past decade has focused on the roles of participants—both student and teacher—and, less frequently, on the differences in those roles. Much of this research has investigated teachers in a less dominant role in discussion, suggesting that both the quality and quantity of students' talk are affected by carefully considered teacher roles (Almasi, 1995; Battle, 1993; Eeds & Wells, 1989; Frank, Dixon, & Brandts, 1998; McGee, 1992; Roser & Martinez, 1985). When working with first graders, McGee (1992) found that the insertion of a well-placed, teacher-framed "interpretive question" at the point at which discussion lags helps bring conversation to the essence of a story. Battle (1993) also found that the teacher contributes to bilingual kindergarten children's collaborative meaning-making by focusing on the content of responses rather than their forms, by encouraging responses throughout the read-aloud event, and by providing multiple invitations for children to speak. Investigating older children, Almasi (1995) reported that student-led discussion groups provided more opportunities than did teacher-led groups for students to work out meanings that were important to them. The critical question may not be whether the teacher should be present or absent in discussion groups, but rather what the target goals for the conversation are.

Other instructional procedures and tools support responses. Over the last decade, as authentic literature gained an increasingly integral role in classrooms, research focused on instructional strategies designed to mediate and sustain literary responses has also increased. Chief among the mediators that have been investigated are literary journals, response frameworks, and response prompts. The findings from a number of investigations of literature journals have converged to suggest that opportunities over time to write about literature in journals support growth in children's responses to literature (Farest & Miller, 1993; Kelly, 1990; Wollman-Bonilla, 1989; Wollman-Bonilla & Werchadlo, 1995). Further, researchers have found that literature journals and open-ended discussion frameworks nurture richer oral discussions of literature (Hubbard, Winterbourne, & Ostrow, 1996; Martinez et al., 1992; Raphael et al., 1992).

Significance of the Review

Over the period of this review, researchers have established a significant body of research on children's responses to literature. Future investigators will be able to build on this foundation as they work for greater understanding of children's literary meaning-making.

The researchers whose efforts are summarized in this review have themselves called for "more" of the many facets of research on response—more comparisons of children's oral and written responses, more investigations of the collaborative nature of literature study in classrooms, more investigations of different learner groups and different genre, more inspection of the contexts for literature study, and deeper understanding of both the participants' and texts' contributions to response. In considering the direction of future research, Rosenblatt (1985) has urged researchers to "reflect on the 'fit' of a problem into a broader perspective related to human development. . . ." (p. 51). We would add that researchers might also reflect on the broader curricular goals for children's literary study. By considering research questions in view of their broadest implications, investigations of the role of literature in classrooms of the twenty-first century are likely to produce teaching effects "that foster the capacity for more and more rewarding transactions between readers and text" (Rosenblatt, 1985, p. 51).

References

Almasi, J. F. (1995). The nature of fourth graders' sociocognitive conflicts in peer-led and teacher-led discussions of literature. *Reading Research Quarterly, 30,* 314–351.

Applebee, A. (1978). *The child's concept of story.* Chicago: University of Chicago Press.

Battle, J. (1993). Mexican-American bilingual kindergartners' collaborations in meaning making. In D. J. Leu & C. K. Kinzer (Eds.), *Examining central issues in literacy research, theory, and practice* (pp. 163–169). Forty-second yearbook of the National Reading Conference. Chicago: National Reading Conference.

Beach, R., & Hynds, S. (1991). Research on response to literature. In R. Barr, M. L. Kamil, P. Mosenthal, & P. D. Pearson (Eds.), *Handbook of reading research* (pp. 453–489). White Plains, NY: Longman.

Bloem, P. L., & Manna, A. L. (1999). A chorus of questions: Readers respond to Patricia Polacco. *Reading Teacher, 52,* 802–808.

Bloome, D., & Bailey, F. M. (1992). Studying language and literacy through events, particularity, and intertextuality. In R. Beach, J. L. Green, M. L. Kamil, & T. Shanahan (Eds.), *Multidisciplinary perspectives on literacy research* (pp. 181–210). Urbana, IL: National Conference on Research in English/National Council of Teachers of English.

Cochran-Smith, M. (1984). *The making of a reader.* Norwood, NJ: Ablex.

Cullinan, B., Harwood, K., & Galda, L. (1983). The reader and the story: Comprehension and response. *Journal of Research and Development in Education, 16,* 29–37.

Eeds, M., & Wells, D. (1989). Grand conversations: An exploration of meaning construction in literature study groups. *Research in the Teaching of English, 23,* 4–29.

Enciso, P. (1994). Cultural identity and response to literature: Running lessons from Maniac McGee. *Language Arts, 71,* 524–533.

Evans, K. S. (1997). Exploring the complexities of peer-led literature discussion: The influence of gender. In J. R. Paratore & R. L. McCormack (Eds.), *Peer talk in the classroom:*

Learning from research (pp. 156–173). Newark, DE: International Reading Association.

Farest, C., & Miller, C. (1993). Children's insights into literature: Using dialogue journals to invite literary response. In D. J. Leu & C. K. Kinzer (Eds.), *Examining central issues in literacy research, theory, and practice.* Forty-second yearbook of the National Reading Conference (pp. 271–278). Chicago: National Reading Conference.

Fish, S. (1980). *Is there a text in this class? The authority of interpretive communities.* Cambridge, MA: Harvard University Press.

Frank, C. R., Dixon, C. N., & Brandts, L. R. (1998). "Dear book club": A sociolinguistic and ethnographic analysis of literature discussion groups in second grade. In T. Shanahan & F. V. Rodriguez-Brown (Eds.), *National Reading Conference Yearbook, 47* (pp. 103–115). Chicago: National Reading Conference.

Galda, L. (1982). Assuming the spectator stance: An examination of the responses of three young readers. *Research in the Teaching of English, 16,* 1–20.

Garrison, B. M., & Hynds, S. (1991). Evocation and reflection in the reading transaction: A comparison of proficient and less proficient readers. *Journal of Reading Behavior, 23,* 259–280.

Goatley, V. J., Brock, C. H., & Raphael, T. (1995). Diverse learners participating in regular education "book clubs." *Reading Research Quarterly, 30,* 352–380.

Hancock, M. R. (1993). Exploring the meaning-making process through the content of literature response journals: A case study investigation. *Research in the Teaching of English, 27,* 335–368.

Hickman, J. (1979). *Response to literature in a school environment, grades K through 5.* Unpublished doctoral dissertation, Ohio State University, Columbus.

Hickman, J. (1981). A new perspective on response to literature: Research in an elementary school setting. *Research in the Teaching of English, 15,* 343–354.

Hubbard, R. S., Winterbourne, N., & Ostrow, J. (1996). Visual responses to literature: Imagination through images. *New Advocate, 9,* 309–323.

Iser, W. (1980). The reading process: A phenomenological approach. In J. P. Tompkins (Ed.), *Reader response criticisms: From formalism to poststructuralism* (pp. 50–60). Baltimore, MD: Johns Hopkins University Press.

Kelly, P. R. (1990). Guiding young students' response to literature. *Reading Teacher, 43,* 464–470.

Kiefer, B. (1988). Picture books as contexts for literary, aesthetic, and real world understandings. *Language Arts, 65,* 260–271.

Leal, D. J. (1992). The nature of talk about three types of text during peer group discussion. *Journal of Reading Behavior, 24,* 313–338.

Lehr, S. (1988). The child's developing sense of theme as a response to literature. *Reading Research Quarterly, 23,* 337–357.

Liaw, M. (1995). Looking into the mirror: Chinese children's responses to Chinese children's books. *Reading Horizons, 35,* 185–197.

Madura, S. (1995). The line and texture of aesthetic response: Primary children study authors and illustrators. *Reading Teacher, 49,* 110–118.

Many, J. E. (1991). The effects of stance and age level on children's literary responses. *Journal of Reading Behavior, 23,* 61–85.

Many, J. E., & Wiseman, D. L. (1992). The effects of teaching approach on third-grade students' response to literature. *Journal of Reading Behavior, 24,* 265–287.

Martinez, M., & Roser, N. L. (1991). Children's responses to literature. In J. Flood, J. M. Jensen, D. Lapp, & J. R. Squire (Eds.), *Handbook of research on teaching the English language arts* (pp. 643–654). New York: Macmillan.

Martinez, M., & Roser, N. L. (1994). Children's responses to a chapter book across grade levels: Implications for sustained text. In C. K. Kinzer and D. J. Leu (Eds.), *Multidimensional aspects of literacy research, theory, and practice* (pp. 317–324). Forty-third yearbook of the National Reading Conference. Chicago: National Reading Conference.

Martinez, M., Roser, N. L., Hoffman, J. V., & Battle, J. (1992). Fostering better book discussions through response logs and a response framework: A case description. In C. K. Kinzer, & D. J. Leu (Eds.), *Literacy research, theory, and practice: Views from many perspectives.* Forty-first yearbook of the National Reading Conference (pp. 303–311). Chicago: National Reading Conference.

McGee, L. M. (1992). An exploration of meaning construction in first graders' grand conversations. In C. K. Kinzer & D. J. Leu (Eds.), *Literacy research, theory, and practice: Views from many perspectives* (pp. 177–186). Forty-first yearbook of the National Reading Conference. Chicago: National Reading Conference.

McGill-Franzen, A., & Lanford, C. (1994). Exposing the edge of the preschool curriculum: Teachers' talk about text and children's literary understandings. *Language Arts, 71,* 264–273.

McGinley, W., & Kamberelis, G. (1996). *Maniac Magee* and *Ragtime Tumpie:* Children negotiating self and world through reading and writing. *Research in the Teaching of English, 30,* 75–113.

McMahon, S. I., Pardo, L. S., & Raphael, T. E. (1991). Bart: A case study in discourse about text. In S. McCormick & J. Zutell (Eds.), *Learner factors/teacher factors: Issues in literacy research and instruction* (pp. 285–296). Fortieth yearbook of the National Reading Conference. Chicago: National Reading Conference.

Morrow, L. M. (1988). Young children's responses to one-to-one story readings in school settings. *Reading Research Quarterly, 23,* 89–107.

O'Flahavan, J. F. (1989). *An exploration of the effects of participant structure upon literacy development in reading group discussion.* Unpublished doctoral dissertation, University of Illinois, Urbana-Champaign.

Purves, A. C., & Beach, R. (1972). *Literature and the reader: Research in response to literature, reading interests, and the teaching of literature.* Urbana, IL: National Council of teachers of English.

Raphael, T. E., & McMahon, S. I. (1994). Book club: An alternative framework for reading instruction. *Reading Teacher, 48,* 102–116.

Raphael, T. E., McMahon, S. I., Goatley, V. J., Bentley, J. L., Boyd, F. B., Pardo, L. S., & Woodman, D. A. (1992). Research directions: Literature and discussion in the reading program. *Language Arts, 69,* 54–61.

Rice, P. S. (2000). Gendered readings of a traditional "feminist" folktale by sixth-grade boys and girls. *Journal of Literacy Research, 32,* 211–236.

Rosenblatt, L. M. (1938/1976). *Literature as exploration.* New York: Noble & Noble.

Rosenblatt, L. M. (1978). *The reader, the text, the poem: The transactional theory of the literary work.* Carbondale: Southern Illinois University Press.

Rosenblatt, L. M. (1985). The transactional theory of literary work: Implications for research. In C. Cooper (Ed.), *Researching response to literature and the teaching of literature: Point of departure* (pp. 33–53). Norwood, NH: Ablex.

Roser, N., Hoffman, J., & Farest, C. (1990). Language, literature, and at-risk children (1990). *Reading Teacher, 43,* 554–559.

Roser, N., & Martinez, M. (1985). Roles adults play in preschoolers' response to literature. *Language Arts, 62,* 485–490.

Roser, N., Martinez, M., Mrosla, H., Junco, C., Gorman, A., & Ingold J. (2000). "What Happens to Book Talk When the Author Joins the Literature Circle?" In T. Shanahan & F. Rodriguez Brown (Eds.), *National Reading Conference Yearbook, 48* (pp. 266–276). Chicago: National Reading Conference.

Short, K.G. (1992). Intertextuality: Searching for patterns that connect. In C. K. Kinzer & D. J. Leu (Eds.), *Literacy research, theory, and practice: Views from many perspectives* (pp. 187–197). Forty-first yearbook of the National Reading Conference. Chicago: National Reading Conference.

Sims, R. (1983). Strong black girls: A ten year old responds to fiction about Afro-Americans. *Journal of Research and Development in Education, 16,* 21–28.

Sipe, L. (1998). Individual literary response styles of first and second graders. In T. Shanahan and F. V. Rodriguez-Brown (Eds.), *National Reading Conference Yearbook, 47* (pp. 76–89). Chicago: National Reading Conference.

Smith, E. B. (1995). Anchored in our literature: Students responding to African American literature. *Language Arts, 72,* 571–574.

Smolkin, L. B. (1995). The literature of the theatre and aesthetic response: Welcoming plays into the world of children's literature. *New Advocate, 8,* 109–123.

Vygotsky, L. (1978). *Mind in society: The development of higher psychological processes.* Cambridge, MA: MIT Press. (Original work published 1969)

Williams, C. L., & McLean, M. M. (1997). Young deaf children's response to picture book reading in a preschool setting. *Research in the Teaching of English, 31,* 337–366.

Wiseman, D. L., Many, J. E., & Altieri, J. (1992). Enabling complex aesthetic responses: An examination of three literary discussion approaches. In C. K. Kinzer & d. J. Leu (Eds.), *Literacy research, theory, and practice: Views from many perspectives* (pp. 283–291). Forty-first yearbook of the National Reading Conference. Chicago: National Reading Conference.

Wollman-Bonilla, J. E. (1989). Reading journals: Invitations to participate in literature. *Reading Teacher, 42,* 112–120.

Wollman-Bonilla, J. E. (1994). Why don't they "just speak?" Attempting literature discussion with more and less able readers. *Research in the Teaching of English, 28,* 231–258.

Wollman-Bonilla, J. E., & Werchadlo, B. (1995). Literature response journals in a first-grade classroom. *Language Arts, 72,* 562–570.

The Impact of Classroom Curriculum on Students' Perceptions of Good Readers and Writers

Sarah J. McCarthey
University of Illinois at Urbana-Champaign

This study is part of a larger project examining the role of student, teacher, peer, and parent perceptions as well as classroom practices in shaping students' identities as readers and writers. In this analysis, I focus on the role of the classroom curriculum in shaping students' perceptions of themselves and their peers as readers and writers.

McKenna, Kear, and Ellsworth (1995) found in a national survey that attitudes toward academic and recreational reading become more negative over the elementary school years and that the least able readers have the most negative attitudes. Other research has supported the finding that voluntary reading is on the decline and that there is a significant decrease in children's motivation for reading as they progress through the elementary grades (Guthrie & Anderson, 1999; Worthy, Moorman, & Turner, 1999). Because motivation and achievement are so closely correlated, this decline in motivation is particularly troubling.

Guthrie and Anderson (1999) identified involvement, curiosity, opportunity for social interchange, challenge, importance, and efficacy as facets of intrinsic motivation for reading, whereas recognition, competition, and grades operate as extrinsic motivators. They suggested that students who read for intrinsic motivations spend more time reading books than do those "who read for grades, competition, and compliance with the demands of a program" (p. 24). Schiefele (1991) found that when students are interested in what they read, they comprehend better and engage in deeper processing of text. Ames (1992) reported that learning is hindered when teachers use evaluations such as ability grouping or public charts of students' scores that highlight comparison among students.

Central to Guthrie and Alvermann's (1999) theory of engagement is the idea that literacy learning must be considered within social and cultural contexts. Students' beliefs about the context can affect their motivation (Bergin & LaFave, 1998). Further, students' perceptions of particular curricular contexts including the amount of teacher feedback, expectations, opportunity, and choice affect their perceptions of ability and achievement (Brattesani, Weinstein, & Marshall, 1984; Weinstein, Marshall, Sharp, & Botkin, 1987). A responsive environment congruent with personal goals and capabilities, one that provides resources and a supportive emotional climate, is essential for optimal performance (Ford, 1992).

Classroom tasks also have an effect on students' motivation. Turner (1995) found that open tasks that allowed choice and problem-solving were more likely

*National Reading Conference Yearbook, **50**, pp. 419–429.*

to facilitate motivation than closed tasks that required one answer and specified procedures. Miller and Meece (1999) found that students preferred high-challenge tasks such as writing essays on topics of their choice, working on research papers, and composing letters to the teacher, over low-challenge tasks such as completing worksheets and doing handwriting exercises. Educators promoting process approaches to writing have been recommending that teachers involve students in authentic tasks that allow students choices over topic, promote communication with real audiences, and encourage teachers and peers to respond to student texts (Calkins, 1986; Graves, 1994; Routman, 1991). Although research suggests that students are more motivated to read and write in classroom contexts that support choice, challenge, collaboration, and problem-solving, elementary-aged children are not necessarily accustomed to discussing the classroom conditions that support their literacy learning or describing themselves as readers and writers. For example, Guice and Johnston (1994) found that many students had rather limited conceptions of how to become better readers and writers, viewing the teacher as the authority and source of motivation, and assessing themselves in quite linear ways such as providing a numerical rating.

Despite research that has documented the importance of teachers nurturing students' intrinsic motivation through practices that support cooperation, choice, and problem-solving, there has been an increasing focus in schools on testing and commercial programs that offer extrinsic rewards (Sailors, Worthy, Assaf, & Mast, 2000). One such program, Accelerated Reading, contains a large collection of trade books, color-coded by reading level, with accompanying comprehension tests for each book. Students read books individually while the teacher monitors a large number of students through computer-assisted assessments. Rewards for reading and passing tests are offered as incentives. Although the creators of the program have argued that students are motivated to read, the extrinsic reward system, the individual and competitive nature of the reading, and the focus on low-level comprehension tests are in direct conflict with research that supports choice, social exchange, and open-ended tasks.

Previous research has provided evidence that the classroom context and tasks affect students' perceptions of their abilities and their motivation to engage in literacy learning. Yet, it is important to understand the implicit messages that are communicated through the enacted, classroom curriculum and to analyze how students see themselves within specific classroom contexts. In this study, I focused on the criteria students used to evaluate their own and their peers' literacy abilities and identified features of the classroom curriculum that contributed to students' perceptions of themselves and others.

Method

I used qualitative methods (Strauss & Corbin, 1990) to explore the ways in which students' perceptions of their abilities to read and write were constructed by the classroom context. Research questions included: (a) what criteria did students use to determine their abilities as readers and writers, (b) what criteria did students use in evaluating their peers' abilities, and (c) what was the role of the curriculum in constructing students' perceptions?

Context

Valley School, located in south central Texas, served inner-city children, suburban children, and rural children: 80% were Latino, 15% were European-American, and 5% were African-American. Over 90% of the students came from low-SES homes, qualifying Valley as a Title I School. The school was focused on the statewide test Texas Assessment of Academic Skills (TAAS) and had implemented the Accelerated Reading Program as the schoolwide reading program. The teacher I selected to observe and interview was a European-American teacher with seven years of experience who valued a literature-based approach to instruction.

The Curriculum

The teacher, Ms. Le Blanc (all names are pseudonyms), described her fifth-grade language arts program as consisting of three components: Reading Workshop, Writing Workshop, and Reading Renaissance, with the Reading Workshop being her priority and the major means for involving students in reading, writing, and discussion. For the Workshop, which departed significantly from the ways many educators such as Atwell (1987) have defined "Reading Workshop," the teacher selected novels that she could read aloud to the class. Her typical sequence was to read one or several chapters of the book aloud and then to lead the students in a discussion of particular aspects of the novels before assigning follow-up activities such as writing responses on class charts or in their notebooks. Two Newbury award winners, *Maniac Magee* by Jerry Spinelli (1990) and *Roll of Thunder, Hear My Cry* by Mildred Taylor (1976) were the novels that comprised the reading workshop portion of the curriculum in January–March. *Maniac Magee* is the story of a homeless, twelve-year-old boy who crosses the boundary between the white West End and the black East End of town. Written by a European-American man, the book focuses on Maniac's attempts to soothe rival factions from the two sides. *Roll of Thunder*, written by an African-American woman, focuses on the struggle of a black family trying to hold onto their land in the South during the Depression. The book portrays the family's defiance of racism amid the turmoil of the time.

The teacher had selected these novels based on her understanding of students' interests, her knowledge of their cultural and social backgrounds, and her own emphasis on books that "deal with race or economics or gender issues." It was important to her to select books that connected to students' lives. Although most of her class was Latino, she chose two books that focused on black-white race relations. She had chosen *Maniac Magee* for the following reasons:

> [The book is about] a boy who has many challenges in his life and has to come up with ways to overcome those challenges. I felt like our students needed to

> know that it's okay to have challenges in your life, that our lives are not perfect. And that especially as a kid, it's okay to have problems, but you need to know how to deal with those problems in a positive way. And the second reason is because it dealt directly with race issues.

She had chosen *Roll of Thunder* not only because it addressed discrimination, but it also showed "generations of strong women…I feel like I just need to bring out different qualities in what girls and women can do." She wanted students to become more aware of social issues and to become more tolerant of one another. She also had an agenda of teaching students to solve problems in nonviolent ways and to have the students develop, as she put it:

> A sense of fairness in the world and seeing people more for who they are than for where they come from or the color of their skin. In both stories, the characters have problems in their lives. They generally tend to solve them positively through actions; actions that would make some changes through law or changing people's ideas of how they think. More non-violent protest. I just want them to get a sense of fairness so they'll think (about) how they treat people and act.

The teacher then designed activities or questions for journals that required students to engage in a range of tasks from asking students to define words, to predicting what would happen next in the book, to connecting issues to their own lives. For example, the journal questions for *Maniac Magee* included "Find legend in the dictionary," "Do you think Maniac will leave the Beals? What would you do?" and "Tell me about a challenge in your own life and how you overcame it." Students also completed charts that listed columns for "main ideas, facts, opinions, and future outcomes" together as a class.

Ms. Le Blanc spent less time on a second aspect of her curriculum, Writing Workshop. She encouraged students to write original pieces when there was time, and students had an option to write a piece to be submitted to NASA for a contest. Shortly after the shootings in Colorado, she gave students the option of writing about their feelings about the incident. About midway through the semester, she introduced students to writing letters and responding to each other. Her emphasis was on communicating to an audience rather than on grammar and mechanics.

The third component of the language arts curriculum was a schoolwide reading program called Reading Renaissance that was part of the commercially available, computerized program, Accelerated Reader. Students took a test the first week of school to determine their reading levels and were placed on a corresponding color. They could select one or two books that were on their color from the school library, which was entirely color-coded. After reading the book, students took computerized tests that checked their comprehension and determined their pass rate. The class received rewards such as pizza parties when all children had passed. Students were required to read their Reading Renaissance (RR) books for 20–30 minutes at home and for 1 hour each day in school. The teacher was required by the school to monitor students' reading and provide feedback to them using Reading Renaissance charts, even though she did not agree with many aspects of the program. Although the teacher did not talk about other practices as part of her language arts program, on occasion I observed students choosing from a list of spelling activities or practicing reading comprehension worksheets that resembled the Texas Assessment of Academic Skills tests.

Student Selection

All 12 students in my sample received free or reduced lunch. Six were from each of the teacher's fifth-grade language arts classes and represented about 20% of the total number of students. The sample reflected the ethnic and cultural diversity of the classroom: seven were Latino/Latina, two African American, one Asian American, one European American, one of mixed Latina and European background. Students represented the whole continuum in terms of success and interest in reading as determined by their "color" ranking on Reading Renaissance and the teacher's rating: three were low, five were average or slightly above average, and four were high achievers. Fewer parents of the low-achieving readers consented to participation.

Data Sources

I spent two mornings a week observing and interviewing students from January to May 1999. I interviewed each student for about 45 minutes three times during the course of the semester. The first interview focused on their family backgrounds, interests in and out of school, their views of themselves as readers and writers, and their conceptions of reading and writing. The second interview focused on students' descriptions of themselves, descriptions of their peers' reading and writing, and opinions of books read within the classroom context. The third interview focused on book selection strategies and perceptions of the schoolwide reading program. As part of the larger study, I collected writing samples from students, interviewed the teacher, and conducted parent interviews.

Analysis

After reading through the interviews of all 12 students, I constructed a profile of each one. The profiles summarized their family background, interest in and habits around reading and writing, perceptions of peers' reading and writing, summaries and attitudes towards books read in class, and their attitudes toward the Reading Renaissance program. I then focused on students' beliefs about their own and others' reading and writing abilities and habits, and derived categories from students' comments. First, I categorized students' comments about reading into the following: identification of color in Reading Renaissance, speed, fluency and expressiveness, and word identification. Next, I categorized students' criteria for assessing others' abilities using the same categories. I then analyzed students' comments about writing and created categories such as expressiveness, details, and imagination. I drew from students' responses to my questions about *Maniac Magee* and *Roll of Thunder, Hear My Cry* for an analysis of students' understandings of and attitudes toward reading workshop.

Results

Criteria for Assessing Good Readers

For the most part, students relied on external criteria to determine their abilities as readers. When asked if they were good readers and how they knew, most students' comments reflected that "the color" they were on in the Reading Renaissance program was the most important indicator of their abilities as readers. The successful readers consistently stated that they were "on a high level," whereas the struggling readers said they were not on a "high color." For example, Daniel's comments represented many of the successful readers' comments when he reported "I'm on the high reading level. I make good grades on the books that I take and are tested on." In contrast, Natalie, like the other struggling readers reported "I'm not on a high level." Sometimes their self-assessments were comparative in nature. For example, Elena compared her reading to Donna's; "She's a good reader because she's on the highest level. My goal is to try and get the same color as she is which is yellow x."

The next criterion for self-assessment was others' perceptions of their reading ability. Thus, students stated that their teacher or friends had provided them with information about their abilities. For example, Antonio stated that "people comment on (my) good reading." Daniel suggested that "One time Ms. Le Blanc said I was the best reader in the class." Amber relied "on a bunch of friends" who told her she was a good reader.

Occasionally, students identified other criteria, but these criteria were almost always in addition to their reading level in RR. For example, two students identified speed in reading and two suggested fluency or expressiveness in reading as important factors in judging their own abilities. Two high-achieving students suggested that their interest in and frequency of engaging in reading contributed to their success. Natalie, a low-achieving ESL student, mentioned the difficulty of identifying words; she stated, "Some words are real hard, most of them are hard" as an indicator of her difficulties in decoding.

Students' perceptions of their peers' reading abilities focused on colors, goals, and points as well. Eight of the 12 students based their judgments about others' reading on their ranking in Reading Renaissance and seemed to equate good reading with achievement of points and goals. For example, one girl identified Daniel and Amber as the best readers "because they usually get the treats for the high goals." Antonio was identified as a strong reader because "he's already in the last reading level, the highest one, and he gets the most points on AR books." Students also saw moving upwards through the colors as a valuable goal. For example, one student was identified as a good reader with the words, "He works his way up the colors."

Students mentioned other criteria such as fluency, expressiveness, interest in books, and length of time to complete books when reflecting on their peers' reading. Jennifer was identified as the best reader "because she has a good accent. And you can hear her clearly. She just makes it sound a little funner." Another student also identified Jennifer as a good reader because "she uses expressions." Some students also referred to the students who tended to read often and to complete many books as good readers. Two students acknowledged that becoming involved in the reading was an indicator of good reading. One student suggested that Jennifer "gets real interested in her books and tells us 'you should read the book because it's really good. It makes you cry and stuff.'" The same student also noted that Amber liked to share what she read with others and became highly involved with the characters, "She cries in some of her books."

The criterion for identifying students who were not good readers, other than being on a lower level, tended to center around their behavior during reading time. For example, Elena stated that Lucas was not a good reader, "He usually plays around during Reading Renaissance. He'll just be talking and he won't read. My teacher will have to get onto him." Jennifer mentioned another low reader who just talked during reading time instead of reading.

Criteria for Assessing Good Writers

In contrast to students' heavy reliance on external "objective" information about reading abilities such as points and reading levels, students' descriptions of themselves and their peers as writers varied and displayed an emphasis on more "subjective" information such as amount of time engaged in writing and interest in writing. For example, Antonio mentioned that good writers are able to write down "anything that comes to their mind" and they write often. Natalie thought Daniel was a good writer because "he always writes stories," and Milton noted that Daniel "likes writing. He writes a lot." Students noted that good writers (including themselves) often created their own stories at home for fun.

Student responses to questions about what makes writing good focused on the quality of writing, including the ability to write in different genres, the use of imagination, and quality of expression. For example, Carmen pointed out that writers "write different kinds of books." Trina found Milton to be a good writer because "when he writes an essay, they (he) always have examples, details, and he adds a lot to it." Lucas noted that good writers are able to "take their expressions out and put them on paper and make them even better." Alan pointed out that good writing had to make sense and include elaboration and description. Handwriting, spelling, and punctuation were identified as aspects that contributed to high-quality writing by some students as well. Antonio summarized many of the qualities of good writing that he observed by pointing out two girls who he thought were good writers, "Johanna and Donna. When Ms. Le Blanc says you only need a paragraph, they write two pages and long stuff. They have nice handwriting. They show good details. They show you can imagine in your mind." Jennifer noted that good writers "have to put some emotion, some feelings, some impressions to make the reader feel (what it is like) to be inside people."

Other students who commented that audience response was central to the writing process echoed the importance of connecting to the readers or listeners. Several of the students noted that they shared their writing with family members, friends, and classmates. They could tell when their writing was good because their parents enjoyed listening to them, but students emphasized the power of their peers' responses. Antonio offered, "I sometimes read out to the class for research and assignments. They (classmates) clap, they like it." Jennifer explained that "they don't really tell me" . . . (but she can tell they like her writing) "Because sometimes their face gets lit up." Some students also identified the role that prewriting strategies played and the need to practice writing in different contexts.

Influence of Classroom Curriculum

Students responded positively to the Reading Workshop in Ms. Le Blanc's class. Their responses to interview questions and their journal writing demonstrated that they understood the content and themes of the two books that were read aloud. All 12 students summarized *Maniac Magee* (Spinelli, 1990) as a story about a boy who experienced living in both the black and white sections of town. Some students saw Maniac as a victim because "they didn't like him because he was white" (Antonio, Latino) and "Maniac was a white boy who just moved to the east side and black people stayed on the west side and they kept making fun of him" (Carmen, African American). Most students saw him as a hero who "didn't see color" (Jennifer, Latina) and could be "friends with all no matter what color they were" (Elena, Latina). Several students identified with Maniac because "he is friends with all different colors. I don't mind if they're white or black or Mexican" (Jennifer, Latina).

Students summarized *Roll of Thunder, Hear My Cry* (Taylor, 1976) as a book about a black family losing its land because of the prejudice of the whites and identified racism as the theme of the book. Several girls identified with Cassie because she "wants to know everything that's going on" (Carmen, African American) and she "asks questions" (Donna, Asian American). Several boys identified with male characters including Jonathan "because he's real calm when Little Man said, 'Why don't you beat him up and stuff?' But he didn't, he tried to solve it in a less violent way. Because I don't really like to fight and stuff" (Antonio, Latino). Alan (African American) identified with Stacy because "he kept on giving things to T.J. and he helped work around the house a lot for Mr. Morrison and his papa."

Several of the students offered evidence of connecting the themes to their own lives. For example, Elena related that she, too, had experienced discrimination when her family had moved from Texas to Minnesota. Carmen identified the racial tensions in the novels as comparable to ones she witnessed in her neighborhood. Daniel wrote a piece about valuing diversity that he shared with the class.

Students' responses, then, indicated that they enjoyed being read aloud to, understood the content, and were able to discuss and relate to major themes from the novels. However, students did not see Reading Workshop as connected to reading. When asked about reading, students' comments always referenced Reading Renaissance. I needed to elicit their responses to the Workshop aspect of the curriculum by specifically asking for their summaries, evaluations, and abilities to relate to characters.

The role of the Writing Workshop was less evident than the other two aspects of curriculum and student responses about writing were not so clearly tied to classroom events. Most of the students who reported that they liked to write also stated that they wrote more at home than in school because there was more time. They often kept journals, wrote letters to family members who lived in other states or countries, or wrote stories and poems that they shared with family members. Yet, the opportunities they did have in the classroom that were more authentic (e.g., writing to a peer) and situated (e.g., responding to the shootings in Colorado) and offered choices seemed to provide them with a view of writing that encouraged fluency and imagination.

Discussion

The multifaceted language arts curriculum in Ms. Le Blanc's classroom was filled with competing norms and goals that influenced the ways in which students perceived reading and writing. Although some aspects of the curriculum were quite structured and constrained such as Reading Renaissance with its color coding, tests, and reward systems, other aspects such as response to literature and writing workshop allowed students opportunities to see reading and writing as more than a set of classroom exercises. The Reading Renaissance program had a powerful influence on students' self-perceptions, as evidenced by students' evaluations of themselves and others based on color codes and achievement of points. The Reading Workshop appeared to have less impact on students' views of who they were as readers.

One possible explanation for the power.of Reading Renaissance in influencing students' self-perceptions includes the visibility of the program. Students received scores on their comprehension of texts through the computerized program, and they were continually reminded of where they were in relation to their peers through the charts and rewards. Despite the teacher's efforts to play down the role of Reading Renaissance, the monitoring she was required to do seemed to highlight the computerized program. This explanation is supported by the research that has found that students are aware of teachers' expectations and that their expectations influence perceptions of their own abilities (Weinstein et al., 1987). A second explanation is that because students were read to (either by the teacher or via the taped version of *Roll of Thunder*) rather than reading the texts themselves, they did not seem to see the Reading Workshop as "reading."

The teacher's valuing of diversity through text and discussion was not fruitless, however. Consistent with other studies focused on the role of multicultural literature in promoting learning (Athanases, 1998; Moller & Allen, 2000), this study suggests that students developed some consciousness of racism as the result of discussing multicultural texts. Some students used the books, activities, and interviews with me to share their personal experiences with racism and to develop appreciation for others from diverse backgrounds.

The specific tasks associated with each of the components of the curriculum can also help account for students' perceptions of themselves and others as readers and writers. The Reading Renaissance tasks closely fit Turner's (1995) and Miller and Meece's (1999) definitions of low-challenge tasks; that is, they required answering specific comprehension questions, were completed alone, and provided only limited opportunities for choice. In contrast, the "Reading Workshop" allowed a larger range of responses that encouraged some problem-solving and opportunities for open-ended responses. The writing activities were by far the most open and challenging, requiring synthesis of information, choice of topic, and opportunities to write to an audience. Students' views of the disciplines seemed to mirror the tasks: they regarded reading, which for them involved low-challenge tasks, as a means of attaining points and rewards. In contrast, they viewed writing, which was filled with challenges and choices, as a discipline dependent upon imagination, audience, and expressiveness.

Although the study suggests that practices associated with Reading Renaissance encourage students to identify themselves and peers in relation to their reading levels, it does not address whether students' motivation to read is increased by providing rewards. More data need to be gathered to establish the program's overall effects on motivation. However, the findings should encourage us to consider some potential dangers associated with the program. For example, the emphasis on comparisons among peers, which is inevitable when charts are publicly displayed, may hinder learning as Ames (1992) found in her study. Students' labeling of themselves and others, something that was pervasive in this study, may result in limiting their understanding of the reading process. Also, the narrow focus on answering comprehension questions in front of a screen may limit students' abilities to become more skilled, connected, and reflective readers and may discourage social exchange (McCarthey, Hoffman, & Galda, 1999). Using narrowly defined computerized programs, even when the teacher does not place a high value on them, may undermine otherwise responsive environments that encourage challenge, provide open-ended tasks, and create opportunities for social interaction (Ford, 1992; Guthrie & Anderson, 1999; Turner, 1995).

A final lesson of the study seems to be that the interactions between classroom curricula and students' perceptions are complex. Even when a teacher values discussion and responsiveness as Ms. Le Blanc did, an externally created program that promises extrinsic rewards may be more powerful than the teacher or others ever imagined. Yet, the impact of the messages the teacher communicated about the value of writing and the negative effects of racism should be underscored for the possibilities of developing more literate, aware students.

References

Ames, C. (1992). Classrooms: Goals, structures, and student motivation. *Journal of Educational Psychology, 84,* 261–271.

Atwell, N. (1987). *In the middle.* Portsmouth, NH: Heinemann.

Athanases, S. (1998). Diverse learners, diverse texts: Exploring identity and difference through literary encounters. *Journal of Literacy Research, 30,* 273–296.

Bergin, D. A., & LaFave, C. (1998). Continuities between motivation research and whole language philosophy. *Journal of Literacy Research, 30,* 321–356.

Brattesani, K. A., Weinstein, R. S., & Marshall, H. H. (1984). Student perceptions of differential teacher treatment as moderators of teacher expectation effects. *Journal of Educational Psychology, 76,* 236–247.

Calkins, L. (1986). *The art of teaching writing.* Portsmouth, NH: Heinemann.

Ford, M. E. (1992). *Motivating humans: Goals, emotions, and personal agency beliefs.* Newbury Park, CA: Sage.

Graves, D. (1994). *A fresh look at writing.* Portsmouth, NH: Heinemann.

Guice, S., & Johnston, P. H. (1994). Assessment, self-assessment, and children's literate constructs. In C. K. Kinzer & D. J. Leu (Eds.), *Multidimensional aspects of literacy research, theory, and practice.* Forty-third yearbook of the National Reading Conference (pp. 72–88). Chicago: National Reading Conference.

Guthrie, J., & Alvermann, D. (1999). *Engaged reading: Processes, practices, and policy implications.* New York: Teachers College Press.

Guthrie, J., & Anderson, E. (1999). Engagement in reading: Processes of motivated, strategic, knowledgeable, social readers. In J. Guthrie & D. Alvermann (Eds.), *Engaged reading: Processes, practices, and policy implications* (pp. 17–45). New York: Teachers College Press.

McCarthey, S. J., Hoffman, J., & Galda, L. (1999). Readers in elementary classrooms: Learning goals and instructional principles that can inform practice. In J. Guthrie & D. Alvermann (Eds.), *Engaged reading: Processes, practices, and policy implications* (pp. 46–80). New York: Teachers College Press.

McKenna, M. C., Kear, D. J., & Ellsworth, R. A. (1995). Children's attitudes toward reading: A national survey. *Reading Research Quarterly, 30,* 934–956.

Miller, S., & Meece, J. L. (1999). Third graders' motivational preferences for reading and writing tasks. *Elementary School Journal, 100,* 19–35.

Möller, K. J., & Allen, J. (2000). Connecting, resisting, and searching for safer places: Students respond to Mildred Taylor's *The Friendship. Journal of Literacy Research, 32,* 145–186.

Routman, R. (1991). *Invitations: Changing as teachers and learners in K–12.* Portsmouth, NH: Heinemann.

Sailors, M., Worthy, J., Assaf, L., & Mast, M. (2000, December). *Judging a book by its color: Students' perceptions of participation in Accelerated Reader.* Paper presented at the meeting of the National Reading Conference, Scottsdale, AZ.

Schiefele, U. (1991). Interest, learning, and motivation. *Educational Psychologist, 26,* 299–323.

Spinelli, J. (1990). *Maniac Magee.* New York: Harper Trophy.

Strauss, A., & Corbin, J. (1990). *Basics of qualitative research.* Newbury Park, CA: Sage.

Taylor, M. (1976). *Roll of Thunder, Hear My Cry.* New York: Bantam.

Turner, J. C. (1995). The influence of classroom contexts on young children's motivation for literacy. *Reading Research Quarterly, 30,* 410–441.

Weinstein, R. S., Marshall, H. H., Sharp, L., & Botkin, M. (1987). Pygmalion and the student: Age and classroom differences in children's awareness of teacher expectations. *Child Development, 58,* 1079–1093.

Worthy, J., Moorman, M., & Turner, M. (1999). What Johnny likes to read is hard to find in school. *Reading Research Quarterly, 34,* 12–27.

The Enactment of an Early Reading Intervention Model in Three Classrooms

Ellen McIntyre
University of Louisville

Sherry Powers
Western Kentucky University

Bill Bintz
University of Kentucky

Elementary teachers and administrators across the country are investigating primary-grade reading instructional models that would best meet the academic needs of their students. Many invite vendors to their buildings to hear pitches for specific programs and learn about the goals, activities, materials, and requirements of those programs. Some programs, such as Success for All (Slavin, Madden, Karweit, Nolan, & Wasik, 1992), are to be adopted by an entire school, whereas others can be adopted by grade levels or classrooms. These programs require the purchase of specialized materials and professional development training on how to use the materials.

Some instructional models such as Four Blocks (Cunningham & Allington, 1994) are not *programs* per se, but are *models* that recommend particular practices without commercial materials. These models often recommend specific strategies and foci for particular amounts of classroom time, and schools hire experts on the model to train teachers. Many of the publishers and authors of both programs and models claim that their programs are research-based with positive results, especially for poor and working class populations.

This clamoring for the best instructional programs or models has caused concern among many educators, including us. In particular, we have worried that teachers are being encouraged to implement instruction that promises results if followed in the recommended ways, without attention to helping teachers make instructional decisions based on the sociocultural context within which teaching and learning happen. Few programs or models address classroom discourse as a powerful variable in what is learned. In most classrooms, most teaching occurs through spoken language (Cazden, 1988). A barrier to school literacy learning is created when teachers fail to build upon the familiar interactional discourse styles of students (Delpit, 1995; Foster & Peele, 2001; Heath, 1983). It may be what teachers say and how they say it in response to their students that affects what

*National Reading Conference Yearbook, **50**, pp. 430–443.*

gets learned more than the organization, structure, activities, or materials around which so many programs and models are written (Castells, 2000).

In our study, we examined one instructional model for struggling readers that we believe holds much promise for helping children become fluent readers in the early grades. The organizational structure, activities, and materials seem theoretically sound. Yet, when we examined the subtle and varied features of the model as it was enacted, we found other more important issues to raise when deciding our reading instructional practices for young children.

Background

In Kentucky, many schools have been given state funds through a competitive grant program to implement reading programs and models for struggling readers in the early grades. Many of the grants have funded commercial programs such as Success for All and some have funded other widely touted models such as Four Blocks. One group of teachers and administrators from several schools read about and discussed early intervention models from Hiebert and Taylor's book *Getting Reading Right from the Start: Early Interventions in Reading* (1994), an edited book containing research study reports of successful interventions. The teachers and principals agreed to adapt one model called "Early Reading Intervention: Supplemental Instruction for Groups of Low-Achieving Students Provided by First Grade Teachers" by Taylor, Strait, and Medo (1994). To the group, this model held the most potential for improving reading achievement of their struggling readers and for sustaining the implementation of the model in the classrooms after the funds were depleted.

We too believed and continue to believe that this model holds potential for improved reading achievement for young children. We were part of a larger study that examined instructional features and student achievement in 12 different early reading programs or models. We included this model in the study because we admired the organizational structure and suggested activities and strategies. This paper will share how we examined instructional features of the models and illustrate how the model was enacted in three different classrooms.

The Model

In this model (adapted from Taylor et al., 1994), teachers identify three to six lowest performing readers in their classroom. They meet with them daily for 45 minutes, focusing on comprehending text, reading and rereading text, word-getting strategies, and writing in response to text. The model recommends how teachers and children spend the 45-minute instructional period: The first 15 minutes is focused on meaning construction as the teachers and children read and discuss a book; then the teacher copies, either on a chart or in small booklets, a portion of the entire book/text to create student texts, and the children read the shortened portion with the teacher. During the second 15 minutes, the goal is getting children focused on print. Children do several more rereadings and some word work (phonics and spelling patterns). During the last 10 to 15 minutes the students write. Then children are to practice the teacher-copied text at school and at home. Common instructional strategies recommended for the lessons include comprehension strategies such as visualization, reciprocal teaching, making connections; fluency strategies such as echo and choral readings of the text; and phonemic awareness and phonics activities such as language play, explanation and demonstration of decoding and encoding, and spelling pattern practice.

The teachers participated in a 3-day summer institute for the model. We refer to this portion of the project as *training* because it lasted only 3 days, and its ultimate goal was to get teachers to learn the model. It was well planned and involved the teachers' active participation in strategy lessons and reflection on what they learned. During the 3-day training institute, the teachers were provided with the theory behind the model and an overview of the model's purposes. Sample lessons were demonstrated with teacher participation and then shown on videotape. Many specific strategies such as those named above were also demonstrated. The teachers received a manual (which they referred to as a "training manual") with all the strategies described and with sample lessons for emergent and beginning readers.

The institute and manual differed from other *training* however, in that teachers were not provided with a script as they often are for the implementation of commercial programs. Rather, teachers were expected to select strategies based on students' needs. One portion of the 3-day institute was dedicated to teaching the teachers the purpose and practice of taking Running Records to observe students' oral reading and the strategies that would build on their strengths.

In addition to the summer institute, the grant funded a *professional development* aspect to the project. We refer to this part of the project as professional development because the focus was on developing teachers' constructions of understandings through dialogue, reflection, and scaffolding by an expert. A literacy expert was hired to come to each school each month to demonstrate potential lessons and act as a coach for implementing the model. Teachers were expected to meet once a month to share insights and issues in after-school meetings. An e-mail discussion group was set up for more communication among teachers. Two Saturdays (one in the fall and one in the spring) were spent revisiting lessons and strategies. The teachers were paid for all extra time spent on the project.

Below is a sample of a lesson taken directly from the manual:

A typical session for emergent readers

First 15 minutes: The teacher will gather the group to a designated spot in her classroom (kept constant for routine and mental planning by the children). If she is working with emergent readers, she begins by reading a predictable book to the group, allowing for spontaneous responses to the book (questions, comments, laughter, etc.) Afterwards, she begins a brief discussion of the book, asking open-ended questions and engaging each child in making a critical statement about the book.

> Second 15 minutes: In this block of time, the teacher will draw children's attention to the print through rereading the text aloud as the children follow along. She may have the children echo read and then participate in a choral reading of the book. Children may take turns reading pages aloud, or the teacher may lead children in a Reader's Theater with the text when appropriate.
>
> Last 15 minutes: In the final block, the teacher selects three or four phonetically regular words from the story and engages the students in phonics activities around those words. For instance, she may choose "bed," "jump," and "fell" from *Five Little Monkeys Jumping on the Bed* (Christelow, 1989) and ask children, "If you can spell 'bed,' can you spell 'red'? 'Led?' 'Ted?'" Finally, she ends the session by telling the children to write a sentence about the story they just read (in reader response fashion), spelling by using the sounds they hear, and assisting those who struggle with this. She then encourages the children to reread the book they studied during independent reading time at school or at home.

In the manual, the teachers were told that the lesson above was only an example of a lesson with emergent readers and that they should adapt the strategies and texts as needed. Sample lessons for beginning and developing teachers were also included.

The Instructional Features

Our study sought to illuminate specific instructional features of the various programs and models we were studying. These features were selected based on numerous studies of effective early reading instruction and prevention (e.g., Clay, 1991). The study team created an observation instrument that asked observers to rate how much time was spent on some features and the quality of implementation of others. Raters scored the instructional features as "high implementation" or "low implementation." Raters were trained using videotapes, and the following features had an interrater reliability of .79 or higher during the training:

1. *Focus on text.* How much time children spend during the lesson focused on print, rather than say, for example, listening, singing, or drawing.
2. *Skills (e.g., phonics) in context.* How much time is spent teaching children skills such as phonics and word recognition in the context of a story, as compared to skills in isolation where children do not connect the skills to reading.
3. *Working on strategies.* How much time children spend practicing the reading strategies that have been explicitly taught.
4. *Connected text.* How much time children spend reading connected text (that is, sentences and stories) rather than individual words.
5. *Talk about text.* How much time is spent on discussion of text ideas.
6. *Risk-taking.* How much the teacher encourages the children to try various strategies when reading rather than a focus on accuracy such that children's reading is impeded.
7. *Meaning-focused.* How much the lessons are focused on constructing meaning when reading, as compared to merely calling off words.

8. *Authentic work.* How much the lesson has children engaged in authentic work, as compared to the kind of work only found in school.
9. *Academic focus.* How much the lesson is academically focused as compared to "just having fun." This does not mean an academically focused lesson is not fun, but it is clear the focus is academic.
10. *Cognitive complexity.* How much the lesson is cognitively complex, rather than on simple ideas or materials too young for the group.
11. *Climate.* How respectful the emotional environment is for the children.
12. *Time usage.* Teaching efficiency; how well the teacher uses time.
13. *Pace.* How well the pace of the instruction appears to be suited to the students. The pace is neither too fast or too slow.
14. *Overall Effectiveness.* The researchers' perception on the overall effectiveness of the lesson observed.

In the larger study, nine teachers implemented the adapted Taylor et al. (1994) model. Classrooms were visited once each fall and once each spring. Two of the authors of this paper had observed in three of the classrooms. McIntyre observed in all three classrooms one time each, in the fall. Bintz observed in the second and third classrooms one time each, in the fall. The first classroom was observed once by a third field researcher. Each of these classrooms were further observed and videotaped in the spring of the school year for the larger study, but these observations are not part of this analysis because our purpose was to show how one model can be enacted quite differently in three different classrooms.

The scores of the instructional features were averaged across all nine classrooms. In comparison to the averaged scores of the other eleven models in the larger study (such as Success for All), this model's average score fell in the middle. When we examined the scores from the fall observations in these three classrooms, we found the feature scores to range from very low to very high with strengths and weaknesses in each classroom. The individual enactments of the model made the scores for our instructional features quite different across classrooms. Table 1 shows these scores by classroom during the fall observations.

In addition to the scores being different, the subtle differences in the way this model was implemented by three different teachers can be shown through our fieldnotes. The notes from each of the following second-grade classrooms were taken in the fall, and the children in each group were all emergent or struggling beginning readers.

School A

> The teacher sits at a table with seven children, four males and three females. The group has been practicing for several days reading a poem from a basal reader selected because most words are decodable. The teacher has duplicated the poem for each child, one line of the poem on each page, and the pages are stapled together in a little book.
>
> The teacher says, "Today is our last day on this story. We get a new one on Monday."
>
> A child says, "The stories are getting harder."

The teacher responds, "You are getting better." She then says, "Let me have your assignment books. Now, first, we are going to do a choral read. Do you remember what a choral reading is?"

A child offers, "We read each page."

"No."

Another child offers, "We read together."

"Yes, we are going to read chorally, then next time we will do an echo reading. Let's read the title. Put your fingers on the words." The children read the title of the poem together. Then the teacher reads the poem, page by page, encouraging the children to read along with her. Four of the children appear to read along, while three do not. The teacher stops periodically to tell the children to follow. After 8 minutes they finish and the teacher says, "Let's take turns."

The first child is given a pointer, and he points to the words and tries to read. He struggles with each word of his sentence: "Max who is six sits up in a tree" except for the word "Max." With a pause before each word, the teacher supplies him with the word.

Table 1

Feature Scores by Classroom

	School A	School B	School C
Time Spent Per Lesson (0–50% low; 26–100% high)*			
Focus on Text	51–70% (HI)	51–70% (HI)	51–100% (HI)
Skills in Context	26–50% (LO)	26–50% (LO)	71–100% (HI)
Working on Strategies	0–25% (LO)	26–50% (LO)	51–70% (HI)
Connected Text	51–70% (HI)	51–70% (HI)	71–100% (HI)
Talk About Text	0–25% (LO)	0–25% (LO)	26–50% (LO)***
Quality of Implementation (1–4 continuum; 1–2 high; 3–4 low)**			
Risk-taking	4-LO	3-LO	2-HI
Meaning-focused	4-LO	3-LO	2-HI
Authentic Work	4-LO	4-LO	2-HI
Academic Focus	1-HI	3-LO	1-HI
Cognitive Challenge	4-LO	3-LO	1-HI
Climate	3-LO	1-HI	1-HI
Pace of Instruction	2-HI	2-HI	2-HI
Overall Effectiveness	4-LO	2-HI	1-HI

*The total time represented in this table does not equal 100% because these features overlap. For instance, the feature "focus on text" can overlap in practice with skills in context, working on strategies and connected text.

**A score of "1" indicates a very high quality of implementation, "2" is high, "3" is low, and "4" is very low.

***This teacher received an estimate of 26-50% time spent on talking about text. Although that is "low" on our scale, it is actually quite appropriate for the lesson. As researchers, we intend to interpret this score as quite good for a 45-minute lesson.

The next child reads fluently, and the third child reads like the first one, waiting for the teacher to provide each word for him. During the round robin reading, those children who are not reading fail to follow the written text, some are not even turning the pages. Two children talk to one another throughout the oral reading exercise. The teacher intervenes often to keep them on task.

After 15 minutes of this sort of reading, the teacher says, "Remember we did some words from our story that were compound words? Do you remember how we found some compound words in our story? See if you can find some words." The children flip through their booklets, and one says, "tiptop."

"What are the two words that make up tiptop? Tip and top" the teacher says.

A child says, "I found one—looking."

"No, remember it must be two little words put together."

"Moonlight," says another child.

"Goodnight," offers another.

The teacher writes these words on the chalkboard as the students say them. (She writes good night as one word.) She then hands out the children's "journals." She tells the children they are to write a sentence using one of the compound words. She reminds them to put the date on their pages.

A child says, "Can I make some cats on the wall?"

The teacher says, "Not until you write your sentence." She asks, "What do all sentences start with?"

A few chant, "Compound words."

"With a capital letter, don't you remember? Your sentences need to make sense. If you use more than one word that is okay. You can't just write a word, you have to write a sentence." The children begin to work. After 10 minutes, two have sentences, two have phrases, two have one word, and one child has nothing on his page. The teacher collects the journals.

In this lesson, we saw *the structure of the model* as demonstrated in the institute and described in the training manual. The lesson has three parts to it: (a) readings and rereadings, (b) word work (compound words), and (c) writing. There was no focus on meaning, as designed by the model, likely because this was the group's "last day on the story." Yet, the painfully slow readings of the text appeared to dismiss meaning-making completely. Particular strategies taught during the institute and described in the manual were employed, such as echo and choral reading, word work, and writing. However, the quality of the enactment caused the lesson to be scored low on our instructional features. The teacher used echo and choral reading in opposite order for scaffolding purposes; her word work was about parts of speech (not suggested by the training or the manual). In addition, she taught incorrect concepts (e.g., good night as one word). The writing assignment seemed contrived. This teacher scored low on features of climate, pace, and overall instruction because she did not address signals from the students that they were bored, having difficulty, or confused. Little was done to guide the reciter or clarify misunderstandings. No instruction was provided for the child who did not complete the written assignment.

School B

The teacher sits at a table with four students, three boys, and one girl. The teacher begins by saying, "I'm always so glad we have this time for reading."

A child says, "Me, too. It's fun."

The teacher responds, "Good. I'm so glad to hear that. Well, then, let's start off this morning like we always do, with a little book chat. This morning we're going to read a book about dinosaurs. One of the reasons I picked this book is because I know all of you like to read about dinosaurs."

A child says, "Yeah, I like dinosaurs."

The teacher says, "Well first we have to put our books together." The teacher has piles of 8½ × 11 pieces of paper stacked in front of her. She distributes these sheets of paper to each child, and gives directions to the group about how to arrange all the sheets into a little booklet. The teacher guides students with comments like: "Let's start putting our booklet together by starting with the cover." Each student creates a booklet that totals 15 pages, each with a line of text and an illustration. The title of the book is *Dancing Dinosaurs* (Deven, 1993), a predictable book with an explicit rhyming scheme.

After all four children have created booklets, the teacher says, "Let's look into our new books to see what interesting things are going on inside." Students spend the next 2 minutes flipping through their books. Two students check to see if all the pages are in the right numerical order.

Finally, the teacher says, "Okay, let's begin. Who wants to read us the title of the story?" One child quickly raises his hand. He reads the title and other words on the page, and then he says something (researcher did not catch) about the letter "s" at the end of some of the different words.

The teacher responds, "Yes, Tim's right. There are some words that have a 's' at the end." The teacher then says, "Did anybody notice that there are two names on the first page? One name belongs to the author, and the other to the illustrator. Does anybody know the difference between the author and the illustrator?"

One child says, "The author is the person who wrote the words, and the illustrator is the person who drew the pictures."

The teacher says, "That's right. Very good." She continues to address words on the book cover. She asks, "Who can find a noun in the title?" Students look at the cover, but are quiet. The teacher adds, "We talked about nouns. Remember, a noun is a person, place, or thing. Do we have any nouns in our title?"

A child says, "Yeah, dinosaur is a thing."

Teacher responds, "Yeah, that's right. Dinosaur is a noun. Can anybody find a verb?" Students look at the cover again, but are quiet. The teacher does not ask the question again.

Then the teacher helps the children use word and picture clues to make and share predictions about the story. She says, "Let's look at some of the words and pictures in our story to see if they give us a clue as to what our story will be about." All four students offer predictions. Afterwards, the teacher says, "Well, let's find out."

Then the teacher asks one student to begin reading the story. The student reads one sentence (page 1). The teacher then asks another student to continue reading from there, and he reads the next sentence (page 2). The teacher stops the reading, and asks, "What time of the day is noonday?" ("noonday" was a word that was in the sentence read by the second student). Students remain quiet.

The teacher explains, "Well, it's 12:00, around lunch time." She says, "Okay, page three is for Emily." This student reads the sentence on the next page. Then the teacher asks the fourth student to read the next page.

The teacher stops the reading, and asks, "Can anybody find any rhyming words on page three?" Students look at the page and offer examples of rhyming

> words such as "do" and "to." Then she then tells the first student to continue reading, and so forth. At different points in the text, the teacher again asks students if they "notice any rhyming words" in the story. The children offer different pairs of rhyming words.
>
> Afterwards, the teacher tells the children to write as many pairs of rhyming words as they can. The children do this and then share their pairs with the rest of the group. These words are unrelated to the text. The teacher listens to the pairs of words and comments briefly about each pair. Then students return their copies of the story to the teacher and go to their desks.

In this lesson we again saw the *structure* of this model put into action. The classroom teacher, rather than an instructional assistant, worked with the struggling readers, as required by the model. The teacher used multiple copies of a text she believed the students can read, and she provided focused and intentional instruction that included (a) the discussion and reading of a book, (b) word analysis activities, and (c) writing. She began by creating a friendly, comfortable and predictable atmosphere for reading by building on student interest in the topic of the book (dinosaurs). Throughout the lesson, her tone was kind and encouraging, resulting in a high score on the climate feature.

For meaning-making, this teacher asked open-ended questions to extend student interest, and she prompted students to make predictions. However, the majority of her lesson's "meaning-focused" time was spent organizing booklets. And the book chat was less a conversation and more an interrogation of book elements (e.g., "Does anybody know the difference between the author and the illustrator?" "Who can find a noun in the title?" "Can anybody find a verb?").

During the reading of the book, the children used round robin reading instead of social reading strategies, resulting in lower scores on risk-taking and meaning-focus. Some of the children were focused on text some of the time, as the teacher used this time to draw children's attention to individual words ("What time of the day is noonday?") and word patterns ("Did anybody notice any rhyming words in the story?"), but this was at the expense of fluency practice, as intended by the model. The teacher continued with word analysis by asking students to create and share examples of rhyming words, but the words were not from the story, resulting in a low score on "skills in context."

Like the previous teacher, this one was also committed to the model and its components as shown by a comment during a follow-up interview. She was asked how closely she believes her instruction followed the model. She said:

> Very closely. I was trying to integrate comprehension, word attack, and fluency all at the same time. . . . I have very positive feelings about this model, like the small group interaction, and integrating comprehension, words, and fluency.

Clearly, this teacher embraced this model. But while the teacher stressed that this model allowed her to "integrate comprehension, word work, and fluency," most of her instruction was focused primarily on word work. This was shown by the difficulty students had responding to comprehension-based questions, such as, "Let's look into our new books to see what interesting things are going on inside." In fact, throughout the lesson the children were more vocal when asked word-based questions than when asked comprehension-based questions.

After the reading, the teacher did not invite students to respond in writing to the text. Rather, as a culminating activity students were simply asked to write new sets of rhyming words.

School C

The six second-grade children gathered at a small kidney-shaped table with their teacher who began the lesson by showing them the cover of the book, *Pigs Aplenty, Pigs Galore!* (McPhail, 1993). She encouraged comments about the book and attempts at reading the title and author. She said, "Let's have a look at it before I read it," and she took the children on a "picture walk" as they studied each brightly colored, funny picture and laughed and made comments.

Then the teacher read the book aloud to the children, allowing them to join in on the rhyming lines. She stopped to define words like, "aplenty" and "galore" and "kilt" during the reading. She allowed and encouraged spontaneous comments about the book, and encouraged them to look closely at subtle signs of humor in the book, such as reading the pizza bill that was for hundreds of dollars or seeing the reflection of the pigs in the bathroom mirror.

After the teacher read the book to the children (with some student-initiated choral reading), the teacher led a discussion. Some of the talk was captured by the researcher. She began by asking, "What did you think?"

A child says, "It was funny!"

The teacher says, "I agree. What made it funny?"

The child says, "Think of all those pigs in *your* house."

Another child takes the book from the teacher and turns to the middle of it, looking for a particular page. When he finds the page, he says, "I like the king and queen pigs. Wow, they're huge!" This continues for about 10 minutes as the children explore the book. One quiet boy says, "He's really nice (meaning the man in the book, the only human character), isn't he? I mean, he let the pigs all stay even though they caused him trouble." The teacher agreed and asked the children how they might have dealt with the problem. After the discussion, The teacher says, "Want to read it?" The children nod and say, "Yes." (It has been about 15 minutes.)

Next, the teacher directs the students' attention to a chart on which she had reprinted the first four pages of the book. She tells the children that she will read the lines first and they will repeat after her. However, they do not wait to echo her reading; some join in attempting to read the text along with her. She allows this, but continues with an additional "choral" reading after her echo reading. One child says, "Let's read it all." The teacher agrees since the words in the book are big enough for the group to see. The children struggle to read most of the text, but seem to follow the teacher's cues as they read (i.e., the teacher's oral reading is just ahead of the children's). Throughout this reading, all the children are engaged, making the effort to read the book. These readings take about 15 minutes.

Afterwards, the teacher tells the children they are going to do some "word work" and she hands out paper and pencils to the group. She begins with "pig" and has children copy it from the chart. Then she asks them to write big, dig, fig, gig, jig, wig, then all of those words with an "s" on the end. Then she says, "Now, I am going to give you some words that are a little harder—you have to change only one letter of each word to make a new word. First, point to your

> word 'big' on your paper." When all have their finger in the correct place, she says, "Now, I want you to write the word 'bag.' It's a lot like 'big,' but one letter is different." This goes on for a few minutes. Three of the children seem to do it quite easily, while two struggle and get assistance from their peers. After they finish, the time is up for the group and the teacher says, apologetically, "Well, we didn't save enough time to write today. Maybe during writing workshop today you could write what it might be like to have a pet pig . . . or something that the book reminds you of."

In this lesson, the teacher again followed the *structure* of the model. She began the lesson with a comprehension focus by showing the pictures, reading aloud, and discussing the text with the children. In fact, nearly half the lesson was focused on comprehension. Her multiple social readings of the text (echo and choral reading) enabled fluent reading in a risk-free way. Whereas her intention was to focus on her reprinted first four pages for intensive reading and rereading, a child suggested they "read the whole thing" and the teacher obliged, following the needs and desires of the students. Her word work was an extension of the words found in the book. Yet, while her writing prompt was more than listing (as in the previous lesson), it was also vague and dismissed, suggesting the teacher may not value that part of the lesson.

Summary and Discussion

It is evident from this study that one instructional model can be enacted differently and with varied student responses even though all teachers followed the implementation "rules" or structure of the model. Additionally, all of these teachers read about the model and participated in the summer training and follow-up professional development (reflection, dialogue, coaching) during the school year. Each teacher bought in to the model; each was selected to be part of the study because of her commitment to the model. And the components of the professional development are those recommended by experts (Anders, Hoffman, & Duffy, 2000). So, why the differences? What did the training and professional development *do* and *not* do?

One of the reasons this study is so complex is because of the promising practices that *were* included in this project. First, the teachers selected a model rather than a program that could be adapted to their individual contexts. Potential lessons and specific strategies were shared in three ways: Demonstrated at the summer institute, observed on videotape with real children, and described in the manual. The follow-up professional development focused on teachers' developing constructions of understanding and provided time for dialogue and reflection. Also, teachers were able to observe an expert demonstrate a lesson with their students with follow-up observation and feedback from the expert. We applaud all these practices.

The project was limited in terms of teacher training. Three days is usually not enough time to changes teachers' thinking about teaching and learning, which might have been necessary in the cases of Teachers A and B in this study. Research has shown that one of the reasons the highly popular Reading Recovery model is effective is due to the extensive professional development of the participants (Shanahan & Barr, 1998).

This project did not focus on the "big picture" of reading instruction (e.g., making sure instruction is enjoyable rather than torturous). We saw children bored and anxious in some classrooms. We saw reading slowed down so much with round robin reading that children could not attend to the print and some seemed afraid to take risks figuring out words. We also saw nonchallenging texts and questions in some classrooms. Little instruction was truly authentic and little real dialogue occurred, aspects of instruction heralded by some as key to the education of children at-risk for school failure (Tharp, Estrada, Dalton, & Yamauchi, 2000).

The varied student responses may have been due to the choices of texts used for instruction. Children in School B appeared to be bored with their predictable texts, whereas in School C the children could not seem to get enough of the quite difficult, but delightful book they were reading, *Pigs Aplenty, Pigs Galore!* (McPhail, 1993). Text choice for beginning and struggling readers is currently a highly debated topic by teachers and researchers. Many instructional models we studied recommend "leveled" texts for children's instruction. Although we agree on the need for text of appropriate difficulty, we do not recommend their use at the expense of boredom.

We also believe that even though this project included some excellent professional development activities such as the dialogue, reflection, and coaching, the focus was still on the implementation of the model over the development of teachers' craft knowledge. Research on teacher competence has shown that teacher expertise contributes most to student achievement (Darling-Hammond, 1995). Gallagher (1998, cited in Gaffney & Anderson, 2000) claimed that teachers need to pay attention to the contextual aspects of what makes a lesson "work" for a particular group of students. She argued that teacher craft knowledge should be the centerpiece of professional development.

The project did not educate teachers about classroom discourse patterns such as mediating the construction of understanding through questioning, modeling, explaining, and scaffolding. It did not focus on how to respond to children's responses. We witnessed lost opportunities for scaffolding children's responses toward deeper understanding or for word identification. Yet, it is teachers' instructional actions (Darling-Hammond, 1995; Duffy & Roehler, 1991) and attention to discourse patterns (Castells, 2000) that appear to lead children to deeper understandings and new skills.

This analysis confirms those who believe a strict comparison of students' achievement in various models may be an inappropriate way of looking at instructional affects. We must look at the specific features of the models and then how each is enacted. We are finding ways to examine scores by teacher and classroom and not just by model name in order to really discern what seems to be most effective in helping struggling readers to achieve. Anders et al. (2000) warn us:

> A "packaging mentality" is sweeping the country regarding teacher education and in-service. School districts are purchasing in-service packages for schools and districts. Why? And with what outcomes? We feel that such a movement might lead some to conduct research on in-service programs comparing method "A" to method "B." In the process of doing this kind of research the teacher becomes subservient to the method. We have made this mistake too often and we are in danger of going down this path again. (p. 723)

It is our hope that more studies like this one can help teachers and administrators rethink pouring money into programs or models without adequate funding spent on increasing teacher knowledge.

References

Anders, P. L., Hoffman, J. V., & Duffy, G. D. (2000). Teaching teachers to teach reading: Paradigm shifts, persistent problems, and challenges. In M. L. Kamil, P. B Mosenthal, P. D. Pearson, & R. Barr (Eds.), *Handbook of Reading Research* (Vol. 3, pp. 719–742). Mahwah, NJ: Erlbaum.

Castells, N. G. (2000). *Early reading: An approach to the knowledge children have and the teachers' teaching strategies.* Unpublished doctoral dissertation, University of Barcelona, Spain.

Cazden, C. B. (1988). *Classroom discourse: The language of teaching and learning.* Portsmouth, NH: Heinemann.

Christelow, E. (1989). *Five little monkeys jumping on the bed.* New York: Clarion.

Clay, M. M. (1991). *Becoming literate: The construction of inner control.* Heinemann.

Cunningham, P. M., Allington, R. L. (1994). *Classrooms that Work: They can all read and write.* New York: Longman.

Darling-Hammond, L. (1995). Inequality and access to knowledge. In J. Banks and C. A. M. Banks (Eds.), *Handbook of research in multicultural education* (pp. 465–483). New York: Macmillan.

Delpit, L.D. (1995). Language diversity and learning. *Other peoples' children: Cultural conflict in the classroom.* New York: New Press.

Deven, M. (1993). *Dancing dinosaurs.* Glenview, IL: Scott Foresman.

Duffy, G. G., & Rohler, L. R. (1991). Teachers' instructional actions. In R. Barr, P. Mosenthal, M. L. Kamil, & P. D. Pearson (Eds.), *Handbook of reading research* (Vol. 2, pp. 667–679). New York: Longman.

Foster, M. L., & Peele, T. B. (2001). Ring my bell: Contextualizing home and school in an African American community. In E. McIntyre, A. Rosebery, & N. Gonzalez (Eds.), *Classroom diversity: Connecting curriculum to students' lives.* Portsmouth, NH: Heinemann.

Gaffney, J. S., & Anderson, R. C. (2000). Trends in reading research in the United States: Changing intellectual currents over three decades. In M. L. Kamil, P. B Mosenthal, P. D. Pearson, & R. Barr (Eds.), *Handbook of Reading Research* (Vol. 3, pp. 719–742). Mahwah, NJ: Erlbaum.

Gallagher, D. J. (1998). The scientific knowledge base of special education. Do we know what we think we know? *Exceptional Children, 64,* 493–502.

Heath, S. B. (1983). *Ways with words: Language, life, and work in communities and classrooms.* New York: Cambridge University Press.

Hiebert, E., & Taylor, B. (1994). *Getting reading right from the start: Effective early literacy intervention.* Boston: Allyn & Bacon.

McPhail, D. (1993). *Pigs aplenty, pigs galore.* New York: Harcourt Brace.

Shanahan, T., & Barr, R. (1998). Reading Recovery: An independent evaluation of the effects of an early instructional intervention for at-risk learners. *Reading Research Quarterly, 30,* 958–997.

Slavin, R. E., Madden, N. A., Karweit, N., Dolan, L., & Wasik, B. (1992). *Success for all: A relentless approach to prevention and early intervention in elementary schools.* Arlington, VA: Educational Research Service.

Taylor, B. M., Strait, J., & Medo, M. A. (1994). Early intervention in reading: Supplemental instruction for groups of low-achieving students provided by first grade teachers. In E. Hiebert & B. Taylor (Eds.), *Getting reading right from the start: Effective early literacy interventions* (pp. 122–136). Boston: Allyn & Bacon.

Tharp, R. G., Estrada, P., Dalton, S., & Yamauchi, L. (2000). *Teaching transformed: Achieving excellence, fairness, inclusion, and harmony.* Boulder, CO: Westview.

Examining the Theoretical Claims About Decodable Text: Does Text Decodability Lead to Greater Application of Letter/Sound Knowledge in First-Grade Readers?

Heidi Anne Mesmer
Virginia Commonwealth University

Decodable text is once again being used in early reading instruction even as researchers debate its usefulness. Some researchers believe that text containing some degree of decodability may be helpful to beginning readers (Adams, 1997; Hiebert, 1998; Juel & Roper/Schneider, 1985). According to others, decodability is not necessary for beginning readers (e.g., Allington, 1997; Routman, 1997). Pikulski (1998) summarized knowledge in this area by asking, "How many studies have been published in which the nature of beginning reading texts is systematically varied and the effects measured?" (p. 30). Others have followed with calls for research (Hiebert, 1998; National Reading Panel, 2000; Snow, Burns, & Griffin, 1998).

This study responds to such calls for research. However, it is not intended to summarily determine whether or not decodable text should be used. Instead, this research focuses on such questions as: "Does decodable text live up to the claims that theorists make about it? Does it do what it is supposed to do?"

Background

This section will only briefly review current literature (for full review see Mesmer, 2001). The first portion of this review examines definitions of decodable text. The second section describes the theoretical purposes of decodable text. The third analyzes studies examining the effects of decodable text on readers and the final section presents a developmental model for the present study.

What Is Decodable Text?

Educators define decodable text by the presence of the following two features: (a) a proportion of words with phonically regular relationships between letters and sounds, and (b) a degree of match between the relationships represented in text and those that the reader has been taught (Allington & Woodside/Jiron, 1998; Groff, 1999; Hiebert, 1998; Stein, Johnson, & Gutlohn, 1999; Willows, Borwick, & Hayvren, 1981).

*National Reading Conference Yearbook, **50**, pp. 444–459.*

In most studies, phonic regularity refers to letter/sound patterns that can be applied to many different words (Hiebert, 1998; Hoffman et al., 1993; Hoffman, Roser, Salas, Patterson, & Pennington, 2000; Juel & Roper/Schneider, 1985; Menon & Hiebert, 1999). A major feature of decodable text, phonic regularity has been assessed using many methods (rating scales, rimes, bigram versatility). However, the simple presence of regular patterns does not necessarily characterize decodability. Instead, decodability is distinguished by the clustering of like words together within specific passages or books (Hiebert, 1998; Juel & Roper/Schneider, 1985). Thus, in decodable text, specific words may not be repeated more often but certain universal word parts are.

Another defining feature of decodable text is a degree of match between letter/sound relationships represented in text and those that the reader has been taught. This feature is called lesson-to-text match. Usually, lesson-to-text match is expressed as a percentage of words matching phonics lessons specified in teacher's manuals. Across studies, decodable text is distinguished from other text by a higher degree of match between words in text and prescribed lessons (Barr & Dreeben, 1983; Beck, 1981; Beck & Block, 1979; Meyer, Greer, & Crummey 1987; Reutzel & Daines, 1987; Stein et al., 1999). A major limitation of work in this area is that the lesson-to-text match feature only takes into account lessons specified in teacher's editions. Actual phonics lessons most definitely take a different form and are crucial to determining actual lesson-to-text match (Ball & Cohen, 1996; Pressley, Rankin, & Yokoi, 1996). The present study inspects the effects of decodable text when actual phonics lessons match text.

What Are Theoretical Purposes of Decodable Text?

To become proficient, beginners must read great amounts of text, yet they are significantly challenged by the task of identifying words in print (Gough & Hillinger, 1980; Gough & Juel, 1991; Juel, 1994). Like all materials with controlled vocabulary, decodable text scaffolds word identification to give readers access to print.

Decodable text is particularly useful because it allows readers to apply phonics instruction as they read in connected text (Adams, 1990; Barr, 1972; Biemiller, 1970; Chall 1967, 1989; Gough & Juel; 1991). This feature of decodable text is especially important because the skills used to learn phonics rules or complete worksheets do not typically generalize to real reading. Reading connected text allows readers to internalize letter/sound knowledge (Adams, 1990; Stahl, Duffy-Hester, & Stahl, 1998).

The supportive features in any text, be they repeated words, supportive pictures, rhyming words, or consistency between letters and sounds, affect that to which beginning readers attend (Adams, 1997). Readers who apply letters and sounds during connected reading must be attending consciously to them; decodable text encourages this attention. It has been argued that the variety of patterns found in nondecodable texts may actually draw readers' attention away from the regularities of the English language (Barr & Dreeben, 1983; Beck, 1981; Beck & McCaslin, 1978; Meyer et al., 1987). When used at the proper developmental juncture, as suggested in this study's model, decodable text may help younger readers use alphabetic knowledge during connected reading.

The Effects of Decodable Text and Instruction on Word-Recognition Strategies

The Juel and Roper/Schneider (1985) study is consistently cited as a source of information on text features and behavior. At three points during a year, these researchers measured the abilities of two first-grade groups, one reading in a decodable text and the other in a high-frequency text. Both received the same phonics instruction. The decodable group performed better on the decoding measure, both at the November/December testing and at the February testing. Also, the decodable group was more successful at reading unknown words from the other group's basal by the end of the year.

The groups did not differ in their abilities to read words from their own basals. For both groups, regularity, repetition, and bigram versatility predicted their abilities to do so but the decodable group was most influenced by regularity. Juel and Roper/Schneider (1985) concluded that text type used during the first two-thirds of the first-grade year contributed to the use of a letter/sound strategy. Text type also facilitated the transfer of letter/sound knowledge through the end of the first grade.

In another study, at-risk students were identified in kindergarten and randomly assigned to either a Code or Context treatment (Felton, 1993). Participants were followed longitudinally for 2 years. Treatments differed by approach to phonics instruction (explicit or implicit) and by text decodability. The Code group outperformed the Context group at the end of first grade both on decoding measures (reading pseudo words) and on spelling. By the end of second grade, the Code group was more skilled at reading real, regular polysyllabic words as well as decoding.

Hoffman et al. (2000) examined how decodability and predictability predicted student accuracy, fluency, and rate within three different instructional treatments. Student accuracy was positively and significantly correlated with decodability indicating that decodability may have assisted students in analyzing words.

A Model Based on Word Identification Phases

Ultimately, most questions of strategies, techniques, and materials do not seek to establish the one method that will work for all children all of the time, but instead relate to developmental points at which strategies may be most effective. This study examined the stages of word recognition at which decodable text may be most useful. Readers in various stages of word recognition are essentially differentiated by the extent to which they apply the alphabetic principle. Prealphabetic readers do not use letter/sound correspondences to recognize words (Ehri & McCormick, 1998). Once readers understand the alphabetic principle, they begin to gradually apply their knowledge in the partial alphabetic stage by using beginning or final consonants. As readers move into full alphabetic reading, they connect all letters in a word with the phonemes that they represent (Ehri, 1991, 1995; Ehri & McCormick, 1998).

Like training wheels on a bicycle, decodable texts are temporary supports that are designed to facilitate future independence. For several reasons, text with some decodability may facilitate readers' transition into full alphabetic reading (Brown, 1999; Mesmer, 1999). A major hurdle for readers at this stage is decoding medial short vowels (Ehri, 1995). Decodable text gives the reader a leg up by presenting phonically regular words. Furthermore, the lesson-to-text consistency may promote expedient application of alphabetic strategies during reading (Adams, 1997; Anderson, Hiebert, Scott, & Wilkinson, 1985; Gough & Juel, 1991; Juel, 1994). Theoretically, the argument for using decodable texts during this transition is clear—at the point when children know enough letter/sound correspondences to apply them to reading but not enough to handle the full range of patterns in English, they may need decodable texts to allow them to practice reading.

The benefits of decodable text critically depend upon an interface between text and instruction. If readers are not taught the letter/sound patterns before they are asked to read them, decodability is not useful. However, attention to what children are taught in actual teacher-delivered phonics lessons has not been controlled or matched to decodability in any known studies.

Purpose

This study manipulated text decodability by coordinating phonics instruction with decodable text, and then measured whether or not participants applied phonics instruction more within a decodable text than a nondecodable text. During the study, all participants received the same phonics instruction, but treatment participants read decodable text and control participants read nondecodable text.

The application of phonics instruction was measured by analyzing oral reading errors and rating them for a match to the print. Each error was assigned a point for each phoneme matching the print. For example, the word "ship" has three phonemes. The error "shop" has two corresponding phonemes and would receive a rating of 2, the error "show" a rating of 1, and the error "got" 0. Errors with two or more phonemes matching the print were called graphically similar. This division corresponds with the developmental juncture of the model. A reader who correctly pronounces 0 or 1 phonemes correctly is most likely a prealphabetic or partial alphabetic reader, using either no alphabetic information or only initial sounds. A reader pronouncing at least two or more phonemes correctly is more likely moving into the full alphabetic phase by using more than an initial or final sound. Children reading decodable text were expected to have a higher percentage of graphically similar errors.

The study explored how decodability would affect readers. The study's purpose related to the theoretical assertions about decodability. Specifically, the study asked whether or not decodable text would result in greater application of phonics instruction. The following specific question guided the study: Do participants reading decodable text apply phonics instruction more during text reading than participants reading nondecodable text as measured by graphically similar errors?

Method

Participants

Two schools in a major metropolitan area in the Mid-Atlantic participated in the study. School I was in a large suburban district with approximately 150 elementary schools. In the three participating first-grade classrooms, teachers regrouped children for reading instruction across classrooms according to reading level. Due to this grouping structure, the classes were reportedly more homogeneous. School II was in a smaller district with approximately 14 elementary schools. Two teachers, one Reading Recovery® trained and the other with a cross-certification in elementary education and ESOL, staffed the participating classroom.

The participating schools and classrooms were similar in a number of ways. Both schools received Title I funding at the schoolwide level, both had large and diverse populations of ESOL students, and both shared similar instructional practices. Teachers used the morning message, shared books, journaling, writer's workshop, and independent reading. Teachers also used a variety of reading materials including literature, big books, and "little books."

The entire sample (*N*=39) was distributed between the two schools. Twenty-three children from School I and 16 children from School II participated in the study. The participants consisted of 23 females and 16 males. Eight participants were Caucasian, 6 African-American, 15 Latino/a, 4 Asian-Pacific Islander, and 6 other. Over half of the children in the study had a home language other than English (*n*=25) and 14 of these children spoke Spanish. All participants were fluent English speakers.

Materials

The Bob Books (Maslen & Maslen, 1987) were chosen as the treatment text because they are highly decodable on four measures—lesson-to-text match, repetition, regularity, and number of syllables. This pronounced decodability made them especially viable for a short-term intervention. The control books included the Dominie Press' Carousel Readers. These texts contained short sentences, many high-content words, print-picture match, and some predictable elements.

During the intervention, each group read 15 books. Three different book sets were used (decodable and control) to insure that children were reading at an instructional level. The researcher analyzed the decodability of books by comparing content words (Clark & Clark, 1977) on lesson-to-text match, phonic regularity, repetition, total number of running words, and number of syllables. For each feature, words were analyzed and book set means compared using *t* tests for independent means (α=.05).

Each content word was analyzed for its match to the letter/sound focus of each lesson delivered by the researcher. The words in text appearing after these lessons were counted as matching. The lesson-to-text feature assumed some previously learned information in lesson-to-text counts because the researcher could not be present for the entire year of instruction. Participants were assumed to have already learned certain relationships when they correctly identified all the words sharing that sound on a preintervention word list. For example, if a student read the short a words "sad" and "bag" correctly on the word list, then the words in text like "hat, pack, and Dan," were assumed in the lesson-to-text match.

The levels of regularity of the words were evaluated using procedures developed by Juel and Roper-Schneider (1985). These researchers used a rating system, a scale categorizing words into three classes, developed by Venezky (1970). Class I words were called Transfer words and contained predictable patterns that could be transferred to the pronunciations of other words (e.g., bag, yell, seat). Class II words were called Association words. These contained frequently occurring but more difficult patterns (e.g., law, that, car). Juel and Roper/Schneider (1985) described these words as containing, l, r, and w controlled vowels, diphthongs, and digraphs. Class III words contained irregular and unpredictable patterns (e.g., come, pear). In the study, each content word was analyzed on regularity. This feature also constituted one of the major differences between the book sets, as it should. Each set of decodable books contained significantly more regular words. The lower ratings on the decodable books indicate higher levels of regularity.

In the areas of lesson-to-text match, regularity and number of syllables the decodable and control texts all differed significantly with the decodable text containing a higher percentage of words matching lessons, more regular words and fewer syllables. In the areas of repetition and number of running words, differences between book sets also existed. Set 1 decodable texts repeated words an average of two more times per book than the control, and Set 2 decodable texts repeated words an average of one more time. By Set 3, the sets did not differ in repetition. Similar differences occurred in the area of total running words. For Set 3 the number of running words in the text did not differ—the expected outcome of the analysis. However, for Sets 1 and 2, the number of running words in the text did differ with the control set containing more words than the decodable texts.

Design

This study used an experimental design. The independent variable was text decodability and the dependent variable was the degree of match between participants' responses and the print. During the study both treatment and control participants received standard phonics instruction delivered by the researcher. Afterwards, the treatment group read decodable text and the control group read nondecodable text. The intervention took place for 15 days. A significant feature of the design was control of actual phonics instruction because no other known study had done this. However, controlling actual phonics instruction required a relatively small sample.

The 39 participants were divided into 10 subgroups containing 4 participants each. One participant was unable to consistently participate in the study and had to be dropped. To increase internal validity, the participants in the ten subgroups were matched on ability. At least two subgroups, randomly assigned to condition, were in each classroom. Participants received phonics instruction within their subgroups. The design directly responded to the literature by contrasting how participants would apply the same phonics instruction in a decodable versus a control context. The design controlled for ability by matching. It accounted for group rivalry and possible control group demoralization by using an alternate text treatment for the control group. Teacher effects were accounted for by matching within classrooms. To control for lessons, the researcher delivered all lessons using a standard format. The book sets were controlled on the two essential features of decodable text as defined by the literature—lesson-to-text match and phonic regularity.

Groups were initially assessed to establish baseline equivalence and to facilitate matching. Children who did not have a firm grasp of the alphabetic principle and firm concept of word were not likely to show any differences regardless of approach and were dropped from the study. Criteria included a minimum score of 20/25 on the letter/sound assessment and 4/6 on the concept of word. The design, procedures, and assessments were informed by a 5-week pilot study involving 17 first graders in two classrooms.

Procedures

Procedures were divided into those employed during the preintervention (14 days), intervention (15 days), and postintervention (2–3 days) stages of the study. Children were given the following preintervention assessments: (a) the Taylor Phonemic Segmentation and Blending Test (Taylor, Harris, & Pearson, 1988), internal consistency/reliability r=.84 (Cronbach's α); (b) a letter/sound recognition assessment based on the work of Bryne and Fielding-Barnsley (1991), r=.65 (Cronbach's α); (c) a concept of word assessment based on the work of Santa and Hoein, (1999), r=.84 (Cronbach's α); (d) the Word Attack Subtest of the Woodcock Reading Mastery Test Form G–Revised; and (e) A word list to verify lesson-to-text match, r=.94 (Cronbach's α).

Using the preintervention assessments, a composite score for each child was derived. Within classrooms, participants were ordered by this composite score. Starting from the top of the list, participants were alternately assigned to groups of four. When the number of students did not match the number of participants needed, participants who least matched the group were eliminated. This resulted in a total of eight participants being eliminated. Ten subgroups or five matched pairs were created as a result.

The degree to which the matching served as a control on ability depended on the number of participants who could be dropped and the homogeneity of the classrooms. The composite scores for Subgroup Pairs 2 and 3 in School I were not as evenly matched as Subgroup Pairs 1, 4, and 5 (see Table 1). This was explained by the fact that only two students could be eliminated in School I and by the fact that participants' abilities were not as homogenous as originally reported. In School II, five students were dropped to arrive at the required 16 students and the resulting Pairs 4 and 5 were very closely matched.

All participants engaged in the phonics lessons. However, the treatment group read decodable text following the lessons. Control participants read nondecodable text following the lessons. The researcher delivered the daily 20-minute lesson which consisted of the following practices: (a) Rereading a familiar book, (b) phonemic awareness activities (segmenting and blending, Elkonin boxes), (c) reading words (sounding and blending), (d) dictated writing, and (e) reading a new book. The lesson components were ordered to scaffold participants' learning. Participants first practiced hearing separate sounds, then decoding words, then encoding the sounds into letters, then reading in context. Instruction within each activity progressed from teacher modeling to group guided practice and to independent practice. During the independent practice, each participant individually completed one or two items within a given activity (e.g., reading words, segmenting words, reading pages). The researcher gave participants specific, corrective feedback. A lesson matrix for each book set included the lesson's sound focus, the books, the words to be used in the modeling, guided practice, and independent practice sections of the phonological awareness, reading words, and writing words activities. Before each lesson, one child from each group individually reread the book from the previous day. On every fourth day, each child reread a book. During this time, data were collected using running record procedures to obtain the total number of graphically similar oral reading errors (Clay, 1985). At postintervention, each oral reading error in each text received a graphic similarity rating as described earlier.

Results

The study examined whether or not participants reading decodable text would apply phonics instruction during text reading more than a control group. Data were analyzed using Analysis of Covariance to compare the two groups. Covariates

Table 1

Subgroup Means of Percentage Correct on Preintervention Assessments

	School I						School II			
Group	1		2		3		4		5	
Treatment	Treat	Con	Treat	Con	Treat	Con	Treat	Con	Treat	Con
Composite Score	74	75	81	75	72	69	57	55	75	74

included scores on the phonemic awareness, letter/sound, and word attack measures. An alpha level of .05 was used with all statistical tests The outcome variable was the number of graphically similar oral reading errors over the entire intervention (i.e., errors with two or more phonemes matching the print, GSEs Total). The GSEs category does not include all substitution errors or those in which only 0 or 1 phonemes match the print. Baseline measures included a phonemic awareness test (segmentation and blending), a letter/sound assessment, and a word attack measure. Table 2 shows the means for treatment and control groups on baseline assessments. All of the participants had very high percentages on the letter/sound assessment. Note also that the results on the phonemic awareness assessment have been reported by total score and by subtest (segmentation and blending) because of the importance of segmenting in full alphabetic reading. Both groups performed better on the blending portion of that test than on segmentation. Table 3 shows participants' mean number of GSEs and adjusted means. A distinct difference exists between the two groups on the number of GSEs; the treatment group almost doubled the number of GSEs made by the control group. The difference is maintained when means are adjusted for phonemic awareness and word attack scores.

Table 4 presents the simple correlation coefficients between participants' GSEs and specific text features that distinguished decodability. These relationships followed predictable patterns. Readers' GSEs positively correlated with lesson-to-text match indicating that as lesson-to-text match increased so did GSEs.

Table 2

Participants' Mean Percentages Correct on Baseline Measures

Measure	Treatment Means	Control Means
1. Phonemic Awareness Total Battery	52.5 (27.9)	40.8 (26.5)
2. Phonemic Awareness Blending	64.2 (29.2)	53.5 (36.1)
3. Phonemic Awareness Segmenting	43.9 (35.7)	31.1 (25.7)
4. Word Attack	33.1 (16. 9)	27.1 (17.9)
5. Letter/sound	97.8 (3.7)	92.8 (23.5)

Table 3

Participants' Mean Number of GSEs Over the Intervention

Measure	Treatment Means	Control Means
Number of GSES total ($\leq$2 phoneme match)	10.3 (8.4)	5.7 (3.7)
Adjusted Number of GSES Total ($\leq$2 phoneme match)	10.6 (8.2)	5.4 (3.8)

Table 4

Pearson Product Moment Correlations Between Participant GSEs and Text Variables

	1	2	4	5
1. GSES	1.00			
2. Lesson to Text	.31*	1.00		
3. Number of Syllables	-.19	-.91*	1.00	
4. Regularity	-.32*	-.97*	.90*	1.00

*Significant at the .01 level.

Readers' total GSEs also negatively correlated with regularity. As text words became more regular, the GSEs increased (more regular words had lower ratings). The number of syllables in text had no obvious relationship to GSEs. The intercorrelations between text features also followed predictable patterns. Regularity and lesson-to-text-match correlated negatively. Regularity ratings decreased as lesson-to-text match increased. A similar relationship existed between lesson-to-text match and number of syllables: as lesson-to text match increased, number of syllables decreased. Finally, regularity and number of syllables were positively correlated, meaning that more regular words contained fewer syllables.

Prior to performing an analysis of covariance, the data were analyzed to insure that the proper assumptions were met. The most important of these was the homogeneity of regression coefficients. Regression coefficients of the covariates (phonemic awareness, letter/sound, and word attack) had to be same for both groups. When controlled for total phonemic awareness, letter/sound, and word attack, groups differed significantly on GSEs [$F(1, 37)=3.82, p>.05$). Thus, the data illustrate that participants reading decodable text did apply phonics instruction more during text reading than participants reading nondecodable text.

Having established a difference between groups, further analysis was undertaken to examine the specific characteristics of decodable text that most affected participants. All decodable and control sets differed significantly on lesson-to-text match, number of syllables, and phonic regularity. When an analysis of covariance was performed including phonemic awareness, letter/sound, and word attack as covariates and lesson-to-text match, regularity, and number of syllables as predictors only regularity significantly affected GSEs [$F(1, 37)=9.04, p>.005$).

The nature of the relationship between the two key decodability features, lesson-to-text match and regularity, made understanding the unique affects of each feature very difficult. Because lesson-to-text match and regularity are so highly correlated with one another (r=-.97), they mask each other's effects. However, when regularity was removed from the analysis, only number of syllables was significant [$F(1, 37)=8.91, p>.05$] and not lesson-to-text match. Therefore, the word-level features phonic regularity and number of syllables were more influential than lesson-to-text match.

Limitations

This study is limited in several respects. First, the intervention phase was 15 days. It is likely that the transition from partial to full-alphabetic reading that is scaffolded by decodable text lasts longer than 15 days. For some participants the affects may have been more pronounced with a longer intervention. Future studies may extend the intervention phase of the study.

Second, a critical component of the intervention was a direct match between the actual phonics lessons and the words in text. For this reason, lessons were tightly controlled and were standardized for both content and format. Despite these controls, the study did not take into account subgroup affects which may have occurred within instructional groups. Finally, the demographics of study participants indicate that these findings best apply to groups with high numbers of fluent English speakers who simultaneously speak a language other than English at home.

Conclusions

Based on this study four conclusions were drawn. The first relates to decodability fulfilling its theoretical purposes. The second discusses the viability of the developmental model. The third conclusion considers how the text features of decodable text affect readers. Finally, connections are made to other studies.

Theory, Reality, and Decodable Text

Does decodable text live up to the claims made about it? Does it do what it is supposed to do? If one of the purposes of decodable text is to assist beginning readers in applying phonics instruction during text reading, then the answer is yes. Participants in this study had oral reading errors that more closely matched the print than nondecodable readers. The design and procedures of the study made two important suggestions about the use of decodable text. First, the coordination between text and actual instruction is crucial. The integration of text with instruction resulted in readers generalizing phonics skills to a reading context. Educators who hope to see readers pay greater attention to letter/sound information as they are reading text may use decodable text along with short, explicit phonics lessons. Second, it is important to note that the participants in this study interacted with many different types of text throughout the school day and only read study texts during the 20-minute intervention phase of the study. This indicates that the textual scaffolds present in decodable text may have affects even when readers use a range of other materials.

The second contribution of this study is related to behavior during connected reading. The outcome measures in this study examined how participants used phonics instruction during real reading, not while reading word lists or decoding in word attack tests. This aspect is important because the very purpose of phonics instruction is that it be used during reading. Finally, the 15-day intervention time suggests that highly decodable text like the Bob Books may be used consistently for an abbreviated period of time to produce effects. These results would support a use of decodable sets containing ten to fifteen books like those decodable books currently being sold.

When Developmentally Might Decodable Text Be Used

The findings offer support for a developmental theory. The readers that participated in this study knew almost all of their letter/sounds. They had some skill in phonemic segmentation and blending, a strong concept of word, and some skill in word attack. The skills of these participants suggest a sketch of who may benefit from decodable text. Certainly readers who possess neither letter/sound knowledge nor a clear concept of word cannot benefit from the decodable text.

Readers should also possess some phonemic segmentation ability. The average first grader scored between 31% and 43% correct on the segmenting portion of the phonemic awareness assessment in this study. If these findings are synthesized with current knowledge of the developmental progression of phonemic awareness, the window of usefulness for decodable text can be further specified. Ability to fully segment phonemes in words appears after rhyme recognition and blending (Schatschneider, Francis, Foorman, Fletcher, Metha, 1999; Yopp, 1988). In one study, kindergartners successfully segmented an average of 9 out of 15 words, or 60% of words (Yopp, 1988). Thus, decodable text may not be useful until children can successfully segment between 37% and 60% of a list of words, a milestone which may occur in either kindergarten or first grade.

Regularity Affects Readers Most

When coupled with explicit phonics instruction, regularity and lesson-to-text match appear to help readers match two or more phonemes to print during connected reading. The number of graphically similar errors correlated positively with lesson-to-text match and negatively with regularity. This suggests that as lesson-to-text match and regularity increased, so did graphically similar errors. Which text features affected readers the most? Of the two key features defining decodability, regularity had a more powerful influence on readers. After regularity, the number of syllables affected readers and finally, lesson-to-text match. Thus, the key component in decodable text is regularity.

Lesson-to-text match defines decodability and yet of the three components it had the least affect on behavior. The finding is puzzling. Practically speaking a child must learn and be taught specific letter/sound knowledge in order to apply it. There are two issues with the lesson-to text construct that obfuscate these findings. First the unique effects of lesson-to-text match are difficult to tease out because of the high correlation between lesson-to-text match and regularity. In this study these two constructs overlap to a high degree but the overlap is necessary because the two features define decodability. Second, the lesson-to-text match construct could be improved. Technically, the crucial match within decodable text is the coordination between the reader and the words in text and not the lessons and the words in text. The focus should be on what has been *learned* as opposed to what has been taught because the two may not always overlap. Although the lesson-to-text match does account for some previously learned information, it was not based on this notion.

Connections with Other Studies

These findings duplicate findings in the Juel and Roper/Schneider (1985) study in two respects. First, these findings suggest that the pairing of text decodability with coordinated phonics instruction affects strategy use more than phonics instruction without coordinated text. However, the findings here add to the previous work because these results apply to strategies used during connected reading. As in the Juel and Roper/Schneider study, both groups of participants in this study had the same phonics instruction but read in different texts. However, in this study, the phonics instruction was more tightly controlled because it was delivered by the same person and actually matched instruction. Second, the influence of text features mirrors earlier findings (Juel & Roper/Schneider, 1985). Using the same rating system (Venezky, 1970) and procedures, regularity again appeared to exert a strong influence on behavior.

The composition of the sample should also be considered in relation to the Juel and Roper/Schneider (1985) study. What are the implications of decodability with children who have a home language other than English? About 30% of the sample in the Juel and Roper/Schneider (1985) was Mexican-American. Although the study does not report the participants' home language, the possibility exists that they spoke Spanish at home. Sixty percent of participants in this study had a home language other than English. Children in both studies were reported to fluently speak English. These findings suggest that decodability may have a different effect on students whose home language is not English.

The intercorrelations between decodability features replicated previous findings. Essentially, the decodable text in this study contained a higher lesson-to-text match, more regular words, and fewer syllables, just like the decodable text used in other studies (Beck & Block, 1979; Beck, 1981; Hoffman et al., 2000; Juel & Roper/Schneider, 1985; Menon & Hiebert, 1999; Meyer et al., 1987; Reutzel & Daines, 1987; Stein et al., 1999). Researchers defining decodability in future studies can trust these features to clearly and strongly operationalize decodability.

Should decodable text be used with beginning readers? This question is beyond the scope of the present research. In fact it is a question that must be answered with consideration of the learner and his or her specific stage of development. The focus of this research relates to theorists' claims about decodable text. At least when it is used for a brief period of time, decodable text appears to fulfill its theoretical purposes. Readers do seem to apply what they know about letter/sounds when they are presented with multiple opportunities to do so in decodable text. Apparently specific text features influence the application of letter/sound information.

Caveats abound. This study does not explore potential negative effects of decodability, which other research has noted (Hoffman et al., 2000). This researcher is reminded of current pharmaceutical advertisements exuberantly touting the medical benefits of wonder drugs and then softly and hurriedly listing the serious potential side-effects. Decodable text is like these wonder drugs. Although it may live up to its intended purposes, it very likely has side effects. As with the proper use of medicines, the proper use of decodable text lies in understanding its purposes, potential side effects, and most importantly the reader with whom it might be used. Many questions related to decodable text still remain unanswered. For example, is there an optimal level of decodability for readers of varying abilities? Do struggling readers need more decodability and other readers need less? Are there differences between readers who are exposed only to decodable text and those exposed to a range of materials including those, which are decodable? Do readers make more errors that reflect inattention to semantics or syntax as they are reading decodable text? Like any strategy, technique, or method, decodability is no panacea. It is simply one of many tools that, when applied properly, may help beginning readers.

References

Adams, M. J. (1990). *Beginning to read: Thinking and learning about print.* Cambridge, MA: MIT Press.

Adams, M. J. (1997). Myths and realities about words and literacy. *School Psychology Review, 26,* 425–436.

Allington, R. (1997). Overselling phonics: Five unscientific assertions about reading instruction. *Reading Today, 15*(1), 15–16.

Allington, R., & Woodside/Jiron, H. (1998). Decodable text in beginning reading: Are mandates and policy based on research? *ERS Spectrum, 16,* 3–13.

Anderson, R. C., Hiebert, E. H., Scott, J. A., & Wilkinson, I. A. (1985). *Becoming a nation of readers: The report of the commission on reading.* Champaign, IL: Center for the Study of Reading.

Ball, D. L., & Cohen, D. K.(1996). Reform by the book: What is—or might be—the role of curriculum materials in teacher learning and instructional reform? *Educational Researcher, 25,* 6–8.

Barr, R. (1972). The influence of instructional conditions on word recognition errors. *Reading Research Quarterly, 7,* 509–529.

Barr, R., & Dreeben, R. (1983). *How schools work.* Chicago: University of Chicago Press.

Beck, I. L. (1981). Reading problems and instructional practices. In G. A. MacKinnon and T. G. Waller (Eds.), *Reading research: Advances in theory and practice* (Vol. 2, pp. 53–93). Academic.

Beck, I. L., & Block, K. K. (1979). *An analysis of the dimensions that affect the development of code-breaking ability in eight beginning reading programs.* Pittsburgh, PA: University of Pittsburgh, Learning Research and Development Center.

Beck, I. L., & McCaslin, E. S. (1978). *An analysis of dimensions that affect the development of code-breaking ability in eight beginning reading programs* (LRDC Rep. No. 1978/6). Pittsburgh, PA: University of Pittsburgh Learning Research and Development.

Biemiller, A. (1970). The development of the use of graphic and contextual information as children learn to read. *Reading Research Quarterly, 6,* 75–96.

Brown, K. (1999). What kind of text—For whom and when? Textual scaffolding for beginning readers. *Reading Teacher, 53,* 292–307.

Chall, J. S. (1967). *Learning to read: The great debate* (2nd ed.) New York: McGraw-Hill.

Chall, J. S. (1989). *The role of phonics in the teaching of reading: A position paper prepared for the secretary of education* (Report No. SC 010 428). Washington, DC: Office of Education Research and Improvement. (ERIC Document Reproduction Service No. ED 328 899).

Clark, H. C., & Clark, E. V. (1977). *Psychology and language.* New York: Harcourt Brace Jovanovich.

Clay, M. M. (1993). An observation Survey. Portsmouth, NH: Heinemann.

Ehri, L. C. (1991). Learning to read and spell words. In L. Rieben & C. A. Perfetti (Eds.), *Learning to read: Basic research and its implications* (pp. 57–74). Hillsdale, NJ: Erlbaum.

Ehri, L. C. (1995). Phases of development in learning to read words by sight. *Journal of Research in Reading, 18,* 116–125.

Ehri, L. C., & McCormick, S. (1998). Phases of word learning: Implications for instruction with delayed and disabled readers. *Reading and Writing Quarterly: Overcoming Learning Difficulties, 14,* 135–163.

Felton, R. H. (1993). Effects of instruction on the decoding skills of children with phonological processing problems. *Journal of Learning Disabilities, 26,* 583–589.

Gough, P. B., & Hillinger, M. L. (1980). Learning to read: An unnatural act. *Bulletin of the Orton Society, 30,* 179–196.

Gough, P. B., & Juel, C. (1991). The first stages of word recognition. In L. Rieben & C. A. Perfetti (Eds.), *Learning to read: Basic research and its implications* (pp. 47–56). Hillsdale, NJ: Erlbaum.

Groff, P. (1999). *Decodable words in reading textbooks: Why they are imperative.* [On-line] Available: http://www.nrrf.org/27_decode_txtbooks.htm.

Hiebert, E. (1998). *Text matters in learning to read* (CIERA Rep. No. 1-001). Ann Arbor, MI: Center for the Improvement of Early Reading Achievement.

Hoffman, J. V., McCarthey S. J., Abbott, J., Christian, C., Corman, L., Curry, C., Dressman, M., Elliott, B., Maherne, D., & Stahle, D. (1993). So what's new in the new basals? A focus on first grade. *Journal of Reading Behavior, 26,* 47–73.

Hoffman, J. V., Roser, N. L., Salas, R., Patterson, E., & Pennington, J. (2000). *Text leveling and little books in first grade reading* (CIERA Rep. No. 1-010). Ann Arbor, MI: Center for the Improvement of Early Reading Achievement.

Juel, C. (1994). *Learning to read and write in one elementary school.* New York: Springer-Verlag.

Juel, C., & Roper/Schneider, D. (1985). The influence of basal readers on first grade reading. *Reading Research Quarterly, 20,* 134–152.

Maslen & Maslen. (1987). *The "Bob" Books, Set 1, 2, & 3.* New York: Scholastic.

Menon, S., & Hiebert, E. H. (1999). *Literature anthologies: The task for first grade readers* (Ciera Rep. No. 1-009). Ann Arbor, MI: Center for the Improvement of Early Reading Achievement.

Mesmer, H. A. (1999). Scaffolding a crucial transition using text with some decodability. *Reading Teacher, 53,* 130–142.

Mesmer, H. A. (2001). Decodable text: A review of what we know. *Reading Research and Instruction, 40,* 121–141.

Meyer, L. A., Greer, E. A., & Crummey, L. (1987). An analysis of decoding, comprehension, and story text in four first-grade reading programs. *Journal of Reading Behavior, 6,* 69–98.

National Reading Panel (2000). *Report of the National Reading Panel: Teaching Children to Read.* Washington, DC: National Institute of Child Health and Human Development.

Pikulski, J. J. (1998). Business we should finish. *Reading Today, 15*(5), 30.

Pressley, M., Rankin, J., & Yokoi, L. (1996). A survey of instructional practices of outstanding primary-level literacy teachers. *Elementary School Journal, 96,* 363–384.

Reutzel, D. R., & Daines, D. (1987). The text-relatedness of reading lessons in seven basal reading series. *Reading Research and Instruction, 27,* 26–35.

Routman, R. (1997). Routman thanks Allington. *Reading Today, 15*(5), 30.

Santa, C. M., & Hoien, T. (1999). An assessment of first steps: A program for early intervention of reading problems. *Reading Research Quarterly, 34,* 54–79.

Schatschneider, W., Francis, D., Foorman, B., Fletcher, J., & Metha, P. (1999). The dimensionality of phonological awareness: An application of item response theory. *Journal of Educational Psychology, 91,* 439–449.

Snow, C., Burns, M. S., & Griffin, P. (1998). *Preventing reading difficulties in young children.* Washington, DC: National Academy of Sciences Press.

Stahl, S., Duffy-Hester, A., & Stahl, K. A. D. (1998). Everything you wanted to know about phonics (but were afraid to ask). *Reading Research Quarterly, 33,* 338–335.

Stein, M., Johnson, B., & Gutlohn, L. (1999). Analyzing beginning reading programs: The relationship between decoding instruction and text. *Remedial and Special Education, 20,* 257–287.

Taylor, B., Harris, L. A., & Pearson, P. D. (1988). *Reading difficulties: Instruction and assessment.* New York : Random House.

Venezky, R. L. (1970). *The structure of English orthography.* The Hague: Mouton.

Willows, D. M., Borwick, D., & Hayvren, M. (1981). The content of school readers. In G. E, MacKinnon and T. G. Waller (Eds.), *Reading research: Advances in theory and practice* (Vol. 2, pp. 95–175). New York: Academic.

Yopp, H. K. (1988).The validity and reliability of phonemic awareness tests. *Reading Research Quarterly, 23,* 159–77.

The Rise and Fall of Multicultural Literature: Conundrums of the California "Canon"

Greta Nagel and Linda Whitney
California State University, Long Beach

Our linked studies investigate the current array of literary works that are included in the core reading lists for California public schools and begin to determine the "story behind the story" as to teachers' actual classroom use of multicultural literature. Study A repeats a research procedure that was conducted twice before. It was reported just over 10 years ago as *An Analysis of the Array of Literary Works in District Core Reading Lists, Grades K–6* (Flood, Lapp, & Nagel, 1991) and 5 years ago as *The California "Canon": Recommendations and Realities* (Nagel, 1996). This current study compares and contrasts the 1999–00 breadth of selections and inclusion of multicultural literature to choices made previously. Study B examines the use multicultural literature in K–6 classrooms. A representative group of K–6 teachers responded to open-ended survey questions to report the titles of multicultural works in classroom use during 1999–00 and to describe the types of classroom activities relating to this literature.

These inquiries have been conducted to determine the level of multicultural literature use within a state context that has undergone many political changes in recent years, including the advent of a new framework and increased legislative and public demands for direct instruction of reading skills and higher standardized test scores. Although the content of these studies relates to only one state, past experience indicates that it has broader implications for many other states. In a popular metaphor that portrays educational policy and procedure as mining, California plays an ongoing role as the "canary" for the nation.

Setting

For more than 20 years, the philosophy expressed within state department publications has pointed to the critical role that can be played by works of literature in "bridging the gap" that separates human beings of different cultures and different values (California Department of Education, 1980). The framework years ago expressed that teachers could help students to respect and appreciate cultural traditions and values unlike their own through books that represented a broad spectrum of minority experience. The document proposed that teachers select books that presented authentic situations and realistic characterizations with language and illustrations that would help youth to develop an awareness of the backgrounds and feelings of people different from themselves. Many would

National Reading Conference Yearbook, ***50***, *pp. 460–470.*

agree that multicultural literature serves as a vehicle for increasing understandings of others, providing information that is seldom provided by face-to-face contacts across races and ethnic groups in our socially separated society (Merriam, 1998; Probst, 1988).

In 1987, the pivotal California framework and *English Language Arts Model Curriculum Guide: Kindergarten through Grade Eight* (California Department of Education, 1987) established the Core Literature program. Their intention was to provide a common literary experience for children in the same grade, investigating works that can bridge the gaps between human beings and show "that some problems in life, and the solutions to them, are shaped by a culture or by individual experience" (California Department of Education, 1987, p. 7). District leaders and committees were to devise grade-level lists of books that would be expected as student readings or read-alouds for all children in that grade. State documents encouraged the use of the *Recommended Readings in Literature, Kindergarten Through Grade Eight* (California Department of Education, 1986) as a possible guide to help find books of literary quality and diversity.

The new *Reading/Language Arts Framework for California Public Schools* (California Department of Education, 1999) is not as forthright about bridging the gap. It presents many standards for Grades K–8, but in discussing literature and literary response makes no mention of culture or multicultural literature as related to classroom practice. What does appear, in the brief section that sets standards for school library media centers, is the following single sentence: "Students should be given access to outstanding examples of multicultural literature across genres to extend literary response and analysis" (p. 247). The message is clear, but no other mention of multicultural literature appears in the context of this framework of several hundred pages.

Data Collection and Analysis

Study A

District core reading lists were requested by letter and by follow-up telephone calls from 24 districts in California (Flood et al., 1991; Nagel, 1996). The selected districts ranged in size and socioeconomic status and represented a full spectrum of urban, suburban, and rural populations in Northern, Central, and Southern California. All lists were entered into a computer program by grade level and alphabetized by title. Lists were then analyzed as to repetitions of titles and authors within and across grade levels, and matched to state lists and materials in order to do multicultural tagging. The districts contacted in 1990 and 2000 were identical. However, the 1996-selected sample of participating districts was similar by attributes of size and location, but they varied as to actual districts contacted. Results were counted and charted by a variety of attributes, including top numbers of selections made for Grades K–6, K–3, and 4–6. Results for 2000 were compared to those of the past two studies.

Study B

Teachers from eleven school districts in Southern California completed an open-ended, 11-item survey that asked about their use of multicultural literature. Their districts represent a wide range of attributes with respect to size, ethnicity, and socioeconomic status and are similar to the core list districts, but the districts are not identical. The 20 participating teachers are students in a rigorous master's degree program in curriculum and instruction. At the time of this inquiry, they were all enrolled in the same course section and made up the entire class. They represent all grade levels, kindergarten through sixth grade, and their service in professional practice ranges from 2 to 6 years. Data gathered from respondents' narrative answers were examined and categorized, then counted, charted, and analyzed (Cox, 1996). The resultant information identified the book titles of literature used, the purposes fulfilled by the literature, the varied activities and uses of the literature, and student/teacher reactions.

Results

Study A

In view of the ongoing repetitiveness of the core selections, readers might interpret that a canon of sorts does exist. It consists of "tried and true" books that are enjoyable, but it is not multicultural. Some titles are extremely popular across districts and grade levels. After examining the lists, for example, one might deduce that any child who has not read *Charlotte's Web* during elementary school is an unusual child indeed.

As in past years, the districts' lists of core literature that were submitted reveal that choices vary greatly in length and content across grades and districts, with as few as four books expected to be read annually in some grade-level situations and as many as 26 in others. Current lists are similar to those from past studies (1991, 1996) in that selected works are all popular books, more than 90% of the entries are narrative fiction, and over 90% of them are stories of Anglo humans or of animals. The copyright dates of frequently selected books are from more than 20, often 30, years ago and books about or by) people of color make up a very small percentage of the whole.

The conduct of the newest study does reveal some differences. One is that in the year 2000, four districts report that they no longer have core lists and five others indicate that their core lists are now the books advocated by the publisher of their selected reading series (Open Court—4; Harcourt Brace—1). Those books were duly entered in the lists. Another difference is that the total list was longer with a broader variety of books entered. Many of them are multicultural in nature, but many were selected by only one district. Books could be selected by fewer districts and still make the top lists. The number of multicultural selections was slightly higher, but the proportion of multicultural works dropped considerably, as indicated in Table 1.

Table 1

Proportions of Titles to Total Core Selections (State Department Recommended Readings Ethnic Designations)

	State Recommended	Districts 1990	Districts 1996	Districts 2000
Black	7.4%	7.0%	7.7%	4.5%
Chinese	1.7%	1.7%	2.4%	1.5%
Hispanic	4.3%	1.4%	2.7%	2.6%
Indian	7.0%	3.5%	4.7%	3.2%
Japanese	2.8%	1.6%	1.6%	1.8%
Korean	.7%	0%	0%	0%
Vietnamese	1.5%	.5%	.5%	.25%

Table 2

Top Twenty-five Selected Core Works, K–6, 1990

Title	Author	How Many
1. *Stone Soup***	Brown	20
2. *Charlotte's Web***	White	18
3. *Mother Goose***	Various	17
4. *Alexander and the Terrible, . . .**	Viorst	16
5. *Sylvester and the Magic Pebble**	Steig	16
6. *Island of the Blue Dolphins***	O'Dell	15
7. *The Little Red Hen**	Galdone	15
8. *Sign of the Beaver***	Speare	15
9. *The Velveteen Rabbit**	Williams	15
10. *Where the Wild Things Are**	Sendak	15
11. *Sarah, Plain and Tall***	MacLachlan	14
12. *James and the Giant Peach***	Dahl	13
13. *Brown Bear, Brown Bear***	Martin	12
14. *Corduroy***	Freeman	12
15. *Caps for Sale**	Slobodkina	11
16. *Lion, the Witch, and the Ward***	Lewis	11
17. *The Three Bears**	Galdone	11
18. *The Three Billy Goats Gruff*	Galdone	11
19. *The Bremen Town Musicians*	Grimm	10
20. *By the Great Horn Spoon***	Fleischman	10
21. *Frog and Toad Are Friends**	Lobel	10
22. *Ira Sleeps Over***	Waber	10
23. *Ramona and Her Father***	Cleary	10
24. *Where the Red Fern Grows***	Rawls	9

*Title remained on two of the three lists over time. **Title continued on all top 25 lists over time.

As Tables 2, 3, and 4 indicate, the most popular current selections are similar, if not identical, to those of the past "Top Twenty-Five Selected Core Works, K–6." Six titles disappeared from top placements in 1996, but returned in 2000, having only moved to lower rankings. Three titles stayed through 1996, but dropped out in 2000. Only two titles have dropped from the list of frequently selected books during the past decade: *The Three Billy Goats Gruff* and *The Bremen Town Musicians.* Two continuing books could be identified as multicultural. They are *Island of the Blue Dolphins* and *Sign of the Beaver.* In addition, in 2000, they have been joined by *In the Year of the Boar* and *Jackie Robinson.* The three upper-grade books link to the designated state Social Studies curriculum. A primary picture book, *Snowy Day,* features a black main character in its simple story. Several multicultural books, expected as part of the district's selected text series, were

Table 3

Top Twenty-five Selected Core Works, K–6, 1996

Title	Author	How Many
1. *Charlotte's Web*	White	14
2. *Brown Bear, Brown Bear*	Martin	12
3. *Mother Goose*	Various	12
4. *The Velveteen Rabbit*	Williams	12
5. *Alexander and the Terrible, . . .*	Viorst	11
6. *Corduroy*	Freeman	11
7. *Island of the Blue Dolphins*	O'Dell	11
8. *Sign of the Beaver*	Speare	11
9. *Where the Wild Things Are*	Sendak	11
10. *Caps for Sale*	Slobodkina	10
11. *Ira Sleeps Over*	Waber	10
12. *Stone Soup*	Brown	10
13. *Very Hungry Caterpillar*	Carle	10
14. *Fables*	Lobel	9
15. *James and the Giant Peach*	Dahl	9
16. *Story of Johnny Appleseed*	Kellogg	9
17. *Lion, the Witch, and the Ward*	Lewis	9
18. *Snow Day*	Keats	8
19. *Bridge to Terabithia*	Paterson	8
20. *Tale of Peter Rabbit*	Potter	8
21. *Where the Red Fern Grows*	Rawls	8
22. *American Tall Tales*	Stoutenberg	7
23. *From the Mixed Up Files of . . .*	Konigsburg	7
24. *Mrs. Frisby and the Rats of NIMH*	O'Brien	7
25. *Ramona and Her Father*	Cleary	7
26. *A Wrinkle in Time*	L'Engle	7

Table 4

Top Twenty-five Selected Core Works, K–6, 2000

Title	Author	How Many
1. *Molly's Pilgrim*	Cohen	11
2. *Snowy Day*	Keats	11
3. *Charlotte's Web*	White	10
4. *Sign of the Beaver*	Speare	10
5. *Ira Sleeps Over*	Waber	9
6. *Island of the Blue Dolphins*	O'Dell	9
7. *Frog and Toad . . . Are Friends*	Lobel	9
8. *Stone Soup*	Brown	9
9. *A Chair for My Mother*	Williams	8
10. *Corduroy*	Freeman	8
11. *Little Red Hen*	Galdone	8
12. *Miss Rumphius*	Cooney	8
13. *Ramona and Her Father*	Cleary	8
14. *Sylvester and the Magic Pebble*	Steig	8
15. *Brown Bear, Brown Bear . . .*	Martin	7
16. *James and the Giant Peach*	Dahl	7
17. *Lion, the Witch, and the Ward*	Lewis	7
18. *There's a Nightmare in My . . .*	Mayer	7
19. *Very Hungry Caterpillar*	Carle	7
20. *Bridge to Terabithia*	Paterson	6
21. *By the Great Horn Spoon*	Fleischman	6
22. *In the Year of the Boar . . .*	Lord	6
23. *Little Engine That Could*	Piper	6
24. *Sarah, Plain and Tall*	MacLachlan	6
25. "Tied for Twenty-Fifth" List	14 books*	5

*This list of 14 titles is not presented in the text of this paper.

selected multiple times, but fell short of making the top list. Series' recommendations can now be very influential, but they, like the other lists, have only a minimal representation of multicultural works.

As mentioned in the section on data collection and analysis, books were counted as multicultural because of state department identification lists. The extent to which they meet high standards for multicultural literature was not examined further in the course of this particular study, even though the authors share many concerns as to the caliber of many works identified as multicultural. Indeed, several works hold potential for promoting misinformation and stereotyping. Popular books, such as *The Sign of the Beaver,* would not meet criteria set by many authorities (e.g., Diamond & Moore, 1995), and their elimination would lower even further the percentages designated as multicultural.

Study B

Responses of individual K–6 teachers tell a slightly different story. They indicated that they do use many works of multicultural literature, as indicated by Table 5.

As Table 6 indicates, a sizeable portion of most teachers' multicultural literature came recommended by their district core lists.

It appears that many practicing teachers also manage to share many multicultural books with their students. The limited number of participants in Study B made an assessment of grade-level popularity unreasonable, but teachers at two or more grade levels often reported using identical key books. They are reported in Table 7.

Teachers report varied activities and uses for the literature as depicted in the lists that follow in Table 8. Written comments of the surveyed teachers revealed that they and their students are enthusiastic about the various purposes fulfilled by the literature. In summary, their remarks fell into the following categories. Students enjoy seeing faces like their own in books; they are interested and engaged

Table 5

Percent of Literature Identified as Multicultural by K–6 Teachers

District	Grade	% of Multicultural Literature from Core Lists
A	3	80
A	6	70
B	K	30
B	1	30
C	2	45
C	3	60
D	1	27.5
E	2	60
E	3	60
F	3	40
F	3	30
F	5	75
G	K	1,000
H	5	80
H	5	50
H	K	100
I	4	25
I	6	45
J	5	30
K	1	15

Table 6

Percentages of Core Literature to Multicultural Literature Used

Grade	Number	Core Literature/Multicultural
K	3	52%
1	3	24%
2	2	53%
3	5	54%
4	1	25%
5	4	59%
6	2	58%

Table 7

Multicultural Titles at More Than One Grade Level

Grades	Title
K, 2	*Amazing Grace*
1, 3	*Everybody Cooks Rice*
2, 3, 5	*Grandfather's Journey*
2, 3, 3, 5	*How Many Days to America*
5, 6	*Number the Stars*
2, 3	*People*
3, 5, 6	*Sadako and the Thousand Paper Cranes*
4, 5, 5, 6	*Sign of the Beaver*
2, 5	*The Little Painter of Sabana Grande*
2, 3, 5	*Too Many Tamales*

by learning about other cultures through literature; the work with literature helps them to open up; students are assisted in learning to walk in another's shoes; and students who speak English as a second language work hard to understand, but are not always clear about the content of the literature.

As one teacher commented, "They like to learn about different cultures, different time periods, and things that they don't know about. They are very attentive during read-alouds and ask many questions." Another teacher said, "When you use a book where their culture is involved, there is a definite pique of interest, smile of recognition, and satisfaction of involvement."

Discussion and Implications

In the past decade, educators' calls for more titles in multicultural literature have been addressed by publishers with an ever-increasing numbers of titles

Table 8

Multicultural Literature Uses Identified

accelerated reader	3	sequencing events	
cause/effect		silent reading	
compare/contrast	3	writing activities	3
describing elements		appreciate differences	
discussion		art extension	
dramatic play	2	celebrate diversity	
ELD	2	compare traditions	
guided reading		explore issues	
individual projects		honor holidays	3
intro. lesson/unit	2	inclusion	
literacy projects		intro. to a country	
literature circles	2	morals	
read aloud	11	multiple perspectives	4
read for enjoyment		social studies	3
read to gain information		science	
response journals	4		
shared reading	2		

each year and recommended book lists and journal articles have promoted quality works throughout the years (e.g., Day, 1994; Schon, 2000). In addition, the demographics of California have continued to change, as predicted. Former minorities are now majorities in most urban centers, and suburban and rural communities have become increasingly diverse. The U.S. census figures (September 2000) indicate that non-Hispanic whites currently make up less than half of the state's population, and numbers for individuals of color will continue to grow to approximately 58% of the total. Unfortunately, the clear call for multicultural literature made by past California Reading Frameworks has been silenced.

It would be reasonable to expect that students of various racial and ethnic groups have characters to identify with in their required classroom literature. It also seems critical that students of other groups have access to those same characters in order to open channels for communication in this era of efforts to defuse school conflict and violence and to promote positive values.

Instead, we are beset by inconsistencies of access to, and use of, multicultural literature for students and teachers. Expectations influence practice, and when state guidelines for multicultural literature diminish and the influence of commercial programs inflates, teachers and students may suffer consequences. Many teachers still, by and large, do what they are told. If they are not *expected* to "bridge the gap" through literature, they forego the opportunity for a variety of reasons that they publicly describe as "time constraints." We may be heartened, nevertheless, by the fact that some teachers do choose multicultural literature in spite of absent mandates. Such individuals are those who often draw upon their own resources to bring multicultural selections to their classrooms. As indicated by the population of Study B, they are often teachers who continue to seek further, quality education for themselves and fulfill roles of leadership in their school contexts.

All educational contexts are, of course, complex. Teachers have access to, and are certainly influenced by, documents and materials beyond the Reading/Language Arts Framework. As previously mentioned, the core book lists are now often supplanted by publishers' recommended readings. The recommendations of the state History/Social Studies framework are certainly influential as well. Samples of these materials reveal lists of suggested materials that are rich with many multicultural titles, but even there, books that are designated as *recommended* are seldom multicultural in nature.

Issues of power and access affect decisions in many ways. Even when multicultural literature is in use, the empathy and identification that come from sharing stories of people of color may not have long-lasting effects. Some students may resist the use of multicultural literature (Beach, 1995), and some conceive of racism as "individual prejudice." If racism exists only on an individual basis, many may avoid equating racism with themselves (Sleeter, 1993). An analysis of the activities reported in Study B shows that even when teachers use multicultural works, they engage students in activities at lower levels of integration of multicultural content (Banks, 2001). Their remarks indicate they tend to use multicultural literature for informative reasons, revealing no evidence of encouraging their students to engage in social action.

Two questions we may very well ask are: (a) Are teachers overlooking the needs of culturally diverse students? and (b) Are required readings no longer fulfilling the role of bridging the gap between cultures for our students? Effective educators can, however, learn to identify and address the issues and effectively promote the use of multicultural literature throughout the curriculum. Teachers must also see its careful and considerate use as expected of them. If state documents, commercial programs, and school administrators do not hold such expectations, it is up to those who care to speak.

References

Banks, J. A. (2001). Approaches to multicultural curriculum reform. In J. A. Banks & C. A. Banks (Eds.), *Multicultural education: Issues and perspectives* (4th ed., pp. 225–246). New York: Wiley.

Beach, R. (1995). *Stances in engagement and resistance in responding to multicultural literature.* Paper presented at the meeting of the National Reading Conference, New Orleans, LA.

California Department of Education. (1980). *English-language arts framework for California public schools.* Sacramento, CA: Author.

California Department of Education. (1986). *Recommended readings in literature, kindergarten through grade eight.* Sacramento, CA: Author.

California Department of Education. (1987). *English-language arts model curriculum guide: Kindergarten through grade eight.* Sacramento, CA: Author.

California Department of Education. (1999). *Reading/language arts framework for California public schools: Kindergarten through grade twelve.* Sacramento, CA: Author.

Cox, J. B. (1996). *Your opinion, please!: How to build the best questionnaires in the field of education.* Thousand Oaks, CA: Corwin.

Day, F. A. (1994). *Multicultural voices in contemporary literature: A resource for teachers.* Portsmouth, NH: Heinemann.

Diamond, B. J., & Moore, M. S. (1995). *Multicultural literacy: Mirroring the reality of the classroom.* White Plains, NY: Longman.

Flood, J., Lapp, D., & Nagel, G. (1991). An analysis of the array of literary works in district core reading lists, grades K–6. In J. Zutell, & S. McCormick (Eds.), *Learner factors/teacher factors: Issues in literacy research and instruction* (pp. 269–279). Chicago: National Reading Conference.

Merriam, A. J. (1998). Literature as window: Developing interracial understanding through fiction. *Journal of Black Studies, 19,* 61–69.

Nagel, G. (December, 1996). *The California canon: Recommendations and realities.* Paper presented at the meeting of the National Reading Conference, Charleston, SC.

Probst, R. E. (1988). Dialogue with a text. *English Journal, 77,* 32–38.

Schon, I. (2000). *Recent children's books about Latinos. Book Links,* 9(6), 37–41.

Sleeter, C. (1993). Advancing a white discourse: A response to Scheurich. *Educational Researcher, 22,* 13–15.

The Impact of Research-Based Reading Instruction on the Beginning Reading Development of a Deaf Child: Perspectives from a Case Study

Diane Corcoran Nielsen and Barbara Luetke-Stahlman
University of Kansas

According to a recent report, many children are considered "at-risk" for having difficulty learning how to read: children of poverty, and those with language, cognitive, learning, and hearing impairments (Snow, Burns, & Griffin, 1998). We have been studying the instructional experiences and the language and literacy development of a such a child, Marcy, from age 4 to age 12. Marcy is deaf. Presented here is a case study of Marcy's first year as a reader.

Although initially it might seem that the literacy development of a deaf child would be very different from that of a hearing child, we would argue that this is not necessarily so, since just like deaf children, many hearing children come to school with limited language development (Hart & Risley, 1995), yet language is the base of reading development. Studying how a deaf child learns to read can help us to better understand how focused instruction in pronouncing and manipulating sounds; and understanding and expressing words, phrases, sentences, and larger units of text helps a beginning reader become more proficient. Research has shown that when deaf children possess phonological awareness and age-appropriate English skills, they read as well as their hearing peers (Paul, 1998).

Research suggests that limited English-language knowledge is at the heart of deaf students' challenge with reading (Lillo-Martin, Hansen, & Smith, 1992) and goes beyond the obvious challenge of acquiring an understanding of the phonological aspects of reading. The bigger challenge is that they do not know linguistic labels for similar words (e.g., broken, smashed), do not comprehend or use figurative English well, and do not use or understand complex English grammar constructions (Paul, 1998). Our experiences tell us that these are the very same challenges for hearing children with limited language development who gain proficiency in decoding words, but struggle with aspects of comprehension despite teachers' efforts to teach comprehension strategies.

The purpose of this study was to examine the language-reading connection and the role of research-based reading instruction within the context of a first-grade deaf child's development as a reader. We drew upon the body of knowledge about reading instruction for beginning readers as our source for "research-based

National Reading Conference Yearbook, 50, pp. 471–482.

reading" instruction. For example, there is a considerable body of knowledge suggesting the need for beginning readers to develop some level of phonemic awareness to begin to decode words (Snow et al., 1998) and certain strategies, such as making the sound/symbol connection explicit with boxes (Clay, 1993) build a bridge between phonemic awareness and decoding words. The research on proficient beginning readers, as summarized by Snow et al. (1998), found that they use multiple word-recognition strategies, have a certain level of fluency and automaticity with words, and monitor their reading as they focus on the ultimate goal: comprehension. Guided reading, a lesson structure which incorporates instruction in strategies targeting goals for beginning readers, is used successfully with beginning readers who are hearing (Clay, 1993), deaf (Luetke-Stahlman, 1999), or bilingual (Lally, 1998) and was the framework for teaching Marcy word-recognition and comprehension strategies.

The questions guiding this case study were: "What strategies did Marcy develop as a beginning reader when taught using techniques commonly used with children who do not have similar language challenges?" and "What instructional experiences impacted Marcy's development as a reader?"

Method

There is no "typical" deaf child. Although it is true that most children with hearing loss have mild impairments rather than prelingual profound losses (Paul, 1998), even children with similar degrees of hearing loss are different. Group research with deaf students is limited since each child is unique in terms of his or her level of English language proficiency due to level of hearing (aided or unaided), type of sign system employed, and proficiency with the chosen sign system. Thus a descriptive case study of one child was appropriate.

Participant

The participant in this study was Marcy, a Bulgarian orphan who was adopted by middle-class parents and came to the United States when she was 4 years old. Born profoundly deaf and not given a hearing aid, Marcy was mute and did not communicate in any way (i.e., verbally or in sign), nor did she have common childhood experiences in her first 4 years of life. English was developed as Marcy's first language because her hearing parents and siblings, one of whom was also deaf, communicated in English as their dominant and home language. Those at home and school communicated using a system of simultaneously spoken and signed English, called Signing Exact English or SEE (Gustason, Zawolkow, & Pfetzing, 1973). SEE was designed to represent the grammar of English in several ways. Different signs are used to represent root words, so that the various pronouns, contractions and verb forms are distinguished visually as different words. That is, unlike other signed inputs, different signs are used for synonyms such as "tree, orchard, and jungle." The SEE system also includes signs that are added to root words or base signs so that inflections (-ing, -s) and derivations ("un" in unhappy, unlike) are produced. The way that SEE is signed is important because of the relationship between morphology and learning to read (Moeller & Johnson, 1988).

Another strategy deaf individuals use is speechreading, sometimes referred to as "lip reading." In general, the ability to speechread correlates with one's English language knowledge. That is, the better a child understands and can predict what a word or phrase is in English, the better he or she is able to see and verify that expectation on the mouth.

Marcy received a cochlear implant (CI) when she was about 4½ years, an age considered late by today's standards. Although initially controversial, this device is a popular option for children (and adults) who have a profound hearing loss and was recently discussed by the National Association of the Deaf (NAD), the leading organization of the deaf community. A section from the NAD (2000) web site position statement on CI devices states, "CI technology continues to evolve, to receive mainstream acceptance, and to be acknowledged as a part of today's reality."

Whereas many profoundly deaf children today receive early childhood intervention, Marcy's first school experience was when she was enrolled in a public, neighborhood school program for deaf preschoolers the day after her arrival in the United States. We will provide a glimpse of Marcy's preschool and kindergarten years as precursors to success in first grade.

Through the preschool and kindergarten years, Marcy was read to by proficient readers who could sign SEE, and she experienced many things one would expect in a family that valued literacy. Marcy's engagement in such activities also supported Chall's (1983) notion of stage theory, that reading develops first from an awareness of the functions of print and later to an awareness of its form. Marcy's task in preschool was to learn to listen to and speak English and to use it in routine conversation. A teacher of the deaf (TOD) and speech/language pathologist (SLP) worked with her daily to do so.

Saturated by visual (signed) and spoken language, often using books as a springboard, and taught how to use assistive listening devices following her CI at age 4½, Marcy began to speak and to sign. Although her world was rich with language and literacy stimulation, a conversation taken from a family videotape around her fifth birthday documents the limitations Marcy faced in expressing herself. When gifts are opened, Marcy signs, "HAVE," and a few seconds later, "ONE," as if to communicate "I have one of these now." By the end of kindergarten, Marcy could produce most phonemes in the initial position in isolated words (e.g., the /b/ in "bat" but not in "grab") and discriminate phoneme pairs. Her score on the receptive Peabody Picture Vocabulary Test (Dunn & Dunn, 1981) was in the fifth percentile, well below average. She did not understand decontextualized English, although her teachers were aware that it was the comprehension and expression of "cognitive-academic" language skill (Cummins, 1984) that was critical to academic success. Using the assessment data, they planned instruction for Marcy's first-grade year.

Instructional Context

Marcy's education resembled that of 80% of deaf students today (Moores, 1999) in that she attended a public school and was one of only a few deaf children in her grade. This neighborhood school is in a Midwestern district serving students from a range of socioeconomic backgrounds.

Throughout her first-grade year, the focus for Marcy was on language and literacy development. She received daily speech/language support and was educated with two deaf peers in the resource room by a TOD where the focus was on reading and math. She was mainstreamed with hearing children for lunch, recess, and "specials." Shared reading was a high priority to the TOD. Mason (1992) noted that during shared reading, adults are able to provide an umbrella of explanation, interpretations, and clarification during "teachable moments." With this information, teachers can make text-to-life and life-to-text connections (Cochran-Smith, 1984) with students, bridging from what they know to new concepts, vocabulary, and grammatical structures, essential for a deaf child or one with limited language.

Team members decided that just like a hearing "at-risk" first grader, Marcy would benefit from the guided reading instruction of a specially trained reading intervention teacher. Thus, Marcy's initial reading instruction came from Barbara, the second author and a deaf educator, trained in the procedures of a reading intervention program similar to Clay's (1993), titled Kansas Accelerated Literacy Learning (KALL) and used in Marcy's school district with "at-risk" hearing first graders. In a study of 758 children, 79% of the children taught one-to-one reached grade level or higher compared to 18% of the children who qualified but did not receive KALL instruction due to a limited number of KALL teachers (Nielsen & Glasnapp, 1999). KALL lessons consist of four parts: rereading an independent level text to promote fluency, assessment of strategy use (running record), word study, and instructional-level reading of narrative and expository text with teacher support to apply a variety of word-recognition and comprehension strategies. Promotion of problem solving and independence are paramount.

Data Sources and Analysis

Barbara, proficient at the SEE-2 sign system, collected much of the data as a participant observer (Bogden & Biklen, 1992) as she taught KALL lessons. The primary sources of data were lesson plans (including daily running records), and detailed fieldnotes from 62 lessons, and videotapes of 15 lessons and family literacy events. Additional sources of data included observations and lessons plans from the TOD, copies of Marcy's IEPs (including annual speech, language and literacy assessments, normed on hearing children), writing and audiotaped language samples.

The first phase of the data analysis involved the authors, one with expertise in reading and the other in deaf education, meeting weekly about what was happening in the lessons. Discussion focused on how Barbara needed to adapt and extend the lessons, devised for hearing children, to meet Marcy's needs. The second phase of analysis was close examination of the lessons, notes, and a subset of the videotapes for patterns, particularly in how Marcy developed word-recognition strategies and what aspects of reading were the most challenging for her. The third level of analysis was an examination of Marcy's achievement on language and literacy tasks in relation to instructional experiences. Barbara checked our thinking with the TOD and the SLP via discussions with them.

Findings and Discussion

Whereas the typical KALL lesson is 30 minutes, Marcy's occurred for 30 to 45 minutes a day, 4 to 5 days a week. Although each session began with Marcy rereading one or two of the books she had recently read, followed by a running record of the last book taught, the lesson focus was on new material. Word study, connected to the new book, focused initially on sight words and an introduction to segmenting and blending new words via writing a sentence and later on orthographic and morphemic aspects of words. Then using the pictures as a springboard, Barbara introduced the new book by engaging Marcy in a discussion of what might be happening and focusing on novel vocabulary or concepts (e.g., "If you eat 'the rest of the bread,' how much is left?"). On the first read, Marcy would try to read the book herself, uninterrupted, and Barbara would take notes of self-corrections or skipped and mis-signed words. This is different from a typical guided reading lesson, but Barbara choose this to decrease Marcy's level of frustration with pronunciation and signing. Early videotaped sessions capture a posture of helplessness, with Marcy often signing and verbalizing, "CAN'T, CAN'T, TOO HARD FOR ME." In the early weeks of lessons, when Marcy skipped or mis-signed a word, Barbara would encourage her to look at the "strategy" chart and try one the strategies she had been taught (e.g., "Does the picture help?" "Look at the first letter."). Many of Marcy's first attempts were guesses based on initial consonants plus picture cues. Over time, Marcy looked less and less at Barbara during this part of the reading session and always choose to both sign and speak the words on the pages. On the second and successive readings, Barbara would stop Marcy at the spots where mis-signed words occurred. If Marcy self-corrected, Barbara would ask her why. In the first few weeks, Marcy was not able to tell her, so Barbara would reinforce a metacognitive approach to reading by suggesting that Marcy probably looked at the picture, read the sentence for meaning clues, or even used sound (e.g., "Beautiful would make sense there but maybe you knew the word was not 'beautiful' because it started with /p/, right?").

Sessions videotaped only a few weeks later show a child turning the pages and attempting to use strategies to figure out unknown words before asking for assistance. Reading the new instructional level text provided Barbara an opportunity to teach Marcy additional word-recognition strategies promoted for hearing children (Clay, 1993) such as searching for a word in a previous context, and skipping then going back to see if she could figure out a challenging word. Adult facilitation in developing multiple word-recognition strategies assisted Marcy's developing ability to problem solve her way through text. After 18 weeks of KALL guided reading lessons, Marcy tested at Peterson's (1991) level 20, a level roughly equivalent to end-of-first-grade-year readers. Thereafter, Marcy's TOD taught the guided reading lessons.

What was happening that allowed Marcy to make such progress? Aspects of a child's language development and features of instruction impact achievement (Snow et al., 1998). An examination of Marcy's development of word recognition and comprehension in relation to her instructional experiences demonstrates this point.

Those working with Marcy knew the research on the reading development of hearing children and believed that the development of phonological awareness should be a priority. They surrounded Marcy with a activities involving rhyming, blending, segmenting, and the imitation of single phonemes modeled by the SLP, often with common objects and children's books. Marcy was engaged in kinesthetic exercises to feel how a particular sound was produced, and she frequently finger-spelled words. The CI gave Marcy *access* to sound, but her brain needed to be trained to *discriminate* what it was hearing. The sounds that Marcy could correctly produce gave adults insight into how well her brain was learning to distinguish sounds.

Ling (1976) explained that even though deaf children may not have the access to sound, they are able to use cues from other sources (e.g., speechreading, articulation training) to discover the relationship between the sound of speech and print. Intelligible speech is not essential for the acquisition of phonological awareness (Lichtenstein, 1985); neither is the ability to hear or speech-read (Bebko, 1998). Deaf students who sign, and those who do not, utilize phonological awareness to distinguish possible letter combinations from implausible ones and to recognize words (Hanson, 1991). This was certainly the case for Marcy.

The work Marcy did with the SLP, starting in preschool, was akin to phonemic awareness and phonics instruction and provided a base for word study work in guided reading lessons. The importance of sound/symbol understanding to word recognition is present in studies with children who are normally developing (Juel & Minden-Cupp, 1999), hearing and language-challenged (Catts, 1991) and deaf (Paul, 1998). Between the SLP and the word study aspects of lessons, Marcy received phonics instruction "first and fast" (Juel & Minden-Cupp, 1999) and regularly applied it with other strategies in reading text.

Barbara documented Marcy's use of strategies by making extensive notes on her lesson plans. Marcy initially decoded unknown words (signed and spoken) by relying on their first letter and possibly picture cues. Her behavior was characteristic of Ehri's (1992) partial alphabetic phase. Explicit instruction assisted her to look at all the aspects of a word as she decoded it. Vowels were extended in pronunciation so she could discern them. A "vowel chart" with key pictures for common ways to say a vowel provided support. Frequently in the early weeks, Barbara would pick a word that Marcy could not sign (read) and "move it to boxes" (Clay, 1993) to help her make sound/symbol associations and to make segmenting/blending concrete. Barbara adapted as necessary since although the

CI provided access to sound, Marcy had trouble identifying some sounds and blending. For example, if Marcy could not produce the correct sound of the letter, Barbara would provide her with a choice ("Does it say /p/ or /t/?"). As Marcy got more adept, Barbara used boxes with more challenging words (bike, bait). In addition, approximately once a week, Barbara would ask Marcy to sound out a specific set of words with the same vowel and ending sound (e.g., moon, soon; sat, mat, pat), and she would chart whether Marcy could (a) sign each word without correctly pronouncing it; (b) sound-it-out, but not able to show comprehension by signing it; (c) do neither; or (d) do both. With this "cloze" set of words, Marcy slowly began to sound out highly similar words and sign them correctly.

Marcy enjoyed word-study activities with Barbara and the SLP, but we remained unsure as if she would ever segment and blend an unknown word on her own. Then on November 10, Marcy came to the sentence, "Wait a minute." She had independently tried two of the strategies on the "strategy chart" (look at the picture; reread the sentence) then looking resignedly at Barbara. she lowered her head and attempted to segment the word, "/w/ /a/ /t/." Barbara sat and waited, a look of encouragement on her face, the same look that had been there many times before. Then, Marcy signed and shouted, "WAIT! IT SAY 'WAIT.'" She smiled broadly, and added, "I FIGURE IT OUT. I DID IT MYSELF." Fieldnotes and videos document that Marcy moved into Ehri's (1992) full alphabetic stage by early December. She commonly segmented words but needed help to blend sounds, a function of her developing speech, according to the SLP.

In mid-December, Marcy was helped to see and use orthographic patterns in unknown words as "chunks" and to blend them, and to "read by analogy" (Gaskins, Ehri, Cress, O'Hara, Donnelly, 1996/97). Barbara and Marcy made a booklet of phonograms, adding new words read in stories to the separate lists on each page of a notebook. Marcy demonstrated the connection between phonograms and rhyming words, but initially matched words by sight as much as sound. For example, one day during this time period she signed, "Look, Mom, that's toot; it rhymes with foot." Sometimes finding words within words that she could pronounce allowed Marcy to sound out words she had been unable to read initially. For example, she found the word "no" in "snow" and knew from the picture that the word had something to do with winter. Saying "no" helped to sound out "know"; finding "now" in the same word, did not. Marcy learned that finding little words within larger words was sometimes helpful. As noted previously, the SEE system has signs for the morphemic units of words which provided Marcy with additional support for decoding and understanding the differences in similar words (e.g., come, comes, coming). The orthography and morphology of words became a key to Marcy's progress in word recognition, and she was able to unlock words with more than one syllable. Fieldnotes and videotaped language samples document that by the end of first grade, Marcy chunked word parts independently, a behavior characteristic of Ehri's (1992) consolidated alphabetic phrase.

Whereas sound/symbol and orthography are valuable sources of information, good readers also use meaning and grammatical structure in dealing with unknown words. Since semantics and syntactics were weak aspects of Marcy's expressive and receptive language, explicit attention was given to them when Marcy got stuck on a word. For example, Barbara showed Marcy how to use a combination of a phonological and syntax cues. Barbara would cover her mouth (so Marcy couldn't lip-read) and say the word, often repeating it a second time in the context of the sentence, and then in isolation again. Sometimes Marcy could "hear" enough of the word that given the pictorial and grammatical context, she would guess it correctly. Other times, if she could not recognize it by "audition only," Barbara would drop her hand and allow Marcy to speech-read. Generally, Marcy could decipher the word in this way, especially if Barbara pronounced it within the short sentence of the story.

As it is for many children, comprehension was a bigger challenge for Marcy than word recognition, and it started at the word level. A difference between Marcy's development of word-recognition strategies and that of a hearing child was that Marcy was reading many words that she had never heard and did not understand. Hearing children with typical preschool language stimulation have a "listening vocabulary" of words they have heard repeatedly. Unlike Marcy, they can focus their cognitive energy on larger units of text than words. Thus, vocabulary instruction became an integral part of each lesson conducted by Barbara, the SLP or the TOD. Language strategies such as defining, giving examples, making associations, and using antonyms or synonyms were used to develop Marcy's understanding of words she encountered in books.

Since Marcy had limited understanding of many words, Barbara in the KALL lesson and the TOD in shared reading taught Marcy to use context as a way to keep "making meaning" in the forefront, even though sometimes Barbara would provide the word for Marcy. For example, Barbara might provide a synonym (e.g., "He was angry; he was [mad]"); an antonym (e.g., "She wasn't hot, she was _____"); a related word (e.g., "She wasn't in the living room, she was in the _____ [kitchen]"; or an analogy or definition (e.g., "People and animals have teeth, but some animals also have _____ [fangs]"), pausing to see if Marcy could supply the missing word. Unfortunately, at least half the time Barbara had to "give" Marcy the word, (e.g., "I think it's either 'corn' or 'can.' What would make sense? How do you know?").

To support Marcy's comprehension beyond the word level, Barbara and the TOD focused primarily at the phase and sentence level by asking Marcy what "under the ground" or "She was hungry" meant. When Marcy did not know or have enough sign to explain, the teacher did so via sign, drawing, demonstration and constant attempts to connect the meaning to something Marcy already knew.

At the end of first grade, Marcy used multiple strategies to unlock unknown words, commonly self-corrected errors, and used semantic and visual cues more than syntactic cues. Even though English (via SEE) was her first language, her syntactic development was significantly behind her hearing peers and thus was not a support system for her at that time. Marcy demonstrated comprehension of a short second-grade narrative passage on the Qualitative Reading Inventory (Leslie & Caldwell, 1990) and scored at the 33rd percentile for vocabulary and 34th percentile for comprehension on a standardized test (MacGinitie & MacGinitie,

1989). On the school district-designed curriculum-based reading assessment, Marcy read authentic passages and answered comprehension questions in writing, blindly scored by teachers using a district scoring rubric. Marcy scored in the "strong performer" range on the narrative task both at midyear and end-of-year testing, as did the majority of other first graders in her school (78% at midyear; 70% at end of year). However, on the expository task she fell into the category of "further development needed" both at the middle and end of the year. In contrast, most of Marcy's hearing peers were judged to be "strong performers." Experiences with expository text expose children to concepts and unique language structures (Pappas, 1993) that Marcy simply could not comprehend at that time. Team members made note of this in the objectives they set for the coming year.

Although her basic conversational abilities in sign and speech improved in first grade, Marcy was still far behind her peers in language. Her conversational speech remained understandable only 50% of the time to an unfamiliar listener. Standardized receptive and expressive language test scores revealed minimal growth. However, her delayed receptive and expressive language abilities did not prevent her from enjoying and learning from shared and guided reading sessions or from being motivated to independently read and enjoy children's literature. Although this may seem surprising, empirical support that limited language skill does not discriminate readers at the *early* stages is available from Huba and Ramisetty-Mikler (1995). However, the relationship between decontextualized English ability and reading achievement has been found to be significant for fourth-grade readers (Tabors, 1996). So while teachers and family celebrated Marcy's progress in first grade, they were very conscious of the challenge that more sophisticated narrative and expository text held for Marcy.

Conclusions

Snow et al. (1998) suggest that children commonly considered "at-risk" of having difficulty learning to read

> do not, as a rule, require qualitatively different instruction from children who are "getting it." Instead, they more often need application of the same principles by someone who can apply them expertly to individual children who are having difficulty for one reason or another. (p. 327)

This was certainly the case with Marcy. We believe she made considerable progress, despite language limitations, for several reasons. First, Marcy's team knew the research on effective reading instruction for hearing children and believed that whereas they would need to adapt and extend it, they *must* provide the same instruction for deaf students. This is not the usual case for deaf students since there is little agreement in the field on how to teach deaf students to read (Paul, 1998) so they do not always get a good base in reading. Thus, phonemic awareness was stressed beginning in preschool, and Marcy was taught using the same word-recognition strategies espoused for hearing children (Clay, 1993; Gaskins et al., 1996/97; Juel & Minden-Cupp, 1999) albeit with additional support via sign, finger-spelling, and kinesthetic attention to sound was essential since her CI allowed her come access to sound, but discrimination of sounds was still a challenge.

Second, the ultimate goal of comprehension of authentic text also drove the team's decisions. Authentic text provides more challenges for all beginning readers than text with controlled syntax and vocabulary. The team felt it was imperative that Marcy approach reading as a problem-solving process from the earliest stages of reading. Thus, they supported her development of strategies for dealing with the multiple levels of authentic text: word, phrase, sentence, and whole text. We believe this is an aspect of Marcy's instruction that is especially relevant for hearing students with language limitations common to children of poverty (Hart & Risley, 1995), since success in reading calls upon strength in decontextualized language understanding (Cummins, 1984; Tabors, 1996). Marcy's team did not assume "understanding." Rather, they targeted aspects of the decontextualized language of authentic text and provided expansions and extensions to direct Marcy's attention to meaning. With such an approach, Marcy developed a questioning stance to reading in first grade which over the years was reinforced by her teachers. Her willingness to ask what something means and to seek solutions to misunderstandings has proven essential to her continued progress as she has moved into more mainstreamed instruction.

Lastly, Marcy's progress as a deaf reader was due in part to the fact that she was *saturated* with language at home and in school, expected to respond, and her first language was English (SEE) rather than the more common Pidgin Signed English, a mix of ASL and English (Paul, 1998). SEE provided Marcy additional support for word recognition and comprehension because of the match between first language (SEE) syntax and morphology and the texts Marcy read. Whereas this was important in dealing with simple first-grade text, it becomes a more critical support as texts get more sophisticated and explains why some deaf students do not achieve reading proficiency commensurate with their peers (Paul, 1998).

In closing, we hope that knowledge of Marcy's beginning reading instruction might assist those teaching hearing students as well as deaf students, since many children have similar challenges at the word, phrase, sentence, and whole-text level in comprehending text. We encourage those teaching children with language limitations to examine the research on effective reading instruction and to note how attention to aspects of language using authentic text can provide a framework for supporting the development of so-called "at-risk" readers.

References

Bebko, J. (1998). Learning, language, memory, and reading: The role of language automatization and its impact on complex cognitive activities. *Journal of Deaf Studies and Deaf Education, 3*(1), 4–13.

Bogden, R., & Biklen, S. (1992). *Qualitative research for education.* Boston: Allyn & Bacon.

Catts, H. (1991). Early identification of reading disabilities. *Topics in Language Disorders, 12,* 1–16.

Chall, J. (1983). *Stages of reading development.* New York: McGraw-Hill.

Clay, M. (1993). *Reading recovery: A guidebook for teachers in training.* Portsmouth, NH: Heinemann.

Cochran-Smith, M. (1984). *The making of a reader.* Norwood, NJ: Ablex.

Cummins, J. (1984). *Bilingualism and special education: Issues in assessment and pedagogy.* Clevedon, Avon, England: Multilingual Matters.

Dunn, L., & Dunn, L. (1981). *Peabody picture vocabulary test.* Circle Pines, MN: American Guidance.

Ehri, L. (1992). Reconceptualizing the development of sight word reading and its relationship to reading. In P. Gough, L. Ehri, & R. Treiman (Eds.), *Reading Acquisition* (pp. 107–144). Hillsdale, NJ: Erlbaum.

Gaskins, I., Ehri, L., Cress, C., O'Hara, C., Donnelly, K. (1996/97). Procedures for word learning: Making discoveries about words. *Reading Teacher, 50,* 312–327.

Gustason, G., Zawolkow, E., & Pfetzing, C. (1973). *Signing exact English.* Los Altamitos, CA: Modern Sign.

Hanson, V. (1991). Phonological processing without sound. In S. Brady & D. Shakweiler (Eds.), *Phonological processes in literacy: A tribute to Isabelle Y. Liberman* (pp. 153–161). Hillsdale, NJ: Erlbaum.

Hart, B., & Risley, T. (1995). *Meaningful differences in the everyday experiences of everyday American children.* Baltimore, MD: Paul H. Brookes.

Huba, M., & Ramisetty-Mikler, S. (1995). The language skills and concepts of early and nonearly readers. *Journal of Genetic Psychology, 56,* 313–331.

Juel, C., & Minden-Cupp, C. (1999). *Learning to read words; Linguistic units and strategies* (CIERA Report No. 1-008). Ann Arbor, MI: Center for the Improvement of Early Reading Achievement.

Lally, C. (1998). The application of first language reading models to second language study: A recent historical perspective. *Reading Horizons, 38,* 267–277.

Leslie, L., & Caldwell, J. (1990). *Qualitative reading inventory.* New York: HarperCollins.

Lichtenstein, E. (1985). Deaf working memory processes and English language skills. In D. Martin (Ed.), *Cognition, education, and deafness: Directions for research and instruction* (pp. 111–114). Washington, DC: Gallaudet University Press.

Lillo-Martin, D., Hansen, V., & Smith, S. (1992). Deaf readers comprehension of relative clause structures. *Applied Psycholinguistics, 13,* 13–30.

Ling, D. (1976). *Speech and the hearing-impaired child: Theory and practice.* Washington, DC: Alexander Graham Bell Association for the Deaf.

Luetke-Stahlman, B. (1999). *Language across the curriculum when students are deaf or hard of hearing.* Hillsboro, OR: Butte.

MacGinitie, W., & MacGinitie, R. (1989). *Gates-MacGinitie reading tests.* Chicago: Riverside.

Mason, J. (1992). Reading stories to preliterate children: A proposed connection to reading. In P. Gough, L. Ehri, & R. Treiman (Eds.), *Reading acquisition* (pp. 215–241). Hillsdale, NJ: Erlbaum.

Moeller, M., & Johnson, D. (1988, November). *Longitudinal performance of deaf students using manually coded English.* Paper presented at the meeting of the ASHA National Conference, Boston.

Moores, D. (1999). Many stories. *American Annals of the Deaf, 144,* 223.

National Association for the Deaf. (2000). *Position statement on cochlear implants.* [Online]. Available: www.nad.org/infocenter/newsroom/position/CochlearImplants.

Nielsen, D., & Glasnapp, D. (1999, April). *The effects of a small group model of reading intervention on the reading achievement of "at risk" first graders.* Paper presented at the meeting of the American Research Association, Montreal.

Pappas, C. (1993). Is narrative "primary"?: Some insights from kindergartners pretend readings of stories and information books. *Journal of Reading Behavior, 25,* 97–129.

Paul, P. (1998). *Literacy and deafness: The development of reading, writing, and literate thought.* Boston: Allyn & Bacon.

Peterson, B. (1991). Selecting books for beginning readers. In D. DeFord, C. Lyons, & G. Pinnell (Eds.), *Bridges to literacy: Learning from reading recovery* (pp. 119–147). Portsmouth, NH: Heinemann.

Snow, C., Burns, M., & Griffin, P. (Eds.). (1998). *Preventing reading difficulties in young children.* Washington, D.C.: National Academy Press.

Tabors, P. (1996, December). *Predicting fourth grade reading comprehension from school age and preschool age data: A preliminary analysis.* Paper presented at the meeting of the National Reading Conference, Charleston, SC.

Teachers' Assessment of Girls' and Boys' Narrative and Persuasive Writing

Shelley Peterson
OISE/University of Toronto

An examination of scores assigned to the writing of elementary school students on provincial, state, and national examinations in Canada and the United States reveals consistent patterns in the distribution of scores assigned to girls' and boys' writing (Alberta Education, 1997; Office of Educational Research and Improvement, 1995; Ohio Department of Education, 2000). Repeatedly, greater percentages of scores showing proficiency or excellence have been assigned to girls' writing, and greater percentages of scores showing the writers' inability to meet grade-level expectations have been assigned to boys' writing.

In an attempt to determine whether similar gender disparities might exist in classroom writing assessment, I examined the relationship between classroom teachers' perceptions of gender differences in students' narrative and persuasive writing and teachers' assessment of the writing. I was particularly interested in cross-gendered writing, that which exhibits characteristics typically attributed to students who are not of the writer's sex. Framed by feminist theory, my study focused on two research questions: (a) What gender characteristics do teachers identify within cross-gendered narrative and persuasive papers written by third- and sixth-grade students as part of a classroom assignment? (b) What are the relationships between teachers' gender perceptions and their scoring of the papers?

Related Research

Gender Differences in Student Writing

Researchers who assessed gender differences in elementary students' narrative writing argue that the social and political realities of girls' and boys' lives lead to differences in their writing. These differences are consistent with the two modes of being in relation to others—masculine independence and objectivity contrasted with feminine connectedness and caring—articulated within feminist theory (Belenky, Clinchy, Goldberger, & Tarule, 1986; Gilligan, 1982). In their analyses of boys' narrative writing, researchers found a limited offering of roles for female characters and a positioning of male characters in powerful, risk-filled roles that required independent problem solving to overcome obstacles, often in violent

*National Reading Conference Yearbook, **50**, pp. 483–494.*

ways (Gray-Schlegel & Gray-Schlegel, 1995–96; Trepanier-Street & Romatowski, 1991; Tuck, Bayliss, & Bell, 1985). These researchers found that the female characters in girls' narratives generally played powerful roles, although some female characters were positioned as submissive to male characters. Violence was an element in some girls' stories. Characters were more likely to resolve conflicts through the creation of alliances with others than through independent, aggressive action, however.

In Knudson's (1992) study of students' persuasive writing at Grades 3, 5, 10, and 12, no gender differences were found in terms of norm invocations (appeals to rules, fair play and reason), positive sanctions (offers of gifts, bargaining, and politeness), requests, and assertions (Knudson, 1992, p. 9). Gender differences were found in an analysis of preschool children's oral persuasion, however (Weiss & Sachs, 1991). In this study, boys tended to use norm invocations to a greater degree than girls did, whereas girls tended to use requests more frequently than boys did.

Teachers' Perceptions of Gender and Their Evaluation of Writing

Research examining the interactions between secondary and postsecondary teachers' gender perceptions and their evaluation of student writing indicated a privileging of the linear, impersonal style traditionally attributed to men's persuasive writing over the contextual and committed style typically attributed to women's persuasive writing (Barnes, 1990; Graham, 1996; Haswell & Haswell, 1995; Roulis, 1995). In Roulis's (1995) study, teachers rated male writers' essays significantly higher in the category of dynamism (strong, aggressive, active, loud), whereas they rated female writers' essays significantly higher in the category of aesthetic quality (nice, pleasant, beautiful, sweet).

The research findings were mixed in terms of teachers' responses to cross-gendered writing. Graham (1996) found that essays written in styles not traditionally associated with students of the same sex as the writer were more likely to receive criticism than those in which gender expectations were reproduced. Teachers in two additional studies (Barnes, 1990; Haswell & Haswell, 1995) favored male writers when assessing cross-gendered writing, however.

The present research extends findings from an earlier study with a similar research design, exploring teachers' perceptions of gender in five narrative pieces written by sixth-grade students (Peterson, 1998). In both studies, I have defined gender as a set of social and cultural expectations for talking, thinking, and acting that are associated with being a girl or a boy. Teachers participating in the previous study felt that sixth-grade students wrote about characters of their own sex. They viewed girls' writing as being organized, detailed, descriptive, and showing a sophisticated use of sentence structure and vocabulary. In contrast, they identified writing that lacked in detail and was poorly developed, in terms of characters, plots, and the use of language, as boys' writing. In spite of the privileging of girls' narrative writing in their identification of gender characteristics, the scores assigned to four of the five papers used in the study showed no significant differences in terms of teachers' perceptions of the writer's sex. These papers conformed to teachers' gender expectations to such a degree that at least 70% of teachers correctly identified the writer's sex.

There was a significant difference in the scoring of a fifth paper that contained characteristics typically attributed to both girls' and boys' narrative writing, however. Teachers who felt that a boy had written the paper assigned lower scores than did teachers who identified the writer as a girl. Gender markers identified by participating teachers varied according to the perceived sex of the writer. Teachers who identified the writer as a girl felt that the story flowed well and that the writer used specific verbs. In contrast, teachers who identified the writer as a boy found the writing to be "choppy," with a paucity of descriptive language.

The present research extends the findings of my previous study through involving teachers of Grades 6 and 3 in the assessment of cross-gendered narrative and persuasive writing.

Method and Analysis

Selection of Writing Samples

My research assistant and I selected three narrative and three persuasive papers from the free-choice writing of an urban third-grade classroom and a corresponding set of six papers from an urban sixth-grade classroom. Because significant differences were found only in the scores of the cross-gendered writing sample in my previous study (Peterson, 1998), we selected cross-gendered papers for the current study. In our selection of papers for the present study, we drew on results of the previous study indicating that teachers based their determination of the writer's sex primarily on the sex of characters in the narrative writing. All of the narrative papers in the current study included protagonists that were not of the writer's sex. In the persuasive writing samples, the writers argued for something that was typically attributed to children of the other sex. The papers were typewritten and had not been edited by adults in order to control for the influence of neatness and handwriting on teachers' identification of gender characteristics.

Procedure

My research assistant and I telephoned 307 third- and sixth-grade language arts teachers in 30 randomly selected urban, rural, and suburban public school districts throughout Ohio. We informed them of the purpose of the study and determined their interest in participating in the study. We sent interested teachers packages containing the six papers written by students at the grade level at which they were teaching, a rating form, and the state scoring guides for student writing. Of those who were sent packages, 52 third-grade teachers and 52 sixth-grade teachers completed and returned the rating forms. Though we kept a record of the sex of the teachers agreeing to participate, we were not able to achieve a balance at either grade level because of the difficulty in identifying male teachers who were willing to participate in the study. Forty-six third-grade teachers were female and 41 sixth-grade teachers were female. Budget restrictions and a move to another country precluded the possibility of redressing this imbalance.

Participating teachers scored the six papers that they received using the state scoring guide (Ohio Department of Education, 1999). This holistic scoring guide uses a 4-point scale with 1 and 2 being below grade-level expectations, 3 being at grade level and 4 being beyond grade level. The rubric addresses the following criteria: relationship to the topic identified in the prompt, use of supporting details, sequencing of ideas/events, word choice, use of complete sentences, usage, spelling, capitalization, and punctuation. Though White (1985) advocated using separate scoring guides for different discourse modes, in order to enhance the validity and reliability of the marking, I chose to use the state scoring guide because the teachers indicated in the telephone conversations that they used this scoring guide to assess their students' classroom writing, regardless of the discourse mode. I felt that the participating teachers' interpretations of the scoring guide's criteria were likely to be more consistent than they would have been if I had introduced new rubrics for the purpose of the study. Teachers identified the sex of the writer (if possible) and identified gender markers within the papers. Attempting to minimize the influence of the research procedure on teachers' evaluation of the writing, I asked teachers to assign a score to the papers before examining the papers for gender markers.

Data Analysis

Quantitative analysis involved obtaining frequencies of teachers' identification of the writer's sex for each writing sample. I used a one-way analysis of variance (ANOVA) to compare the means of the scores assigned to each of the writing samples in terms of the teachers' perceptions of the writer's sex. I conducted a multivariate analysis of variance (MANOVA) of the mean scores assigned to all of the narrative papers and all of the persuasive papers at each grade level. Because there were so few male teachers in the study, I did not identify differences between male and female teachers' scores.

My graduate research assistant and I categorized the gender characteristics (gender markers) that teachers identified within each paper using two features drawn from Roulis's research on teachers' responses to male and female students' essays: (a) aesthetic quality (emotional, pleasant, optimistic, committed), and (b) dynamism (aggressive, active, strong). We also used two features from my previous study: (c) matching the writer's sex with that of characters in narratives, and (d) demonstration of the writer's competence (Peterson, 1998). Throughout the analysis process, my research assistant and I worked independently and then compared our analyses, clarifying our rationales for particular categorizations when disagreements arose until we reached consensus. We then calculated the percentage of gender markers attributed to girls and those attributed to boys within each gender marker category at each grade level.

Results

Gender Characteristics Identified by Teachers

Matching the writer's sex with that of characters in narratives. The character's sex was used most frequently by participating teachers to determine the sex of the writers of the narrative papers. At the third-grade level, 41% of gender markers used to identify writers as boys and 23% of gender markers used to identify writers as girls were based on the character's sex. These percentages were higher at the sixth-grade level: 48% of gender markers identifying male writers and 53% of gender markers identifying female writers.

The resulting accuracy in identifying the writer's sex was low in comparison to that of my previous study because the papers in the present study were selected for the mismatch between the writer's and the character's sex. Teachers' accuracy ranged from 52.8% for third-grade persuasive paper #1, written by a girl, to 0% for sixth-grade persuasive paper #1, written by a girl.

Teachers' uncertainty about the sex of the student writers ranged from 5.8% for sixth-grade narrative #1, written by a boy, to 69.2% for sixth-grade persuasive paper #2, written by a girl. Greater percentages of teachers were uncertain about the sex of the writers of the persuasive papers than of the narrative papers.

Aesthetic quality. Teachers highlighted the aesthetic qualities of the writing when they perceived the writer to be a girl. Fifty-eight percent of third-grade teachers' gender markers and 23% of sixth-grade teachers' gender markers identifying writers as girls addressed the aesthetic qualities within the narrative papers. None of the gender markers used to identify writers as boys dealt with aesthetic qualities of the writing. Included within this category were happy endings, expressions of emotion, such as "fell to her knees crying," and evidence of caring and collaboration. In third-grade narrative #2 about a mouse who moved to the city and could not find a home until a grandmother, concerned that he would catch a cold, invited him in, seven female teachers identified the happy ending as an indicator of a girl's writing. Four female teachers associated the inclusion of details about the grandma's caring about the mouse with girls' writing, as well. The writer was a boy.

Teachers' perceptions of the writer's sex varied, depending on their interpretation of the emotional depth within the writing. Seven female teachers felt that the emotion expressed in the final sentence of sixth-grade narrative #1, "and her mom said, 'You should know home is where the heart is,'" was typical of a female writer. In contrast, a sixth-grade female teacher stated that the story was not emotional. She used the explanation, "boys don't pick emotional issues" to support her identification of the writer as a boy.

Gender markers used to identify the writers of the persuasive papers also associated aesthetic qualities with girls' writing. Sixty-two percent of gender markers used by third-grade teachers and 80% of gender markers used by sixth-grade teachers to identify female writers highlighted the passion and commitment of the writers in presenting their arguments. None of the gender markers identifying writers as boys referred to aesthetic qualities. Two female third-grade teachers correctly identified the writer of persuasive paper #3 as a boy, for example, explaining that "a girl would have given feeling reasons" to support the argument. Another female teacher found the writing to be "factual and analytical, with no emotionalizing or appealing to the listener."

Dynamism. Teachers in both grades positioned boys as the writers of more violent, action-filled and aggressive writing. These qualities were present in 59% of the third-grade gender markers and 9% of the sixth-grade gender markers used to identify writers of the narrative papers as boys. One sixth-grade teacher associated the female character's "getting smart with the teacher" with girls' writing in narrative #1 about a girl who was kicked out of school because she wore her headphones to school. The teacher's perception was incorrect, as the writer was a boy. Otherwise, there were no gender markers within the category of dynamism used to identify writers as girls.

Teachers perceived characters' actions differently depending upon their positioning of the writer as a boy or a girl. Two female third-grade teachers who felt that the writer of third-grade narrative #2 (about the mouse trying to find a home) was female described it as "mellow and sweet." Two female teachers felt that there was less violence than there would have been if a boy had written the story. A male teacher stated that "boys would have had the cat eat the mouse." One female teacher who correctly identified the writer as a boy thought the story was "spooky" and noted the action and the "chasing" as masculine gender markers. A male teacher also felt there was action in the story, a characteristic he attributed to narratives written by boys.

The third-grade writers of two persuasive arguments used in this study promised that being given a computer or a trampoline would help them to "stay out of trouble." This was the predominant gender marker that female and male third-grade teachers used to identify the writers of the two papers as boys. As a result, 77% of the gender markers within persuasive writing at the third-grade level referred to the dynamism of the writing. One teacher associated the plea for a more lenient school attendance policy in sixth-grade persuasive paper #2 with the "discipline problems prominent in males." Participating teachers did not otherwise use dynamism as a feature to determine the sex of the student writers of persuasive papers.

Demonstration of writer's competence. With few exceptions, teachers participating in this study characterized girls as being more competent narrative writers than boys. After the match between the character's and the writer's sex, the greatest percentage (34%) of gender markers used to identify sixth-grade narrative writers as boys referred to the writer's incompetence. In contrast, 13% of gender markers at the sixth-grade level and 19% of gender markers at the third-grade level referred to the writer's competence when identifying writers as girls.

Participating teachers described papers whose writers they perceived to be girls as interesting, complete, and "showing a lot of thought." They also associated the use of sophisticated vocabulary with girls' writing.

Teachers' perceptions of the writer's competence appeared to be contingent on their perception of the writer's gender. In one narrative, for example, two female sixth-grade teachers who thought the writer was a girl found evidence of "good spelling" and "details," whereas a female teacher who thought the writer was a boy felt that there was a "lack of description" and "short sentences." Another female teacher found the ending weak, explaining that "boys have more problems with conclusions."

At the sixth-grade level, the perception of girls as better writers than boys was carried into participating teachers' assessment of gender markers within the persuasive papers. The one gender marker referring to girls' competence as persuasive argument writers was positive. A female teacher explained that the argument in persuasive paper #1 "started forcefully and ended nicely." In contrast, 90% of gender markers used to identify male writers referred to mechanical errors or the limitations in the supporting details within the persuasive papers. One female teacher, referring to persuasive paper #2, explained, "most students who write so poorly are boys." Only one female sixth-grade teacher commended a writer perceived as a boy on the effectiveness of the argument. This teacher felt that the writer of persuasive paper #1 provided "good points."

At the third-grade level, participating teachers' perceptions of girls' and boys' relative competence in their persuasive writing were mixed. Thirty-one percent of the gender markers associated with girls' persuasive writing and 14% of the gender markers associated with boys' persuasive writing referred to the writer's competence. In persuasive paper #1, a male third-grade teacher, perceiving the writer to be a boy, felt that the writer "presented convincing aspects as to why he wants a trampoline. He used a very logical approach." In contrast, a third-grade female teacher who felt that the writer of the paper was a girl found "good explanations for each reason given to get a trampoline." The uneven perceptions of girls' and boys' writing competence was evident in gender markers identified in persuasive paper #2, as well. One female third-grade teacher felt that the writer presented a weak argument whereas another female teacher assessed the argument as being "supported by clever details." Both teachers perceived the writer to be a boy.

Teachers' gender perceptions and their evaluation of student writing. The highest mean scores for 6 of the 12 papers were assigned by teachers who were uncertain of the writer's gender. Scores for a narrative and persuasive paper at each grade level ranged from 1 to 4. For 3 other papers at each grade level, the scores ranged from 1 to 3 and for 1 paper at each grade, the scores ranged from 2 to 4.

A one-way analysis of variance (ANOVA) comparing scores assigned by teachers who perceived the writer to be a boy, those who identified the writer as a girl, and those who were uncertain of the writer's sex showed no significant differences for any of the papers, nor did an orthogonal planned contrast between scores assigned by teachers who identified the writer as a girl or a boy. Participating teachers did not consistently score the writing of one sex higher than that of the other across all of the writing samples.

In a comparison of the means of the three narrative scores and of the three persuasive scores by a multivariate analysis of variance (MANOVA), I found a significant effect of discourse mode at the third-grade level, $F(3, 49)=10.48, p<.001$. Mean scores of the three persuasive papers were significantly higher than mean scores of the three narrative papers. At the sixth-grade level I also found a significant effect of discourse, $F(3, 49)=109.48$, $p<.001$. At this grade level, the three narrative papers received higher scores, however. This finding is particularly interesting at the sixth-grade level, as the same student wrote persuasive paper #1 and narrative #3. As shown in Table 1, the mean of scores assigned to her narrative writing was 3.19. The mean of scores assigned to her persuasive writing was 2.02.

Discussion

A shared perception of gender differences in student writing was evident in the third- and sixth-grade teachers' descriptions of gender markers within the

Table 1

Means of Scores Assigned to Writing Samples

Writing Samples	Mean Scores Assigned to Writing samples	*SD*
Grade 3		
Girl		
Narrative #1	1.92	.65
Boy		
Narrative #2	1.89	.68
Narrative #3	2.77	.61
Girl		
Persuasive #1	3.10	.45
Persuasive #2	2.04	.59
Boy		
Persuasive #3	2.56	.83
Grade 6		
Boy		
Narrative #1	2.08	.56
Narrative #2	3.27	.72
Girl		
Narrative #3	3.19	.56
Persuasive #1	2.02	.54
Persuasive #2	1.25	.62
Boy		
Persuasive #3	2.67	.64

narrative papers used in this study. These differences were consistent with researchers' analyses of elementary students' narrative writing (Gray-Schlegel & Gray-Schlegel, 1995–96; Trepanier-Street & Romatowski, 1991; Tuck et al., 1985). As in my previous study (Peterson, 1998), participating teachers' descriptions of the writing varied according to their perception of the writer's sex. The teachers foregrounded certain features that confirmed their identification of the writer as a girl or a boy and overlooked other features indicating that a student of the other sex had written the paper.

Predominant among the identified differences in teachers' description of gender markers within the writing samples was the match between the writer's and the protagonist's sex. The third- and sixth-grade teachers felt that girls emphasized aesthetic qualities, such as interpersonal relationships and emotion, in their writing. This perception contrasted with a view of boys as writers who emphasized dynamic qualities, such as aggression and action. In their identification of gender markers within the writing samples, teachers at both grade levels privileged girls' writing over boys' writing in terms of the use of writing conventions, details, and vocabulary.

Participating teachers' perceptions of gender characteristics of student writing were consistent with gender differences foregrounded within feminist theory (Belenky et al., 1986; Gilligan, 1982). The aesthetic qualities that teachers in this study attributed to girls' writing reflect a view of feminine values and ways of thinking that develop out of women's participation in nurturing, relationship-oriented roles within the domestic sphere. In contrast, the dynamic qualities that teachers ascribed to boys' writing are consistent with a view of masculine ways of being that develop out of men's participation in a competitive environment beyond the domestic sphere.

With one exception, these gender perceptions were consistently reproduced in teachers' identification of gender markers within the persuasive papers used in this study, as well. The exception arose in third-grade teachers' perceptions of boys' and girls' competence in presenting a convincing argument. Like the secondary and postsecondary teachers participating in previous research (Barnes, 1990; Graham, 1996; Haswell & Haswell, 1995; Roulis, 1995), some third-grade teachers in the current study privileged masculine styles of persuasive writing. They described persuasive writing that they perceived to have been written by a boy as logical and well developed with strong supporting details. In this respect, the third-grade teachers reproduced the perception held by secondary and postsecondary teachers within previous studies that masculine writing styles were better suited to the persuasive discourse mode than were feminine writing styles. Other third-grade teachers in this study described persuasive papers that they perceived to have been written by girls as logical and containing strong supporting details, however. It appears that they carried their perceptions of girls as more competent narrative writers into their assessment of persuasive writing.

There was no evidence of gender bias in teachers' scoring of the cross-gendered classroom writing samples used in this study. In this respect, the results of this study of classroom teachers' assessment of students' classroom writing were inconsistent with the results of large-scale examinations of elementary student writing at the provincial, state, and national levels (Alberta Education, 1997; Office of Educational Research and Improvement, 1995; Ohio Department of Education, 2000). The privileging of girls' writing that was evident in the scores assigned to writing assessed in large-scale evaluations and in the third- and sixth-grade teachers' qualitative descriptions of the classroom writing samples used in this study did not appear to a significant degree in the teachers' scoring of the classroom writing.

There was a significant difference in the scores assigned to the narrative writing and the persuasive writing samples at each grade level. Third-grade teachers scored the persuasive writing samples significantly higher than they scored the narrative writing samples. The opposite was true for the scores that sixth-grade teachers assigned to writing samples at their grade level. In this study, the discourse mode appeared to have a greater effect on teachers' evaluative responses to the writing than did the gender characteristics of the writing.

Research Limitations

The limitations of the study center on the sample teacher population, the selection of the scoring guide and the influence of the gender identification process on the teachers' scoring of the writing. The sample size, smaller than anticipated when the study began, limits the widespread generalizing of these results. Large percentages of participating teachers were uncertain of the writer's gender of many of the papers, and there was an imbalance in the identification of the writer's sex for other papers. These imbalances limited comparisons of scores according to teachers' perceptions of the writer's sex. Future research studies might address this limitation by comparing the scores assigned to cross-gendered narrative and persuasive papers whose writers are identified for half of the participating teachers as boys and for the other half of teachers as girls. Modifying the research study design in this way would also address the possible influence of being asked to identify the writer's sex on teachers' scoring of the writing.

Of great significance to the widespread use of this study's results is the paucity of data showing male teachers' gender perceptions. The lack of success in achieving a balance in female and male teachers' participation in the study has a great impact on the results of a study of gender perceptions, as comparisons of male and female teachers' scoring of classroom writing cannot be made with any degree of reliability. Further research with a determined focus on examining the gender perceptions of male teachers and their evaluation of students' narrative and persuasive writing is needed to redress this imbalance.

My decision to use the state scoring guide contributed to greater consistency in teachers' scoring of the selected papers because of teachers' widespread use of the scoring guide across the state. The limitations of the scoring guide presented corresponding limitations to the validity of the findings, however. The criteria in the scoring guide are relatively superficial, as they focus more on writing conventions and organization of ideas than on the content of the writing. In addition, criteria such as "relationship to the topic identified in the prompt" and "use of supporting details" are more appropriate to the assessment of expository writing than to narrative writing. For this reason, the validity of scores assigned to the narrative writing in this study is limited. In a forthcoming study, I intend to use discourse-specific scoring guides that have been developed by the provincial ministry of education for use by teachers in the Canadian province in which I currently reside.

The finding of significant differences in the scores assigned to persuasive writing as compared to narrative writing leads to questions about teachers' expectations and classroom practices in teaching and assessing the two kinds of writing at each grade level. Further research might examine the standards that teachers at various grade levels use to evaluate writing across discourse modes.

Implications for Practice

The findings of this study indicate a need to rethink the criteria used in assessing student writing across discourse modes. The state scoring guide used in this study appeared to be based on a view of "good" writing as that which participating teachers attributed to girls' writing. Equity and consistency may have been compromised in the assessment of the writing because the scoring criteria did not encompass the values of feminine and masculine writing styles within the two discourse modes.

The consistency with which participating teachers associated indicators of writing competence in the selected papers with girls' writing leads to questions about the degree of objectivity that is possible in writing assessment. In a search for more equitable approaches to writing assessment, teachers will need to embrace and celebrate girls' and boys' writing styles. Teachers might begin by examining their own beliefs, expectations, values, feelings, and experiences regarding gender in student writing. What gender patterns have teachers and students observed in their own and others' writing over the years? What kind of feedback do teachers give to students of their own and the other gender when responding to student writing? What alternatives to dominant gender discourses do students embed within their writing? How do teachers respond to writing that does not conform to stereotypical gender patterns? Thoughtful consideration of questions such as these will bring teachers' implicit expectations for gender-related writing characteristics to a conscious level where their possible influences on consistency and equity in writing assessment can be addressed.

Author Note

This research was supported by an Elva Knight Grant from the International Reading Association. I am grateful to participating teachers for their involvement in this study.

References

Alberta Education. (1997). *Achievement testing program provincial report.* Edmonton, AB: Author.

Barnes, L. L. (1990). Gender bias in teachers' written comments. In S. L. Gabriel & I. Smithson (Eds.), *Gender in the classroom: Power and pedagogy* (pp. 140–159). Urbana and Chicago: University of Illinois Press.

Belenky, M. F., Clinchy, B. M., Goldberger, N. R., & Tarule, J. M. (1986). *Women's ways of knowing: The development of self, voice, and mind.* New York: Basic Books.

Gilligan, C. (1982). *In a different voice: Psychological theory and women's development.* Cambridge, MA: Harvard University Press.

Graham, M. B. (1996). Rejecting tradition: Females and males at risk. *The Writing Instructor, 15,* 117–129.

Gray-Schlegel, M., & Gray-Schlegel, T. (1995–96). An investigation of gender stereotypes as revealed through children's creative writing. *Reading Research and Instruction, 35,* 160–170.

Haswell, R. H., & Haswell, J. E. (1995). Gendership and the miswriting of students. *College Composition and Communication, 46,* 223–254.

Knudson, R. E. (1992). *An analysis of persuasive discourse: Learning how to take a stand.* Paper presented at the meeting of the National Reading Conference, San Antonio, TX.

Office of Educational Research and Improvement, U.S. Department of Education. (1995). *Windows into the classroom: NAEP's 1992 writing portfolio study.* Washington, DC: Author.

Ohio Department of Education (1999). *Scoring guide: Writing.* <www.ode.state.oh.us/proficiency/sample_tests/sixth-6ptman02.pdf>. Columbus, OH: Author.

Ohio Department of Education. (2000). *Ohio sixth-grade proficiency test results: Gender and ethnic March 2000 test administration.* Columbus, OH: Author

Peterson, S. (1998). Evaluation and teachers' perceptions of gender in sixth-grade student writing. *Research in the Teaching of English, 33,* 181–208.

Roulis, E. (1995). Gendered voice in composing, gendered voice in evaluating: Gender and the assessment of writing quality. In D. L. Rubin (Ed.), *Composing social identity in written language* (pp. 151–185). Hillsdale, NJ: Erlbaum.

Trepanier-Street, M., & Romatowski, J. A. (1991). Achieving sex equity goals: Implications from creative writing research. *Educational Horizons, 70*(1), 34–40.

Tuck, D., Bayliss, V., & Bell, M. (1985). Analysis of sex stereotyping in characters created by young authors. *Journal of Educational Research, 78*(4), 248–252.

Weiss, D. M., & Sachs, J. (1991). Persuasive strategies used by preschool children. *Discourse Processes, 14,* 55–72.

White, E. M. (1985). *Teaching and assessing writing.* San Francisco: Jossey-Bass.

Reaching Understandings of Literature and Life: The Unfolding Responses of a Child with Hearing Loss

LaFon Louise Phillips
Tucson Unified School District

Children's drawings, with their characteristic simplicity, directness of expression, and *joie de vivre*, have been a source of great pleasure, curiosity, and perplexity throughout my career as a teacher of hearing-impaired children. However, it was not until 1992 with the arrival of a new group of kindergarten students that possibilities for examining children's drawings in response to literature began to take form in my mind. During this time, Hickman's (1979) observation that young children's literary response drawings tend to "collect" items and ideas nudged me to question whether or not this was true of my own students' visual responses. From the adult perspective, this statement could be an accurate description of such pictorial content. However, it seemed to me that in the case of my students' literary response drawings, there was more to the subject than met the eye. Therefore, in the spring of 1994, I undertook a reader response study that focused upon an aesthetic approach to the exploration and teaching of literature through the sign systems of language, drama, and art.

The theoretical perspectives underlying this investigation (and the literature-based sociosemiotic curriculum of my classroom) are the transactional theory of literature as conceptualized by Louise Rosenblatt (1938/1983, 1978) and the semiotic processes of signification and transmediation put forth by C. S. Peirce (Deely, 1990; Merrell, 1995).

In *Literature as Exploration* (1938/1983), Rosenblatt challenged the New Critics' emphasis upon text and literary form and called instead for a focus upon the reader and the act of reading. In her initial conceptualization of a transactional theory of literature, Rosenblatt proposed that a literary text is simply symbols on a page and that the literary work, or "poem" as she later designated it, exists only in the "live circuit between the reader and the text" (p. 25). In recognizing and explicating the active and creative nature of the reading process, Rosenblatt suggested that the literary experience should be phrased as a transaction between reader and text. This co-emphasis upon reader and text was elaborated in Rosenblatt's later work *The Reader, the Text, the Poem* (1978), wherein she characterized the reader's transaction with text not as a unilinear action, such as text acting on reader or reader acting on text but as a "situation, an event at a particular time and place in which each element conditions the other" (p. 16).

Rosenblatt also delineated the nature of the reader's relationship to text during various kinds of reading events, and she contended that, depending upon the

National Reading Conference Yearbook, ***50***, *pp. 495–506.*

reader's purpose, the reader assumes different stances in his or her transaction with literary text. These stances, which can be placed along a continuum from more efferent to more aesthetic, indicate the focus of the reader's attention while reading and also the reader's readiness to respond in a particular way. In an *efferent* reading stance the primary focus of the reader is upon what he or she will carry away from the reading, the information that will remain as the residue of the reading. In contrast, the primary focus of the reader involved in an *aesthetic* reading stance is upon his or her experience of the literary work and the savoring of the images, thoughts, and emotions evoked as a result of the literary experience.

These crucial insights, in conjunction with Peirce's concepts of the role of the triadic sign in the chain of semiosic signification and transmediation (Deely, 1990; Merrell, 1995; Siegel, 1995) provided the interpretive lens for this study. Other influential theoretical concepts underlying my study are found in the work of Dewey (1934), Arnheim (1969), Gardner (1980, 1990), Goodman (1976, 1978), and Lowenfeld and Brittain (1987).

As distant teachers, these theorists guided my creation of a learning environment in which my students were encouraged to use the sign systems of language, drama, and art in the course of responding to and reflecting upon their aesthetic experiences of literature. In my classroom, this process began with my oral reading of picture books to the class. My particular style of reading might be characterized as an "interpretive presentation" of text as it involves an active use of facial expression, gesture, body movement, and physical contact with listeners in addition to the use of intonational features of pitch (the rise and fall of the voice in speech), stress (accent or loudness), and juncture (pause).

In the course of each read-aloud experience my students' actions and comments about a story often indicated some of the avenues that we might take to extend their initial responses and understandings. Quite often, these extensions included dramatizing stories, participating in choral readings or choral responses, drawing or painting visual responses, talking about specific aspects of stories or illustrations, singing, puppetry, readers' theater or mime. For an in-depth discussion of the sociosemiotic framework underlying this curriculum, see Phillips (1999).

Method

The purpose of this paper is to report on my 5-year, longitudinal, teacher research investigation into young, "oral" hearing-impaired children's responses to literature through the sign systems of language, drama, and art. Conducted in a public school special education program in Tucson, Arizona, this study focused upon nine children with hearing loss who remained in an ongoing, oral language literature group for 5 years.

This study provided multilayered insights relative to my questions concerning the role of literature in my classroom and in the lives of my students; the role of dramatization in these children's constructions of literary meaning; the visual and verbal content of their literary response drawings and dictations; and, the patterns and changes found in these students' artistic and verbal responses to literature over the course of time.

The data collected for this inquiry were generated as part of a daily class activity that was referred to as "literature group." During "literature group," students participated in "literary events" that involved listening to orally read texts and responding to literary experiences through drama, language, and art. At various points during each classroom literary event, students always responded to the stories under consideration by drawing pictures and dictating statements to accompany their visual responses. The student dictations served a dual purpose in this study as a source of data and as a means of member checking (Lincoln & Guba, 1985) to verify, correct, and/or expand upon children's verbal statements.

The primary data sources informing this study consisted of children's drawings (*n*=559) and dictated response statements (*n*=559) that were collected throughout the investigation. Secondary sources of data included students' literature response portfolios containing group and/or individual projects, and miscellaneous student artifacts such as written documents, charts, webs, sketches, or notes. Other data included transcribed audio recordings of group literature discussions and teacher fieldnotes.

The data generated during this investigation were examined with various purposes in mind: to gain deeper understandings of my students as individuals and as members of a learning community; to guide my decisions and actions as a teacher and, to generate possible answers to my research questions. This multiplicity of purpose meant that these data were being examined on an ongoing basis throughout the course of the investigation.

During the first three semesters of the literature group data collection period, no attempts were made to categorize students' drawings or dictations. These data were pasted onto color-coded sheets of paper and maintained chronologically in separate student notebooks. As a body of work, these data gave me a general feel for how individual students were responding to their literary experiences. They also gave me a sense of the differences and commonalities of these responses. Therefore, at the end of the first data collection period, I analyzed each of the collected drawings for pictorial content and the accompanying dictations for verbal content. These preliminary analyses indicated one strong commonality in students' drawings and yielded 12 tentative categories of verbal response discussed in the next section.

This process of analysis was repeated at the end of the second literature group data collection period. At that time, the first set of data was re-coded to determine whether or not the data "fit" into their assigned categories. Then the second set was coded with the result being that both sets of data fit easily into the previously constructed categories of response. The next step in my analytical process involved tallying the occurrences of these responses and determining the percentage of each type of response in each set of data. These sets of data were then compared against one another in order to determine if there were any patterns of change evident between the sets of data. These comparisons revealed a steady pattern of visual response in my students' drawings and significantly changing patterns of verbal response in their dictated statements.

In addition to being examined for patterns of collective response, these accumulated data were also examined for indications of themes or patterns in individual response, patterns that might identify characteristic responses of individual students. One of these unique themes of individual response will be explicated in this report following a review of the broad findings.

Results

Research findings indicated a steadfast pattern of visual literary response on the parts of my students, that is, these children *depicted story characters* (94% of 559), *story settings* (3%), or *something else* (3%) in responding to literature through the sign system of art. Patterns of verbal response were found in the accompanying dictated statements for these drawings as well. In these statements, students focused upon giving *explications of story characters' actions and feelings* (41% of 559), *retellings of story events* (22%), *synopses of story events* (20%), *evaluative statements* (6%), *identifications of items in drawings* (4%), *combined synopsis/retellings of story events* (4%), or *other* types of comments (1%). Further analyses of these data revealed a strong, humanist focus upon what I term "matters of the heart" at the intersections of these visual and verbal literary responses.

Within these patterns of collective literary response, uniquely characteristic and focused themes of personal response were found as well. This individuality of response became manifest over the course of time as each of the study participants actualized her or his unique potentials as a meaning maker of literature through the sign systems of language, drama, and art.

One of the meaning-makers was Jenna, whose personal themes of response led her to actualize her potentials as a *contemplator of human emotion* and *explorer of personal identity*. Jenna's quest to make meaning of life and literature is the subject of a case study presented next.

Jenna: Actualizing Self as a Contemplator of Emotion and Explorer of Identity

Rosenblatt (1983) held that "to the great majority of readers, the human experience that literature presents is primary [and that] for them the formal elements of the work—style and structure, rhythmic flow—function only as a part of the total literary experience" (p. 7). This majority of readers, she suggested, is seeking "to participate in another's vision—to reap knowledge of the world, to fathom the resources of the human spirit, [and] to gain insights that will make his [or her] own life more comprehensible" (p. 7).

This path of understanding is one that was evidenced strongly in Jenna's explorations of human emotion and identity via literary transaction. These interwoven themes of understanding will be traced in two chronologically ordered descriptions of Jenna's visual and verbal responses to literature. To that end, the first presentation offers a selected set of literary responses that highlight Jenna's meaning making in the area of human emotion and feelings.

Jenna: Contemplator of Human Emotion and Feelings

In actualizing herself as a contemplator of feelings and emotion via multifaceted transactions with literature, Jenna "appropriated symbol systems as metaphorical vehicles with generative syntax" (Tierney, 1997, p. 296) that afforded her new possibilities for engagement with self, others, and the world. These multisymbolic, personal and social literary transactions allowed Jenna to explore and express her evolving understandings of a range of human emotion that are exemplified in her responses to the stories of *Babushka Baba Yaga* (Polacco, 1993), *Fritz and the Beautiful Horses* (Brett, 1981), *Big Anthony and the Magic Ring* (dePaola, 1979), *The Rag Coat* (Mills, 1991), and *Mary Todd Lincoln* (Anderson, 1991).

In the spring of her first-grade year, Jenna drew a picture of the heartbroken Russian grandmother from the story of *Babushka Baba Yaga* (Polacco, 1993). In the verbal response for this drawing, Jenna stated that the grandmother, "Baba Yaga was very sad because her heart was very, very heavy. Her friends made her sad because she was ugly [and then] Baba Yaga kissed the baby [good-bye]."

In her visual and verbal responses to this story, Jenna was focusing upon the grandmother's feelings of anguish and heartache brought about by village gossip that the "horrible, wicked Baba Yaga . . . is ugly . . . a hag . . . evil and hateful!" (Polacco, 1993).

Likewise, in the fall of her second-grade year, Jenna depicted the solitary, sobbing figure of the main character in *Fritz and the Beautiful Horses* (Brett, 1981). In the verbal description of this drawing, Jenna stated that, "Fritz saw the horses and the children on the horses. Fritz was sad. The citizens laughed at Fritz because they thought he was ugly."

In these responses, Jenna was focusing upon the feelings of pain and rejection felt by a homely, outcast pony who suffered the jeers and laughter of the arrogant citizens of a city famous for its beautiful horses.

In the fall of Jenna's third-grade year, her literature group read the tale of *Big Anthony and the Magic Ring* (dePaola, 1979). In this story, the plain-looking and always-bumbling Big Anthony pilfers Strega Nona's magic ring and transforms himself into "Handsome Big Anthony." In this new state of being, he attends a village dance where all of the ladies compete for his attention until he is forced to escape and return to his former self. In her visual response, Jenna depicted a scene in which the smiling character of Bambolona is handing a flower to Big Anthony. Jenna's written response for this drawing, "Bambolona gave Anthony a flower because she like's Anthony when he [is] plain" is a thoughtful inference that Bambolona's tender feelings for Anthony were not predicated upon his outer physical appearance.

In the spring of Jenna's third-grade year, her literature group read *The Rag*

Coat (Mills, 1991), which tells the story of an orphaned child's patchwork coat. Jenna's drawing in response to this story showed a sobbing child alone in the woods and her written response stated:

> I feel sorry for mina because her father died that summer. And she dosen't have a coat ethier. And I feel sad when other kids make fun of her. Kids feel angry or sad when other people tease them. when she ran into the wood's she felt better. Then she told stories about the rags to the other kids. [child's spelling from the original]

In these responses, Jenna was focusing upon the feelings of pain, sadness, loss, and rejection felt by the bereaved character who was taunted by her classmates for wearing a "ragcoat" to school. Jenna's comments about the emotional effects of mean-spirited teasing revealed her thought-out understandings of this cruel behavior.

During her fourth-grade year, Jenna and her classmates read the biography of *Mary Todd Lincoln* (Anderson, 1991). In her responses to the first chapter of this book, Jenna depicted an angry confrontation between Mary Todd and her stepmother and she wrote that, "I think that Mary was angry because everyone stared at her. And she was guwachy [grouchy]. Then she ask her mom if she can change her dress after breakfast."

In her responses, Jenna was focusing on Mary's feelings of anger and humiliation when her family was startled by a "fashion-statement" dress that she wore to breakfast. This story event led Jenna to speculate that Mary's anger was brought about by the stares of her family.

Jenna's focus upon human actions, feelings, and emotions was one that she and her classmates expressed consistently in their visual and verbal literary responses throughout the course of this investigation. As a result, many of their literary responses bore a strong resemblance to one another.

However, the above-described literary responses were unique in that they cloaked Jenna's never-mentioned understandings of the effects of social rejection. The motivation underlying Jenna's interpretive focus for these particular stories will become evident in the following recollection.

Jenna: A remembrance. My first encounter with Jenna took place during student registration in August before entering first grade. On that day, she was accompanied by her parents who protectively held her hands as they squeezed through the doorway of my classroom. While her father went through the rituals of introduction, Jenna and her mother stood by quietly until he turned to them and prompted Jenna to "Say hello to Mrs. Phillips!"

Despite previous knowledge of Jenna's medical history, the first sight of her malformed face struck a strong chord of compassion and sympathy within me. However, over the course of our 5-year relationship, the exterior aspect of Jenna's being would become virtually unnoticeable by me as her inner beauty and strength of character became apparent. Now, 7 years later, a discussion of her appearance is important only because of the light that it may shed upon Jenna's transactions with literature during this period of her life.

By 7 years of age, Jenna had undergone more than 20 operations to correct a variety of congenital craniofacial abnormalities. During her elementary school years, another surgery was performed in an effort to deepen her eye sockets and to give greater form to the wide nasal bridge that accentuated her red-streaked, protuberant eyes.

In the early years of her schooling, Jenna's demeanor remained quiet and reserved to the extreme. However, with the passage of time she became increasingly comfortable in the special education setting to the point that she became the acknowledged classroom leader. This was due largely to her role as the "peacemaker" in a close-knit but sometimes contentious group of children whose feuds and friendships waxed and waned over the course of this investigation.

Jenna's philosophy and practice of pacifism sometimes masked the import of her literary responses. The previously discussed literary responses give credence to Rosenblatt's (1983) contention that talking about emotional matters in terms of situations in a book make "it easier for the reader to bring his own inner problems into the open, and to face them or seek the help of others without embarrassment of explicit self-revelation" (p. 205).

Jenna's visual and verbal responses focusing upon the actions and feelings of these story characters suggested that she was engaging in a transactional process of response and interpretation through which her unconscious understandings were being transformed into "conscious, social, moral, and intellectual meanings" (Holland, 1975, p. 17). In Bettelheim's (1989) view, transactions of this nature allow children to *feel* which stories are true to their inner situations of the moment and then through gradual processes of recognition and apprehension, they come to an increasing awareness of what stories have to offer them in terms of greater personal understandings.

From this perspective, Jenna's focus upon the emotional distress felt by Babushka Baba Yaga, Fritz, Mary Todd, and Minna suggested that she was identifying (in the literary sense of the word) with these characters' feelings of personal rejection. In expressing her awareness of these characters' feelings through art and language, Jenna was calling upon her own painful experiences of the world and perhaps coming to a better understanding of herself and others.

Jenna's enduring interest in these "matters of the heart" was closely related to the theme of response manifested in her transactions with "family-" and "Asian" related literary texts. This second theme of personal response will be traced in a presentation of Jenna's explorations of familial and cultural identity via transactions with literature.

Jenna: Explorer of personal identity. In February 1996, Jenna's literature group reread the story of Patricia Polacco's father, *My Ol' Man* (1995), in conjunction with *My Rotten Redheaded Older Brother* (Polacco, 1994) and *Firetalking* (Polacco, 1994), which is an autobiographical account of Polacco's life. At the conclusion of these readings, Jenna and her classmates created their own "Photograph Albums" of the various members of Patricia Polacco's family. In the course of this work, Joey exclaimed, "1948! That's when Indians and cowboys was here

. . . and Japanese . . ." At which point Jenna quietly but firmly interjected, "I'm not Japanese. I don't speak Japanese. I speak Cantonese. . . . My dad was in Hong Kong and he decided to marry. He went to Saigon, Vietnam, [where my mother was and] then they both marry together and they decided to come to Arizona because they like the United States. And they want me to go to school and learn."

In this brief exchange, Jenna outlined her family origins in the event that Joey might be under the mistaken impression that she was of Japanese descent. Jenna's account of her parents' marriage and immigration to the United States revealed the strong sense of pride that she felt for her family and their cultural heritage.

This sense of familial pride was evidenced again in Jenna's subsequent visual and verbal literary responses to this theme study where she depicted an inverted version of the different branches of her ancestry and explained, "This is my family. This is my grandparents and they're married. This is my mom and dad and they're married. Here's my brother and my sister. That's me. We're Chinese and that's our Chinese names. My Chinese name is Sukwon."

Although Jenna was familiar with the typical genealogical format, her decision to situate her maternal and paternal grandparents along the baseline of this drawing lendt a strong emphasis to their roles as co-founders of Jenna's family. This visual response and Jenna's careful explication of the different familial relationships and reiteration of the fact that, "We're Chinese and that's our Chinese names" seems to validate Holland's (1975) notion of "an identity principle of continuity" (p. 175), a principle he described as follows:

> The individual (considered as the continuing creator of variations on an identity theme) relates to the world as he does to a poem or a story: he uses its physical reality as grist with which to re-create himself, that is, to make yet another variation in his single, enduring identity. (p. 128)

In accordance with this viewpoint, re-creations of self through literary experience may be an inevitable form of response because, "We can really know those words only from inside our own mental processes" (Holland, 1975, p. 221) and we cannot examine texts apart from our own personal and inner re-creations of them. In a like vein, Scholes (1989) suggested that, "Reading is not just a matter of standing safely outside texts, where their power cannot reach us. It is a matter of entering, of passing through the looking glass and seeing ourselves on the other side" (p. 27). He contended:

> When we become aware of ourselves, we are already thoroughly developed as textual creatures. What we are and what we may become are already shaped by powerful cultural texts . . . [and that] we cannot start ourselves over as blank pages but must go on writing the texts of ourselves from where we find ourselves to be. (p. 27)

In April of her third grade year, Jenna's passages through a looking glass of "Cinderella" stories allowed her to recognize herself anew and to write the important texts of her life. These literary looking glasses included *Cinderella* (Andreas, 1954), *Princess Furball* (Huck, 1989), *The Rough-Face Girl* (Martin, 1992), *Yeh-Shen* (Louie, 1982), *Cinderella Penguin* (Perlman, 1992), and *Prince Cinders* (Cole,

1987). After our reading of the Chinese Cinderella story, *Yeh-Shen* (Louie, 1982), Jenna's literature group spent several days reading portions of this story together and creating time-line responses that explicated the events of Yeh-Shen's life.

Jenna's first time-line drawing depicted Yeh-Shen's father in the middle of the page with his wives and their respective daughters on opposite sides of him. According to Jenna's dictation, "This picture is before when Wu and Yeh-Shen's mother died. I drew the fish right behind Yeh-Shen because Yeh-Shen loved her fish. When I was drawing I forgot to make Chinese eyes for Yeh-Shen's family." The portrait-like quality of Jenna's first response drawing and her statement that she forgot to make "Chinese eyes" for some of the family members pointed to her focus upon achieving realistic likenesses of these characters.

Jenna's second time-line drawing that she entitled, "Yeh-Shen as a Girl" was highly realistic in depicting Yeh-Shen's Asian appearance. Jenna's dictation for this drawing states that, "When Yeh-Shen's a girl she have to live with her stepmother. The stepmother wants Yeh-Shen to work, but Yeh-Shen doesn't want to work." Interestingly, Jenna's response drawing of Yeh-Shen as a girl was remarkably similar to a self-portrait that she created during this same time period. The strong similarity between Jenna's self-portrait and that of Yeh-Shen suggested that Jenna was communicating, through the sign system of art, a variation of her "single, enduring identity" (Holland, 1975, p. 128).

In her fourth time-line responses to this story, Jenna stated, "Yeh-Shen was sad because her fish is no longer alive. She stand on her knees and started crying and the wise man came and told her about the death of her friend. The wise man told her that the bones [of her fish] had spirits." Jenna's visual response to this event included a depiction of the spiritual being who informed Yeh-Shen of the death of her fish that contrasted vividly with that of book illustrator, Ed Young. Unlike Young's amorphous being, Jenna's wise man exhibited strong Asian facial characteristics which bore out her sustained focus upon realism of physical appearance in these particular response drawings.

At the conclusion of this literary theme study, Jenna and her classmates were asked to draw pictures of their favorite Cinderella stories. Jenna's drawing was surprising in that she had sectioned off her paper and drawn *all* of the characters in individual boxes. Jenna's explanation for this decision was that, "They're all my favorites. Yeh-Shen because she's Chinese like me. The Rough-Face Girl when she went into the lake and she was beautiful. Cinderella Penguin because I like penguins and they live in Antarctica. Princess Furball because I like all of the dresses. Cinderella because I like the magic when it was midnight and she ran home. Prince Cinders . . . I like his story because it was funny."

Jenna's reasons for liking each of these stories seemed to substantiate Holland's (1975) view that, "each reader creates from the literary work a psychological process in himself. We say we get absorbed in the act of reading or watching a film or play, but to speak of being 'absorbed' by a book puts the metaphor the wrong way around. It is not the book that absorbs us; it is we who absorb the book" (p. 18).

Jenna's "absorption" and appreciation of these different literary texts revealed several facets of her identity as a reader. She liked the story of *Yeh-Shen* (Louie, 1982) because Yeh-Shen is Chinese; she liked the transformation of *The Rough-Face Girl* (Martin, 1992) into a beautiful maiden; she enjoyed the story of *Cinderella Penguin* (Perlman, 1992) because of her liking for penguins; she admired the different dresses worn by *Princess Furball* (Huck, 1989); she appreciated the magic of *Cinderella* (Andreas, 1954), and the humor of *Prince Cinders* (Cole, 1987). However, if the order of these stories was of any significance, it appears that Jenna's themes of personal concern, that is, her focus upon personal identity and physical appearance were given primacy in this series of texts: "Yeh-Shen because she's Chinese like me" and "The Rough-Faced Girl when she went into the lake and she was beautiful."

Discussion

Jenna's actualizations of self as a contemplator of emotion and explorer of identity via literary transaction was a circuitous path of realization that allowed her to reach greater personal understandings of the world within the context of literature. In responding to literature through the sign systems of art and language, Jenna was able to focus upon the texts of characters' lives and come to greater understandings of herself and her experiences of the world. Throughout the course of this 5-year investigation, Jenna expressed these understandings *only* within the context of literary response. However, after her transition to middle school she began to articulate issues related to her physical appearance and social isolation to the counselor of hearing-impaired students.

At my request, this counselor wrote a brief reflection about Jenna's thoughts and feelings on these issues:

> October: Throughout the first eight weeks of middle school Jenna has been confronted with the grim realities of immense numbers of students, a six-class schedule, and the anonymity of those who are judged to be "different." She has been well-prepared for these challenges by her family's support but she is still somewhat isolated and lonely for friends.
>
> Jenna has concentrated on doing well in school but is expressing, for the first time [in the course of a 6-year relationship], that she is bothered by the appearance of her face. She has commented that she sometimes eats alone during lunch. One topic that she has brought up several times in the past few weeks is the possibility of starting an Asian Club. Jenna has remarked that there are "a lot of Asian students" at school and that a club would be a "good thing." She sees the prospect of a club as a refuge from the wall of indifference and glances out in the school hallways. In her mind, the only place she has been accepted and loved on a deeper level has been at home. I think that she views the possibility of a roomful of Asian students as the next best thing to being at home because they surely would understand her more than the others.

These insightful comments reveal Jenna's strength of character in the face of the harsh realities of her life in the environs of school. They also reveal the source and nurturance of this inner strength, the warm and loving family whose eyes see the true beauty that is within Jenna's being. I would suggest that Jenna's strength of character was nurtured also by her thoughtful explorations of literature that allowed her to revise her conceptions of the world and her place within it.

Implications

One implication to be drawn from these research findings is that children's literature is a medium of exploration through which readers may explore and become aware of potentialities for thought and feeling within themselves (Rosenblatt, 1938/1983). This is possible because bodies of literature record "the depths and heights of the human experience [and] can develop compassion by educating the heart as well as the mind" (Huck, Hepler, & Hickman, 1987, p. 317). In educating the hearts and minds of learners, literature allows for the consideration of new ideas and the development of personal insight and understandings as readers' imaginations are captured and enriched through their personal and social experiences of literature.

These findings suggest that the realization of the potentialities of literature to entertain, enlighten, inform, educate, and edify the mind and the heart may be accomplished through an aesthetic stance or attitude. This stance allows learners, such as Jenna, to consider personally meaningful lines of thought as they transact with stories and reflect upon their literary experiences.

Finally, these findings advance the thought that the different expressive potentialities of art, drama, and language allow learners, such as Jenna and her classmates, to think critically and reflectively upon their personal and social experiences of literature and life and to accomplish a "greater complexity of thought and the consideration of new connections and ideas" (Short & Kauffman, 2000, p. 60) that would not have been possible in a single sign system alone.

References

Anderson, L. (1991). *Mary Todd Lincoln: President's wife.* New York: Chelsea House.

Andreas, E. (1954). *Cinderella* (R. Ives, Ill.). New York: Grosset & Dunlap.

Arnheim, R. (1969). *Visual thinking.* Berkeley: University of California Press.

Bettelheim, B. (1989). *The uses of enchantment.* New York: Vintage.

Brett, J. (1981). *Fritz and the beautiful horses.* Boston: Houghton-Mifflin.

Cole, B. (1987). *Prince Cinders.* New York: Putnam.

Deely, J. (1990). *Basics of semiotics.* Bloomington: Indiana University Press.

dePaola, T. (1979). *Big Anthony and the magic ring.* USA: Harcourt Brace Jovanovich.

Dewey, J. (1934). *Art as experience.* New York: Capricorn.

Gardner, H. (1980). *Artful scribbles: The significance of children's drawings.* New York: Basic.

Gardner, H. (1990). *Art education and human development.* Los Angeles: Getty Center for Education in the Arts.

Goodman, N. (1976). *Languages of art: An approach to a theory of symbols* (2nd ed.). Indianapolis, IN: Hackett.

Goodman, N. (1978). *Ways of worldmaking.* Indianapolis, IN: Hackett.

Hickman, J. (1979). *Response to literature in a school environment, grades K–5.* Unpublished doctoral dissertation. Ohio State University, Columbus.

Holland, N. (1975). *5 readers reading.* New Haven, CT: Yale University Press.

Huck, C. (1989). *Princess Furball* (A. Lobel, Ill.). New York: Scholastic.

Huck, C. S., Hepler, S., & Hickman, J. (1987). *Children's literature in the elementary schools* (4th ed). Ft. Worth, TX: Holt, Rinehart & Winston.

Lincoln, Y. S., & Guba, E. (1985). *Naturalistic inquiry.* Beverly Hills, CA: Sage.

Louie, A. (1982). *Yeh-Shen: A Cinderella story from China.* New York: Sandcastle.

Lowenfeld, V., & Brittain, W. L. (1987). *Creative and mental growth* (8th ed.). New York: Macmillan.

Martin, R. (1992). *The rough-face girl* (D. Shannon, Ill.). New York: Putnam.

Merrell, F. (1995). *Peirce's semiotics now.* Toronto: Canadian Scholars' Press.

Mills, L. (1991) *The rag coat.* USA: Little, Brown.

Perlman, J. (1992). *Cinderella Penguin or the little glass flipper.* New York: Puffin.

Phillips, L. (1999). *Pathways to understanding: Children with hearing loss respond to literature through language, drama and art.* Unpublished doctoral dissertation. University of Arizona, Tucson.

Polacco, P. (1993). *Babushka Baba Yaga.* New York: Philomel.

Polacco, P. (1994). *Firetalking* (L. Migdale, Ill.). New York: Owen.

Polacco, P. (1994). *My rotten redheaded older brother.* New York: Simon & Schuster.

Polacco, P. (1995). *My ol' man.* New York: Philomel.

Rosenblatt, L. (1938/1983). *Literature as exploration* (4th ed.). New York: Modern Language Association of America.

Rosenblatt, L. (1978). *The reader, the text, the poem: The transactional theory of the literary work.* Carbondale: Southern Illinois University Press.

Scholes, R. (1989). *Protocols of reading.* New Haven, CT: Yale University Press.

Short, K., & Kauffman, G. (2000). Exploring sign systems within an inquiry curriculum. In M. Gallego & S. Hollingsworth (Eds.), *What counts as literacy: Challenging the school standard* (pp. 42–61). New York: Teachers College Press.

Siegel, M. (1995). More than words: The generative power of transmediation for learning. *Canadian Journal of Education, 20,* 455–475.

Tierney, R. (1997). Learning with multiple symbol systems: Possibilities, realities, paradigm shifts and developmental considerations. In J. Flood, S. Heath, & D. Lapp (Eds.), *Handbook of research on teaching literacy through the communicative and visual arts* (pp. 286–298). New York: Simon & Schuster Macmillan.

"I Did Not Plan Ahead": Preservice Teachers' Concerns Integrating Print-Based Literacy Lessons with Computer Technology

Janet Richards
University of Southern Mississippi

> Information technology . . . particularly the Internet . . . can help you gain knowledge. But first you need to know how to use it. And even if you know the basics, if you're not using the Internet to its fullest potential, you're likely missing out. (Goldsborough, 2000, p. 14)

> When I met my second grade students' classroom teacher one of my first questions was, "Do you use the computers in your room and access the Internet very often?" To my surprise she answered, "Not very often." (preservice teacher's case, November 2000)

Until recently, the term "literacy" referred to the ability to read and write (Messaris, 1997). Now, literacy is defined as a multitude of interconnected proficiencies, including accessing information through electronic databases, critically interpreting facts on the Internet, and connecting and comparing ideas offered in print and electronic text (Reinking, Labbo, & McKenna, 1997).

Broadened conceptions of literacy are vigorously endorsed by exemplars listed on *The National Council of Teachers of English/International Reading Association Standards* (Farstrup & Myers, 1996) and benchmarks established by the American Library Association (1998). Defining information literacy as "the ability to find, evaluate, and use information effectively" (American Library Association, 1991, p. 152), the American Library Association suggests that teachers can and should support students' literacy learning "regardless of the medium . . . print, visual, video, audio, or electronic" (Rafferty, 1999, p. 23). In addition, recently released National Technology Standards for Teacher Preparation Programs recommend that preservice teachers learn to weave technology with content lessons in authentic classroom situations (U.S. Department of Education, 2000).

In response to National Standards and acknowledging expanded definitions of literacy, I now require preservice teachers in my three field-based literacy courses (language arts, reading methods, content reading) to integrate computer technology with their K–8 reading lessons at every relevant opportunity. Through such connections, I hope to develop my preservice teachers' recognition, expertise, and passion for what is possible when printed text and electronic forms of learning and communication are combined.

Studies that examine computer activities in classrooms have been limited (Kamil & Intrator, 1998). Moreover, research has overlooked preservice teachers

National Reading Conference Yearbook, **50**, *pp. 507–518.*

as one of the many interacting variables that might influence technology initiatives (Reinking & Watkins, 2000). Yet, what preservice teachers learn and perceive about using technology in authentic school contexts has the capacity to positively or negatively impact their use of computers throughout their professional lives (U.S. Department of Education, 2000). Therefore, "pursuing such knowledge [about preservice teachers] is increasingly important given the growing availability and use of technology in schools" (Reinking & Watkins, 2000, p. 387).

In order to determine my preservice teachers' reflective thinking and concerns as they addressed the complexities of supporting and augmenting their students' literacy instruction through computer activities, I decided to conduct a systematic qualitative inquiry. I wanted to add relevant, essential, pragmatic, field-based information that has been omitted from the literature. In addition, I hoped to enhance my own pedagogy by ascertaining exactly what types of problems my preservice teachers experienced as they extended their literacy lessons beyond conventional approaches to reading instruction.

Context and Participants

Three School Contexts for the Study

I conducted the study in three schools (names used here are pseudonyms), all located within the same school district in south Mississippi. Bay View Primary School is a 40-year-old K–3, arts-based school. Bay View was "wired" 2 years ago to accommodate use of computers throughout the school. There are one or two outdated, donated computers with printers in each classroom. The computers often are "sluggish" or do not work at all. Because of electrical wiring difficulties, Internet access is sporadic.

Students at Bay View attend a computer lab 30 minutes a day, four times a week. The lab is staffed by two assistants who monitor the K–3 students as they work through self-paced tutorials in reading, math, and language arts. Keyboarding instruction is not offered. There is no "resident computer expert" (e.g., a classroom teacher, media specialist or computer teacher) at Bay View who can assist teachers or students when they wish to expand their computer expertise, or remediate a computer malfunction.

First Street Upper Elementary School (Grades 4 and 5) is over 60 years old and also recently was "wired" for computer use. As is the case in Bay View Primary School, many of the donated computers in First Street School are old, react "sluggishly," and malfunction often. There are also some recently purchased computers in each classroom. Students attend a 40-minute computer lab 5 days per week where they work through self-paced tutorials. Keyboard instruction is not offered to students. As is the case in Bay View School, there is no "resident computer expert" at First Street School.

Louis Middle School (Grades 6–8) was recently constructed and contains "state-of-the art" computer hardware, software, and essential electrical wiring. All classrooms have at least 4 new computers with printers, and the media center contains 10 new computers. Ten more computers were recently purchased with grant funds. The librarian/media specialist in charge of the center is highly knowledgeable about all aspects of computer applications. As the "resident expert," she holds an "open door" policy regarding the use of the media center and provides superb computer instruction for students, teachers, and even preservice teachers if they ask for help. Teachers and students are welcome to visit the media center at any time to use the computers as a whole-class activity or on an individual basis. In addition to the considerable ongoing computer activities in the media center, eighth-grade students receive 55 minutes of keyboarding instruction from a certified computer teacher 5 days per week throughout the school year.

The Preservice Teachers and their Teaching Schedule

The 58 preservice teachers in the study were enrolled in one of three literacy early-field programs (i.e., prior to student teaching). Twenty-nine preservice teachers in a required 6-semester-hour reading/language arts block reported to Bay View Primary School (Grades K–3) two mornings a week (8:00–10:45 a.m.) during the fall semester. On Monday mornings, with my guidance and support, the preservice teachers worked with small groups of students (the same students throughout the semester). The preservice teachers' lessons centered around use of quality children's literature, reading, writing, and arts connections (e.g., creative book-making, drama enactments, mural constructions, music), promoting students' strategic reading through reading comprehension strategies, and integrating reading instruction with computer technology. On Wednesday mornings, I offered demonstration lessons and lectures and led seminar discussions.

Ten preservice teachers enrolled in a 3-semester-hour content-reading class required for education majors seeking a concentration in reading reported to First Street Upper Elementary School (Grades 4 and 5) two mornings a week during the spring semester (9:25–10:40 a.m.). On Tuesday mornings, the preservice teachers offered literacy lessons in science, social studies, or language arts classes to small groups of students (the same students throughout the semester). The lessons centered around the use of strategies to promote students' comprehension of content text, writing in duel entry diaries, linking literacy with the arts (e.g., drama enactments, music, dance, mural constructions), and relevant use of computers to enhance reading instruction (e.g., locating information about text authors; researching why Plymouth Rock was moved from its original location; comparing and contrasting facts and details about Egyptian pyramids, oceans, and the solar system).

Nineteen preservice teachers studying content-reading methods reported to Louis Middle School (Grades 6–8) two mornings a week during the fall semester (9:25–10:40 a.m.). Working in science, social studies, or language arts classrooms, these preservice teachers followed the same schedule and lesson formats as the preservice teachers at First Street Upper Elementary School, including the use of computers to enhance and optimize students' content-literacy instruction.

Writing Teaching Cases

The preservice teachers also wrote two teaching cases describing their reflective thinking, concerns, and problems as they addressed the intricacies of devising and offering print-based literacy lessons augmented by computer technology. One case was written at mid-semester and the second case was written 2 weeks before the end of the semester (see Richards & Gipe, 2000, for information about writing teaching cases).

Conceptual Framework for the Inquiry

Four literatures informed my inquiry: (a) tenets of social constructivism which suggest that language reveals individual's knowledge, perceptions, and beliefs (Goetz & LeCompte, 1984); (b) ideas from discourse analysis that describe written texts as true reflections of human experiences (Gee, Michaels, & O'Connor, 1992); (c) premises from social constructivism which suggest that as human beings encounter problems that emerge through circumstances, they move to resolve those problems through thoughtful reflection and action (Woods, 1992); and (d) Heideggerian phenomenology that seeks truth within the context of human experience (Rennie, 1999). In addition, I was mindful of traditions from hermeneutics which "indicate that the same text can be read [and interpreted] in a number of different ways" (Tappan & Brown, 1992, p. 186).

Questions Guiding the Inquiry

The preservice teachers' cases served as the main data source for the inquiry. Therefore, I sought to answer the following questions: (a) What themes are visible in the preservice teachers' cases? (b) Are the case themes related to the primary, upper elementary, or middle schools in which the preservice teachers worked? (c) Does the content of the cases illuminate instructional gaps or shortcomings that I, as program supervisor, need to remedy? (d) Are the implications of the research germane to teacher education and school districts?

Method

I examined 58 cases written by the 29 preservice teachers in the Bay View School, 20 cases written by the 10 preservice teachers in First Street Upper Elementary School and 38 teaching cases authored by the 19 preservice teachers in Louis Middle School (total = 116 cases).

First, I collated the cases according to the three teaching contexts in which the preservice teachers worked. Then, following analytic induction methods (Bogdan & Biklin, 1992), I read and reread the cases, identifying and coding the encompassing themes (e.g., "students' lack of keyboarding skills," "misuse of CD-ROM applications"). The coding process allowed the data to emerge (Maxwell, 1996; Miles & Huberman, 1994). I also interviewed the preservice teachers and scrutinized my observation fieldnotes (10 observations for each preservice teacher) and the preservice teachers' weekly dialogue journal entries in order to cross-check and triangulate different types of data that focused on the same phenomenon (Gordon, 1980). As a validity and member check of the accuracy of my judgment, the preservice teachers read and gave their approval of the manuscript.

Analysis revealed that the 58 cases written by the 29 preservice teachers enrolled in the combined reading/language arts block in Bay View Primary School (Grades K–3) portrayed three dilemmas associated with linking literacy lessons with computer activities. These three issues were: (a) preservice teachers' use of computer technology in ways that were not meaningfully integrated with literacy instruction (24%/14 cases), (b) preservice teachers' insufficient planning and preparation pertinent to the use of computer technology (25.9%/15 cases), and (c) computer technology malfunctions and glitches (50%/29 cases).

Analysis of the 20 cases authored by the preservice teachers at First Street Upper Elementary School (Grades 4 and 5) revealed four dilemmas. These four dilemmas were: (a) preservice teachers' use of computer technology in ways that were not meaningfully integrated with literacy instruction (14%/3 cases), (b) preservice teachers' insufficient planning and preparation pertinent to the use of computer technology (14%/3 cases), (c) computer technology malfunctions and glitches (30%/6 cases), and (d) students' lack of keyboarding skills (40%/8 cases).

Examination of the 58 cases written by the preservice teachers at Louis Middle School (Grades 6–8) revealed two dilemmas: (a) preservice teachers' use of computer technology in ways that were not meaningfully integrated with literacy instruction (39%/15 cases) and (b) preservice teachers' insufficient planning and preparation pertinent to the use of computer technology (60.5%/23 cases). The following cases (written by the preservice teachers) portray these themes.

Concerns of the Preservice Teachers

Concern #1: Preservice Teachers' Use of Computer Technology in Ways That Were Not Meaningfully Integrated with Literacy Instruction

"I Didn't Expect This!" First, my fifth graders and I completed the text chapter on the heritage and culture of the Mississippi Natchez Trace. We read about the Choctaw Indians and viewed photographs of Native American artifacts, like tomahawks and flint arrow points. The text also discussed how wagons were pulled by mules 100 years ago. We used the SQ3R strategy (Robinson, 1961), and the students really did nicely turning the subtitles and first sentence of every paragraph into questions. After we completed the chapter, I assembled my group of eight students around the only computer in the classroom. I had brought in what I thought was a wonderful interactive CD-ROM video. It depicted horses native to the American West. The video is designed so that viewers can manipu-

late the horses' tails, hooves, movements, and so on, and the scenery, such as barns, trees, mountains, pastures, and fences. The students loved it and we stayed at the computer for about 25 minutes. Only later did I find out that there were concerns about my linking the content of the text with a computer activity.

When the lesson was over, the classroom teacher asked me, "Didn't you realize that the other students in the room were angry because they didn't get to use the computer?" She also said, "You were on the computer too long. Your students needed to be reading." Then, she told me, "I think that the *game* you brought in had nothing to do with the text chapter."

I have to rethink everything about the lesson. I know that my students absolutely loved the computer venture. It was the very first time I ever linked a reading lesson with technology and I thought the connection helped to reinforce what my students read in the chapter. It also helped my students visualize horses and their surroundings. And, I noticed that the students who had some difficulties reading the text especially were enthralled with manipulating the pictures on the computer screen. What went wrong?

Concern #2: Preservice Teachers' Insufficient Planning and Preparation Pertinent to the Use of Computer Technology

The Name Game." I teach in a first-grade classroom once a week. Last week we were reading the story *Luke's Quilt* (Guback, 1984). It is about a girl who lives in Hawaii. While searching on the Internet, I found this web site <http://www.hisurf.com/hawaiian/names.html> where you could type in your English name and you get a translation of your name in Hawaiian. I was so excited with my find that I could not wait to share it with my students.

We all sat around the computer and I pulled up the web site. First, we used the Hawaiian dictionary and found out how to say, "I love you." So far, so good! We decided to try my name first. I typed in "Patti," hit enter, and came up with my Hawaiian name, "Pakelikia."

We decided to try "Bria" next. I typed in her name and hit enter and up came "Palaina."

Ashley was next so I typed in her name and hit enter and . . . nothing! This little box popped up that said, "Sorry this name is not in our data base." I certainly did not expect this and I had to think quickly. I had what I thought was a great idea. "Let's try your middle name," I said.

Ashley looked happy, but when she tried to tell me her middle name it made no sense. I was already thinking to myself that if I had trouble with the name Ashley, I was in for it with my next two students, Darian and Gavin. My assumptions were correct. Their names were not in the database. My nice project had turned into an ordeal and a disaster.

What I should have done was tried to find all of the students' names prior to the lesson. It did not even occur to me that I could not find certain names. I did not plan ahead. I just assumed that my wonderful idea would turn out fine.

Concern #3: Computer Technology Malfunctions and Glitches

"Blank Screens." When I met my second-grade students' classroom teacher one of my first questions was, "Do you use the computers in your room and access the Internet very often?" To my surprise she answered, "Not very often."

Of course I decided to link my print-based literacy lessons with computer technology literacy activities as often as I could. Therefore, as a postreading activity last week, I planned to help my students find information on the Internet about the author of our story. From Day One, two fully equipped computers were in the classroom and I wanted to make good use of them.

As I was setting up my supplies for the lesson, I told the teacher that we would be using the Internet. She said, matter of factly, "The computers are out, but I have a set of encyclopedias." I asked, "Why aren't they working?" She answered, "I don't know. I only complete a form and turn it into the office. They handle it from there. It's not just me either. Three or four other teachers can't use their computers either. They've been out for a week or longer."

I went to the office to inquire about the problem and the secretary said, "I'm not familiar with that particular concern, but a man comes to the school once every other week and works on computer difficulties. It sounds like a wiring problem if four computers are out."

I was really upset because I did not have a back-up for a postreading strategy. I did not know what to tell the students. Should I have tried to look up the author in the encyclopedia? I doubt if I could have found the information. I was in a panic, but I did not want my students to know that I was upset. Should I have tried to "plug in" another postreading strategy?

Reflecting on my dilemma, I could have asked the classroom teacher if we could go to another teacher's room and use the computers. I could have gone to the school library. I bet they have computers there. A little prior planning on my part would have saved the end of the lesson and kept me from a panic attack.

Concern #4: Students' Lack of Keyboarding Skills

"Having Computers in Classrooms Isn't Always the Answer." I work with seven sixth graders every week, linking content-reading lessons with writing, and connecting our lessons to technology. After completing a chapter about the State of Mississippi, I decided to have my students create an imaginary brochure, describing the interesting sights and activities in the state. First, I had the students create their brochures on paper. Then, all eight of us (seven students and me) sat around the three computers in the room. As three students typed their brochures, the other four watched. Can you already figure out that I had problems? Here is what happened. First, the four students who were watching their peers type got bored and began to disturb the other students in the room. Then my professor came in to observe and she looked at my students transferring their writing to the computer. "Why did you have them compose first on paper?" she asked.

I had to reply, "I don't know. I never thought of having the students compose directly at the computer." Then, my professor looked carefully at the students' writing. Here is how Mary's brochure looked on the computer screen:

(1) We can go swimming.
(2) We have beaches.
(3) It is warm here.

"Why is Mary typing a list, rather than a complete descriptive paragraph?" asked my professor. Again, I had no clever answer.

The following week, I presented a process writing strategy (Richards, in press) to my students. They loved it! First, they created a semantic map of their ideas and then they transformed the ideas in their semantic maps into category columns (e.g., ideas that were related to one another were grouped together, such as all of the interesting places to visit in Mississippi).

We were ready now to get to the computers. I left four of my students sitting in a semi-circle. Their task was to read the next chapter in their book. I took the remaining three students with me to the computers. I expected them to really zoom along with their writing. Instead, each student typed in a laborious, slow way. They used only one hand and rested their other hand in their laps. Two just used their index fingers to type. "Come on," I said. "Let's get going. We need to move along so the others can type too."

"We can't type," said Jennie. "Why can't you type?" I asked. "You all go to the computer lab and get 45 minutes of computer instruction everyday." "Yeah, but we don't learn how to type," replied Carey.

These incidents have let me know that there is more to linking literacy lessons with computers than just sitting kids down in front of computer monitors. Using the computers actually slowed up my students' efforts at composing brochures. How do other teachers handle this?

Findings and Discussion

It must be acknowledged that the findings of this inquiry cannot be generalized to other preservice teachers and teaching contexts. To a great extent, school contextual influences determine what preservice teachers learn and perceive important, and what problems they encounter (Richards, Moore, & Gipe, 1996/1997). In addition, it must be noted that I directed the preservice teachers to confine their case writing only to the problems they experienced as they integrated their literacy lessons with technology. Their technology accomplishments are not part of this inquiry.

Despite the lack of generalizability, the research provides some intriguing narrative evidence that supports teaching cases as windows into preservice teachers' lived experiences and realities. Analysis of the preservice teachers' cases highlighted concerns about integrating literacy lessons with computer technology in three different teaching contexts. Therefore, in this particular inquiry, cases served as valuable data.

The findings of the inquiry indicate that school context accounted for 50% of the preservice teachers' concerns at Bay View Primary School and 70% at First Street Upper Elementary School. In particular, antiquated computers and inadequate wiring served to exacerbate the preservice teachers' frustrations and problems as they worked to augment their literacy lessons with computer technology activities. Further, the lack of a "resident computer expert" at Bay View and First Street Upper Elementary prohibited the preservice teachers (and classroom teachers and students) from being able to seek help when necessary (see the case, "Blank Screens"). In addition, although students' lack of keyboarding skills was not a problem to the preservice teachers at Bay View School, it was a concern for the preservice teachers at First Street Elementary School (i.e., 40% of the cases). It is not surprising that the preservice teachers at Bay View School did not consider students' lack of keyboarding skills as problematic. Most K–3 students are not expected to be proficient typists, and in all probability, the preservice teachers did not plan for these younger students to engage in e-mail, word processing, or Internet research activities. On the other hand, the preservice teachers working in First Street Upper Elementary School were concerned about their students' lack of keyboarding skills. In fact, most of the preservice teachers assumed that the fourth- and fifth-grade students at First Street School would be able to type (see the case, "Having Computers in Classrooms Isn't Always the Answer"). In actuality, experts disagree about the age at which students should receive keyboard lessons (Leu & Leu, 1997). According to Westreich (2000) keyboarding should be taught by fourth grade "in order to take maximum advantage of technology. By this age . . . students have made the transition to formal operations and are capable of making abstract connections between symbol systems and thought processes" (p. 23).

Across the three teaching contexts, 23 cases out of 116 written by the preservice teachers described using computer technology in ways that were not meaningfully integrated with literacy instruction. Forty-one cases out of 116 discussed the preservice teachers' inadequate planning and preparation for their computer activities (total = 64 cases/55%) (see cases, "I Didn't Expect This!" and "The Name Game"). As supervisor in charge of these literacy programs, I must accept responsibility for the two issues that directly relate to guiding preservice teachers' professional development. I assumed that the preservice teachers were knowledgeable about ways to integrate computer technology with print-based literacy lessons and I left it to their judgment to choose appropriate software and computer applications that would complement and extend narrative and content text. Certainly, the preservice teachers' lack of prior planning and preparation correlate with their understandable lack of overall teaching experience (Byra & Coulon, 1992). My preservice teachers are consistently well prepared for their print-based literacy lessons because I emphasize the connections between preparation for teaching reading, teaching effectiveness, and student achievement (Peterson, 1978). Yet, I overlooked the import of carefully planning computer initiatives.

Implications for School Districts and Teacher Education

This research indicates that school districts and university supervisors must work in concert in order to provide optimum opportunities for preservice teachers (and classroom teachers and students) to become proficient in utilizing all aspects of electronic communication in classroom settings. The inquiry spotlights the importance of schools providing the best computer equipment and technology support systems they can afford. Studies indicate a positive relationship between pupil expenditures and student achievement (Fortune & Spofford-Richardson, 2000). Often, students and teachers at Bay View and First Street Schools could not use their classroom computers because they were not in working order. In addition, wiring problems and lack of a "resident computer expert" prohibited the preservice teachers, students, and classroom teachers from achieving their full potential and goals. "Integrating technology with instruction requires that teachers, . . . administrators [and school district officials] deal with a variety of technical, curricular, financial, and other obstacles" (Reinking & Watkins, 2000, p. 387). It is clear that simply having computers available in classrooms does not mean that instruction will be powerfully transformed (Reinking et al., 1997).

The study also pinpointed significant variations in the computer instruction offered to upper elementary students (Grades 4 and 5) and middle school students (Grades 6–8) in the same school district. Forty percent of the cases authored by the preservice teachers at First Street Upper Elementary School discussed problems revolving around students' lack of keyboarding skills. On the other hand, preservice teachers working in Louis Middle School did not consider their students' keyboarding abilities to be an issue. It is intriguing to note that although students at First Street Upper Elementary School visit the computer lab 5 days per week, they do not receive keyboard instruction. In contrast, eighth-grade students at Louis Middle School receive daily keyboarding instruction and all sixth- to eighth-grade students receive individual computer instruction from the media specialist, if they choose. This considerable discrepancy in instruction is, in all probability, related to school district policies and guidelines that consider eighth-grade students developmentally mature enough to receive and benefit from keyboarding lessons.

The inquiry also offers practical information to literacy teacher educators who increasingly will require their preservice teachers to implement technology in field-based courses. Specifically, the inquiry accentuates gaps in course instruction that I, as supervisor must take steps to remediate. Clearly, I must become more "computer literate" so that I can model appropriate use of computer software and supply relevant readings for my preservice teachers relating to selection and use of suitable computer software. I also need to emphasize to my preservice teachers the importance of carefully planning and preparing for computer endeavors.

Finally, the inquiry shows that simply requiring preservice teachers in field-based courses to integrate literacy lessons with technology without considering their school context and determining what preservice teachers already know about computers will, in all likelihood, prove less than satisfactory. Scholars have "argued that schools often intentionally or unintentionally subvert any possibility that new technology will transform existing instructional practices" (Reinking & Watkins, 2000, p. 387; also see Papert, 1993). The results of this research indicate that we (the school district and I) unintentionally inhibited the preservice teachers' successful implementation of technology. In this case, Leu's (2000) cautions about the possible negative consequences of rapidly infusing technology with literacy instruction without careful planning proved correct. The lessons I learned through this research may prove helpful to other teacher educators who wish to support preservice teachers as they integrate print-based literacy lessons with computer technology.

References

American Library Association (1998). *Information power: Building partnerships for learning.* Chicago: Author.

Bogdan R., & Biklin, S. (1992). *Qualitative research for education* (3rd ed.). Needham Heights, MA: Allyn & Bacon.

Byra, M., & Coulon, S. (1992). Preservice teachers' in class behaviors: The effects of planning and not planning. (ERIC Document Reproduction Service No. ED 371 355)

Farstrup, A., & Myers, M. (Eds.). (1996). *Standards for the English language arts.* Urbana, IL and Newark, DE: National Council of Teachers of English and International Reading Association.

Fortune, J., & Spofford-Richardson, S. (2000). A critique of methods used to answer the question: Does money make a difference? *Research in the Schools, 7*(2), 21-31.

Gee, J., Michaels, S., & O'Connor, C. (1992). Discourse analysis. In M. LeCompte, W. Millroy, & J. Preissle (Eds.), *The handbook of qualitative research in education* (pp. 227-229). New York: Academic.

Goetz, J., & LeCompte, M. (1984). *Ethnography and qualitative design in educational research.* New York: Academic.

Goldsborough, R. (2000, October/November). Using the net to learn the net. *Reading Today,* p. 14.

Gordon, R. (1980). *Interviewing: Strategies, techniques, and tactics.* Homewood, IL: Dorsey.

Guback, G. (1984). *Luke's quilt.* New York: Greenwillow Books.

Kamil, M., & Intrator, S. (1998). Quantitative trends in publication of research on technology and reading, writing, and literacy. In T. Shanahan & F. Rodriguez-Brown (Eds.), *National Reading Conference Yearbook, 47* (pp. 385-396). Chicago: National Reading Conference.

Leu, D. (2000). Literacy and technology: Deictic consequences for literacy education in an information age. In M. Kamil, P. D. Pearson, & R. Barr (Eds.), *Handbook of reading research* (Vol. 3, pp. 77-92). Mahwah, NJ: Erlbaum.

Leu, D., & Leu, D. (1997). *Teaching with the Internet: Lessons from the classroom.* Norwood, MA: Christopher Gordon.

Maxwell, J. (1996). *Qualitative research design: An interactive approach.* Thousand Oaks, CA: Sage.

Messaris, P. (1997). Introduction. In J. Flood, S. Brice Heath, & D. Lapp (Eds.), Handbook of *research on teaching literacy through the visual and communicative arts* (pp. 3-5). New York: Simon & Schuster, Macmillan.

Miles, M., & Huberman, A. (1994). *Qualitative data analysis: An expanded sourcebook* (2nd ed.). Thousand Oaks, CA: Sage.

Papert, S. (1993). *The children's machine: Rethinking school in the age of the computer.* New York: Basic Books.

Peterson, P. (1978). Teacher planning, teacher behavior, and student achievement. *American Educational Research Journal, 15,* 417-132.

Rafferty, C. (1999). Literacy in the information age. *Educational Leadership, 57*(2), 22-25.

Reinking, D., Labbo, L., & McKenna, M. (1997). Navigating the changing landscape of literacy: Current theory and research in computer-based reading and writing. In Flood, J., Heath, S. B., & Lapp, D. (Eds.), (1997). *Handbook of research on teaching literacy through the communicative and visual arts.* New York: Simon & Schuster, Macmillan.

Reinking, D., & Watkins, J. (2000). A formative experiment investigating the use of multimedia book reviews to increase elementary students' independent reading. *Reading Research Quarterly, 35,* 384-419.

Rennie, D. (1999). Qualitative research: A matter of hermeneutics and the sociology of knowledge. In M. Kopola & L. Suzuki (Eds.), *Using qualitative methods in psychology* (pp. 3-13). Thousand Oaks, CA: Sage.

Richards, J. (in press). Steps to independent writing. In J. Gipe, *Multiple paths for corrective reading* (5th ed.). Scottsdale, AZ: Merrill.

Richards, J., & Gipe, J. (2000). *Elementary literacy lessons: Cases and commentaries from the field.* Mahwah, NJ: Erlbaum.

Richards, J., Moore, R., & Gipe, J. (1996/1997). Preservice teachers in two different multicultural field programs. The complex influence of school context. *Research in the Schools, 3*(2), 31-53.

Robinson, F. (1961). *Effective study.* New York: Harper & Row.

Tappan, M., & Brown, L. (1992). Stories told and lessons learned: Toward a narrative approach to moral development and moral education. In C. Witherell & N. Noddings (Eds.), *Stories lives tell: Narrative and dialogue in education* (pp. 171-192). New York: Teachers College, Columbia University.

U.S. Department of Education (2000). *National Educational Technology Standards (NETS) for Teacher Preparation.* Washington, DC: Author.

Westreich, J. (2000). High-tech kids: Trailblazers or guinea pigs? In D. Gordon (Ed.), *The digital classroom: How technology is changing the way we teach and learn* (pp. 19-29). Cambridge, MA: Harvard Educational Letter.

Woods, P. (1992). Symbolic interactionism: Theory and method. In M. LeCompte, W. Millroy, & J. Preissle (Eds.), *The handbook of qualitative research in education* (pp. 337-404). New York: Academic.

What Does It Take to Reform Instructional Practices?

Emily M. Rodgers, Susan Fullerton, and Diane DeFord
Ohio State University

It is perhaps more true today than at any time in our history that all citizens, not just a privileged class, are expected to become literate (Walmsley & Allington, 1995). Yet recent reports and initiatives indicate that reading achievement among children in the United States is at an unacceptably low level (National Education Goals Report, 1995). In response, the Clinton administration awarded over $200 million in 1999 between 13 states in the form of Reading Excellence Grants to support reading initiatives. Presumably these plans will help realize the President's goal of developing a nation of readers who can read "independently and well" by the end of third grade.

However, the decision to allocate over $200 million to various statewide reading initiatives is a questionable one given all that we know about the tendency of educational reform efforts to fail (Fullan, 1993; Wilson & Daviss, 1994). In fact, the prognosis for change is bleak; failure is even predictable (Sarason, 1990). According to Fullan (1991), the complexity and intractability of problems in education make it difficult for reform to occur. As a result, reform efforts are usually directed at changing things that do not matter instead of targeting "fundamental instructional reform" (Fullan, 1993, p. 46). Without a shift, educators are doomed to enact one idea after another with little hope that the new program will be sustainable for more than a few years.

This study takes up Fullan's challenge to target fundamental instructional reform in order to bring about real change. In this case, change was needed in the way Reading Recovery (RR), an intervention for first-grade students at risk of literacy failure, was being delivered. RR was originally introduced to Midwest City Schools about 14 years previously and since then about 20 other school districts in the state have also adopted it.

Analyses of data at the end of the 1998–99 school year revealed that the children in the Midwest City Schools district were not faring as well in RR as the children in other districts around the state. In this district, only about 37% of the students had made sufficient progress in the program to reach the average reading and writing levels of their peers in 1998–99. Both the university faculty and school district literacy leaders agreed that the teachers involved with the program in Midwest City Schools needed more support in order for change to occur. Therefore, we collaborated with the district literacy leaders and 30 RR teachers in 26 city

*National Reading Conference Yearbook, **50**, pp. 519–531.*

schools to design a complex model of professional development with the aim of bringing about fundamental change to instruction.

Two questions were posed in this study: (a) What is the nature of change, if any, within a multidimensional model of professional development. Change was defined in three ways: the progress of students in 1998–99 compared to 1999–00; the teachers' perceived effectiveness in key areas of teaching; and actual changes in teaching practice. (b) How are these changes brought about?

These questions are significant because they address the challenge of change in education and may provide insight in to what it takes to reform educational practices.

Theoretical Background

This study is situated within a theoretical frame that views learning as a sociocultural process. We understand that knowledge is constructed within a social milieu as the learner interacts with others (Vygotsky, 1978) and that language is a critical tool for this process (Luria, 1979). Having opportunities to collaborate with peers or more knowledgeable others is the process by which learners move through a zone of proximal development to actual development (Vygotsky, 1978).

In order to create fundamental changes to instruction, as Fullan challenged, we designed professional developmental experiences that would provide opportunities for the teachers, school district literacy leaders and faculty members to have multiple conversations around shared teaching experiences. We expected new understandings to develop as a result of these opportunities to collaborate with peers around conversations about instruction.

Method

We used a qualitative case study approach to describe the nature of change within a multidimensional model of professional development involving collaboration between university faculty, school district personnel and RR teachers. The purpose of the case study approach is to gather comprehensive, systematic and in-depth information about each case (Patton, 1990).

Data were also collected on the progress of the students who received RR. These data were not used to evaluate the effectiveness of the program but to compare the progress of the RR students during the year of the study (1999–00) to the previous school year.

Participants

Five university instructors, two school district personnel (Teacher Leaders) and 30 RR teachers in 26 schools all situated in a large midwestern city and teaching within an urban school district ("Midwest City Schools") participated in this collaboration.

The teachers. Two-thirds of the teachers held Masters' degrees in education, and their teaching experience ranged from 5 to 32 years with an average of 16.9 years. These teachers worked for half their day as RR teachers and the other half of their day as either Title One teachers in kindergarten to Grade 3 or as classroom teachers.

The Teacher Leaders. The main role of the Teacher Leaders was to provide professional development to the 30 RR teachers in their district and to train new RR teachers. Both Teacher Leaders in this study had at least 10 years experience in their role.

The university faculty. The university faculty were regularly involved in training RR Teacher Leaders and providing professional development workshops to trained Teacher Leaders.

The RR students. In order to look for differences in the students' literacy achievement we compared the progress of the 1999–00 cohort of RR students (the year of the study) to those RR students served during the previous year.

The random samples. Each year, the Teacher Leaders drew a random selection of 100 first graders from the schools in the district where there was RR. Students who received RR were excluded as well as students in self-contained special education classes. Special Education students who were mainstreamed in first-grade classrooms were included in the sample. These random samples were used to determine the average band performance of the RR students' peers and did not serve as a control group to compare performance. Table 1 provides descriptive data of the four groups.

Students were selected for RR based on their stanine scores on the six literacy tasks of *An Observation Survey* (Clay, 1993). At each school, classroom teachers' rank ordered their students from highest to lowest according to their evaluation of their students' literacy achievement. RR teachers tested approximately the lowest 20% of these students using the *Observation Survey.* In each building, the students with the most number of stanine ones on the six tasks were selected for RR service.

The maximum length of a RR program is 20 weeks. By that time, one of five possible decisions are made:

Discontinued. A student whose program was discontinued was one who had developed a repertoire of reading and writing strategies comparable to average students in their classrooms. This may have occurred in fewer than 20 weeks. When a RR teacher decided, in consultation with the classroom teacher, that a student had reached reading and writing levels comparable to the average of the class, a different RR teacher readminstered *The Observation Survey* to the student. Using those results, that RR teacher evaluated whether the student was indeed working at an average level and made the decision to discontinue the program or not. The next lowest student was then selected to replace that student.

Recommended action. The student received the program for 20 weeks but

Table 1

Description of RR Students and Random Samples (RS) for 1998 and 1999

	1998–1999				1999–2000			
	RR		RS		RR		RS	
	n	%	*n*	%	*n*	%	*n*	%
Sex								
Male	288	59%	37	51%	174	54%	44	51%
Female	198	41%	32	46%	146	46%	42	49%
Total	486		69		320		86	
Lunch Costs								
Free	402	83%	54	78%	214	67%	46	53%
Reduced	22	5%	4	6%	20	6%	11	13%
Regular	39	8%	11	16%	73	23%	27	31%
Unavailable	21	4%	0	0%	13	4%	3	3%
Total	484		69		320		87	
Race/Ethnicity								
Asian	11	2%	2	3%	2	1%	2	2%
African–American	324	67%	45	65%	172	54%	44	51%
Hispanic/Latino	11	2%	0	0%	5	2%	3	3%
White	138	28%	22	32%	140	44%	36	41%
Other/Multi	1	0%	0	0%	1	0%	2	2%
Total	485		69		320		87	

Note. RR students were excluded from the random samples.

had not reached an average level of performance to qualify as "discontinued." At this point, another intervention was recommended (e.g., placement in special education) for that student. The next lowest student was then selected to replace that student.

Moved. The student moved from the school before the end of his or her program. The next lowest student was then selected to replace that student.

Incomplete program. The student was still in RR at the end of the school year because time ran out to complete the program. These programs were categorized as "incomplete."

None of the above. The student was removed from RR before 20 weeks as a result of a decision made by someone other than the RR teacher. The parent may have requested the removal or a team of educators may have made the decision due to unusual circumstances (e.g., placed back in kindergarten, or removed from RR due to excessive absences from school). These programs were categorized as "none of the above." The next lowest student was then selected to replace that student. This was a rare decision made in unusual circumstances.

Data Collection

Glesne and Peshkin (1992) recommend the use of "multiple data collection methods" (p. 24) and note that three data gathering techniques have dominated: participant observation, interviewing, and document analysis.

Data to describe teacher change. The authors also took part in the study, so we fully participated as observer-participants. Individually, we collaborated with the Teacher Leaders to conduct school visits and to lead group sessions for the RR teachers.

The 30 teachers were divided into two groups. Each group met four times throughout the year for day-long group professional development sessions to discuss literacy learning theory, analyze videotapes of their own teaching and to view and discuss two lessons taught by RR teachers behind a one-way mirror. During the lesson, the rest of the teachers observed from the other side of the mirror and took part in "collaborative inquiry" (Lindfors, 1999) alternately led by one of the university instructors and one of the Teacher Leaders.

We kept fieldnotes during these group sessions and wrote summaries afterwards that described shifts in the teachers' learning and areas where follow up was needed. These notes were shared among the Teacher Leaders and university faculty while the study was ongoing.

Teachers also received individual school visits between the first and second group sessions and the third and fourth group sessions. Typically during school visits, a university instructor, paired with a Teacher Leader, to observe a RR teacher teach a lesson. Following the lesson, there were two levels of debriefing. Whoever led the observation of the lesson also debriefed with the teacher once the lesson was finished. Afterwards, the university instructor and Teacher Leader debriefed together about how the school visit had been conducted. Fieldnotes describing the teaching during the school visits and areas of focus during the debriefing with the teacher were kept and were used by Teacher Leaders and university participants to guide decision-making in terms of areas of focus for subsequent group professional development sessions.

Semi-structured and structured interviews with teachers were videotaped at the conclusion of the study to determine shifts in learning as identified by the teachers. These findings were triangulated with fieldnotes from school visits and group sessions and with surveys given to teachers before and after the study. The Teacher Leaders and university instructors took part in an unstructured focus group interview to discuss shifts that they had made in their own teaching as a result of participating in this study.

At the beginning and end of the study, teachers completed a survey using a Likert Scale format to indicate the strength of their effectiveness on 20 areas of teaching.

Data to describe student change. These data were collected by RR teachers (with the supervision of the Teacher Leaders) for all children served during both school years. At year-end, the data were sent to the RR National Data Evaluation

Center (NDEC) for analysis. Each year, data were also collected on random samples of first-grade students from the same schools to establish an average band of performance (+ or - .5 *SD* of the mean text reading level of the random sample). This comparison score range was used to validate the discontinuing decisions made by the Reading Recovery teachers. Students whose programs were discontinued would be expected to have scores that fell within the average band of a random sample of their peers. This process is in keeping with the annual collection and analysis of data in which RR teachers take part. These data, described below, include results on a literacy survey and changes in classroom reading group placement.

An Observation Survey of Early Literacy Achievement (Clay, 1993) was administered at the beginning and end of the school year to chart the progress of the RR and random sample students. Data were collected on the six tasks: Letter Identification, Word Knowledge, Concepts About Print, Writing Vocabulary, Hearing and Recording Sounds in Words, and Text Reading Levels. For the purposes of this study, we will focus on changes occurring in text reading.

Classroom teachers reported the reading-group placement (low, low middle, upper middle, or high) of each RR student at two points in time: fall and end of year.

Findings

We conducted a qualitative case study about the professional development of teachers. The data regarding student progress were not used to evaluate the effectiveness of RR. They are intended as another data source to inform our questions about the kinds of changes that occur when a multidimensional model of professional development is used.

Student Progress

We looked for evidence of the RR students' literacy progress by comparing their progress to the RR students from the previous year, on measures of *An Observation Survey* (Clay, 1993). We also charted changes in their reading group placements over the school year.

Percentage of discontinued programs. The percentage of students whose programs were discontinued increased slightly to 44% in 1999–00 after the study, from 39% in 1998–99 (see Table 2).

Average text reading levels. An examination of average text reading levels (TRL) for 1998–99 and 1999–00 for RR students whose programs were discontinued provides more evidence of the RR students' progress.

Table 3 shows that both cohorts of RR students in 1998 and 1999 made similar gains on the Text Reading Level measure; starting the year approximately below a level one text reading level and ending the year at about a text reading level 16. These findings provide evidence that RR teachers did not simply lower their

Table 2

Program Outcomes for All RR Students

	n	Discontinued	Recommended	Incomplete	Moved	None of Above
1998	486	39%	21%	29%	8%	4%
1999	320	44%	22%	20%	8%	6%

Note. Percentages reflect the whole population of RR students, whether they received a full program or not.

Table 3

Average Text Reading Levels (TRL) at Fall and End of Year (EOY) for Students Whose Programs Were Discontinued and the Average Band of the Random Sample (RS)

Year	*n**	Fall TRL		*n*	EOY TRL		RS Average Band
		M	*SD*		*M*	*SD*	
1998	173	.6	.9	184	15.7	3.8	9.8–18
1999	136	.8	.9	142	16.1	3.6	14.1–23.4

*Fewer RR students were served in 1999 because the number of RR teachers decreased from one year to the next.

standards to discontinue programs, thereby accounting for a greater percentage of students discontinuing. Standards remained the same and fell within the average band performance of a random sample for the district.

In 1998–99, the end-of-year text reading level of 99% (*n*=182) of all students whose programs were discontinued, fell within or above the random sample average band. 16% (*n*=15) of students who were recommended for another intervention fell within the average band as well as 14% (*n*=19) of students whose programs were incomplete at the end of the year.

By comparison, during the year of the study, the percentage of discontinued students whose end-of-year text reading level fell within or above the district average band, fell to 85% (*n*=121). The text reading levels of the other discontinued students (*n*=21) fell below the random sample's average band. It appears that 15% of the discontinued students did not make it into the average band for text reading level at the end of the year. This finding may be explained by the fact that the average band of the random sample was quite a lot higher in 1999–00 making it more difficult for students to fall within that range.

Changes in reading group placement. The progress of RR students whose programs were discontinued is also reflected in changes in their reading group placement throughout the year (Table 4). At the beginning of the study almost all

Table 4

Comparison of Changes in Reading Group Placement for Discontinued Students and Random Sample from Fall to End of Year (EOY) in 1998–1999 and 1999–2000

			n	Low	Low Middle	Upper Middle	High
	Discontinued	Fall	181	90%	9%	1%	0
1998		EOY	185	3%	17%	53%	27%
1999	RS	Fall	68	41%	29%	13%	16%
		EOY	58	26%	17%	24%	33%
	Discontinued	Fall	137	92%	8%	0	0
1999		EOY	143	9%	20%	58%	13%
2000	RS	Fall	84	26%	27%	20%	26%
		EOY	68	21%	15%	24%	41%

RR students had been placed in the lowest reading group in their classrooms. By the end of the year, 71% had been moved into the upper middle and high reading groups where none of them had been placed at the beginning of the year. By comparison, nearly as many students in the random sample remained in the lowest reading group placement at the end of the year.

This trend is comparable to the previous year, 1998–99, in which 90% of RR students whose programs were discontinued were originally placed in the lowest reading group and 1% was placed in the upper to high reading groups. By the end of the year, these percentages flip-flopped with 3% in the lowest reading group and 80% in the two highest groups.

This change in rank is notable given that longitudinal research on low progress students has demonstrated that class rankings tend to remain the same throughout the elementary grades (Juel, 1988; Wells, 1986). These findings appear to be corroborated here in the relative stability of the random samples' rankings throughout the year.

Discussion of Changes in Student Progress

We examined the literacy progress of the RR students as one way of describing the nature of change in a multidimensional model of professional development. We found a modest increase in the number of students who were discontinued from the program. These discontinuing decisions were validated by corresponding changes in reading group placement (changes made by the classroom teachers) and by the fact that the average text reading level at year-end remained about the same for both cohorts. These findings suggest that discontinuing decisions cannot be explained by a lowering of standards from one year to the next.

A confounding finding was that 85% of the discontinued students in 1999 scored within or above the random sample's average band for text reading level compared to 99% in the previous year. This decline may be explained by the fact that the average band in 1999 was very high with the range set from 14.1 to 23.4.

In the next section, we will discuss changes in teaching practices that occurred throughout the course of this study and we will offer a theory about how we think these changes may have come about.

Changes in Teaching—"What" Changed?

The data collected on teaching within this study included transcriptions of video tapes of teachers' reflections about the year, observer and instructor notes of discussions of lessons conducted taught behind the one-way glass during group sessions, and discussion points from records taken during school visits. Teachers involved in the study evaluated the sessions and discussed their learning in a survey given before and at the completion of the study. The transcripts of teachers discussing their year of professional development were transcribed and coded. Information from notes of school visits and professional development sessions where lessons with children occurred were used to provide evidence to support teacher statements about what changed, and what areas they wanted to become more effective in as they taught. We sought to find synchronicity across these sources of data.

Extending theoretical understandings about teaching procedures. During the semi-structured interviews at the conclusion of the study teachers were asked to talk about if and how the professional development experiences had impacted their teaching. Even though the teachers were very experienced, they talked mainly about teaching "procedures." However, we noted that these conversations went beyond a discussion about "how" to carry out a procedure to linking the procedure to new theoretical understandings. For example, they did not just talk about how to build a core of sight words for reading but they discussed the need for a student to become fluent with everything that he knew, from sight words in reading, to writing words he knew, to recognizing letters quickly.

In another example, one teacher talked about how she was getting better at providing book introductions before the student read the story aloud to her:

> A teacher who did fourth grade work on summarizing helped me to recognize the potential of making book introductions more concise. Then [the Teacher Leader] came to visit, and gave me a better perspective on what I was saying, and thinking about who is telling the story rather than just giving an overview. Then, in continuing contact [group professional development sessions], we talked about Pat's New Puppy, talked about how there are two different things going on: the description of the dog and what happened in the park [knowing] that helps the child read the text.

According to their self-reports, the teachers extended their theoretical understandings about teaching procedures as they tried new techniques. These self-reports were confirmed by our fieldnotes during the individual school visits and during the group sessions. For example, one entry following a school visit suggests that we (the Teacher Leader and university faculty member who conducted the visit) saw evidence that the teacher was linking knowledge about a teaching procedure (building a sight vocabulary for reading) to a theoretical understanding of how it would impact the child's processing:

> The teacher analyzed that by using known words in writing and building a reading vocabulary, the child could read more fluently and would not need to reread so much to self-correct—this was getting in the way of the child's fluent reading. (Fieldnote entry, School visit, October 18.)

Extending theoretical understandings about instructional language. Teachers also stated that these professional development experiences helped them learn how to use specific language to teach more effectively. Again, this discussion went beyond "what to say" when teaching to why and how to use language effectively. They felt that they recognized the importance of being more explicit with their instructional language and that this in turn helped their students make links across the lesson components. For example, when a student came to a difficult word in the text while reading, the teacher supported his visual analysis by telling him, "This is just like what we were doing with the magnetic letters on the board [looking for known parts, substituting onsets and rimes]."

In concert with this awareness of the need to use more explicit instructional language, teachers demonstrated a growing ability to put this into practice when we worked with them during school visits and the group sessions.

Extending theoretical understandings about teaching. The teachers also felt they had become more effective in linking theoretical understandings to their teaching practices. For example, rather than teaching word families they were now teaching their students how to manipulate onsets and rimes to derive new words. This meant that that they were teaching in a more generative way and departing from a focus on item knowledge.

They also felt that they were more effective in teaching consistently and early on for behaviors such as achieving one-to-one correspondence in reading and monitoring known words while reading. They linked this emphasis to a theory that these behaviors needed to be secure before teaching strategies such as searching for more information at difficulty or self-correcting. One teacher noted that she thought these early behaviors were already in place and it was not until a school visit that she realized they were not controlled as well as she thought.

Changes in Teaching—How the Changes Occurred

Teachers reported their instructional language had become more explicit. They also reported changes in how to use procedures more thoughtfully and effectively, and how to make learning more generative for children by making their teaching decisions more powerful (addressing what the child needs most in daily lessons).

Demonstrating. Overwhelmingly, teachers found "demonstrations" to be the most powerful in taking on something new or redirecting their own practice, and they valued the conversations they had during professional development sessions and the help they gained from contact with other teachers who were more expert than themselves during school visits. School visits were noted often for their contribution to their work with children, helping them to become more effective with their children and more powerful in making powerful decisions. As one teacher stated, "So many of us are alone. There is no one to bounce ideas off of. If someone is in the building working with you, they teach, you watch; you teach; they watch." Teachers noted that demonstrations provided by either the Teacher Leader or university faculty were important whether given during school visits, group sessions when lessons were taught behind the one way mirror, or as topics were revisited after lessons in the professional development sessions. These demonstrations helped the teachers reflect on their own teaching in light of their observations and conversations.

These opportunities to see as well as talk about teaching around real examples of their students, were considered a dynamic in their own learning. As one teacher reported, "Behind the glass [when lessons were taught behind the one-way mirror during group sessions] clears up ideas we might have about procedures, 'I thought you had to do it THIS way.' Something always gets sorted out!"

Seeking improvement. However, although these teachers felt they had made shifts in their teaching, they always were seeking more ways to improve. They always wanted to get better. They asked questions like "How can we get more links across the lesson?" Areas for growth seemed to crop up even as they reflected on their own growth: "It's a problem getting down notes, knowing what to get down, what things should we be watching for? How do we note it to help our teaching?" As one teacher noted, "Teacher talk, I can't stress it enough. The hardest thing to get is language. There are still words in my vocabulary that I'm trying to purge!"

Dialoguing. At the end, they talked about how this year had provided more professional contact than ever before. They felt that having trainers (university faculty) as well as their Teacher Leader on visits or during the group sessions enabled them to really reflect on their practice and on their students. "The dialogue was sometimes 1:1 or 2:1. However it happened, all of the talk focused on YOUR student and how to achieve gains, that was invaluable to us!" In all instances, the teachers reported shifts in learning while simultaneously talking about critical moments in their work with children and the value of problem-solving with other teachers. The words of these teachers indicate a possible model through which to see the evolution of change in teaching (see Figure 1).

For these RR teachers, the power was in demonstration and conversation. The demonstrations they gave and received, and the conversations they had, aided them in taking on new theoretical understandings and integrating new learning with their previous experiences and practical notions of theory. As they observed teaching in action while talking, they learned to reason through their own

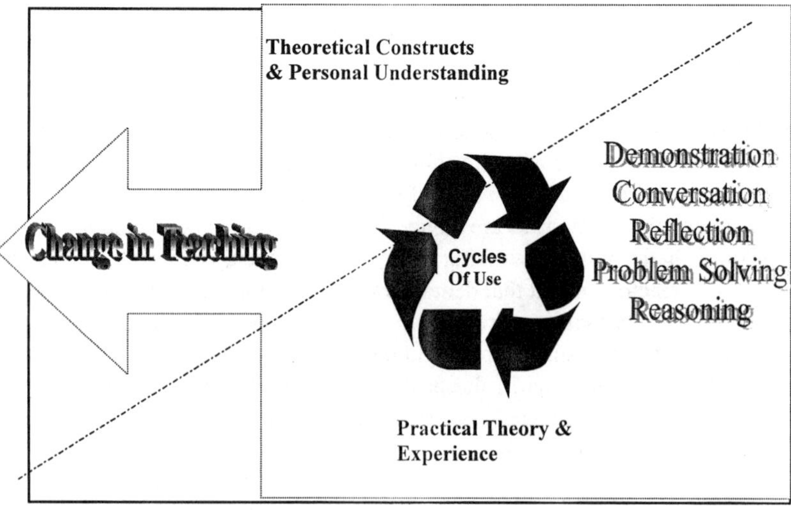

Figure 1. Evolution of change in teaching.

rationales and those of others. Critical learning moments (usually occurring as a result of a demonstration by a more expert other) seemed to provide momentum for their growing understanding; teachers tied their new knowledge to the powerful moments that continued to serve them as exemplars. As teachers revisited the topics most critical to teaching in professional conversations and engaged in additional cycles of use, they gained greater theoretical understanding. In this way, they extended their own practical theories, created more complex experiential networks, and understood new theoretical constructs.

Discussion

Traditional attempts to reform educational practices have been delivered using a divergent forces model. In that model, professional development is delivered separately at the school, district, and university levels. In our model to influence fundamental instructional change, we brought together school district and university personnel to deliver professional development for teachers within a collaborative model incorporating individual, paired, and group demonstration, conversation, reflection, problem-solving, and reasoning. Our diagram (see Figure 1) suggests that fundamental change to instruction occurs as these forces, or shared experiences, converge and build upon each other.

No claims are being made for systemic change or long-term effects of our work. Clearly, for the teachers, learning was ongoing. Although the data suggest changes in student progress, the changes were small, and we recognize that continued collaboration might be needed to maintain the impact on instruction and have a greater impact on student progress.

References

Clay, M. M. (1993). *An observation survey of early literacy achievement.* Portsmouth, NH: Heinemann.

Fullan, M. (1991). *The new meaning of educational change.* New York: Teachers College Press.

Fullan, M. (1993). *Change forces: Probing the depths of educational reform.* Bristol, PA: Falmer.

Glesne, C., & Peshkin, A. (1992). *Becoming qualitative researchers.* New York: Longman.

Juel, C. (1988). Learning to read and write: A longitudinal study of fifty-four children from first through fourth grade. *Journal of Educational Psychology, 80,* 437–447.

Lindfors, J. (1999). *Children's inquiry: Using language to make sense of the world.* New York: Teachers College Press.

Luria, A. (1979). *The making of mind.* Cambridge, MA: Harvard University Press.

National education goals report: Building a nation of learners (1995). Washington, DC: U.S. Government Printing Office.

Patton, M.Q. (1990). *Qualitative evaluation and research methods.* New York: Sage.

Sarason, S., (1990). *The predictable failure of educational reform.* San Francisco: Jossey-Bass.

Vygotsky, L. (1978). *Mind in society: The development of higher psychological processes.* Cambridge, MA: Harvard University Press.

Walmsley, S., & Allington, R. (1995). Redefining and reforming instructional support programs for at-risk students. In R. L. Allington & S. A. Walmsley (Eds.), *No quick fix: Rethinking literacy programs in America's elementary schools.* New York: Teachers College Press.

Wells, G. (1986). *The meaning makers: Children learning language and using language to learn.* Portsmouth, NH: Heinemann.

Wilson, K., & Daviss, B. (1994). *Redesigning education.* New York: Holt.

Redesigning America Reads: A K-3/University Collaboration

Pamela Ross
San Diego State University

In October 1996, Congress approved a bill to substantially increase Federal Work Study funds, earmarking the increase for university students to serve as America Reads tutors for elementary school children 5–8 years of age. Under the umbrella of the America Reads Challenge, millions of dollars have been allocated for use by university campuses nationwide to provide literacy tutoring to schools. However, no funding for infrastructure and few guidelines for implementation or evaluation accompany the program. Despite these limitations, preliminary research on America Reads programs has been highly positive both for those tutored (Morrow & Woo, 1998) and for the tutors themselves (Adler, 1999; Fitzgerald & Wolery, 1998; Gambrell, Dromsky, & Mazzoni, 1998). However, managing an America Reads program on a shoestring budget is a challenge, and innovation is a necessity since external resources must be identified for training, coaching, and monitoring. Many programs struggle to provide tutor training, support mechanisms for tutors, and/or monitoring systems for those tutored.

This paper describes the approach to the America Reads Challenge developed at a large, urban university in southern California involving 70 tutors and several hundred children in 12 urban schools. Following a brief overview of the program's successive approximations during its first 3 years of operation, the paper chronicles the process used at the end of Year 3 to reinvent content and delivery based on collaboration between K–3 teachers and university faculty. It further documents the degree to which the redesigned program was subsequently implemented at participating sites in Year 4.

Program Overview

Background

Research indicates that successful literacy tutoring programs require a structure for providing ongoing training and coaching of tutors, quality materials for tutoring, consistent service to the students being tutored, and monitoring of students' progress (Erickson & Anderson, 1997; Neumann, 1994; Pinnell & Fountas, 1997; Schine, 1997; Wasik, 1998a). Key components of successful tutoring programs include use of simple diagnostic tools such as word lists, running records and phonics inventories, as well as structured tutoring sessions incorpo-

*National Reading Conference Yearbook, **50**, pp. 532–543.*

rating the reading and rereading of children's literature, writing activities, phonemic awareness activities and work on letter-sound correspondences (Invernizzi, Juel, & Rosemary, 1997; Juel 1996; Pinnell, Lyons, DeFord, Bryk, & Seltzer 1994; Pinnell & Fountas 1997; Wasik 1998a; Wasik & Slavin, 1993).

Year 1

Mindful of these guidelines, faculty and staff at a large southern California university, representatives from the California Literature Project, and school district staff in two districts serving highly diverse populations, formed an America Reads partnership in spring 1997. Approximately $250,000 in work-study money was committed to the project for 1997–98. During this first year, in addition to being work-study eligible, potential tutors were required to complete a detailed application describing special qualifications to serve as a tutor. Staff in the Financial Aid Office reviewed applications and scored them based upon educational goals, tutoring experience, and experience working with children. Acceptable candidates were referred to a school district where they were interviewed by the site coordinator before being hired. At the last minute the university supplied funding for a 3-unit tutor-training course spread over two semesters developed by the researcher and three instructors. However, due to inadequate notice about its existence, enrollment was not mandatory. Ultimately, over 160 undergraduate tutors worked with over 1,000 children in 26 schools within two school districts; just over half of the tutors enrolled in the tutor training course at some point during the year.

Year 2

In the second year of the program (1998–99), nearly 1,000 children in 25 schools had contact with 110 America Reads Tutors. Tutors were required to enroll in the 3-unit tutor training course on developing and enhancing literacy skills in children. In addition, tutors were supported by two graduate student coordinators who conducted on-site visitations, met with district staff, offered ad hoc training sessions, and provided office hours for tutors seeking individualized help. A reading coordinator at each site monitored the mechanics of time cards, placed tutors with teachers, established tutoring schedules, and served as a liaison between tutors, the district, and the tutor-training coordinator. Coordination meetings involving university faculty, financial aid staff, and district reading coordinators took place at least twice each semester. A handbook was compiled containing general information about the program, tutor responsibilities, and procedures related to time cards. The university provided some additional funding for America Reads activities, training, and coordinators.

The tutor training course focused on an introduction to the reading process, simple diagnostic tools, and a variety of literacy strategies such as guided reading, shared reading, language experience (writing), repeated readings, reciprocal questioning, think-alouds, K-W-L, phonemic awareness/phonics activities, and use of predictable books. In general, the content of the course matched the key components for tutoring sessions recommended in the literature as well as instructional approaches for struggling readers supported by research. Students were required to keep a reflective journal containing lesson plans and to complete a case study on one child. Tutors worked 10–20 hours a week, had considerable latitude in development of lessons, and were encouraged to experiment with strategies. Although reading coordinators at each site made classroom assignments, ultimately, in most cases, classroom teachers used guidelines provided by the university to determine which children would be tutored. Students tutored had to be between 5 and 8 years of age, considered by their teachers to be at risk of failing in reading, and could not be involved in Reading Recovery. Tutors were encouraged to work one-to-one with children on a regular basis, but they were allowed to work with small groups (up to three students) if the host teacher so desired.

Year 3

As the university coordinator, I conducted a study of teacher perceptions and practices using surveys and interviews in spring 1999 and fall 2000 (Ross, 2000). Although the results revealed an overall positive response to the America Reads program, the use made of the tutors and the content of tutoring varied widely from classroom to classroom. Although the majority of teachers (90%) assigned tutors to work on a one-to-one basis at least part of the time, many teachers (49%) also assigned tutors to work with pairs of children, or in small groups of no more than three (47%). Almost a third reported that tutors also functioned as aides, working with groups of more than three during the reading rotation established by the teacher. Sometimes tutors worked with all children on a specific task such as computer-based phonics lessons, listening to oral reading, or working on proofreading skills during writing. Contrary to expectation, tutors were placed predominantly in grades two and three rather than in kindergarten and first-grade classrooms.

Most teachers (60%) indicated that they had little or no contact with the site coordinator and reported no contact with the university tutor-training coordinator. Awareness of the training provided by the university for the tutors was high (86.6%), and one-third of the tutors did discuss the course with their teachers. Despite this awareness, 60% of the teachers said they had never seen the course syllabus or the program handbook. Of a list of strategies drawn from the tutoring course outline, teachers identified six strategies that were employed by more than 50% of tutors: guided reading (84%), shared reading (70%), phonemic awareness activities (65%), phonics activities (62%), repeated readings (59%), and language experience (51%).

About 40% of teachers made no attempt to monitor the progress of the children in their classrooms as a result of tutoring. However, even in the absence of hard data, the majority of teachers (66%) believed that the America Reads program had substantial impact on the achievement of the recipients. Suggestions for improving the program centered on building better communication between the university and host teachers and on ways to enhance tutor training. Teachers also mentioned conflicts between tutors' university course schedules and the block of time normally dedicated to literacy instruction in the elementary classroom. As a result of this study, I decided to redesign the tutoring program with the help of participating teachers, site coordinators, and course instructors.

Redesign of the Program

Focus Groups

Although during its first 3 years our America Reads program was based on paradigms for successful tutoring, the implementation of the plan was hampered by lack of communication between university and school personnel, inconsistent site coordination, and absence of a monitoring system for student progress. In the spring of 2000, I, along with an Americorps Vista volunteer conducted focus groups (Stangor, 1998) with participating teachers and site coordinators at 14 of the schools engaged in the program. These focus groups were designed to inform teachers about the components of the existing program, present data about the nature of successful tutoring programs similar to America Reads, and solicit ideas about how to redesign and implement a program based on sound principles without creating significant additional burdens for teachers and coordinators.

The first part of the 60-minute informal group meetings established common ground for discussion. The university coordinator and research assistant discussed current practices at the site related to tutor placement, selection of children receiving tutoring, assistance provided to tutors at the site such as training or materials, monitoring of tutors and of progress of children tutored. The information generally verified findings from surveys completed in spring 1998 and one-to-one interviews conducted in fall 1999 (Ross, 2000). In almost every case, the site coordinator interviewed and placed the tutors in classrooms. Once assigned to classrooms, teachers selected children who would receive tutoring based on the DRA (an informal reading inventory), language skills, informal observations, and a variety of other variables. Tutors were thinly spread, working in from one to as many as eight classrooms; on the average, though, they worked in three different rooms. Training was provided by teachers only in one or two instances, although several sites reported that teachers provided some materials for their tutors. The only monitoring of tutors reported was related to attendance. No official system for monitoring the progress of children who participated in the program was evident. Most sites reported that teachers monitored progress as a part of their general student assessment. Overall, the degree of knowledge about the purpose of the program, its organization, and the expectations that the university had for its implementation was very discouraging.

Following these informal discussions of practices related to the America Reads program, the facilitator presented some data about the program including: (a) an overview of the current program, its purposes, training, coordination and management; (b) data gathered through teacher surveys and interviews in Years

2 and 3 that indicated wide variation in the implementation of the program from site to site; and (c) a summary of research findings about the structure and delivery of successful tutoring programs.

The second portion of the meeting was organized around focus questions that concentrated on soliciting input to help redesign the program. Guiding questions included items related to: (a) the feasibility of developing and implementing a more theoretically sound approach to tutoring; (b) ways to improve training; (c) ways to increase teacher communication with site coordinators, tutors, and other university personnel; (d) possible approaches to monitoring student progress; and (e) willingness to participate in a more tightly structured program.

Fieldnotes from the focus groups were entered into the computer and analyzed for themes. From this analysis, the need surfaced for increased involvement of site coordinators both in tutor assignments and monitoring of student progress. Teachers and site coordinators requested that the university conduct preliminary interviews with tutor candidates before assigning them to a school site for further screening. During the interview process, it was suggested that potential tutors sign an agreement to enroll in the tutor-training course at the university. Verification of availability to tutor in the morning at least two days a week was also recommended.

Teachers requested that tutor training concentrate in greater depth on fewer strategies and techniques. Strategies based on Reading Recovery such as the use of running records, reading of familiar and unfamiliar texts, and emphasis on developing the child's use of the language cueing systems were generally seen as good approaches for the content of tutoring sessions. Other suggestions for enhancing tutor training included more exposure to basic reading terminology and improving phonics background knowledge of tutors. A simple weekly tutor-teacher log was recommended to enhance communication between teachers and tutors concerning the content of sessions. Informal evaluations such as the use of word banks, running records and journals were seen as possible ways to monitor progress of children. However, some teachers expressed unwillingness to participate in the program if revisions required substantial amounts of their time for coordination.

Following the focus group meetings, revised program guidelines (see Figure 1) were developed with the help of teacher volunteers for later presentation to all site coordinators at a general meeting in June 2000. A tutor-teacher log was developed containing a checklist of strategies used by the tutor, a record of books read with the child, and a place for tutor and teacher comments. Based on the coordination demanded by the new guidelines, it was determined that in order to allocate sufficient resources to each site, fewer schools and tutors would need to be involved in the program. A target of 60–80 tutors placed in twelve sites was set by the university. School sites were given the opportunity to decline participation in the program under the new guidelines. Since none of the sites voluntarily withdrew from the program, I reviewed the demographic, socioeconomic status, and student achievement profiles in school-site report cards (available on line through the county office of education). The 12 sites with the greatest achievement gaps were offered the program; the remaining sites were put on a waiting list pending any changes in resource allocations. The guidelines were implemented during the summer of 2000.

Evaluation Surveys

In fall 2000, teachers and site coordinators participating in the redesigned program completed a two-part, 22-item survey to determine the degree to which new guidelines were being implemented. Part A of the survey contained 13 Likert Scale items and four open-ended questions intended for all teachers. Questions related to (a) consistency of tutor contact with children, (b) use made of tutors by teachers, (c) match between strategies employed by tutors and school curriculum, (d) effectiveness of the monitoring system for student progress, and (e) level of

Selection of Tutors

1. University staff will conduct a paper screening of applicants followed by face to face interviews.
2. Only those tutors deemed good candidates given the new guidelines will be sent to school sites for further screening.

Nature of the Tutoring Sessions

1. Tutors must be available at least *two* and preferably *three* days a week.
2. Tutors should work consistently *one-to-one* with at least *the same four children* for *an entire semester.*
3. Children receiving tutoring must be *5–8 years of age.*
4. Tutor *placements* should be limited to *1–2 classrooms.*
5. Tutors should tutor each child *20–30 minutes each session.*
6. Tutors should employ strategies they have learned in their University course during tutoring.

Placement of Tutors in the Classroom

1. America Reads tutors may not be utilized as classroom aides.
2. Site coordinators in consultation with school administrators will determine classrooms to receive tutors.
3. Site coordinators in consultation with teachers will determine children to receive tutoring based upon appropriate assessments.

On-Site Support for Tutors

1. Site coordinators in consultation with teachers will help provide appropriate materials for tutoring.
2. Materials should be in a centralized location easily accessible to tutors.

Communication

1. Tutors and teachers will communicate using a standard vehicle developed for the program (tutor/teacher log).
2. Progress of children tutored should be monitored by the teacher in a simple but standardized way.
3. Continuing tutors who have already completed training need to be introduced to the new form of communication.

Figure 1. Revised program guidelines.

communication among partners. The open-ended questions provided opportunities for teachers to describe strengths and weaknesses of the program, generate suggestions for further improvement, or make other comments related to the program. Five additional Likert Scale questions (Part B) required direct comparisons of the program before and after the redesign and were intended only for teachers who had hosted tutors for at least 2 years.

Surveys were distributed to and collected from the school sites by the tutor-training coordinators within a 2-week period in November. A total of 46 out of 77 surveys were returned for a response rate of 60%. Of these, a subset of 24 teachers compared previous experience to the current year. Statements for open-ended questions were analyzed and response categories were developed for each. In some cases, multiple responses to questions were supplied by teachers. For these items, all nonredundant responses were tallied and results reported as a percentage of the total number of responses rather than as a percentage of the teachers who gave a specific response. All results are reported descriptively.

Survey Results

A summary of current findings and a comparison of these where appropriate to Year-3 research results follows. Teachers were asked to rate the tutors in terms of reliability, professionalism, potential for teaching, and overall quality on a scale of 1 to 5. Results indicated that teachers were very favorably impressed with the quality of the tutors. Table 1 summarizes these ratings which show substantial increases over the previous year in three of the four areas. The distribution of tutors across grade levels showed a modest shift indicating 35% of tutors were concentrated in lower primary grades (K–1) compared to 28% the previous year. Teachers also indicated that in 100% of cases tutors worked "always" or "most of the time" with the same children, and a greater percentage (89% vs. 68%) worked

Table 1

Teacher Ratings of Tutor Quality

	High (4–5)		Average (3)		Low (1–2)	
Variable	1999–2000	2000–2001	1999–2000	2000–2001	1999–2000	2000–2001
Reliability	74%	85%	14%	5%	12%	9%
Professionalism	88%	88%	8%	5%	4%	7%
Potential for Teaching	77%	92%	17%	5%	4%	2%
Overall Quality	77%	88%	17%	10%	6%	2%

with children either one-to-one, in pairs, or in groups of no more than three. However, 21% of teachers still reported that tutors worked with groups of more than three children at least part of the time. New guidelines for the program required tutors to work one-to-one with at least four children in a classroom before providing instructions to pairs or small groups of students. In 68.3% of classrooms, this was apparently the case. However, 31.7% of tutors saw fewer than four children in a classroom individually.

Teachers continued to report varying degrees of familiarity with the tutor-training course syllabus and program handbook, although the number reporting no knowledge at all of these items dropped from 60% to 37%. In addition, 89% of teachers believed the match between tutor strategies and the school curriculum was good compared to 60% the year before. Contact between teachers and site coordinators also seemed to have improved substantially. Those interviewed in fall 1999 said contact was limited to once or twice a semester, if at all. Data collected from the new survey indicated 61% interacted with their site coordinator at least once a week and 82% at least twice a month. On the other hand, 75% of teachers reported no contact with the tutor-training coordinator. Finally, 41.9% of teachers found that the introduction of the teacher-tutor log enhanced communication with tutors and 53.8% felt it improved their ability to monitor the progress of child receiving tutoring.

Analysis of the responses to the four open-ended questions revealed gains in program integrity. A total of 45 comments related to strengths were coded. Program strengths most frequently cited included provision for one-to-one instruction (28.8%), supplemental help for teachers (17.7%), and tutor training (28.8%). These same strengths were among those most frequently mentioned the previous year with a 10% increase in comments related to tutor training reflected in current data. Representative statements included such remarks as: "I really can't tell you how much I appreciate this great program. America Reads allows me to give at-risk students the one-to-one teaching strategies they need." "The training is excellent; tutors follow through on strategies that I use myself." "Tutors are optimistic, enthusiastic, and have a great desire to help children."

Weaknesses of the program most frequently mentioned (28 coded responses) included teacher-tutor communication (35.7%), inconsistency of tutors (17.9%), and tutor schedules (14.3%). Once again, similar response patterns emerged prior to program redesign, although some slight increases in concerns related to scheduling, teacher-tutor communication, and inconsistency of tutors emerged this year. On the other hand, lack of familiarity with training declined from 17% to 7% as a concern. Typical issues are reflected in comments such as: "There is no real time to talk to the tutor—I'm teaching and she's tutoring." Teachers also made statements that indicated tutoring was "occasionally inconvenient because kids missed other instruction." Concerns about scheduling are summed up by one teacher who complained, "Available tutor hours can be difficult to work around. I'd like to have tutors work less time per day, maybe 90 minutes during the literacy block, but work for a longer duration, September through the end of second semester." The latter remark has much to do with the fact that tutors may work up to 20 hours per week, depending on the limitations of their Federal Work Study award, and exit the program at the conclusion of the university semester in May.

Suggestions for improving the program (22 coded responses) included better communication between university, site coordinators, and tutors (22.7%); enhanced training (13.6%); and teacher-tutor communication (13.6%). Requests for more tutors were reflected in 18% of remarks. The majority of "other" comments (69.6% of 23 coded responses) were devoted to a variety of kudos for the program such as "great program," "keep it up," "wonderful program," and so on. An illustration of these sentiments can be seen in the following statement made by one teacher: "I feel the program is beneficial to the students, especially for kids struggling in reading. They need the extra one-to-one help that is oftentimes impossible for the teacher to provide, as least on a consistent schedule."

Finally, direct comparisons of years three and four based on Part B of the survey are reported in Table 2. These findings are encouraging as approximately 50%–60% of respondents thought the program had improved since the redesign in the areas of tutor qualifications, tutor schedules, teacher-tutor communication, teacher knowledge about tutor lesson content, and university-school site communication.

Discussion and Conclusions

Results of previous research on the university's America Reads program raised serious concerns about program delivery and quality. These concerns led to an attempt to redesign the program within parameters acceptable both to teachers and the university. From the university perspective, effective program content and delivery are essential to maximize impact on student achievement. At the same time, program guidelines cannot place unrealistic demands on the teachers who support initiatives like America Reads without undermining the endeavor's success. Dialog during the focus groups revealed a strong need for improved communication between the university and the schools. Bringing site coordinators together for occasional meetings with the university team was insufficient to promote such communication. Site visits during the focus groups appeared to be

Table 2

Comparison of Program Years 3 and 4

Teacher Perception	Improved	Neutral	Not Improved
Tutor Qualifications	52.1%	34.8%	13%
Tutor Schedules	62.4%	37.5%	0%
Teacher/Tutor Communication	62.4%	20.8%	16.6%
Teacher Knowledge About Tutor Lessons	54.1%	37.5%	8.4%
University/School Site Communication	50.0%	41.7%	8.3%

an effective way to raise teacher consciousness about the goals of the program, the nature of the training, and appropriate tasks for tutors. This consciousness may have helped influence the improvements noted in the survey in both the placement of tutors in early primary grades as well as the tutor assignments to tasks once in the classroom.

As liaisons between the university and the school, tutor-training coordinators make periodic site visits to meet with and observe tutors. Presently, each coordinator monitors six sites, rotating through them on a fixed schedule. Despite these efforts, the university coordinators appear to be invisible to teachers. Periodic site visits unrelated to tutor supervision might need to become part of the routine. This might require more tutor-training coordinator positions.

It was reasonable to expect that the redesigned program would produce improvements in tutor quality; a better match between tutor hours and school needs; a better match between training and school curriculum; more one-to-one instruction; and greater communication between site coordinators and teachers, teachers and tutors, and the university and school sites. University screening and interviewing of candidates should have helped insure selection of more appropriate tutors who would enroll in training and be available during hours and days requested by teachers. Improvements in all these areas were in fact noted. However, it appears that we still have a distance to cover to close the gaps. Too many tutors still work with groups larger than desired and do not work with enough children individually. Some of this may be an artifact of the number of hours spent in classrooms by tutors each week (up to 20). Because they work around their university course schedule, tutors are often unable to stay and confer with their host teachers. Despite deep concerns about lack of teacher time to meet with tutors, teachers offered a certain degree of resistance to developing procedures for monitoring them. During the focus groups, use of e-mail and dialog journals were explored with teachers but rejected as too time consuming. Face to face conferences, although difficult to document, are probably the most expedient method of communication. However, a significant number of teachers complained that tutor schedules did not permit this luxury. The tutor-teacher log shows some promise, although it is probably too soon to tell if this is the answer. Further time will reveal its usefulness.

Many educators suggest that in order to effectively tutor students in reading, extensive training for volunteer tutors is necessary (Juel, 1994; Roller; 1998). However, few experimental studies have examined the impact of volunteer tutoring programs on achievement relative to the intensity of tutor training (Shanahan, 1998; Wasik, 1998b). A recent longitudinal study (Baker, Gersten, & Keating, 2000) researched the effects of SMART, a volunteer tutor program intentionally designed to place minimal demands on teachers whose students were being tutored and requiring little training and supervision of tutors. The program employs successful adult members of the business community as tutors and currently serves more than 7,000 children in the state of Oregon. Children in the experimental sample (N=43) were individually tutored an average of 30 minutes twice a week during both first and second grade. Results indicated that when achievement gains of participants were compared to students in a comparison group deemed similarly at risk of failure as well as to a group of average students who received no tutoring, those tutored made greater growth on measures of word reading, reading fluency, and word comprehension. Significant differences for passage comprehension were not found. Compared to programs that provide more extensive training, SMART appears to have a similar impact on student achievement. Although the researchers assert "less may be more," it is important to note that despite the progress made by students, their mean posttest scores on subtests of the standardized instrument employed placed them at the 30th percentile. Given what we know about the ever-expanding gap between good and poor readers over time (Stanovich, 1986), these findings are both intriguing and disturbing. They point to the highly complicated nature of research in the area of tutoring programs for at-risk and struggling readers as well as the vicissitudes of interpreting results.

Considering the magnitude of America Reads and the dozens of other tutoring programs at work across the nation, potential impact of these endeavors on achievement in K–3 classrooms is substantial and largely undocumented. Therefore, now that we have achieved a degree of standardization in the delivery of the program, our future research will focus on student achievement gains as a result of tutoring by well-trained America Reads tutors. Pre/post test scores on the DRA and several other variables for K–3 children who have received tutoring will be compared to those of a control group with similar pretest scores who did not participate in the program and received no other extra support. Research on tutoring programs needs to be encouraged if we are to develop procedures that are fiscally parsimonious and optimize long-term, measurable impact within the real world constraints of delivering and monitoring one-to-one instructional models.

References

Adler, M. (1999). *The America reads challenge: An analysis of college students' tutoring* (CIERA Report No. 3-007). Ann Arbor: University of Michigan.

Baker, S., Gersten, R., & Keating, T. (2000). When less may be more: A 2-year longitudinal evaluation of a volunteer tutoring program requiring minimal training. *Reading Research Quarterly, 35,* 494–519.

Fitzgerald, J., & Wolery, R. (1998, December). *An exploratory close-up look of two tutors.* Paper presented at the meeting of the National Reading Conference, Austin, TX.

Erickson, J., & Anderson, J. (Eds.). (1997). *Learning with the community: Concepts and models for service-learning in teacher education.* Washington, DC: American Association for Higher Education.

Gambrell, L., Dromsky, A., & Mazzoni, S. (1998, December). *Tutor successes and frustrations.* Paper presented at the meeting of the National Reading Conference, Austin, TX.

Invernizzi, M., Juel, C., & Rosemary, C. A. (1997). A community volunteer tutorial that works. *Reading Teacher, 50,* 304–311.

Juel, C. (1994). At-risk university students tutoring at-risk elementary school children. In E. H. Hiebert & B. M. Taylor (Eds.), *Getting reading right from the start* (pp. 39–61). Boston: Allyn & Bacon.

Juel, C. (1996). What makes literacy tutoring effective? *Reading Research Quarterly, 31,* 268–289.

Morrow L., & Woo, D. (1998, ??). *The effect of "America reads" tutoring on achievement and attitude of children.* Paper presented at the meeting of the National Reading Conference, Austin, TX.

Neumann, A. (1994). *Volunteer tutor's toolbox.* Newark, DE: International Reading Association.

Pinnell, G. S., & Fountas, I. C. (1997). *A coordinator's guide to help America read: A handbook for volunteers.* Portsmouth, NH: Heinemann.

Pinnell, G. S., Lyons, C. A., DeFord, D. E., Bryk, A. S., & Seltzer, M. (1994). Comparing instructional models for the literacy education of high-risk first graders. *Reading Research Quarterly, 29,* 9–39.

Roller, C.M. (1998). *So . . . what's a tutor to do?* Newark, DE: International Reading Association.

Ross, P. (2000). America reads: Teachers' perception of the program. In T. Shanahan & F. V. Rodriguez-Brown (Eds.), *National Reading Conference Yearbook, 49* (pp. 500–510). Chicago: National Reading Conference.

Schine, J. (Ed.). (1997). *Service learning: Ninety-sixth yearbook of the National Society of the Study of Education.* Chicago: University of Chicago Press.

Shanahan, T. (1998). On the effectiveness and limitations of tutoring in reading. In P. D. Pearson & A. Iran-Nejad (Eds.), *Review of research in education* (pp. 217–234). Washington, DC: American Educational Research Association.

Stangor, C. (1998). *Research methods for the behavioral sciences.* Boston: Houghton-Mifflin.

Stanovich, K. E. (1986). Matthew effects in reading: Some consequences of individual differences in the acquisition of literacy. *Reading Research Quarterly, 21,* 360–406.

Wasik, B. A. (1998a). Using volunteers as reading tutors: Guidelines for successful practices. *Reading Teacher, 51,* 562–570.

Wasik, B. A. (1998b). Volunteer tutoring programs in reading: A review. *Reading Research Quarterly, 33,* 266–292.

Wasik, B. A., & Slavin, R. E. (1993). Preventing early reading failure with one-to-one tutoring: A review of five programs. *Reading Research Quarterly, 28,* 178–200.

Of Virgins, Blank Slates, and Gurus: An Interpretive Case Study of Elementary Teachers Implementing Peer Discussion

Mary S. Rozendal and Janice F. Almasi
University at Buffalo, State University of New York

Peer discussion is an instructional approach used for developing comprehension and critical thinking about texts. As an instructional approach that differs from traditional patterns of classroom interactions, the implementation of peer discussion involves a process of teacher learning. The purpose of this investigation was to understand how elementary teachers implement peer discussion of text in their classrooms. Twelve teachers and two university professors engaged in a teacher study group that met 11 times during 1½ school years. The group met to learn about peer discussion and to problem-solve issues and concerns that arose as teachers began using the approach in their classrooms. In this study we looked specifically at the teachers' individual and group development for factors that both contributed to and inhibited the implementation of peer discussion.

Theoretical Framework

The rationale for this study is based on prior research that indicates teachers find peer discussion valuable but difficult to implement in their classroom. Peer discussion is grounded in the sociocultural theories of learning and this foundation further supports its use. Therefore, we highlight prior research that demonstrates the potential for using teacher study groups to support teachers through the difficulties of implementing peer discussion. This study looks at the beginnings of an intervention that engaged teachers in a study group about peer discussion as they began to use the approach in their classrooms.

Peer Discussion

Typical classroom discussions are often structured according to the Initiate-Respond-Evaluate (IRE) participation structure in which the teacher's role is central, and student participation is contingent on teacher permission to respond (Cazden, 1986, 1988). Although some IRE classroom interactions support student learning (Cazden, 1986, 1988; Wells, 1993), often students are cognitively disengaged and passive (Doise & Mugny, 1984; McMahon & Goatley, 1995). In contrast, peer discussion provides a decentralized context in which small groups of

National Reading Conference Yearbook, 50, pp. 544–557.

students collaboratively interpret and construct meaning about texts (Almasi, 1996). Instead of merely responding to the teacher, students initiate topics of conversation (cf. Commeyras, 1994; Commeyras, Sherril, & Wuenker, 1996) and assume a variety of dynamic roles (Mannheim & Tedlock, 1995).

When IRE participation structures are diminished and students are provided opportunities for decentralized participation in peer discussion, research has reported cognitive, social, and affective benefits for students' development (Almasi, 1995; Alvermann, O'Brien, & Dillon, 1990; Eeds & Wells, 1989; Goatley, Brock, & Raphael, 1995; Leal, 1992; Many & Wiseman, 1992; Martinez, Roser, Hoffman, & Battle, 1992; McGee, 1992; McMahon, 1996; Slavin, 1990). Commeyras and DeGroff's (1998) survey of 1,482 literacy professionals (school principals, library-media specialists, reading specialists, middle and high school English teachers, K–5 elementary teachers and reading/language arts teacher educators) revealed that these benefits have convinced most literacy professionals (95%) that peer discussion is valuable and most (77%) are interested in using it with their students. However, it is still quite rare in classrooms. Only 33% of the literacy professionals in the survey reported actually using peer discussion frequently in their classrooms. This raises the question why peer discussion, a practice that demonstrates significant educational value and is highly regarded by literacy professionals, is not implemented more widely.

There are several reasons for the lack of implementation. Providing for peer discussion means the teacher must relinquish some of the control within classroom discussions (Cazden, 1986). This proposition can be very threatening or intimidating even for teachers who are interested in utilizing the approach. In addition, it takes time for students to learn how to interact successfully within peer-discussion groups. The lengthy developmental period means that initial discussions may not be successful, causing many teachers to abandon the practice before it becomes successful (Gilles, Dickinson, McBride, & Vandover, 1994; Roller & Beed, 1994). Ongoing staff development as in teacher study groups holds the potential for supporting teachers through the difficulties of implementation. However, a teacher study group also entails a developmental process as teachers improve their abilities to learn in a discussion format and construct their own understandings about using peer discussion in their classroom (Short et al., 1992). This study examines the teacher and study group development that supported teachers' initial attempts to implement peer discussion of text into their classroom reading instruction.

Sociocultural Theories

The guiding principles of peer discussion are rooted in sociocultural theories of development that maintain children learn the intellectual rules, procedural rules, and social conventions of discussion by observing and participating in them (Vygotsky, 1978). Social learning environments enable learners to observe and interact with more knowledgeable others as they engage in cognitive processes they may not be able to engage in independently. Learning in these social environments may occur incidentally as learners observe the cognitive and social processes of their peers, or learning may be more direct when teachers or peers function as more knowledgeable others to scaffold learning. Through scaffolding learners become capable of achieving more than they could have independently (Rogoff, 1990; Vygotsky, 1978). As a result of incidental learning or scaffolded instruction learners gradually internalize higher cognitive functions, such as interpreting literature or monitoring one's comprehension. Peer discussions provide a social environment in which students can observe the cognitive and social processes of their peers and begin to use the strategies they observe for interpreting literature and interacting with one another in a productive manner.

Just as students learn in social contexts, teachers' learning of new instructional approaches, such as peer discussion, must be supported through social interactions and ongoing experiences with new instructional techniques (Englert & Tarrant, 1995; Lave, 1996). Learning is also a social process for teachers where they enter and participate in communities of practice (Lave, 1996). Teachers are increasingly viewed as collaborators in constructing models of teaching and learning (Santa Barbara Classroom Discourse Group, 1992). This perspective diverges from traditional, externally mandated staff development. Richardson and Anders (1994) assert that "the very process of group conversation about teaching and schooling will have more effect on classroom practices than structural change or mandated behavior" (p. 213). By participating in ongoing collaborations with researchers (as in teacher study groups), teachers feel more empowered to make and sustain changes in their instruction, they incorporate current research on learning and instruction, and they support their colleagues' efforts to do the same.

Teacher Study Groups

Research has shown that teacher study groups can be an effective means of staff development and support for teachers trying to implement new instructional practices (Fullan, 1991; Hargreaves, 1994; Short et al., 1992; Sparks, 1988). Systematic reflection in study groups that includes dialogue and consideration of everyday practice helps improve instruction (Clift, Veal, Johnson, & Holland, 1990; Richardson & Anders, 1994; Wells, & Chang-Wells, 1992). It is this type of staff development that supports long-lasting educational change (Englert, Tarrant, & Rozendal, 1993; Fullan, 1991). Teachers are able to bring instructional concerns and problems to the other members of their own learning community in order to problem-solve and improve their practice (Laird et al., 1994).

In this study group teachers were working together to create meaning for themselves about peer discussion. Oja (1989) characterized the development of study groups by adapting Loevinger's (1976) stages of ego development, that is, development where individuals create meaning of an experience. Oja used four stages to describe group development: (a) the self-protective, (b) the conformist, (c) the conscientious, and (d) the autonomous. According to Oja in the self-protective stage, study groups are beginning to develop an identity, but the process involves protecting the individuals in the group. This stage is characterized by the fear that mistakes made by teachers will put them in a negative position with their administrators. There is little efficacy and participants blame factors outside of themselves when the process breaks down. Valentino (1998) found that teachers in study groups at this stage met for less than an hour, did not complete outside reading assignments for group discussions and had limited sharing of ideas.

In the conformist stage there is a strong bond where members have a sense that they need to belong. Because of this need participants avoid conflict by avoiding contentious topics and they keep interactions friendly and congenial (Little, 1982; Rozendal, 1996). At this stage, there are strong leaders and strong followers with followers making efforts to avoid conflict with the leaders. In addition, there is a sense that group members are just "putting in their time," and whereas little work is done to bring new ideas to the group, few ideas from the group discussions are applied to the classroom. Participants in study groups at this stage may experience frustration with the group, but will not air their concerns for fear of being ostracized (Valentino, 1998). Many study groups find themselves in these two stages in the first year of meeting as a group in which a period of introduction and transition takes place before the group begins working toward its goals (Hamilton & Richardson, 1995; Rozendal, 1996; Valentino, 1998).

More self-aware and self-critical study group members characterize the third stage, the conscientious stage. Groups at this stage are aware of successes and setbacks because participants have developed self-reflection and personal efficacy. Groups have clear objectives for their activities, have developed a guiding sense of purpose, and are driven by intrinsic rewards rather than extrinsic validation. Valentino (1998) notes that study groups in this stage do not focus on things that are out of their control such as time constraints or parental issues, but focus instead on instructional factors they can control in the classroom.

The autonomous stage is the stage in which all participants are working toward the same objectives. The other participants recognize each member as bringing important knowledge, skills, and abilities to the group so all are respected. Conflicts are expected to arise, but the mutual respect supports working through any conflicts. Groups at this stage also have a strong sense of interdependence among participants that allows study groups to succeed.

The developmental characteristics of teacher study groups help us to understand the learning process that is involved as teachers engage in staff development efforts that are valued for supporting lasting change. Research has shown that peer discussion is an instructional approach that requires time to implement (Gilles et al., 1994; Roller & Beed, 1994). Thus, to understand the factors that support and inhibit teachers as they learn to implement peer discussion in their classrooms, we must examine their development in the context of the study group where their efforts are supported. Two research questions guided our investigation: (a) How did the study group develop in the first year and a half of meetings? (b) What were the attributes of the teachers' development as they began to implement peer discussion?

Method

This interpretive case study (Merriam, 1998) was designed to analyze, interpret, and theorize about how teachers begin to implement peer discussion into their literacy instruction. Descriptive data were analyzed to develop conceptual categories that illustrate and extend our understanding of how teachers constructed their knowledge in the study group and applied that knowledge to their classroom instruction.

Participants

Of the 12 teachers in the study group, 9 were elementary school teachers (3 fourth-grade, 3 third-grade, and 3 second-grade teachers) and 3 were reading specialists at a suburban K–4 elementary school on the East Coast. The school is located within a district that ranks consistently as one of the highest achieving school districts in the state and contains over 10,000 students. The majority of the students in the school are Caucasian and are from middle- and upper-middle class backgrounds. Two university professors joined these teachers in regular teacher study group meetings that examined the use of peer discussion in classrooms. Seven of the teachers volunteered to engage in research activities such as videotaping their peer discussions, observing one another's peer discussions, and participating in demonstration lessons (see Table 1). Although data collected at the study group meetings include all 12 teachers, we were only able to collect and examine additional data relating to the development of the 7 project teachers for this report.

Table 1

Research Participants

Teacher	Grade-Tenure Status	Experience with Peer Discussion
Mrs. Brown	2nd—untenured	Novice
Mrs. Fitzpatrick	2nd—tenured	Novice
Former journalist and middle school teacher		
Mrs. Davidson	3rd—tenured	Novice
Mrs. Huizen	3rd—tenured	Novice
Mrs. Williams	3rd—tenured	Novice
Grade-level team leader		
Mr. Danson	4th—tenured	Novice
Mrs. St. James	4th—tenured	Experienced
Grade-level team leader		

Note: All names of teacher participants are pseudonyms.

Data Sources

Data sources included observational fieldnotes, videotapes, transcripts of peer discussions of text, interviews with teachers, and artifacts. Artifacts from peer discussions included: written products produced either during or following peer discussion, teacher lesson plans, and teacher memos. Both formal and informal interviews were conducted. Formal interviews were phenomenological (Seidman, 1998) in that they were aimed at gaining information that established the context of the participant's experience with peer discussion, reconstructing details of the participant's experience within the context, and enabling participants to reflect on the meaning of the peer discussion experience for them. Sample questions included, "How did you come to be interested in peer discussion?" "Why are you interested in focusing on peer discussion in your classroom?" "Tell me about the role of peer discussion in your classroom." "Tell me about how peer discussion operates in your classroom." "Tell me about your best/worst experiences with peer discussion." All formal interviews were audiotaped. Informal interviews occurred "on-the-fly" throughout the year as we saw teachers in the hallways or after observing them as they implemented peer discussions in their classrooms. Fieldnotes were taken to capture the essence of these conversations. Data were also gathered during teacher meetings in the form of observational fieldnotes and audiotapes of study group meetings. All audio- and videotapes were transcribed in their entirety.

Data Gathering Procedures

The peer discussion study group met regularly for over 1 year. During the 1998–99 school year, the group met four times from April to June. During the 1999–00 school year, the group met seven times from September to June. During these meetings, the group identified issues and concerns with implementing peer discussion and shared their experiences. Fieldnotes were taken from each study group meeting, and those meetings from 1999–00 were audiotaped and transcribed in their entirety. At the conclusion of each meeting, the group members who were interested in studying their own teaching more closely signed up for scaffolded assistance in the form of demonstration lessons, co-teaching, observations, or videotaping. Because teachers chose the type of activities in which they wanted to participate, the number of peer discussions videotaped, demonstration lessons performed, co-teaching opportunities, and observations varied from teacher to teacher.

Data Analysis Procedures

Data were analyzed using inductive methods (Erickson, 1986). Throughout the data gathering process we made analytical memos regarding hunches and interpretations. Activity codes (Bogdan & Biklen, 1998) were used to identify phases of peer discussion implementation and affiliated teacher behaviors. Videotapes, transcripts, fieldnotes, and analytic memos were examined and reexamined and coded to reflect phases of teacher implementation, teachers' thinking about their use of peer discussion, and regularly occurring behaviors. A domain analysis (Spradley, 1980) was conducted to determine the characteristics and attributes of teachers in various developmental phases.

Results and Discussion

Similar to other beginning study groups (Hamilton & Richardson, 1995; Rozendal, 1996; Valentino, 1998) the study group development was characterized by the first two stages of Oja's (1989) development stages. Within the group, however, the teachers' development varied. We first report the characteristics of the study group and then examine individual teacher characteristics as they began implementing peer discussion in their classroom. The examination reveals a reflexive relationship between teacher development and the study group development.

Study Group Development

Study group meetings evolved over the year as teachers and researchers negotiated their roles and clarified their purposes for the group. The group exhibited many of the characteristics of Oja's (1989) first two stages of development, the self-protective and the conformist stages. As characteristic of the self-protective stage, members were reluctant to share the peer discussion activities they were trying in their classrooms with each other and with the researchers. They shared ideas from outside sources rather than from their personal experiences trying peer discussion thereby incurring minimal risk of criticism by the other members in the group. Similarly, as characteristic of the conformist stage, participants attended meetings only for the allotted time, remained friendly toward other members in the group, and followed two conversational leaders, Mrs. Browne and Mrs. Fitzpatrick. These leaders were both novice teachers in terms of peer discussion experience and Mrs. Browne was also the only untenured teacher. Though these findings are consistent with other initial study group findings, in order to further understand the study group development we also examined the participants' developmental characteristics.

Individual Characteristics

As the 1999–00 school year began, we found that the teachers quickly aligned themselves into one of two groups—those with little or no experience implementing peer discussion, and those with extensive experience implementing peer discussion. The groups reflected teachers' individual development in regards to using peer discussion but did not reflect their general teaching experience. Novices included young, untenured teachers such as Mrs. Browne who referred to herself as a "peer discussion virgin" (Fieldnotes, 12/7/99) and veteran teachers such as Mrs. Huizen who thought of herself as a "blank slate" (Interview Transcript, 11/19/99). Mrs. St. James, a veteran fourth-grade teacher who had been implementing peer discussion for over 10 years, was aware that she was at a different stage than most of the other teachers and felt that "everybody, I think, thinks like 'Oh, she knows everything. . . .'" (Interview Transcript, 1/6/00). In fact, the novice teachers often referred to Mrs. St. James and us (the university researchers) as "gurus." In the remaining discussion we have chosen to use the teachers' native term (Spradley, 1980) rather than researcher-imposed labels.

Our analysis revealed that teachers in these two groups reflected phases of development that had common and contrasting features associated with them. Novice or "virgin" teacher attributes included a fear of failure, the need to provide scaffolding for students to maintain a semiotic presence, and resistance. Experienced or "guru" teacher characteristics included possessing expert attributes, transferring conversational control to students, and maintaining a lifelong learning stance.

Fear of failure. The "virgins" seemed to feel that they had to understand the concept of peer discussion fully before they could attempt it. It seemed that these teachers feared failure. They did not want to be observed doing a poor job. When asked in an interview why she had not tried peer discussion, Mrs. Huizen responded, "It's in my *head* to try it . . . I *will* try it. I, you know, but I want to *learn* more about it, too. I don't, I want to do this *right*. I don't want to just jump in, which I've, we've done with other things" (Interview Transcript, 11/10/99).

In addition, teachers needed to feel that their initial attempts with peer discussion were conducted in personally safe situations. Personally safe situations included only trying peer discussion with their top reading groups, watching demonstration lessons by a researcher, and co-teaching initial lessons with a researcher. During study group meetings teachers repeatedly requested to be told exactly how to begin doing peer discussions and to see videotapes that showed examples of how to start. In addition, they requested modeled lessons with their students and co-teaching during initial attempts to use peer discussion. In December, when we had convinced several of the teachers that we needed to videotape their groups in their initial discussions to document students' cognitive and social growth and development, they began with their "high" reading group students and created discussion contexts that were highly scaffolded for students. Mrs. Huizen embodied the perception that peer discussion is only for good readers when she stated, "I think it'll be good because a lot of [my] kids...are pretty solid readers so we can focus a little more on discussions and less on the 'teaching of reading'" (Interview Transcript, 11/10/99).

Resistance. Resistance by the novice teachers to implement peer discussion was not directed at the intervention or at the research project, but indicated that teachers were either not ready or able to make changes to their instruction (Friend & Cook, 1996). This created a personal tension that teachers welcomed, but were not eager to resolve. Mrs. Huizen commented, "I hesitated to agree to this [research project] because it puts pressure on *me*. You know it's easy to say I'm not interested, but I *want* pressure on me, but I don't want to be overwhelmed either.

So, I'm just gonna take it at my own pace and see what happens" (Interview Transcript, 11/10/99).

A common feature was the political tension associated with teaching in a high-achieving district. Both "virgins" and "gurus" noted that their days began well before the children arrived and ended long after the children departed. They commented frequently about not having enough time and worried about the state's new English Language Arts exam given to fourth graders. Mrs. Williams, a veteran third-grade teacher, noted that "teaching just isn't fun anymore" (Interview, 2/10/00), and Mrs. St. James noted, "This time problem is a big, big, big problem. . . . I'm doing less [professional] reading now than I did. And it's not, it's because I'm spending more time on keeping records, on making files, on a lot of stuff that, you know, is very time consuming" (Interview Transcript, 1/6/00).

Although both groups of teachers clearly felt pressured, they differed in how they went about implementing peer discussion while under this pressure. The "virgins" sought ways of easing into the peer discussion experience as indicated by Mrs. Huizen's desire to "take it at my own pace." Initially they resisted all attempts to videotape or observe them implementing peer discussion. Many referred to the fact that they were untenured or preparing for the English Language Arts exam as reasons for why they could not implement peer discussion. The resistance and attempts to locate blame on outside factors is consistent with the initial self-protective stage of the study group's development (Oja, 1989).

In contrast, Mrs. St. James (the "guru"), a fourth-grade teacher whose students would be taking the new state English Language Arts exam, never used the school's imposed exam preparation as an excuse not to engage her students in peer discussion as the "virgins" had done. Instead, she saw it as a vital aspect of her curriculum that could not be eliminated. Mrs. St. James invited us to videotape months before the other teachers. She was eager to critique her own work either by chatting informally with us while the students were discussing, or by viewing videotapes of the discussions in the evening. She was also much more comfortable with the language of peer discussion and was able to identify the titles and authors of books on peer discussion that she had read whereas the "virgins" used the more generic term, "research," to explain why they valued the notion of peer discussion. When pressed to identify what she meant by "research," Mrs. Huizen remarked, "I have no idea (laughs). I knew you were gonna ask me that. I don't know where I read that—somewhere. Somewhere" (Interview Transcript, 11/10/99).

Conversational control. Even though the "virgins" made statements such as, "I would rather children generated their own discussion about their books" (Mrs. Huizen Interview Transcript, 11/10/99), they found it difficult to relinquish the discussion totally to the students. Their interpretation of peer discussion seemed to rely primarily on the teacher's physical absence from the group. To retain control and compensate for their physical absence the teachers designed highly scaffolded situations in which they were not present physically, but semiotically (cf. Almasi, Russell, Guthrie, & Anderson, 1998). They accomplished this semiotic presence by: (a) providing students with teacher-generated open-ended questions to help foster discussion rather than permitting students to set their own discussion agenda and (b) assigning roles to the students while they discussed. Mr. Danson, aware that he was in a novice phase of implementing peer discussion, referred to the assigning of roles to students as "peer discussion for the anal retentive."

Mrs. St. James's response to conversational control was to be analytic about turns and roles within the discussion groups. Fieldnotes from her 11/15/99 interview indicate that she had recently begun doing peer discussion with expository text and noted that she felt like she did too much of the talking. She noticed that the students were answering questions and that it was more answering than discussing. She commented, "It really wasn't discussion. People shared information they found in a book. They all had their own little thing. Maybe I was rushing." The ability to step back and analyze classroom contexts and tasks is one of the attributes of expert teachers.

In addition, Mrs. St. James was willing to release responsibility to the students. She stated in her interview, "I think [the students] know I expect a lot from them. They're expected to work hard and persevere." When asked about a good experience she had with peer discussion, she replied, "When I can just look over here, and they have started without me. They're over here talking about their stuff" (Interview Transcript, 11/15/99).

Interactions Between Individual and Group Development

Mrs. St. James's excitement for implementing peer discussion in the classroom did not translate into leadership in the study group. Instead we found there was an interesting interaction between teachers' individual development and the development of the study group as teachers constructed meaning about the peer discussion instructional approach.

As the group began exhibiting aspects of Oja's (1998) conformist stage characterized by strong leaders and followers, Mrs. St. James, the "guru," did not take on a leadership role. Within the study group, Mrs. St. James engaged in a self-imposed silence whereas the "virgins" were quite active. When asked to problem-solve issues around implementing peer discussion, these teachers discussed information gathered from outside sources (i.e., conferences or inservices) rather than ideas tried with their own students. Fieldnotes of 11/23/99 indicate teachers' uptake on discussion ideas involved "other people's ideas rather than taking up issues of implementation in their classroom." These solutions were superficial to teachers' classroom experiences and did little to address real classroom concerns.

When asked about her participation in the study group, Mrs. St. James shared that she felt the other teachers might feel threatened or feel that she was a "know-it-all." She noted that she was trying to be quiet and felt that the others did not always trust the validity of her comments (Mrs. St. James's Interview Transcript, 1/6/00). We never noticed any behaviors that might indicate that the "virgins" felt this way. On the contrary, Mrs. Browne (a "virgin") asked us whether Mrs. St.

James would be willing to share one of her videotapes with the study group and explain how she started peer discussions in her classroom. When we told Mrs. St. James this, she bashfully agreed to share her videotape, however, she still was sensitive to others' perceptions. Similarly, novice teachers who viewed themselves as "blank slates" looked to researchers to give them information rather than negotiate uncertain ideas they brought to the group. In this way, there was a reflexive component to the development of individual teachers and the study group itself. Advanced study group development involves self-aware, self-critical, and self-reflective teachers who are addressing mutual concerns and problems. This requires teachers to bring experiences and problems to the group. "Virgins" did not have personal experiences or problems to bring to the study group until they were willing to try peer discussion, and Mrs. St. James was unwilling to share her experiences. Therefore, the beginning study group itself provided a limited resource to support teachers' implementation of peer discussion and personal and group development was slow.

Conclusions

This examination of the initial year of the peer discussion study group begins to document the process involved as teachers develop along with their study group. The slow development of both the novice teachers' use of peer discussion in their classrooms and the study group itself is important to understand since we need to know why study groups, that provide such a strong support to teachers over time, begin with such hesitation. Very little research on study groups answers the questions about why such groups begin slowly, but eventually become a powerful context for teacher learning and development. This study begins to understand some of the questions but several limitations remain.

First, her peers characterized only one teacher in the study as a "guru." As more teachers in the group work through the process of trying peer discussion with their students and sharing their experiences and concerns, we will be able to understand the developmental process of implementing peer discussion in classrooms and see if similar expert characteristics emerge. This requires more longitudinal study in which the development of the study group is also examined. Second, most teachers in this study group were at an early point in time of their learning about peer discussion and the differences between the teachers that reflect the early stages of development in comparison to the "guru" teacher were extrapolated rather than traced. Further research is needed to better understand their development over time.

Finally, this is the case of one set of teachers and one study group. The in-depth examination of this group provides insights into one group of teachers; however, these results cannot be generalized. More research is needed that looks at teachers participating in different study groups to better understand general patterns of development in such groups and to understand more general needs of teachers using peer discussion in their literacy instruction.

The results of this study provide evidence that teacher growth, like that of emergent readers, is developmental. Their initial attempts at implementing new instructional methods such as peer discussion involved approximations of more advanced techniques and required a safe environment in which to try them. As we continue to study the growth of these teachers we anticipate a more refined picture of their development, but it is clear that such a picture is critical if we are to understand how teachers make new approaches such as peer discussion part of their classroom instruction.

References

Alvermann, D. E., O'Brien, D. G., & Dillon, D. R. (1990). What teachers do when they say they're having discussions of content area reading assignments: A qualitative analysis. *Reading Research Quarterly, 25,* 296–322.

Almasi, J. F. (1995). The nature of fourth graders' sociocognitive conflicts in peer-led and teacher-led discussions of literature. *Reading Research Quarterly, 30,* 314–351.

Almasi, J. F. (1996). A new view of discussion. In L. B. Gambrell & J. F. Almasi (Eds.), *Lively discussions: Fostering engaged reading* (pp. 2–24). Newark, DE: International Reading Association.

Almasi, J. F., Russell, W. S., Guthrie, J. T., & Anderson, E. (1998, December). *Scaffold to nowhere? Appropriated voice, metatalk, ad personal narrative in third graders' peer discussions of informational text.* Paper presented at the meeting of the National Reading Conference, Austin, TX.

Bogdan, R. C., & Biklen, S. K. (1998). *Qualitative research in education: An introduction to theory and methods* (3rd ed.). Boston: Allyn & Bacon.

Cazden, C. B. (1986). Classroom discourse. In M. C. Wittrock (Ed.), *Handbook of research on teaching* (3rd ed., pp. 432–463). New York: Macmillan.

Cazden, C. (1988). *Classroom discourse: The language of teaching and learning.* Portsmouth, NH: Heinemann.

Clift, R., Veal, M. L., Johnson, M., & Holland, P. (1990). Restructuring teacher education through collaborative action research. *Journal of teacher education, 41*(2), 52–62.

Commeyras, M. (1994). Were Janell and Neesie in the same classroom? Children's questions as the first order of reality in story book discussions. *Language Arts, 71,* 517–523.

Commeyras, M., & DeGroff, L. (1998). Literacy professionals' perspectives on professional development and pedagogy: A national survey. *Reading Research Quarterly, 33,* 434–472.

Commeyras, M., Sherrill, K. A., & Wuenker, K. (1996). Trusting students' questions about literature: Stories across contexts. In L. B. Gambrell & J. F. Almasi (Eds.), *Lively discussions: Fostering children's engagement with text* (pp. 73–896). Newark, DE: International Reading Association.

Doise, W., & Mugny, G. (1984). *The social development of the intellect.* New York: Pergamon.

Eeds, M., & Wells, D. (1989). Grand conversations: An exploration of meaning construction in literature study groups. *Research in the Teaching of English, 23*(10), 4–29.

Englert, C. S., & Tarrant, K. L. (1995). Creating collaborative cultures for educational change. *Remedial and Special Education, 16,* 325ff.

Englert, C. S., Tarrant, K. L., & Rozendal, M. S. (1993). Educational innovations: Achieving long-lasting curricular change through extended collaboration and reflective practice. *Education and Treatment of Children, 16,* 441–473.

Erickson, F. (1986). Qualitative methods in research on teaching. In M. C. Wittrock (Ed.), *Handbook of research on teaching* (3rd ed., pp. 119–161). New York: Macmillan.

Friend, M., & Cook, L. (1996). *Interactions: Collaboration skills for school professionals* (2nd ed.). White Plains, NY: Longman.

Fullan, M. G. (1991). *The new meaning of educational change.* NY: Teachers College Press.

Gilles, C., Dickinson, J., McBride, C., & Vandover, M. (1994). Discussing our questions and questioning our discussions: Growing into literature study. *Language Arts, 71,* 499–508.

Goatley, V. J., Brock, C. H., & Raphael, T. E. (1995). Diverse learners participating in regular education "Book Clubs." *Reading Research Quarterly, 30,* 352–395.

Hamilton, M., & Richardson, V. (1995). Effects of the culture in two schools on the process and outcomes of staff development. *Elementary School Journal, 95,* 367–385.

Hargreaves, A. (1994). *Changing teachers, changing times: teachers' work and culture in the postmodern age.* New York: Teachers College Press.

Laird, J., Crawford, K. M., Ferguson, M., Kauffman, G., Schroeder, J., & Short, K. (1994). Teachers as collaborators for an inquiry-based curriculum. *Teacher Research, 1,* 111–121.

Lave, J. (1996). Teaching, as learning, in practice. *Mind, Culture, and Activity, 3*(3), 149–164.

Leal, D. (1992). The nature of talk about three types of text during peer group discussions. *Journal of Reading Behavior, 24,* 313–338.

Little, J. W. (1982). Norms of collegiality and experimentation: Workplace conditions of school success. *American Educational Research Journal, 19,* 325–340.

Loevinger, J. (1976). *Ego development: Conceptions and theories.* San Francisco: Jossey-Bass.

Mannheim, B., & Tedlock, D. (1995). Introduction. In D. Tedlock & B. Mannheim (Eds.), *The dialogic emergence of culture* (pp. 1–32). Urbana: University of Illinois Press.

Many, J. E., & Wiseman, D. L. (1992). The effect of teaching approach on third-grade students' response to literature. *Journal of Reading Behavior, 24,* 265–287.

Martinez, M., Roser, N. L., Hoffman, J. V., & Battle, J. (1992). Fostering better book discussions through response logs and a response framework: A case of description. In C. K. Kinzer & D. J. Leu (Eds.), *Literacy research, theory, and practice: Views from many perspectives.* Forty-first yearbook of the National Reading Conference (pp. 303–311). Chicago: National Reading Conference.

McGee, L. (1992). An exploration of meaning construction in first graders' grand conversations. In C. K. Kinzer & D. J. Leu (Eds.), *Literacy research, theory, and practice: Views from many perspectives.* Forty-first yearbook of the National Reading Conference (pp. 177–186). Chicago: National Reading Conference.

McMahon, S. I. (1996). Student discussions about texts: Why student-led groups are important. In L. B. Gambrell & J. F. Almasi (Eds.), *Lively discussions: Creating elementary classrooms that foster engaged reading* (pp. 224–247). Newark, DE: International Reading Association.

McMahon, S. I., & Goatley, V. J. (1995). Fifth graders helping peers discuss texts in student-led groups. *Journal of Educational Research, 89*(1), 23–35.

Merriam, S. B. (1998). *Qualitative research and case study applications in education.* San Francisco: Jossey-Bass.

Oja, S. N. (1989). *Collaborative action research: A developmental approach.* London: Falmer.

Richardson, V., & Anders, P. (1994). A theory of change. In V. Richardson (Ed.), *Teacher change and the staff development process: A case in reading instruction* (pp. 199–216). New York: Teachers College Press.

Rogoff, B. (1990). *Apprenticeship in thinking: Cognitive development in social context.* New York: Oxford University Press.

Roller, C. M., & Beed, P. L. (1994). Sometimes the conversations were grand, and sometimes . . . . *Language Arts, 71,* 509–515.

Rozendal, M. S. (1996). *The development and dynamics of intersubjectivity: A sociocultural examination of a beginning teacher study group.* Unpublished doctoral dissertation, Michigan State University, East Lansing.

Santa Barbara Classroom Discourse Group. (1992). Constructing literacy in classrooms: Literate action as social accomplishment. In H. Marshall (Ed.), *Redefining learning: Roots of educational restructuring.* Norwood, NJ: Ablex.

Seidman, I. (1998). *Interviewing as qualitative research: A guide for researchers in education and the social sciences* (2nd ed.). New York: Teachers College Press.

Short, K. G., Crawford, K., Kahn, L., Kaser, S., Klassen, C., & Sherman, P. (1992). Teacher study groups: Exploring literacy issues through collaborative dialogue. In C. K. Kinzer & D. J. Leu (Eds.), *Literacy research, theory, and practice: Views from many perspectives.* Forty-first yearbook of the National Reading Conference (pp. 367–377). Chicago: National Reading Conference.

Slavin, R. E. (1990). *Cooperative learning: Theory, research, and practice.* Englewood Cliffs, NJ: Prentice-Hall.

Sparks, G. M. (1988). Teachers' attitudes toward change and subsequent improvements in classroom teaching. *Journal of Educational Psychology, 80*(1), 111–117.

Spradley, J. P. (1980). *Participant observation.* Orlando, FL: Harcourt Brace Jovanovich.

Valentino, L. R. (1998). *Teacher study groups: A case study of teacher groups and their influence on teachers' attitudes toward student achievement and social justice issues.* Unpublished doctoral dissertation, University of California at Los Angeles.

Vygotsky, L. S. (1978). *Mind in society: The development of higher psychological processes.* Cambridge, MA: Harvard University Press.

Wells, G. (1993). Reevaluating the IRF sequence: A proposal for the articulation of theories of activity and discourse for the analysis of teaching and learning. *Linguistics and Education, 5,* 1–37.

Wells, G., & Chang-Wells, G. L. (1992). *Constructing knowledge together: classrooms as centers of inquiry and literacy.* Portsmouth, NH: Heinemann.

Successful Middle School Reading Intervention: Negotiated Strategies and Individual Choice

Brenda A. Shearer
University of Wisconsin, Oshkosh

Martha Rapp Ruddell
Sonoma State University

Mary Ellen Vogt
California State University, Long Beach

The purpose of this investigation was to examine the effects of a year-long reading intervention program with 17 middle school students experiencing difficulties in literacy development. As we sought to establish an effective model of intervention we became convinced that traditional long-term pullout models of literacy intervention not only denied struggling readers access to a rich core curriculum, but that the positive effects from these programs were small at best, and often nonexistent (Allington & Walmsley, 1995). Instead, we were guided by theory that views language and literacy development as a constructive, social process (Rosenblatt, 1978, Vygotsky, 1986) in which learners negotiate meaning through transactions with text and with each other. We decided to investigate the effects of an intensive, year-long middle school intervention model that incorporated strategy instruction within a student-led, modified reciprocal teaching format (Palinscar & Brown, 1984).

Theoretical Background and Rationale

In a study of struggling middle school readers, Vogt (1997) found that adolescents who struggled with literacy had experienced difficulty with reading since the beginning of their schooling, supporting findings of earlier investigators such as Kos (1991) and Meek (1983). Further, Vogt found that many of the adolescents adopted complex strategies to avoid reading aloud in class and often acted out or withdrew. Typically, these students had poor grades, low self-esteem, limited phonics skills, and little interest in school or extracurricular activities. Because most professed to have no problems with literacy, they had little hope of improving their reading ability and profoundly disliked reading.

Consistent with the findings of Stanovich (1986), Vogt (1989) also discovered a number of incongruities between both preservice and inservice teachers' attitudes and practices relative to high and low achievers. Higher functioning stu-

National Reading Conference Yearbook, 50, pp. 558–571.

dents spent more classroom time engaged in silent versus oral reading. They were provided with more instructional time, more opportunities to engage in higher levels of thinking and strategic learning, and more independent research and synthesis projects. Teachers asked these students questions requiring higher levels of thinking followed by more wait time. Such discrepancies in opportunity and instruction may indeed help to explain the "Matthew Effect," an assertion by Stanovich (1986) that relative to literacy development, "The rich get richer, and the poor get poorer."

Several short-term, intensive reading intervention models (12–16 weeks) for younger students have shown considerable promise. The goal of these programs was to rapidly accelerate achievement and return children to their regular classrooms (Pikulski, 1994; Taylor, Short, Frye, & Shearer, 1992). There are, however, few replicable models for middle school students (Cooper, 1999). Although there is no set of instructional techniques that is effective all of the time for all students, Pikulski (1994) uncovered a number of common characteristics in effective intervention for young children. Successful models shared the belief that reading for meaning was the primary goal. Such programs provided intervention with small pupil-to-teacher ratios in sessions that were frequent, regular, of sufficient duration, and fast-paced. Writing was used to facilitate reading.

A growing body of evidence supports the instruction of strategic reasoning for reading delayed adolescents (Anderson, Chan, & Henne, 1995; Cooper, 1999). For example, incorporating elements of reciprocal teaching in reading instruction with struggling readers has been shown to enable students to build their repertoire of strategies and to use those strategies in increasingly flexible ways (Palinscar & Brown, 1984; Vogt, 1998). In the reciprocal teaching model, students read passages paragraph by paragraph or in designated chunks. During reading, students support one another in learning and developing proficiency in four basic strategies associated with comprehension: predicting, questioning, clarifying word meanings and ideas, and summarizing. As students progress through sections of text, the teacher provides individualized guidance and feedback through modeling, coaching, and explaining. Other students in the group are encouraged to react to their peers by adding comments, clarifications, or questions. Gradually, the responsibility for instruction shifts to the students, with the teacher observing and providing needed guidance. As students gain understanding of the unique processing of their peers, discussions become more interactive, focusing on strategy application.

Researchers and practitioners agree that when students are provided with explicit instruction and modeling in effective group processes (Au, 1993) and given specific tasks and guidelines, student-led discussions can be both productive and powerful. Reading class, then, becomes what Patterson, Cotten, Kimball-Lopez, Pavonetti, and VanHorn (1998) describe as a complex adaptive system in which meaning-making systems emerging in a classroom may at times include only students, with the teacher often outside the system boundaries. It is no surprise, given the litany of ways instruction is differentiated for high- and low-achieving students, that the majority of students in traditional remedial reading programs receive little opportunity for the kinds of interaction advocated by these researchers.

Another important discovery is that although struggling middle school readers are able to identify CVC (consonant, vowel, consonant) words, many experience difficulty identifying polysyllabic words (Shefelbine, 1995; Vogt, 1998). These students often lack the ability to distinguish morphemic elements or to recognize logical syllabic units. However, Shefelbine's method of teaching older students to identify polysyllabic words suggests that students can acquire this ability rapidly.

Research confirms that lower-achieving students possess more limited vocabularies than high-achieving students, and that knowledge of word meanings and the ability to use language effectively have a marked impact on academic success and literacy development (Graves, 2000). Educators recognize the importance of helping struggling readers develop self-learning systems for acquiring new vocabulary. The positive effects of approaches such as Vocabulary Self-Collection (VSS) (Haggard, 1982; Ruddell, 2000), an instructional method in which students nominate a list of words to study and engage in interactive, constructivist, social processes to support word learning, confirm the efficacy of using social interactions to facilitate vocabulary acquisition.

Recent research examining the effects of social interactions on vocabulary acquisition have yielded the following conclusions: (a) High levels of student interaction in conjunction with vocabulary study extended teacher-student discussions and were more effective than definition-only study (Stahl & Vancil, 1986); (b) students who were allowed to choose their own words for study chose words of "significant difficulty," but words not as domain specific as teacher-selected words (Fisher, Blachowicz, Costa, & Pozzi, 1992); (c) students engaged in self-collection and interactive instruction assumed ownership of learning and enjoyed being in a position of self-determination (Ruddell & Shearer, 1999); and (d) students contributed more of their own background knowledge to discussion and remembered words longer when learning words of their choice.

Elements within the intervention that we used reflected the knowledge of what works in successful models of intervention (Pikulski, 1994). These elements included instructional practices that advocated the primacy of meaning while providing direct multisyllabic word-identification strategies in and out of context. Further, the model was designed to move quickly into at-grade-level material, involve ownership by students and parents, and include self-assessment and goal-setting (Vogt, 1998). VSS was an integral component of the intervention because of its demonstrated ability to support students' growth as independent word learners with heightened word awareness (Haggard, 1982; Ruddell, 2000). Because research confirms the power of journal writing to enable students to keep running accounts of their progress and knowledge (Zinsser, 1988) and to explore ideas and issues in relationship to what they know and what they are learning, writing was imbedded in the intervention through journaling. Reading logs were included as an additional means for students to record and assess their reading over the school year.

Method

Context of the Study

The middle school intervention study was conducted with students in a small Midwestern, rural community throughout the 1998–99 school year. All 17 participants were Caucasian, representative of the predominately white, middle-class culture of the community. The population of seventh- and eighth-grade students in the district typically includes approximately 130 students at each grade level. Students in both seventh and eighth grades receive literacy instruction in two separate 43-minute developmental reading and language arts classes, with approximately 20–25 students per class. Although Title I services are available in the elementary school (Grades K–4), no services are available for middle and secondary students who do not qualify for special education services. At the beginning of the 1998–99 school year, a university reading professor was hired by the superintendent to design, implement, and teach a middle school intervention program during the last three 43-minute class periods, 5 days a week.

Participants

Students were selected through a two-tier process. At the beginning of the school year, teachers in reading and language arts were asked to identify students from the previous year whose reading appeared to be significantly delayed relative to their peers. All forty students nominated by their teachers were individually tested using the Woodcock-Johnson Psycho-Educational Battery. An informal reading inventory and an informal self-evaluative interview were used to provide more specific insight into individual reading processes for purposes of instruction. Eleven eighth-grade students and six seventh-grade students who were reading at least 2 years below grade level (on either word-identification or comprehension subtests of the Woodcock-Johnson PEB) at the beginning of the school year were identified and selected to participate in the program. Each of the three small groups of middle school students (one group of six eighth graders, one group of five eighth graders, and one group of six seventh graders) received 43 minutes of daily reading intervention in place of their regular developmental reading class and an additional 20 minutes of daily independent reading practice outside of the classroom.

Components of the Model

Ten Minutes of Daily Practice in Multisyllabic Word Analysis

Because 15 out of the 17 students were able to decode CVC words but had difficulty analyzing and identifying polysyllabic words, the early weeks of the program included 10 minutes of daily instruction and practice in word-chunking techniques, adopting the methods developed by Shefelbine (1995) and used in the Read-2-Succeed model (Vogt, 1998). Shefelbine's model begins by teaching students a system to pronounce one-syllable nonsense words following the CV or CVC pattern. The rules students are to memorize and state are, "One vowel at the end is long," and "One vowel not at the end is short." Students practice memorizing and using these rules and applying them to nonsense chunks such as the following: *su, suf, uf* or *ab, fa, fab,* moving rapidly back and forth within each three letter combination. It is important to note that these synthetic exercises are used only the first few days of the year. As soon as students were able to apply these rules flexibly, they began to use chunking procedures on specific word parts, such as *ment, anti, der, er, -ible, -able, mid,* and on polysyllabic words, such as, *digestible, reinforcement, instructionally, standardization, distribution,* and *consultation.* From the beginning, our model supported the application of these chunking procedures in classroom reading sessions. After approximately 6 weeks, our intervention model eliminated the 10-minute word drills and applied Shefelbine's procedures only during interactions with connected text. The 10 minutes previously allocated to out-of-context word chunking was then used for journaling and VSS discussions. The word-identification strategies were then incorporated in the reciprocal teaching model as another means to negotiate through text. Again, students became facilitators, models, and coaches for one another. Often, if a student was struggling to chunk a work in context, a group member, who had not been prompted by the teacher to do so, approached the board and demonstrated how to chunk the word.

Thirty-three Minutes of Peer-Mediated Reciprocal Teaching Techniques

Strategies identified by researchers as those consistently used by proficient readers: predicting, summarizing, clarifying, and questioning, were explicitly introduced, modeled, and reinforced entirely within the context of connected text. In addition to the Reciprocal Teaching strategies, students were encouraged to share personal connections and reactions to ideas and events in the text.

During the first several months, students were given Reciprocal Teaching Cue Cards to facilitate discussion. The cards were adapted from card prompts developed by teacher Sue Mowrey in 1991. Students were required to select a card and model the strategy it described during the discussion of the paragraph or chunk of text assigned. After each student performed the task on the cueing card, the other students were encouraged to add to the discussion by helping, coaching, modeling, teaching, and offering their own questions related to the strategy.

The cue cards contained the following role prompts:

1. Predictors: "I wonder ____." "I predict ____."
2. Questioners: "I'm curious about ____." "I wonder ____." "Who? What? When? Where? Why? How?"
3. Clarifiers: "This is confusing." "I need to (reread, slow down, look at the pictures, chunk word parts, etc.)." "I'm thinking the word might be ____ because ____." "What I'm thinking is ____, but ____." "The problem is ____." "This doesn't make sense. I need to ____."
4. Summarizers: "In my own words, so far, this is about ____ ." "The main

point is ____." "Overall, this is about ____." "I think the author is telling us ____." "So far, this has happened ____."

Initially, the teacher and the students took turns serving as group leader, assigning roles, and monitoring responses. Gradually, as students became comfortable with the elements of reciprocal teaching, they assumed responsibility for vocabulary and word-identification instruction, and negotiation of meaning. The student who led the group determined the discussion format and decided whether or not cueing cards and/or journaling would be used. Although the basic structure followed the reciprocal teaching model, after several months students no longer relied on the strategy cueing cards and rapidly switched roles, acting as both tutor and tutee within the same lesson. The cueing model was, however, available on a wall chart for referral.

Writing was often used in conjunction with reading. Two to three times a week, students recorded their summaries, questions, clarifications, predictions, and personal reactions as they read and used the notes in discussion. Among the unusual aspects of the program was the selection of at-or-above grade-level reading material for instruction. As actual grade-level content area text pieces, such as Social Studies reading assignments, were incorporated in the intervention, it became apparent that intervention must include more challenging material. These struggling readers needed to progress rapidly to at-or-above grade-level materials if they were to make the gains necessary for academic success. To accomplish this goal, a wide variety of expository text material in a number of content areas, difficult narrative selections (such as Edgar Allen Poe's short story, *The Black Cat*), short mysteries, and news articles were included in the intervention. Often several choices were made available to the group and students would select the next piece for the group to read.

Periodic Self-Analysis and Goal-Setting

Journaling, peer interaction, individual conferences with the teacher during reading, and informal surveys helped students reflect on and identify their metacognitive processing, their strengths and weakness, and their individual goals. They identified the specific processes they would employ to meet each goal and engaged in self-evaluation of progress through periodic discussions with the teacher.

The Vocabulary Self-Collection Strategy

To foster long-term acquisition and development of vocabulary, each student selected one word per week (Mondays) to contribute to the class list. These included words they wanted to learn, were important to them, or for which they had interest or curiosity. Students then told: (a) where they found each word, (b) what they thought it meant, and (c) why they thought it was important for the group to know. The teacher also selected a word and modeled the three steps. Both students and teacher entered the group's words in their journals. This list became the class spelling and vocabulary list for the week. Vocabulary study during the week included discussions to clarify words and to use and record meaningful sentences for each. Students were tested on their ability to spell each word correctly on Fridays. They were also asked to write an explanation of its meaning, and demonstrate the ability to use it meaningfully in writing. The group spent up to 10 minutes daily (during the time previously devoted to isolated word chunking) focusing on one or two of the chosen words and engaging in a variety of activities, including discussions that engaged students in: (a) using the words in meaningful ways, (b) connecting the words with individual experience, and (c) associating them with content concepts. Often, group mapping and webbing were used to extend and explore the concepts. Both teacher and students kept learning and reflective journals. Every 3 weeks students were tested on a random selection of five words from the lists their class developed.

Independent Reading

Because they were reading extremely challenging text during classroom sessions, students were also required to read at the independent level for an additional 20 minutes daily outside of school to promote fluency and interest in recreational reading. Students were instructed that such reading was not to include homework or assignments from programs such as Confirmation classes, but rather from books or magazines that were of interest to them. Parents, students, and the teacher monitored the reading through a daily reporting system. The daily recording sheets required a full parent signature verifying the number of minutes and the material read. The teacher also kept a daily log verified by a family member. Student logs reflected selections from sporting, hunting, and teen-directed magazines, as well as romance and adventure novels, biographies of Tiger Woods and other sports heroes, inspirational books, and poetry. As students entered the classroom and submitted their logs, they and the teacher informally shared information about their independent reading with the group. This at-home aspect of the intervention added an additional 20 minutes daily to the 43-minute in-school intervention, in effect, boosting the time spent on focused literacy engagement to over an hour per day.

Data Sources

Woodcock-Johnson Psycho-Educational Battery—Revised

Alternate forms of the Woodcock-Johnson Psycho-Educational Battery were used pre and post treatment to assess achievement in Word Identification and Passage Comprehension. A follow-up test was administered to all 17 participants in May 2000, 1 year after the completion of intervention, to ascertain whether gains attributed to the intervention program had been sustained.

VSS Scores and Scores on Weekly Language Arts Spelling Tests

End-of-week and 3-week-interval VSS test results were analyzed to determine short and long-term retention of word meanings and spellings. Weekly VSS test scores (based on percent correct) over a 9-week period were recorded and compared to spelling test scores (percentages) during the same 9-week period from the commercially prepared spelling program used in the students' language arts classes.

VSS Word List Selections

Lists of the words selected each week were examined to determine the progression of difficulty in words selected, the contexts in which the words occurred, the relationship of the words to content areas and to personal experience, and the reasons for word selections.

Journal Entries

Each week, the students and their teachers recorded in their journals reflections related to any aspect of the VSS. Journal entries of both teacher and students were analyzed to determine students' reactions to the VSS instructional approach, their attitudes toward vocabulary learning, and their reflections on themselves as learners.

Informal Data Used for Instructional Planning

Several informal measures provided insight into students' instructional needs and progress. An informal reading inventory was administered to students at the beginning of the school year to help the teacher understand individual reading behaviors. Informal assessment occurred daily, through teacher observation within the context of the instruction. The group often discussed ways to improve their interactions. Periodically, the teacher met with individual students to engage them in self-assessment and to set goals. These informal data sources were used to plan and adjust instruction.

Results

Woodcock-Johnson Psycho-Educational Battery—Revised

Scores on the Woodcock Johnson Psycho-Educational Battery—Revised (Table 1) revealed an average gain of 5.3 years in Word Identification and 4.4 years in Comprehension for the eleven students in Grade 8, and an average gain of 4.8 years in Word Identification and 4.1 years in Comprehension for those in Grade 7. Students were retested a year after the treatment ended to find out of if the gains held. As Table 1 indicates, scores on Passage Comprehension and Word Identification follow-up tests for both seventh- and eighth-grade intervention students remained relatively stable. Wilcoxson T test was used to compare treatment gain scores with those obtained in follow-up testing. The data revealed no significant differences in scores on Word Identification or Passage Comprehension for either group of students, indicating that the gains from the treatment persisted.

Comparison of VSS Scores and Scores on Weekly Language Arts Spelling Tests

A 9-week comparison of means of participants' scores (based on percent correct) on weekly spelling tests in Language Arts class and scores on their weekly VSS spelling tests confirmed that students performed significantly better on self-selected VSS lists than on the teacher-selected commercial program ($N=17$, $M=-.178$, $SD=.126$, $P=0.000$). A test of skewedness was applied to the two sets of percentage scores to verify the normality of distribution, a potential problem with small sample size and tests of unequal item numbers. The skewedness (-.924) was less than twice the standard error of measurement (.550). Thus, the distribution can be considered normal. In addition, periodic testing of randomly selected VSS words revealed that students scored as well on review tests as they did on their weekly tests.

Table 1

Pre- and Post-Treatment Grade-Level Means on the Woodcock-Johnson Psycho-Educational Battery—Revised Word-Identification and Passage-Comprehension Subtests

	M	Range	*SD*	*SE*
Grade 8 *N*=11				
Word ID Pretest*	6.2	4.0–10.4	1.799	0.542
Word ID Posttest**	11.5 (+5.3)	8.9–16.9	2.434	0.734
Word ID 1 yr. Follow-up***	11.7 (+0.2)	9.2–16.8	2.153	0.649
Comprehension Pretest*	6.4	4.4–8.1	1.168	0.352
Comprehension Posttest**	10.8 (+4.4)	9.0–13.2	1.379	0.416
Comprehension Follow-up***	11.2 (+0.4)	10.0–13.6	1.130	0.341
Grade 7 *N*=6				
Word ID Pretest⁺	3.9	3.3–4.6	0.459	0.188
Word ID Posttest⁺⁺	8.7 (+4.2)	7.1–11.4	1.509	0.616
Word ID 1 yr. Follow-up⁺⁺⁺	9.6 (+0.9)	6.7–10.7	1.483	0.606
Comprehension Pretest⁺	5.4	4.0–7.3	1.219	0.498
Comprehension Posttest⁺⁺	9.5 (+4.1)	9.0–10.9	0.789	0.322
Comprehension Follow-up⁺⁺⁺	10.3 (+0.7)	9.2–11.0	0.791	0.323

*Actual grade level = 8.1. **Actual grade level = 8.9. ***Actual grade level = 9.9.
⁺Actual grade level = 7.1. ⁺⁺Actual grade level = 7.9. ⁺⁺⁺Actual grade level = 8.9.

Analysis of Word Selection

As shown in Table 2, students chose difficult words. A sampling of words from Week 5 included content area words such as *geothermal* and *quadrilateral,* as well as more general words such as *conceive, mundane,* and *tedious.* When Dole, Sloan, and Trathen (1995) used VSS as a single text comprehension strategy, they found that teacher selected words improved comprehension more than student selected words. They attributed this to the fact that students in their study selected words from the piece primarily because they were unknown while teachers selected words more central to understanding the text. However, we discovered that when VSS is used in a comprehensive spelling/vocabulary program to help students become independent, enthusiastic word learners, and word-selection processes are modeled and discussed, student choices reflect a much broader set of criteria. In examining the sources of the words selected, it became apparent that students found words in school, at home, in music, from magazines and conversations, and that a number were key content area concepts. Their remarks

Table 2

Examples of Students' VSS Word Entries from Week 5

Word	Where the Word Was Found	Rationale for Selecting the Word
oblivious	In the mysteries we're reading.	It's an interesting real-life word. It has the *ious* pattern. Sometimes we all act that way.
tedious	In our reading book about Washington, D.C.	It has a cool meaning; we should know what it means.
aisle	In the Scholastic Book order.	It has a tricky spelling.
dupe	My Mom used it talking about being tricked.	I asked her what it meant. It's interesting and useful.
geothermal	In Science World magazine.	It's going to be really important in the future. We're looking to use it instead of fossil fuel.
determination	My Mom said I needed to have it to ride my horse.	Because it's something everybody needs.
conceive	In Science World magazine.	I heard it before. It's tricky to spell.
mundane	In the Shania Twain song, "Honey I'm Home." She's describing her job.	No one could tell me what it meant, so I looked it up. School's like that sometime.
lacquer	Dad told me to use lacquer for my LSAV in Tech. Ed.	It's unusual. When I saw how it's spelled. I couldn't believe my eyes.

Other words from Week 5: significant, quadrilateral, international, recapitulate, distribution, pinnacle, cantaloupe, hoarse, electronics, impossible, abbreviate.

also reflected a curiosity and word awareness not present at the beginning of the program. Many engaged family members and friends in discussions of word meanings and made use of references, such as the dictionary. Several students made highly personal connections to words they selected.

VSS Journal Entries

As 69 student journal entries reacting to VSS were examined and analyzed, patterns of responses emerged. Statements were classified into six categories: noticing, choosing, using metacognition, valuing, learning, and transforming. Two researchers classified each statement independently, using a single-code, forced-choice model. Discussion was used to reach consensus on their final categorization. Explanations of the categories and sample student responses for each are as follows:

1. *Noticing: What makes a word good?* In this category, students described how they chose the words used for VSS. One student wrote, "I pick a word that is hard to spell and has a tricky definition—that's not too difficult and not too easy and has more than one meaning."

2. *Choosing: What do I like about choice?* One student responded, "I think we should keep on being able to pick our own words because then we will want to study them more efficiently. If we get something handed or picked out by a teacher, we don't want to study something we don't like."

3. *Using Metacognition: What are my strategies?* In this category, student journal entries described the strategies they used to learn new words. A typical response includes the following, "I have been learning more and asking more about what the word is. If I find a word I don't know what it means, I ask for help or I look it up in the dictionary."

4. *Valuing: Why is this important?* Students gave highly personal reasons why VSS was important to them. For example, one student, who struggled with spelling on all of his seventh-grade written assignments, valued the way VSS word analysis helped him meet what he perceived to be the spelling expectations of his Middle School content area teachers. "All that matters is if we can spell or not. All I want is to spell right."

5. *Learning: How am I improving?* Journal entries in this category included self-evaluation. "I never thought that I could ever do better in reading. Now I can find the syllables and sound them out."

6. *Transforming: How am I changing the way in which I see the world?* Student journals reflected high levels of word awareness and curiosity about unknown words. "I hear words from all over the place. I mean there are millions of words just sitting out there I don't know." "I heard three of our words used this week. Mr. D used the words *mortal* and *intriguing* to describe the Civil War. My pastor used *aerobic* when I was at Confirmation last night."

These coded journal entries revealed: (a) Students contributed their background knowledge to discussion and remembered words longer, (b) students reported noticeable transfer to general reading and writing ability, (c) students greatly enhanced their ability to acquire vocabulary as self-learners, and (d) students were more word aware and intrinsically interested in vocabulary acquisition.

Discussion

The importance of this study lies in its contribution to the knowledge about effective middle school intervention. A variety of data sources confirm that this intervention resulted in average gains of over 4 years in reading for the seventh- and eighth-grade student participants. Moreover, follow-up testing 1 year later reveals that these sizable gains are lasting.

This program builds on previous studies that emphasize student ownership (Anderson et al., 1995). Clearly, the students in this study became the complex adaptive system Patterson et al. (1998) describe. Students' peer coaching responses, knowledge of their own metacognition, ability to pin-point the needs of their peers and to provide the necessary scaffolding at the teachable moment all demonstrate that teachers need not fear allowing students to assume ownership of their learning.

Contrary to the notion that low-achieving students lack motivation and interest in reading, all seventeen students in this study consistently fulfilled their 20-minute at-home reading obligation, rarely failing to return their signed logs, and often reading beyond the time required. They engaged in animated discussions of their reading, particularly with students who shared their interests. The success of this aspect of the intervention reflected a shared commitment among students, parents, and teacher.

The rate at which these students acquired the ability to identify polysyllabic words both in and out of context was one of the unanticipated outcomes of the study. By adapting Shefelbine's methods to connected text, students were able to abandon the synthetic approach after a brief period. Although student responses during reciprocal teaching, VSS, and in journal writing strongly suggest transfer of learning, the exact nature of this process requires further investigation.

Among the most important aspects of this study was VSS and its powerful and lasting impact on comprehension, word awareness, and facilitation of independent vocabulary acquisition. Word lists demonstrate that when given the opportunity to select their own words, students will consistently choose important, challenging, interesting words. In addition, comparative test scores reveal that they will devote more effort to learning self-selected words than to the traditional commercial word lists imposed on them.

Several aspects of this middle school intervention model warrant further investigation. There is a need to implement similar models in a variety of settings and with greater numbers of students. Systematic data collection including transcripts will yield valuable insight into the dynamics of student -led literacy intervention as students move beyond the highly structured reciprocal teaching model. Applying and extending the model in an integrated language arts block would enable investigators to increase and evaluate the role of writing in more meaningful ways. An investigation of the impact of non-traditional roles for students and teachers relative to the intervention process and outcomes would also be of interest. Finally, the apparent positive effects of VSS to increase word awareness of low-achieving students and its impact on their literacy achievement merit further research attention. This study suggests great promise and direction for further investigation of these components and their apparent ability to produce rapid and sizable gains in reading proficiency for struggling middle school students.

References

Allington, R., & Walmsley, S. (Eds.). (1995). *No quick fix: Rethinking literacy programs in America's elementary schools.* Newark, DE: International Reading Association.

Anderson, V., Chan, C., & Henne, R. (1995). The effects of strategy instruction on the literacy models and performance of reading and writing delayed middle school students. In K. A. Hinchman, D. J. Leu, & C. K. Kinzer (Eds.), *Perspectives on literacy research and practice.* Forty-fourth yearbook of the National Reading Conference (pp. 180–196). Chicago: National Reading Conference.

Au, K. H. (1993). *Literacy instruction in multi-cultural settings.* New York: Harcourt Brace Javanovich.

Cooper, J. D. (1999). *Project Success: An intervention model for grades 3–6.* Paper presented at the meeting of the Research Institute of the California Reading Association, Long Beach, CA.

Dole, J. A., Sloan, C., & Trathen, W. (1995). Teaching vocabulary within the context of literature. *Journal of Reading, 38,* 452–461.

Fisher, P. J. L., Blachowicz, C. L. Z., Costa, M., & Pozzi, L. (1992, December). *Vocabulary teaching and learning in middle school cooperative literature study groups.* Paper presented at the meeting of the National Reading Conference, San Antonio, TX.

Graves, M. F.(2000). Vocabulary program to complement and bolster a middle-grade comprehension program. In B. M. Taylor, M. F. Graves, & P. Van den Broek (Eds.), *Reading for meaning: Fostering comprehension in the middle grades* (pp. 116–135). New York: Teachers College Press.

Haggard, M. (1982). The Vocabulary Self-Collection Strategy: Using student interest and word knowledge to enhance vocabulary growth. *Journal of Reading, 27,* 203–207.

Kos, R. (1991). Persistence of reading difficulties: The voices of four middle school students. *American Educational Research Journal, 28,* 875–895.

Meek, M. (1983). *Achieving literacy: Longitudinal studies of adolescents learning to read.* London: Routledge & Kegan Paul.

Palinscar, A. M., & Brown, A. (1984). Reciprocal teaching of comprehension fostering and monitoring activities. *Cognition and Instruction, 1,* 117–175.

Patterson, L., Cotten, C., Pavonetti, L., Kimball-Lopez, K., & VanHorn L. (1998). The shared "ah-ha experience": Literature conversations and self-organizing complex adaptive systems. In T. Shanahan & F. V. Rodrigeuez-Brown (Eds.), *National Reading Conference Yearbook, 48* (pp. 143–156). Chicago: National Reading Conference.

Pikulski, J. J. (1994). Preventing reading failure: A review of five effective programs. *Reading Teacher, 48,* 30–39.

Rosenblatt, L. M. (1978). *The reader, the text, the poem: The transactional theory of literary work.* Carbondale: Southern Illinois University Press.

Ruddell, M. R. (2000). *Teaching content reading and writing* (3rd ed.) New York: Wiley.

Ruddell, M. R., & Shearer, B.A. (1999, December). *The vocabulary self-collection strategy*

(VSS) in a middle school reading intervention program. Paper presented at the meeting of the National Reading Conference, Orlando, FL.

Shefelbine, J. (1995). *Syllabic unit approach.* Paper presented at the meeting of the Asilomar Regional Reading Conference, Monterey, CA.

Stahl, S. A., & Vancil, S. J. (1986). Discussion is what makes semantic maps work in vocabulary instruction. *Reading teacher, 40,* 62–67.

Stanovich, K. (1986). Matthew effects in reading: Some consequences of individual differences in the acquisition of reading. *Reading Research Quarterly, 21,* 360–407.

Taylor, B. M., Short, R. A., Frye, B. J., & Shearer, B. A. (1992). Classroom teachers prevent reading failure in low achieving first grade students. *Reading Teacher, 45,* 941–945.

Vogt, M. E. (1989). *The congruence between preservice teachers' and inservice teachers' attitudes and practices toward high and low achievers.* Unpublished doctoral dissertation, University of California, Berkeley.

Vogt, M. E. (1997). *Intervention strategies for intermediate and middle school students: Three models (that appear) to work.* Paper presented at the meeting of the Research Institute of the California Reading Association, Anaheim, CA.

Vogt, M. E. (1998). *Read-2-Succeed: an intervention model for middle school students.* Paper presented at the meeting of the Research Institute of the California Reading Association, Santa Barbara, CA.

Vygotsky, L. (1986). *Thought and language.* Cambridge, MA: MIT Press.

Woodcock, R. W., & Johnson, M. B. (1989, 1990). *Woodcock-Johnson Psycho-Educational Battery-Revised.* Allen, TX: DLM Teaching Resources.

Zinsser, W. (1988). *Writing to learn.* New York: Harper & Row.

Using E-Mail to Facilitate Dialogue Between High School Students and Preservice English Methods Students

B. Joyce Stallworth
University of Alabama

English classrooms must be alive, inclusive, authentic, and meaningful for all students (Gallo, 1992); therefore, English teachers must make wise decisions based on students' interests, needs, and experiences. Such decisions can increase the likelihood that students will find some pleasure and enjoyment in reading and will want to read more. Operating from this perspective, a high school English teacher, her intern, and a teacher educator designed a project that included e-mail as one vehicle for engaging high school students and preservice English teachers in purposeful dialogue about *Ironman* (Crutcher, 1995), a contemporary young adult novel. The overarching purpose of the project was to involve preservice teachers and 10th-grade students in an active process of reading, writing, and talking about quality literature. E-mail was one tool used to facilitate engagement between the students and preservice teachers.

With the guidance of Anita, the inservice teacher, and Helen, the teacher intern, 11 preservice English teachers and I participated in conversations via e-mail and activities during class related to *Ironman* (names of all participants mentioned are pseudonyms). The novel was new to Anita, all of her students, and 9 of the preservice teachers. Helen and I had studied the novel in a young adult literature course. Although most of the high school students were adept at using e-mail, they had never participated in purposeful dialogue with university students. Therefore, studying the process and the outcomes was a way to investigate a different use of e-mail in a specific context to determine its impact on how high school students and preservice teachers with whom they communicated would respond to a contemporary young adult novel.

Integrating Technology

Technology is a powerful tool for learning, communicating, and collaborating in classrooms. Successful use of technology can encourage students to define problems, ask questions, participate in dialogue with others inside and outside the school, and assess progress by self-reflection (Corl, 1996). Technology can also enrich the learning environment by instantaneously connecting classrooms to outside resources, experts, new curricula, and communication avenues (Russel, 1995; Zehr, 1998). These connections result in more engaged learning by more

National Reading Conference Yearbook, **50**, *pp. 572–583.*

active students, increased contributions by students to the classroom knowledge base, increased relevancy of learning activities, and increased technological skills for learners and educators (Bosch & Cardinale, 1993). A growing number of schools and teacher education programs are recognizing that e-mail, the Internet, and discussion groups can be used to provide opportunities for flexible, student-centered learning among students at different levels and in different locations. Further, a growing body of research is focused on the outcomes of efforts to bring students in K–12 classrooms together in online learning communities with those training to become teachers (Bradley, 1998; Means, 1994). However, a report from the Office of Technology Assessment (1995) suggested that teacher educators do not sufficiently model appropriate uses of computers, e-mail, and the Internet for instructional purposes in courses or in fieldwork. Also, the instructional technology provided to preservice teachers tends to focus more on simple applications and less on newer, more sophisticated tools such as electronic networks, discussion groups, e-mail, and integrated media. Therefore, more research is needed to investigate these advanced applications in specific contexts.

Literacy Learning

Integrating technology into instruction is one way to encourage active literacy engagement. Kinzer and Leu (1997) discussed the importance of technology in the teaching and learning of literacy, suggesting that English teachers must become more insightful about technology in order to understand how various applications can support literacy instruction. Noden and Vacca (1994) specifically suggested that e-mail and discussion group communication can facilitate important literacy learning opportunities for students by making reading and writing authentic. Such exchanges are authentic "talk." One project described by McKeon (1997) focused on preservice teachers' discussions with fourth graders about the trade books the fourth graders were reading. The project was successful because students were involved in an active process of language use and learning; important learning connections were made; and the e-mail partners came to know each other socially as they shared information, asked questions, and responded to literature. A similar project from the Kentucky Telecommunications Writing Project connected students in different schools with each other for e-mail conversations about books they were all reading (Bell, Cambron, Rey-Barreau, & Paeth, 1995). Such applications are consistent with many of the standards outlined by the National Council of Teachers of English (1996), including a need to enhance students' abilities to use a variety of technological resources to gather and synthesize information and to create and communicate knowledge. More collaborative efforts that involve the integration of technology will be necessary to create authentic learning opportunities and to facilitate active student engagement in 21st-century classrooms (Office of Technology Assessment, 1995).

Using Young Adult Literature

Teachers must facilitate students' active engagement in reading, speaking, writing, and listening tasks (Atwell, 1998). When students actually read, comprehend, and respond to good literature that they enjoy, they develop and practice literacy skills. Support for this position includes research by Reed (1994), who concluded that the young adult novel specifically (a) helps improve the reading skills of adolescents; (b) encourages adolescents to read more books, thereby improving their abilities to read; (c) allows teachers to incorporate more books of interest to adolescents into the curriculum, thereby avoiding the nonreading curriculum or workbooks and lectures; and (d) facilitates the development of an inclusive curriculum.

Applebee's (1989) study investigating the most frequently used book-length titles revealed the need for expanding the literature curriculum given the diversity in this country's student population and the quality literature routinely omitted. Research has suggested that one goal in selecting literature must focus on helping all students see their realities reflected in the texts used in schools (Richard & Ernst, 1993; Rogers & Soter, 1997). When students can make personal connections, learning becomes much more authentic, exciting, meaningful, and fun for them (Bushman & Bushman, 1997).

Research Questions

Given these lines of inquiry, it seemed that one way of helping English teachers create effective and authentic learning environments would involve exploring how the use of technology could facilitate high school students' literacy engagement and enhance their abilities to make connections with literature. This classroom research was designed to investigate the use of technology in a very specific way. The research questions that guided the study were: (a) How did e-mail dialogue influence 10th-grade students' understanding of, responses to, and enjoyment of *Ironman;* (b) what did the preservice teachers learn about effective teaching using e-mail; and (c) what were the participants' perceptions of the academic outcomes of electronic dialogue?

Method

Setting and Participants

The study took place over a 7-week period at an urban high school in a midsized city in the southeast of the United States. Pairs of 10th-grade students enrolled in a regular English class were randomly assigned to one preservice teacher from an English methods course. The high school class consisted of 25 students. The demographics were as follows: 10 black and 1 white male students, 13 black and 1 Asian female students. Anita and Helen, the teacher and intern, were both white. There were 11 preservice teachers, 10 white women and one white man. I, a black female teacher educator, also participated in the project and was paired with three students. The preservice teachers were each paired with two students.

Procedures

Copies of the novel *Ironman* were purchased for all participants. Helen developed the 5-week unit that used the novel as the major literature focus as part of her requirements for the internship. Before the project began, permission forms were sent to all students' parents/guardians and all agreed to allow their children to participate. The project began with three training sessions in the high school computer lab 2 weeks prior to the beginning of the unit. The purpose of these sessions was to prepare the high school students to use e-mail appropriately. They were assigned e-mail addresses and given opportunities to practice sending and receiving e-mails. Training for the preservice teachers was also important because as the adult respondents in the conversations, they were responsible for ensuring that communication remain professional, ethical, purposeful, and meaningful. A common session among all participants was included that focused on e-mail etiquette and ethics.

All participants communicated on four separate occasions during the week prior to the beginning of the unit. Topics included favorite novels (or short stories, poems, plays), favorite authors, hobbies, school activities, and other interests. These sessions were very structured in order to set an appropriate tone for the 5-week project. An opening breakfast in the classroom ended the preparation and began the unit. During this breakfast, the preservice teachers, Anita, and I participated in prereading activities that included Helen's brief description of the book's author, the completion of an anticipation guide (Vacca & Vacca, 1999), and the e-mail partners' small-group discussions of issues related to today's high school (e.g., violence, relationships, sports and other extracurricular activities, peer pressure) that are also issues with which the characters in the novel are grappling.

Over the weeks, topics for e-mail dialogue emerged as Anita and Helen assigned various reading and writing tasks associated with the novel and other class activities. All participants read the novel and discussed it via e-mail, and the preservice teachers and I made six classroom visits. The visits consisted of the following: three times for simply reading aloud, discussing the novel in small groups, and working on during-reading activities; two times for more reading and working with our e-mail partners to develop ideas and to practice for their project presentations. The last visit was to participate with the high school students in their final presentations. We set three as the minimum number of e-mails per week; however, this goal was not always met. We did not set a minimum length but encouraged the preservice teachers to write at least one paragraph each time, as we expected their writing to serve as models for the students, both in form and in content.

As the e-mail dialogue progressed, the major roles for the preservice teachers were as online tutors, mentors, and fellow learners. They asked and answered questions; checked vocabulary assignments; discussed literary elements, including themes, symbols, characters, and setting; offered responses and advice on reading and studying; read their e-mail partners' papers before the assignments were due; participated with their partners in final projects; and offered additional information and assistance as students worked through assignments and activities.

Data Analysis

Data sources included the e-mail transcripts, teachers' and students' weekly journal reflections, students' final projects, focus-group post-interviews with selected students and preservice teachers, teachers' fieldnotes, and project surveys. The high school students also completed a pre- and post-survey focused on their reading preferences and the use of young adult literature. E-mail transcripts were coded and chunked into categories that illuminated the research questions (Miles & Huberman, 1984). The other data were also coded and chunked into the emerging categories to illuminate the research questions. As themes emerged during the categorizing of data, memos were used to construct initial propositions then a preliminary summary. Debriefing sessions were conducted during class to ensure continuously that the project was meeting its major goals. The teacher and the teacher intern critiqued the preliminary summary to ensure that the reporting of the project events had credibility, dependability, applicability, and confirmability (Lincoln & Guba, 1985). A final summary was completed during the summer after the spring project was completed. Results discussed here focus primarily on the e-mail transcripts and the focus-group post-interviews.

Results

General Findings

Benefits for participants. This was our first attempt at using e-mail for such specific purposes. Although logistics and time for adequate responses were major constraints, the project was successful based on feedback from the participants. The high school students benefited because they had additional help with their class work. For example, Shurrun stated on one of her last e-mails to her partner Staci, "Thanks for taking the time to help me. I know you must be busy with your college stuff so I just wanted to thanks for helping me. I liked talking about the book. I learned a lot about writing in the e-mails" (note: all of the students' e-mails are reproduced verbatim except that names have been changed). The students looked forward to sending and receiving messages from their university partners. Aletia told her e-mail partner Amber, ". . . just having a teacher other than Mrs. D. to talk to is a lot of fun. I felt good when I had e-mails waiting for me on the computer." After I informed my partners that I would be in South America for a week during the project and could not e-mail them, Quisha e-mailed me the following message:

> B. J. B. J. B. J. B. J. B. J.!!!!!!!!!!!!
> Oh no! Your are going where, when, how long?!?!? Who on earth will I have to

> E-Mail !?! Well I hope you have a good time and enjoy your self. I am really enjoying Ironman. Anyway I hope you get this E- Mail before you leave, so I'll here from whenever you get back. Have a safe trip!
> Quisha

Andy participated in the last focus group interview. He stated:

> I liked talking on the computer. I don't have a computer at home so school is the only place I can use it. I am glad we had time before school also. Thc labs get so busy that nobody can spend long. Having the time for just us was good because I know I was gonna have a letter from Mary on Wednesdays and Fridays.

Margo also expressed her enjoyment with using e-mail in one of her last e-mails to Shellie:

> Dear shellie,
> It has been good chating to you threw the computer. I like you, you have a nice personality. Thank-you you have been a good listener. well I guess I have to go see you again hopefully.
> your penpal, margo

The students took pride in their work, especially their final projects from *Ironman.* They were excited about practicing for their final presentations and were glad the university students came to their practices. Benita made the following comment during the focus group interview:

> No one has ever took the time to come to our classroom before. The advanced kids get to do stuff all the time. So we were happy that we got to go to lab each week to talk to people from the university. It was fun doing our play in the auditorium to.

The groups' final projects ranged from readers' theater productions, to explorations of metaphors using PowerPoint, to rap songs created to illustrate themes in the novel.

The university students also benefited because they gained more confidence in their abilities to work successfully with urban students. Working in depth with two students helped them see that students are individuals with unique characteristics even when they belong to the same ethnic group and are from the same socioeconomic backgrounds. They gained new insights about the power of working with students individually and in small groups. Lauren, a white woman from a small town in rural Alabama, commented that she was amazed at what the students could do if given the chance. During one of our last discussions in methods class, she reflected: "If only we could have a teacher for every five students. We could see some real progress." Most of these preservice teachers had also had very limited experiences working with students who were not from white middle-class backgrounds. From this, I learned the importance of purposefully structuring opportunities for my preservice teachers to cross borders. These preservice teachers learned why teachers must hear their students' voices and understand their perspectives.

Preservice teachers' roles and responsibilities. The preservice teachers successfully negotiated their diverse roles as tutors, mentors, and fellow learners. As tutors and mentors, they were able to use their background knowledge, understanding of reading strategies, and experiences as avid readers to guide these high school students who struggled with reading and other literacy tasks. For example, competencies in the preservice teachers' content area literacy course, a required education course, included knowledge of and ability to use specific literacy strategies for before, during, and after reading. The preservice teachers were able to practice teaching these strategies to their students because part of the process of guiding the students through the reading was demonstrating to them how to use these specific literacy strategies. Linda, one of the preservice teachers, spent a significant amount of time teaching her students how to use the reading strategy DR-TA (Tierney & Readence, 2000). Linda was amazed that the strategy actually worked. She commented: ". . . it was great when Jamie finally extracted from the novel all of the complex sources of Bo's anger. I know that using DR-TA helped her critically reflect and understand his anger." Linda connected theory and practice. This was one of the several unexpected but important outcomes of the project.

As fellow learners, the preservice teachers were able to experience a new novel. Most of them had had very little knowledge of contemporary young adult literature as their regular university literature classes had included only traditional works. Therefore, although their knowledge of literature was more sophisticated than the high school students', their knowledge of literature written specifically for young adults was not developed. They had to read and develop their perspectives on the novel's purpose, themes, and meanings. They also had to understand the author's approach to form, point of view, and tone. Thus, the project was also a useful exercise for the preservice teachers' development as teachers and learners. As a result of the project, three of the preservice teachers took the elective course we offer in young adult literature in a subsequent semester.

Findings Related to the Research Questions

How did e-mail dialogue impact 10th-grade students' understanding of, responses to, and enjoyment of Ironman? The students had concrete ideas to share about the novel. They were motivated to read about characters with whom they could relate. For example, in a message to Pam, Mark stated: ". . . the book has a lot of cursing in it that's what make it funny. . . . It's good, but it has its low points were it makes you look inside to see where you stand." The students enjoyed updating us on their reading and demonstrating their understanding of the novel, as some of their responses illustrate:

> Jessica,
> I think that the book is down to earth will alot of it's lyrics. And I think Ms. U [teacher intern] is doing a great job at making us learn about the book by giving

> us activities to do while reading in class. Today we are doing colages with magazines and different books to express what might cause anger.
> Anisha
>
> Ms. S.,
> I have not wrote in a long time. I am typing you to give you an update on Iroman. This book is very intresting and I think that teenagers should read it. This book is about anger, a enemy that lives inside teenagers that make them do things to hurt people and theirselves, oh no the bell just rung I have to go, type later.
> Sherry

In my response to Sherry noted below, I responded specifically to what she had to say and tried to prompt her to think about other characters. I also reminded her about our ongoing work with grammar:

> Sherry,
> I am glad that you are enjoying *Ironman.* I believe the book has much to say to all of us about managing our anger and managing relationships. I really enjoyed reading the book also. Bo has to overcome so much. I like the way that he is so committed to his athletic event. I can't imagine all the training he has to do. What other characters in the book do you like? We will continue to work on your writing and grammar. Remember that "theirselves" should be "themselves" and use "have written," not "have wrote."
> Ms. S.

Readers will note the many grammar and usage problems in the students' e-mails. We tried not to emphasize these problems, but they were too common to overlook and had to be addressed occasionally as discussed later. We were pleased that the students could engage in conversations about the novel and had original ideas to share.

What did the preservice teachers learn about effective teaching using e-mail? The preservice teachers consistently said that the combination of e-mail dialogue and classroom visits was most useful. All agreed that meeting the students first was very necessary. Taking the time to find out about their lives helped them as the project progressed. Three preservice teachers noted frustration with their partners' lack of writing skills. These preservice teachers believed that they had spent too much time trying to decipher what the students were trying to communicate. They did realize, however, that poor literacy skills are a reality among the students with whom we were working. Nine of the preservice teachers believed they had learned from the project, as e-mail dialogue was a useful way to help the students work through the novel and develop their literacy skills. Two of them believed that the e-mail dialogue was useful for the high school students but less so for themselves.

What were the participants' perceptions of the academic outcomes of electronic dialogue? The students did well on the unit test, and their final project performances were outstanding. All of the students responded on the posttest and in interviews that the additional assistance from the university students aided their understanding of the novel. Anita and Helen noted that the students were more engaged and focused because they knew that the university students would expect them to be ready to discuss the novel each week. Further, the students' writing skills improved as a result of the electronic dialogue. The preservice teachers and I made conscious efforts to help the students use correct grammar without criticizing them because we did not want them to stop communicating. However, we addressed the problems with them using a variety of methods consistent with Weaver (1996). The verb phrase "have wrote," as in Connie's beginning to an e-mail message with "Sorry I havent wrote since last week," was a grammar problem that is entrenched in their dialect. We consistently used "have written" in our responses and informed Helen and Anita that we saw this problem in most of the students' writing. Although we sometimes corrected their errors explicitly, we also used the strategy of simply restating correctly sentences that contained errors in the e-mails. Also asking them to elaborate in their responses helped them to begin using more complex sentences rather than the short, choppy, simple sentences they were accustomed to using.

When we reviewed their writing assignments, we used "Track Changes" in Microsoft to point them to sections that needed revising. Although we made suggestions, we did not do the revising for them. We guided them in the use of dictionaries and other reference materials. Most of their grammar and usage problems seemed to result from their home dialect, and grammar worksheets had had little impact on these writing problems. However, as Elbow (1997) suggests, their writing improved throughout the course of the project because they were writing to a real audience and for an authentic purpose. We were models for them, and the dialogue made sense to them.

Discussion and Implications

I am an advocate of using young adult literature in the high school classroom. There are many excellent young adult novels that should be integrated into the curriculum. Often, preservice teachers are only exposed to works from the traditional canon and fail to understand that these are not always developmentally appropriate for young adults. They often go into their first years of teaching using literature they were taught in college and do not realize that students could also benefit from literature containing plots consistent with their experiences, themes of interest to them, main characters who are young adults, and language that corresponds to their own language (Bushman & Bushman, 1997). The preservice teachers saw, as Donelson and Nilsen (2001) suggested, that students are motivated to read when they see characters and situations reflecting their own experiences. Comments from two of the preservice teachers illustrate these discoveries about young adult literature:

> As a result of reading *Ironman* and working with these kids, I have learned so much about integrating young adult literature into the English classroom. The students had such insight about Bo and really seemed to identify with him.

> Their e-mails were filled with references to themes and symbols in the novel. They had something to say which was exciting to see. I didn't realize the value of using YA lit. I know that it is just a matter of putting the time and effort into researching and reading and developing activities. Cheryl
>
> *Ironman* was an excellent choice for these 10th graders. I have witnessed students in other placements who hate reading. They are not motivated to read something that they don't understand. These students had the opportunity to read quality literature that they actually understood and enjoyed. Integrating YA literature into the curriculum increases students' motivation to read. Helen

There is room in the English curriculum for traditional literature, multicultural literature, contemporary literature, and young adult literature.

The project was personally beneficial to me as a teacher educator because it was an opportunity to integrate technology in an authentic context, extend my work with area English language arts teachers, and promote field-based preparation of preservice teachers. The results of this project have informed revisions in my methods course and facilitated more extensive collaboration with other English language arts teachers, their students, and my preservice teachers. For example, the preservice teachers must demonstrate their abilities to use technology and work with students in different group settings during their required 90 hours of clinical experiences attached to the methods course. They must also complete 15 hours of service with a teacher at our Professional Development School, a rural Title One school in the area. The purpose is simply to provide as many opportunities as possible to infuse technology into instruction and to involve them in meaningful work with students from different backgrounds and in different contexts. This approach is consistent with research (Balli & Diggs, 1996) contending that preservice teachers must incorporate technology into practical field experiences in order to enhance their understanding of how technology can support teaching and learning.

This project incorporating e-mail as one vehicle for teaching and learning literature was exciting and beneficial but also time consuming and logistically difficult. It was positive because the purposeful dialogue led the university students to new insights about guiding students individually and meeting them where they are and led the high school students to deeper understanding of literature. It was challenging first because we used class time for the six visits (the class time coincided with my Tuesday/Thursday 75-minute methods course). We sometimes met in class for 30 minutes then drove to the school; other times we met for the entire 75 minutes with the students. Secondly, responding to and guiding the students online was often difficult because of our busy schedules and multiple responsibilities. However, preservice teachers, inservice teachers, and teacher educators must continue to explore ways to infuse technology into education and ensure that the applications remain collaborative, student centered, relevant, and focused on curriculum.

This project was purposefully planned to enhance students' engagement with this novel. Anita, Helen, and I concluded that the e-mail dialogue and interactions encouraged the students to be more accountable and served as an incentive for them actually to read and respond. These students had not experienced much school success and had no previous opportunities to interact with university students in this more personal way. However, designing a project to study the differences between teaching a similar unit with and without e-mail dialogue may provide more insights about the effectiveness of using e-mail in a similar context.

Finally, other projects should be designed and studied in an effort to increase the use of technology, young adult literature, and opportunities for communication among secondary students and preservice teachers. Future research should investigate (a) the relationship between online communication in the language arts classroom and secondary students' growth in very specific areas such as grammar, usage, and writing; (b) how classroom visits and face-to-face encounters enhance the beneficial effects of the e-mail dialogue; and (c) other methods for extending the use of technology to improve interdisciplinary collaboration.

References

Applebee, A. (1989). *A study of book-length works taught in high school English courses.* Albany, NY: Center for the Study of Teaching and Learning of Literature.

Atwell, N. (1998). *In the middle: New understandings about reading, writing, and learning* (2nd ed.). Portsmouth, NH: Heinemann.

Balli, S., & Diggs, L. (1996). Learning to teach with technology. A pilot project with preservice teachers. *Educational Technology, 36,* 56–61.

Bell, N., Cambron, D., Rey-Barreau, K., & Paeth, B. (1995). *Online literature groups.* Paper presented at the meeting of the National Council of Teachers of English, San Diego, CA.

Bosch, K. A., & Cardinale, L. (1993). Preservice teachers' perceptions of computer use during a field experience. *Journal of Computing in Teacher Education, 10,* 23–27.

Bradley, A. (1998). Building a better teaching force: Everyone can raise their hands. *Education Week, 18,* 45–47.

Bushman, J., & Bushman, K. (1997). *Using young adult literature in the English classroom* (2nd ed.). NJ: Merrill/Prentice Hall.

Corl, S. F. (1996). *Novices on the net: An introduction to education class uses e-mail and the Internet.* Paper presented at the meeting of the National Council for Occupational Education, St. Louis, MO.

Crutcher. C. (1995). *Ironman.* NY: Bantam Doubleday Dell.

Donelson, K., & Nilsen, A. (2001). *Literature for today's young adults* (6th ed.). Needham Heights, MA: Allyn & Bacon.

Elbow, P. (1997). Grading student writing: Making it simpler, fairer, clearer. *New Directions for Teaching and Learning, 69,* 127–140.

Gallo, D. (1992). Listening to readers: Attitudes toward the young adult novel. In V. Monseau & G. Salvner (Eds.), *Reading their world: The young adult novel in the classroom* (pp. 17–27). Portsmouth, NH: Boynton/Cook.

Kinzer, C., & Leu, D. (1997). The challenge of change: Exploring literacy and learning in electronic environments. *Language Arts, 74,* 126–136.

Lincoln, Y., & Guba, E. (1985). *Naturalistic inquiry.* Thousand Oaks, CA: Sage.

McKeon, C. (1997). *Investigating a literature-based electronic-mail collaborative.* Unpublished manuscript, Kent State University.

Means, B. (1994). *Technology and education reform.* San Francisco, CA: Jossey-Bass.

Miles, M., & Huberman, A. (1984). *Qualitative data analysis.* Thousand Oaks, CA: Sage.

National Council of Teachers of English. (1996). *Standards for the English language arts.* Urbana, IL: Author.

Noden, H., & Vacca, R. T. (1994). *Whole language in middle and secondary classrooms.* New York: HarperCollins.

Office of Technology Assessment. (1995). *Teachers and technology: Making the connection.* Washington, DC: U.S. Government Printing Office.

Reed, A. (1994). *Reaching adolescents: The young adult book and the school.* New York: Macmillan College.

Richard, K., & Ernst, G. (1993). Understanding the other, understanding myself: Using multicultural novels in the classroom. *Clearinghouse, 67,* 88–90.

Rogers, T., & Soter, A. (Eds.). (1997). *Reading across cultures.* Urbana, IL: National Council of Teachers of English.

Russel, A. L. (1995). Stages in learning new technology: Naïve adult e-mail users. *Computers in Education, 25*(4), 173–178.

Tierney, R., & Readence, J. (2000). *Reading strategies and practices: A compendium.* Boston, MA: Allyn & Bacon.

Vacca, R., & Vacca, J. (1999). *Content area reading: Literacy and learning across the curriculum* (6th ed.). New York: Addison Wesley Longman.

Weaver, C. (1996). *Teaching grammar in context.* Portsmouth, NH: Boynton/Cook.

Zehr, M. (1998). Changing the way teachers teach: Away from the chalkboard. *Education Week, 18,* 41–43.

Children's Motivation to Read Following Reading Recovery

Michael A. R. Townsend
University of Auckland

Jane E. Townsend
Stanhope Road School

Kyung Ja Seo
University of Auckland

More than two decades have passed since Reading Recovery was first introduced into Auckland classrooms (Clay, 1979). The program is now firmly established throughout New Zealand and has expanded overseas. In spite of its widespread use in classrooms around the world, the effects of the program are still being investigated. This study is concerned with the long-term motivational outcomes of the program.

Recent research on motivation has indicated that children's attitudes, values, and beliefs about reading play a significant role in the acquisition of reading skill (Cramer & Castle, 1994; Turner & Paris, 1995). Thus, educators need to be concerned with what children choose to read, their persistence in reading, the effort given to reading, the use they make of their reading skills, their enjoyment of reading, and their personal beliefs about their competency in reading (Elley, 1992; Gambrell & Morrow, 1996). A successful reading program is one in which children learn to read, but also one in which children value reading as an activity, use their reading skills in a variety of contexts (both work and leisure), and feel confident about reading. These are all issues of motivation (Pintrich & Schunk, 1996).

A number of current theories of motivation suggest that a child's self-perceived competence as a reader, and the value that the child has for reading tasks, are major determinants of motivation and engagement. For example, Eccles and her colleagues (Eccles, 1983; Wigfield & Eccles, 1992) proposed an "expectancy-value" theory of motivation in which motivation for an academic task is a function of expectations concerning the likelihood of success or failure on the task, and the perceived value or relative attractiveness of the task. There is empirical support for both of these motivational functions in reading. Students who believe that they are capable and competent readers are more likely to have higher achievement on a reading task than those who do not hold such beliefs (Paris & Oka, 1986). Furthermore, students who have higher task value for reading show greater effort and purpose than those who do not (Ames & Archer, 1988; Dweck & Elliot,

National Reading Conference Yearbook, **50**, pp. 584–596.

1983). In brief, there is a convergence of theoretical opinion and empirical research to suggest that higher motivation to read is associated with more positive self-concept as a reader and higher task value for reading.

The research just noted suggests that studies of the motivational outcomes of Reading Recovery, when addressed within an expectancy-value theoretical perspective, should include measures of self-concept and task value. A number of instruments are currently available for measuring students' general attitude toward reading (e.g., McKenna & Kear, 1990; Tunnell, Calder, Justen, & Phaup, 1988), as well as several that measure the specific dimension of self-concept (Harter 1981; Henk & Melnick, 1995; Pintrich & DeGroot, 1990). However, a recently developed instrument, the "Motivation to Read Profile" (Gambrell, Palmer, Codling, & Mazzoni, 1996) includes quantitative scales of both self-concept and task value in reading for primary school children. Before the study reported here, this instrument had not been used in research in New Zealand.

Some researchers in New Zealand have been concerned with the relationship between reading skill and self-concept (e.g., Chapman, Tunmer, & Ryan, 1997; Chapman & Tunmer, 2000), but only one local study has systematically addressed the motivational effects associated with Reading Recovery. Wade and Moore (1998) assessed 121 ex–Reading Recovery children from 13 schools in Victoria, New South Wales and in New Zealand, in Years 5 or 6, some 4 or 5 years after having participated in the program. The assessment included a standardized measure of reading comprehension, and an overall rating of self-perceived reading skill (a single item in which children checked whether they were poor, weak, good, or brilliant at reading). It also included an "Attitudes to Reading" Likert scale measure, consisting of 12 items (e.g., "Reading is very important," "Watching TV is better than reading," "Reading is enjoyable"), scored on a 5-point scale (from strongly agree to strongly disagree). Scores on all measures were contrasted with the scores of 121 classmates of the Reading Recovery children who had "mainly average or below average" (Wade & Moore, 1998, p. 99) reading skills for their class in Year 1, but who had not participated in the program. Results indicated that ex–Reading Recovery children had significantly greater reading comprehension (by approximately 1 year of reading age), and were significantly more positive about reading than their classmates who had not participated in the program. Additionally, the ex–Reading Recovery children viewed themselves more positively as readers. These results are noteworthy given the length of time that had elapsed since the program, and the fact that the comparison children were initially a more able group of readers.

Some aspects of the study, however, limit the conclusions that may be drawn concerning motivation in the New Zealand context. No indication was given of how many of the children in the sample were from New Zealand schools. Further, the reliability and validity of the attitude scale were not reported nor were details of its construction. Finally, concerns may be expressed about the comparison group. Wade and Moore (1998) ignored gender in forming their comparison group. Given that girls typically have higher reading achievement (Wilkinson, 1998), more positive attitudes toward reading (McKenna, Kear, & Ellsworth, 1995), and higher task values for language-related activities (Townsend & Hicks, 1997; Wigfield & Eccles, 1992), it is appropriate that gender be included in the design of such research. Further, the comparison and Reading Recovery groups were quite dissimilar in reading ability. A more sensitive analysis would follow from a comparison of Reading Recovery children with a group of children similarly at risk of reading failure, as well as a group of children with average reading ability.

In summary, there is a need to examine the effects of Reading Recovery in terms of motivational outcomes, particularly self-concept and task value. In view of the uncertainty over the longevity of the reading skill effects usually assessed, it is also important that the motivational effects be explored in groups of children who have been discontinued from the program for varying lengths of time, and for groups of children varying in similarity to those receiving the program. There is also a need to supplement formal assessment with the informal assessment knowledge held by teachers about their children. The one study in this area (Wade & Moore, 1998) has critical weaknesses in regard to the features just mentioned. Thus, the major purpose of the present study was to examine motivation for reading in two groups of children, currently in Years 4, 5, or 6 at school yet previously assessed as at risk of reading failure after their first year of school. One group consisted of children who had been successfully discontinued from the Reading Recovery program, whereas the other group consisted of children assessed as initially eligible for the program but unable to participate because of lack of places. These two groups were contrasted with a third group of children, a random sample of those who were not assessed as candidates for the program (i.e., average readers). Based on research that indicates positive effects of Reading Recovery on reading skill, and the positive relationship between skill and motivational outcomes, it was anticipated that children successfully discontinued from the program would be more similar in motivation for reading to average readers than to children who were eligible for Reading Recovery but who did not participate in the program. As a secondary issue, the study was also designed to provide some evidence about reading skill as measured by formal and informal means. Finally, the study allowed an examination of whether the magnitude of any residual program effect was affected by whether the children had been in the program 2, 3, or 4 years earlier.

Method

Participants

Participants were 103 children in Year 4 (n=38), Year 5 (n=40), or Year 6 (n=25) at two schools in Auckland classified as decile 3 (i.e., among the lowest one-third in socioeconomic status in the country). There were 36 children who had completed Reading Recovery at age 6 (the Reading Recovery group), 31 children who had been tested as eligible for Reading Recovery but who had not gained a place in the program (the Non–Reading Recovery group), and 36 children who were making good reading progress at age 6 and were not considered as candidates for the program (the Random group). There were 63 boys and 40 girls.

Instruments

All children completed the 10-item Reading Self-Concept and Reading Value scales of the Motivation to Read Profile (Gambrell et al., 1996), as well as a 12-item Attitude to Reading scale (Wade & Moore, 1998). All scales reached acceptable internal consistency reliability (Cronbach alphas of .80, .77, and .74 were obtained for the three scales, respectively).

All teachers completed a 10-item questionnaire of their perceptions of each child's classroom reading. Six of these items assessed motivation for reading (involvement in instructional reading, motivation in the class reading program, motivation for independent reading, level of home reading, independent use of books to locate information, and engagement in informal discussions with peers or teacher about books), and had a reliability index of .89. The remaining four items measured essential aspects of reading skill (general reading level, knowledge of strategies, level of decoding skills, and ability to retell a story in sequence), and had a reliability index of .83. The questionnaire also asked teachers to provide descriptive data from class records of the reading age of the child (and how obtained), and the average reading age, and range, of the class as a whole. It also invited teachers to write any comments they wished to make about the child's reading skills or motivation. This questionnaire was developed following open-ended interviews with a number of primary school teachers across several schools to determine what aspects of children's reading motivation and behavior were of most concern in making decisions about classroom instruction.

Procedure

Two neighboring primary schools that operated a Reading Recovery program were invited to participate in the study. School records were searched to identify all current pupils in Years 4, 5, and 6 who had received a program of Reading Recovery in Year 2 and had been successfully discontinued (the Reading Recovery group). These records were also searched for current same-gender classmates of the Reading Recovery children who had also been assessed as eligible for Reading Recovery but had not been able to join the program because of limited places (the Non–Reading Recovery group). It was possible to locate a match for 31 of the 36 children (indicating that the schools tested approximately twice as many pupils as they could take into the program). All of these children had completed the Observation Survey of reading skills in Year 2, a set of measures including Letter Identification, Concepts about Print, Word Recognition, Reading Age, Writing Vocabulary, Dictation, and Book Level. (The records from Year 2 contained no formal assessments of motivational factors, thus it is not known whether there were initial differences in motivation between these groups.) Finally, one current same-gender classmate of each Reading Recovery child was selected randomly from the remaining children in the same grade level (the Random group).

Both schools had administered the standardized Progressive Achievement

Tests of Reading in Comprehension and Vocabulary (Reid & Elley, 1991) earlier in the current school year, thus providing current measures (obtained from school records) of reading skill for the children now in Years 4, 5, and 6. Complete data sets were collected for all 103 children (except for 2 children, 1 at each school, whose records did not contain the PAT Vocabulary test).

The measures of current motivation to read and attitude toward reading were administered by the authors to small groups of 4 to 6 children in sessions lasting approximately 20 minutes. The participants' teachers completed the Teacher Questionnaire for each of the students in the study. An analysis of the open-ended written comments made by teachers at the end of the Teacher Questionnaire followed the procedures recommended by Strauss and Corbin (1990). Comments were classified according to an orthogonal matrix consisting of affect (positive or negative) and domain (reading motivation or reading skill). Comments for 10 children were coded independently by all authors, resulting in 100% agreement.

Results

Early Reading and Gender Effects

Preliminary *t*-test analyses revealed no significant differences between the Reading Recovery and Non–Reading Recovery groups in age and the seven reading measures in the Observation Survey undertaken when the children were in Year 2 (age 6 years). Further preliminary analyses involving Group × Year Level × Gender multiple analyses of variance (MANOVA) were also undertaken to examine possible gender effects associated with the major variables of the study. Not unexpectedly, there were significant effects for gender on two measures (girls had higher PAT comprehension scores and greater motivation as judged by their teachers). However, because most measures showed no gender effects, and there were no interaction effects, gender was not included in any further analyses.

Current Reading

How well were the children reading at the time of the study? Although the major focus of the study was on motivation, there were three sources of information about the current reading skills of the children. First, age percentile scores on the standardized PAT Comprehension and Vocabulary tests administered in the current year were subjected to separate 3 (Group) × 3 (Year Level) factorial analyses of variance. There were significant main effects for Group in both the Comprehension and Vocabulary scores, but no significant Year Level or interaction effects. Tukey comparisons indicated that children in the Random group had significantly higher comprehension and vocabulary skills than children in either the Reading Recovery or Non–Reading Recovery groups (see Table 1). However, reading comprehension was also significantly higher in the Reading Recovery group than in the Non–Reading Recovery group. The vocabulary scores of these two groups were similar.

Second, teachers' ratings of reading skill as assessed by four items on the Teacher Questionnaire were combined and again examined in a Group by Year Level factorial analysis of variance, revealing only a significant main effect for Group (see Table 2). Teachers rated the reading skills of the Random group significantly higher than either the Reading Recovery group or the Non–Reading Recovery group, whereas these latter groups did not differ. Inspection of the individual items suggested that those reflecting general level of ability and decoding skill appeared to differentiate the Random group from the other two groups. Interestingly, although the two remaining groups had similar mean scores, teach-

Table 1

Mean Reading and Motivation Scores of Children in the Reading Recovery, Non–Reading Recovery, and Random Groups

	Group					
	Reading Recovery		Non–Reading Recovery		Random	
	M	*SD*	*M*	*SD*	*M*	*SD*
Reading Age Percentiles						
Comprehension	31.81	20.94	18.90	14.24	49.36	26.75[1]
Vocabulary	20.91	16.67	21.07	15.86	44.64	22.35[2]
Motivation						
Self-Concept	28.47	4.58	29.55	5.28	32.42	4.41[3]
Task Value	31.50	4.91	33.45	4.09	33.69	4.34[4]
Attitude	48.36	6.27	46.35	6.69	50.25	7.79[5]

[1]Group $F(2, 94)=14.44$, $p<.001$: Random>RR ($p<.05$); RR>NRR ($p<.05$). [2]Group $F(2, 92)=16.86$, $p<.001$: Random>RR ($p<.05$); RR=NRR. [3]Group $F(2, 94)=5.76$, $p<.01$: Random>RR ($p<.05$); RR=NRR. [4]Group F not significant. [5]Group F not significant.

Table 2

Teacher Mean Estimates of Reading Age, Skill, and Motivation for the Reading Recovery, Non–Reading Recovery, and Random Groups

	Group					
	Reading Recovery		Non–Reading Recovery		Random	
	M	*SD*	*M*	*SD*	*M*	*SD*
Reading Age	9.03	1.37	8.64	1.41	10.17	1.76[1]
Reading Skill	11.67	2.75	11.25	2.70	14.92	2.73[2]
Motivation	16.22	4.28	16.00	3.77	19.89	3.69[3]

[1]Group $F(2, 94)=15.23$, $p<.001$: Random>RR ($p<.05$); RR=NRR. [2]Group $F(2, 94)=19.68$, $p<.001$: Random>RR ($p<.05$); RR=NRR. [3]Group $F(2, 94)=10.74$, $p<.001$: Random>RR ($p<.05$); RR=NRR.

ers rated the ability to retell a story in sequence somewhat higher in the Reading Recovery group than the Non–Reading Recovery group. It should be noted that across the sample the mean rating by teachers was slightly above the mid-point of the scale.

A third estimate of current reading skill across the three groups came from the reading ages provided by the teachers (see Table 2). The overwhelming majority of teachers (98%) reported using running records on a prose inventory of graded passages to make this assessment. The Group × Year Level analysis of variance revealed a significant main effect for Group, with the mean reading age for the Random group being higher than that for either of the other two groups. However, the somewhat higher mean reading age (approximately 5 months) in the Reading Recovery group was not statistically greater than that of the Non–Reading Recovery group. As expected, there was a significant effect of Year Level, with the mean reading age increasing across Years 4, 5, and 6, but the interaction effect was not significant.

In sum, although the mean scores for reading skills were generally higher for the Reading Recovery children than for the Non–Reading Recovery children, only reading comprehension was significantly higher. However, scores of both of these groups were below those of their average peers. These differences did not depend on the time elapsed since being in the program.

Motivation for Reading

Scores on the three motivation measures administered to the children (Self-Concept, Value, Attitude) were examined in separate Group × Year Level factorial analyses of variance. Children appeared to have a moderately high self-concept for reading in so far as the mean score on the Self-Concept scale was considerably higher than the mid-point of the scale. The analysis of variance showed a significant main effect for Group (see Table 1), and Tukey comparisons revealed that self-concept was higher in the Random group than either of the remaining groups, which were not significantly different. There were no Year Level or interaction effects.

The children also appeared to have a high value for reading, with the mean score again being substantially above the mid-point of the scale. There were no significant differences between the means for the three groups, nor were there any Year Level or interaction effects.

Finally, the children also reported a very positive attitude to reading, with the mean score being well above the mid-point of the scale. Again there were no significant differences between the mean scores of any of the groups, nor Year Level and interaction effects.

In brief, these measures obtained directly from the children revealed very positive motivation toward reading that appeared relatively uninfluenced by the reading group or year level of the children. Although the more capable readers (the Random group) were higher in self-concept than the children in the other two groups, all three groups were similarly positive in their value for reading and attitude toward reading.

The children's motivation for reading was also assessed from the teachers' perspective using six items in the Teacher Questionnaire (see Table 2). In contrast to the students' very positive assessment of their motivation, the teachers appeared only mildly positive in rating their students' motivation, with a mean score only fractionally higher than the mid-point of the scale. In the analysis there was a significant effect for Group, with the Random group being seen by their teachers as significantly higher in motivation for reading than the two other groups. This significant effect appeared to stem from teachers' higher assessments for independent reading and the amount of home reading in the Random group.

Finally, further insights came from 130 teacher comments made about 48 children on the Teacher Questionnaire. Most comments (89%) could be classified according to whether they were positive or negative, and about reading skill or reading motivation. Teachers made almost twice as many comments about motivation as reading skill, and they were somewhat more likely to make positive rather than negative statements. In terms of the three groups, 58 comments were made about a total of 20 children in the Reading Recovery group; 27 comments were made about 13 children in the Non–Reading Recovery group; and 35 comments were made about 15 children in the Random group. The pattern of comments about motivation was similar across groups; teachers were likely to be positive. However, comments about reading skill varied across the groups: Teachers were less likely to make positive comments about the reading skills of children in the Non–Reading Recovery group, and more likely to make negative comments about the reading skills of children in the Random group.

These results may suggest that children in the Non–Reading Recovery group had lower levels of reading skill than their classmates, making positive comments less likely. This view was supported by a preponderance of statements that expressed low expectations for these children (e.g., "I keep him in a lower group so he doesn't need to compete with more dominant children"), or that explicitly identified a weakness in reading (e.g., "Has difficulty understanding what she reads"). Children in this group received only two positive comments about their reading skill ("Fluent at this [lower] level" and "He has been having some success lately"). They did, however, receive several positive comments about motivational factors such as enjoyment ("he enjoys reading to me"), persistence ("always has a book in her desk"), and effort ("makes some effort at SSR now"). In contrast, children in the Reading Recovery group received almost three times as many positive comments, including comments about motivation (e.g., "Tries very hard," "Enjoys stories at a higher level," "Very confident") and reading skill (e.g., "Beginning to read more independently," "Reading fluently," "Shows good comprehension"). Even allowing for more comments about children in the Reading Recovery group than in the Non–Reading Recovery group, the comments were markedly more positive in the former group.

The higher incidence of negative comments about the reading skill of children in the Random group may be a function of teachers holding higher expectations for regular children in the classroom, thus increasing the likelihood of comments about the need to improve. Some support for this was found in examples of comments made about these children: "Makes careless errors that go uncorrected," "Is not working to potential," "Needs to concentrate."

Discussion

The results of this study do not unequivocally support the expectation that reading motivation in ex–Reading Recovery children would be more similar to average readers than to other children at risk of reading failure. However, there is evidence to suggest that motivation to read is quite positive in children who have participated in the Reading Recovery program. This latter conclusion is supported from several sources of information. On self-report scales of reading self-concept, reading value, and attitude about reading, the ex–Reading Recovery children had moderately high motivation. Teacher ratings of the motivation of these children were also moderately positive, as were the informal comments made by teachers about the children. These results are consistent with the positive outcomes reported by Wade and Moore (1998) for ex–Reading Recovery children in New Zealand and Australia. The results also suggest that the teachers of these children have involved them in reading instruction that encourages effort and persistence, as well as beliefs about personal competency and an enjoyment of the activity (Cramer & Castle, 1994; Gambrell & Morrow, 1996; Turner & Paris, 1995). These beliefs and attitudes are important for sustaining active lifelong literacy.

These positive motivational outcomes must be qualified in two ways. First, the children who had experienced Reading Recovery did differ in some ways from the average readers in their classrooms. Although both groups were similarly positive in their value for reading and their attitude toward reading, the self-concepts of the more competent readers were higher, and the teacher ratings of the motivation of average readers were also higher than those of the ex–Reading Recovery children. The more positive finding for more able readers is consistent with other research carried out in New Zealand at earlier (Year 2 and Year 3) levels (Chapman et al., 1997). It is likely that these differences were implicated in the teachers' recognition of motivational differences between these two groups in the current study.

This consistency in findings across different research samples, at different age levels, and using different measures, strengthens the argument that children who have experienced Reading Recovery do not develop the same level of perceived competency as average readers, at least not during the primary school years. This conclusion has significant implications for children who experience early reading difficulties. Stanovich (1986) has argued that these difficulties in reading may result in general behavioral, cognitive, and motivational deficits, or "negative Matthew effects" (p. 360). It should be noted, however, that there is little evidence of a Matthew effect in the current study. The self-concepts and motivation of the ex–Reading Recovery children were still relatively positive, even though lower than for the average readers.

The second qualification about the positive motivational results is that the ex–Reading Recovery children did not appear dissimilar to the children, also at risk of reading difficulties, who did not participate in the program. There were no significant differences between these two groups in reading self-concept, reading value, attitude to reading, or teachers' ratings of motivation, although informal teacher comments did appear more positive about children in the ex–Reading Recovery group. It might be expected that as children develop skill in reading there would be concomitant growth in various factors of motivation, including self-concept, self-efficacy, expectations, and attitude (Borkowski, Carr, Rellinger, & Pressley, 1990). The finding of little measurable effect on motivation to read in these children who had experienced Reading Recovery is different to that found by Wade and Moore (1998) for whom the contrast group was more skilled in reading than the contrast group in the current study. However, the current results are consistent with the findings of Chapman et al. (1997) using a contrast group identified as "having some reading problems but not placed in Reading Recovery." There are no apparent reasons for the differences in these findings, although the number of children in the Chapman et al. study was relatively small. There is clearly a need for further research on this issue, using more closely matched groups and a methodology that would examine changes in motivational outcomes associated with the nature of the instruction that children experience. In this regard, the limitations of the Motivation to Read Profile (Gambrell et al., 1996) must also be acknowledged. Although this instrument was selected, in part, because of its appeal to teachers and school administrators, it may lack sufficient depth to assess complex issues of self-concept and task value, particularly when used with children unknown to the examiners.

The results just discussed were not affected by whether the children had experienced Reading Recovery 2, 3, or 4 years earlier. As noted earlier, much of the success of the Reading Recovery program has come from an analysis of gains made during the program, but there is debate about whether the program results in sustained reading skill. Although some research suggests that the reading skill effects are still apparent 3 years after the program (Lyons, Pinnell, & Deford, 1993; Pinnell, 1989), other research suggests that within a year the residual effects of the program are quite small (Center, Wheldall, Freeman, Outhred, & McNaught, 1995; Glynn, Bethune, Crooks, Ballard, & Smith, 1992). It is possible that any parallel effects for motivation have also diminished within 2 years of discontinuation. It should be noted, however, that the current study was not designed to measure motivational patterns at the end of the program. Thus, it is impossible to tell whether motivation increased as a function of the program, and then decreased, or whether the program had little effect on motivation at all. This remains an issue for further research.

Few gender effects were apparent in this study. As expected from previous literature on children at risk of reading difficulty (Wilkinson, 1998), more boys than girls participated in the Reading Recovery program, and girls had higher scores on standardized measures of reading than did boys. Girls were also judged higher in motivation by their teachers, although they were not significantly different on any of the other measures in this study. These results are consistent with other research that indicates that motivation is multidimensional and that different patterns of gender effects occur across different dimensions of motivation (Wigfield, 1997). However, none of these gender effects was associated with whether or not children had participated in the Reading Recovery program. This suggests that whereas educators should remain concerned about the distinct educational difficulties experienced by boys (Mullis, Campbell, & Farstrup, 1993), the results do not suggest a need for different kinds of assistance.

One of the major limitations of this study, and indeed of many studies in this area, is the difficulty in attributing causal effects to the program. For example, children in the current study had had 2, 3, or 4 years of schooling since being on the program. It is possible that experiences during this time may have shaped their current reading skills and motivation. Indeed, their intervening teachers would probably make such a claim even though there are serious difficulties in addressing the needs of these children through regular reading instruction. Whether the answer is to provide ongoing specialist assistance to the children when they return to the classroom, or to alter the method of instruction, remains an important research question. Allied to this problem is our lack of understanding of the processes and mechanisms that mediate the relationships among instruction, learning, and motivation in the classroom. An intensive longitudinal research program involving observation and assessment both during the program and at times of transition in and out of it, including measures of early motivation not possible in this retrospective study, would provide valuable insights.

A central assumption of this study was that growth of motivation in reading, as reflected in reading self-concept, reading value, and attitude to reading, is reciprocally determined in interaction with the acquisition of reading skill. This assumption runs counter to the belief that reading instruction should focus on developing positive attitudes toward reading "even if this means reducing the attention to word analyses skills" (Saracho & Dayton, 1991, p. 44). However, there seems little doubt about the importance of motivation to the acquisition and practice of reading skills. For this reason it is important that we increase our concern about the ways in which motivation is implicated in reading success, especially for those children at risk of failure in the early school years. An assessment of motivation should become routine in the evaluation of reading programs.

References

Ames, C., & Archer, J. (1988). Achievement goals in the classroom: Students' learning strategies and motivation processes. *Journal of Educational Psychology, 80,* 260–267.

Borkowski, J. G., Carr, M., Rellinger, E., & Pressley, M. (1990). Self-regulated cognition: Interdependence of metacognition, attributions, and self-esteem. In B. F. Jones & L. Idol (Eds.), *Dimensions of thinking and instruction* (pp. 53–92). Hillsdale, NJ: Erlbaum.

Center, Y., Wheldall, K., Freeman, L., Outhred, L., & McNaught, M. (1995). An evaluation of Reading Recovery. *Reading Research Quarterly, 30,* 240–263.

Chapman, J. W., & Tunmer, W. E. (2000). Early reading related skills and performance, reading self-concept, and the development of academic self-concept: A longitudinal study. *Journal of Educational Psychology, 92,* 703–708.

Chapman, J. W., Tunmer, W. E., & Ryan, H. A. (1997, July). *Reading for self-concept and self-concept for reading: The development of reading self-concept and its relation to early reading achievement.* Paper presented at a conference on "Reading on Track: Research Results for Teaching Reading," Massey University, Palmerston North, New Zealand.

Clay, M. M. (1979). *The early detection of reading difficulties.* Auckland: Heinemann.

Cramer, E., & Castle, M. (Eds.). (1994). *Fostering the love of reading: The affective domain in reading education.* Newark, DE: International Reading Association.

Dweck, C., & Elliot, E. (1983). Achievement motivation. In E. M. Hetherington (Ed.), *Handbook of child psychology: Vol. 4. Socialization, personality and social development* (pp. 643–691). New York: Wiley.

Eccles, J. (1983). Expectancies, values and academic behaviors. In J. T. Spence (Ed.), *Achievement and achievement motives* (pp. 75–146). San Francisco: Freeman.

Elley, W. B. (1992). *How in the world do students read?* Hamburg, Germany: International Association for the Evaluation of Educational Achievement.

Gambrell, L. B., & Morrow, L. M. (1996). Creating motivating contexts for literacy learning. In L. Baker, P. Afflerbach, & D. Reinking (Eds.), *Developing engaged readers in home and school communities* (pp. 115–136). Hillsdale, NJ: Erlbaum.

Gambrell, L. B., Palmer, B. M., Codling, R. M., & Mazzoni, S. A. (1996). Assessing motivation to read. *Reading Teacher, 49,* 518–533.

Glynn, E., Bethune, N., Crooks, T., Ballard, K., & Smith, J. (1992). Reading Recovery in context: Implementation and outcome. *Educational Psychology, 12,* 249–261.

Harter, S. (1981). A new self-report scale of intrinsic versus extrinsic orientation in the classroom: Motivational and informational components. *Developmental Psychology, 17,* 300–312.

Henk, W., & Melnick, S. A. (1995). The Reader Self-Perception Scale (RSPS): A new tool for measuring how children feel about themselves as readers. *Reading Teacher, 48,* 470–482.

Lyons, C. A., Pinnell, G. S., & DeFord, D. E. (1993). *Partners in learning: Teachers and children and Reading Recovery.* New York: Teachers College Press.

McKenna, M., & Kear, D. J. (1990). Measuring attitude toward reading: A new tool for teachers. *Reading Teacher, 43,* 626–639.

McKenna, M., Kear, D. J., & Ellsworth, R. A. (1995). Children's attitudes toward reading: A national survey. *Reading Research Quarterly, 30,* 3934–956.

Mullis, I. V. S., Campbell, J. R., & Farstrup, A. E. (1993). *NAEP 1992: Reading report card for the nation and the states.* Washington, DC: U.S. Department of Education.

Paris, S. G., & Oka, E. R. (1986). Self-regulated learning among exceptional children. *Exceptional Children, 53,* 103–108.

Pinnell, G. S. (1989). Reading Recovery: Helping at-risk children learn to read. *Elementary School Journal, 90,* 161–184.

Pintrich, P. R., & DeGroot, E. V. (1990). Motivational and self-regulated learning components of classroom academic performance. *Journal of Educational Psychology, 82,* 33–40.

Pintrich, P. R., & Schunk, D. H. (1996). *Motivation in education.* Englewood Cliffs, NJ: Prentice Hall.

Reid, N. A., & Elley, W. B. (1991). *Progressive Achievement Tests of Reading.* Wellington: New Zealand Council for Educational Research.

Saracho, O. N., & Dayton, C. M. (1991). Age-related changes in reading attitudes of young children: A cross-cultural study. *Journal of Research in Reading, 14,* 33–45.

Stanovich. K. E. (1986). Matthew effects in reading: Some consequences of individual differences in the acquisition of literacy. *Reading Research Quarterly, 21,* 360–406.

Strauss, A., & Corbin, J. (1990). *Basics of qualitative research: Grounded theory procedures and techniques.* Newbury Park, CA: Sage.

Townsend, M. A. R., & Hicks, L. (1997). Classroom goal structures, social satisfaction and the perceived value of academic tasks. *British Journal of Educational Psychology, 67,* 1–12.

Tunnell, M. O., Calder, J. E., Justen, J. E., & Phaup, E. S. (1988). Attitudes of young readers. *Reading Improvement, 25,* 237–242.

Turner, J., & Paris, S. G. (1995). How literacy tasks influence children's motivation for literacy. *Reading Teacher, 48,* 662–673.

Wade, B., & Moore, M. (1998). Attitudes to reading: A longitudinal study of the effectiveness of Reading Recovery. *New Zealand Journal of Educational Studies, 33,* 95–106.

Wigfield, A. (1997). Reading motivation: A domain-specific approach to motivation. *Educational Psychologist, 32,* 59–68.

Wigfield, A., & Eccles, J. S. (1992). The development of achievement task values: A theoretical analysis. *Developmental Review, 12,* 265–310.

Wilkinson, I. A. G. (1998). Dealing with diversity: Achievement gaps in reading literacy among New Zealand students. *Reading Research Quarterly, 33,* 144–167.

Commonplace Books, Commonplace Practices: Literacy and Giftedness in a Complex World

Ruth F. Wiebe
Simon Fraser University

Just as each of us has one body with many members,
and these members do not all have the same function,
so we who are many form one body,
and each member belongs to all the others.
We have different gifts . . . (Paul, Romans 12: 4–6a)

It is time for us to incorporate, to bring into the collective body, individual potential. I do not mean the breathless worship of transcendent heroes constructed within our competitive systems. To honor ability with exorbitant positional or material reward is to suggest that giftedness resides within the individual as property. I am speaking of something else entirely. When we come together in deepest humility, with a firm commitment to the impossibility of individual completeness, and an organizing celebration of the potential of community, we begin to create spaces for the construction, nurturing, and sharing of difference. Recognizing that giftedness arises always and only within the context of complex relations, we embrace our interdependence and freely bring that which is uncommon about us, weakness, strength, perception, ability, disability, into the common place where it is valued, interpreted, and used in the body corporate.

In this essay, I revisit the understandings of giftedness that infused my childhood community, drawing implications for educators in terms of such pathologies as learning disabilities. As mother, researcher, teacher, and writer, I move among modes, narrative, reflective, and expository, to consider hermeneutically connections between lived experience and more traditionally constructed knowledge. Finally, I suggest particular practices, commonplace practices, that celebrate and nurture giftedness-within-community.

The data that form the core of this paper are drawn from a variety of sources, collected through various methods. Formally conducted over the course of 1 year, my study with Alison involved taped interviews, reciprocal response journals, and reflections on her own writings. She did read this account and concurred with its conclusions. The story of Robert was developed through several interviews. Maureen was twice a student of mine over a 3-year period; her story was gathered through interviews, through my reading of her assignments and journals, and through narrative reflection. In the stories of James, of Tristan, and of the sixth-grade classroom, I took the role of participant-observer. They were recorded in my

National Reading Conference Yearbook, ***50****, pp. 597–609.*

own commonplace book following experiences in the classroom. All names have been changed.

Exploring Notions of Sameness

There is evidence that along with global urbanization has come the greatest cultural homogeneity since prehistoric times (Bowers, 1993). Satellite-facilitated telecommunications ensure the availability of pop culture in West Vancouver's mansions and the favellas of Rio. A computer virus initiated in the Philippines has impact on individuals in multiple nations. World religions are being encouraged toward the politically benign "god-as-you-perceive-him-or-her-to-be." To be noted as "educated" anywhere implies an ability to communicate, and perhaps to think, in English.

School systems align with this trend: No matter where I pose the question, "What is the one thing that 'successful' schools must do?" adults respond, "teach children to read." UNICEF (2000) includes literacy among its goals and strategies. Traditionally oral cultures are moving in this direction as well (Carlson, Carlson, Thom, & McHalsie, 1996).

The implications of this are profound for, though with homogeneity comes increased efficiency and ability to communicate broadly, there is an accompanying vulnerability that must also be considered. Just as the alignment of computer platforms has made us globally susceptible to viruses, so uniformity in thinking patterns limits our resistance to unpredictable factors. With literacy comes an altered relation with our surroundings (Abram, 1997; Bowers, 1993). No longer dependent upon our senses for the location of food sources, and no longer requiring sentient vigilance in ensuring safety from predators, we can focus consciousness on text-based activities. As our livelihoods become ever more dependent upon information processing, this distancing-from-the-world increases.

As an individual charged with children's literate development, it concerns me that I may be fostering this dissociation. I must bear this in mind, infusing literate activities with those who require bodily connection with surroundings. But there is another, perhaps more pressing concern: What happens when children are unable to make the requisite separation? For some, the cause may be environmental. Having grown up in situations in which food and safety are scarce, their senses are engaged by survival concerns. For others, it may be a matter of sensation. Hypersensitive to environmental stimuli and, therefore, deeply connected bodily to surrounding events, they may not be able to separate consciousness long enough to engage in reading.

Consider Robert's story. As a child, he loved to construct things mechanical. Unable to learn to read, at the age of 10 he left school for the family farm, all the while developing his skills as a metal worker. Later he became a trucker. One of the most frustrating events was having his rig off the road for extended periods of time while the universal joint was replaced. Eventually, through visualization, he "walked his way" through the problem and developed a wrench that would exert leverage at just the right points, dislodge the u-joint and shorten the repair time significantly. After successfully marketing this tool, he invented many more. At age 70, he sold his multimillion dollar corporation. He never learned to read or write.

We may think that such stories are byproducts only of the long-past. Tristan is a seventh-grade student in our neighborhood school. He cannot read and has great difficulty attending to instruction. But he loves the stage and is active in local theater. Recently, his class was discussing the effects of advertising. Tristan stood up and improvised an entertaining and insightful 10-minute monologue of an advertising executive convincing teens to take up smoking. Much of his time is spent with a learning assistance teacher, working through a torturous list of decontextualized literacy lessons. Despite his known gifts, his disability has become the organizer of his school day.

The move toward "sameness" that most troubles me is this societal expectation that all must conform through schooling. I agree with Schmitt (1994) when he says that there are more creative ways of addressing the particular characteristics associated with what we have come to call learning disabilities. He considers his own dyslexia a kind of gift that allows him to experience the world with great visual intensity. Grandin (1995) writes of her autism not as a disability in understanding human relationships but as an extreme ability in understanding the minds of animals. Both have come to see their "disabilities" as differences that function positively within society, a view that I do not see supported in schools.

In Search of Difference

Today, as I enter this particular sixth-grade classroom, I am struck by apparent sameness. Though ethnic diversity is present, clothing and casual conversation reveal a common set of values. I am here to focus on reading assessment. The teacher and I take a running record of each child's oral reading behaviors, discuss with each child the strategies that he or she is using in solving reading problems, and leave each with a response assignment. By the time I leave, I have begun to ascertain differences: some are struggling with the English language itself, others are battling the mysteries of print, one is partially blind, another has been pathologized as hyperactive. In response to the story, some write paragraphs, others itemize events; some draw stick figures, others create elaborate drawings, one makes a chart, others create webs. Despite their outward similarity, I quickly know that these children are quite diverse. And we have just begun. Though we have learned a great deal, we still know nothing about these students' attitudes, perceptions, backgrounds, or passions.

For though they are trying hard to look and act just like the idealized Western 11-year-old, it is in the development of personal uniqueness that their strength will lie. And it is in the sharing of that uniqueness, the celebration and nurture of it, that a strong community will grow. Superficial similarity may remain but it is imperative that these students come to understand the importance of their own giftedness and the processes by which it is developed and expressed in concert with friends.

I was raised in Community. Though quite liberal in comparison with the very traditional Mennonite communities of eastern North America, our small colony might be judged as fostering religious and social homogeneity. And yet, in forming a committed community, it was recognized that what would hold us together were not our similarities but our differences: the distinct abilities, insights, perceptions, and perspectives that each of us embodied. We equated these with giftedness, not in the "school sense" as a socially constructed "category created by tests and measurements" (Pinar, Reynolds, Slattery, & Taubman, 1996, p. 463) implying exceptional ability, but as a set of characteristics enacted, concurrently, within each-of-us-within-the-group as complex interactions worked to build society.

The Community and Giftedness

When I was born, it was assumed that, should I choose to participate, eventually the community would know particular gifts because of my presence. As these would arise concurrent with the needs of the community, they would never be known as "my" gifts. But they were not wholly the community's either because without me these particular gifts would be absent. They were, then, situated neither in me nor in the community, but in the inclusive relationship that existed between us. The same could be said for every member. In each person, gifts developed within the interactions that comprised the community. Giftedness infused and co-specified the context within which it grew.

Because they were all necessary, no gift was to be considered less or more important than any other gift. If the community were healthy, and focused on living within the largess of God, needs would be met. If the community were selfish or materialistic, or began to arrogantly deem some members more significant than others, gifts would not arise and the group would become spiritually and emotionally needy. It was incumbent upon the community, then, to maintain both its relationship with God and an atmosphere of nonjudgmental love among members. My forebears lived together in this way for centuries, denying the comforts of "the world," accepting as sufficient the giftedness that became apparent within the group.

Sometimes gifts came in unexpected forms. It was accepted that each person, in as much as he or she brought unique gifts, also was a unique gift. All children, aging parents, the handicapped, the dying were considered contributing members. It was up to the community to incorporate members' particular experiences into the common construction of knowledge and belief.

The implications of this were many. As children, although we were encouraged to act in socially normed ways, we were also encouraged to be aware of and thankful for those characteristics about ourselves and our friends that were different from everyone else. As we grew older, we were encouraged to develop and freely contribute our special skills and insights. We were consciously taught not to expect to do everything on our own but, in humility, to rely on the giftedness of our neighbors as they relied on ours. And we were taught not to judge the importance of gifts, but to interpret even those that were hardest to accept as having a potential for positive impact.

A Historical Perspective

All of this developed neither quickly nor in isolation. The meanderings of my people began in sixteenth-century Holland. As the humanistic followers of Menno Simons, they were driven from their homeland because they challenged the authority of the Pope. They fanned out through Prussia, only to be sent to horrific deaths by the leaders of the Protestant Reformation. They kept on moving. At various times, splinter sects would escape the persecution by finding their way to America: the Pennsylvania "Dutch," the Amish, the Huldemanne. The New World became a common knot for the disparate strands forming the tapestry of this earthy people.

Another such knot was formed on the vast Ukrainian steppe. Farming communally on prime bottomland, villages grew affluent and large. Within a hundred years, the Mennonite presence in Russia filled two massive colonies in the watershed of the Dnieper River. Some leaders became concerned that people had grown dependent on their wealth. A schism developed and, after giving dire warnings of materialism and impending judgment, one group moved south into the Crimean Peninsula and, from there, to the United States. In the 1870s, this rather narrow strand rested in Kansas, the birthplace of my mother's parents.

My father's family stayed in the colonies until, property confiscated by the various armies of the Revolution, they escaped by train in 1926. Ten years after their penniless arrival in Canada, my grandfather and three of his sons had managed to buy a square half-mile of stumpy land. Across the road, one set of cousins did the same and, down and up the connecting roads, other sets, until an area of about 10 square miles was owned by relatives and friends. Central to that community stood the church and the cooperative store. My family's land abutted the store along the north side of the main road, and was equally divided into four narrow, deep farms. Uncle Abram was the oldest of the sons. Brusque and entrepreneurial, he was credited with having bribed the officials who finally allowed the family to leave the Ukraine. He was also a skilled builder who ran the lumberyard and was responsible for additions to family houses and barns. While everyone assisted, he oversaw all construction. A successful farmer, he provided nieces and nephews with summer work. No one expected him to be sociable, however; his efficiency in farming and building was matched by a lack of diplomacy in his relations with others. Uncle Jacob, on the other hand, was friendly and conversational. To him fell the sale of crops, the purchase of supplies, and other business negotiations. The first to hold an "outside" job, he led the way for others. Aunt Martha was gifted in terms of hospitality, continually welcoming strangers and neighbors to her table. As children, we ran through her kitchen, stole from her pantry, explored her attics, and thumped noisily down her scarred staircases. In contrast, children would not consider entering Aunt Frieda's porch, let alone that stark and spotless kitchen. Everyone acknowledged, however, the superiority of the milk that came freely from her whitewashed barn. Grandfather was quite elderly. No longer capable of heavy work, he tended the family orchard. My mother, with imagination and a Canadian education, cited Tennyson and read to us the writings of Lewis Carroll. My father was sent to university, becoming a lay minister. While he studied, my aunts, uncles, and mother tended our farm.

All of this I came to know because we spent so much authentic time together, in common spaces, doing common things, differently. We gathered in groups to sing, to study scripture, to pray, to play. We ate together at weddings and celebrations and picked berries together through the hard heat of July. At Christmas, the massive feasts were combined with hours of stories, songs, and performances. We came to know, deeply, each other's dislikes and preferences, strengths and weaknesses. And in all of that, we constructed our selves as we constructed our community. The processes were inseparable.

The differences I experienced among the adults of my community enriched my learning, providing optional pathways and multiple tools as I began to develop agency and identity. My father paved the way for those who chose higher education. My uncles assisted in setting up businesses. Our mothers provided a variety of role models: some held jobs outside the home; others ran farms; still others spent most of their time keeping house. The willingness of adults to contribute diversely facilitated our resilience in light of sweeping cultural change. We children became extremely adaptable, moving out of our village into myriad positions in cities around the world. We could not have done this if we had not been taught to value personal difference.

Announcing the Common Place

With this in mind, I return to the sixth-grade classroom. Today, I hope to create locations that will open their eyes and mine to the gifts we bring to this group. The story, a fairy tale set in China, recounts how the daughter of an emperor sets out to protect a precious tree by building a wall. Over the years, as her concurrent love and anxiety grow, she orders the wall to be raised. Eventually, this wall cuts off sun and rain, and the tree dies, leaving the princess with only a handful of fruit. Realizing her folly, the princess plants the seeds of the final cherries, hoping they will grow. She vehemently promises that there will be no more walls.

After reading and processing the story, we begin to get at the theme. No one seems to connect with questions about having felt overprotected but, with a slight shift in focus, the stories begin to come: It turns out that, although few of them have felt restricted by protection, many of them have felt the need to protect. They chat with each other about their connections, scratch their ideas onto one side of their papers, discuss this web with a friend, and then begin to draft a story. Later, some of them read their stories to the class. Chris tells about the mint-condition, first-edition comic collection he is building. He cannot afford classics, so he is calculating which new ones might be valuable in the future, purchasing them at first-issue prices, storing them in special cases, and never reading them. We learn from Tanjeet that she received a special doll from her grandmother who has since died. She feels the threat of younger sisters who want to play with this special toy. This reminds Darren of a stuffed bear he received for this first birthday. One by one, the stories emerge, their stories of the things they value, the efforts they go to protect them, the intricacies of family. The murmurs begin: I have a toy like that, too; my brothers are always getting into my stuff; you have *that* comic?; can I see your hockey cards some time? A few of them conclude that overprotectiveness has cost them the joy of the item itself. Keith had a fish that he hid in a closet to protect it from his cat. It died, he thinks, for lack of sunlight and friendship. Jonathan writes that his love of skateboarding is dying because his anxious mother will not let him go alone to the skateboard park. A classmate invites him to use his front yard ramp.

Before our time is up, we are beginning to talk about our lives beyond the facade of sameness. We are beginning to form humanizing connections.

I know we have much further to go.

I have been here before with my eldest child.

Alison and Commonplace Practices

From the time Alison was born, I could sense the unease in her. As she grew older, she bit, hit, and fought at the slightest provocation. Her tantrums and resistance would cause all of us pain. Alison's best times were when she was alone paging through a catalogue or magazine.

Kindergarten and the primary grades were chaos. She screamed and bashed, was bullied, ran from classrooms, shook with terror. Still, she managed her academic learning and everyone felt assured that the rest would come. I worked hard to "help" her look like everyone else. My major hope was that through a combination of cajoling and force I would somehow be able to normalize her: She would no longer destroy pretty classrooms but would go to school quietly, sit in restaurants, visit like other children did. My efforts failed. Over the years we settled into an uneasy truce, broken by passionate battles. For the most part, however, Alison existed in silent isolation.

At some point during those years, Alison became a reader. She surrounded herself with a growing library, spent hours sequestered in her room, and continually carried a shopping bag of stories. One day, as part of an assignment in a literary response course I was taking, I asked her what she was reading. Among other titles, she mentioned *Middlemarch* (Eliot, 1872/1981). She was 15. Taken aback, I explored further and discovered that she was working her way through complex works of literature, a different title for each day of the week, with systematic habits of record-keeping and insightful response. Five years of data testified that I had missed much about this child.

Reciprocal Response Journals

With encouragement from my professor and classmates, I began to read with her, hoping to get a clearer picture of Alison's view of the world. I had previously learned that asking her for an opinion resulted in a mere shrug and "I don't know . . . I don't want to talk about it . . ." I asked her if she would like to read with me and we decided to work our way through *The True Confessions of Charlotte Doyle* (Avi, 1990). After reading each of four sections, we wrote personal responses. In addition, we wrote a prediction of each other's response. Several things became evident during this joint exploration. First, Alison's predictions of my responses were much more accurate than mine were of hers. Given her great fascination with the study of history, I predicted that she would write rather clinically about the adventure within the plot, about the historical setting and associated events, in short, that she would read efferently rather than aesthetically.

She did not. Rather, she wrote in direct response to the emotions of the main character, identifying with Charlotte's nervousness in meeting new people, the vulnerability caused by her aloneness at sea, and the anxiety she felt when anticipating her return to her family: "She wants to be her own person." Alison predicted, correctly, that my response would connect Charlotte's nervousness with her own, and that I would question the wisdom of the parents in sending an unescorted adolescent on an ocean voyage.

Through her responses, I learned that Alison was able to anticipate my locations of connection much better than I was able to predict hers. Clearly, I needed to know her better. As we continued our work together, it became apparent that discussion in response to reading provided a location for deeper conversations than we had ever experienced before. Though I had thought she often read superficially, with neither analysis or connection, one day she spoke at length about the changing role of women in Western society. She also talked about peer pressure: "I make my own decisions. If it's not something I want to do and I've made my mind up about it, I'm going to be adamant about it." For the first time, I could see that what I had interpreted as her "blind stubbornness" also had positive potential. She told me that she had learned to listen to the ideas of other people, to compare them with her own ideas, and to change her mind when she needed to. She was also becoming reflective about her passion for history. When she was young, she simply memorized facts; now she was learning that "facts" are open to interpretation: "I know in Socials Studies that I know the right answer and sometimes I have to be willing to get the answer wrong in order to be able to understand other's views on things. And I also learned that people's views change—they aren't going to be the same, year after year."

And so, by initiating a commonplace location through the character of Charlotte Doyle, we began, in Alison's words, "a habit of talking about things." I learned that many of my assumptions about her were false. She did feel deep positive emotions even though she did not express them readily. She did have an understanding that changing one's opinion in light of other people's ideas was different from bowing to peer pressure. She could consider the perspective of others if given time and support.

Discussion of Personal Connections

Jane Eyre (Bronte, 1874/1992), her favorite novel, was our next topic of discussion. Through it, I learned about what Alison calls her "dark side," that tendency to become angry and disoriented, and then to withdraw. It was something she did not want to talk about, something she was "trying hard to forget." Our conversation, then, was short. This was a book that she loved but was uncomfortable discussing. We left it for another time.

Next, we went on to *Nobody Nowhere* by Donna Williams (1992). Here, in response to Williams's description about clouds of light, Alison first told me about her tendency to sit in class and "watch the air . . . it looks like the snow on the television. . . . I like watching it when I get bored." Whereas I had known that she was hypersensitive to sound, this comment convinced me that she perceived light more acutely, as well. I mentioned this conversation to one of our district psychologists. "I think she might have Asperger's," she said.

Interpreting Asperger's Syndrome

The journey through medical pathologizing is never a pleasant one, but through it I have gained an appreciation of the giftedness that is inherent in my daughter's syndrome. Like other children who share her perceptual profile, she is able, given time and silence, to explain the intricacies of social situations. In the moment, however, she is often distracted because of her intense hypersensitivity to sound, light, and touch. She finds it painful to be in large groups, and avoids environmental noise as much as possible. At the same time, her hypersensitivity gives her a more acute appreciation of nature. She is the one who points out the songs of new birds in the yard, predicts that it will soon be raining because "the air is already beginning to fall," and, in her learned capacity for controlling chaos, reminds us of appointments and birthdays. Her special giftedness helps to meet these needs in us. In turn, we provide her with space to manage her anxieties, express her opinions, and spend hours alone, reading. She attends university now, has learned to drive and, with our help, entertain. We are constructing community.

James and Commonplace Practices

James was a student who taught me much about giftedness and community. Coming into the library in September of the fifth grade, he announced that he did not need a book because he "couldn't read anyway." Instead, he wanted to make a copy of the funeral mask of Tutankhamen: did I know of any pictures and where might they be? A few weeks later I saw an astonishingly beautiful and accurate clay rendition of the famous mask standing in the office window.

James's artistic ability was not limited to copying. With creativity and thought he completed assignments through sculpture, drawing, or painting. For someone so young, his work was commanding and was often featured at local art shows. Nevertheless, though he had received several years of learning assistance, he could not read or write beyond a first-grade level.

Literary Response Groups

By sixth grade, James's reading and writing had improved little, though his artistic talents had continued to develop. His classroom teacher and I decided to set up a group that would look at a variety of ways of responding to reading. Our hope was that, as curiosity and experimentation deepened, our students would begin to construct a learning community that was not only inclusive of, but also dependent upon, a variety of perceptual and representational styles. James was concerned. He could not read well and wanted nothing to do with a literature group. With the assurance that much of the text could be read to him, either in class or at home, and that he could represent his knowledge, images, and feelings in any way he liked, he agreed to participate. After several sessions, he was surprised to find that he enjoyed the group and that his contributions during discussions were considered astute. With our guidance, the group decided to create a joint response in the form of a video. James, always imaginative, contributed to discussions about the script while others recorded the words. He took leadership in constructing a set, something that would have been quite difficult for the group to accomplish without him. As they worked, they talked about their lives, their interests, their fears. Gradually, they came to rely on and to know each other in deeper ways, interpreting the text, their lives, and the script as one event in the construction of self and of knowing. Ironically, with literacy no longer the privileged mode, James's reading and writing skills grew markedly. As he drew others' ideas and they scripted his, he came to see relationships that he had somehow missed. He needed this location that nurtured and valued his differences as strengths, rather than focused on them as weaknesses.

Maureen's Commonplace Book

Maureen is learning to construct these sorts of learning locations. As a teacher of students with special needs, she would like other teachers to care about her students as much as she does, but often she feels that they are attempting to distance themselves. She wants to help them see the giftedness of her students, but realizes she must first see it herself.

She begins by keeping a commonplace book (Sumara, 1996). In it she records her conversations with teachers, her observations of her students, and her rather lengthy notes about Jerry, a young boy with severe speech difficulties. She includes poetry linking his difficulties with speech and her struggles with voice. She records her frustrations as a single mother, coming home to make dinner and finding no vegetables other than a lone onion. She writes about the guilt in not being able to meet the needs of her students, her own children, her self. Somewhere in this process she comes to empathize with the classroom teachers who, too, have no tools for meeting her expectations of them.

As the semester progresses, Maureen begins tape-recording Jerry's few words and playing them back so that he can hear the sound of his own voice. He makes a tape for our class and we respond. Maureen incorporates sections of the transcripts and our matching responses into her commonplace book. She also plays the tape during a staff meeting, talking about Jerry's struggles and the significance of his progress. She tells the staff about his strengths: he is able to write on the computer now and, with her, has developed an ability to create poetry. She reads it to them and goes on to talk about the tools she is learning for supporting students with special needs; she asks if anyone is interested in exploring these with her. Two teachers respond. Using their various strengths they too begin forming a community.

It is through the writing of her life in her commonplace book that Maureen has developed the voice she craved. This location of intertextual interpretation (Pinar et al., p. 436) has woven the seemingly disparate threads of her life into a single, completely new, fabric.

In the complexity of the classroom, it is difficult to think in terms of focusing on developing uniqueness. Society, after all, has asked us to work toward homogeneity. Mandated outcomes and standards, developed over fears of inequities within the public school system, regulate the content of student learning and investigation. We are pushed toward developing independent, as distinct from interdependent, learners. In attempting to achieve an atmosphere of professional accountability, ministries of education issue standardized measurements. We are attempting to manage the perceived complexity of human relations by imposing objectification. It is easy to assess student learning based on progress against a list of skills and standardized measures. It is easy, through criterion referencing, to impose the definition of powerful learning before it is lived. It is much more difficult to ascertain whether, as literate beings, we are developing our collective ability to participate in the type of communication that constructs knowledge from unique, diverse perspectives.

I am concerned about our tendency to reduce complexity. Theorists speculate that decreasing the number of agents, or variables, within a dynamical system reduces the ability of the system to adapt to changes in the environment (Waldrop, 1992). Our world population is undergoing unprecedented shifts. In years to come, our collective ability to produce food, protect species, and adapt to crowded conditions will demand creativity of thought (Bowers, 1993). Although many of us espouse a belief in the importance of interdependence, I wonder whether we may have a very narrow vision of what interdependence might mean. Mostly we think of it as involving people who are relatively homogeneous in terms of perception and cognition. If we take into account what complexity theorists have to say, however, we must consider that diversity in sensing, perceiving, and acting is the normal and necessary result of the co-evolutionary process that ensures our survival as a species (Waldrop, 1992, pp. 320–322). As educators, then, we become mindful of the need to create locations that will invite the mutual sharing of significantly different ways of being. Only then can we begin a truly humanizing discourse of the sort promoted by Freire (1993), not through standardizing curriculum outcomes or strategies, but through supporting children and teachers in forming and communicating their own interpretations within a context of genuine interest and concern.

As teachers, it is important that we create spaces for the evolution of unpredictable knowledge. Reading response represented in commonplace books and practices announces a location for diverse perspectives to be generated, experienced, valued, and co-developed. Complexity is celebrated and contained, held continually on that edge of chaos and order.

Conclusion

As we address issues of complexity, survival, and community, must we consider that those characteristics we have collectively labeled as learning disabilities are constructed within our cultures because, at some deep, unadmitted, preconceptual level, we know that it is in difference that our continuation as a species rests? Perhaps some primal memory warns us that we need multiple perceptual profiles—someone needs to hear, smell, see, with greater acuity than the rest of us. Just as we need highly literate people, we need people like Robert who remain highly mechanical, and people like James who remain highly visual, and people like Alison who stay attuned with our natural space. We need musicians who will express understanding in nonstatic ways and artists who will enact thought nonlinguistically. We need gifted environmentalists to remind us that humans interact not only with each other but with all species, with the matter we have been and will be again. Lewis (1946/1997, p. viii) asserted that as we move toward cultural sophistication, individuals will become less alike, while depending upon each other more. Maturated diversity, rather than undeveloped sameness, is characteristic of a healthy, educated community. Socialization is interpreted not as a process of conformity but as the process of learning collectively to nurture, value, and exercise the individuality evolving within the wholeness of relations among members. We need to know that there is something individual, unique, that arises in us-within-the-community and that in this difference lies our legitimate reason for participating.

It is in the common place that we come to know and construct that which is uncommon. It is there that we begin to catch glimpses of what might be if we were to somehow commit to the symphony that is humanity. Let us teach our children to expect that place.

References

Abram, D. (1997). *The spell of the sensuous : Perception and language in a more-than-human world.* New York: Vintage.

Avi. (1990). *The true confessions of Charlotte Doyle.* New York: Avon.

Bowers, C. A. (1993). *Education, cultural myths, and the ecological crisis : Toward deep changes.* New York: SUNY Press.

Bronte, C. (1874/1992). *Jane Eyre.* London: Penguin.

Carlson, M., Carlson, K., Thom, B., & McHalsie, A. (1996). *Spoken literature : Stó:lo oral narratives.* [On-line]. Available: http://web20.mindlink.not/stolo/

Eliot, G. (1872/1981). *Middlemarch.* London: Penguin.

Freire, P. (1993). *Pedagogy of the oppressed.* New York: Continuum.

Grandin, T. (1995). *Thinking in pictures and other reports from my life with autism.* New York: Vintage.

Lewis, C. S. (1946/1977). *The great divorce.* London: HarperCollins.

Pinar, W. F., Reynolds, W. M., Slattery, P., & Taubman, P. M. (1996). *Understanding curriculum : An introduction to the study of historical and contemporary curriculum discourses.* New York: Peter Lang.

Schmitt, A. (1994). *Brilliant idiot: An autobiography of a dyslexic.* Intercourse, PA: Good Books.

Sumara, D. (1996). *Private readings in public.* New York: Peter Lang.

UNICEF (2000). *Core messages and strategies in education.* [On-line]. Available: http://www.unicef.org/pdeduc/education/about.htm.

Waldrop, M. M. (1992). *Complexity : The emerging science at the edge of order and chaos.* New York: Touchstone.

Williams, D. (1992). *Nobody nowhere.* Toronto: Doubleday Canada.

Linking Literacies of Yesterday and Today with Literacies of Tomorrow: A Coda to the National Reading Conference's 50th Annual Meeting

Peter B. Mosenthal*

Syracuse University

> . . . a system is like the tail of truth, but truth is like a lizard; it leaves its tail in your fingers and runs away knowing full well that it will grow a new one in a twinkling.
>
> —Ivan Turgeney to Leo Tolstoy (1956; cited in Boorstin, 1983, p. 81)

A Tale of Old

Trying to recapture memories in history is not unlike Turgeney's capturing the tail of a lizard; one is left holding the tail while the animal continues on through time. And so it is with National Reading Conference (NRC). The 50th Annual Meeting of NRC has come and gone; the spirit of NRC has redefined itself as it continues its ontogeny at the 2001 meeting in San Antonio, Texas. All that remains are remnants of the tail (tale).

The tale is one that had both important stagehands as well as actors. Figured prominently in the former were the remarkable Area Chairs who oversaw the submission and review process for the Conference. These included: Cynthia Lewis and Heriberto Godina (Area I: Children's, Young Adult and Adult Literature); Patricia R. Schmidt (Area II: Literacy Processes: Long-Standing NRC Emphasis: Elementary,Secondary); Jodi Holschuh (Area III: Literacy Processes: Long-Standing NRC Emphasis: College/Adult Reading); Janice F. Almasi (Area IV: Literacy Processes: Focusing on Pre-School, Early Childhood and Elementary-Age Learners); Elizabeth Moje and LeeAnn Sutherland (Area V: Literacy Processes: Middle School, High School, and Adult Learners); Lesley Mandel Morrow (Area VI: Learning/Teaching Processes); William H. Rupley (Area VII: Teacher Education—Early Childhood/Elementary); William Dee Nichols (Area VIII: Teacher Education, Middle School/Secondary); Kelly Chandler (IX: Emergent Literacy); Virginia Goatley and Vanessa Machado (Area X: Special Populations); Georgia Earnest García (Area XI: Literacy and Language Diversity); Anne McGill-Franzen (Area XII: Assessment, Evaluation, and Policy Issues); and Dennis Mike (Area XIII: Technology and Media). Also of tremendous help were Judi Burnison and Crissy Coit from NRC Headquarters and the many reviewers who so graciously gave of their time and talents.

*NRC Program Chair 2000.

*National Reading Conference Yearbook, **50**, pp. 611–614.*

Other individuals who contributed significantly behind the scenes included members of the NRC Executive Board (Taffy E. Raphael [President], Deborah R. Dillon [Vice President Elect], Lee Gunderson [Secretary], and Peter Dewitz [Treasurer]), as well as Board Members (Richard Beach, Elfrieda H. Hiebert, Georgia Earnest Garcia, Douglas Hartman, Donald Leu, and Lesley Mandel Morrow). Significant others who helped implement the organization's agenda were Beth Roberts (Parliamentarian); Norman A. Stahl (Historian); David Reinking, Donna E.Alvermann, and Cynthia R. Hynd (Editors of the *Journal of Literacy Research*);Timothy Shanahan and Flora V. Rodriguez-Brown (Editors of the *NRC Yearbook*); and Cynthia Brock and Mary Rozendal (Newsletter Editors).

Yet another group of individuals who deserve recognition for advancing NRC's programmatic causes were the Committee Chairs (Lesley Mandel Morrow [Albert J. Kingston Award], Maureen McLaughlin [Ethics], Jeannie Steel and Riita Liisa Körkeamaki [International]; Arlette Ingram Willis [Multicultural and Diversity Issues]; Barbara Kapinus [Policy and Legislative]; Susan B. Neuman [Publications]; Maribeth Scmitt [Student Outstanding Research Award]; Michael Kamil [Technology] Laurie MacGillivray [Critical Spaces]; Trika Smith-Burke [Distinguished Educator Award]; Susan McMahon and Jeanne Paratore [Early Career Achievement Award]; Laura Roehler [Ed Fry Book Award]; Kathryn H. Au [Long Range Planning]; Doug Hartman [Oscar Causey Award]; and Dana L. Grisham and Deborah Tidwell [Field Council]. Acknowledgments also must be given to John McEneaney for maintaining NRC's web site and Barbara Guzzetti for maintaining NRC's listserve.

Overall, there were 488 submissions to this conference. This included 148 round tables, 70 joint round tables, 158 paper-sessions, 57 alternative sessions, and 55 symposia. Given that this was the 50th Anniversary Conference, a special effort was made to include as many participants as possible; as such, 85% of the submissions were accepted. The raw number of submissions and percent accepted by Area were as follows (from lowest to highest number of submissions): 7/100% (Area 3), 14/86% (Area 9), 18/100% (Vice President's Area), 25/88% (Area 8), 25/92% (Area 12), 25/92% (Area 13), 28/75% (Area 2); 31/87% (Area 1); 41/80% (Area 10), 41/80% (Area 11), 43/84% (Area 4), 48/83% (Area 6), 53/85% (Area 5); and 89/69% (Area 7).

The 978 registered participants had the opportunity to hear Susan Hynds (Middle Ground: Literacy for Social Action in the Middle Grades) open with the First Plenary session on Wednesday. Becky Barr (The Bridging of Cultures: How Can Inquiries by Outsiders Inform Educational Practice?) gave the Oscar Causey Address on Thursday morning. On Thursday afternoon, Taffy E. Raphael (Literacy Teaching, Literacy Learning: Lessons from Book Club Plus) gave the Presidential Address. On Friday, Carl A. Grant (Reconceptualizing Literacy in Multicultural Terms: Taking Issue with Commonplace Notions of Print, Pedagogy, and Epistemology) presented the Second Plenary Address. On Saturday, Karen K. Wixson teamed with Sheila W. Valencia (Policy That Makes a Difference: Reading Performance and Practice) to present the Review of Research Address.

Eight Study Groups were run in the morning to extend participants' insights into current issues. Among these were the following (along with the organizer of each study group): (1) America Reads Challenge Programs (Abha Gupta); (2) Learning to Read and Spell (Linnea C. Ehri); (3) Teacher Education Research (Sheila Cohen); (4) Instructional Text and the Beginning Reader (Heidi Anne E. Mesmer); (5) Reading/Literacies Clinics (Barbara Laster and Penny Freppon); (6) Reading Initiatives and the Research Community (Kathleen Heubach); (7) Literacy Learning Through Technology (Greg Brooks); and (8) Addressing Policy, Practice, and Research Issues Associated with High-Stake Standards Assessment (Michael D. Hardt).

A sample of the many exemplary sessions is the following. The History of NRC: The Past 50 Years (Deborah R. Dillon, Chair); Discussing Issues Regarding the Connection between Technology and Literacy (Dennis G. Mike, Chair); Using Reading Research to Make Laws (Kenneth S. Goodman, Chair); The RAND Reading Study Group: Charting the Course for a National Research Agenda in Skillful Reading (Anne Sweet and Catherine Sweet, Co-Chairs); National Commission on Excellence in Elementary Teacher Preparation for Reading Instruction: Findings, Implications and Recommendations (Cathy M. Roller, Chair); Seeing Worlds in Grains of Sand: Cases, Complexity and Cognitive Flexibility in the Teachers Learning Collaborative (Rand Spiro, Chair); Augmenting the Canon: Promoting Multicultural and Multi-ethnic Literature in Diverse Classrooms (Arlette Willis, Chair); Putting Students First in the Context of Current Political and Educational Agendas (Cathy Collins Block and Michael Pressley, Co-chairs); Later Literacies: A Panel Discussion on the Politics of Adolescent and Adult Literacy (Elizabeth Birr Moje); Building Connections Between Home and School to Strengthen a Preschool Literacy Intervention Program (David B. Yaden, Jr., Chair); The CIERA School Change Project (Year 1): Implementing Research-Based Reading Program Reform in High-Poverty Elementary Schools (Deanna Birdyshaw, Chair); Entering the Media Millennium: Media Literacy Practices and Research (Ann Watts Pailliotet, Chair); Cross-Disciplinary Perspectives on Children's and Young Adult Literature (Cynthia A. Lewis, Chair); Understanding the History of Reading Histories: The Cyclical Nature of Reading Reform (Chair, Gerry Giordano);Instructional Research on Reading: Final Report on the Work of the National Reading Panel (Michael L. Kamil, Chair); Examining Key Issues in Second-Language Acquisition (Eurydice B. Bauer, Chair); Phonological Awareness and Reading: Issues in Development and Instruction (Michael D. Hardt, Chair); The New Millenniums Plus Fifty: Where Are We Going and How Will We Get There? (Lenore H. Ringler, Chair); and the National Reading Conference Oral History Project (Norman A. Stahl and James R. King, Co-Chairs).

In addition to such fine sessions, there were many opportunities for participants to share ideas. Included among these was the Wednesday night's Plenary Speakers' Recognition Reception, Thursday night's President's Reception, Friday night's Champagne Reception and Semi-Centennial Anniversary Dinner, and Saturday's Vital Issues in the President's Suite.

As has been NRC's long-standing tradition, numerous awards were presented to give recognition to excellence in research and service. The recipients and their awards were as follows: Michael Pressley, Oscar Causey Award; Albert J. Kingston Award, Lee Gunderson; Student Outstanding Research Award—Rebecca Rogers, Early Career Achievement Award—Elizabeth B. Moje, Ed Fry Book Award, "Inside City Schools: Investigating Literacy in Multicultural Classrooms," Sarah W. Freedman, Elizabeth R. Simons, Julie S. Kalnin, Alex C. Reno, and the M-Class Team. NRC is honored to make these awards to such exceptional Individuals.

A Tale of New

With partial credits to the tale of NRC 2000 etched above, there is still the ontogeny of the "lizard" itself to consider. Although NRC has not grown extensively in membership the past several years, it has grown enormously more complex. In short, it has greatly expanded its mission and its membership. While the organization once served as an incubation for new research ideas in reading, the mission has shifted to transforming those ideas into socially responsive agendas—agendas set to promote equality, equity, fairness, access, opportunity, and critical knowledge in literacy research, practice, policy, and technology. The membership, which once was largely white male professors, has expanded to include individuals and groups representing numerous educational professions (e.g., researchers, teachers, administrators, reading specialists) as well as diverse races, ethnic groups, ESL groups, and geographical communities.

In light of this complexity, the NRC Board is in the process of updating and refining its By-Laws and its Policy and Procedures Handbook. In so doing, the Board is attempting, with the help of the NRC membership, to redefine NRC's operative structure, moving the organization from one that largely responds to key policy issues to one that helps to inform and set such issues. Concomitantly, the Board is currently considering how the organization can provide much more training for future literacy researchers and teachers so that they are able to conceptually grasp not only the lizard's tail, but the whole of the lizard.

Indeed, this is a time when every Educational Week features a major story about reading or literacy at the local, state, or national level. The challenge for NRC is not how these issues should shape NRC but how NRC should shape these issues. Hopefully, in the next 50 years, NRC will be in a position to undertake this shaping. How effective it is in this pursuit, time and a tail (tale) will tell.

Reference

Boorstin, D. (1983). *The discoverers.* New York: Vintage.

Program Listings by Presenter
National Reading Conference
Scottsdale, Arizona, December 2000

Abadiano, Helen R., Catherine Kurkjian, Central Connecticut State University; **Kenneth J. Weiss,** Nazareth College of Rochester. *Computer-Based Text Analysis: Its Potential as a Medium for Exploring Aesthetic and Efferent Reader Response.*

Ackerman, John M., Northern Arizona University. *Spatial Practice in Everyday Life.*

Adams, Marilyn, Bolt, Beranek, Newman (BBN Technologies); **Richard L. Allington,** University of Florida; **Rep. Linda Gray, Sen. John Huppenthal,** Arizona State Legislature. *Using Reading Research to Make Laws.*

Adams, Mary Lou, Holt, Rinehart and Winston. *Enduring Literacy Issues: Stories of Readers Learning to Teach.*

Afflerbach, Peter, University of Maryland/College Park. *A Strategic Perspective on Critical Reading.*

Aguilar, Jill A., USC Rossier School of Education. *Listening to Graffiti: Political and Pedagogical Implications.*

Albers, Peggy M., Georgia State University. *Multiculturalism and Diversity in Caldecott Award-Winning Literature, 1970–2000.*

Albright, Lettie, Ohio University. *Learning Geography through Picture Books: A Study of Reading Aloud to Seventh Graders in Inclusive Classrooms.*

Allen, Diane D., University of North Texas; **Rebecca A. Swearingen,** Southwest Missouri State University. *Linking Preservice Literacy Teachers to the Profession through Mentoring by Inservice Teachers.*

Allen, Diane D., Jeanne B. Cobb, University of North Texas. *Social Interaction of Highly Effective Non-Educator Literacy Tutors AND Using the Coaching Model with Teachers Working with Pre-Service Tutors.*

Allen, JoBeth, University of Georgia. *Cultural Memoirs as a Tool for Culturally Responsive Preservice Teacher Professional Development: Perspectives from University Literacy Methods Course Instructors.*

Allington, Richard L., University of Florida; **Patricia A. Edwards,** Michigan State University; **Anna M. Duffy-Hester,** University of North Carolina/Greensboro; **Robert Rueda,** University of Southern California. *The Past, Present and Future of Research with Special Populations.*

Allington, Richard L., University of Florida. *Counteracting the "Teacher Stuplification Movement."*

Almasi, Janice F., Mary S. Rozendal, SUNY/Buffalo. *Of Virgins, Blank Slates, and Gurus: An Interpretive Case Study of Elementary Teachers Implementing Peer Discussion.*

Almasi, Janice F., SUNY/Buffalo; **William S. Russell,** New York Institute of Technology. *Positioning for Power: When Scaffolding Does Not Lead to Dialogism.*

Alvermann, Donna E., Margaret C. Hagood, Alison Heron, Preston Hughes, Kevin Williams, University of Georgia. *Changing Understandings of Popular Culture and Critical Media Literacy Instruction.*

Alvermann, Donna E., University of Georgia; **Susan Hynds,** Syracuse University; **Bettina Fabos, Cynthia A. Lewis,** University of Iowa; **Margaret Finders,** Purdue University; **Robert Jimenez,** University of Illinois/Urbana; **Larry Mikulecky,** Indiana University; **Eliane Rubinstein-Avila,** Harvard University; **William Stroud,** Urban Peace Academy. *Later Literacies: A Panel Discussion on the Politics of Adolescent and Adult Literacy.*

Anders, Patricia L., University of Arizona. *Portfolios as an Option: Making the Process Meaningful for Students.*

Anderson, Diane D., Swarthmore College. *Learning for Life: What Students and Staff Members Learned when They Mentored One Another and Negotiated Campus Resources.*

Anderson, Jim, Gabriella Minnes-Brandes, Thomas Wong, University of British Columbia; **Mitzi Lewison,** Indiana University; **Rise Paynter,** Binford Elementary School. *Journal Writing as a Reflective Tool in Teacher Education: Problem Sharing, Problem Posing, Problem Solving from Multiple Perspectives.*

Anderson, Nancy, Texas Woman's University. *Understanding Effective Professional Development to Transform Learning.*

Anderson, Rebecca S., Bauer, John F., University of Memphis. *Out with the Old: Restructuring a University Reading Center.*

Apol, Laura, Aki Sakuma, Tracy Reynolds, Bette Shellhorn, Yahya Kurniawati, Sheryl Rop, Michigan State University. *"When Can We Make Paper Cranes?": Examining Pre-Service Teachers' Resistance to Critical Readings of Children's Literature.*

Appleman, Deborah, Carleton College. *Multiple Theories, Multiple Worlds: Teaching Literary Theory to Adolescents.*

Appleman, Deborah, Carleton College. *Unintended Betrayal: Dilemmas of Representation in Research with Youth.*

Asbury, Elizabeth Brown, Rutgers University. *Processes of Teacher Change: Three Case Studies of Primary Teachers Learning to Implement Guided Reading Instruction.*

Ash, Gwynne Ellen, Margaret C. Hagood, University of Georgia/Athens. *Of Rats and Researchers: Possible Unintended Motivational Consequences of Classroom-Based Literacy Intervention Research.*

Ash, Gwynne Ellen, University of Georgia. *Assuming Ethical Stances: Middle School Teachers' Perceptions of their Role in the Literacy Development of Struggling Readers.*

Askew, Billie J., Texas Woman's University; **Melissa Draper, Denise Duncan,** Richardson I.S.D.; **Teddi Fulenwider,** Mesquite I.S.D.; **Robyn Kordick,** Little Elm I.S.D.; **Sara Scheuermann, Patricia Vollenweider,** Arlington I.S.D. *Developing a Model of Professional Development to Support Early Literacy Classrooms.*

Bainbridge, Joyce, University of Alberta. *Understanding the Role of Children's Literature in a Post-Colonial Culture.*

Baker, Elizabeth (Betsy), Judy M. Wedman, Kyeong-Hee Rha, University of Missouri/Columbia. *Developing Kidwatching among Preservice Literacy Teachers Using Digital Portfolios.*

Balajthy, Ernest, SUNY/Geneseo. *Unpacking Exemplary Early Reading Instruction.*

Baldwin, Shelia C., Monmouth University. *Initial Teaching Experiences through Service Learning: Preservice Teachers' Reflections.*

Ballenger, Cindy, Graham and Park Schools and the Cheche Konnen Center at TERC. *"The Librarian Said There Weren't Any Wrestling Books There": Issues of Relevance in Children's Literature.*

Banning, Marlia E., Northern Arizona University. *Unlearning Privilege.*

Barber, Liz, Virginia Tech; **Kathy Husted,** Lynchburg College. *Catching the Kids Who Fall Through the Cracks: Literacy Tutoring, Teacher Education and Professional Development.*

Barksdale-Ladd, Mary Alice, Paula Leftwich, University of South Florida; **Anne McGill-Franzen,** University of Florida. *The Lived Experience of Intermediate and Adolescent Public School Students.*

Barksdale-Ladd, Mary Alice, University of South Florida. *Literacy Educators' Perspectives on Addressing Racism in Literacy Teacher Education.*

Barnes, Charline J., University of Northern Iowa. *The E-Mail Literacy Conversations Projects.*

Barone, Diane M., University of Nevada/Reno. *Convergence in Learning: A Study of First-Grade Literacy Learning in an At-Risk School.*

Barone, Diane M., University of Nevada/Reno. *Revisioning: Multiple Positions of a Parent, Student, and Researcher in Response to Classroom Context.*

Barone, Diane M., University of Nevada/Reno; **Lea M. McGee,** University of Alabama. *Case Studies of Young Children's Literacy Development: What We Learned Then, What We Know Now.*

Barr, Rebecca, National-Louis University. *The Bridging of Cultures: How Can Inquiries by Outsiders Inform Educational Practice?*

Barrera, Rosalinda B., Robert T. Jiminez, University of Illinois/Urbana-Champaign. *What Bilingual Teachers Have to Say Concerning the Literacy Development of Latino Students.*

Bauer, Eurydice B., M. Kristiina Montero, University of Georgia. *Reading vs. Translating: A Preschool Bilingual's Interpretation.*

Baumann, James F., Barbara Bradley, Elizabeth Carr Edwards, George Font, George G. Hruby, University of Georgia. *Teaching Generalizable Vocabulary-Learning Strategies: A Critical Review of the Literature.*

Baumann, James F., Elizabeth Carr Edwards, George Font, Stephen F. Olejnik, University of Georgia; **Cathleen Tereshinski,** Clarke County (GA) School District; **Edward J. Kame'enui,** University of Oregon. *Teaching Morphemic and Contextual Analysis to Fifth-Grade Students.*

Beach, Richard W., University of Minnesota. *Students' Use of Critical Discourse Analysis to Analyze Viewer/Reader Stance in a Media Studies Course.*

Bean, Rita M., Gregory A. Morris, Allison Swan, R. Tony Eichelberger, University of Pittsburgh. *Critical Features of a Staff Development Program: Improving Literacy Achievement of Primary Students.*

Bean, Thomas W., University of Nevada/Las Vegas; **Nicole Rigoni,** Centennial High School. *The Impact of a Multicultural Young Adult Novel on Intergenerational Dialogue Journal Discussion.*

Begoray, Deborah, University of Manitoba. *Through a Class Darkly: The Challenge of Implementing Viewing and Visually Representing Approaches in a Canadian Middle School.*

Belshe, Paulette G., University of Oklahoma. *Young Children's Self-Perceptions of Competency in Literacy during One-on-One Instruction.*

Benton, Ronald E., University of Texas/Austin. *Combining Voices: When Writers Work Together.*

Bernhardt, Elizabeth, Stanford University. *Progress and Procrastination in Second-Language Reading Theory-Building.*

Berninger, Virginia, University of Washington. *Developmental Changes in the Contribution of Morphological Awareness to Reading Comprehension.*

Birdyshaw, Deanna, CIERA/University of Michigan; **Lisa Sensale,** CIERA/Michigan State University. *The Role of Professional Development in the Development of a School-Wide Assessment System.*

Bishop, Rudine Sims, The Ohio State University. *Children's Literature and Literacy Education.*

Blachowicz, Camille L., Peter J. Fisher, Mary Kay Moskal, National Louis University. *Everybody Reads: Researching Fluency Development in Second-Grade Classrooms.*

Black, Wendy, Illinois State University. *Analyzing Discourse Analysis: Examining a Process of Retrospective Miscue Analysis with a Fourth-Grade Reader.*

Black, Wendy, Illinois State University; **Sarah Costello,** Tuscon Unified School District; **Simone Gers, Lori Grimm,** Pima Community College; **Yetta M. Goddman, Gopa Goswami, Eric Paulson,** University of Arizona. *Research Implications of Retrospective Miscue Analysis: Struggling Readers Revaluing Themselves and Their Reading.*

Blair, Heather, Kathy Sanford, University of Alberta. *Boys and Literacy: A Conflict in the Making.*

Blanton, William E., University of Miami; **Woodrow Trathen, Linda Pacifici,** Appalachian State University. *Effects of Participation in the Fifth Dimension on Children's Comprehension of Written Directions.*

Block, Cathy Collins, Texas Christian University. *It's Not Scripted Lessons but Challenging and Personalized Interactions that Distinguish Effective from Less Effective Primary Classrooms.*

Boothroyd, Kimberly A., University of New Hampshire. *Teachers Write to Teach Elementary Writers.*

Boyd, Fenice B., University of Georgia. *Struggling Readers and Writers' Concessions while Studying Multicultural Literature.*

Brantley, Diane K., University of Nevada/Las Vegas. *America Reads: Co-Construction of Knowledge in a One-on-One Tutoring Situation.*

Brenner, Devon, Mississippi State University, **Kevin Dupre,** University of Southern Mississippi. *Efferent, Aesthetic and Critical: Reciprocity Between Transactional Theory and Critical Literacy.*

Brink, Beverly, Washington State University/Vancouver; **Dana L. Grisham,** San Diego State University. *Voices from the Northwest.*

Broaddus, Karen, Emma Savage-Davis, Karen Santos, James Madison University. *Literacy, Diversity, and Special Needs in Adolescent Literature: A University Collaboration in Preservice Teacher Education.*

Brock, Cynthia H., University of Nevada/Reno. *Using Positioning Theory to Explore an English Language Learner's Opportunities for Literacy Learning in a Mainstream Classroom.*

Bronkhorst, John, Harry Paus, Ludo Verhoeven, University of Nijmegen/Netherlands. *Multimedia and Enhanced Learning in Preservice Education.*

Brooks, Wanda, University of Pennsylvania. *Culturally Relevant Literature: Middle School Students Respond to African American Fiction Novels.*

Browne, Susan, University of Pennsylvania. *Responding to Culturally Relevant Text in a Community Based Literary Club.*

Brozo, William G., University of Tennessee; **Jack Cassidy,** Texas A&M University/Corpus Christi. *"I Know the Difference Between a Real Man and a TV Man": Exploring Positive Male Values through Literature in a Junior High School in the "Hood."*

Bruning, Roger H., Mary Jane White, Christy A. Horn, University of Nebraska/Lincoln. *Implicit Beliefs about Writing.*

Buly, Marsha Riddle, Western Washington University. *Reading below the Bar: A Diagnostic Study of Fourth-Grade Students Who Did Not Meet the Standard.*

Burnison, Judi, NRC Executive Director. *Behind the Scene Scoops: The Past Ten Years with NRC.*

Bus, Adriana, University of Leiden; **Elizabeth Sulzby,** University of Michigan/CIERA. *Parental Strategies to Engage Young Children in Book Reading.*

Campbell, Ellen, State College Area School District; **Karen Morris,** Pennsylvania State University. *Through Technology Integration.*

Cantrell, Susan, Georgetown College; **Polly Page,** Kentucky Department of Education; **Cary Pappas, Mary C. Shake,** University of Kentucky; **Lynne A. Smith,** Northern Kentucky University; **Melinda Willis,** Morehead State University. *A State-Wide Literacy Agenda: The Kentucky Reading Project.*

Carlisle, Joanne F., Northwestern University. *The Relationship of Different Aspects of Morphological Awareness and Literacy-Related Abilities.*

Caron, Thomas, Marshall University; **Joan E. Hughes, Sharman Oliver,** CIERA/Michigan State University. *Expanding the Learning Environment: Increased Scaffolding through Hypermedia.*

Carr, Kathryn, Kitty Brant, Central Missouri State University. *An Action Research Study*

Group Designed to Change Writing and Reading Instruction through A School-University Partnership.

Carr, Linda M., South Colonie CSD and SUNY/Albany. *Early Literacy Assessment: Influences on Teacher Knowledge and Instructional Practice.*

Carr, Sharon M., National-Louis University. *First Graders Using Imagery to Construct Meaning while Listening to Stories Being Read.*

Carroll, Maureen, University of California/Berkeley. *Cartwheels on the Keyboard: The Role of Technology in an Elementary Classroom.*

Cervetti, Gina, Stephanie Davis, Michigan State University. *The Residual Effects of Summer School: Looking at Remedial Programs up Close and Personal.*

Chambliss, Marilyn J., University of Maryland/College Park. *Are Trade Books an Improvement over Textbooks for Primary-Age Children?*

Chandler, Kelly, Syracuse University; **Lois Pangburn,** Mapleton Elementary School. *Thinking Aloud with Feedback: E-Mail Conversations about Teaching between a First-Grade Teacher and a Methods Instructor.*

Chapman, Marilyn L., University of British Columbia. *Learning/Writing Science: A Case Study of a Third-Grade ESL Classroom.*

Chapman, Valerie G., University of Memphis. *Phonemic Awareness Enhanced through Social Interaction in a Primary Classroom.*

Ching, Stuart, Northern Arizona University; **Jaan Pataray-Ching,** University of Nebraska/Lincoln. *Cultural Traveling Through Children's/Adolescent Literature: Cross-Generational Memory Bridging Home and School.*

Cobb, Jeanne B., University of North Texas. *The Effects of Using Manipulatives and Instructional Activities Incorporating Play on the Metacomprehension Strategies of Elementary-Aged Children.*

Cohen, Sheila, Ellen Jampole, SUNY/Cortland. *Voices from the East.*

Coke, Pamela K. Ames, University of Iowa. *Literacy Education Tomorrow: Linking Theory and Practice Through First-Year Teachers.*

Coleman, Janet, Jeanne B. Cobb, Diane D. Allen, University of North Texas. *Linking College Students with At-Risk Children through Effective Training in an America Reads Program.*

Collins, Jim, Mark Jury, Peter H. Johnston, SUNY/Albany/CELA; **Cheryl Dozier,** University of Albany. *Instructional Interactions between Tutors and their Middle-School Students: Sources and Consequences.*

Collins, Kathleen M., Monmouth University/New Jersey. *Creating a Multicultural Preservice Curricula: Documenting the Change Process.*

Collins, Kathleen M., University of San Diego. *"Why is science like another language?" Multiple Literacies and the Social Construction of Ability.*

Colvin, Carolyn, University of Iowa. *Gender and Media Literacy.*

Compton, Donald L., University of Colorado/Boulder. *Modeling At-Risk First-Grade Children's Response to Basic Word Reading Instruction.*

Compton-Hall, Margaret, Texas Woman's University, **Susan H. Gooden,** University of Southern Indiana; **Denese Jones,** University of Kentucky; **Sherry W. Powers,** Western Kentucky University. *Finding Our Own Paths by Guiding the Paths of Others: Mentoring Relationships in Literacy Research.*

Condon, Mark, University of Louisville. *Portfolios and State Standards for Teachers.*

Condon, Mark, University of Louisville; **Michael McGuffee,** Arbor Lake Publications. *Real-e-Publishing: Using Web Resources to Help Developing Readers Publish.*

Conley, Mark W., Michigan State University. *Narrative Admissions Essays for Teacher Preparation Programs: What Can They Tell Us?*

Cook, Leslie Susan, University of Georgia. *Sounds of Deep Waters: Listening, Learning, and Becoming in the World of Research.*

Cooper, Paula K., Salem Grade School. *Orthographic Development in Early Readers.*

Cooter, Robert B., Jr., Southern Methodist University; **Kathleen S. Cooter,** Texas Christian University; **William J. Webster,** Dallas Public Schools. Perfil de Lectura y Escritura de Dallas (The Dallas Literacy Profile): *Review of a Benchmark-Based Alternative Assessment Instrument for Urban Classrooms.*

Costello, Paula, SUNY/Albany. *Multiple Discourses, Multiple Identities: Investment and Agency.*

Cotton, Carol, Joan Parker-Webster, Leslie Patterson, Leigh Van Horn, University of Houston. *Multiple Texts: The Art and Science of Reconstructive Analysis.*

Cowan, Kay W., Walker County (GA) Schools. *The Composing Processes of the Middle School Student: An Examination of the Visual and Verbal Connections of Writing.*

Cox, Kathleen E., John T. Guthrie, University of Maryland. *Influences of Conceptual Instruction on Engaged Reading and Conceptual Learning From Text.*

Craig, Holly K., Julie A. Washington, Carol M. Connor, University of Michigan. *Similarities and Differences in Language Production of African American Children among Reading, Writing, and Oracy Contexts.*

Crumpler, Thomas P., Illinois State University. *Process Drama and the Range of Children's Response to Literature: An Ethnographic Study.*

Cuban, Sondra, Harvard University (NCSALL). *Before Days: Women in a Library Literacy Program in Hilo, Hawai'i Talk Story.*

Cunningham, James W., Stephanie A. Spadorcia, University of North Carolina/Chapel Hill; **Karen A. Erickson**, University of New Hampshire; **David A. Koppenhaver,** Gustavus Adolphus College. *Do Rigby PM Books Have More High Frequency Words or More Decodable Words than Other Books Leveled for Use in Reading Recovery?*

Dalton, Bridget, University of Guam; **Dana L. Grisham,** San Diego State University. *Myths and Realities of Publishing Online: Are We Taking Advantage of the Medium?*

Damico, James L., Joan E. Hughes, CIERA/Michigan State University. *Case of Karen: An Individual RCE Distance Learner.*

Dandridge, Jennifer, Michigan State University/CIERA. *Gender and Reading.*

Dantas, Maria Luiza, California State University/San Marcos. *You go to b ab t rod the 16 levo [You got to be able to read the 16 Level]: Derek's Literacy Learning Story in First Grade.*

Davis, Lyle Hull, Joanne F. Carlisle, Northwestern University. *Rimes, Rhyme, Reading and Spelling: Rime-Based Analogy Training for Children with Good and Poor Phonological Awareness.*

Davis, Rachel T., University of Georgia. *Sister Group: Documenting Experiences of African American Females as They Participate in a Book Club.*

Deal, Debby, George Mason University. *Interpreting Literacy Events During Science Instruction: The View From a Fifth-Grade Classroom.*

DeFord, Diane E., The Ohio State University. *Theory and Research behind the Literacy Collaborative as a Professional Development Program.*

Degener, Sophie, Harvard Graduate School of Education. *Critical Family Literacy in the United States.*

Dewitz, Peter, Somerset County (MD) Schools. *Initiating and Sustaining District-Wide Literacy Reform.*

Diaz-Gemmati, Griselle M., National-Louis University. *"And Justice for All": Using Literature and Writing to Confront Racism.*

Dickinson, Sherry C., SUNY/Albany. *Learning to Read Through the Shadows: Case Study Portraits of Two Emotionally and Behaviorally Disordered Struggling Readers.*

Dillner, Martha, University of Houston/Clear Lake. *Teacher Education and Critical Literacy.*

Dimitriadis, Greg, University at Buffalo; **George G. Kamberelis,** Purdue University. *"Working the Hyphens" at a Local Community Center.*

Donovan, Carol A., Joan Primeaux, University of Alabama; **Laura B. Smolkin,** University of Virginia. *Supporting Struggling Readers Expository Text Comprehension through Information Book.*

Donovan, Carol A., University of Alabama. *The Complexity of K–5 Children's Story and Information Writing in One Elementary School: Comparisons Across Gender, Genre, and Grade Levels.*

Dougherty, Abby, Jane West, Agnes Scott College; **Jeannie Oakley,** Holsenbeck School, **Penny Oldgather,** University of Georgia. *The Children's Thinking Project: A Tool for Understanding Social Constructivism.*

Dozier, Cheryl, Jennifer Grand, SUNY/Albany; **Peter H. Johnston,** SUNY/Albany/CELA. *Reflective Inquiry: Building Productive Instruction for Struggling Middle School Students.*

Dozier, Cheryl, Jennifer Grand, Susan Garnett, Melinda Teter, Stehpanie DeInnocentiis, SUNY/Albany. *Case Studies of Three Struggling Middle-School Students.*

Draper, Roni Jo, University of Nevada/Reno. *How Secondary Preservice Mathematics, Science, and Social Studies Methods Textbooks Support Content-Area Reading and Writing Instruction: A Qualitative Content Analysis.*

Dreher, Mariam Jean, Ann Dromsky, University of Maryland/College Park. *Increasing the Diversity of Young Children's Independent Reading.*

Dressman, Mark, University of Illinois/Champaign; **Joan Parker Webster,** University of Houston. *Description, Prescription, or Cultural Reproduction? The Function of Rosenblattian Criticism in Reader Response Research and Teaching.*

Dubert, Lee A., Pete Erickson, Pat Louderback, Boise State University. *Secondary Reading Improvement Study.*

Duffy-Hester, Ann M., Terry S. Atkinson, University of North Carolina/Greensboro. *Learning to Teach Struggling (and Non-Struggling) Elementary School Readers: An Analysis of Preservice Teachers' Personal, Professional, and Practical Knowledges.*

Duffy-Hester, Ann M., University of North Carolina/Greensboro. *Supporting Teacher Researchers in Literacy Education: Possibilities and Pitfalls.*

Duke, Nell K., CIERA/University of Michigan; **Victoria Purcell-Gates,** Michigan State University. *Explicit Explanation/Teaching of Informational Text Genres: A Proposed Model for Research.*

Dunlap, Kristy L., George Mason University. *Learning To Teach Literacy during High-Stakes Testing: Perceptions of Interns and Mentors in Professional Development Schools.*

Dunsmore, KaiLonnie, Carol Sue Englert, Michigan State University. *Emergent Literacy, Expository Writing, and Scientific Discourse: How Young Children Develop Competency in Expository Genre Forms.*

Dunston, Pamela J., Kathy N. Headley, Clemson University. *Competency or Discourse? A Comparison of Two Models for Teacher Education.*

Dymock, Susan J., University of Waikato. *The Effects of Sustained Silent Reading on Reading Comprehension: A Review of the Research.*

Edmondson, Jacqueline, Penn State University. *Prairie School: Literacies and Politics in Rural Minnesota.*

Edmondson, Jacqueline, University of Minnesota/Morris. *Purse Strings: Control of Research Agendas and Distribution of Results.*

Edwards, Patricia A., Jennifer C. Dandridge, Brigette B. Laier, Gwendolyn Thompson McMillon, Michigan State University/CIERA. *Using Parent Stories to Foster the Instructional Change Process in an Urban Elementary School.*

Ehri, Linnea C., CUNY Graduate School; **Michael L. Kamil,** Stanford University; **S. Jay Samuels,** University of Minnesota; **Timothy Shanahan,** University of Illinois/Chicago; **Joanna Williams,** Columbia University; **Dale Willows,** University of Toronto. *Instructional Research on Reading: Final Report on the Work of the National Reading Panel.*

Elish-Piper, Laurie A., Northern Illinois University. *Critical Issues Related to Portfolio Assessment in Graduate Reading Programs.*

Ellis, Monica, University of Winnipeg. *One Teacher's Perceptions of the Communication Strand in the Mathematics Curriculum.*

Elsacker, Willy van, Ludo Verhoeven, University of Nijmegen/The Netherlands. *Home and School Predictors of Reading Comprehension, Reading Strategies, and Reading Motivation of Third- and Fourth-Grade Students in Multilingual Classrooms.*

Elster, Charles, Purdue University. *Young Children Reading Poems and Stories.*

Enciso, Patricia E., The Ohio State University. *"Can We Take a Moment?": Teachers and Children's Adaptations of a Prescribed, Externally Assessed Reading Program.*

English, Carmen Urdanivia, Myers Elementary School. *Students Create their Own History through Community Photographs and Family Interviews: Perspectives from a 5th-Grade ESOL Teacher.*

Erickson, Joan L., Karen Hux, Nancy J. Manasse, University of Nebraska. *The Impact of Speech Recognition on the Writing Difficulties of Three Students.*

Evans, Karen, Marquette University. *Gender and Discussion.*

Everson, Michael, University of Iowa. *Reading in Non-Roman Orthographies: Research for the New Millennium.*

Fairbanks, Colleen M., University of Texas; **Mary Arial Broughton,** Texas Woman's University. *Reading the Silences: Early Adolescent Girls' Negotiations of Self in a Reading/Language Arts Classroom.*

Falk-Ross, Francine C., Northern Illinois University. *Expanding Language Routines in Literacy Activities for Students with Reading Disabilities.*

Fang, Zhihui, University of Florida. *Examining Upper Elementary Students' Discursive Power in Science: A Language-Based Perspective.*

Fang, Zhihui, University of Florida. *Teaching and Learning in A Multigrade Classroom: A Naturalistic Study.*

Farnan, Nancy, Douglas Fisher, San Diego State University. *Voices from the West.*

Fazio, Michelle M., Angela McNulty, Reba Powers, Texas A&M University/Commerce. *Best Practice: A Collaborative Effort among Reflective Literacy Educators Utilizing Technology To Enhance Preservice Teacher Education.*

Fazio, Michelle M., Texas A&M University/Commerce. *The Impact of Constructive Comprehension and Metacognitive Strategy Instruction on Preservice Teachers During the First Semester of Field-Based Student Teaching: Phase II of a Longitudinal Study.*

Fearn, Leif, San Diego State University. *Speaking, Reading, and Writing English as a Second Language.*

Fecho, Bob, Leslie S. Rush, University of Georgia. *Getting Beyond the "Grr, Grr, Grr, Grr" Stage: Working through Threat in a Critical Inquiry Classroom.*

Ferdig, Richard E., P. David Pearson, CIERA/Michigan State University. *The Potential and Demands of Technology-Supported Scaffolding Environment: Examining Scaffolding in the Reading Classroom Explorer.*

Ferdig, Richard E., Patricia Norman, Laura R. Roehler, CIERA/Michigan State University. *Scaffolding through Multiple Conversations: A Case Study of Elementary Education Teacher Candidates.*

Fey, Marion, SUNY/Geneseo. *A Narrative Review of the Teacher Research on Gender and Post-Typographical Text.*

Fey, Marion, SUNY/Geneseo. *Gender and Post-Typographical Text.*

Fielding, Linda, Carolyn Colvin, Michael Prier, Chinatsu Sazawa, Heather Williams, University of Iowa; **Priscilla Gomez-Stream, Laura Smith,** Iowa City Community Schools. *Voices in Silence: Pre- and In-service Teachers Discuss the Use of Gay/Lesbian Texts in the Public School.*

Finders, Margaret, Purdue University. *Critical Media Literacy and Teacher Education: Practical and Impractical Views.*

Fine, Joyce C., Florida International University/Miami; **Deborah Eldridge, Alene Smith, George Gonzalex, Mirian Belmuth,** Hunter College; **Amy Seely Flint, Christine**

H. Leland, Indian University; **Denise Littleton, Mona Bryant-Shanklin,** Norfolk State University; **Shane Templeton, Diane M. Barone, Cynthia H. Brock,** University of Nevada/Reno; **James V. Hoffman,** University of Texas/Austin; **Miriam G. Martinez, Janis M. Hormon, Wanda B. Hedrick, Susan K. Strecker, Bertha Perez,** University of Texas/San Antonio; **Rachelle Loven,** University of Sioux Falls. *National Commission of Excellence in Elementary Teacher Preparation for Reading Instruction: Findings, Implications and Recommendations.*

Finkbeiner, Claudia, Christine Koplin, University of Kassel/Germany. *ABC's Model: An Autobiographic and Biographic Approach toward Raising Cultural Awareness.*

Fives, Helenrose, Patricia A. Alexander, Michelle M. Buehl, University of Maryland. *Teaching as Persuasion: Approaching Classroom Discourse as Refutational Text.*

Flint, Amy Seely, Katie Van Sluys, Julie Enyeart, Debbie East, Yi-Hsuan Lo, Indiana University. *"Maybe You Could Put 'To Be Continued . . .' ": Examining Interactions and Engagement during Author's Circle.*

Flint, Amy Seely, Mitzi Lewison, Katie Van Sluys, Indiana University. *Interruptions and Transformations: Investigating Critical Literacy in Elementary Classrooms.*

Flood, James, Diane Lapp, Douglas Fisher, San Diego State University. *At-Home Reading in Kindergarten and First Grade.*

Foote, Martha M., Carole Walker, Texas A&M University/Commerce; **Catherine K. Zeek,** Texas Woman's University. *Teachers' Transactional Inquiries into Literacy Practices: A Sociocultural Exploration.*

Forbes, Rosalie, Barabara Lukas, National-Louis University; **Bill M. Ware,** Freeport Public School District; **Donald C. Parker,** Harlem Public School District; **Evelyn A. O'Connor,** New York University School of Education; **Connie M. Briggs,** Emporia State University. *Using Reading Recovery Program Data to Inform District Curricular Decisions.*

Forbush, Lisa, Princess Anne Primary School/Maryland. *Reading Reform in the Primary Grades.*

Francis, Michelle Andersen, University of Georgia. *Students' Beliefs about Vocabulary in Relation to their Performance on Vocabulary and Reading Comprehension Tasks.*

Freppon, Penny, University of Cincinnati. *Where Are the Reading Clinics and What Are their Salient Features?*

Fry, Edward, Rutgers University; **Jaap Tuinman,** Open Learning Agency, **Lenore H. Ringer, M. Trika Smith-Burke,** New York University; **P. David Pearson,** Michigan State University/CIERA; **Jerome C. Harste,** Indiana University; **James V. Hoffman,** University of Texas; **Gerald G. Duffy,** Michigan State University; **Robert J. Tierney,** University of British Columbia; **Donna E. Alvermann,** University of Georgia; **Rebecca Barr,** National-Louis University; **James Flood,** San Diego State University; **Jane Hansend,** University of Virginia; **Richard Allington,** University of Florida; **Kathryn H. Au,** University of Hawaii; **Martha Rapp Ruddell,** Sonoma State University; **Linda B. Gambrell,** Clemson University. *The New Millennium Plus Fifty: Where Are We Going and How Will We Get There?*

Fullerton, Anne, International Reading Association. *Changing Roles of Authors, Editors, Publishers in Online Journals.*

Fullerton, Susan, Diane E. DeFord, The Ohio State University. *The Nature of Teacher-Student Interactions in Reading Recovery Lessons: Conversations before Writing.*

Gaffney, Janet S., University of Illinois/Urbana-Champaign; **Jeanette M. Methven,** California State University/Fresno. *Assisting Older Students to Read Expository Text: A High-Impact Tutorial Intervention.*

Gaffney, Janet S., University of Illinois/Urbana-Champaign; **Ted Dawson,** Vail School District/Tucson, AZ. *Coaching Early Literacy Volunteers: Form Follows Function.*

Gallego, Margaret A., Carla Mathison, San Diego State University. *Reading between the Lines: The Relationship Between Narrative and Expository Text in Student Content Understanding.*

Gambrell, Linda B., Clemson University; **Kim M. Bobola,** Montgomery County (MD)

Public Schools. *Exploring Connections Across the Integrated Language Arts: Discussions, Writing, and Reader Response.*

Ganske, Kathy A., Rowan University. *Exploring the Relationship Between Orthographic Knowledge and the Writing of At-Risk Students.*

Garcia, Georgia Earnest, University of Illinois/Urbana-Champaign. *A Theoretical Discussion of Young Bilingual Children's Reading (Preschool–Grade 3).*

Garmon, M. Arthur, Western Michigan University; **Troy V. Mariage,** Michigan State University. *Collaborative Structures that Animate Literacy Learning: Points of Entry for School-Wide Reform in an Underachieving Rural PDS.*

Gavelek, James R., Oakland University. *Whither Thematic Instruction?*

Gentile, Claudia, Educational Testing Service. *New Modes of Writing Assessment: Using Integrated Reading/Writing Essays to Measure Student Growth.*

George, MariAnne, Rochester Community Schools and Oakland University; **Kathy Highfield,** Holly Area Schools and Oakland University; **Marcella Kehus,** Berkley Schools and Oakland University; **Andrew Topper,** Grand Valley State University. *Seeing Worlds in Grains of Sand: Cases, Complexity and Cognitive Flexibility in the Teachers Learning Collaborative.*

Gilbert, Susan N., Gary B. Morrman, Linda C. Pacifici, Appalachian State University. *Designing, Implementing and Evaluating Web-Assisted Instruction.*

Gill, Sharon Ruth, University of Akron. *Of Paradigms, Thomas Kuhn, and the Field of Reading.*

Gioia, Barbara, The Sage Colleges; **Peter H. Johnston,** SUNY/Albany. *Beating the Odds: Literacy Learning and Teaching with the Deaf.*

Giorgis, Cyndi, University of Nevada/Las Vegas; **Gloria Kauffman,** Duffy Elementary School/Tucson Unified School District. *Potential for Talk: Supporting Students, Responses to Literature.*

Gnadinger, Cindy M., University of Louisville. *Teaching the Zone of Proximal Development: Assisted Reading Performance in Kentucky's Multi-Aged Classrooms.*

Goatley, Virginia J., Kimberly Anderson, Vanessa-Larae Machado, SUNY/Albany/CELA; **Rebecca Rogers,** Washington University/St. Louis, *Written Representations of Student Achievement in Integrated Social Studies/Language Arts Classrooms.*

Godina, Heriberto, Carolyn Colvin, University of Iowa. *A Methodological Perspective On Mexican Background Adult/Student Literacy: Research and Reflection in Progress.*

Godina, Heriberto, Lee Ann Schrage, University of Iowa. *Language Loss in the Rural Midwest: German/English and Spanish/English Subtractive Bilingualism.*

Goetze, Sandra K., Barbara J. Walker, Oklahoma State University; **Ronald D. Kieffer,** University of North Dakota; **Dana L. Grisham,** San Diego State University, **Linda J. McElroy,** University of Science and Arts in Oklahoma. *On-line Apprentices: Preservice Teachers Learning to Integrate Technology within Reading Methods Courses.*

Goetze, Sandra K., Oklahoma State University. *Children's Literacy Perceptions as They Authored with Hypermedia.*

Grace, Ted, Syracuse University. *Comparing the Oral and Written Narrative Development of 4th- and 5th-Grade African American Students in an Urban Setting.*

Gray, Esther, Illinois State University. *Inquiring Into the Process of Examining Reading and Writing as Semiotic Practices in a Third-Grade Inquiry-Based Curriculum.*

Greene, Sarah, Larry Ferguson, Pennsylvania State University. *Through Collaborative Assessment.*

Greenman, Gretchen G., Raquel J. Schmitt, Mary S. Rozendal, SUNY/Buffalo. *Reading Instruction in the Inclusion Classroom: Research-Based Practices.*

Gregory, Anne E., Maribeth Cassidy Schmitt, Purdue University. *A Qualitative Exploration of Children's Developing Metacognitive Knowledge.*

Greybeck, Barbara J., Texas A&M International University. *A Comparison of Text Comprehension in English and in Spanish: A Study of Bilingual Sixth Graders in Mexico.*

Griesel, Patricia, Patricia L. Anders, University of Arizona; **Shelley Ann Maxfield,**

Pima Community College. *Teacher and Student Actions to Construct Biology Literacy at a Community College: A Bounded Case Study.*

Grisham, Dana L., San Diego State University; **Beverly Brink,** Washington State University/Vancouver. *Teachers Reflect on the Reform Movement and Its Impact on Their Practice.*

Gritsavage, Margaret, Arizona State University. *An Integrative Review of Survey Research on Gender and Computer Text.*

Gritsavage, Margaret, Arizona State University. *Gender and Literacy Autobiography.*

Groth, Lois A., George Mason University. *Kindergartners' Discussions of Their Own Original Texts.*

Guice, Sherry L., South Colonie Central Schools/Albany. *Reconstruct, Reflect, Refine: Returning to the Classroom Twelve Years Later.*

Gunderson, Lee, University of British Columbia. *Unsung Heroes of NRC.*

Gunning, Thomas G., Central Connecticut State University. *Assessing the Difficulty Level of Reading Material in the Primary Grades: A Study in Progress.*

Gutierrez, Kris, University of California/Los Angeles. *Using Cultural-Historical and Activity Theory to Expose Minimalist Approaches to Literacy.*

Guzzetti, Barbara J., Arizona State University. *A Critical Review of the Qualitative Research on Gender and Electronic Text.*

Guzzetti, Barbara J., Arizona State University. *A Critical Review of the Literature on Gender and Literacy Autobiography.*

Hagood, Margaret C., Donna E. Alvermann, University of Georgia. *Media Literacies: Varied but Distinguishable.*

Hall, Kathy, Leeds Metropolitan University/UK. *Co-Constructing Literacy in A Multi-Ethnic Primary Classroom in England: An Ethnographic-Sociocultural Perspective.*

Hall, Kathy, Leeds Metropolitan University/UK; **Mohsin Zulfiqar,** Leeds Local Education Authority. *Supplementary Schooling in England: A Case Study of Oppositional Pedagogy?*

Hammons, Jean E., M. Jane Greenewald, University of Wisconsin/La Crosse. *A Descriptive Analysis of Coaching Notes and Written Feedback Used to Scaffold Preservice Teachers' Tutoring of At-Risk Primary-Level Readers.*

Hansen, Jane, University of Virginia. *Teachers Write and Self-Evaluate to Become Better Teachers of Writing.*

Harmon, Janis M., University of Texas/San Antonio. *Teachers' Beliefs and Practices of Vocabulary Instruction with Social Studies Textbooks in Grades 4–8.*

Harrison, Colin, University of Nottingham; **Wendy Kasten,** Kent State University, **Nancy Knapp**, University of Georgia; **Barbara P. Laster,** Towson University; **Janet C. Richards,** University of Southern Mississippi; **Mary Beth Sampson,** Texas A&M University/Commerce. *Ethicals Perspectives 2000.*

Hartman, Douglas K., University of Pittsburgh. *Choosing and Representing: Temporal and Thematic Patterns from a Longitudinal Study of Urban Teenagers.*

Hayes, Monie, University of Iowa. *Gender and Writing.*

Hayes, Nancy M., Ellen E. Fairchild, University of Iowa. *Adult ESL Learners and Tutors at (Literacy) Work: Two Case Studies.*

Hearne, Elizabeth, University of Illinois. *Children's Literature and Library Science.*

Hefflin, Bena R., University of Pittsburgh. *Multicultural Children's Literature: Its Use by Teachers, Preservice Teachers, and University Professors.*

Henderson, Susan D., Georgia State University, The Atlanta School. *One Teacher's Use of Scaffolding in a Multiage Preschool Class: Supporting the Dynamic Dance of Literacy.*

Henry, Justina, Barbara Joan Wiley, The Ohio State University. *Inside a Literacy Collaborative Classroom: Teaching for Shifts in Student Learning.*

Hiebert, Elfrieda H., University of Michigan; **Jacalyn M. Colt**, St. Vrain Valley (CO) School District. *An Early Reading Intervention and a District: Change Over a Decade.*

Hill, Margaret, University of Houston/Clear Lake. *Critical Incidents that cause the Shift from Teacher-Centeredness to Student-Centeredness.*

Hillinger, Michael, LexIcon Systems. *Developing Web-Based, Virtual Worlds for Teaching Literacy Skills.*

Hinchman, Kathleen A., Syracuse University. *Jared's Insight: "Doesn't Columbine Have Something to Do with Literacy?"*

Hittleman, Daniel R., CUNY/Queens College. *Portfolios and Multiple Measures of Student Performance: Links to NCATE and IRA Expectations.*

Ho, Hsiang-ju, SUNY/Buffalo. *Literature-Based Instruction in a Taiwanese Primary-Grade Classroom.*

Hoffman, James V., Elizabeth U. Patterson, Lori C. Assaf, Misty W. Sailors, Marg A. Mast, Jason McCoy, University of Texas/Austin. *The Year 2000 Basals: Decodability, Predictability, and Engagingness.*

Hollie, Sharroky, University of Southern California. *African American Students as Standard English Language Learners: An Alternative Approach.*

Hollingsworth, Sandra, Developmental Studies Center/Oakland, CA; **John Shefelbine,** California State University/Sacramento. *Teaching Upper Grade Students to Read: The Next Frontier.*

Holschuh, Patrick, Jodi, Betty Hubbard, Michelle Francis, Sally Randall, University of Georgia. *Epistemological Beliefs Development in a Learning-to-Learn Course: A Study of Epistemic Nudging.*

Hruby, George G., University of Georgia. *A Review and Discussion of the Neuroscience Research on Reading: Cautions and Caveats.*

Huang, Jingzi (Ginny), Monmouth University/New Jersey. *Literacy across the Curriculum: Implications of New Jersey Core Curriculum Content Standards.*

Hubbard, Betty, Michelle Fancis, Leslie S. Rush, Cynthia R. Hynd, University of Georgia. *Student and Professor Perceptions of Learning in Large Lecture Classes.*

Hughes, Marie T., Janette K. Klingner, Michele Mits Cash, University of Miami. *Professional Development Programs in Reading: A National Survey of District Directors.*

Humphrey, Kathy, Ingham Intermediate School District. *Summer School Reading Interventions: The Problem, the Context, and the Methods.*

Hutzel, Laura N., Lois K. Haid, George Mason University. *Relationship between Elementary School Principal Involvement In and Success of a Reading Professional Development Effort.*

Hynd , Cynthia R., University of Georgia. *Sharing an Editorial Perspective.*

Hynd, Cynthia R., Betty Hubbard, Jodi Patrick Holschuh, University of Georgia. *College Students' Beliefs about Author Credibility: The Case of History.*

Iannone, Patrick V., Marshal University; **Laura Payne-Bourcy,** Syracuse University. Literacy Research and the Internet: *Understanding Qualitative Data Collection in Cyberspace.*

Invernizzi, Marcia, CIERA/University of Virginia. *Book Buddies in the Bronx: Testing a Model for America Reads and National Service.*

Ivey, Gay, University of Maryland/College Park. *Expertise with Teaching Struggling Readers.*

Ivey, Gay, University of Maryland/College Park. *Giving Struggling Young Adolescent Readers a Fighting Chance.*

Jacobson, Erik H., University of Massachusetts/Boston. *Critical Literacy in Japanese Adult Education*

Jacobson, Julie K., San Diego City Schools; **James Flood, Diane Lapp,** San Diego State University. *The Effects of Topic Familiarity on Second Language Acquisition.*

Janisch, Carole, Texas Tech University. *Young Readers' Academy: Opportunities for Conversations about Literacy Teaching and Learning.*

Jaynes, Carolyn, Michigan State University/CIERA; **Barbara M. Taylor,** University of Minnesota/CIERA. *The CIERA School Change Project: Student Reading Growth in Year One.*

Jenkins, Christine A., University of Illinois/Urbana-Champaign. *YA Literature with Gay/ Lesbian Content: From "Search and Destroy" to Find and Use.*

Jenkins, Christine A., University of Illinois/Urbana-Champaign; **Dan Hade,** Pennsylvania State University; **Theresa Rogers,** University of British Columbia. *Turning Back to Go Forward: Representing and Reading "the Truth" in Landmark Historical Literature for Young People.*

Johnson, Brian Walker, Principia College. *Teacher Development and Metacomprehension Instruction: Growth in Confident Practice.*

Johnson, Peter, SUNY/Albany/CELA. *Being Fully Literate—or Not.*

Johnston, Francine R., Dixie Massey, University of North Carolina/Greensboro. *Analysis and Comparison of Assignments in Seven Spelling Programs.*

Johnston, Peter H., University at Albany/CELA; **Susan Leyden,** University at Albany and Skidmore College. *Teachers' Descriptive Assessments of their Students' Literacy Development in a High Stakes Testing Environment.*

Jones, Deneese, University of Kentucky. *Teachers' Beliefs and Practices Prior to and after Reading Interventions.*

Joshi, R. Malatesha, Texas A&M University; **P. G. Aaron,** Indiana State University. *Word Familiarity as a Confounding Factor in Spelling: Implications for Spelling Assessment and Instruction.*

Juel, Connie, Harvard University; **Tim Konold, Jennifer Kovak, Beth Morris, Marlie McKinnon, Cecilia Minden-Cupp,** University of Virginia/CIERA. *Preschool: How Haunting the Impact by the End of First Grade?*

Jury, Mark, SUNY/Albany. *Logging Differences: Reading and Writing Contradictory Texts of Timber Workers.*

Kagan, Jennifer, LeMoyne College. *Understanding the Secondary Conditions of Dyslexia: An Intergenerational Study.*

Kamil, Michael L., Helen S. Kim, Stanford University. *Children's Preferences, Motivation, and Learning in Electronic and Multimedia Texts.*

Kaplan, Diane S., Texas A&M University. *Preservice Reading Teachers' Self-Awareness of Past Learning and Development as Motivation for Continued Learning: A Conditional Relationship.*

Karchmer, Rachel A., Virginia Commonwealth University. *Changing Instruction: How Teachers Understand Literacy in the Internet-Connected Classroom.*

Karchmer, Rachel A., Virginia Commonwealth University. *How the Career of Teaching is Altered by Internet Use: Important Teacher Education and Staff Development Issues.*

Kaser, Sandy, Tucson Unified School District. *Exploring Identity through Responses to Literature.*

Kaste, Janine A., Georgia State University. *Walking the Culturally Responsive Talk: Two Preservice Teachers' Practices for Promoting Literacy in the Middle Grades.*

Kauffman, Gloria, Tucson Unified School District. *Exploring Children's Views of Themselves as Learners in an Inquiry-Based Curriculum.*

Kaufman, Douglas K., University of Connecticut. *Teachers Write to Teach Writing Teachers.*

Kealy, William A., Florida State University. *Advantages of Spatially Organized Displays for Processing Related Texts.*

Kehus, Marcella J., Oakland University. *An Online Discourse Community of Adolescent Writers.*

Kelly, Patricia R., San Diego State University. *A Follow-Up Study of One English Language Learner.*

Kidd, Julie K., Sylvia Y. Sanchez, Eva K. Thorp, George Mason University. *Facilitating Language and Literacy Development through Projects: An Applied Internship in Diverse, Mixed-Age Classrooms.*

Kim, Hae Won, Chung-ang University; **Sandra Twardosz,** University of Tennessee/Knoxville. *Effects of Independent Reading Time in Day Care Classrooms.*

Kim, Youb, Karen Lowenstein-Damico, P. David Pearson, CIERA/Michigan State University. *The Role of Written Language Activities in the Development of Second Graders' Oral Language Proficiency.*

Klenk, Laura, SUNY/Buffalo. *"I'm Gonna Beat You": The Discourse of Kindergartners during Unsupervised Literacy Tasks.*

Kletzien, Sharon B., Robert J. Szabo, West Chester University. *Elementary School-Age Children's Genre Preferences.*

Knapp, Nancy F., University of Georgia. *From the Parents' Perspective: A Summer Family Reading Apprenticeship Program for Delayed and Novice Readers.*

Kolloff, Penny, Illinois State University. *Taking an Introspective Look at Our Actions, Reactions, and Emotions.*

Koppenhaver, David A., Gustavus Adolphus College; **Karen A. Erickson,** University of New Hampshire; **Stephanie A. Spadorcia, James W. Cunningham,** University of North Carolina/Chapel Hill. *Do Basal Readers with "Decodable Text" Support Onset-Rime Decoding Instruction?*

Korkeamäki, Riitta-Liisa, University of Oulu/Finland. *Modeling Literacy Behavior for Information Text in Finnish Primary Schools.*

Korkeamäki, Riitta-Liisa, University of Oulu/Finland; **Mariam Jean Dreher,** University of Maryland. *Play as a Medium of Learning Literacy in a Finnish Kindergarten.*

Koziol, Steven, Michigan State University. *The Gap Between Writing Assessment and Programmatic Writing: The Case of Admissions Essays for Teacher Preparation Programs.*

Krol-Sinclair, Barbara D., Chelsea (MA) Public Schools; **Michelle Pierce,** Boston University. *For Our Children and for Ourselves: Assessing Literacy Change in Parents Participating in an Intergenerational Literacy Project.*

Kucan, Linda L., Bethany College. *Transcript Analysis Project (TAP): An Opportunity for Student Teachers to Engage in Practical Inquiry into Classroom Discussion.*

Kuhn, Melanie, University of Georgia. *A Comparative Study of Small Group Fluency Instruction*

Kulesza, Dorothy L., University of Nevada/Las Vegas. *The Role of Elementary School Reading Specialists: Their Responsibilities, Instructional Practices, and Impact on Children.*

Kurkjian, Catherine M., Sue Chase, Central Connecticut State University. *Impact of the Internet as a Tool in Supporting Inservice and Preservice Teachers in Literature Circles.*

Labbo, Linda D., M. Kristiina Montero, University of Georgia. *Computer Center Conversations: Analyzing the Purpose and Quality of Children's and Teachers' Talk during Literacy-Related Work in a Kindergarten Classroom Computer Center.*

Labbo, Linda D., Steve Stahl, Kay Stahl, University of Georgia. *I Feel Like Such an Expert Now: Exploring the Use of Interactive Case-Based CDs on University Students Expertise in Administering and Analyzing K–5 Reading Diagnostic Instruments.*

Labbo, Linda D., University of Georgia. *Kids' Snapshots and Chats as a Tool for Culturally Responsive Literacy Tutoring and Professional Development: Perspectives from Preservice Student Interns in the Field.*

Laidlaw, Linda D., York University; **Ruth Wiebe,** Simon Fraser University. *Commonplace Books, Commonplace Practices: A Complex Approach to Literacy Education.*

Lapp, Diane, Douglas Fisher, James Flood, Kelly Goss, San Diego Unified School District; **Nancy Frey,** San Diego State University. *An Investigation of Teacher and Parent Perceptions Regarding the Effectiveness of Class Size Reduction (CSR) and other Related Factors on the Literacy Development of Children.*

Lapp, Diane, Douglas Fisher, James Flood, Nancy Frey, San Diego State University. *Grading: How Do Elementary School Teachers Evaluate Student Performance.*

Laster, Barbara P., Towson University. *What Parents Learn at Reading Clinics.*

Lazar, Althier M., West Chester University. *Building Passion for Literacy Teaching in Urban Communities: A Case for Reforming Preservice Teacher Education.*

Leavell, Alexandra G., Raquel Oxford, Amy White, University of North Texas; **Sheila Maher,** Creekview High School. *Content Literacy in the High School: Students and Teachers' Perceptions of the Benefits of and Obstacles to Systematic Strategy Usage in Social Studies and Science.*

Lee, Elizabeth A., Monique Bournot-Trites, University of British Columbia. *Becoming Fluent Readers in A Second Language: Student Tutoring and French Immersion Students.*

Leftwich, Stacey, Rowan University. *Making a Connection: Using the ABC's Model to Help Preservice Teachers Implement Culturally Diverse Literature in their Future Classrooms.*

Leland, Christine H., Jerome C. Harste, Indiana University. *Teacher Education and Critical Literacy.*

Lenski, Susan Davis, Illinois State University. *Acknowledging Paradoxes: "Thinking the World Together."*

Lenski, Susan Davis, Illinois State University; **Catherine Zeek,** Texas Woman's University. *Voices from the Midwest.*

Lenski, Susan Davis, Illinois State University. *Untangling the Web: Netsearch Strategies of Experienced Researchers.*

Leroy, Carol A., University of Alberta. *Gender, Power and School-Based Literacy: Conversations with Inner-City Boys.*

Leslie, Lauren, Marquette University; **JoAnne Caldwell,** Cardinal Stritch University. *Validation of Think-Alouds as Online Measures of Comprehension.*

Leu, Jr., Donald J., Syracuse University. *Building Online Learning Communities.*

Leu, Jr., Donald J., Syracuse University. *New Literacies in the Classroom: A Study of Literacy Events Appearing on Classroom Web Pages.*

Levin, Frances A., New Jersey City University. *Literacy Intervention in Academic and Content Reading: Study Skills, Metacognition, and a Teamed Approach.*

Lewandowski, Rosemarie V., Union County College. *Reading, Drawing, Thinking, Talking: Exploring Images with Community College Developmental Readers.*

Lewis, Cynthia, University of Iowa; **Jean Ketter,** Grinnell College. *Encoding Youth: Popular Culture and Multicultural Literature in a Rural Context.*

Linder, Patricia E., Martha M. Foote, Texas A&M University/Commerce. *Home Is Where it Starts: Preservice and Mentor Teachers' Awareness of the Influence of Family on Literacy Learning.*

Lipson, Marjorie Y., James H. Mosenthal, Jane E. Mekkelsen, Barbara J. Russ, Susan A. Sortino, University of Vermont. *Consolidating our Understanding of Contexts and Practices for Success: Contrasting Successful and Less-Successful Schools.*

Lloyd, Carol, University of Nebraska/Omaha. *Moving Beyond the Scrapbook to Critical Reflection in Portfolios.*

Lonigan, Christopher, Florida State University. *Development and Promotion of Phonological Sensitivity in Preschool Children At-Risk for Reading Difficulties.*

López-Robertson, Julia M., Tucson Unified School District. *Literacy Instruction in a Primary Bilingual Classroom.*

Lowenstein-Damico, Karen, Youb Kim, P. David Pearson, CIERA/Michigan State University. *The Role of Written Language Activities in the Development of a Fifth-Grade ESL Student's Oral Language Proficiency.*

Lu, Lucia Y., Clark Atlanta University. *Semiotics for Early Intervention.*

Luse, Elizabeth A., Texas Woman's University. *From Student Teaching to Teaching Students: Teacher Language During Storybook Reading.*

Lyons, Carol A., The Ohio State University. *Learning to be more effective: The Role of the Coach.*

Macaul, Sherry L., University of Wisconsin/Eau Claire. *The State of Media Literacy Standards and Assessment.*

Macaul, Sherry L., University of Wisconsin/Eau Claire. *Viewing Circles in Elementary/ Middle-Level Classrooms.*

MacGillivray, Laurie, Jill Aguilar, Nancy Walker, CIERA/University of Southern California. *School Literacies and Dominant School Discourses: Latina Educators and Academic Success.*

MacGillivray, Laurie, Nancy Walker, Jill Anguilar, CIERA/University of Southern California. *Literacy Learners as Literacy Teachers: Then and Now.*

Mack, Patti, Penn State University. *An Ethnographic Case Study in the Elementary Classroom: Dialogic Language, Discourse, and Technological Composition.*

MacLeod, Elaine R., University of Southern California/Los Angeles. *Teacher Initiated Practices which Foster Children's Growth as Writers: A Perspective from a Primary Classroom.*

Madrigal, Patricia, Anamarie Tam, Susie Altamirano, CIERA/University of Southern California. *Building Links Between Home and School.*

Madrigal, Patricia, CIERA/University of Southern California; **Maria Izquierdo,** 9th Street School/Para Los Ninos. *Building Partnerships with Parents.*

Maimon, Lia F., University of Bridgeport. *A Theoretical Conceptualization as a Basis for a Pragmatic, Agenda-Driven Literacy Theory and Practice.*

Mallette, Marla H., Southern Illinois University; **John E. Readence, Marilyn McKinney,** University of Nevada/Las Vegas; **Margaret M. Smith,** Clark County School District, Las Vegas, NV. *Understanding Preservice Teachers and Researchers' Knowledge through the Lens of their Beliefs.*

Maloch, Beth, Vanderbilt University. *The Use of Meta-linguistic Techniques to Scaffolds Students' Appropriation of Exploratory Talk: One Teacher's Role in Literature Discussion Groups.*

Maniotes, Leslie Kuhlthau, University of North Carolina/Greensboro. *Comprehension Difficulties and Students' Perceptions of the Reading Process.*

Many, Joyce E., Georgia State University. *What Occurs during Instructional Conversations in Literature Circles and Interdisciplinary Units?: An Examination of Teacher and Peer Scaffolding.*

Manyak, Patrick C., University of Southern California. *Negotiating Life and Literacy in a First-Grade English Immersion Class.*

Manyak, Patrick C., University of Southern California. *Legitimate Peripheral Participation, Classroom Literacy, and Latina/o Children.*

Mariage, Troy V., Michigan State University; **M. Arthur Garmon,** Western Michigan University. *The Impact of Project PREPARE on the Teaching and Learning of Literacy: Teacher Change and Student Achievement.*

Marshall, James, University of Iowa. *Young Adult Literature and English Education.*

Martin, Debra Bayles, San Diego State University. *Using the Triple-Transfer Lesson Plan to Guiding Teachers' Reflection Before, During, and After Instruction: What Are The Effects?*

Martinez, Miriam G., University of Texas/San Antonio; **Nancy L. Roser,** University of Texas/Austin. *A Review of Research on Children's Responses to Literature.*

Martínez-Roldán, Carmen M., University of Arizona. *Thinking through Discourse: Learning in Two Languages in Small Group Literature Discussions.*

Martínez-Roldán, Carmen M., University of Arizona/Tucson. *The Power of Children's Dialogue: The Discourse of Latino Student's in Small Group Literature Discussions.*

Mathis, Janelle B., University of North Texas. *Literacy Learning with Culturally Relevant Hispanic Children's Literature.*

Matthews, Mona W., Georgia State University. *Peers Learning with Peers: An Investigation* *of How the Children in One First-Grade Interacted as they Worked Together during Literacy Events.*

McCallister, Cynthia A., New York University. *Intentionality in Pedagogy and the Interpretation of "Difference."*

McCarthey, Sarah J., University of Illinois/Urbana-Champaign. *Constructing Self-Perceptions from Reader Response and "Reading Renaissance."*

McCollum-Clark, Kim, Millersville University. *Silent Partners: Consensus Building for English Language Arts.*

McCormack, Rachel L., Massachusetts Public Schools/Plymouth; **Jeanne R. Paratore,** Boston University. *"Hey, I Can Read This Book without Even Looking!": A Reading Teacher's (Swift) Intervention Using Grade-Level Texts with Struggling First-Grade Readers.*

McDaniel, Julie E., Cecil G. Miskel, Celia H. Sims, University of Michigan. *The Effect of Interest on Decisions: Influence and Domination in the Reading Policy Network.*

McElroy, Linda J., University of Oklahoma. *Conversations Among Multiple Voices: Examining Preservice Literacy Teachers' Sense of Self as a Literacy Teacher Through Collaborative and Person Inquiry.*

McEneaney, John E., Oakland University. *Web-Based Path Assisted Learning: The Web PAL Model.*

McEneaney, John E., Oakland University. *Redefining Literacy and "Reader Friendly" Text in an Online Writing Environment.*

McGee, Lea M., University of Alabama. *Toward the Alphabetic Principle: A Case Study.*

McGivern, Lynne, Mario Lopez, Lee Gunderson, University of British Columbia. *Exploring the Assessment of Primary ESL Students.*

McHill-Franzen, Anne, University of Florida/Gainesville; **Rebecca Rogers,** Washington University/St. Louis; **Vanessa Machado, Maureen Hogan,** SUNY/Albany. *How to Represent Learning that Isn't on the Test? The Researchers and Collaborating Teachers' Dilemma in an Interdisciplinary Project.*

McIntyre, Ellen, Cindy M. Gnadinger, University of Louisville; **Karen Miller**, Roby Elementary; **Gayle Moore,** LaGrange Elementary. *A Model for the Relationships among Instructional Practice, Families' Funds of Knowledge, and Young Children's Achievement.*

McIntyre, Ellen, University of Louisville. *The Effects of Reading Intervention Models.*

McIver, Monette C., University of Colorado/Boulder. *Teachers as Writers: The Impact of a Teacher-Writing Group on Classroom Instruction.*

McKenna, Michael C., Georgia Southern University; **Etta Young, Judy Gatliff,** Burke County (GA) Public Schools. *Creating and Using Talking Documents with Struggling Second-Grade Readers.*

McKinney, Marilyn, Peggy Perkins, John Unger, Susan P. Miller, Sandra J. Odell, University of Nevada/Las Vegas. *Learning to Teach Literacy in Urban Schools: Changing Beliefs.*

McLellan, Meredith, Andrea McPherson, Spartan Village Elementary School. *Instructional Context and Expectations for Second Language Learners.*

McMahon, Susan I., National-Louis University/Center on English Learning and Achievement; **Janice Strop,** Center on English Learning and Achievement; **Linda Gordy,** Cardinal Stritch University/Center on English Learning and Achievement. *Developing an Integrated Curriculum and Its Influence on Student Achievement.*

Medina, Carmen, The Ohio State University. *Jerry Springer Meets La Curandera: Fifth Graders' Use of Drama to Interpret Latina Literature.*

Meredith, Kurt, Jeannie Steele, University of Northern Iowa; **Sona Kikusova,** Comenius University. *Literacy and Constuctivism for Early Childhood Education in an Emerging Democracy.*

Mesmer, Heidi Anne E., Virginia Commonwealth University. *How and When Might Text Decodability Influence First-Grade Readers?*

Meyer, Ricahrd J., University of New Mexico; **Yetta M. Goodman,** University of Arizona; **Diane Stephens,** University of South Carolina; **Randy Bomer,** Indiana University; **Peggy M. Albers,** Georgia State University; **Leslie Patterson, Denise McDonald,** University of Houston; **Shirley Ernst,** Eastern Connecticut State University; **Kathy Whitmore,** University of Iowa. *Teaching Teachers to Teach Reading: Issues, Dilemmas, Perspectives, and Possibilities.*

Meyer, Richard J., Leila Flores-Duenas, Pamel Rossi, Mary Louise Sena, Janet Lear, University of New Mexico. *Teaching Today for Teachers Tomorrow: Preservice Teachers' Preparation for Teaching Reading and Subsequent Practices as Student and Inservice Teachers.*

Michelson, Nancy L., Salisbury State University; **Concetta Busick**, Dorchester County Public Schools. *When Strategic Teaching Isn't Enough: A Case Study of Struggling Readers Left behind in a High School Reading Intervention.*

Mike, Dennis G., Buffalo State College. *A Classroom Study of Computer Mediated Word Recognition.*

Miller, Cynthia, University of Iowa. *After the Romance: Reading Young Adult Novels on Teen Pregnancy.*

Miller, Samuel D., University of North Carolina/Greensboro. *Partners-in-Reading.*

Miller, Teresa, University of Pennsylvania. *Response of Literature Discussion Groups to Culturally Relevant Children's Literature in the Kindergarten Classroom.*

Minden-Cupp, Cecilia, CIERA/University of Virginia. *Interactions of Adult Influences on Elementary Students' Literacy Learning.*

Moje, Elizabeth Birr, University of Michigan. *Toward Secondary, Content-Literacy Pedagogy.*

Moje, Elizabeth Birr, University of Michigan. *Merging Official and Unofficial Literacies: Personal and Political Dilemmas.*

Möller, Karla J., JoBeth Allen, University of Georgia. *Connecting, Resisting, and Searching for Consensus: A Tale of Two Authors.*

Möller, Karla J., University of Georgia. *Realizing the Possibilities: Accepting and Creating Opportunities for Collaborative Writing and Publication.*

Monaghan, E. Jennifer, CUNY/Brooklyn College; **Douglas K. Hartman,** University of Pittsburgh. *Undertaking Historical Research in Literacy: Some Pleasures and Perils.*

Monzo, Lilia D., Laurie MacGillivray, CIERA/University of Southern California. *Gender, Culture, and Literacy: Competing Discourses in Latina Mothers' Talk.*

Moore, Ramona C., Western Washington University. *"So, Why Do We Have to Use Books?": Teaching High School Reading through Multiple Literacies.*

Moore, Sharon Arthur, Peoria (AZ) Unified School District. *Images of Teachers and Schools in Children's Literature.*

Moore, Sharon Arthur, Linda R. Bromert, Peoria (AZ) Unified School District. *After L.E.A.P: A Longitudinal Examination of Participants in A Literacy Intervention Program.*

Moore-Hart, Margaret A., Peggy Liggit, Peggy Daisy, Theresa Cyrnkovich, Eastern Michigan University. *Fostering Science Literacy Performance through an Interdisciplinary WET Program for Preservice Teachers and Elementary Students.*

Morgan, Brian, SUNY/Buffalo. *Making Progress: Perceptions of Affect and Literacy.*

Morris, Darrell, Appalachian State University. *Early Steps: Replicating the Effectiveness of a First-Grade Reading Intervention Model.*

Morrow, Lesley Mandel, Rutgers University. *Creating Quality Interactive Television: Coordinating Staff Development and Graduate Courses in Literacy.*

Morrow, Lesley Mandel, Rutgers University. *Visualizing the Setting: Looking Inside the Classroom.*

Morrow, Lesley M., Melissa Collucci, Adah Razdin, Rutgers University. *Staff Development: A Means to Promote Exemplary Instruction in the Integrated Language Arts.*

Morrow, Lesley M., Michael Smith, Mary Silver, Rutgers University; **Diane Tracey,** Kean University; **Jean Vorrhees,** New Jersey State Department of Education. *The NJ GAINS Project: Gaining Achievement in the New Standards: Teachers and Parents as Partners.*

Morton, Beth E., Peabody College/Vanderbilt University. *Locating Knowledge through Discourse Analysis: Power, Language and Race in a Seventh-Grade Language Arts Classroom.*

Morton, Mary Lou I., Nancy Williams, University of South Florida. *Critical, Collaborative Questions about Reading Instruction: The Restructuring of Professional Educators.*

Mosenthal, James H., Marjorie Y. Lipson, University of Vermont. *The Relationship of Reform in Student and Teacher Assessment to Teachers' Intelligent Action.*

Moss, Barbara, University of Akron. *Learning and Nonfiction Trade Books in Reading Workshop.*

Mueller, Faye L., WestEd. *Looking Closely at Underachieving Ninth-Grade Students' Academic and Leisure Reading.*

Mulcahy-Ernt, Patricia I., University of Bridgeport. *Linking Pre-Service English Language Arts Teachers to Alternative Ways of Knowing Literature through Media Responses.*

Munoa, Candace B., Janet R. Young, Timothy G. Morrison, Brigham Young University. *Literacy on Prime Time Television.*

Murrill, Leslie D., Roanoke College; **Rosary V. Lalik,** Virginia Polytechnic Institute and State University. *Evolution Toward Community: Bringing Progressive Literacy Instruction into City Schools.*

Myers, Jamie M., Pennsylvania State University. *Literacy as Context Awareness, Not Textual Reproduction.*

Nagy, William, Seattle Pacific University. *Changes in Relationships among Orthographic, Phonological, and Morphological Variables and Reading Fluency and Comprehension after a Balanced, Integrated Reading-Writing Intervention.*

Neuman, Susan B., University of Michigan; **Donna Celano,** Temple University. *Access to the Integrated Language Arts: The Growing Knowledge Gap.*

Neuman, Susan B., University of Michigan. *The Ecology of Literacy: Recognizing Societal Fault Lines and Outlining Strategies for Improving Equal Access to Reading and Writing Resources.*

Newsome, Faye, Alice Lloyd College. *Student Achievement in Reading Intervention Classrooms.*

Nichols, William Dee, Jeanneine Jones, Dawson Hancock, Karen Wood, University of North Carolina/Charlotte. *Exploring the Relationship between Teacher Reported Instructional Design and Students' Perceptions of How They Learned: Why Are Students Task Oriented Learners?*

Nielsen, Diane Corcoran, Barbara Luetke-Stahlman, University of Kansas. *A Deaf Child's Receptive and Expressive English Language and Reading Development, Preschool through Sixth Grade: Insights for Language Challenged Children.*

Nierstheimer, Susan L., Illinois State University; **Carol J. Hopkins,** Purdue University. *Using Preservice Teachers' Written Reflections to Identify Experiences that Lead to Personal Growth in Understanding Literacy Teaching and Learning.*

Nierstheimer, Susan L., Illinois State University. *Fighting Images with Words: Identifying Students' Beliefs and Practices through Our Own Stories.*

Nixon-Ponder, Sarah, Southwest Missouri State University. *Using Popular Culture Media for Literacy Instruction and Critical Thinking Enhancement in K–12 and Teacher Education.*

Norton, Bonny, University of British Columbia. *Archie Comics: A Window on Gender, Literacy, and Popular Culture.*

Norwood, Rachel, University of Georgia. *From the Beginning: A Research Apprentice Learns in Collaboration with a Mentor Professor.*

Oates, Scott Forbes, University of Wisconsin/Eau Claire. *Articulating School and Everyday Literacies.*

O'Brien, David G., Deborah R. Dillon, Kerry A. Hoffman, Michele Pittard, Joy Seybold, Ling Wang, Stephen A. Wellinski, Purdue University. *A Discourse Community of Teachers Engaged in Professional Development Academies and Inquiry Projects Tied to State Performance Based Licensure.*

O'Brien, David G., Purdue University. *Media Literacy: "At-Risk" Adolescents as Literate Intellectuals.*

O'Brien, David G., Purdue University. *Tensions of Researching and Advocating for "At-Risk" Youth.*

O'Day, Shannon A., Georgia State University. *Creative Drama as a Literacy Strategy: Teachers' Use of a Scaffold.*

Orellana, Marjorie Faulstich, Northwestern University. *Mediating Mediation: Immigrant Children as Language Brokers or "Para-phrasers."*

Osborn, Jean, University of Illinois/Urbana-Champaign. *The NRC and Reading Standards.*

Overturf, Brenda J., Jefferson County Public Schools. *Developing Teachers' Knowledge of Middle-Level Reading within a Social Constructivist Professional Development Perspective.*

Pailliotet, Ann Watts, Whitman College. *A Synthesis of the Literature on Gender and Post-Typographical Text: Insights Across Methodological Approaches.*

Pailliotet, Ann Watts, Whitman College. *Issues in Media Literacy Research and Instruction.*

Pak, Yoon, University of Illinois/Urbana-Champaign. *Biography as History: Exploring Asian American Educational Experiences through Literature in the History of Education Classroom.*

Palmer, Rosemary, Roger A. Stewart, Boise State University. *Nonfiction Trade Book Use in Primary Grades: A Case Study of One School.*

Pantaleo, Sylvia J., Queen's University. *Exploring Teachers and Teacher-Librarians' Knowledge and Use of Canadian Children's Literature.*

Pappas, Christine C., Maria Varelas, University of Illinois/Chicago; **Anne Barry,** Jungman Elementary School; **Amy O'Neill,** Alexander Hamilton Elementary School. *The Development of Science Discourse Genres in a Primary-Grade Integrated Science-Literacy Unit on States of Matter: An Analysis of Intertextuality.*

Paris, Scott G., P. David Pearson, Michigan State University/CIERA. *Reprise: What Have We Learned about the Efficacy of Summer Reading Programs?*

Paris, Scott G., University of Michigan/CIERA; **Joseph Martineau,** Michigan State University. *Does Summer School Close the Performance Gap for Low Achieving Students in the Primary Grades?*

Passman, Roger, Texas Tech University. *We Get to Ask Our Questions: People, Place, and Time, A Framework for Developing Self-Questioning Engagement with Non-Traditional Text.*

Patberg, Judythe P., Eileen M. Carr, University of Toledo. *Thinking Works: The Effects of a Professional Development Program on Teachers' Attitudes and Instruction.*

Paterson, Patricia O., Georgia State University/Atlanta. *Conversations in Classrooms: Student Negotiation of a Literary Text in Student-Led Discussion Groups.*

Patterson, Elizabeth U., University of Texas/Austin. *On the Wings of Words: A Life History of Bill Martin, Jr.*

Pattnaik, Jyotsna, Central Missouri State University and Utkal University. *The ABC's Model: A Report from Cross-National Research.* **Paul, Carol,** State College Area School District; **Amy Taylor,** Pennsylvania State University. *Through Curricular Invention.*

Pavonetti, Linda M., Kathy Brimmer, James F. Cipielewski, Oakland University. *Accelerated Reader: What Are The Lasting Effects on the Reading Habits of Middle School Students Exposed to Accelerated Reader in Elementary Grades?*

Payne-Bourcy, Laura, Syracuse University. *Chris' Cloak: Life as a Discourse Chameleon.*

Pearson, P. David, Michigan State University/CEIRA. *Views on the Relationship between Oral and Written Language Development.*

Pearson, P. David, Michigan State University/CIERA. *Relationships between Student Growth and Classroom Practices in Summer Reading Programs.*

Pearson, P. David, Michigan State University/CIERA; **Debra Peterson,** University of Minnesota/CIERA; **Loukia K. Sarroub,** Michigan State University/CIERA. *Overview of the CIERA School Change Project and Changes at the School Level in Year One.*

Peck, Sharon M., SUNY/Albany. *Impacting Change in Early Literacy Instruction: Listening to Teachers' Perspectives.*

Pederson, Rod, Jamie Myers, Pennsylvania State University. *Through Contesting Discourse.*

Pederson, Rodney W., Pennsylvania State University. *Critical Literacy and Second Language Learning: A Question of Identity.*

Pennington, Christina, Clemson University. *Finding the Link Between the University and the Classroom through Preservice Teachers' Voices.*

Peterson, Cynthia L., David Caverly, Susen Cusenbary, Thomas Mandeville, Sheila A. Nicholson, Sharon O'Neal, Southwest Texas State University; **Wesley Hoover,** Southwest Educational Development Lab. *When They Still Can't Read: A Framework for Looking at Struggling Secondary Readers.*

Peterson, Shelley L., OISE/University of Toronto. *Teachers' Perceptions of Gender in the Evaluation of Student Narrative and Persuasive Writing.*

Phelps, Stephen, Buffalo State College. *Implementing Early Literacy Assessment through Collaborative In-Service.*

Phillips, LaFon, Tucson Unified School District. *The Unfolding Themes of Self-Realization in the Literary Responses of Young Children with Hearing Loss.*

Phillips, Linda M., Stephen P. Norris, Connie A. Korpan, University of Alberta. *Texture and Structure of Media Reports of Science: University Students' Interpretations and Their Need to Understand the Metadiscourse of Science.*

Picard, Theresa M., University of Connecticut. *The Development of an Instrument Used to Determine Children's Self-Efficacy towards Reading.*

Pinnell, Gay Su, The Ohio State University. *Acquiring Conceptual Understandings and Knowledge.*

Pitcher, Susan, Bloomsburg Central School District. *Buddy Can You Spare a Dime: Funding of the Most Important Literacy Research in America.*

Potter, Christine L., University of Iowa. *Teacher Education Today: Linking Theory and Practice through Preservice Teachers.*

Powell, Becky, Georgetown University. *A State-Wide Bill Supporting Early Literacy.*

Powers, Sherry W., Western Kentucky University. *Classroom Features of Reading Intervention Models.*

Powers, Sherry W., Western Kentucky University. *Ways of Talking: The Effect of Teacher Discourse on an Appalachian Student During Writing Conferences.*

Pressley, Michael, University of Notre Dame. *Historical and Contemporary Perspectives Concerning First-Grade Instruction: Which Ideas Will Survive in Light of New Analyses.*

Pritchard, T. Gail, University of Alabama. *Dialoguers and Lurkers: Electronic Discussions among Preservice Content Area Literacy Students.*

Quatroche, Diana J., Patricia J. Wheeler, Indiana State University. *Reflection on Practice: Pre-Service Teachers Meet the Standards Based on Challenge.*

Ranck-Buhr, Wendy, San Diego State University. *Testing the Water: Attitudes and Career Choices of America Reads Tutors.*

Raphael, Lisa M., Kristen M. Bogner, Michael Pressley, University of Notre Dame. *How Do First-Grade Teachers Motivate Their Students to Do Things Literate?*

Rasmussen, Jean M., Carolyn Colvin, University of Iowa. *"But They're Supposed to Know How to Read": Student Teachers Negotiating the Teaching of Literature and the Teaching of Reading in the Secondary Language Arts Classroom.*

Readence, John E., University of Nevada/Las Vegas. *Research Priorities in Adolescent Literacy.*

Reinking, David, Linda D. Labbo, University of Georgia; **Michael L. Kamil,** Stanford University; **Donald J. Leu, Jr.,** Syracuse University. *Discussing Issues Regarding the Connection between Technology and Literacy.*

Reinking, David, University of Georgia. *Adolescent Literacy for a Post-Typographic World.*

Rhodes, Carole S., Adelphi University. *Preparing Suburban Pre-Service Students to Work in Urban Schools.*

Rhodes, Carole S., Adelphi University. *Transcending Technology: Autobiographical Perspectives.*

Richards, Janet C., University of Southern Mississippi. *"Do You Have Any Advice for Me?": Novice and Experienced Preservice Teachers' Journal Conversations in Two Field-Based Literacy Methods Courses.*

Richards, Janet C., University of Southern Mississippi. *"I'm Not a High Tech Whiz Kid!": Preservice Teachers' Quandaries and Accomplishments Linking Text-Based Literacy Lessons with Computer Technology.*

Richgels, Donald J., Northern Illinois University. *A Kindergarten Classroom as Case Study: The Functions of Writing in an Exemplary Kindergarten.*

Ridgeway, Victoria Gentry, Chris Peters, Clemson University; **Janis Harmon,** University of Texas/San Antonio; **T. Gail Pritchard,** University of Alabama. *Conversations in the Round Revisited: A Comparison of Electronically and Non-Electronically Mediated Discussion Groups.*

Risko, Vicki, Vanderbilt University; **Kathy Roskos,** John Carroll University; **Carol Vukelich,** University of Delaware. *Reflection and the Future Teacher of Reading: Multiple Views, Multiple Implications.*

Robbins, Mary E., Debbie Price, Sam Houston State University. *Primary Teachers' Perceptions of Instructional Change in Literacy.*

Roberts, Theresa A., California State University/Sacramento. *Preschool Letter-Name Instruction Can Enhance Early Word Learning.*

Robinson, Ethel, Syracuse University. *Home-School Perspectives of Middle-Income African Americans and their Impact on Early Literacy Development.*

Robinson, Richard D., University of Missouri/Columbia. *The National Reading Conference and Its Historical Place in the Field of Literacy Education: A Reflection.*

Rodgers, Emily M., Susan Fullerton, Diane E. DeFord, The Ohio State University. *What Does it Take to Reform Instructional Practices?*

Rogers, Rebecca, Washington University/St. Louis. *Ethnographic Intentions: Multi-Vocal Representations in an Ethnographic Case Study.*

Rogers, Rebecca, Washington University/St. Louis; **Cheryl Dozier,** SUNY/Albany. *Inviting Parents into the Conversations.*

Romeo, Lynn, Monmouth University. *Literacy Exploration Labs: Authentic Middle School Classroom Environments for Integrating Literacy and Science.*

Romeo, Lynn, Monmouth University; **Kristie Andres,** Mill Lake School. *"Electronic" Reading Buddies: Graduate Students and 3rd Graders Respond to Literature.*

Rosemary, Catherine A., Dale Whittington, John Carroll University. *Preventing Reading Failure in Grade Four: Effects of the First Three Years of Kindergarten Literacy Intervention.*

Roskos, Kathy, John Carroll University. *The Role of Play in Literacy Development and Learning: The Way Forward.*

Ross, Pamela, San Diego State University. *Redesigning America Reads: A K–3 University Collaboration.*

Rowe, Deborah, Vanderbilt University. *Power, Identity, and Instructional Stance in the Writers' Workshop: Sociocultural Perspectives on the Learning and Teaching of Writing in Elementary Classrooms.*

Rowe, Deborah, Alyson Bass, Vanderbilt University. *Appraising an Examination of Young Children's Use of Drama and Dramatic Play in Response to Literature.*

Rozendal, Mary S., SUNY/Buffalo. *Positioning in Special Education Literacy Instruction: Forging an Entrance into the Print World.*

Ruan, Jiening, Oklahoma University; **Beverly Cox,** Purdue University. *Orthographical Impact on Young Children's Spelling Development.*

Rueda, Robert, Laurie MacGillivray, Lilia Monzó, University of Southern California; **Angela Arzubiaga,** University of California/Los Angeles. *Reading Engagement and Motivation to Read: A Multilevel Approach.*

Rush, Leslie S., University of Georgia. *Reading between the Lines: Critical Literacy in a Tutoring Setting.*

Rush, Leslie S., University of Georgia. *Teaching and Writing in Tandem: Where Do I Stand in All of This?*

Sampson, Mary Beth, Wayne M. Linek, I. LaVerne Raine, Texas A&M University/Commerce. *Examining the Literacy Beliefs and Change Processes of Reading Specialists in a Field-Based Teacher Education Program: Critical Dissonance Factors.*

Sarroub, Loukia K., Michigan State University. *Problematizing Gender and Ethnicity: Representation in Ethnography.*

Scharer, Patricia L., Gay Su Pinnell, Sharan A. Gibson, Peg Gwyther, The Ohio State University. *Improving Student Achievement through Effective School-Home Kindergarten Literacy Programs.*

Scharer, Patricia L., Karin L. Dahl, The Ohio State University. *Spelling Achievement in Whole Language First Grades.*

Schmitt, Maribeth Cassidy, Purdue University. *Metacognitive Strategy Knowledge: Comparison of Former Reading Recovery Children and Their Current Elementary Classmates.*

Semali, Ladislaus M., Pennsylvania State University. *Explorations of Transmediation in a Media Literacy Classroom.*

Semali, Ladislaus M., Pennsylvania State University. *The Hidden Curriculum of Critical Media Literacy: Myths, Barriers and Future Directions.*

Sensale, Lisa, Sapna Vyas, P. David Pearson, Michigan State University/CIERA. *Student and Parent Views of an Assessment System: Are Their Questions about Student Progress Getting Answered?*

Shannon, Patrick, Penn State University. *Market Madness: An Overview of Neoliberal Agendas in Education.*

Shearer, Brenda A., University of Wisconsin/Oshkosh; **Martha Rapp Ruddell,** Sonoma State University; **MaryEllen Vogt,** California State University/Long Beach. *Successful Middle School Reading Intervention: Negotiated strategies and Individual Choice.*

Short, Kathy G., University of Arizona. *Literacy Instruction within Literature-Rich Classrooms.*

Sims, Celia H., Cecil G. Miskel, Julie E. McDaniel, University of Michigan. *The Influence Tactics of Interest Groups and National Reading Policy.*

Sipe, Lawrence R., University of Pennsylvania. *A Content Analysis of Picture Storybooks for Teaching Art History.*

Sipe, Lawrence R., University of Pennsylvania. *Peter Rabbit Goes Downtown: Urban Children's Responses to a Literary Classic.*

Skinner, Charlotte A., Arkansas State University. *Written Response to Multiethnic Picture Books by Mainstream Respondents.*

Smith Bass, Alyson, Peabody College/Vanderbilt University. *Teacher Book Selection Decisions for Emergent Readers in a Literature-Based Reading Program.*

Smith, Sally A., CUNY/College of Staten Island. *"Would I Use This Book When I Teach?": White, Female Education Students Examine Their Beliefs about Teaching In Multicultural Context.*

Smith, Susan S., Drake University; **Patricia L. Bloem,** Cleveland State University; **Alan Crawford,** California State University; **Samuel R. Mathews,** University of West Florida; **Sarah Nixon-Ponder,** Southwest State University. *Language and Literacy Instruction: An International Perspective.*

Smith, Susan S., Drake University. *The Challenges Facing Implementation of the Emergent Literacy Paradigm.*

Smith-Burke, M. Trika, New York University; **Susan L. Lynaugh, Diane Montminy,** East Central Consortium/St. Johnsbury, VT. *Patterns of School Change in Early Literacy Instruction: A Regional Case Study of the East Central Consortium in Vermont.*

Soler, Marta, CREA/Barcelona. *A Social Model for Adult Education in Spain.*

Spadorcia, Stephanie A., University of North Carolina/Chapel Hill. *Analyzing the Word-Level, Sentence-Level, and Passage-Level Demands of Easy Books of Interest to Adolescent Readers.*

Spencer, Vicky G., George Mason University. *Yours, Mine, and Ours: The Evolution of a Classwide Intervention for Enhancing Reading Comprehension within an Inclusive Elementary Social Studies Classroom.*

Stadler, Sue E., Purdue University. *Kindergartners' Utilization of Grapho-Phonological Information for Reading and Writing Continuous Text.*

Stahl, Katherine A. D., University of Georgia and Clarke County Public Schools; **Steven A. Stahl,** University of Georgia/CIERA. *The Measurement of Sequencing Skill in Reading Comprehension.*

Stahl, Norman A., Northern Illinois University. *Challenges of Portfolios from Faculty and Administrative Perspectives.*

Stahl, Norman A., Northern Illinois University. *Conducting Organization Histories: NRC as a Case Study.*

Stahl, Norman A., Northern Illinois University. *Historical Roots of Current Literacy Debates.*

Stahl, Steven A., Alicia A. McCartney, University of Georgia. *The Effects of Explicit Phonics Instruction and Text Decodability in First Grade.*

Stallworth, B. Joyce, University of Alabama. *Using E-Mail to Facilitate Dialogue between 10th Graders and Preservice English Majors.*

Stevens, Lisa, University of Nevada/Las Vegas. *Reflective Teaching as Social Practice.*

Stevens, Lisa, University of Nevada/Las Vegas. *What Happens after the Dust Settles?: Examining Dimensions of Content Area Teacher Change after a Staff Development Project Ends.*

Steward, Darrel, University of Pennsylvania. *Nightjohn—Venue for Social Change.*

Strecker, Susan K., Wanda B. Hedrick, University of Texas/San Antonio. *A Comparative Study of Preservice Teachers Serving as Reading Tutors in Two Different Settings.*

Stuart, Denise H., Cleveland State University. *A Study of Fifth-Grade Students' Use of Peer-Led Discussion in Literature Clubs of an Urban Gifted and Talented Program.*

Sturtevant, Elizabeth G., George Mason University. *Contradictions of High Stakes Assessment.*

Sturtevant, Elizabeth G., George Mason University; **Gay Ivey,** University of Maryland; **Patricia L. Anders,** University of Arizona. *Adolescent Literacies: Multiple Perspectives on What Is Important, What Is Challenging and What Should be Done to Improve Teaching and Learning.*

Sulentic, Margaret-Mary, University of Southern Mississippi. *The Importance of Audience Purpose: A Case Study of a Fifth-Grade Writer.*

Sweet, Anne P., RAND/OERI; **Mike Timpane,** RAND. *The RAND Reading Study Group: Charting the Course for a National Research Agenda in Skillful Reading.*

Tam, Anamarie, CIERA/University of Southern California. *Latino Teacher Beliefs and Their Impact in a Preschool Setting.*

Tam, Anamarie, Joan Massa, CIERA/University of Southern California. *Building Partnerships with Teachers.*

Tao, Liqing, Western Kentucky University. *A Reality Check On Content Area Reading Instruction: Do Our Teachers Need Assistance in Facilitating their Students' Learning in Content Areas?*

Tao, Liqing, Western Kentucky University. *Electronic Pen-Pals: How Second Graders Converse Via Electronic Communication Over Authentic Classroom Learning Tasks.*

Taylor, Barbara M., University of Minnesota. *Highly Accomplished Primary-Grade Teachers in Effective Schools.*

Taylor, Barbara M., University of Minnesota/CIERA; **Kathleen Clark,** University of Minnesota/CIERA; **Suzy Knezek,** Michigan State University/CIERA. *The CIERA School Change Project: Changes at the Classroom Level in Year One.*

Taylor, D. Bruce, University of Iowa. *Sticks and Stones: The Discourse and Labeling of Readers.*

Thomas, Heather, Ithaca City Schools. *Nicholas' Advice: "You Just Do It. That's All."*

Thomas, Karen F., Lauren Freedman, Western Michigan University. *What I Didn't Learn: PreService Literacy Education of Secondary Teachers.*

Thomas, Karen F., Western Michigan University. *Issues in the Recruitment and Retention of Minority Literacy Educators.*

Tidwell, Deborah, University of Northern Iowa. *What Teachers Learn from Writing Authentic Anecdotal Records.*

Toll, Cathy, Illinois State University. *Washing the Students Clean—Do We? Should We?*

Torgesen, Joseph, Florida State University. *Is Articulatory-Level Stimulation Critical for Remediation of Severe Reading Difficulties: Results from an Intensive Intervention Study with Older Children.*

Townsend, Michael A., Jane Townsend, University of Auckland. *Motivation to Read in Ex-Reading Recovery Children in New Zealand.*

Tracy, Pamela, The Ohio State University. *Of Blue Fizzy Pens and Body Gel: The Politics of Playing "Girl" in Upper Elementary Reading Lessons.*

Triplett, Cheri Foster, University of Georgia. *Toward a Grounded Theory of Dialogic Responsiveness in Early Childhood Literacy Learning.*

Valencia, Sheila W., Pamela Grossman, Nancy Place, Susan Martin, Laura Adriance, University of Washington. *Beginning Teachers and Curriculum Materials: Navigating the Terrain.*

Valencia, Sheila W., University of Washington. *The Development of Reflective Practice: From Teacher Education to Beginning Teaching.*

VanOrder, Allyson, Jerome Zutell, The Ohio State University. *Extending Developmental Spelling Research: A School-Wide Assessment: Cross-Sectional and Longitudinal Changes, Primary Grades.*

Verhoeven, Ludo, University of Nijmegen/Netherlands. *Early Literacy Intervention for At-Risk First-Grade Students: Integrating Effective Classroom Instruction.*

Vogt, MaryEllen, California State University/Long Beach; **Thomas W. Bean,** University of Nevada/Las Vegas; **Donna Ogle,** National Louis University; **Martha Rapp Ruddell,** Sonoma State University; **Brenda Shearer,** University of Wisconsin/Oshkosh. *Teachers' Perceptions and Innovative Practice.*

Vogt, MaryEllen, Jana Echevarria, California State University/Long Beach; **Deborah Short,** Center for Applied Linguistics/Washington, DC; **Randy Gibson,** Hill Middle School/Long Beach. *The Sheltered Instruction Observation Protocol (SIOP): Improving Language, Literacy, and Content Learning for English Language Learners.*

Vukelich, Carol, University of Delaware; **Mary F. Roe,** University of Oregon. *Tutoring the Reading Tutor: A Case Study.*

Vyas, Sapna, P. David Pearson, Michigan State University/CIERA; **Deanna Birdyshaw,** University of Michigan/CIERA. *The Changing Views of School Personnel.*

Wade, Suzanne E., University of Utah. *Critical Discourse Analysis of Preservice Teachers' Discussions on the Internet.*

Waff, Diane, School District of Philadelphia. *Social Vision and Social Change: Critical Inquiry in a Multicultual Classroom.*

Wagner, Richard, Florida State University. *Estimating the Effects of Instruction in Phonological Awareness on Reading Growth: A New Meta-Analysis.*

Walker, Carolyn Ann, Linda E. Martin, Sherry Kragler, Ball State University. *From Author's Chairs to Organization: An Investigation of Teacher Change in a Long-Term Writing In-Service Project.*

Walker, Nancy, University of Southern California; **John E. Readence,** University of Nevada/Las Vegas; **Brenda A. Shearer,** University of Wisconsin/Oshkosh; **Kathy Neal Headley,** Clemson University; **Carole S. Rhodes,** Pace University; **Elizabeth U. Patterson,** University of Texas at Austin; **Ann L. Loranger,** University of New Hampshire; **Laurie A. Elish-Piper,** Northern Illinois University; **Martha Rapp Ruddell,** Sonoma State University; **James R. King,** University of South Florida; **Norman A. Stahl,** Northern Illinois University. *National Reading Conference Oral History Project.*

Wallis, Judy, Spring Branch Independent School District; **Catherine Kell, Linda Sievert, Rick Hy, Mary Gregory,** Maple West Elementary. *Raising Readers and Writers Across the Grades: Case Studies of School-Based Literacy Teams.*

Walpole, Sharon Arthur, Johnson School. *The Place and Characteristics of Comprehension Instruction K–3: Read-Aloud or Student Reading, Language Arts or Content Area Literacy.*

Wasik, Barbara A., Mary Alice Bond, Johns Hopkins University. *Getting the Most out of a Book: Teacher Training and Interactive Book Reading.*

Wedman, Judy M., Elizabeth Baker, Kyeong-Hee Rha, Laurie H. Kingsley, University of Missouri/Columbia. *What is the Relative Value of Multimedia Portfolio Cases to a Literacy Methods Course: Who's Learning What and How?*

Weisberg, Renee, Beaver College. *Implementing an Intervention Program for At-Risk First Graders: Negotiating Boundaries between Programmatic Principles and Instructional Practices.*

Weiss, Mary, Joann Cruce, Central Missouri Regional Professional Development Center. *Increasing the Effectiveness of State-Supported Professional Development.*

Wellinski, Stephen A., Kerry A. Hoffman, Michele Pittard, David G. O'Brien, Purdue University. *(Re)Constructing Preservice Teachers' Beliefs about Literacy and Learning in their Content Area Classrooms.*

Wharton-McDonald, Ruth, University of New Hampshire. *Doing It All: How Exemplary Teachers Use Research-Based Practices to Meet Individual Student Needs.*

Wickstrom, Carol D., Texas Woman's University. *Learning from the Past: Teaching in the Present.*

Wickstrom, Carol D., Texas Woman's University. *Preservice Teachers' Portfolio Conferences: Conversations that Self-Assess or Conversations that Identify Course Contents.*

Wiencek, B. Joyce, Oakland University; **Laurie Kaufman,** Madonna University. *Capturing the Range of Writing Development in First Grade.*

Williams, E. Jane, The Ohio State University. *The Impact of Literacy Collaborative Training on Literacy Achievement.*

Willis, Arlette Ingram, Julia L. Johnson, University of Illinois/Urbana-Champaign. *Using Multicultural Literature in a Culturally Diverse High School Classroom.*

Willson, Victor L., William H. Rupley, Daniel F. Brossart, Texas A&M University. *Nomographic versus Ideographic Modeling of Reading Development in Children: Issues and Recommendations.*

Wilson, Elizabeth K., B. Joyce Stallworth, University of Alabama; *Kimberly Callison,* Holt High School; **Kathy Shaver,** Alabama Consortium for Educational Renewal. *Literature, Literacy, and Legacy: Teaching* The Watsons Go To Birmingham—1963 *at a Professional Development School.*

Windsor, Louise, Westover Elementary School/Maryland. *Reading Reform in Grades 3, 4, and 5.*

Wiseman, Donna L., Northern Illinois University. *Synthesizing the Issues and Trends of Using Portfolios in Graduate Reading Programs.*

Wold, Linda, University of Chicago. *An Examination of Teacher's "Learning to Act" on Reflection.*

Wolf, Shelby A., Monette C. McIver, University of Colorado/Boulder. *"That Dog Won't Hunt!": Exemplary School Change Efforts to Match Kentucky's Writing Reform.*

Wolf, Shelby A., University of Colorado/Boulder. *"Only Connect!" Cross Cultural Connections in the Literary Engagement of a Preservice Teacher and the Child Who Taught Her.*

Woo, Deborah, Rutgers University. *Focusing on Exemplary Literacy Instruction through the Integration of the Language Arts.*

Wood, Jeffery W., Indiana University. *Reading The Research: An Analysis of Qualitative Research.*

Wood, Julie M., Harvard University. *They've Got Mail: Struggling Readers/Writers Publish and Communicate Using the Web.*

Wood, Julie M., Harvard University. *Using Technology for Clients' Authentic Literacy Learning.*

Worthy, Jo, Kathryn Hooper, University of Texas/Austin. *Preparation and Supervision for Tutors in Three America Reads Programs.*

Worthy, Jo, Misty W. Sailors, Lori C. Assaf, Marg A. Mast, University of Texas/Austin. *Accelerated Reader: Help or Hindrance to Improving Reading Attitudes and Achievement.*

Xu, Shelley Hong, Texas Tech University. *Perservice Teachers' Developing Understandings of Diversity: The ABC's Model and Teaching African American Students.*

Xu, Shelley Hong, Texas Tech University. *Whose Popular Culture?: Teachers Explore Making Connections of Diverse Students' School and Home Literacy Experiences.*

Yaden, Jr., David B., Susie Altamirano, Danny Brassell, Patricia Madrigal, Joan Massa, Anamarie Tam, University of Southern California/CIERA. *Four-Year-Olds Emergent Literacy Growth in Spanish and English during Preschool and the Impact of Transition to Public Schooling.*

Yaden, Jr., David B., University of Southern California/CIERA. *Uncovering the Unconventional: Glimpses into How Preschoolers Think about Reading and Writing.*

Yoon, Jun-Chae, University of Georgia. *Critical Memoirs: Literacy Practices in Dark Times.*

Young, Josephine Peyton, Arizona State University. *Creating Spaces for Exploring Gender in Texts.*

Young, Josephine Peyton, Arizona State University. *Flirting with Gender Identities: Middle School Students Define and Question Practices of Gender Through Media, Community, and Other Texts.*

Zecker, Liliana B., DePaul University; **Betina Plaza de Arrúe,** Comunidad Educativa San Judas Tadeo. *Emergent Literacy Development across Languages and Genres: Some Universals among Monolingual Spanish- and English-Speaking Kindergartners and First Graders in the U.S. and Argentina.*

Zhang, Yuanzhong, University of Arizona and Hunan XU Teli Institute of Education/China; **Yueh-nu Hung,** University of Arizona; **Wenjun Lin,** University of Arizona and Taiwan Provincial Institute of In-service Teacher Education. *Making Sense of Nonsense out of Context: A Study of Meaning Conjecture in Reading Chinese.*

Zipes, Jack, University of Minnesota. *Children's Literature and Literary Criticism.*

Zutell, Jerome, Allyson VanOrder, The Ohio State University. *Extending Developmental Spelling Research: A School-Wide Assessment: Cross-Sectional and Longitudinal Changes, Upper Elementary Grades.*